THE EDINBURGH EDITION
OF THOMAS REID

General Editor
Knud Haakonssen

1 *Thomas Reid on the Animate Creation: Papers Relating to the Life Sciences*, Paul Wood (ed.) 1995.

2 *An Inquiry into the Human Mind on the Principles of Common Sense*, Derek R. Brookes (ed.) 1997 (hardback), 2000 (paperback).

3 *Essays on the Intellectual Powers of Man*, Derek R. Brookes and Knud Haakonssen (eds.) 2002.

4 *The Correspondence of Thomas Reid*, Paul Wood (ed.) 2002.

5 *Thomas Reid on Logic, Rhetoric and the Fine Arts: Papers on the Culture of the Mind*, Alexander Broadie (ed.) 2004.

6 *Thomas Reid on Practical Ethics*, Knud Haakonssen (ed.) 2007.

7 *Essays on the Active Powers of Man*, Knud Haakonssen and James A. Harris (eds.) 2010.

8 *Thomas Reid on Society and Politics*, Knud Haakonssen and Paul Wood (eds.) 2015.

9 *Thomas Reid on Mathematics and Natural Philosophy*, Paul Wood (ed.).

10 *Thomas Reid and the University*, Alexander Broadie and Paul Wood (eds.).

THOMAS REID ON SOCIETY AND POLITICS

PAPERS AND LECTURES

EDITED BY
Knud Haakonssen and Paul Wood

The Pennsylvania State University Press
University Park, Pennsylvania

First cloth edition published in 2015 in the United States by
The Pennsylvania State University Press
USB 1, Suite C, University Park, Pennsylvania 16802

First published in the United Kingdom in 2015 by
Edinburgh University Press Ltd

Typeset in Times New Roman
by R. J. Footring Ltd, Derby, and
printed and bound in Great Britain by
CPI Group (UK) Ltd, Croydon CR0 4YY

Cataloging information for this title is available at the Library of Congress.

ISBN 978 0 271 07076 6

The Pennsylvania State University Press is a member of the Association of American University Presses.

It is the policy of The Pennsylvania State University Press to use acid-free paper. Publications on uncoated stock satisfy the minimum requirements of American National Standard for Information Sciences—Permanence of Paper for Printed Library Material, ANSI Z39.48–1992.

Contents

Acknowledgements

The editors are grateful to Aberdeen University Library for permission to publish the manuscripts included in this volume. They would also like to acknowledge the assistance of David Armitage, Alexander Broadie, John Cairns, Roger Emerson, James Harris, Julian Hoppit, Michael Lobban, Michael Quinn, Michael Seidler, M. A. Stewart, Carl Wennerlind, Richard Whatmore and Donald Winch, who generously responded to our queries regarding matters of fact and interpretation. Knud Haakonssen would like to thank the Swedish Collegium for Advanced Study (Uppsala) and the Max-Weber-Kolleg für Kultur- und Sozialwissenschaftliche Studien (Erfurt) for institutional support during work on this book. Paul Wood would like to thank the Reading Room Manager, Michelle Gait, and the staff of the Wolfson Reading Room, Special Collections Centre, University of Aberdeen, for their help and cheerful support; Mathieu Robitaille, Tiffany Gunton and Sara Siona Régnier-McKellar, who provided research assistance at various points during the preparation of this volume; and the Social Sciences and Humanities Research Council of Canada for the funding which supported his editorial work on this book.

Erfurt and Victoria
January 2014

The Manuscripts and Editorial Principles

The manuscripts that we have transcribed and publish in this volume belong to the Special Collections Centre in the Sir Duncan Rice Library, University of Aberdeen. Most of the manuscripts are part of the Birkwood Collection, while the remainder are found in a significant collection of Reid's papers given to the Library in 1980. Details of the physical state of each manuscript and authorial revisions and annotations are given in the Textual Notes. All of the manuscripts in the Birkwood Collection have been digitised and are available on the website of the Library (http://www.abdn.ac.uk/diss/historic/Thomas_Reid).

It appears that Reid himself organised his papers thematically, for among the manuscripts now located in the bundle MS 2131/4/III/12–23c there is an uncatalogued wrapper labelled 'Politicks' in Reid's hand. This wrapper was used to keep together the papers related to Reid's politics lectures now found in the MS 2131/4/III/1–23c sequence. After Reid's death, his colleague George Jardine arranged all of the surviving manuscripts into ten topical groups, and the wrappers for these ten parcels are now kept in the box containing the manuscripts catalogued as MS 2131/8/I–VII. The wrappers themselves are uncatalogued. A transcription of them will be published in volume 10 of the Edinburgh Edition of Thomas Reid. In addition to the original wrappers there is an equivalent set created in the nineteenth or twentieth century. This second set of wrappers has labels written in ink that are transcriptions of Jardine's labels affixed to the original wrappers. Despite these efforts to arrange the manuscripts into topical groups, the thematic ordering of Reid's papers has in fact been significantly disturbed at various points, so that their catalogued order in many cases bears little relationship to their original intellectual order. Moreover, Reid himself reworked material with revisions, deletions, insertions and additions written in margins or inter-lined in the original text. He also used blank parts of paper for miscellaneous notes of little or no relevance to the original text of the document. His writing paper was typically a sheet that was folded and refolded to form an approximately octavo-sized quire of four leaves held together with a small string (which often has broken, leaving the leaves free to migrate elsewhere or be lost entirely). All these factors conspire to make our reconstruction of Reid's lectures on politics subject to some uncertainty and to leave several gaps in it. We can only confirm what George Jardine wrote on the label of the relevant bundle (Wrapper B):

> This Parcel Contains Heads of Lectures on Pneumatology, Ethicks & Politicks which seem to have been delivered the first Session Dr. Reid Taught in Glasgow College. To which so many additional Notes & Illustrations have been made in Succeeding years that they cannot easily be put in exact order.

The papers that Reid presented to the Aberdeen Philosophical Society and the Glasgow Literary Society, included in Part Three of this volume, pose less of an editorial challenge than his lecture notes that make up Part Two. While not in all cases without problems for modern editors, these papers were sufficiently polished to be read aloud. The reading notes transcribed in Part One are the least problematic from an editorial point of view, even though they sometimes raise serious issues of interpretation.

Our aim in transcribing the manuscripts included in this volume has been to provide accurate and easily readable texts, while preserving the integrity of Reid's writing. Because most of the manuscripts contain numerous deletions, insertions, corrections and the like, the creation of such texts is not a straightforward process. We have therefore adopted the following principles in order to achieve our editorial end:

1. We have made no attempt to normalise Reid's erratic spelling and punctuation, except where the spelling was clearly mistaken or its eccentricity too distracting.

2. In our transcriptions, words or characters which are missing because of damage to the manuscript or are judged to have been inadvertently omitted by Reid are enclosed thus: '‹ ›'. Illegible letters or words are indicated thus: '‹?›'.

3. Any characters written as superscripts are here printed not raised.

4. In Reid's manuscripts, he typically overlines for emphasis, and we have reproduced the relevant words or passages in italics without editorial comment.

5. We have silently normalised Reid's contractions and abbreviations where no modern equivalent exists, or where they are not self-explanatory or readily pronounceable by the modern reader. Thus, on page 3, line 1, we have not expanded 'Aug' because it is still recognised as an abbreviation for 'August', but on the next line we have normalised Reid's contraction 'Cha' because it does not obviously stand for 'Charles'. We have also silently expanded some of Reid's contractions in the interests of readability. For example, on page 3, line 6, we have normalised Reid's 'Art' to 'Article' because it occurs in a reading context. But where contractions occur in the context of a reference (as on page 10, line 1), we

have usually left them unexpanded because their meaning will become obvious from the information supplied in our explanatory notes.

6. We have silently omitted repetitions of words or phrases, catchwords and any material deemed to have been mistakenly included in the manuscripts.

7. Folio/page breaks are indicated by a vertical line, '|', in the text. In the page margin at the line in which Reid began a new folio or page, the manuscript number is printed together with the folio or page number. There are two types of manuscript numbers in the volume, respectively of these forms: 2131/2/II/14 and 3061/3. The former type always has the first four digits (2131) in common and these are left out in the marginal printing. The manuscript number is followed, after a comma, by an indication of the folio or page number in the original manuscript; in the case of unpaginated manuscripts, we give the folio number and the side – recto 'r' or verso 'v' – of the folio. The folio/page indications should allow the reader to follow the way in which we have arranged the manuscripts that remain from Reid's lectures on politics. As mentioned, Reid often used the same sheet of paper for different purposes, and it has therefore been necessary to divide a number of manuscripts. Conversely, the rejoining of manuscripts that cohered originally has meant that their folios/pages are printed here in an order different from that in which they happen to have been preserved.

8. In the transcriptions of Reid's manuscripts we have added line numbers. These are used for reference to the Textual and Editorial Notes (see points 9 and 10 below). In cases where the line numbers coincide with the manuscript numbers (cf. point 7 above), the line number is not included.

9. Variants in Reid's manuscripts are recorded in the Textual Notes, and these are keyed to the relevant texts using page and line numbers (that is, '18/32' in the Textual Notes refers to p. 18, l. 32 in this volume). In these notes, editorial comment is in italics and Reid's wordings are in roman typeface. Instances where Reid has changed an unfinished text by superimposing a letter or word over what he had originally written, or revised a phrase in the course of his initial writing, have been used in our transcriptions but have *not* been recorded in the Textual Notes. We have also not recorded those instances where Reid has merely gone back and corrected his spelling or grammar, or supplied a missing character or word. Variants are indicated in the following manner. In MS 2131/4/III/3 (p. 32, l. 13 below), for example, Reid initially wrote 'something in the Nature of it', then deleted 'the Nature of', leaving as his final formulation 'something in it'. Reid's change is recorded in the Textual Notes thus: something in it] something in the Nature of it.

Reid often failed to replace deleted material with a new word or phrase. These cancellations have been identified and recorded in the Textual Notes.

In recording Reid's revisions we have made a distinction between insertions and additions. Where Reid has indicated where to place additional material in the text (typically with a '^'symbol below the line) we have used the annotation '*inserted*'. Where Reid has not indicated where to place additional material with a symbol, we have used the annotation '*added*'.

In ambiguous cases we have specified the revision using the normal convention illustrated above. Where Reid has written his insertion or addition in the margin of the page, we have noted the location of the insertion or addition in our annotation.

10. The Editorial Notes preceding the Textual Notes contain translations of Latin passages, and the details of papers and books Reid quotes from or refers to in his texts. In many cases we have also referred to literature which we have no direct evidence that Reid used, but which we believe is a help to the reader in understanding which subjects Reid was addressing. Detailed commentary on the contents of the manuscripts has been confined to our editorial introduction.

The Editorial Notes are indicated in Reid's texts by asterisks * and are keyed to the texts using the same convention as that employed in the Textual Notes.

Where known, life dates for all figures active prior to 1800 mentioned in the notes to the Introduction and the Editorial Notes are given in the Index of Persons and Titles.

Index of Manuscripts

1. Birkwood Collection, Aberdeen University Library

2. Special Collections, Aberdeen University Library

Introduction

Knud Haakonssen and Paul Wood

1. Thomas Reid: The Politics of a North Briton

Dugald Stewart's influential depiction of Thomas Reid as a thinker living 'in the obscurity of a learned retirement', distanced from 'the political convulsions which Europe has witnessed for a course of years', has long masked the fact that throughout Reid's career he was deeply engaged with many of the pressing social, economic and political issues that preoccupied his contemporaries across the Atlantic world. While Stewart was understandably anxious to present Reid's philosophical legacy without reference to the political and cultural conflicts in Britain caused by the French Revolution, Stewart's predicament in Edinburgh at the turn of nineteenth century led him to create a portrait of Reid that does not do justice to the full range of Reid's activities or the scope of his intellectual enterprise.[1] For, as Reid's correspondence reveals, he gave serious thought to matters of social and economic policy at various points during his long career, and he was an active participant in both the anti-slavery movement and the meetings held in Glasgow to express support for the early, moderate phase of the French Revolution. Moreover, the papers we publish in this volume cast Reid in a very different light from that found in Stewart's biography because they illustrate how his responses to the political, economic and social problems confronting Britain in the second half of the eighteenth century were informed by the theoretical ideas that he refined and systematised in the classrooms of King's College Aberdeen and the University of Glasgow.

Reid's mature thinking about politics, the economy and society took shape in the distinctive milieu of the north-east of Scotland. As a boy, he experienced at first hand the political and religious divisions that plagued the north-east, as well as Scotland more generally, in the first half of the eighteenth century. His extended family was split between those loyal to the Hanoverian and Presbyterian settlements and those who were Episcopalians with Jacobite sympathies. His mother, Margaret, was the daughter of David Gregory of Kinnairdy and Gregory's second wife, Isabel Gordon. The offspring of Gregory's first wife, Jean Walker

[1] Dugald Stewart, *Account of the Life and Writings of Thomas Reid* (1803), p. 2. On Stewart's *Account* see Paul Wood, 'The Hagiography of Common Sense: Dugald Stewart's *Account of the Life and Writings of Thomas Reid*'.

were, Reid later recalled, 'torries & Episcopalians', whereas Isabel and her children 'were zealous Presbyterians', like the Reids. The tensions resulting from these conflicting allegiances left a permanent mark on the family and, on occasion, led to somewhat strained relationships between the direct descendants of Gregory's two wives.[2] Aberdeen was also still scarred by the Jacobite rising of 1715 when in April 1722 Reid was sent to study at the Aberdeen Grammar School before entering Marischal College the following October. The north-east was a hotbed of Jacobitism, with the Old Pretender, James Francis Edward Stuart, being proclaimed as James III and VIII in Aberdeen on 20 September 1715. The patron of Marischal College, the tenth Earl Marischal, George Keith, was one of the leading supporters of the would-be king, and most of those teaching at Marischal and King's came out on the side of the Jacobite cause. Once the rebellion was quashed in 1716, the Hanoverian regime moved swiftly to remove those implicated in the abortive rising. Royal Commissions of Visitation, convened in 1716 and 1717, found that eight of the ten members of King's College and six of the seven members of Marischal were Jacobites. They were all replaced by men loyal to the Hanoverians, and Keith was stripped of his patronage of the college his family had founded.[3] The new cadre of regents and professors who lectured at King's and Marischal after the colleges reopened in 1717 effected significant changes to the curricula, which were to prove beneficial to students such as Reid. Reid's regent, George Turnbull, began his brief career at Marischal in 1721 and, over the course of the next six years, did much to transform the teaching of the *cursus philosophicus*. Through Turnbull, Reid was introduced to such canonical writers on politics and natural law as Hugo Grotius, Samuel Pufendorf, Richard Cumberland, Thomas Hobbes and John Locke, and probably also the works of James Harrington and Old Whigs such as Robert Molesworth.[4]

[2] See Reid's account of his visit in 1736 to his cousin David Gregory, in Reid to James Gregory, 24 August 1787, in Reid, *Correspondence*, pp. 189–90.

[3] On the '15 see Daniel Szechi, *1715: The Great Jacobite Rebellion*. For specific information about Aberdeen, see Alistair Tayler and Henrietta Tayler, *1715: The Story of the Rising*, pp. 52, 128–32; and Kieran German, 'Jacobite Politics in Aberdeen and the '15'.

[4] On Turnbull's teaching at Marischal College see Paul Wood, *The Aberdeen Enlightenment: The Arts Curriculum in the Eighteenth Century*, pp. 40–49. For the graduation thesis Turnbull published when Reid received his MA in 1726 see George Turnbull, *Education for Life: Correspondence and Writings on Religion and Practical Philosophy*, pp. 59–74. See also George Turnbull, *The Principles of Moral and Christian Philosophy* (1740), vol. I, pp. 226–29, on the 'science of politics', and Turnbull's commentary in Johann Gottlieb Heineccius, *A Methodical System of Universal Law: Or, the Laws of Nature and Nations Deduced from Certain Principles, and Applied to Proper Cases* (1738), for an extended exposition of his political principles; cf. the interpretation in Knud Haakonssen, *Natural Law and Moral Philosophy: From Grotius to the Scottish Enlightenment*, pp. 85–99.

While Reid studied divinity at Marischal from 1726 to 1731, he was exposed to the political realities of Scottish academic life when he participated in the election of the College Rector. During the late 1720s rectorial elections at Marischal were a microcosm of the struggle for power and influence in the political nation at large between two rival factions of Whigs: the Squadrone, led by the first Duke of Montrose, James Graham, and the first Duke of Roxburghe, John Ker, and the Argathelians, led by the second Duke of Argyll, John Campbell, and his brother Archibald, Lord Ilay. After Marischal reopened in 1717, the Squadrone controlled the college. In 1726, however, the party suffered a reverse when the Argathelian Patrick Duff was elected Rector. In 1729 Reid was chosen as a procurator to represent the student 'nation' of Angus and he voted for the successful Argathelian candidate, Duff's cousin, William Duff of Braco.[5] During the course of the election, Reid met the local clergyman, the Rev. John Bisset, who was appointed by Reid and his fellow procurators to serve as an assessor alongside the new Rector. We do not know what transpired between Reid and Bisset in 1729, but in 1737 they became bitter antagonists when Reid became entangled in the ecclesiastical politics surrounding the issue of church patronage.

We know almost nothing about Reid's involvement with political and social matters in the years immediately following his departure from divinity school, although a hint of his interest in politics comes in a list of books he apparently wanted to read dating from January 1736, which included the Scottish Catholic historian Thomas Innes' controversial *A Critical Essay on the Ancient Inhabitants of the Northern Parts of Britain, or Scotland* (1729) and a Tory political pamphlet by the Scottish Scriblerian John Arbuthnot.[6] Willingly or not, Reid was drawn on to the local political stage the following year, when he was presented to the parish of New Machar by King's College Aberdeen.[7] The issue of who had ultimate control over the appointment of parish ministers in Scotland had become a matter of controversy following the passage of the Act of Patronage of 1712, which restored the right of a patron, rather than the congregation, to install a minister. Initially patrons tended to consult with local presbyteries and parishioners in order to avoid undue conflict, but the right of patrons was insisted on by Robert Walpole's managers of Scotland after 1725, the second Duke of Argyll and

[5] Roger L. Emerson, *Professors, Patronage and Politics: The Aberdeen Universities in the Eighteenth Century*, pp. 45–51; 'Minutes of the Rectorial Elections, Marischal College, 1723–1860', Aberdeen University Library (henceforth AUL), MS M 104, entry for 1 March 1729. The student body at Marischal was divided into four 'nations': Angus, Buchan, Mar and Moray.

[6] Reid, *Correspondence*, p. 325.

[7] In what follows we draw on Andrew L. Drummond and James Bulloch, *The Scottish Church, 1688–1843: The Age of the Moderates*, pp. 38–44.

Argyll's brother the Earl of Ilay. Their uncompromising stance sparked a conflict within the Kirk which led to the secession of the Rev. Ebenezer Erskine and a number of like-minded ministers opposed to patronage, and to numerous disputed clerical appointments across Scotland.

In the north-east, a dispute took place at New Machar in 1728 when John Bisset was succeeded by Thomas Reay, the choice not of the congregation but of the patron, King's College. Having been installed by a 'riding committee', Reay subsequently did little to win over his parishioners and he was dismissed in September 1736 'for immorality and for deserting his charge'.[8] Bisset meanwhile had attacked the right of patrons in two pamphlets and, when Reay left the parish in disgrace, Bisset marshalled opposition to the principle of patronage and to the choice of Reid by King's as Reay's replacement. Even though Reid was militantly opposed by the elders of the parish he was ordained as the new minister in May 1737, largely because he had the backing of prominent members of the local social and political elite, as well as of the Aberdeen Town Council. Bisset and his allies in the Popular Party within the Kirk thus suffered a humiliating defeat in this affair, and Bisset's resentment was such that once Reid began to attend the meetings of the Presbytery of Aberdeen in 1737, Bisset absented himself from them for the rest of his life.[9]

Reid had many responsibilities as a parish minister, ranging from preaching and catechising to enforcing discipline among his flock.[10] From the pulpit, he spoke to his parishioners not only about religious themes but also about social and political issues, including vagrancy, the curbing of immorality and, during the '45, their obligation to remain loyal to the Hanoverian state. Within the parish, he was obliged to deal with practical matters such as the policing of sexuality, as well as the management of the poor. Because of the administrative structure of the Church of Scotland, ministers were involved in the affairs of the Kirk more generally through their presbyteries and synods, and, periodically, the General Assembly. Reid was active in the upper tiers of Kirk government, serving a six-month term as the Moderator of the Presbytery of Aberdeen in 1742–43 and of the Synod of Aberdeen which met in October 1743. In addition, he was sent as a representative to the General Assembly in 1738, 1741, 1743, 1745 and 1747. Meetings of the Presbytery usually dealt with relatively mundane managerial problems like assigning substitute preachers to fill in for sick or absent ministers,

[8] Hew Scott and John Alexander Lamb, *Fasti Ecclesiae Scoticanae: The Succession of Ministers in the Church of Scotland from the Reformation*, vol. VIII, p. 66.

[9] Bisset died in 1756. Our summary of Reid's installation at New Machar is based on the detailed account in Paul Wood, *The Life of Thomas Reid: The Culture of the Mind.*

[10] The following paragraph summarises the extended discussion in Wood, *The Life of Reid.*

whereas the Synod tackled weightier, and occasionally controversial, questions of social and ecclesiastical policy. Reid served on various committees convened by the Synod of Aberdeen, most notably a committee struck in 1749 to consider changes to the Scottish Poor Law. Reid took the lead in drafting a revised set of regulations governing the relief of the poor and the control of vagrants which were favourably received by the Synod, but the proposed reforms were opposed by the landed interest in Aberdeenshire and subsequently shelved as a consequence.[11]

Over the course of the fourteen years Reid attended the meetings of the Synod he was also called upon to intervene in a number of disputed settlements when the skirmishes over church patronage escalated in the 1740s, and he was expected to implement in his parish the directives passed by the Synod, including those to raise funds to support the Aberdeen Infirmary and the work of the Scottish Society for the Promotion of Christian Knowledge (SSPCK) in the Highlands and Islands. The latter initiative, taken in 1748, was especially contentious given that the work of the SSPCK to 'Christianise' the Highlands was intended to consolidate the power of the Hanoverian–Presbyterian nexus in areas of the north and west of Scotland by rooting out the remaining vestiges of Catholicism, Episcopalianism and Jacobitism. In promoting the SSPCK Reid was thus effectively acting as an agent of the British state, and he likewise acted in this capacity when the Synod declared fast days to mark the suppression of the '45. On these occasions Reid celebrated the virtues of the Hanoverian regime, and he had earlier gone so far as to declare a fast day in the parish in December 1745 in order to exhort his parishioners to remain steadfast in their loyalty to King George II, the Whig government in London and the Presbyterian settlement in Scotland. Yet even if Reid could on occasion be a defiantly loyal North Briton, he was nevertheless on reasonably friendly terms with those whose allegiances differed from his own, as can be seen in the fact that he was willing to give overnight shelter at the manse in New Machar to the Jacobite Robert Hepburn of Keith during the '45.[12]

By the time Reid was elected as a regent at King's College Aberdeen on 25 October 1751, he had gained considerable practical experience in the political and social realms through his activities as a parish minister. Unfortunately, there is no record of what he may have read on politics or public policy during his years at New Machar. However, his first graduation oration, delivered in April 1753, tells us that he based his first set of politics lectures on Xenophon, Plato and Aristotle among the ancients, and, among the moderns, Machiavelli, Harrington,

[11] On Reid's involvement in Poor Law reform see also Alexander Gordon to William Grant, 7 February 1750, and Reid to Alexander Gordon, 7 February 1750, in Reid, *Correspondence*, pp. 6–8.

[12] Reid to John Robison, 12 April 1792, in Reid, *Correspondence*, p. 227.

Hume and, especially, Montesquieu.[13] Since it is reasonable to assume that he was introduced to the political writings of Xenophon, Plato, Aristotle, Machiavelli and Harrington in the 1720s, while he was a student at Marischal College, it would seem that he probably first read Hume's *Essays, Moral and Political* (1741–42) and Montesquieu's *L'Esprit des loix* (1748) while he lived in New Machar.[14] Reid may well have revised the scope and contents of his politics course after delivering his first oration, because in the spring and summer of 1753 he spearheaded a complete overhaul of the curriculum at King's.[15] Apart from Reid's first graduation oration, little evidence survives regarding his teaching prior to the reform of the curriculum, so we cannot be certain about the extent to which his politics course changed in the wake of the restructuring of the *cursus philosophicus*. What we do know is that, after 1753, students in their fourth and final year covered 'the Philosophy of the Human Mind and the Sciences that depend upon it', including 'Logic, Rhetoric, The Laws of Nature and Nations, Politicks, Oeconomicks, the fine Arts and natural Religion'.[16] In this connection it should be noticed that Reid emphasised the coherence of all branches of philosophy, which was one of his premises for retaining the unitary regenting curriculum; he argued that the feature which made intellectual endeavours into philosophical disciplines, or 'sciences', was a self-conscious dependence upon a common set of 'axioms or common notions' in argumentation, and by this criterion politics was a 'science', he said.[17]

As a regent, Reid taught the whole of the three-year philosophy course, which meant that he subsequently lectured on politics on only three occasions, in 1756, 1759 and 1762. However, when switching to Glasgow's specialist professorship in moral philosophy in 1764, he clearly continued where he had left off in Aberdeen. In the more extensive treatment of politics required in his new position, Reid not only developed the substantive themes represented by his earlier reading and teaching, he also set out his 'axiomatic' approach at the very beginning of these lectures, as we see in the manuscripts printed in Part Two of this volume.

Outside of the classroom, Reid commented on legal, social and economic matters in the Aberdeen Philosophical Society or Wise Club (*fl.* 1758–73), of

[13] Thomas Reid, *Philosophical Orations*, oration I, para. 11; the *Orations* are reproduced in Reid, *University*.

[14] Although it is likely that Reid was introduced to Xenophon by his regent, George Turnbull, a brief set of reading notes from Xenophon's *Oeconomicus* dating from September 1750 survives; see AUL, MS 2131/3/II/4. Presumably by April 1753 Reid had also read Hume's recently published *Political Discourses* (1752).

[15] On these reforms see Wood, *The Aberdeen Enlightenment*, ch. 3.

[16] Anon., *Abstract of Some Statutes and Orders of King's College*, [1754]), pp. 13, 19; in Reid, *University*.

[17] See Reid, *Philosophical Orations*, oration II, paras 19–20.

which he was a founder member.[18] The Society is best known as a venue for criticism of the writings of David Hume, thanks to the publications of Reid and his fellow members James Beattie, George Campbell and John Gregory. But the discussions and discourses of the participants in the Wise Club ranged far more widely than is commonly recognised and dealt with topics in literary criticism, rhetoric, the anatomy of human nature, natural history, language, natural philosophy, medicine, morals, mathematics, history, education, politics and political economy.[19] Reid's papers on topical economic and social issues and on the English and Scottish legal systems will be analysed in detail below. Here it should be emphasised that he was not alone in addressing such subjects. During the six years that Reid was active in the Society, Robert Traill discoursed on Jean-Jacques Rousseau's *Discours sur l'origine de l'inégalité* (1755), while members also proposed questions on the origin of civil government, the use of agrarian laws to enlarge the population, the national debt, the utilisation of machines and the price of labour, the apparent conflict between slavery and good government, the Poor Law, the relationship between civil and natural law, the state of the British coinage, justice and the courts, and the advantages and disadvantages of commerce.[20] Many of these questions – and the conversations they prompted – show that Reid and the early members of the Society were committed to effecting social and economic improvement, be it in Scotland or Britain more generally. Moreover, they shared their commitment to the improving ethos with their patrons in the north-east, notably James Ogilvy, Lord Deskford, who was a significant improver in his own right and who did much to promote the advancement of the Scottish economy through his work on the Board of Trustees for Fisheries, Manufactures and Improvements in Scotland and as a Commissioner for the Forfeited Estates. Reid was also a member of the Gordon's Mill Farming Club (1758–64), a grouping which reflected the preoccupation with agricultural improvement of Reid's patron from the 1730s onwards, Archibald Grant of Monymusk.[21] Through his participation in these two clubs, Reid was at the heart of the circle of improvers who sought to transform the economic and social conditions of the north-east of Scotland.

[18] On the Society see H. Lewis Ulman (ed.), *Minutes of the Aberdeen Philosophical Society, 1758–1773*.

[19] See Ulman's editorial introduction to *Minutes of the Aberdeen Philosophical Society*, pp. 59–63, and Paul Wood's entry on the Society in the online edition of the *Oxford Dictionary of National Biography*.

[20] Ulman, *Minutes of the Aberdeen Philosophical Society*, pp. 81, 83, 191–3 (questions 27, 32, 39, 43, 45, 50, 52, 55, 57 and 58).

[21] J. H. Smith, *The Gordon's Mill Farming Club, 1758–1764*.

In 1762 Reid was introduced through Deskford to another prominent Scottish improver, Henry Home, Lord Kames, who soon became Reid's correspondent, friend and patron. Thanks to the combined political clout of Deskford and Kames, Reid succeeded Adam Smith as the Glasgow Professor of Moral Philosophy in 1764, despite the opposition of the Professor of the Practice of Medicine and lecturer on chemistry, Joseph Black, and the Professor of Law, John Millar, who were both close associates of Smith and powerful figures within the College.[22] While maintaining a deferential stance towards his predecessors, Reid's public lectures on moral philosophy differed significantly in terms of content, balance and overall structure from those given by Francis Hutcheson and Smith.[23] Whereas Smith followed the precedent set by previous occupants of the Glasgow chair and covered natural theology, ethics, natural jurisprudence and politics in his course, Reid restructured the moral philosophy curriculum. He adopted a tripartite division in his lectures, which were now organised under the heads of pneumatology, ethics and politics, and spent the bulk of his classroom time anatomising the intellectual and active powers of the human mind.[24] Having dealt with the science of the mind and, briefly, natural theology, he turned to what he called 'speculative' and 'practical' ethics, before concluding with lectures on politics, which he likewise divided into two parts. The first focused on 'the various Forms of Government their Causes & Effects', while the second was devoted to 'Police', which he defined as 'those Regulations which are common to Different forms of Government for Promoting Religion Virtue Education, Arts & Sciences Agriculture Trade Manufactures & for Regulating the Arms and Finances of the State and other Objects of that kind which are not essential to the being of a State or Government but conducive to its well being and Security'.[25]

Reid delivered this course of lectures until he retired from teaching and left the course to his assistant and former student, Archibald Arthur, in 1780. However, nearly all of Reid's lecture notes that have survived from the course stem from his first two years in Glasgow, and it is mainly on this basis that we have made our reconstruction. Despite their often fragmentary character as preserved, the lectures are of central importance for our understanding of Reid as a thinker

[22] For the details of Reid's election to the Glasgow chair see Paul Wood, '"The Fittest Man in the Kingdom": Thomas Reid and the Glasgow Chair of Moral Philosophy', pp. 289–91.

[23] In his first lecture at Glasgow Reid paid fulsome tribute to Smith and praised Francis Hutcheson. He also said to his students: 'I shall be much obliged to any of you Gentlemen or to any other, who can furnish me with Notes of his [Smith's] Prelections whether in Morals Jurisprudence, Police or in Rhetorick'; AUL, MS 2131/4/II/9, p. 1 (original pagination).

[24] Wood, '"The Fittest Man in the Kingdom"', pp. 279, 280, 285, 286, 292–93; Reid, *Practical Ethics*, pp. 1–16.

[25] Reid, *Practical Ethics*, pp. 15–16.

and as a central figure in the Scottish Enlightenment. The lectures provide clear evidence for considerable continuity between Reid's earlier political interests while in Aberdeen and the more elaborate standpoints he developed in Glasgow in the second half of his life. At the same time, the lectures demonstrate a clear systematic intent, and they do in fact offer a framework both for his reading and for, so to speak, all the special topics that he dealt with at greater length in the various discourses and other papers that we present in this volume.

The paucity of documentary evidence makes it impossible to reconstruct the precise development of Reid's political and economic ideas while he lived in the north-east of Scotland. We are better able to map the trajectory of his thinking about politics and economics after his move to Glasgow because most of his surviving manuscripts and correspondence date from after 1764. Furthermore, we can also trace at least some of his reading thanks to the preservation of the 'Professors Receipt Books', which list the books borrowed from the university library by each of the Glasgow professors from 1751 to 1789.[26] In general terms, the library records tell us that, of the 615 books (459 titles) Reid took out in the period 1767–89, forty-two (9%) were on history, nineteen (4%) on politics, thirteen (3%) on natural law, seven (2%) on political economy and four (under 1%) on law. These figures roughly correspond to those obtained when we survey the 106 sets of reading notes found among Reid's extant manuscripts. Of these notes, there are four sets (4%) from works on politics, three (3%) from books on history and one each (1%) from writings on natural law and political economy. When compared with his reading in other fields, such as moral philosophy, the natural sciences and mathematics, the numbers for natural law, political economy and law are small. Nevertheless, it is striking that he was better read in politics and history than might otherwise be expected and that his reading of historical works was almost as extensive as that of books on religion or philosophy. Moreover, the chronological pattern of his borrowing is surprising, given that it would be reasonable to assume that the bulk of his reading was prompted by his teaching. In fact, he apparently had little time for reading while he was lecturing, because the majority of the books he borrowed were taken out after he retired from the classroom in the spring of 1780. His borrowings of works on natural law, however, constitute an exception to this pattern, since he borrowed almost all of the natural law books recorded in the 'Professors Receipt Books' before 1780, which suggests that his reading on the subject was primarily related to his teaching. This

[26] 'Professors Receipt Book, 1770–[1789]', Glasgow University Library (henceforth GUL), Spec. Coll. MS Lib. (uncatalogued). For a preliminary survey of Reid's reading see Paul Wood, 'A Virtuoso Reader: Thomas Reid and the Practices of Reading in Eighteenth-Century Scotland'. We draw on this study in what follows.

is consonant with the impression that natural law was a subject that Reid first took a serious interest in when he had to meet the requirements of the Glasgow chair.[27]

The sets of reading notes published in Part One of the present volume well illustrate the range of texts on history, politics and political economy that Reid consulted in Glasgow, as well as the issues that preoccupied him when thinking about these topics. For example, his notes from the founding charter of Pennsylvania and William Penn's pamphlet *The Frame of the Government of the Province of Pennsilvania in America* (1682) dating from 1768 register his view of the growing tensions between Britain and its American colonies precipitated by the Sugar and Stamp Acts of 1764 and 1765. In a letter written to his old friend Andrew Skene in December 1765, Reid commented on the deep division within the merchant community in Glasgow over the hostile American reaction to the Stamp Act but he did not spell out what his own position on the matter was. However, we know from his lectures on practical ethics that he rejected the Lockean premise of the argument that there should be 'no taxation without representation' used by the American colonists to question the legitimacy of the Stamp Act, and his reading notes clearly indicate that he believed both that the British Parliament had authority over the government in Pennsylvania (and, by extension, the other colonies) and that Parliament had a right to levy taxes without consulting the colonists.[28] Otherwise there is surprisingly little evidence regarding Reid's reaction to the unfolding situation in the American colonies, apart from a passing reference to the beneficial effect the repeal of the Stamp Act had on trade in Glasgow and a brief paragraph in a letter to Lord Kames dating from the end of February 1778 in which Reid was critical of the conciliatory stance towards the colonists adopted by Lord North in a speech to Parliament earlier that month.[29]

Reid's remarks suggest that his response to the American Revolution was the same as that of his friends among the Moderates in the Church of Scotland such as Alexander Gerard, who, in a published Fast Day sermon delivered on 26 February 1778, defended 'the generous spirit of British liberty' against those who had used the slogan 'no taxation without representation' in order to foment rebellion in

[27] Cf. Reid, *Practical Ethics*, pp. xxxii–xxxiii. One natural law text that Reid borrowed on a number of occasions and in various editions in the late 1760s and through the 1770s was Hugo Grotius's *De jure belli ac pacis libri tres* (1625).

[28] See Reid to Andrew Skene, 30 December 1765, in Reid, *Correspondence*, p. 46; Reid, *Practical Ethics*, pp. lxxiii, 158–59, 302–3, n24; see below, pp. 3–5.

[29] Reid to David Skene, 25 February 1767, and Reid to Lord Kames, 27 February 1778, in Reid, *Correspondence*, pp. 57, 98 and 291 n. We also know that he intended to read, or perhaps had read, William Barron's *History of the Colonization of the Free States of Antiquity, applied to the Present Contest between Great Britain and her American Colonies* (1777); for evidence, see our textual note to AUL, MS 2131/4/III/13 below, pp. 221–22.

the American colonies. In his sermon Gerard argued that the colonists' objection to the taxes levied by the British government was misplaced because 'taxes are encroachments upon liberty, not by their being imposed upon persons without their own consent, but only … when they are excessive, or when they are grossly unequal, or when there is no security against their becoming such', and in doing so he echoed the point Reid insisted on in his lectures on practical ethics.[30] Moreover, Reid's opposition to the American cause also meant that he was at loggerheads with local evangelical clergymen affiliated to the Popular Party. The evangelicals were bitterly opposed to the policies and politics of the Moderates, with the Popular Party being a powerful force in Glasgow and the west of Scotland for much of the eighteenth century.[31] Leading figures among the 'high flyers' in the Glasgow area, such as the Rev. William Thom of Govan, urged their parishioners to support the American colonists, with Thom being a particular thorn in the side of Reid and his fellow professors because of his attacks on the teaching and curriculum at Glasgow University published in the 1760s.[32] Responses to the American conflict were thus interwoven not only with differences of political principle but also with the divisive ecclesiastical politics which plagued the Kirk throughout the middle decades of the eighteenth century.

Reid's reading notes on Penn's pamphlet also register his fascination with Harringtonian republicanism and with Montesquieu's tripartite classification of the different forms of government.[33] Moreover, Montesquieu's admiration for the British constitution informed Reid's own understanding of the superiority

[30] Alexander Gerard, *Liberty the Cloke of Maliciousness, both in the American Rebellion and in the Manners of the Times* (1778), pp. 10, 13. The response of the Moderates to the American conflict is discussed in Richard B. Sher, *Church and University in the Scottish Enlightenment: The Moderate Literati of Edinburgh*, pp. 262–76.

[31] Reid had little time for the brand of Calvinism championed by the Popular Party. Writing to Andrew Skene, Reid said that 'the common people here [i.e. in Glasgow] have a gloom in their countenance which I am at a loss whether to ascribe to their religion or to the Air and Climate'. He added: 'there is certainly more of religion amon‹g› the common people in this town than in Aberdeen and although it has a gloomy Ent‹h›usiastical Cast, yet I think it makes them tame & sober'; Reid to Skene, 14 November 1764, in Reid, *Correspondence*, p. 38.

[32] On the Popular Party's support for the American colonists see Robert Kent Donovan, 'The Popular Party of the Church of Scotland and the American Revolution', and Jonathan M. Yeager, *Enlightened Evangelicalism: The Life and Thought of John Erskine*, ch. 7. For the Rev. William Thom, see Robert Kent Donovan, 'Evangelical Civic Humanism in Glasgow: The American War Sermons of William Thom', and Richard B. Sher, 'Commerce, Religion and the Enlightenment in Eighteenth-Century Glasgow', pp. 342–45.

[33] Reid's study of various republican governments (as well as his obsessive eye for detail) is in evidence in his brief, undated set of notes from Gasparo Contareni's *De magistratibus & republica Venetorum libri quinque* (1592); see below, p. 19.

of the British political system, as can be seen in Reid's lectures on politics.[34] Reid's conviction that Britain was the only nation to enjoy true liberty meant that he was especially receptive to the message of another continental admirer of the British constitution, the Genevan politician and theorist Jean Louis De Lolme, whose analysis of the balanced structure of the English system followed that of Montesquieu. The three sets of notes from De Lolme's *The Constitution of England* (1775) transcribed in Part One show that Reid studied closely De Lolme's explanation of how the constitutional checks and balances between the interests of the crown, the nobility and the people served as the ground for English liberty, as well as De Lolme's specific historical claim that the introduction of the feudal system by William the Conqueror eventually led to the emergence of political liberty in England because feudalism united the nobles and people against the King.[35] Other delineations of the feudal system appear among Reid's reading notes, most notably the accounts of feudalism found in George Lyttelton's *The History of the Life of King Henry the Second* (1767–71) and William Robertson's *The History of the Reign of the Emperor Charles V* (1769). Around the time that Reid took his notes from Lyttelton and Robertson in the late summer of 1769, he was also reading a number of works dealing with British history, including Hume's *History of England*, Robertson's *History of Scotland*, and *A General History of England* (1747–55) written by the nonjuror and Jacobite Thomas Carte. Why he was doing so remains unclear. But it is significant that he was immersing himself in some of the key texts in the emerging genre of philosophical history, and his study of these historians strongly suggests that he shared their interests.[36] Moreover, his engagement with history points to the fact that his anatomy of the mind was firmly grounded on an empirical foundation derived from his extensive reading in history, natural history and the literature on travel.[37] The same can also be said of his science of politics.

Reid's reading notes from books on political economy illustrate important facets of his thinking on the subject. First, his notes from Sir James Steuart's *The*

[34] See p. 51, and Reid, *Philosophical Orations*, oration. I, para. 11, where Reid tells his audience that Montesquieu 'is especially worthy of being called a Briton because he has taught us very fortunate people, who are blessed with a political state excelling all other political states, whether revealed by history or painted by the imagination, to know and to appreciate these good things of ours'.

[35] See pp. 16–18. De Lolme's work was first published in French in 1771. The 1775 English edition incorporated various textual changes and three new chapters; see David Lieberman's introduction to Jean Louis De Lolme, *The Constitution of England; or, an Account of the English Government*, p. xx.

[36] On Thomas Carte as a historian see Paul Kléber Monod, 'Thomas Carte, the Druids and British National Identity'. Carte's interest in the development of political institutions, religion, manners and customs was characteristic of the genre of philosophical history.

[37] Wood, 'A Virtuoso Reader', pp. 59, 60.

Principles of Money Applied to the Present State of the Coin of Bengal (1772) reflect his curiosity about coinage, which is first mentioned in a letter to Lord Kames dating from December 1762. Reid there told Kames that he had 'met lately with a manuscript Table of Scotch money, shewing the proportion of a pound scotch to a pound weight of Silver ever since the twelth [*sic*] Century', and suggested that if such a table had not already been published it would be worth doing so 'in the transactions of some of your learned Societies'.[38] In addition Reid investigated the history of English coinage from the time of the Norman Conquest to the reign of Elizabeth I, as can be seen in his notes from Martin Folkes's *A Table of English Silver Coins from the Norman Conquest to the Present Time* (1745).[39] It is also the nature of money that is the subject of the only surviving evidence of Reid's engagement with Smith's *Wealth of Nations*, namely, some brief paraphrases from Smith's discussion of the subject.[40] Thus, although his undated paper on the state of coinage in Britain delivered to the Glasgow Literary Society (to be discussed below) was undoubtedly prompted by the widespread concern in the 1770s with the problem of the shortage and debasement of small copper and silver coin, the paper was also rooted in his long-standing historical interest in such matters.[41]

Secondly, Reid's notes from Steuart's *The Principles of Money* register his high regard for Steuart as a political economist. A few months after the publication in early 1767 of Steuart's magnum opus, *An Inquiry into the Principles of Political Oeconomy*, Reid wrote to David Skene, 'I have gone over Sir James Stewart's great Book of Political Oeconomy, wherein I think there is a great deal of good Materials; carelessly put together indeed; but I think it contains more sound principles concerning Commerce & Police than any book we have yet had'.[42] Beyond this general assessment, we unfortunately do not know the specifics of what Reid made of Steuart's *Inquiry* because either he did not take reading notes when he first encountered the work or his notes have not survived. We therefore have no indication of how Reid viewed the details of Steuart's account of the three primary sectors of the economy (agriculture, trade and manufactures), money,

[38] Reid to Kames, 29 December 1762, in Reid, *Correspondence*, p. 22. Earlier in the month, Reid and his fellow members of the Aberdeen Philosophical Society discussed a question proposed by Thomas Gordon, 'Whether the current coin of the nation ought not to be debased by alloy or raised in its value so as there shall be no profit made by exporting it?'; Ulman, *Minutes of the Aberdeen Philosophical Society*, pp. 112–13, 193.

[39] See p. 20.

[40] See p. 65.

[41] For Reid's paper, see pp. lxxxi–lxxxiv and 96–106.

[42] Reid to David Skene, 14 September 1767, in Reid, *Correspondence*, p. 60.

credit or taxation, even though it is reasonable to assume that Reid took on board some of Steuart's ideas when considering these subjects.

A third point that emerges from Reid's reading notes is his fascination with political arithmetic and the use of quantitative reasoning in economics. As a natural philosopher Reid adopted a rigorously quantitative approach to the study of the material world, and a similar impetus to reduce economic phenomena to 'number, weight, and measure' is in evidence in his writings on political economy.[43] While any discussion of coinage might be said to have an inescapable quantitative dimension, the same does not hold true of the analysis of the economy in much of the literature published in the eighteenth century. Hence Reid's brief note on Ange Goudar's estimate of the physical size and population of France is best seen as symptomatic of his broader interest in the field of political arithmetic, which was defined by Charles Davenant as 'the art of reasoning by figures, upon things relating to government'. According to Davenant, political arithmetic encompassed the study of revenue, trade and population, and these topics, coupled with a quantitative approach to their investigation, figure prominently in Reid's extant writings.[44] For instance, his paper 'Whether By proper Laws the number of Births in every parish might not be doubled, or at least greatly increased?' is a clear example of the genre of political arithmetic, insofar as it takes up the issue of population and utilises the work of Edmond Halley and the Comte de Buffon on bills of mortality in order to calculate the 'normal' rate of population growth.[45] In the lectures on 'oeconomical (household) jurisprudence', Reid sets the population issue in the context of the 'oeconomy of nature' and the discussion of polygamous versus monogamous marriage. Also there, he was interested in

[43] On Reid as a natural philosopher see Paul Wood, 'Thomas Reid and the Culture of Science'; see also Wood's forthcoming edition of Reid's manuscripts on natural philosophy, *Thomas Reid on Mathematics and Natural Philosophy*. One of the earliest exponents of political arithmetic, Sir William Petty, wrote that in studying the economy 'I have taken the course (as a Specimen of the Political Arithmetick I have long aimed at) to express my self in Terms of *Number*, *Weight*, or *Measure*; to use only Arguments of Sense, and to consider only such Causes, as have visible Foundations in Nature'; see Petty's preface to his *Political Arithmetick* (1690) in Petty, *The Economic Writings*, vol. I, p. 244. See also Julian Hoppitt, 'Political Arithmetic in Eighteenth-Century England', and Joanna Innes, *Inferior Politics: Social Problems and Social Policies in Eighteenth-Century Britain*, ch. 4.

[44] Charles Davenant, 'Discourses on the Public Revenues, and on the Trade of England', in Davenant, *The Political and Commercial Works* (1771), vol. I, p. 128. Compare with John Arbuthnot, 'An Essay on the Usefulness of Mathematical Learning', in George A. Aitken, *The Life and Works of John Arbuthnot*, pp. 421–22, where Arbuthnot affirms that political arithmetic 'is the true political knowledge' (p. 422).

[45] See pp. 88–92. The use of bills of mortality to calculate population was closely associated with the work of the founders of political arithmetic in seventeenth-century England, John Graunt, Sir William Petty, Gregory King and Edmond Halley.

comparative demographic facts, drawing on Montesquieu, as well as Engelbert Kaempfer's account of Japan.[46]

Reid's interest in the widely debated problem of the national debt also manifests his predilection for quantitative analysis. His surviving lecture notes tell us, for example, that he was familiar with Andrew Hooke's *An Essay on the National Debt, and National Capital*, wherein Hooke proclaimed that 'Political Arithmetic is not barely a speculative Amusement, as 'tis generally esteemed, but, when rightly apply'd, has a better Claim to be rank'd among the Sciences than many other Branches of Literature thus dignify'd', and went so far as to assert that the method he had followed in calculating the size of the national debt in relation to the wealth of the nation was 'perfectly *Newtonian*'.[47] We do not know what Reid made of these claims, but he was evidently impressed enough with the overall argument of Hooke's *Essay* to recommend it to his students. Reid also read two subsequent and highly important exercises in political arithmetic by Richard Price dealing with the national debt and related issues, *Observations on Reversionary Payments* (1771) and *An Appeal to the Public, on the Subject of the National Debt* (1772). Writing to Price in 1772 or 1773, Reid said that the *Observations* was 'a Work … I value highly' and noted that 'I have not yet had leisure to examine your Sentiments upon the National Debt, with the Attention I would wish'. Nevertheless, the latter book prompted the comment that the British government 'may receive great aid in the Matter from those who have entered most deeply into the Science of Numbers' and he observed that 'it is much to the Honour of Science, & ought to draw more Respect to it than it commonly meets with in this Age of Dissipation that even the most abstract parts of it are found of so great utility in the affairs of Life'.[48] Reid's comments give us some sense of why he regarded political arithmetic as a valuable branch of the science of politics, namely because it provided the kind of quantitative and hence objective factual knowledge that could be used as the basis for the formulation of sound economic and social policies. And in thinking this, Reid gave expression to the 'quantifying spirit' that gave rise to the increasing use of mathematical methods

[46] See Reid, *Practical Ethics*, Sections VI and XIV, especially pp. 69 and 116–26 and the references in notes 11–12, p. 270. For the demographic details, see p. 125; cf. Montesquieu, *The Spirit of the Laws* (1748), book XVI, ch. 4, and Engelbert Kaempfer, *Histoire naturelle, civile, et ecclesiastique du Japon* (1732), vol. I, p. 308. See also the further discussion below, pp. lxix–lxxvii.

[47] For the reference to Hooke, see p. 62; Andrew Hooke, *An Essay on the National Debt, and National Capital: Or, the Account Truly Stated, Debtor and Creditor* (1751), pp. viii (of the Preface), and p. 52.

[48] Reid to Price, [1772/73], in Reid, *Correspondence*, pp. 63–64.

in order to understand and control the economy and society more generally during the Enlightenment.[49]

Like King's and Marischal, the College in Glasgow boasted a professorial club, the Glasgow Literary Society, founded in January 1752. Following Reid's move to Glasgow in the summer of 1764, he was elected as a member of the Literary Society on 9 November, having been nominated at the first meeting of the session the previous week.[50] Whereas the Wise Club was made up of a relatively homogeneous and harmonious group of men linked to Lord Deskford, the Literary Society was a far more volatile body, whose members were divided by university politics and the politics of the nation at large.[51] Given that Reid was a leading figure in the College faction opposed to the policies of the Principal, William Leechman, he was inevitably drawn into conflict with some of his fellow members of the Society, most notably in the 1770s, when the faculty was at war over the issue of the administration of the University accounts. The minutes of the Society are missing for the period February 1773 to November 1776, which suggests that meetings were either suspended or especially fractious, and there were further skirmishes in late December 1778 and early January 1779, when a heated dispute arose over whether to adjourn the Society over the New Year period. Reid and three of his colleagues formally dissented from the majority decision to do so, and they met independently on 1 January 1779 to hear a paper by the College librarian (and later Reid's assistant and successor), Archibald Arthur, on 'the dispersion at Babel'. At the following meeting, on 8 January, involving the whole of the group, there was a disagreement over who should take the chair as president, with Arthur squaring off against the Humanist William Richardson over who should do so. After a lengthy and acrimonious intervention by the Professor of Natural Philosophy, John Anderson, who was allied with both Reid and Arthur, the meeting finally proceeded and there were no serious disruptions within the Society from then onwards.[52] Moreover, despite the fact that Anderson and Reid were close friends until their relationship cooled in the 1780s, they also fell out at the Society, as did Reid and John Millar, who, as mentioned earlier, opposed Reid's appointment to Glasgow and held different philosophical views,

[49] Reid's view of the practical utility of mathematics was much the same as that of his teacher Colin Maclaurin; see Judith V. Grabner, 'Maclaurin and Newton: The Newtonian Style and the Authority of Mathematics'. For the broader European context see especially Frängsmyr et al. (eds), *The Quantifying Spirit in the Eighteenth Century*.

[50] 'Laws of the Literary Society in Glasgow College', GUL, MS Murray 505, p. 16.

[51] On the Glasgow Literary Society and Reid's involvement in it, see Paul Wood, 'Thomas Reid, Natural Philosopher: A Study of Science and Philosophy in the Scottish Enlightenment', pp. 175–87, 385–87; see also Kathleen Holcomb, 'Thomas Reid in the Glasgow Literary Society'.

[52] 'Laws of the Literary Society in Glasgow College', GUL, MS Murray 505, pp. 76–77.

but who was broadly in the same party political camp as Reid.[53] The meetings of the Glasgow Literary Society were thus highly politicised and often contentious, unlike those of the Wise Club, and there was far less consensus among the members about the social, political and economic topics that Reid addressed in his contributions to the Society.

In the years immediately after Reid's retirement from teaching in 1780, his energies were largely taken up with the composition of his two volumes of *Essays*. Nevertheless, we know from the Professors Receipt Books that he read more widely than he was previously able to do and his borrowings increased through the 1780s over what they had been in the previous decade, to reach a maximum of sixty-six titles in 1787.[54] In the years 1780–89, he borrowed some fifteen books on history, nine on politics and three each on political economy and law.[55] The history titles are drawn from a mix of genres, although he continued to be interested in philosophical history and took out works by his Glasgow colleague John Millar, Voltaire, Adam Ferguson and Gilbert Stuart. His reading in politics was decidedly Whiggish in orientation, for it included a striking number of works on republicanism, *An Essay on the Right of Property in Land* (1781) by his former student and successor as regent at King's William Ogilvie, the collected political works of Andrew Fletcher of Saltoun and Francis Blackburne's *Memoirs of Thomas Hollis, Esq.* (1780).[56] His correspondence also tells us that in 1793 he read Mary Wollstonecraft's *A Vindication of the Rights of Women* (1792), which he recommended to Dugald Stewart with the comment, 'I think a Professor of Morals may find some things worthy of his attention, mixed, perhaps, with other things which he may not approve of'.[57] Of the trio of books on political economy, two were notable works by Scots, *An Historical and Chronological Deduction of the Origin of Commerce* (1764), by the Aberdeen-born Adam Anderson, and John Campbell's *Political Survey of Britain* (1774), while the books on law were a miscellany that included Gabriel Bonnot de Mably's *Le Droit public de l'Europe, fondé sur les traités* (1746).

[53] For an example of a heated exchange between Reid and Anderson, see Wood, 'A Virtuoso Reader', pp. 47–48. On Millar's likely opposition to Reid's appointment, see Paul Wood, '"The fittest Man in the Kingdom"', p. 291. On the philosophical differences, see Knud Haakonssen, *Natural Law and Moral Philosophy*, pp. 180–81. On the Society disputes between Reid and Millar, see John Craig, 'Account of the Life and Writings of John Millar, Esq.', in John Millar, *The Origin and Distinction of Ranks: Or, an Inquiry into the Circumstances which Give Rise to Influence and Authority, in the Different Members of Society* (1806), pp. lxi–lxii.

[54] Wood, 'A Virtuoso Reader', p. 55.

[55] 'Professors Receipt Book, 1770–[1789]'.

[56] See also Reid to William Ogilvie, 7 April 1789, in Reid, *Correspondence*, p. 204.

[57] Reid to Stewart, 21 January 1793, in Reid, *Correspondence*, pp. 231–32.

Following his retirement from the classroom, Reid was heavily involved in various local philanthropic enterprises. In the summer of 1786, for example, he helped to manage subscriptions collected at Glasgow's Tontine coffee house for a proposed monument to honour the Dissenter and noted prison reformer John Howard. Reid himself contributed two guineas to the fund (which was one of the largest amounts subscribed in Glasgow), but the scheme proved to be an abortive one because Howard personally intervened to put a stop to it.[58] Significantly, one of the other subscribers who also contributed two guineas was David Dale, the Glasgow merchant and founder of New Lanark (1784), who was active in some of the other philanthropic projects that Reid participated in.[59] The following year, Reid was appointed to the managing committee of the charity that promoted the construction of the Royal Infirmary, which gained its royal charter in December 1791 and eventually opened its doors to the sick poor in 1794. Reid served the Infirmary in a number of different official roles; he personally donated £100 to the institution and visited the wards, where he also gave small amounts of money to needy patients.[60] In promoting the Royal Infirmary Reid worked closely with his University colleague, the Professor of Logic and Rhetoric George Jardine, and, periodically, with Dale, who, like Reid, supported the Infirmary from the outset.[61] In 1790, Reid was a founding member and the first President of the Glasgow Society of the Sons of Ministers of the Church of Scotland, a body intended to provide financial relief to the sons of clergymen in need.[62] And in the same year a Humane Society was established in Glasgow for the treatment of those 'drowned, or otherwise suffocated'. Both Reid and Dale were involved in the Society, as was their mutual friend, the University Lecturer on Materia Medica and later Chemistry, Dr Robert Cleghorn. Reid was, for a time, one of the Directors.[63]

At the national level, Reid was a supporter of the campaign to abolish slavery. Reid affirmed in his Glasgow lectures on practical ethics the principle that there is a 'Natural Equality of Men' and that 'None ‹are› naturally born to be

[58] Reid to the Committee of the Subscribers to the Design of Erecting a Statue to Mr Howard, 28 August 1786, in Reid, *Correspondence*, pp. 186–87 and 304n.

[59] On Dale and New Lanark, see Ian Donnachie and George Hewitt, *Historic New Lanark: The Dale and Owen Industrial Community since 1785*.

[60] Wood, 'Thomas Reid, Natural Philosopher', pp. 188–89.

[61] On the early history of the Royal Infirmary, see Moses Steven Buchanan, *History of the Glasgow Royal Infirmary, from its Commencement in 1787, to the Present Time* (1832).

[62] Martin J. Clelland, *Historical Sketch of the Glasgow Society of the Sons of Ministers of the Church of Scotland, Instituted Anno 1790*, pp. 31, 99; see also John M'Caul to Thomas Reid, 24 July 1792, in Reid, *Correspondence*, p. 230.

[63] Wood, 'Thomas Reid, Natural Philosopher', p. 188

slaves'.[64] Presumably he had said much the same thing in his lectures at King's College; among the first cohort of students he taught there was the abolitionist the Rev. James Ramsay, who later published *An Essay on the Treatment and Conversion of African Slaves in the British Sugar Colonies* (1784) and various pamphlets related to the anti-slavery campaign. Although no letters between the two apparently survive, we know that they kept in touch, for in 1785 Reid sent Ramsay a presentation copy of his *Essays on the Intellectual Powers of Man*.[65] Reid thus had personal contact with those leading the fight against slavery in England, and there is little doubt that he welcomed the formation of the London Abolition Committee and similar groups elsewhere in 1787 and 1788. The London Committee and its affiliates circulated petitions opposing the slave trade in most major urban centres in Britain, including Glasgow, and duly presented them to Parliament. We do not know if Reid signed the Glasgow petition, but he was a signatory of one forwarded by the University to the Commons in the spring of 1788. He reported to his kinsman Dr James Gregory that 'Our University has sent a petition to the House of Commons, in favour of the African slaves' and expressed the hope that 'yours [i.e. Edinburgh] will not be the last in this humane design; and that the Clergy of Scotland will likewise join in it'.[66] Even though there was widespread popular support for the abolitionists' cause, William Wilberforce's efforts in the House of Commons to pass legislation banning the slave trade failed in 1789, and, despite attempts to revive the legislation in the years that followed, it was not until 1807 that slavery was finally outlawed. Nevertheless, Reid and his colleagues at the University of Glasgow continued to back abolitionism by awarding Wilberforce an honorary LLD in 1791 and again petitioning Parliament in 1792 to legislate against slavery.[67]

When writing to James Gregory about the anti-slavery initiatives in Scotland in 1788, Reid quipped that 'I comfort my grey hairs with the thoughts that the world is growing better, having long resolved to resist the common sentiment of old age, that it is always growing worse'.[68] His optimism was soon to be sorely tested by the onset of the French Revolution. Reid was closely connected personally

[64] Reid, *Practical Ethics*, p. 46. Reid deals at some length with slavery as an issue in moral and legal theory in the lectures on 'domestic oeconomy'; see Reid, *Practical Ethics*, pp. 71 and 132–35, and, for the intellectual context, the notes pp. 241–43 and 275–77.

[65] Reid to John Bell, 27 June 1785, in Reid, *Correspondence*, p. 177.

[66] Reid to Gregory, [late February 1788], in Reid, *Correspondence*, p. 197, 307n. At the meeting of the General Assembly of the Church of Scotland held in May 1788, a resolution condemning the slave trade was passed, although the Assembly voted against petitioning Parliament; see the *Scots Magazine* 50 (1788), pp. 305–6.

[67] Wood, 'Thomas Reid, Natural Philosopher', p. 190, and the references cited there.

[68] Reid to Gregory, [late February 1788], in Reid, *Correspondence*, p. 197.

and politically to those who initially welcomed the events of 1789, the most prominent being Richard Price. Reid's correspondence with Price began in the early 1770s and, notwithstanding their differences over the American conflict, the two men clearly had great respect for one another. Reid sent presentation copies of his two *Essays* to Price, while Price reciprocated by sending Reid a copy of his controversial tract, *A Discourse on the Love of Our Country* (1789).[69] Reid would have been sympathetic to Price's comparison between the Glorious Revolution and the events unfolding in France, although he would have rejected the parallel drawn in the *Discourse* between the Revolution of 1688–89 and the American War of Independence.[70] Reid probably also read Edmund Burke's riposte to Price, *Reflections on the Revolution in France* (1790), given that Burke had served a term as Rector at the University of Glasgow from 1783 to 1785 and prior to 1789 had, like Reid, been affiliated to the Foxite Whigs. We have indirect evidence on what he would have made of Burke's *Reflections* in a letter later written by his old Aberdeen friend William Ogilvie to James Mackintosh. Mackintosh's *Vindiciae Gallicae: A Defence of the French Revolution and its English Admirers* (1791) was widely regarded in Whig circles as being one of the most cogent answers to Burke to appear in the heated public debate sparked by the publication of the *Reflections*. Reid apparently regarded the *Vindiciae Gallicae* in this light, for Ogilvie reported to Mackintosh that Reid had read the work and 'was struck with admiration on reading that Essay, and used frequently to speak of it as one of the most ingenious works of the kind that he had ever met with'.[71] In the tumultuous years after 1789, then, Reid remained true to the Whig principles that he shared with Price and Mackintosh and from which Burke had lapsed.

In Glasgow, Reid was known to be one of a phalanx of Foxite Whigs at the University that included his colleagues John Anderson, Robert Cleghorn,

[69] Reid to John Bell, 27 June 1785 and 21 February 1788, in Reid, *Correspondence*, pp. 177, 195; Price to [James Wodrow], 20 January 1790, in Price, *The Correspondence of Richard Price*, vol. III, pp. 269–71. Price also refers favourably to Reid's *An Inquiry into the Human Mind, on the Principles of Common Sense* (1764) and *Essays on the Intellectual Powers of Man* (1785) in the third edition of *A Review of the Principal Questions in Morals* (1787); see Price, *A Review*, pp. 279–82.

[70] Richard Price, *A Discourse on the Love of our Country* (1789), in Price, *Political Writings*, pp. 195–96.

[71] The undated text of Ogilvie's letter to Mackintosh (which Mackintosh apparently received in 1805) is transcribed in *Memoirs of the Life of the Right Honourable Sir James Mackintosh*, vol. I, pp. 380–81. Ogilvie was told about Reid's enthusiasm for the *Vindiciae Gallicae* by Reid's daughter Martha, who cared for her father after the death of her mother in April 1792. Cf. James Mackintosh, *Vindiciae Gallicae. Defence of the French Revolution and its English Admirers, against the Accusations of the Right Hon. Edmund Burke* (1791), in Mackintosh, *Vindiciae Gallicae and other Writings on the French Revolution*; and Knud Haakonssen, *Natural Law and Moral Philosophy*, ch. 8.

George Jardine and John Millar and his son James.[72] All of these men were early supporters of the French Revolution, and they were joined, at least initially, by Reid's assistant, Archibald Arthur.[73] Millar, Jardine and Reid subsequently became members of the Glasgow Friends of Liberty, which met in 1791 to commemorate the storming of the Bastille on 14 July 1789. Reid agreed to act as a steward at their celebratory dinner on the condition that 'no unfavourable Reflection direct or oblique either on the Constitution or present Administration, of Great Britain was to be heard', and his name was used in newspaper announcements of the meeting. As he told an unidentified Catholic correspondent, in doing so he 'meant nothing more, than to own my self not ashamed to be thought a friend to the French Revolution, & thought no Mortal needed to take offence at this'. But such was the temper of the times that he 'received an Anonymous letter in a feigned hand professing friendship, and great Surprize *that my Name should appear at the bottom of an Advertisement calling together a set of political Madmen and Blackguards; and acquainting me that the time is fast approaching when I and some of my brethren will repent the steps we have taken*'.[74] Reid was not intimidated by the threatening letter and attended the meeting which, *inter alia*, toasted the King and royal family of Britain, as well as the French National Assembly, and expressed the hope that 'the free constitution of Great Britain and Ireland flourish and prosper to the latest posterity'.[75] Nor did Reid waver in his support for the Revolution. In 1792 he contributed to a subscription fund launched in Glasgow to support the French National Assembly, much to the horror of James Beattie's friend Robert Arbuthnot, who wrote to Beattie in August 1792, 'Were you not sorry when you heard that your worthy and venerable friend, Dr. Reid, was so weak as to remit money to the National Assembly?'[76] In reply, Beattie commented darkly that 'I am not greatly surprised at what you tell me of our friend at Glasgow. He is very much a man of speculation, and I believe not a little of a republican. In matters of science he is extremely acute, but knows not much of the world; and though well acquainted with man's general nature, sees but a little way into the characters of individuals'. And, after recounting an anecdote to illustrate Reid's obsession with the details of Harrington's *Oceana*, he observed

[72] Bob Harris, *The Scottish People and the French Revolution*, p. 25.

[73] William Richardson, 'An Account of some Particulars in the Life and Character of the Author', in Archibald Arthur, *Discourses on Theological and Literary Subjects* (1803), pp. 512–14. Richardson almost certainly exaggerates the rapidity with which Arthur (and Reid) became disillusioned with the course of the French Revolution.

[74] Reid to ?, [July/August 1791], in Reid, *Correspondence*, p. 224.

[75] See the report of the meeting in the *Edinburgh Evening Courant*, no. 11,415, 16 July 1791.

[76] Henry W. Meikle, *Scotland and the French Revolution*, p. 75, n3; Margaret Forbes, *Beattie and His Friends*, p. 272.

that 'I am told that republican (I should rather say *levelling*) principles are very prevalent in the College of Glasgow'.[77]

By mid-1793 Reid and his colleagues were the target of more than the private criticism of erstwhile friends and associates. In August and September of that year the *Glasgow Courier* printed a series of letters by 'Asmodeus' which attacked the 'democrats' in Glasgow and its University for being sympathetic to the French cause and for espousing republicanism. At one point Asmodeus remarked that 'Beings of my order, Mr. Editor, are incapable of procreating flesh and blood; but were I a mortal and a father, I would certainly prefer finishing my son's education at a brothel, to a school where his political principles were likely to be contaminated', and 'Asmodeus' complained bitterly about 'the glaring impropriety of employing men of Republican principles as teachers in the seminaries of this kingdom'. At the end of the series, Asmodeus cast generalities aside and singled out Millar and Anderson in particular as being guilty of 'impertinence and folly'.[78] It is in this context that Reid's discourse to the Glasgow Literary Society on 28 November 1794, 'Some Thoughts on the Utopian System', must be read.[79] We will be discussing the argument of this discourse below, but we want here briefly to consider the significance of the textual changes made to the paper when it was repackaged for publication in the *Glasgow Courier* on 18 December 1794 under the title 'On the Dangers of Political Innovation', since this sheds further light on the historical circumstances in which Reid's discourse was composed.

According to Henry Meikle, who was unaware of the much larger manuscript from which the published paper was cut, the article constitutes a political volte-face. Reid, Meikle writes, 'bowed to the storm' of the reaction in Britain to the Terror and the increasingly violent course the Revolution in France had taken after the execution of Louis XVI and Marie Antoinette in 1793.[80] Meikle's interpretation is, however, problematic for a number of reasons. First, we cannot be certain about the extent to which Reid was involved in the publication of the article. Both the *Glasgow Courier* and Reid's colleague William Richardson, writing ten years later, maintained that the text was published with Reid's consent. While this may be true, it is also misleading. Insofar as Richardson was not

[77] Beattie to Arbuthnot, [*c.* 10 August 1792], in Beattie, *The Correspondence of James Beattie*, vol. IV, p. 174.

[78] Anon., *Asmodeus; or, Strictures on the Glasgow Democrats. In a Series of Letters, Several of which were Lately Published in the Glasgow Courier* (1793), pp. 3, 4, 24; on p. 24 'Asmodeus' also refers to a number of specific individuals who cannot be readily identified.

[79] 'Minutes of the College Literary Society, 1790–99', GUL, MS Gen. 4, p. 8.

[80] Meikle, *Scotland and the French Revolution*, pp. 155–56.

a member of Reid's immediate political or social circle, there are good grounds to doubt his motives, not least because in making the statement he was attempting to conceal the degree to which Reid and his anointed successor, Archibald Arthur, welcomed the French Revolution in its initial moderate, reformist phase.[81] While it is likely that Reid gave his permission for excerpts from his discourse to appear in print, we simply do not know who was responsible for choosing those excerpts or who gave them their politically charged title. Secondly, as indicated, Meikle did not know of and had not read the whole of Reid's discourse from which the article was excerpted. If he had, he would have seen that the published text was carefully crafted to advance the political agenda of the *Glasgow Courier*. When the *Courier* first appeared, in September 1792, it self-consciously maintained a neutral political stance and included articles sympathetic to reformist causes as well as others critical of such causes, for example calls for the abolition of the slave trade. Yet by late 1792 its political posture had altered dramatically, for the paper was now militantly opposed not only to the French Revolution but also to the reformist politics it had earlier countenanced.[82] Reid's warning in the article against revolutionary action and his remarks on peaceful reform could be seen as signalling a political change of heart, and one that was consistent with the shifting politics of the *Glasgow Courier*. However, when these passages are read in the context of Reid's discourse as a whole, we see that his political principles remained the same until the end of his long life. What had changed were the historical circumstances he was confronted with. We will return to this point below.

2. Reid's Glasgow Lectures on Politics

Reid lectured on politics both in Aberdeen and Glasgow, but the surviving record of his teaching of the subject at King's College is very limited. The main source is the brief discussion in each of the orations that he delivered at the graduation of his class. As we mentioned above, we have evidence of some of his reading, and we can trace elements of his early teaching in the surviving notes from

[81] Richardson, 'An Account', in Arthur, *Discourses*, pp. 514n, 518. Earlier printed versions of the paper do not bear the title given by Richardson: 'Observations on the Danger of Political Innovation, from a Discourse delivered on the 28th November 1794, before the Literary Society in Glasgow College, by Dr. Reid, and published by his consent'. Compare *Glasgow Courier*, 18 December 1794, and [Robert Cleghorn], *Sketch of the Late Thomas Reid, D.D. Professor of Moral Philosophy in the University of Glasgow* (1796), p. 9. As we have seen, Robert Cleghorn was one of Reid's closest political associates; he was also Reid's personal physician during his final illness.

[82] Harris, *Scottish People*, pp. 51–53.

his Glasgow lectures, mainly specific topics and authors but also method of presentation. In his Aberdeen period, he was particularly inclined to arrange his material in sequences of 'principles' or 'axioms', and some of the papers thus arranged are among the notes for his Glasgow lectures.[83] However, while we have such evidence of continuity in the development of Reid's teaching of politics, the bulk of the surviving material and its arrangement stems from his time in Glasgow. What we present in this volume is, therefore, a reconstruction of his teaching in Glasgow, where politics formed part of his course in moral philosophy from when he started lecturing in the academic year 1764–65 until his retirement from the classroom in the early summer of 1780. What we can reconstruct is his initial course, for nearly all the surviving notes are from 1765 and 1766, with only a few later items. If this was a book about Reid, rather than one presenting his own writing, we could have incorporated material from the fairly copious student notes that have survived, some of which stem from later years in his teaching career.[84] However, this would present issues of interpretation and editorial procedure foreign to the Edinburgh Edition of Reid's own work. In effect, then, the lectures in this volume represent Reid's teaching in the first two years of his tenure at Glasgow. They must, therefore, be seen in the context of his overall teaching at the University but, at the same time, they provide a systematic framework both for his reading, the evidence of which we print in Part One, and for the particular topics discussed in the discourses and other essay-style papers that we print in Part Three. It is a remarkable fact that Reid's students had at least some introduction to all the topics that he elaborated in the more advanced papers for his colleagues and peers.[85] The modern reader can now follow the same paths.

The lectures on politics formed the final section of Reid's general course on moral philosophy. As we have explained in greater detail elsewhere, Reid's course

[83] See note 23/11 to the lectures, p. 160, for an explanation of Reid's 'axiomatic' method. For Reid's teaching of politics at Aberdeen, see Wood, *The Aberdeen Enlightenment*, pp. 34–35, 46–47, 66–68.

[84] Of the known surviving sets of student notes from Reid's lectures, those most directly relevant to an understanding of his teaching of politics are:

Robert Jack. 'Dr. Reid's Lectures, 1774–1776', GUL, MSS Gen. 116–18.

George Baird. 'Notes from the Lectures of Dr. Thomas Reid, 1779–1780'. 8 vols. Mitchell Library, Glasgow, MS A104929.

For a complete list of the sets of student lecture notes see Kurtis G. Kitagawa, 'Not Without the Highest Justice: The Origins and Development of Thomas Reid's Political Thought', pp. 378–79. Kitagawa makes extensive use of the student notes.

[85] For some evidence of Reid's student audience, see Haakonssen's Introduction to Reid, *Practical Ethics*, pp. xxvii–xxx.

had three parts: pneumatology, practical ethics and politics.[86] Of these, pneumatology was by far the most extensive, reflecting Reid's primary concern with the philosophy of mind in the widest sense. The final monuments to this part of Reid's teaching endeavour were his *Essays on the Intellectual Powers of Man* (1785) and *Essays on the Active Powers of Man* (1788), which he composed on the basis of his lectures and the papers given to the Aberdeen Philosophical Society and the Glasgow Literary Society. The two other parts he left unpublished, but practical ethics, which was largely a course on natural jurisprudence, has been reconstructed in an earlier volume of the Edinburgh Edition, and politics follows in Part Two of the present volume. Reid's lectures began around 10 October and finished in late May or early June. In 1764–65, the first part, pneumatology, ended around the beginning of March; practical ethics ran until the middle of April; and politics ended the course on 17 May. In later years, he added material and appears not to have completed the course until the beginning of June.[87] In the approximately five weeks available for politics, Reid would have given around twenty-five lectures. In his 'Heads of Lectures on Politicks' at the beginning of the sequence of manuscripts there are in fact twenty-five 'Heads', but the available material does not allow us to infer that he devoted one lecture to each topic.

The 'Heads' show that Reid devised his lectures on politics as a systematic introduction to the subject. The arrangement was very much his own, and there is here a clear difference between politics and natural jurisprudence. The latter was a subject that had become a well-defined academic discipline during the preceding century, and as part of this development it had acquired a rich textbook literature that, so to speak, codified the subject.[88] In his lectures on natural jurisprudence Reid largely followed the pattern that had been laid down by Samuel Pufendorf and adapted by Francis Hutcheson.[89] With politics it was very different. The idea of a 'science of politics' was, of course, a leading topic of debate in the Enlightenment, not least in Scotland once Hume began to publish, and this debate was reflected in many ways also in academic teaching, not least in lectures on natural jurisprudence, as we see also in the case of Reid. However, it would be a long

[86] See Introduction to Reid, *Practical Ethics*, pp. xxx–xxxii and liv–lvi; Wood, '"The Fittest Man in the Kingdom"', pp. 292–93.

[87] For evidence of Reid's teaching schedule, see the Introduction to Reid, *Practical Ethics*, pp. xxvi–xxvii and lxxvii (n195), where the uncertainty concerning the dates is explained.

[88] See Haakonssen, 'Enlightenment and the Ubiquity of Natural Law'; Haakonssen, 'Natural Jurisprudence and the Theory of Justice'; Haakonssen, 'Natural Jurisprudence and the Identity of the Scottish Enlightenment'.

[89] The discovery of this use of the natural law systematic was in fact an important guide to the reconstruction of the lectures in the Edinburgh Edition of *Practical Ethics*.

time before politics acquired a commonly accepted identity so as to become a standardised academic discipline with its own textbooks. Reid was therefore more or less left to his own devices in constructing his course, and his arrangement is best seen as a contribution to the wider debate about the identity of politics as one of the moral sciences.

At the most basic level Reid characterised his subject as both a 'science' and an 'art'. As such, it has to be understood in terms of two fundamental distinctions that he draws repeatedly. One is between 'political jurisprudence' and 'politics'; the other is the subdivision of 'politics' into 'the Constitution of a State' and 'police'.[90] The former distinction may sound very much like modern philosophy's separation of normative and scientific disciplines, but this is deceptive. Political jurisprudence was part of what Reid called 'practical ethics', a discipline that considered agency, or 'praxis', in three different forms, in accordance with the Pufendorfian scheme. The first was the isolated individual in abstraction from social relations, that is, in the 'state of nature'; the second was the person in interaction with others in familial, productive and social life; and the third was the agent in the relations of political life, including the collective agency of political society. In each of these categories agency was analysed in terms of the offices or roles that the acting persons had, where 'office' meant the duties and rights that pertained to a given role, though, in the parlance of the time, the Latin *officium* was often rendered as 'duty'. 'Duty' thus became an ambiguous word, referring both to the wider 'office' and to the particular duties that were part of an office. Accordingly, in one's 'office' as a natural human being one had duties to oneself (self-preservation, self-development, et al.); in the wide variety of social offices (spouse, parent, employer, neighbour, etc.) one had duties to others; and, finally, there were duties within states between rulers and ruled, and externally between states; this was political jurisprudence, which included the law of nations.

The discipline of practical ethics provided a comprehensive catalogue of humanity's many offices and in this way it gave guidance for how we should behave. However, it is misleading to see this as normative in the sense of modern moral philosophy. When Reid deals with moral obligation, it is as part of his 'theory of the mind'; that is, it is an explanation of how the human mind functions when it binds the person to be obliged, and it is therefore more like what today is called moral psychology. But the duties of our offices that make up practical ethics are not derived from one or more prescriptive rules or laws of ethics, such as a Kantian imperative or a utilitarian maximisation calculus. Reid himself characterised practical ethics as a classificatory discipline that mapped the offices

[90] For the subdivision of 'politics', see pp. 22, 25–26, 54–55.

of life, and the aim was to do this so that people could understand their roles and by understanding them perform them. This applied also to politics:

> What more can be desired in order to the greatest happiness of Society, than that its Members, in their several Departments, should go on to old Age in the Way they ought to go? … The Materials [i.e. the Members] of the Political Fabrick must be formed to fit the places for which they are destined.[91]

In other words, there was an underlying assumption of the objective rightness of the duties of our offices. The closest we come to an analogy with a meta-ethical argument in the modern sense is that the objective system of the moral world is providentially arranged just like the objective structure of the physical world.[92] In that sense one can say that our duties and rights are derived from the overall happiness or goodness that is the ultimate goal of the Creation.

It was political jurisprudence as part of practical ethics in this meaning that formed the defining *contrast* to the art or science of politics in Reid's thought. Basically politics had as its object the provision of the means for the fulfilment of the duties specified in political jurisprudence. Considered as a science, politics made this provision by explaining the institutions that were suited to make different kinds of societies internally and externally secure (i.e. forms of government and the actions of government), and analysing the practical means of making life within such societies as good – 'happy' – for the conduct of human offices as possible (social and political economy). Considered as an art, politics was the actual practice of participating in the political process informed by the science.

With this structure of providing means to presupposed ends, Reid's notion of politics might be considered closer to certain modern forms of normative moral and political reasoning than the prima facie 'normative' discipline of political jurisprudence (and practical ethics in general). However, despite his insistence upon the importance of keeping political jurisprudence and politics apart, he himself described the most important part of political science as the specification of the 'end' of government, namely 'the good and happiness of the Governed'. It is also in these terms that we can make sense of why Reid himself had problems keeping the two disciplines separate in practice, as he indeed acknowledged. In fact, he found it so problematic that he apparently moved material between the two parts of his lectures.

91 See p. 144; and see Reid, *Active Powers*, pp. 281–82.

92 For this common mode of reasoning, see J. B. Schneewind, 'The Divine Corporation and the History of Ethics'.

The source of the problem is that our offices in life often have so many constituent parts that it is difficult to distinguish the offices from the means of fulfilling them. Consequently, the same act of government may be evaluated either in terms of justice or in terms of police: 'The same Question may be considered either in a political or in a Moral Light‹.› Instance Tolleration of those who are not of the established Religion' (26). The example that Reid hints at is that of the Dissenters from the Church of England after the Restoration in 1660, who might be tolerated as a matter of their right to a free conscience, or as a prudent policy to maintain civic peace. Another example of this problem arises over laws that provide for the punishment of children for the crimes of their parents; such laws 'are either unjust, or they are to be considered as acts of police, and not of jurisprudence, and are intended as an expedient to deter parents more effectually from the commission of the crime'.[93] It is especially problematic for Reid's distinction between political jurisprudence and politics that the political means to the fulfilment of our offices may be *constitutive* of a certain office in such a way that they must be presupposed for that office's normative status. Thus, in the case of the 'office' of being a party to a commercial contract, the person concerned needs a proper understanding of the price of the things that are the object of the contract; this requires a measure of value, which entails money or the like; and that again presupposes government policy on monetary matters. In short, Reid is well aware of the difficulties in maintaining a clear distinction between political jurisprudence and politics, and we are going to return to these problems. Nonetheless, his basic intention is clear. Political jurisprudence, as a part of practical ethics, analyses and systematises the common offices of life with their rights and duties, while politics is the science that explains the means to secure the fulfilment of those offices and the art that shows how to implement those means.

Politics itself is divided into constitutional theory, broadly conceived, and the making of policy (social, economic, educational, foreign, military, etc.), which in the language of the time was called 'police'.[94] This division, which is basic to Reid's lectures on politics, is an echo of the traditional Aristotelian distinction between living and living well:

> The chief ends of Political Society Security from forreign Enemies and the maintenance of Peace and justice among the Subjects, these Ends are to be attained by a proper form and Model of Government. But there are also Subordinate ends of Political Society the attainment of which tho not necessary to

[93] Reid, *Active Powers*, p. 71. This remark is made in the context of a different discussion.

[94] We return to the concept of police below, pp. liii–liv.

> the being or continuance of it may yet conduce greately to its well being and Prosperity. The proper means of Promoting these are likewise an object of the Science of Politicks. (55)

Constitutional theory addresses two problems:

> First a Constitution or form of Government being given to point out the Natural Effects and Consequences of that Constitution whether for Instance it will be lasting or of short duration, whether powerfull against forreign Enemies or weak and Easy to be conquered, whether internally quiet and pe‹a›ceable or turbulent and Seditious, whether the Subjects will be oppressed or enjoy the common Rights and Liberties which mankind are entitled to. (54)

What Reid had in mind was an analysis of historically given constitutions, and he covered this topic through an extensive discussion of the British constitution and a less extensive one of the French. But before doing so, he took a different approach to forms of government. Instead of starting from de facto governments, he proposed to ask how government should be formed in order to secure the fundamental ends of political governance:

> The second Problem is‹,› having given the End for which a Constitution of Government is intended‹,› to point out that Constitution or Model of Government which will most effectually promote and secure this end. It is very obvious that the End of Government ought to be the good and happiness of the Governed. And therefore every Form or Model of Government if we judge of it by the moral Standart is to be more or less approved of according as it tends more or less to promote this end. (54–55)

At first sight, this might seem to be an endorsement of an imagined ideal society as the measure of a good constitution. But both the phrase 'most effectually promote' and Reid's actual practice in the lectures show otherwise. The speculative constitution on which he spent the most time and obviously was most taken with was that of James Harrington's Oceana. Yet Harrington's imagined republic was not Reid's morally ideal society. For Oceana was based upon private property in land, which Reid considered to be, in purely moral terms, the main source of corruption in a society. In his view, corruption could be avoided only in the entirely propertyless Utopia of Thomas More. Nevertheless, Reid admired Harrington's Oceana, because it was the means that would 'most effectually promote' the ends of political government, or at least one such aim, namely a certain basic degree of equality among citizens that would come about by the redistribution of land and open rotating access to public offices. How this squares with his endorsement of a Whig idea of the existing British constitution remains to be seen. First we must sort out the idea of political science upon which Reid based his political views. In the lectures, as these have been preserved, this is somewhat sketchily drawn up, but it is possible to suggest the general line of argument.

As we have seen, politics is an explanatory science that inquires, on the one hand, 'what are the Causes that produce such or such Events in Society; or on the other hand what are the Effects and consequences that follow from such or Such Constitutions‹?›' (71–72). As with all systematic thought, according to Reid, such an inquiry must operate with certain basic principles:

> Every Science must be grounded on certain principles & if Politicks can be at all reduced to a Science, as I doubt not but it may, there must be certain first Principles from which all our Reasonings in Politicks are deduced as there are certain first Principles or Axioms in Mathematicks upon which all our Reasonings in Mathematicks are built, and as there are in Morals certain first Principles, as we have had occasion to shew, upon which our Reasoning in the Science of Morals are built. (26–27)

These principles are assumptions about the general features of human nature and human interaction without which it is impossible to recognise life-forms as human. Reid lists a dozen such principles in his lectures, but makes it quite clear that the list is not exhaustive. The principles are common empirical observations about humanity and the field is open to discovery and revision in light of experience. Hence he cannot mean that politics should be an axiomatic *system*, and we must in fact understand the formalistic language of axioms and deductions rather loosely. As Reid says elsewhere, reasoning in politics is probabilistic (and often analogical). What he means by a 'science' of politics is perhaps best shown through his rejection of two imagined objections to such a project. The first objection is to the effect that explanations of human behaviour presuppose a necessary connection between motives and actions, something that Reid, as a libertarian of the will, rejected. He puts this objection aside by suggesting that it is equally destructive for a determinist idea of political science. Since we can never be certain that we know all of the motives for human behaviour, we cannot be certain that we have the right causes to explain the behaviour that we are investigating. Our uncertainty in reasoning about human matters is the same whether we see the uncertainty as metaphysical (i.e., as a matter of the free will) or as epistemic (i.e., as a matter of ignorance about human motivation). As Reid observes: 'the uncertainty of the Event to us will be the same when it proceeds from causes or motives that are unknown as when the motives do not necessarly produce the Action' (28).

However, the issue of freedom versus determinism is in fact irrelevant to the possibility of political science, for this is based upon the above-mentioned common assumptions about how people in general act, not upon causal inferences about individuals and their particular actions. In this way Reid meets the second objection to the possibility of a science of politics, namely that political phenomena are so dependent upon the particular character of political agents that general propositions are impossible. To the contrary, he suggests:

> we may form much more certain conclusions with regard to the conduct of a body of Men united in political Society than with respect to the conduct of an individual.… It is from this Uniformity of Character in a Multitude of Men notwithstanding of the Diversity of the Individuals of which it is composed, that all General Principles in Politicks are derived. (30)

It is not surprising that Reid at the end of these arguments refers to Hume's essay 'That Politics May Be Reduced to a Science'. Evidently they had much the same idea of what such a science should look like, and both set aside the metaphysical issue of determinism or libertarianism as irrelevant in this connection. But despite these notable similarities, the two thinkers drew very different inferences from their political science when it came to the practice of politics. Hume's (considered) political stance has felicitously been characterised as 'sceptical Whiggism',[95] but while Reid certainly was a Whig, his position might better be described as moral Whiggism.

As a science that explains how certain means lead to certain ends, politics is also, as we have mentioned, a practice or an 'art' of how to do things. In keeping with tradition, Reid invokes the analogy between the human and the political body in order to compare politics to medicine:

> Politicks has a like Relation to States & to Government as the Science of Medicine has to the human Body, and the Politician is the State Physician. He knows wherein the Sound & healthfull Constitution of the State consists. When any disorder appears in it he can judge by the Symptoms what is the cause of that disorder and he knows what are the Remedies and can pre‹s›cribe for them with great probability of Success. (26)

In the lectures, Reid gives a sketch of one sound constitution, the imaginary one of Harrington's Oceana, and a health report on actually existing constitutions,

95 See Duncan Forbes, *Hume's Philosophical Politics*, ch. 5.

mainly that of Great Britain, a report that is deeply influenced by Montesquieu and weaves together explanation of function and diagnosis of disorder.[96]

Reid belonged squarely in the tradition of Commonwealthmen that he had first encountered in the classroom of George Turnbull in the 1720s.[97] It is, however, remarkable that he kept this particular republican faith for the duration of his long life. Reid was certainly aware of, and contributed to, the new Scottish discourse on the history and theory of civil society and its development of political economy, just as he took seriously the natural jurisprudence of duties and rights. In the end, however, these lines of thought had to be made compatible with his republican values. This is clearly reflected in his academic tuition, where we find extensive analyses of Harrington. The immediately most striking feature of Reid's lectures on Harrington is his fascination with the baroque labyrinth of rules and regulations in Oceana, and one cannot help but get the feeling that this may have been a pedagogical device for stirring the imagination of his young listeners, to whom the Harringtonian world of rotating offices, balloting and associated ceremonial must have been very odd. However, when read against the background of Reid's ideas on the social formation of character, it seems obvious that he was trying to convey some basic moral and political principles, especially the importance of institutional machinery as the framework for politics, the republican principle of the non-hereditary nature of political authority, the principle of a minimal equality among participants in the political process and – Harrington's most original contribution to political theory, in Reid's opinion – the close link between property and political power. Indeed, for such a government as that of Oceana to last, it would have to make high moral demands:

> Requires the preservation of Morals. the Suppression of Luxury. The inspiring the people with a Spirit of Liberty‹,› of Zeal for the Government‹,› of Moderation in the Use of Riches‹,› of Respect to the Laws & Magistrates. (42)

This point is significant for it also indicates just how qualified Reid's appreciation of Harrington was. Reid did not think that Oceana in fact would meet these demands, and for two reasons. First, he did not think that Harrington had established that there was always a clear connection between property and power, so that curbing the inequality of ownership through an agrarian law might not bring about

[96] There is a heading for More's Utopia in the lectures (p. 43) but no notes have survived. Presumably Reid gave his students a shorter version of the analysis he presented in his Utopia discourse to the Glasgow Literary Society many years later (see pp. 134–54).

[97] See p. xvi above. For the Commonwealth tradition, see the classic treatments in Caroline Robbins, *The Eighteenth-Century Commonwealthman*, and J. G. A. Pocock, *The Machiavellian Moment*, part 3. For the presence of the tradition in Aberdeen, see the references in note 4 above.

the desired reform of political morality. More especially, Harrington had lived too soon to know that there were forms of property other than real estate that were intertwined with politics in ways unimaginable in his time. Reid was, of course, thinking of the moneyed interest that the growth of commercial society had created. Secondly, Reid questioned whether Oceana did enough to provide moral education for its citizens. Implicit in these criticisms is a much more fundamental rejection of Harrington. The old English republican had devised an institutional machinery that took for granted that humanity was morally flawed and had to be contained by rules and regulations that balanced interests. This was precisely what Hume liked about him. In contrast, Reid thought of humanity as morally perfectible and therefore considered political government to be a prime means in the open-ended process of moral training. The implication was that the basis for political legitimacy was morality, not property, and more particularly equal opportunity for moral betterment. This implication was drawn most explicitly in Reid's last political statement, his paper on the Utopian system delivered to the Glasgow Literary Society. But it is also clearly behind the way in which he dealt with Harrington in his lectures in the 1760s. This is not to say that Reid was disingenuous in his praise of Harrington, for the latter's ideas had a pedagogical role:

> If the Oceana of Mr Harrington is considered in itself onely, or if it were once established in a Nation sufficiently enlightned, & not prejudiced against this or in favours of another form of Government. I conceive it to be the best model of Republican Government that has ever been proposed. (43)

The principles of Harrington are excellent, but in reality nations are not enlightened and without parochial prejudices. They need moral education. What is more, actual nations already have a constitution, and here Harrington can be used as a diagnostic tool.

However, Reid's *medico-politicus* needed further tools for his state doctoring. Reid went on to explain the constitutional contrast to Oceana, namely pure monarchy. This was clearly a shorter section in the course of lectures than that devoted to Harrington. It was substantially based upon Montesquieu's account of monarchy, using France as the main historical manifestation of this form of government. In the manner of Montesquieu, Reid explained the importance of rule by means of law and institutions, the symbolic politics in the role of the absolute monarch, the central role of a hereditary nobility in Court culture, the desire for military glory, the emphasis on culture and learning and the lack of emphasis on commerce. However, what interested him most of all was Montesquieu's mode of explaining the differences between the three basic forms of government – republic, monarchy and despotism – in terms of their different 'principles' – respectively, virtue, honour and fear. Reid understood this as an interaction between the principle that dominated in a people and the principle by which government was conducted:

> every Government that is secure and lasting must be in some degree adapted to the principles by which human creatures are commonly influenced in their conduct, so there are some Governments that are more adapted to one principle of human Nature others to another. That Principle which is peculiarly adapted to the Nature of the Government will always be cherished by that ‹government› and the natural tendency of the Government will be to mould Men into that Character and temper which agrees best with the Nature of the Government‹.› On the other hand the More that Principle, that temper and Character prevails which is suited to the Nature of the Government, the more smo‹o›thly & easily will the wheels of Government move. (45–46)

Using this framework derived from Montesquieu, Reid honed his tools for the analysis of Britain that was to come.

Despotism with its 'principle' of fear was easily dismissed for its arbitrariness, lack of institutional structure and dependence upon one person, who was himself at the mercy of the uncontrolled power inherent in the government, a kind of many-layered mutual fear. The 'principle' of republican government, virtue, is stated in terms that clearly foreshadow the paper on the Utopian system, namely the key concepts of liberty and the common good:

> in a Republick the great End of the Government is the common good of the Whole and the Preservation of civil Liberty. That Spirit therefore in the Subjects which is best adapted to this form of Government is the Love ‹of› their Constitution and the love of Liberty and of the Laws‹;› this the true Spirit of a free Government and while this Spirit prevails the Government will be well administ‹e›red and powerfull against its Enemies. &c Sparta. Athens. Rome. (46)

Against the background of these two forms of government and their principles, despotical fear and republican virtue, Reid states his view of monarchy and its guiding principle of honour. It is a remarkable exercise. Reid begins in the mode of Montesquieu by seeing honour as an *Ersatz* morality in the upper social ranks, a replacement of virtue and a moral shallowness that ultimately is self-interested. However, he then broadens his target from honour to politeness. While acknowledging that 'nothing tends more to promote peace harmony and good will in Society than a polite and obliging behaviour in men towards one another', he insists that 'this amiable Quality does not always proceed from the principles of true Virtue & humanity‹;› it is often the offspring of Vanity and the desire of Esteem' (47). It seems that Reid was here criticising something much wider than the morals of the nobility in a monarchy, such as France. It is in fact difficult not to read these remarks as strictures upon the pervasive cultivation of politeness as the preeminent social virtue among the Enlightenment intelligentsia.[98]

Having presented the pure constitutional types with some remarks on their historical approximations, Reid turned to the mixed constitution of Great Britain, which seems to be the topic to which he devoted the most time in the lectures. He gave a detailed factual account of how the main parts of the political system functioned, in which he paid special attention to Scotland. To some extent influenced by Montesquieu's discussion in *L'Esprit des loix* and drawing on his knowledge of British constitutional history, Reid combined different lines of analysis.[99] First, there is the ancient idea of the mixed constitution of King, lords and commons. Secondly, there is the division into separate functions for the three constituent parts of the sovereign power: the judicial, the legislative and the executive. The latter, the functional analysis, was the vehicle for much of the explanation of how institutions functioned, while the former, the mixed constitution, was the framework for considering the political process. In keeping with the terms in which Hume in particular had analysed the British constitution in the wake of the Glorious Revolution, Reid dealt with the balance of powers between Crown and subjects, and with the changing balance among the latter, between nobility and commons as matters of their respective 'interests'. He subscribed to the common view that the interest of the nobility, hence of the House of Lords, was dwindling in importance, so that the real constitutional balancing act was that of the Crown versus the House of Commons. In this, again following a general trend in the debate, Reid saw the growth of commerce and with it the emergence of a new factor, that of the financial sector or the 'moneyed interest', as of great importance.[100] All of this then provided the framework for his analysis of the changing system of parties and factions.

[98] It is not difficult to imagine what Reid thought of Bernard Mandeville's suggestion that 'public virtue' originates in 'private vice', but as a matter of fact he only ever mentions Mandeville once in his published works (*Active Powers*, p. 353) and rarely in the manuscripts. Reid would have appreciated Rousseau's indictment of the shallowness of modern *mores*, but his main interest in Rousseau was elsewhere, as we shall see in our discussion of the paper on the Utopian system (p. xcix).

[99] Montesquieu, *The Spirit of the Laws*, book XI, ch. 6.

[100] In *Active Powers* Reid offered a brief analysis of the desire for money as an 'acquired desire', as distinct from natural desires. He condemned the former as 'not only useless, but hurtful and even disgraceful' (p. 105). However, since he took this desire to be very strictly for money for its own sake, not as a means to anything else, it is not obvious that he intended a total rejection of the capitalist mentality. Contrast Giovanni Grandi, 'Hume and Reid on Political Economy'.

In his discussion of the role of parties, Reid was taking up one of the key factors in English and subsequently British politics of the preceding century, and here his factual analysis shaded over into ideological argument and critique. This was a debate in which sectional interests dogmatically were taken to mean a denial of the public interest, so that parties identified through their interests were seen as 'factions' dangerous to the common weal. This highly loaded language was applied to the binary power situation that was emerging with the diminishing significancc of the Lords. The problem that the political debate had to come to terms with was that the two supposedly contrary interests, that of the 'Court' and that of the 'Country' as represented in the Commons, in fact were intertwined and mutually dependent and were becoming more so for every year of increasing commercial and military ambition. The result was a hybrid government establishment, and this was cultivated and maintained by the party that historically was identified with the cause of the Commons, the Whigs, especially under the leadership of the long-serving first minister, Robert Walpole. One effect of this was a political battle about the identity of Whiggism and about the true interest of 'the Country', in which traditional Commonwealthmen carried the radical flag; another was the alienation from the political mainstream of a fringe of Tories concerned about the erosion of their traditional role of supporting the Crown on the basis of the power of the nobility. In this situation one of the great political operators of the time emerged to prominence, namely Henry St John, Lord Bolingbroke, on whom Reid spent some time in the lectures.

In the 1730s Bolingbroke tried to fuse the more or less radical Whigs and the renegade Tories into a new party based on his idea of the true Country interest,[101] which for him encompassed subscription to the Revolution principles of 1688, ancient constitutionalism, (quasi-Harringtonian) ideals of land ownership and political authority. But, first and foremost, the Country interest was defined by its sharp opposition to the 'Court', that is, the establishment Whigs in government. They were seen to stand for the 'corruption' of British politics by their creation of the new system of deficit financing of large government, including military adventures overseas, the consequent dominance of the 'moneyed interest' and the Crown's control over Parliament through the disposal of offices. Part of this political rhetoric was the opposition between 'party' and 'faction', the former being defined by the pursuit of the 'common good', the latter by that of sectional interests. However, part of Bolingbroke's story was that parties had mostly been transient formations to meet particular political crises, and only factionalism had given them life beyond this. This was the case with the Tory and the Whig parties,

[101] Henry St John, Viscount Bolingbroke, *Dissertation upon Parties* (1734).

which were now irrelevant. The drift of this argument was that a party that had a grip on the truly common good was a party of the whole country and thus not a party, except to the extent that it was resisted by a cabal of 'Court' interests, that is, a faction.

This debate about parties was primarily an English debate. In Scotland it developed somewhat differently and Reid explained this to his students by reference to a pamphlet by the Edinburgh philosopher William Cleghorn (50). Much like Bolingbroke and many others, Cleghorn made the point that a party that has the universal common good of the community as its aim is one to end all parties, and he maintained that the Whigs were precisely such a party. But in Scotland the Jacobites had, of course, retained a continuous influence until the debacle of the insurrection in 1745, and the important party division was therefore Whig versus Jacobite, not Whig versus Tory. This was again closely connected with associations of political and religious 'parties' that were different from those in England. Here the notes indicate that Reid went through all the main groups and their political associations of the seventeenth century, ending by pointing out that since the revolution of 1688, it was 'Torry & Jacobite & High Church' on one side and 'Anticourtier, Whig Revolutioner Low Church or Dissenter' on the other; while in Scotland it was 'Jacobite & Episcopalian' versus 'Revolutioner & Presbyterian', where 'Revolutioner' meant people maintaining the principles of the constitutional settlement after 1688.

Finally, Reid refers to Hume's contribution to this debate (50). Hume had analysed party politics in the *Essays*, especially in 'Of Parties in General', 'Of the Parties of Great Britain', and 'Of the Coalition of Parties'. Here one of Hume's central points was a rejection of Bolingbroke's whole idea of a politics beyond parties. In view of human fallibility, it was an illusion to think of a public interest that could set aside the pursuit of particular interests; the public interest was the balancing of particular interests and it was futile, if not dangerous, to attempt any calibration of the relative worth of the latter. Accordingly, like it or not, parties were for Hume integral to the British political system, and the task of the science of politics was to explain why they came about and how they functioned.

Reid's own attitude to the complicated constitutional situation in Britain is relatively clear from his lecture notes. He agreed with Hume that it was in 'the Nature of the Constitution' that parties arose, and that for two reasons. First, there were people who sought the public interest but they would have different ideas of what it was; secondly, there would be people who would look after themselves by seeking office and benefits from government. These two factors led to the 'Country' and 'Court' parties, by which Reid presumably simply meant governed and government. Parties arising for other reasons were 'accidental', that is to say, they arose due to special historical circumstances. The same applied to alliances between parties, especially between political and religious groups. It is in this connection that he lists all the parties, political and religious, English and Scottish, of the seventeenth and eighteenth centuries: all of these groupings were products of historical accident. In addition to the natural parties of governors and governed, there were factions: 'Jacobites a Faction Revolutioners Not so'. The reason would seem to be that Jacobites rejected the constitution, whereas 'Revolutioners' upheld the principles of the constitution (49–50).

Reid told his students that the British constitution 'is more admirably fitted for preserving the liberty of the Subject than any other form of government that ever existed, or even any model that ever was proposed even the Oceana itself'. It was integral to this liberty that 'there is no Restraint upon a calm and candid Philosophical Discussion of the Principles of our happy Constitution, nor even on pointing out the Defects and weak sides of it that those who have it in their Power may apply the proper Remedies' (51–52).

This was just as well, for the professor was in fact very critical of that constitution. Although he thought that the formation of two parties was a natural effect of the constitution, he clearly saw this as problematic. Keeping the balance of the constitution was, he said, 'a ticklish thing', and what he meant was that the power of the Crown was an unstable factor. It depended upon the personal ability of the King, his longevity, his personal connections to other monarchs, the civil list at his disposal; in short, the reasons traditionally marshalled by British republicans of the Commonwealth tradition. To these considerations Reid added one more: 'The House of Commons may be weakened by the Inequality of the Representative' (49). So already in his lectures in the mid-1760s Reid seems to have expressed himself in favour of electoral reform. In addition to the 'ticklish thing' of maintaining its balance, the constitution fostered a corrupt electoral system due to the influence of the Court – this was standard Commonwealth fare. Last but not least, 'The British Constitution has a tendency to a Corruption of Morals & seems to have no sufficient provision against that'. He details this with an extraordinary indictment of British public culture: the corroding example of Court culture and of political fraud, the proliferation of oaths, 'the Profanation of the Sacrament' by its being made a requirement by the 1673 Test Act for holding public office, the degeneration of free speech to 'Libertinism', the contempt for religion and clergy, the growth of city living, the commercialisation of all aspects of life.[102] How can all of this be checked, he asked? Would proper Church discip-

[102] In keeping with republican tradition, Reid thought of rural life as the best nursery for good morals in the general population. At the same time, he kept a long distance from Rousseau's rejection

line serve like the censorial power of the ancient republics? Could the clergy be trusted with such power in view of the tendency to corruption in both the Church of England and that of Scotland? What he wished was to see rural life encouraged and made free and independent (presumably of remaining feudal restrictions), for that form of life 'tends to preserve the Morals of a People'. Clearly Reid was here combining traditional Commonwealth criticism of commercial society as it was developing in Britain with the moral (and religious) criticism that characterised his consideration of the Utopian system many years later. Just as he rejected the moral standing of politeness, as we have seen, so with modern sociability. Unless these sentiments arose from a sense of duty, they were just emotive states. Or, as he put it when criticising Hume in *Essays on the Active Powers*,

> Good breeding is a very amiable quality; and even if I knew that [a] man had no other motive to it but its pleasure or utility to himself and others, I should like it still, but I would not in that case call it a moral virtue.[103]

Having dealt with constitutional theory and practice in the first part of his lectures on politics, Reid turned in the second part to a wide range of subjects that in the language of the time was called 'police', and which had been thus labelled in the lectures of Reid's predecessor, Adam Smith, as well as by himself once, in the general introduction to the whole of his course on moral philosophy.[104] However, it is worth noting that in the politics lectures themselves Reid never used this or any other unitary title for this part of his course. The topics dealt with were united purely by functional considerations; they were the functions of government that were 'secondary' and 'subordinate' to the 'primary' and 'principal' ends of internal and external security. As we have mentioned, these 'secondary and Subordinate Ends of Political Society are whatever may render the Society more happy and flourishing' (65). It would therefore be a mistake to think that there necessarily is some sort of systematic coherence in the subjects. Reid did not seem to think of them as forming a scientific discipline, and, as he pointed out, 'I cannot pretend to enumerate all these [subordinate ends] far less to insist upon them' (55). We may extend this consideration even further. When Reid had discussed the first three policy areas – population, national virtue and learning – and turned to the areas that his contemporaries (and he on a few

of civilisation; see p. 51.

[103] Reid, *Active Powers*, p. 305.

[104] See Reid, *Practical Ethics*, p. 16, and see also p. 95; Adam Smith, *Lectures on Jurisprudence*, (A) i.3–4 and vi.1–171, (B) 5, 203–307 and 326–33. For an overview of eighteenth-century ideas of 'police', see L. J. Hume, *Bentham and Bureaucracy*, ch. 2.

occasions elsewhere) called political economy, he never gave them such a title. While he clearly thought that national riches, commerce, money, interest, trade, banking, credit et al. were related subjects, we have no solid reason to believe that he saw them as making up a coherent science with a common set of principles. This is not to say that, according to Reid, we could not – or should not – think systematically about each of them in the same way as we could think about any other subject matter. But there is at least no clear evidence to suggest that Reid saw political economy as a particular discipline. In fact, he said, these subjects formed a field that 'is indeed so copious a Subject and has been so little handled in a Systematical way that it is difficult to reduce it in to method'. However, in order 'to prevent Embarrassment', he had at any rate 'endeavoured to give a Distinct notion of what is understood by Riches' (65–66). With this particular subject he did indeed proceed in his quasi-axiomatic manner, which, as we mentioned, seems to have appealed to him mainly in his Aberdeen years. In trying to imagine Reid's perspective on these questions of the coherence of his subject and the way to analyse it, we have to remember that even as Reid began his lectures in Glasgow, it would be two years before the publication of Sir James Steuart's *An Inquiry into the Principles of Political Oeconomy* and eleven years before Smith's *Wealth of Nations*, and while there was plenty of writing on political economy, as Reid was well aware, it is understandable that he was missing something that was 'in a Systematical way'.[105]

The first of Reid's subordinate policy subjects in the lectures, population, was one he had dealt with a few years earlier in a paper to the Aberdeen Wise Club, 'Whether By proper Laws the number of Births in every parish might not be doubled, or at least greatly increased?' This discussion goes far beyond the lecture notes, and we refer to our analysis of the paper and its context in the next section of the Introduction.[106] The second subject, national virtue, was, he said, to be understood in the present context not as a matter of moral perfection and of religion, but as a purely political matter of 'how far Virtue is necessary or conducive towards making men good citizens or good Members of a State' (56). Here Reid returned to Montesquieu's triad of fear in despotism, honour in monarchy, and virtue in republican government, specifying what he himself meant by the last:

[105] Even while singing the praises of Steuart's *Inquiry* a few months after its appearance in 1767, Reid complained of its lack of organisation; see his letter to David Skene, quoted p. xxvii above. Concerning Reid as a pioneer in lecturing on political economy, see Nagao, 'The Political Economy of Thomas Reid', pp. 23ff.

[106] See pp. lxix–lxxvii and Reid's paper on pp. 88–92.

The means of promoting and preserving Virtue in a State

1 Good Education. Publick Schools properly endowed and provided.
2 Execution of the Laws against Vice and Immorality.
3 Zeal & Strictness of Life in the Ministers of Religion & Magistrates
4 Care of the Army and Navy. (57)

In other words, he here dealt with topics that were related to his criticism of contemporary Britain and were later spelled out in his Utopia paper, except that the list includes military training as part of civic education. The martial side of traditional republicanism is otherwise virtually absent from Reid's work.

In the surviving manuscripts, there are no notes on the third topic of Reid's lectures on policy matters, namely learning. He combines it with 'arts' and with 'knowledge', and it is clearly different from 'education'. He also suggests, like Hume, that learning, in contrast to commerce, may be encouraged under monarchical government. So we may guess that he told his students about the civic importance of philosophy, literature and the arts, in the wide meaning of these terms that was common in the eighteenth century.

Turning to Reid's substantial series of lectures on topics in political economy, we note how he compensated for the lack of systematic treatments that he perceived in the existing literature by employing some basic organising principles to create an elementary systematics for his students. He adopted Aristotelian concepts to distinguish: first, between natural and artificial riches; secondly, between natural and artificial 'traffick' (exchange); thirdly, by implication, between natural and artificial markets; and fourthly, between natural and artificial value (59, 66–67, 72, 74). This is the basis for a four-stage theory of the emergence of commerce which he sketched in the lectures and later elaborated in the preamble to his discourse on interest.[107] This extended use of the natural–artificial distinction inevitably reminds the reader of Reid's well-known criticism of Hume's theory of justice as an artificial virtue, a matter we return to shortly.[108] There are in fact connections of interest, for all the distinctions mentioned have reference to the intentionality with which human behaviour is taking place; in the case of economic behaviour, the relevant intentions concern the satisfaction of our desires. Natural riches are the things that the natural world spontaneously provides for the satisfaction of humanity's needs to live and pursue ('increase') its happiness, in other words food, shelter, materials for tools and so on. 'But the far greatest part of what

[107] See pp. 66–67, 117–25. The four-stage structure is more explicit in the lectures, but the discourse adds more detail.

[108] See Reid, *Active Powers*, pp. 301–28.

may be called Riches is produced by human Labour & Industry', in other words by intentional exertions on the materials provided by nature (57). Since humans in general cannot satisfy their own needs individually, exchange ('bargain') of the riches produced by labour is always a feature of human life, and as long as such exchange is for the sake of the person's own needs, it is natural. When the exchange is aimed at using goods as the means of acquiring other goods, then they are 'commodities' and the transaction is 'artificial', that is, 'commerce' (66–67). This leads to Reid's concept of value. If we imagine individuals living in an 'unsocial State' without any exchange with others, then things would have value only in terms of the desires of each individual. This is radically different in all social states, where there is exchange. When the goods being exchanged are considered to be the equivalent of the means of maintaining the labourer who produces such goods, then the value is 'natural' (72–74).[109] Natural value is distinguished from 'market value', which represents yet another shift in intentionality, namely one in which the intentions of those involved interfere with each other, so that the outcome, market value, is divorced from any specific human intention. Market value becomes the price of things, and price is the ever-shifting balance between the desires of buyers and sellers. Reid sees this process of commercialisation of society as happening in four steps:

> The Steps by which Artificial Traffick or the Profession of Merchants is introduced into Society. 1 Labour assorted into particular Trades and Arts which are made distinct Professions. As Shoe makers Weavers Taylors Blacksmiths farmers and the like‹.› The Advantage of this to Society‹.› 2 Markets or Fairs for the Sale of those several Commodities. 3 Merchants who buy at one Market and carry to another‹.› 4 Manufacturers who hire artificers to work for them. The last state most favourable to Commerce‹;› it multiplys professions, makes men more dexterous and Skillful in their several Professions more laborious and produces better commodities. Gives rise to the Invention of Machines, & the multiplication of them by which more work is done with the same Quantity of Labour‹.›[110]

Elsewhere in the lectures, as we have seen, he acknowledged the importance of the emergence of a capitalist class of financiers and investors, the 'moneyed

[109] It is clear that Reid includes in the maintenance of the labourer those who are dependent upon him: family and servants.

[110] See p. 67. In the lecture on price from 25 March 1765, Reid stressed the surplus productivity associated with the first step here, the division of labour; see pp. 70–71.

interest', within commercial society, something that he later spelled out in his paper on interest (128–29).

Reid's stadial account of the development of commerce has some similarities with that of Adam Smith in his lectures at Glasgow and, later, in *The Wealth of Nations* (1776). It was part of what Smith called 'the natural course of things'.[111] Both Reid and Smith formulated their accounts of commerce within the framework provided by one of their main natural law sources, Pufendorf.[112] This is underlined by the fact that they both first dealt with the subject as part of the theory of contract in their lectures on natural jurisprudence and then moved it to their lectures on 'police'.[113] Natural-law theorists analysed social life in general by means of the concept of contracts, and this included economic phenomena. However, early modern natural law was by no means a unitary doctrine, and there were as many ideas of contractualist explanation as of natural law. So although Reid, like many other Enlightenment thinkers, made use of natural law's topics and their systematic arrangement, one cannot infer from this that he shared the philosophical ideas of the natural-law author in question.[114] The stadial theory of commerce is an interesting case in point. For Pufendorf, all social relations were analysed in terms of the fulfilment of obligations to a superior. To show this, he put forward a series of states of nature, ranging from the completely abstract pre-moral and isolated human being whose humanity consisted in nothing more than the capacity for obligation to natural law, through the (also abstract) state of the individual among other individuals, to the pre-civil state and, finally, the state of nature among civil states.[115] These states of nature are not a sequence in either a temporal or a logical sense, but overlapping ways of describing human nature and human relations. The conditions thus described include the pre-civil practice

[111] See Adam Smith, *An Inquiry into the Nature and Causes of the Wealth of Nations* (1776), book III, ch. 1, section 8 (p. 380).

[112] In this connection Reid's other main reference, Hutcheson, plays no obvious role.

[113] In Reid's case, he seems to have moved his actual notes from the natural jurisprudence of contract to the later lectures. See note 69/21, pp. 187–88, for our explanation of this situation. In the case of Smith, the earliest record of his lectures, from around 1753–55, shows that he dealt with value and price in the mode of natural jurisprudence as part of contract, but in the extensive notes of his lectures in 1762–63 and (probably) 1763–64, the economic material that eventually was developed into *The Wealth of Nations*, constituted nearly all of 'police'. see Smith, 'The Anderson Notes', pp. 469–70; Smith, *Lectures on Jurisprudence*, (A) vi.7–171 and (B) 205–70.

[114] See references in note 88 above.

[115] See Haakonssen, 'Natural Law and Personhood: Samuel Pufendorf on Social Explanation'; Fiammetta Palladini, 'Pufendorf Disciple of Hobbes. The Nature of Man and the State of Nature: The Doctrine of *socialitas*'. For some of the several formulations of Pufendorf's complex ideas of the state of nature, see Pufendorf, *The Law of Nature and Nations* (1672), II.1–2 and VII.1.

of being under obligations, to the family, clan or tribal leader. One of the many sources of conflict and, consequently, of the need for obeisance to authority is commercial exchange, and it is due to the inefficiency of the pre-civil authorities that the sovereign political state is necessary in order to secure peace, including commerce. In other words, in Pufendorf's theory the focus is on the creation of political obligation through contract, and to the extent that this is successful, the variety of cultural exertions that humanity is capable of, including commerce, will flourish.[116] The drift of important strands in the Enlightenment's political theory was to intertwine these two lines of argument by setting the contract aside, so that political obligation became a result of the historical development of social, including commercial, relations. The most famous version of this transformation of the natural-law account – specifically of the inversion of Pufendorf's intentions – is the four-stage theory of Adam Smith, which Smith had developed in his lectures at Glasgow during the 1750s and '60s. But neither in this nor in any other regard do we have any hard evidence that Reid had access to notes from his predecessor's lectures, although he had welcomed such information, as we mentioned above.[117] What Reid did have access to was the pioneering formulation of the four socio-economic stages by Lord Kames (Henry Home) in the second edition of his *Essays on the Principles of Morality and Natural Religion* (1758) and, especially, his *Historical Law-Tracts* (1758).[118] More generally this type of analysis was in the air, as we see from John Dalrymple's *General History of Feudal Property in Great Britain* (1757), the (posthumously published) work of Turgot and other French suggestions.[119]

However, these recent and contemporary theories were concerned with the history of property, especially landed property, and how it related to the history

[116] For a different view, see Istvan Hont, *Jealousy of Trade*, ch. 1. On obligation in Pufendorf, see Ian Hunter, *Rival Enlightenments*, pp. 154–63. For passages in Pufendorf that could be used in stadial accounts, see especially Pufendorf, *Law of Nature*, IV.4, V.1 and VII.1.

[117] See p. xxii, note 23, above. Surviving student notes from Smith's lectures were not published until the 1890s; further ones were so in the 1960s. They are now to be found in Smith, *Lectures on Jurisprudence.*

[118] Home, *Essays on the Principles of Morality and Natural Religion* [1751], third edition (1779), pp. 47–48; Home, *Historical Law-Tracts* (1758), pp. 77–80 (note), 92–93 and tract III, *passim.*

[119] John Dalrymple, *An Essay Towards a General History of Feudal Property in Great Britain* (1757), pp. 86–88. In contrast to Kames and Smith, Dalrymple does not mention commerce as a distinct fourth stage.What he has to say about commerce as an activity is to do with the hindrances in feudal law to commerce in land, which is also the main emphasis in Kames' discussion. For Turgot, see the manuscripts translated in Ronald L. Meek (ed.), *Turgot on Progress, Sociology and Economics.* For a comprehensive overview, see Ronald L. Meek, *Social Science and the Ignoble Savage*, chs 3–4.

of political authority. In fact Kames – let alone Dalrymple – did not have a great deal to say about commerce as such. In contrast, Reid's stadial theory had its origins within contract theory, for his focus was on exchange; it is a stadial theory of commerce. Reid's concern was to show that the profound changes in values between societies at different stages were compatible with a basic morality that was universal to humanity, in fact the common moral sense of humanity. The point of his stadial theory was that the universality of morality was underlined by its discernible presence across the deep differences between social stages. We see this dramatically argued in the preamble to his paper on the taking of interest on money, where he insists that the diametrically opposed attitudes to this practice in different stages of the history of social living shows 'no change in mens moral Sentiments in Ancient and in modern times' (125). The implication is that there are basic moral sentiments that remain constant underneath the more superficial sentiments that shift with time and circumstance.

This is the deepest reason for his insistence upon the need for a theory of natural value, despite the problems in such an idea. The natural value of commodities in exchange is 'that which enables those that produce them by their Labour to purchase all the Conveniencies and Accommodations of Life which labourers of that kind are by the Customs & Opinions of the Countrey entitled to' (59). However, this is obviously a standard that varies considerably across time and from society to society, as Reid explains at length. Nevertheless, it is a guide to values that are invariable, namely humanity's sense of injustice. The science of politics and economics will explain how things are valued in given societies, and this will inform our common sense of right and wrong:

> When … we here enquire into the natural Measure of the Price of things in Society it is that we may be able to determine more justly the limits of right and wrong in those Contracts wherein a price or Value is put upon things. It can admit of no doubt, that a Man taking advantage of the Ignorance or Necessity of another may take an unreasonable or exorbitant Price and thereby Injure his Neighbor; even the civil Laws of all Nations suppose this and allow redress for such injuries. But it is impossible to determine when we injure others in this way without knowing upon what principles the Natural and Reasonable Price depends & how it is measured.

It is for this reason that when it comes to the basic economic issues of value and price in commercial society, 'It is difficult … to separate the Provinces of Morals and Politicks' (71–72).

We may further illuminate the relationship between these two 'Provinces' by considering it in light of the later paper on the Utopian system, in which Reid imagined the abolition of private property. This would remove the source of conflicting interests which was the basis for artificial exchange, the commodification of humanity's riches, market value and everything that followed from this. If we place this Utopian economy in the scheme of economic ideas outlined above, we see that it would rest on the natural value of labour and on natural exchange and consequently be stable and open to control by government. As we will explain when analysing Reid's discourse on the Utopian system (xcix), this control would consist of the moral assessment of the contribution of each labourer to the common good. This is the important point for comparison between the economy of Utopia and the market economy of commercial society. The latter cuts the direct link between, on the one hand, intentional behaviour and, on the other, social and economic outcome, typically market price, which is the unintended outcome of the behaviour of individuals acting on their separate intentions. The problem is that such market phenomena as prices are difficult to accommodate within Reid's moral theory. Unless an action sprang from a regard for its inherent moral value and hence was done as a duty, it had no moral value.

This was at the heart of his criticism of Hume, who, in Reid's eyes, had divorced justice from any genuine moral motive. According to Hume, the rules of justice had come about unintentionally and were then maintained for non-moral reasons of expediency that, so Reid believed, Hume mistook for moral reasons – an artificial construct of mere utility. The parallel between justice understood in this way and the economic market would seem to imply that market behaviour and its results would constitute an amoral sphere in human life, an unintended outcome of sundry non-moral motives. However, we do not find that Reid drew this inference. On the one hand, he was clearly unnerved by several aspects of the modern market economy, as can be seen in the strictures upon contemporary Britain that he put forward in his lectures and in his Utopia discourse, where he would indeed draw out the full political consequences of his moral theory, which amounted to the rejection of commercial society. However, as we shall see, this was a purely philosophical thought experiment explicitly abstracted from the political realities of the day. On the other hand, Reid clearly saw the benefits of the emerging capitalist economy and endorsed its main instruments, including paper money, credit, interest and banking, as we see in both the lectures and the discourses. When he did address the question of how the utility of this political economy is related to morals, he dealt with individual intentional actions, namely the taking of interest on money, which he suggested was not injurious in commercial society, in contrast to pre-commercial society. He did not explain whether and how the market could be subject to moral judgement, or whether it was simply a matter of utility and thus, in his eyes, amoral.

However, irrespective of Reid's Utopian moral perspective, his task in the lectures was to explain the principles of the economy as it was, and this would in any case be relevant also for Utopia, for although it had abolished domestic commerce, it would have to take part in external trade in the international marketplace. In fact, much of Reid's account of commerce was concerned with foreign trade, where his mercantilist approach could be taken without regard to his concern about commercial society as a domestic political culture. Reid accordingly gave a general account of the main topics in political economy that followed upon his four-stage explanation of commercial society: price, money, credit, banking and so on. On some of these topics the discourses provide fuller and more detailed ideas, and much of our analysis of them is to be found in the next section. Here we shall note that on the points where we can check, the lectures give evidence of a strong continuity in Reid's economic views. The ideas of riches, money, credit and trade that we find in the paper on credit from the Aberdonian period (1761) are present in the Glasgow lectures. The theory of price that is applied in the paper on the warehousing of grain and in the paper on taking interest on money (both 1778) is clearly and in some respects more systematically outlined in the lectures. As we have seen, in the latter Reid explains the various factors that might influence market price to deviate from the natural price, such as the psychology of market operators (expectations, hopes and fears, etc.), physical facilities (storage), alternative resources, and political interference in the form of taxes and other impositions. Whenever there is 'artificial traffick', fluctuations of market prices will occur, and this necessitates the use of a common and stable measure of value.

In order to serve as a common measure of value for the purpose of facilitating the exchange of goods, a substance has to have some inherent value that is readily recognised. Traditionally gold and silver had been accepted as having such value, owing to their relative scarcity and durability, as well as the value added through the labour of mining and refining them, plus the fact that their quality was ascertainable. When the security of quality is reinforced through stamping and coining, we have money. The implications of this dual view of money as at once the facilitator of the exchange of commodities and itself a commodity of inherent value were drawn out with some force in Reid's lectures. First, the value of money could not be a matter of the caprice of political rulers, whether in the form of legislation fixing the value or in the form of debasement of the coin. Nor could money function properly if its value was not protected against the interference of private individuals (clipping, washing, etc.) and special measures had to be taken to deal with the diminution by wear and tear, which was the subject of one of Reid's papers in the Glasgow Literary Society. In an argument similar to one that was stated in much greater detail by Adam Smith,[120] Reid maintained that money, as itself a commodity among many others and subject to trade, could not be the same as the riches of a nation, as mercantilist theory would have it. Consequently national wealth was not protected by prohibitions on the export of bullion, nor was there any point in trying to keep money in the country by minting it out of base metals that nobody abroad would want.

Reid also told his students not to believe in the quantity theory of money that had recently been stated by, among others, Hume. This was the idea that there is a direct relationship between the quantity of money and the prices of commodities, so that an increase in the supply of money leads to a similar increase in prices. In the very brief surviving lecture notes, the reasons for this rejection are not indicated, but they are in the Aberdonian discussion paper on credit (63–64 and 80–81). There the argument is admittedly not entirely clear because Reid seems to have taken the quantity theory of money to be an implication of the mercantilist equation of wealth and money. Nevertheless, his rejection of this composite idea did fall into two more or less distinct parts: first, the suggestion that wealth – both individual and national – consists of much more than money; and secondly, the suggestion that there are other determinants of price than money, such as (other) commodities that are available for consumption and exchange. In the lectures, the idea of wealth as money and the quantity theory of money are clearly distinguished, so presumably the reason for rejecting the latter remained something like the plurality and complexity of the determinants of price.

The quantity theory of money was associated with critical concern about paper money, or credit, on the part of several of Reid's contemporaries, notably Hume. The core of the concern was that if the quantity of money determined prices and costs, then the growth of the money supply by means of paper credit would drive up price inflation. Reid, however, argued that paper money was simply an extension of metallic money, and since the latter had no direct correlation with price, nor did the former. In this regard the lectures give a briefer version of the argument in the paper on credit.

The remaining topics in Reid's plan of lectures are so briefly indicated in the surviving notes that any attempt at analysis would be purely speculative. What is more, the available discourses and other manuscripts do not provide any clues as to what he may have said in the remainder of his course. Barring new discoveries of manuscripts, we shall never know from his own pen what Reid thought about overseas trade and colonies; army, navy and militia; the raising of public revenue; and associated issues.

[120] Smith, *Lectures on Jurisprudence*, (A) vi.127–71, (B) 244–70; Smith, *Wealth of Nations*, IV.i.

3. Reid's Discourses and Papers on Political Economy, Police and the Law

With the exception of two papers on aspects of the law and one on political theory, Reid's discourses and contributions to the Aberdeen Philosophical Society (Wise Club) and the Glasgow Literary Society all addressed topical social, economic or political questions. Reid's manuscript on paper credit is a case in point. Against the backdrop of continuing anxiety about the level of the national debt and a brief crisis in public finance precipitated by fears of a war with Spain, both John Gregory and David Skene proposed questions on economic matters that were taken up in meetings of the Wise Club in early 1761.[121] Skene's question, 'Whether Paper Credit be beneficial to a Nation or not', was discussed in his absence on 24 February 1761. Because Reid had recently been elected President of the Club, it fell to him to draw up an abstract of the conversation that had taken place.[122] The manuscript transcribed below (79–83) does not appear to be a copy of Reid's abstract, but rather a draft of his contribution to the discussion.[123] Precisely why Skene came up with this question remains something of a mystery. We know from his surviving papers that he was interested in the debate between David Hume and Robert Wallace over the economic benefits of banks and paper credit and it may be that he was also aware of the controversy that occurred in 1759 and 1760 in Ireland over this issue.[124] The republication of an edition of John Law's *Money and Trade Considered: With a Proposal for Supplying the Nation with Money* (1705) by the Foulis Press in 1760 might also have triggered

[121] On the financial crisis of 1761 see Hoppit, 'Financial Crises in Eighteenth-Century England', pp. 45, 48–49. Gregory posed the question, 'What are the Natural Consequences of high national Debt & whether upon the whole it be a benefite to a Nation or not?', which was addressed by the Wise Club on 13 January 1761; see Ulman, *Minutes of the Aberdeen Philosophical Society*, pp. 99, 192.

[122] Ulman, *Minutes of the Aberdeen Philosophical Society*, pp. 99, 100, 192. A similar question had been debated in the Select Society of Edinburgh three times in 1755 and once in 1759: 'Whether the Numbers of Banks now in Scotland be useful to the trade of the Country? And Whether paper credit be advantageous to a nation?' Skene and his fellow members of the Wise Club probably knew about these discussions through Lord Deskford, who became a member of the Select Society in 1755.

[123] Another version of Reid's manuscript in a different hand survives among David Skene's papers. Comparison between the two versions indicates that AUL, MS 2131/2/II/16 is a preliminary draft of a text that Reid most likely read to the Wise Club. See David Skene, 'Notes of Discourses in the Philosophical Society of Aberdeen', AUL, MS 540, fols 28r–29r.

[124] David Skene, 'Extracts from Mr Wallace's Characteristics of the present Political State of Great Britain', in Skene, 'Literary Essays', AUL, MS 475, pp. 89–96; the 'Extracts' are undated. Skene's summary of the views of Hume and Wallace is noticed by Hont, *Jealousy of Trade*, p. 279. Searching Eighteenth Century Collections Online for works published in 1760 using the keyword 'credit' yields a number of Irish pamphlets on the subject of banks and paper credit.

the question.[125] Whatever the motivation, Skene's question prompted Reid to summarise his thoughts regarding the long-standing dispute concerning the use of paper instruments of credit.

Reid's manuscript incorporates a number of ideas that he presumably put forward in his lectures on political economy at King's College and that he subsequently developed in Glasgow. First, the manuscript shows that Reid recognised the important role played by credit in the economies of commercial societies. Social and economic historians have recently begun to explore the ways in which credit functioned during the early modern period.[126] Unfortunately, less attention has been paid to how credit was theorised in the writings of political economists and other commentators in the seventeenth and eighteenth centuries, and it is difficult within the present framework to assess whether or not Reid's analysis of how credit arises in tandem with exchange and facilitates economic growth was in any way distinctive. Earlier authors cited elsewhere by Reid such as Charles Davenant likened credit to a 'huge engine' driving trade and filling the coffers of government with much-needed revenue, while at the same time emphasising the fickle nature of both public and private credit.[127] Reid's remarks in this manuscript register these common perceptions of the centrality and caprice of credit, but he seems to go beyond such standard views in emphasising that credit, like commerce, is a 'necessary Consequence' of the formation of human societies.[128]

Secondly, in acknowledging the pivotal role of credit in our social and economic relations, Reid followed John Law, George Berkeley and Robert Wallace in highlighting the benefits of the circulation of paper instruments of credit, including the use of paper money. Law, for example, had argued for the superiority of paper money over silver coin as a medium of exchange and insisted that economic prosperity in Scotland depended upon the stimulus provided by the utilisation of paper money.[129] Berkeley likewise promoted the advantages to be gained by the employment of paper credit and echoed Law in holding that 'paper hath in many

[125] Philip Gaskell, *A Bibliography of the Foulis Press*, p. 237. The Foulis Press had already published an edition of this title in 1750.

[126] See, for example, Julian Hoppit, 'Attitudes to Credit in Britain, 1680–1790'; Craig Muldrew, *The Economy of Obligation: The Culture of Credit and Social Relations in Early Modern England*; Margot C. Finn, *The Character of Credit: Personal Debt in English Culture, 1740–1914*; Carl Wennerlind, *Casualties of Credit: The English Financial Revolution, 1620–1720*.

[127] Davenant, 'Discourses on the Public Revenues', in Davenant, *The Political and Commercial Works*, vol. I, p. 151; compare Daniel Defoe, *An Essay upon Publick Credit*, third edition (1710), especially p. 6.

[128] See below, especially p. 82.

[129] [John Law], *Money and Trade Considered* (1705), pp. 84–110.

respects the advantage above coin, as being of more dispatch in payments, more easily transferred, preserved, and recovered when lost'.[130] Wallace for his part did not dwell on such practical considerations. Instead, he focused on the benefits to the nation of using paper money and affirmed that 'there is an absolute necessity for Paper-credit' because once 'a spirit of industry is … raised, it may require a larger circulation of specie to support it, than the gold or silver in the country can supply'.[131] In agreeing with Law, Berkeley and Wallace, Reid was implicitly positioning himself in the debate over the merits of paper credit that played out in Scotland following the publication of Hume's *Political Discourses* in 1752. In his essays 'Of Money' and 'Of the Balance of Trade' Hume questioned whether the use of paper credit was as advantageous as its advocates had made out. According to Hume a reliance on paper credit undermines the economic competitiveness of a nation by driving up the cost of provisions and labour, erodes the foundations of the economy by preventing the accumulation of bullion and enslaves a country to the vagaries of public and private credit.[132] Hume's criticisms were subsequently restated in a more polemical form in an anonymous pamphlet published in 1755 variously attributed to Hume's friend Patrick Murray, fifth Lord Elibank, and to another Scot, Alexander Montgomerie, tenth Earl of Eglinton.[133] The author blamed the stagnation of trade and manufactures and the slow pace of agricultural improvement in Scotland on the use of bank notes, which, he said, had 'sunk the intrinsic value of our money, and introduced all the real inconveniencies of plenty of money, without the smallest advantage to any individual but the bankers themselves'. Relying on Hume's 'maxim' that 'the price of labour and commodities is always regulated by the quantity of money circulating in a state', the author contended that paper money had inflated wages and food prices and thereby caused the decline of trade because Scottish goods were too expensive. He concluded that the only Scots who were untouched by the deterioration of the economy were the bankers responsible for issuing the notes, and he therefore called for the regulation of banks and asked 'the landed gentlemen, farmers, and manufacturers' of Scotland to refuse to accept or circulate paper money.[134]

[130] George Berkeley, *The* Querist (1735–37 and 1750), in *The Works of George Berkeley, Bishop of Cloyne*, vol. VI, p. 123 (query 226).

[131] [Robert Wallace], *Characteristics of the Present Political State of Great Britain*, second edition (1758), p. 30.

[132] Hume, *Essays Moral, Political and Literary*, pp. 284–85, 316–20.

[133] Anon., *Essays. I, On the Public Debt. II, On Paper-Money, Banking, &c. III, On Frugality* (1755). Elibank publicly disowned the essays on paper money and frugality in the 'Advertisement' to Murray, *Thoughts on Money, Circulation and Paper Currency* (1758).

[134] Anon., *Essays*, pp. 20, 21, 23, 26.

Reid's reply to the arguments of Hume and his fellow critics of paper credit is the third noteworthy feature of this manuscript. For Reid's defence of paper credit rests on his rejection of what has become known as the quantity theory of money, and this manuscript contains the earliest statement of Reid's objections to one of the 'False Notions concerning Money' that he later attacked in his Glasgow lectures on politics (63–64). The origins of the quantity theory of money can be traced back to the sixteenth-century writings of Jean Bodin and Bernardo Davanzati, but it is more closely associated with the work of Locke, Montesquieu and Hume.[135] Given the pervasive influence of Montesquieu on Reid's political thought, it is not surprising that Reid's formulation of the basic principle of the quantity theory – the 'Maxim' that 'the Money that circulates is the representative of all the Commodities of a Nation and is equal to them in value' – is taken from Montesquieu's *L'Esprit des loix*.[136] Although Reid's initial formulation of the theory was less clear than one could have wanted, his counterargument that there is no strict linear relationship between money and prices is simple and to the point, and his examples also illustrate his view that the wealth of a nation (or an individual) ought not to be equated with the amount of bullion held.[137] And in denying that paper credit functions exactly like specie in raising prices, Reid echoed Wallace's response to Hume that prices rise because of the increase in trade prompted by the circulation of paper money rather than the stimulus of the paper money itself and that the benefits of greater trade outweigh the disadvantage of higher prices.[138]

The fourth and final aspect of Reid's manuscript to be noted is his view on how the 'Spirit of Trade' transforms society.[139] Reid's remarks suggest that he was thinking of this transformation within the framework of a stadial history of society, as this history was being developed on the basis of figures such as Pufendorf and Montesquieu. Moreover, the claim that commerce 'seems to alter the very Nature of right and wrong' (82), as instanced in attitudes towards usury,

[135] For the history of the theory see Hugo Hegeland, *The Quantity Theory of Money: A Critical Study of Its Historical Development and Interpretation and a Restatement*.

[136] See p. 80; compare Montesquieu, *The Spirit of the Laws*, book IV, ch. 22 (p. 399). See also John Locke, *Some Considerations* (1696), in Locke, *Locke on Money*, pp. 264–66, and David Hume, 'Of Money', in Hume, *Essays Moral, Political and Literary*, p. 290.

[137] Below, pp. 80–81. Sir James Steuart likewise rejected the quantity theory of money; see Steuart, *An Inquiry* (1767), vol. I, pp. 394–414, and Skinner, 'Money and Prices: A Critique of the Quantity Theory'. Concerning the problem with Reid's formulation, see note 80/27, p. 190, to the 1761 paper and note 64/2, p. 183, to the lectures.

[138] See p. 81; compare Wallace, *Characteristics*, pp. 29–31. Wallace does not, however, make the point that the creation of paper credit also creates an equivalent level of debt.

[139] See pp. 79–80, 82–83.

is striking, not least because it prefigures the argument of his discourse on usury given to the Glasgow Literary Society in March 1778 (117–34). We will return to both of these issues in greater detail below.

Towards the end of Reid's year-long term as President of the Wise Club, a meeting convened on 24 November 1761 at which the group addressed a question posed by Thomas Gordon, 'Whether Slavery be in all cases inconsistent with good Government?' During the course of the conversation, a further question arose which was reserved for a future gathering, namely 'What are the best expedients for preventing an extravagant rise of servants wages, and for obliging them to bestow their labour, when agriculture and manufactures require it?' This question was subsequently discussed on 12 January 1762, with Reid as the outgoing President asked to draw up an abstract. This abstract was eventually read on 9 February, and the paper was 'appointed to be recorded when he found it convenient'.[140] There is no evidence in the Club's minutes that he ever did so. The manuscript dealing with this question that is transcribed in Part Three (83–86) may be Reid's abstract, but we incline to the view that Reid used the manuscript as the basis for his oral contribution to the discussion that took place at the January meeting.

Part of Gordon's abstract of the conversation prompted by his question on slavery survives. It shows that the members of the Wise Club apparently all agreed that 'slavery is now justly exploded in all European governments', and that they specifically endorsed Montesquieu's condemnation of slavery in *L'Esprit des loix*.[141] But even though slavery had disappeared in Europe, there was still the need for the 'inferior laborious services of society [to] be performed' and this meant that the work previously done by slaves was now done by individuals whose services were secured through 'voluntary contract'. The sense of the meeting was that this situation could be exploited by both labourers and masters, with labour in the mid-eighteenth century holding the upper hand. The view was expressed that 'the servile part are presently the objects of just complaint, having by a certain management got their wages extravagantly augmented, while their petulance & negligence is arrived at a greater height than it was ever known before'.[142] The members noted that there was a shortage of agricultural labour because labourers

[140] Ulman, *Minutes of the Aberdeen Philosophical Society*, pp. 106, 107, 108, 193.

[141] Gordon, 'Questions Discussed by the Aberdeen Philosophical Society', AUL, MS 3107/2/4, p. 119. The meeting did, however, recognise that a form of public servitude would be an appropriate punishment for criminal offences (pp. 119–20), an idea still endorsed thirty years later by Reid in his paper on the Utopian system; see p. 148.

[142] Gordon, 'Questions Discussed by the Aberdeen Philosophical Society', AUL, MS 3107/2/4, f. 121.

were being drawn to the towns by the high wages paid in manufactures, and that the current wage levels in manufacturing were having an adverse effect on commerce because the goods produced were too expensive to compete in markets elsewhere. Consequently, 'most people of public spirit' recognised the need for laws regulating wages, and it was thus felt appropriate that the Club should reflect further on the question that they had been led briefly to consider.[143]

This discussion in the Wise Club points to the serious problems affecting the Scottish economy in the early 1760s. As the members suggested, there was in fact a labour shortage in the agricultural sector, which led not only to wage demands that employers found excessive but also to militancy and occasional violence among farm workers.[144] Wages were also on the rise in manufacturing. At the beginning of the decade there were not enough workers to meet demand and those in work organised themselves into unions to hold out for better wages. As a result, Scottish goods were relatively expensive and hence uncompetitive in overseas markets.[145] Exasperated by the behaviour of the labouring classes, farmers, land owners and manufacturers turned to the law to keep wages in check. In Scotland the Commissioners of Supply (a body made up primarily of Justices of the Peace and men of landed property) had the power to set wages and the duration of contracts, and they were increasingly drawn into the struggle between workers and employers.[146] Moreover, the issue of escalating wage demands attracted attention in the popular press, in part because reports appeared in the *Scots Magazine* and other prints of meetings held by members of the landed interest in Stirlingshire and elsewhere to come up with a set of regulations that would govern the wages of labouring servants throughout Scotland.[147] Nor were Aberdeen and the north-east immune to this contest between labourers and their employers, as can be seen in a memorial prepared in 1762 by the woollen manufacturers of Aberdeen in which they attacked the 'Cabals and Societys' of workers that pushed for unreasonably high wages and whose protection made their members 'lazy and indolent & indifferent about their work'.[148] Reid's manuscript on servants' wages thus needs to be read in the context of the earlier conversation on the topic in the Wise Club, as well as the general economic climate in Scotland *circa* 1760.

143 Gordon, 'Questions Discussed by the Aberdeen Philosophical Society', AUL, MS 3107/2/4, f. 122.

144 Christopher A. Whatley, *Scottish Society, 1707–1830: Beyond Jacobitism, Towards Industrialisation*, pp. 210–11; Malcolm Gray, 'The Social Impact of Agrarian Change in the Rural Lowlands', pp. 57–62.

145 Whatley, *Scottish Society*, pp. 82–85.

146 Whatley, *Scottish Society*, pp. 147, 210–11.

147 *Scots Magazine* 22 (1760), pp. 445, 551, 646; *Edinburgh Magazine* 4 (1760), pp. 441–42.

148 Quoted in Whatley, *Scottish Society*, p. 84.

Reid's analysis rests on two basic principles, one explicitly stated and one assumed but not articulated in the text. The first principle, which he formulates at the outset, is that prices (and hence wages) are a function of supply and demand. Here Reid may be indebted to Pufendorf and other writers in the natural-law tradition. The second principle, which remains unstated, is that the economy needs to be managed by government. There is no suggestion that Reid or any of his colleagues in the Wise Club questioned this assumption, which was a commonplace prior to the publication of Adam Smith's *Wealth of Nations* in 1776. Nor did they apparently have any reservations about recommending that the wages of servants and labourers should ideally be kept low as a matter of sound economic policy or 'police', as opposed, for example, to Hume's position that high wages served as an incentive for the industriousness of workers.[149] As for Reid's analysis itself, his overall argument is largely unremarkable, apart from his suggestion that the army should be disbanded in times of peace so that the soldiers could be employed as servants, and his endorsement of the view previously expressed in the Club that criminals could be punished by being put into servitude.[150]

An engagement with matters of police is also in the foreground of Reid's paper on the question he posed for discussion by the Wise Club, 'Whether by the encouragement of proper laws the number of births in Great Britain might not be nearly doubled, or at least greatly increased?'[151] The manuscript transcribed in Part Three (which Reid prepared for the meeting held on 8 June 1762) is best understood in relation to a number of different but overlapping contexts. The first is the development of political arithmetic during the course of the eighteenth century.[152] As we have noted above, Reid's penchant for quantitative reasoning in the natural sciences manifested itself in his interest in the writings of earlier political arithmeticians such as William Petty, who led the way in attempting to provide reliable numerical estimates of the size of the population of major urban centres such as London on the basis of parish bills of mortality. The ground-breaking work of Petty and his friend John Graunt in turn provided the inspiration for Edmond Halley's influential study of the bills of mortality

[149] Hume, 'Of Commerce', in Hume, *Essays Moral, Political and Literary*, pp. 265–66; A. W. Coats, 'Changing Attitudes to Labour in the Mid-Eighteenth Century', pp. 39–40; M. G. Marshall, 'Scottish Economic Thought and the High Wage Economy: Hume, Smith and McCullogh on Wages and Work Motivation', pp. 312–15; Ann Firth, 'Moral Supervision and Autonomous Social Order: Wages and Consumption in Eighteenth-Century Economic Thought'.

[150] See pp. 85, 86.

[151] Ulman, *Minutes of the Aberdeen Philosophical Society*, pp. 110, 193. Reid's wording of the question in his manuscript differs from that in the minutes of the Society.

[152] The link between political arithmetic and demography is emphasised in Andrea A. Rusnock, 'Biopolitics: Political Arithmetic in the Enlightenment'.

for the city of Breslau (now known as Wrocław), which he used to calculate the life expectancy of different age groups within the population in order to determine prices for life insurance.[153] The researches of Petty, Graunt and Halley subsequently gave rise to the quantitative analyses of the population carried out on the continent by such figures as Leibniz, Johann Peter Süssmilch and Buffon, as well as to Robert Wallace's actuarial scheme for the Fund for the Widows and Children of the Ministers of the Church of Scotland established by an Act of Parliament in 1744 and the Rev. Alexander Webster's Scottish census of 1755.[154] South of the Tweed, political arithmeticians were hampered by the unreliability of the bills of mortality and the repeated failure of efforts to improve the recording of population data.[155] Nevertheless, the debate over the size of the population in England initiated by the clergyman William Brakenridge and carried out in the pages of the *Philosophical Transactions* in the years 1755–57 showed that the research programme initiated by Petty, Graunt and Halley was still ongoing. As a regular reader of the *Philosophical Transactions*, Reid was undoubtedly familiar with the details of this debate.[156]

The second context for Reid's paper is mercantilism. Political arithmeticians were typically motivated to study demography because they shared the mercantilist belief that the wealth and power of a nation rested on a sizeable and growing population. More people meant more hands to work, a larger military and increased government revenues through taxation. Petty, for example, affirmed that 'Fewness of people, is real poverty; and a Nation wherein are Eight Millions of people, are more than twice as rich as the same scope of Land wherein are but

[153] Edmond Halley, 'An Estimate of the Degrees of the Mortality of Mankind, Drawn from the Curious Tables of the Births and Funerals at the City of Breslaw; with an Attempt to Ascertain the Price of Annuities upon Lives' (1693); Halley, 'Some Further Considerations on the Breslaw Bills of Mortality' (1693). On the pioneering work of Petty, Graunt and Halley see, for example, James Bonar, *Theories of Population from Raleigh to Arthur Young*, pp. 67–120; Terence Hutchison, *Before Adam Smith: The Emergence of Political Economy, 1662–1776*, pp. 42–46.

[154] Charles Emil Stangeland, *Pre-Malthusian Doctrines of Population*, pp. 206–9, 213–23; Mary Pickard Winsor, 'Robert Wallace: Predecessor of Malthus and Pioneering Actuary', pp. 215–24; *Scottish Population Statistics: Including Webster's Analysis of Population, 1755*, edited by James Gray Kyd. The Widows' Fund was initially proposed in 1742 and a revised version of the scheme was adopted by the General Assembly of the Church of Scotland in 1743. For the 1744 Act see 17 George II c. 11. On Colin Maclaurin's role in the establishment of the Widows' Fund, see Grabner, 'Maclaurin and Newton', pp. 155–58, and the references cited there.

[155] D. V. Glass, *Numbering the People: The Eighteenth-Century Population Controversy and the Development of Census and Vital Statistics in Britain*, pp. 15–21.

[156] See D. V. Glass, *The Population Controversy*, which reprints the relevant articles from the *Philosophical Transactions* by Brakenridge and his critics.

Four'.[157] Halley likewise believed that a nation should support a large population. He observed that his data showed that a shortage of subsistence limited the number of marriages, which, in turn, lowered the birth rate. He found this aspect of the story told by the bills of mortality especially problematic because he maintained that 'the Strength and Glory of a King' rests on 'the multitude of his Subjects'. Halley therefore suggested that 'Celibacy ought to be discouraged', laws put in place to promote large families and 'effectual Care' taken 'to provide for the Subsistence of the Poor, by finding them Employments, whereby they may earn their Bread, without being chargeable to the Publick'.[158] Similar mercantilist schemes to manage the size of the population were proposed in Britain during the first six decades of the eighteenth century, notably by Josiah Tucker, whose writings Reid read. In *The Elements of Commerce, and Theory of Taxes* (1755), Tucker outlined a system of police which, he argued, would stimulate population growth. First and foremost, Tucker urged the government to pass laws that would encourage marriage across the social ranks. Furthermore, he recommended that legal measures be taken to facilitate the immigration of 'wealthy and industrious Foreigners'. He also thought that laws should be put in place to 'promote Industry and discourage Vice' because for him a greater degree of industriousness and the improvement of morals in society would both contribute to an increase in population. Lastly, he emphasised that his set of recommendations were all interconnected, since they reflected the fact that 'the several Parts of the great Commercial System … mutually support and strengthen each other … inasmuch as populous[n]ess hath a natural Tendency to promote Industry and good morals, – and these in their Turn as naturally create Populousness'.[159]

In Scotland, the mercantilist point that 'every state is rich and powerful, in proportion to the number and industry of its inhabitants' prompted the author of the anonymous *Essays* published in the same year as Tucker's *Elements* to propose an experiment whereby a tax would be levied in Aberdeen and the shire in order to raise a fund of £1500, which would then be used to provide £50 to 'thirty young industrious farmers, or tradesmen, in different parishes' to enable them to marry. If this experiment continued for three years, the author was confident that after twelve years there would be an additional thousand hands available for work in the area, which meant that labour costs would fall and the production of

[157] Sir William Petty, *A Treatise of Taxes & Contributions* (1696), in Petty, *Economic Writings*, vol. I, p. 34.

[158] Halley, 'Some Further Considerations', p. 656.

[159] Josiah Tucker, *The Elements of Commerce, and Theory of Taxes* (1755), pp. 16–40, quotes from pp. 30, 40. On Tucker's *Elements* see George Shelton, *Dean Tucker and Eighteenth-Century Economic and Political Thought*, ch. 6.

commodities would increase. And if the proposal were to be applied throughout Britain, the author predicted that the nation would 'very soon become the richest, happiest, and most powerful state in *Europe*' thanks to the improvements in commerce and manufactures and the greater military might brought about by the 'swarm of people' that 'marriage, under these encouragements, would necessarily produce'.[160]

A third context for Reid's manuscript is Christian apologetics. The interaction of demography and the defence of Christianity can be seen clearly in John Graunt's *Natural and Political Observations ... upon the Bills of Mortality* (1662). In his discussion of the London bills of mortality Graunt addressed the question of how long it would take for the number of inhabitants of London to double, and affirmed that the population would do so in seven or, if there were an outbreak of the plague, eight years. On the basis of this estimate, he inferred that

> According to this proportion, one couple, *viz. Adam* and *Eve*, doubling themselves every 64 years of the 5610 years, which is the *Age* of the World according to the *Scriptures*, shall produce far more People than are now in it. Wherefore the World is not above 100 thousand years older, as some vainly imagine, nor above what the *Scripture* makes it.[161]

A similar defence of the veracity of Scripture based on an estimate of the rate at which the human population grows is to be found in Matthew Hale's *The Primitive Origination of Mankind* (1677). Building on the work of Graunt, Hale contended that notwithstanding a number of significant 'checks' or 'correctives' affecting the size of human populations, the natural rate of population growth was such that the earth would be completely overstocked if the world were truly eternal. Moreover, Hale asserted that both the operation of the 'checks' on population growth and the roughly equal number of males to females found in the human species were evidence of 'the wise Providence of God'.[162] These points were later taken up by John Arbuthnot and William Derham in their highly influential formulations of the argument for design. Arbuthnot's argument rested on two demographic facts. First, he said there was 'an exact Balance ... maintained, between the Numbers of Men and Women'. For him, this was significant because mortality rates for males were greater than those for females. However, having examined the records

[160] Anon., *Essays*, pp. 28–30, quotes from pp. 28, 30.

[161] John Graunt, *Natural and Political Observations ... upon the Bills of Morality* (1662), in Petty, *The Economic Writings of Sir William Petty*, vol. II, p. 388. Graunt's figure for the age of the world was taken from the work of the Dutch scholar Joseph Justus Scaliger.

[162] Sir Matthew Hale, *The Primitive Origination of Mankind, Considered and Examined according to the Light of Nature* (1677), pp. 203–40; for his use of Graunt see pp. 205–6, 213.

of christenings in London he pointed to a second fact, namely that more males were born annually than females. According to Arbuthnot, these facts were clear evidence of the Divine hand at work in human affairs, insofar as God evidently wanted to guarantee an equal number of males and females for the purpose of reproduction. And to reinforce his argument, Arbuthnot invoked the calculus of probabilities to show that the probability of both facts was extremely low, which he took as proof that these two features of human populations were the products of design rather than chance.[163] In his enormously popular *Physico-Theology*, first published in 1713, Derham drew on Graunt and Arbuthnot to assert that the ratio between males and females illustrates God's providential design.[164] Moreover, he generalised Hale's claim that there are various 'checks' on the growth of the human population in affirming that God manages the numbers of each animal species to ensure that a balance in nature is maintained so that overpopulation does not occur.[165] Demography and natural theology thus became intertwined during the course of the late seventeenth and early eighteenth centuries.

Lastly, Reid's paper on increasing the birth rate in Britain needs to be read in the context of the general debate over whether the ancient or the modern world was more populous.[166] In the *Lettres persanes* (1721) Montesquieu reiterated the view initially put forward by the peripatetic Dutch scholar Isaac Vossius that since classical antiquity the earth had become progressively more depopulated. Through the epistolary exchanges of the characters Rica (who first raises the issue) and Usbek, Montesquieu suggested that the human population had shrunk during the course of history due to such physical causes as pestilence, disease and periodic geological catastrophes, as well as moral causes like changes in divorce law, the acceptance of polygamy, the enslavement of African blacks, the spread of Islam and Christianity, political institutions, colonisation and the manners and customs of the various peoples across the globe.[167] Montesquieu later returned to the topic in *L'Esprit des loix*, where he enumerated some of the same physical and moral causes in explaining the depopulation of Europe and advised that European states needed to adopt legislation that would promote population

[163] John Arbuthnot, 'An Argument for Divine Providence, Taken from the Constant Regularity Observ'd in the Births of Both Sexes' (1710–12).

[164] William Derham, *Physico-Theology: Or, a Demonstration of the Being and Attributes of God, from his Works of Creation* (1732), pp. 175n–76n. Arbuthnot's paper was also used in another important natural theology text of the period, Bernard Nieuwentyt's *The Religious Philosopher: Or, the Right Use of Contemplating the Works of the Creator* (1718–19), vol. I, pp. 318–25.

[165] Derham, *Physico-Theology*, pp. 168–71, 177–79.

[166] On this debate, see Sylvana Tomaselli, 'Moral Philosophy and Population Questions in Eighteenth-Century Europe' and F. G. Whelan, 'Population and Ideology in the Enlightenment'.

[167] Montesquieu, *Persian Letters*, pp. 148–66 (letters 108–18).

growth.[168] Famously, Hume was not persuaded by Montesquieu's reading of the demographic history of humankind. In 'Of the Populousness of Ancient Nations' (1752), Hume dismissed out of hand the 'extravagancies of VOSSIUS' and used Montesquieu's claim that in the eighteenth century 'the earth support[ed] barely a fiftieth part of the population that it had in Caesar's day' as a starting point for a detailed reconsideration of the question.[169] While recognising that '*particular physical* causes' like venereal disease and smallpox were relevant to his inquiry, Hume nevertheless focused on the role played by moral causes in determining the size of human populations and emphasised that 'if every thing else be equal, it seems natural to expect, that, wherever there are most happiness and virtue, and the wisest institutions, there will also be [the] most people'.[170] For Hume, there was no doubt that the moderns were superior to the ancients measured according to these criteria, not least because the moderns enjoyed all of the advantages resulting from greater individual liberty, political stability, polished manners and the progress of trade, manufactures and industry. He therefore concluded that since the evidence for the size of the population in classical antiquity was unreliable, it was far more reasonable to think that the numbers of humankind had in fact increased rather than declined. But Hume was quickly challenged by his colleague in the Philosophical Society of Edinburgh, Robert Wallace, whose *A Dissertation on the Numbers of Mankind* (1753) defended the view that depopulation had taken place since classical times.[171] Although Wallace agreed with Hume that moral causes were paramount in setting population levels, he put forward a diametrically opposed assessment of the respective merits of the ancient and modern worlds. He maintained that the simplicity of taste and manners that characterised life in the ancient Mediterranean world, including Greece and Italy, especially prior to the conquests by Rome, was conducive to population growth, whereas the luxury and corruption which he thought disfigured life in modern European societies led to moral and physical corruption and hence to a gradual decline in the numbers of humankind.[172]

These various debates and discussions had already been in the background of Reid's lectures on police; in his manuscript on population they are registered

[168] Montesquieu, *The Spirit of the Laws*, book XXIII.

[169] Montesquieu, *Persian Letters*, p. 150; Hume, *Essays Moral, Political and Literary*, p. 380.

[170] Hume, *Essays Moral, Political and Literary*, pp. 379, 382.

[171] Wallace had earlier read a paper on the population of ancient Greece and Rome in the Philosophical Society; see Winsor, 'Robert Wallace', pp. 217–18.

[172] See Robert Wallace, *A Dissertation on the Numbers of Mankind in Ancient and Modern Times* (1753), pp. 32–79, for evidence of the superior populations of the ancient world, followed by extensive analyses of the physical and moral causes of this situation, beginning with an overview, pp. 79–83.

in full. His starting point is the mercantilist belief that the power and wealth of a nation are related to the size of its population, with the rider that the 'number of hands' must be 'properly directed' (89). Consequently, the management of the population was for him, as for the mercantilists, an important aspect of police and, especially, the promulgation of laws to promote marriage.[173] Echoing Halley, Tucker and many others, Reid called for legislation that would enhance the attractions of the marital state by rewarding and supporting procreation and by punishing those who remained single or who indulged in extramarital sex. He nevertheless struck a new note in his treatment of this issue, in that he indicated that different policies must be adopted to encourage marriage in the upper and lower ranks of society. Among the wealthy, Reid saw luxury as the main obstacle to marriage and he therefore suggested that unmarried men in the upper ranks of society be taxed and excluded from public office.[174] However, Reid thought that marriage rates in the upper ranks were less significant than those among the poorer sort because the wealthy 'do not make the twentieth part of a State', whereas 'the poor people who must beget labouring hands … are most wanted and make … 19/20 parts of the whole'.[175] Hence his proposals for the promotion of marriage among the labouring poor were more elaborate than those he outlined regarding the better sort. And it is here that we see his experience in administering poor relief at New Machar surface, insofar as he recommends that a 'publick fund' be established to assist the poor and that the decisions about those eligible for support be made by 'The Overseers of the Parish or a Jury'. This aspect of his scheme was clearly modelled on the administrative structure of the old Scottish Poor Law. Furthermore, his first-hand knowledge of how the Poor Law was applied in practice undoubtedly led him to state that the labouring poor ought to have a legal right to support, because poor relief in eighteenth-century Scotland was commonly perceived to be a matter of individual Christian charity rather than a social relationship involving rights and duties set by law.[176]

Reid's paper also displays his mathematical turn of mind and his engagement with political arithmetic. In the eighteenth century, disputes in demography were extremely difficult to resolve due to the unreliability of the available data and the

[173] Compare Reid's Glasgow lectures on politics, p. 55. Presumably Reid also touched on the question of population in his politics lectures at King's College.

[174] See p. 89. Compare Tucker, *The Elements*, p. 17; Josiah Tucker, *A Brief Essay on the Advantages and Disadvantages which Respectively Attend France and Great Britain, with Regard to Trade*, third edition (1753), pp. 127–32.

[175] See p. 90; compare Wallace, *Characteristics*, p. 121, on the importance of the lower orders. Reid elsewhere in this manuscript (p. 91) suggests that luxury also affects the lower ranks of society.

[176] See p. 90; Rosalind Mitchison, *The Old Poor Law in Scotland: The Experience of Poverty, 1574–1845*, pp. 46–48.

fact that there were no standardised procedures used to calculate population size or growth. His observation that 'it would be of use have some standard by which we might Judge whether a State is upon the increase or decrease in population' was thus an apposite one regarding contemporary population estimates as well as the debate over the numbers of humankind in the ancient and modern worlds.[177] Moreover, his attempt to provide a measure for population change not only points to his familiarity with the work of political arithmeticians like Halley and Buffon but also reflects the principle he enunciated in his 'Essay on Quantity' that quantitative reasoning can be utilised legitimately only in fields where the objects of study can be measured with precision. Thus, even though populations were 'capable of More and Less' and hence potentially susceptible to quantitative analysis, he evidently felt that the lack of an agreed measure of changes in population size was a problem in political arithmetic that needed to be rectified.[178]

Lastly, Reid's discussion of what he calls 'the rate of the natural increase of Mankind' and the 'impediments which check and restrain the natural inclination of mankind to pair' reveals his indebtedness to those writers whose interest in demography was framed by their religious concerns. Given that the human population would double naturally in the space of twenty-five years, Reid recognised that there must be some limits on population growth in order to prevent the overpopulation of the earth.[179] His use of the terms 'check' and 'restraint' follows the language employed by Hale and Derham in their analyses of the factors which controlled the numerical increase of humankind and his remarks on the natural limit on the fertility of the earth in the last paragraph of the manuscript suggest that he knew Robert Wallace's critique of utopian thinking in Wallace's recently published *Various Prospects of Mankind, Nature and Providence*.[180] Moreover, the phrase 'the Proportion of Males & females' in Reid's concluding paragraph implies a familiarity with John Arbuthnot's paper

[177] See p. 91. Both Hume and Wallace recognised that such problems bedevilled the debate over whether the earth was more densely populated in classical antiquity or in the modern era.

[178] Thomas Reid, 'An Essay on Quantity; Occasioned by Reading a Treatise, in which Simple and Compound Ratio's Are Applied to Virtue and Merit' (1748), pp. 505–20 (quote at pp. 512–13). A critical edition of this text will appear in the Edinburgh Edition *Thomas Reid on Mathematics and Natural Philosophy*.

[179] Estimates of the rate of natural population growth varied widely in the eighteenth century. Reid seems to have taken his figure of twenty-five years from Benjamin Franklin; see Franklin's *The Interest of Great Britain Considered ... To which are Added, Observations Concerning the Increase of Mankind, Peopling of Countries, &c.* (1760), pp. 23, 56. It is possible but not likely that Reid took the figure from Ezra Stiles' *Discourse on the Christian Union* (1761), which discussed population growth in the American colonies.

[180] Robert Wallace, *Various Prospects of Mankind, Nature and Providence* (1761), esp. pp. 115–16, 122.

in the *Philosophical Transactions* discussed above, while his assertion that 'the Intention of Providence must be that Mankind should never exceed' a set number of people shows that he believed that the facts of human demography illustrated God's wise providential governance of the natural order. Like other works on population written in the period, Reid's manuscript thus blends together natural theology with political arithmetic and police.

As we have already noted, Reid's papers on aspects of the law are somewhat anomalous with respect to his other contributions to the Wise Club analysed above because the questions that inspired them were not prompted by topical issues in mid-eighteenth-century Britain. The question 'Whether the determination by unanimity or a majority in Juries is most equitable?' was proposed by David Skene and discussed by the Club on 9 March 1762.[181] As was customary in the Society, Skene recorded the conversation and prepared the abstract for the question. Reid's manuscript, therefore, must have been written for another purpose and most likely served as the basis for his own contribution to the discussion on 9 March.[182] What is immediately striking about his response to the question is that it is framed in terms of an explicit contrast between the jury systems used in England and Scotland, with Reid admitting at the outset that 'I know not Whether my Judgment in this Question be in any degree influenced by an attachment to the Laws of my Country'.[183] His preference for the Scottish system was echoed by all of the other members of the Club present and his arguments against the English system were basically the same as those of his colleagues, although many of the details found in the manuscript were probably unique to Reid.[184] His point that a collective decision is commonly regarded as being more trustworthy than one taken by an individual was apparently not raised or addressed at the meeting, but we note that it fits into his general theory of reasoning that he elaborated in *Essays on the Intellectual Powers*. The deliberation of a jury is a form of probable, as distinct from demonstrative, reasoning and, more particularly, reasoning from testimony.[185] Reid seems not to have considered a problem that provoked some disagreement, namely whether it was equitable to have criminal cases involving capital punishment decided by a simple majority, as was the practice in Scotland.

[181] Ulman, *Minutes of the Aberdeen Philosophical Society*, pp. 108, 193.

[182] For Skene's abstract see Skene, 'Literary Essays', AUL, MS 475, pp. 17–22 (pagination in the original).

[183] See p. 86. Adam Smith made a similar contrast between English and Scottish juries and expressed a strong preference for the latter. See Smith, *Lectures on Jurisprudence*, (A) v.37–41 and (B) 73–74.

[184] Compare Skene, 'Literary Essays', pp. 17–19.

[185] Reid, *Intellectual Powers*, pp. 555–62, especially 557–58; cf. Reid, *Inquiry*, pp. 190–95.

At least one member of the Society insisted that in such cases there should be a greater majority than one, even though most of his colleagues thought that a simple majority decision was acceptable.[186] Unfortunately, we do not know what Reid's view of this issue was, nor do we know whether he believed that the Scottish legal system was in need of reform as one or more of his fellow members of the Club evidently did.

Alexander Gerard's question 'Whether it be best that Courts of Law and Courts of Equity were different, or that the same court had the power of determining either according to law or equity as circumstances require?' generated a prolonged conversation within the Aberdeen Philosophical Society that continued over meetings held on 25 January and 8 and 22 February 1763.[187] No other question addressed by the Society led to such a lengthy discussion, although it is not clear why it did so. Gerard's question may have originated in his reading of Francis Bacon, for in *De augmentis scientiarum* (1623) Bacon stated that courts of law should be sharply distinguished from courts of equity on the ground that 'if there be a mixture of jurisdictions, the distinction of cases will not be retained, but discretion will in the end supersede the law'.[188] The issue was of some moment in the English legal system since the Court of Chancery dealt exclusively with matters of equity, whereas other courts were taken up with the common law. In Scotland, there was no such separation. The Court of Session was a court of both law and equity, and this mixing of jurisdictions was defended by Lord Kames in his *Principles of Equity*, first published in 1760.[189] Thus Gerard's question, like the one posed by Skene, highlighted the differences between the English and Scottish legal systems and, in doing so, invited the members of the Society to judge which of the two systems was preferable.

Even though Reid was present at the meeting of the Wise Club held on 25 January 1763, he may well have contributed little to the initial discussion of Gerard's question because his manuscript dealing with the question is dated February 1763 (92). The manuscript indicates that he was not interested in the kinds of technical legal details which preoccupied Kames, which suggests that his reflections had their origins in domains like politics and practical ethics rather

[186] Skene, 'Literary Essays', p. 21.

[187] Ulman, *Minutes of the Aberdeen Philosophical Society*, pp. 114, 115, 193.

[188] Francis Bacon, *The Philosophical Works of Francis Bacon Baron of Verulam, Viscount St. Albans, and Lord High Chancellor of England*, p. 620.

[189] On the Court of Session see, for example, Andrew McDouall, *An Institute of the Laws of Scotland in Civil Rights: With Observations upon the Agreement or Diversity between them and the Laws of England* (1751–52), vol. II, pp. 516–17; Henry Home, Lord Kames, *Principles of Equity* (1760), pp. xiii–xvi. Cf. David M. Walker, 'Equity in Scots Law', and Ian Simpson Ross, *Lord Kames and the Scotland of his Day*, ch. 12.

than the law. Instead, he was more concerned with clarifying the different senses in which justice and equity can be said to be in conflict, and with the related constitutional issue of the relationship between the courts and the legislature. The first sense he identified is where a court makes a decision, based on the principles of equity, which contradicts 'the meaning and intention of the Law'. He maintained that such decisions transcend the limitations on the power of the courts because the power to alter the laws of the land rests solely with the legislature. Clearly he was worried that decisions of this sort subverted the proper constitutional relationship between the legal and legislative arms of 'a free Government' like that of Britain (93). Secondly, he believed that where the law is silent it is legitimate for both higher and lower courts to make judgements based on the principles of equity, on the ground that judgements of this type are no more than 'Supplements to the Law' (93–94). Thirdly, he also granted that courts should be able to make decisions 'which are grounded upon the reason and intendment of the Law although not within or contrary to the letter of it'. Here he acknowledged that interpretation is needed to apply general statements like those of the law to specific actions. And for Reid, the interpretive gap between the general and the particular can be bridged only by considering the intentions of human agents and by invoking considerations of equity. This point led him to reflect on the common law courts of England, which he criticised for their legal 'Chicanery' and for an unwarranted degree of power lodged with juries precisely because the judgements of these courts were not governed by the principles of equity (94–95). It followed that, for Reid, the legal system in Scotland was superior to that in England since the Scottish Court of Session combined justice and equity within its jurisdiction.

Reid's papers on the law are historically significant not so much for the details of the arguments found therein but for their defence of the merits of the Scottish legal system. It has been suggested that there was wide recognition in the eighteenth century of the need for Scottish law and legal institutions to be modernised in order to keep pace with the social, political and economic changes brought about by the Union of 1707.[190] Reid's patriotic defence of the Scottish jury system and the hybrid nature of the Court of Session would thus seem to put him at odds with the majority of Scots jurists in the period, including his patron and friend Lord Kames. Nevertheless, we believe that Reid (like Kames) is best described as a 'North Briton' in the eighteenth-century sense of that term.[191] Scottish Whigs, such as Reid, welcomed the Parliamentary Union because the political and economic assimilation of Scotland within the new British polity

[190] Colin Kidd, *Union and Unionisms: Political Thought in Scotland, 1500–2000*, pp. 178–90.
[191] Cf. Colin Kidd, 'North Britishness and the Nature of Eighteenth-Century British Patriotisms'.

brought with it the advantages of the mixed English constitution and a more advanced commercial economy. Reid's paeans on the virtues of the British constitution speak to the common perception among his Scottish contemporaries that it was thanks to the Union that the Scots enjoyed the benefits of English liberties, as well as the material prosperity fostered by the gradual disappearance of the last remnants of outmoded Scottish feudal institutions. But even though Reid and his fellow Scottish Whigs were 'Anglocentric' and assimilationist in outlook, they also stoutly defended the distinctiveness of the Church of Scotland in its Presbyterian guise, and were sympathetic to traditional cultural forms like Scots vernacular poetry even while they endeavoured to eliminate Scotticisms from their prose.[192] On the evidence of Reid's papers on the law, it appears that he viewed the Scottish legal system as a constitutive part of the North British identity insofar as that system, like the Kirk, was guaranteed its distinctiveness by the Union settlement.[193] Paradoxically, he can thus be seen as a legal nationalist before legal nationalism.[194]

During Reid's thirty-two years as a member of the Glasgow Literary Society, we know that he gave at least twenty discourses and handled eleven discussion questions. Of these, one discourse and six questions dealt with political, economic and social topics.[195] Unfortunately, the papers Reid prepared to open the discussion of the questions 'What are the most proper Means to be used by a State in order to prevent the necessarys of life from rising to too high a price' and 'Whether Paper Credit is beneficial or hurtful to a trading Nation' have not survived.[196] The former question, which he addressed on 30 January 1767, was most likely prompted by the spike in food prices in 1765–66, which led to serious rioting in Glasgow in 1767.[197] The latter question, which he had already discussed in the Wise Club in 1761, was the basis for a conversation in the Literary Society which took place on 1 May 1767, just as it was taken up in his lectures on police at the time (67–68). Given his onerous college duties, it is conceivable that he returned to this question in order to save preparation time, although it is also possible that he believed the

[192] See Kidd, 'North Britishness', pp. 365–66.

[193] The same can be said for the Scottish university system.

[194] Compare Kidd, *Union and Unionisms*, pp. 173–78.

[195] See the list in Appendix III of Wood, 'Thomas Reid, Natural Philosopher', to which must be added a question on paper credit from 1767.

[196] 'Laws of the Literary Society in Glasgow College', GUL, MS Murray 505, pp. 20–21, 23. Reid's paper on the question discussed 1 April 1768, 'Whether the Supposition of a tacit Contract at the beginning of Societies is well founded', is reproduced in Reid, *Practical Ethics*, pp. 136–43.

[197] A. J. S. Gibson and T. C. Smout, *Prices, Food and Wages in Scotland, 1550–1780*, p. 173; Whatley, *Scottish Society*, p. 207.

issue was still pertinent in the aftermath of the international banking crisis that had occurred in 1763.[198]

Reid subsequently addressed monetary matters in his undated paper on the question 'What are the bad consequences of the Diminution of our Coin by wearing? and what the means of preventing those Consequences?' The state of both silver and gold coin was a matter of widespread concern in Britain from the late 1750s onwards, since much of the coinage in circulation was below its regulation weight or otherwise adulterated.[199] A limited number of new silver coins – shillings and sixpence pieces – had been minted for the Bank of England in 1757–58 for private distribution, but otherwise little new silver coin was issued by the Mint. By the early 1770s there was such a shortage that some commentators likened the situation to the dark years of the early 1690s, when silver coin was in such a perilous state that the English government had to undertake a complete recoinage.[200] Moreover, figures such as Matthew Boulton attributed the financial crisis affecting banks and private credit that occurred in 1772 in part to the corrupt state of the gold coin.[201] Parliament responded by passing three pieces of legislation: 'An Act for the better preventing the counterfeiting, clipping, and other diminishing the Gold Coin in this Kingdom' in 1773, followed by 'An Act to prohibit the Importation of light Silver Coin, of this Realm' and 'An Act for applying a certain Sum of Money, for calling in, and recoining, the deficient Gold Coin of this Realm' in 1774.[202] Since the minutes of the Glasgow Literary Society

[198] Hoppit, 'Financial Crises', pp. 49–50.

[199] On the state of the British coinage, see John Craig, *The Mint: A History of the London Mint from A.D. 287 to 1948*, ch. 14; Albert Feavearyear, *The Pound Sterling: A History of English Money*, pp. 168–72; Thomas J. Sargent and François R. Velde, *The Big Problem of Small Change*, pp. 299–301; George Selgin, *Good Money: Birmingham Button Makers, the Royal Mint, and the Beginnings of Modern Coinage, 1775–1821*, ch. 1.

[200] Craig, *The Mint*, p. 246; [William Beldam], *Considerations on Money, Bullion and Foreign Exchanges; Being an Enquiry into the Present State of the British Coinage; Particularly with Regard to the Scarcity of Silver Money* (1772), pp. iii, v; Anon., *A Letter to the Members in Parliament, on the Present State of the Coinage: With Proposals for the Better Regulation thereof* (1771). On the recoinage of the mid-1690s, see Ming-Hsun Li, *The Great Recoinage of 1696 to 1699*.

[201] Craig, *The Mint*, p. 242. On the financial crisis of 1772, see Hoppit, 'Financial Crises', pp. 45, 51–54.

[202] 13 George III c. 71, 'An Act for the better preventing the counterfeiting, clipping, and other diminishing the Gold Coin in this Kingdom'; 14 George III c. 42, 'An Act to prohibit the Importation of light Silver Coin, of this Realm, from Foreign Countries, into Great Britain or Ireland; and to restrain the Tender thereof beyond a certain Sum'; and 14 George III c. 70, 'An Act for applying a certain Sum of Money, for calling in, and recoining, the deficient Gold Coin of this Realm; and for regulating the Manner of receiving the same at the Bank of *England*; and of taking, there, on Account of the Deficiency of the said Coin, and making Satisfaction for the same; and for authorising all Persons to cut and deface all Gold Coin, that shall not be allowed to be current by his Majesty's Proclamation', in Owen Ruffhead, *Statutes at Large* (1786), vol. VIII, pp. 261, 347–48, 364. See also

are almost entirely missing for the period February 1771 to May 1775, we cannot be certain about the dating of Reid's manuscript on light coin. However, we think that the paper dates from the early 1770s, and was most likely prompted by the widespread anxiety about the debased nature of British coinage and by the discussions in Parliament surrounding the three Acts.[203] The fact that Reid repeatedly refers to Sir James Steuart's extended treatment of money and coin in *An Inquiry into the Principles of Political Oeconomy* but not to Adam Smith's analysis of the subject in the *Wealth of Nations* also strongly suggests that the paper was written after 1767 but before 1776. Our dating of the paper is also influenced by the fact that Reid had addressed this topic and made substantially the same points in his undergraduate lectures, at least by 1765–66.[204] In addition, his reading of Steuart's *The Principles of Money* in May 1773 points to a renewed interest in coinage in the early 1770s. Given the historical context and the evidence provided by both the text itself and his reading notes, we conclude that Reid's manuscript was most probably composed in 1772 or 1773, or perhaps 1774 at the latest.

In the lengthy 'Preamble' to his paper, Reid recapitulates the basic elements of the theory of money that he outlined in his politics lectures in order to make one main point, namely that in order to facilitate commerce modern European states had all opted to employ gold or silver coins whose face value was guaranteed by a 'publick Stamp' which vouched for both the weight and the fineness of the metal.[205] However, in doing so, they faced two practical problems: deterring the unscrupulous from tampering with the coinage and preventing coins from wearing through use. And, as Reid noted, neither problem had been solved by the British government or any other European state. Of these two problems, he clearly regarded the loss of weight over time as the more serious one because metal coin inevitably wears and the resultant circulation of light coin was detrimental to the economy in a number of ways. As mentioned above, the matter of worn coin had recently been explored by Sir James Steuart, but Reid went far beyond Steuart in his detailed discussion of the deleterious economic consequences of a debased coinage.[206] Perhaps the most striking feature of Reid's discussion is his

the 1774 Parliamentary report on the state of the gold coin in William Cobbett and T. C. Hansard, *Cobbett's Parliamentary History of England, from the Earliest Period to the Year 1803. From which Last-Mentioned Epoch it is Continued Downwards in the Work Entitled, 'The Parliamentary Debates'* (1806–20), vol. XVII, pp. 1327–30.

[203] The extant minutes of the Glasgow Literary Society while Reid was a member cover the periods November 1764 to January 1771, November 1771, February 1773, November 1776 to May 1779 and November 1794 to April 1800.

[204] See pp. 63–64.

[205] See pp. 96–101.

[206] See pp. 101–3; compare Steuart, *An Inquiry*, vol. I, pp. 540, 553–7.

assertion that once it becomes public knowledge that the coins in circulation are under-weight, the debasement of a nation's coinage 'has a tendency to go on with an accelerated Motion, like a Stone going down hill'.[207] Reid thus agreed with those who maintained that Britain faced an economic crisis because the coin was in the same debased state as it had been prior to the Great Recoinage of 1696, although the remedy he proposed to avoid such a crisis was radically different from what the English government had undertaken some eighty years earlier.

The most novel aspect of Reid's paper on coinage is his proposal that over the long term the British government should abandon the attempt to guarantee the weight of the silver coin in circulation because the problems associated with trying to do so were insuperable. However, as a first step towards this long-term solution he suggested that Parliament should pass a law requiring that 'in all time to come no man shall be obliged to take money in payment that is deficient in weight'.[208] Even though such a law would have meant that the exchange of silver money would entail weighing the coin used, he believed that people would become adept at assessing the weight of coin and that light coin would inevitably find its way back to the Mint to be recoined because it would otherwise be refused in cash transactions. Moreover, he argued that if such a law were to be passed, it would reduce the price of an ounce of silver bullion to make it equivalent to that of an ounce of silver coin, which was not the case by the early 1770s. In doing so, the law would indirectly ensure that there was a regular supply of silver to the Mint and that the coin in circulation was of the correct weight. Consequently, money in Britain would genuinely be 'a proper Measure of the price of things', whereas in its current debased state it was not.[209] The primary ends of 'coinage by tale' – guaranteed fineness and weight – would thus be achieved by the expedient of a simple piece of legislation, while a costly wholesale recoinage like that previously undertaken would, according to Reid, be avoided. And given that he thought that the clipping of coin in the late seventeenth century and the Great Recoinage of 1696 had both contributed to the high level of public debt in Britain, his scheme had much to recommend it, because it avoided significant public expenditure and remedied the problem of debased coin.[210] Reid's proposed response to the coinage crisis was, however, at odds with the recommendations of prominent political

[207] See p. 103.

[208] See p. 103. Reid here echoes John Locke's *Further Considerations concerning Raising the Value of Money* (1691), in Locke, *Locke on Money*, vol. II, pp. 418–19.

[209] See p. 105.

[210] See p. 106. The one problem he saw with his scheme was that debtors would find their debts increased by 5%, and he suggested that they be protected in the legislation on coinage that he envisaged; see p. 106.

economists like Steuart and the views of MPs. For in 1773–74, legislation passed by Parliament initiated a recoinage of gold coin in order to combat clipping but signally failed to address the decrepit state of silver coinage in the realm.

The problems of police related to the regulation of food prices that Reid addressed in 1767 were thrown into even sharper relief when climbing grain prices, lower wages and food shortages caused widespread hardship and renewed social unrest in Scotland in the period 1771–73. The new Corn Law passed in 1773 did nothing to solve the problem of providing subsistence for the labouring poor. If anything, the law made matters worse in Scotland because it allowed the importation of oats and oatmeal only at a price that was higher than it had been under the previous Corn Law.[211] Merchants in Glasgow were heavily involved in the lobbying of MPs that took place when the new legislation was passed in 1773, and they were again active in 1777 when a bill was proposed to regulate the import and export of corn in Scotland.[212] On 8 April 1777 the MP for Ayrshire, Sir Adam Fergusson, moved to table a bill that would amend the 1773 Corn Law as it applied to Scotland. At the request of Parliament, Fergusson, along with the Lord Advocate, Henry Dundas, and the MP for the Glasgow Burghs, Lord Frederick Campbell, drafted a bill which was given a first reading in the Commons on 16 April and a second on 28 April. The draft legislation was then printed on 1 May and circulated among the counties and burghs of Scotland for comment; it was resolved to delay further discussion of it until the next session of Parliament.[213] Before the draft had been printed, news of the proposed legislation reached Glasgow, where the Lord Provost called a meeting of 'the merchants, traders, and principal manufacturers' of the city. The group met on 25 April to voice their opposition to Fergusson's bill, which they feared would lead to higher grain prices.[214] A committee was struck to muster support for the position taken by the Glasgow merchants, and the committee members issued a *Memorial for the Merchants, Traders and Manufacturers of Glasgow*, dated 2 May 1777, summarising

[211] Gibson and Smout, *Prices, Food and Wages*, pp. 173–74; Whatley, *Scottish Society*, pp. 208–10. The price for oats was set at sixteen shillings per quarter; see 13 George III c. 43.

[212] On the lobbying of the Glasgow merchants in 1773 and 1777, see Bob Harris, 'Parliamentary Legislation, Lobbying and the Press in Eighteenth-Century Scotland', pp. 85–87.

[213] *Scots Magazine* 39 (1777), pp. 569–75, at p. 569; Harris, 'Parliamentary Legislation', p. 86; Julian Hoppit (ed.), *Failed Legislation, 1660–1800: Extracted from the Commons and Lords Journals*, pp. 444–45 (reference number 118.038). For the draft bill see 'A Bill to Amend and Render more Effectual so much of Two Acts, Made in the Thirteenth and Fourteenth Years of the Reign of His Present Majesty, as Relates to the Regulating the Importation and Exportation of Corn, in that Part of Great Britain called Scotland', in Sheila Lambert (ed.), *House of Commons Sessional Papers of the Eighteenth Century*, vol. XXVIII, pp. 88–101.

[214] Implicitly, the Glasgow merchants were worried by the possibility of further food riots.

their objections to the draft legislation. Copies of the *Memorial* were forwarded to various Scottish newspapers for publication and to a committee of the Convention of Royal Burghs, which ordered that the *Memorial* be printed and sent to all of the Scottish MPs, the royal burghs and the manufacturing towns of Scotland.[215]

The Glasgow *Memorial* proved to be highly controversial because it criticised Fergusson's bill for favouring the landed interest in Edinburgh and the east of Scotland on the grounds that the bill vested the power of regulating the corn trade in the Court of Session and Court of Exchequer, as had been the case prior to 1773, and used the price of corn and oatmeal in Edinburgh as the standard for the rest of Scotland, even though prices were typically lower in Edinburgh than elsewhere. Furthermore, the authors of the *Memorial* objected to the fact that the bill set too high a price threshold for the importation of oatmeal and urged that it was in the interest of the nation to allow 'the free importation of provisions, or at a low limited price', since this would ensure a plentiful supply of cheap food and allow 'manufactures [to] flourish'.[216] A flurry of pamphlets responding to the *Memorial* appeared and the landed interest held a series of meetings in November and December 1777 in Banffshire, Ayrshire and Edinburgh.[217] Because lower grain prices were the likely result of freer trade, landowners vigorously attacked the position articulated by the Glasgow merchants, as well as sections of the 1773 Corn Law. For example, a committee drawn from an informal group of representatives from most of the counties in Scotland that met in Edinburgh in November 1777 took aim at the Law and declared that 'the warehousing of either grain or meal for re-exportation is highly prejudicial to the true interest of this country, and to the exportation of the native produce: [and] That as the warehousing of oatmeal never hath been allowed, it ought not to be agreed to;

[215] *Scots Magazine* 39 (1777), pp. 569–73. For the Glasgow *Memorial*, see also the 3 July 1777 issue of the *Weekly Magazine, or Edinburgh Amusement* 37 (1777), pp. 1–5. The argument of the *Memorial* regarding the 1773 Corn Law is couched in the language of 'North Britishness' explored by Kidd in his article with that title. The position taken by the Glasgow merchants was endorsed by 'W.C.' in 'A Peep at the Corn Bill', which appeared in the 29 May 1777 issue of the *Weekly Magazine, or Edinburgh Amusement* 36 (1777), pp. 293–94.

[216] *Scots Magazine* 39 (1777), pp. 572–73. The argument made by the Glasgow merchants that manufactures flourish when food prices are low was challenged by Sir James Steuart; see Steuart, *An Inquiry into the Principles of Political Oeconomy* (ed. Andrew Skinner), vol. I, pp. lii–lv, and vol. II, pp. 737–38. Steuart maintained that high food prices promoted industriousness and hence stimulated both agriculture and manufactures.

[217] *Scots Magazine* 40 (1778), pp. 6–8. For examples of the pamphlets critical of the Glasgow *Memorial*, see anon., *Considerations on our Corn-Laws and the Bill Proposed to Amend them* (1777); anon., *Corn-Bill Hints, in Answer to the Memorial for the Merchants, Traders and Manufacturers of the City of Glasgow* (1777); and anon., *Essay on the Corn Laws* … (1777).

and the warehousing of other grain ought to be prevented if possible'.[218] The landowners were thus not merely opposed to the relaxation of restrictions on the grain trade, for they now wanted the repeal of the provisions in the 1773 Corn Law which permitted the warehousing of grains other than oats. This new challenge to the Glasgow merchants was particularly unwelcome because their commercial prospects were already grim due to the American War. Consequently, they began a subscription in early December to fight Fergusson's bill, and the counties of Argyll and Dumbarton, along with several burghs and towns, rallied behind them. In the end, the intense lobbying by the Glasgow merchants succeeded in killing the bill, for it did not resurface in the Commons before Parliament was prorogued by George III in early June 1778.[219]

Reid's paper on the question 'Whether the Storing or Warehousing foreign Grain or Meal for reexportation be highly prejudicial to the interest of this Country and whether it ought to be prevented if possible', which he 'illustrated' at the meeting of the Glasgow Literary Society held on 30 January 1778, defends both the warehousing provisions in the 1773 Corn Law and the position taken in the Glasgow *Memorial* regarding the grain trade.[220] As Reid reported to Lord Kames in late February, his paper focused on 'a Clause of the last Corn Act about Warehousing Grain, a Clause which some meetings of the Landed Gentlemen have resolved to be prejudicial to the Country, I think unjustly'.[221] Significantly, Reid's colleague John Millar had already read a discourse to the Society 'On the Expediency of restraining the importation of foreign Grain or bestowing a bounty upon the exportation of what is produced at home' in November 1777.[222] Hence it is unclear whether Reid thought that his paper simply supplemented what Millar had to say on the topic, or whether he set out to challenge the argument that Millar

[218] See the report in the *Scots Magazine* 40 (1778), p. 8. A committee comprised of landowners and Justices of the Peace in Banffshire expressed the same view in that issue (p. 7).

[219] *Scots Magazine* 40 (1778), p. 8.

[220] 'Laws of the Literary Society in Glasgow College', GUL, MS Murray 505, pp. 62–63. For the warehousing provisions, see 13 George III c. 43, 'An Act to Regulate the Importation and Exportation of Corn', in Ruffhead, *Statutes at Large*, vol. VIII, pp. 222–28 (at p. 223). For another perspective on the context for Reid's paper see Hont, *Jealousy of Trade*, pp. 403–19. Reid's paper is noted on p. 412, n58.

[221] Reid to Lord Kames, 27 February 1778, in Reid, *Correspondence*, p. 97.

[222] 'Laws of the Literary Society in Glasgow College', GUL, MS Murray 505, pp. 57–58. The wording of the title of Millar's discourse suggests that he followed Adam Smith in recommending that all restrictions on the import and export of corn be removed, just as he followed Smith's general argument for commercial liberty. See John Millar, *An Historical View of the English Government* (1787), vol. IV, pp. 713–18. For Smith's analysis see his 'Digression concerning the Corn Trade and Corn Laws', in Smith, *Wealth of Nations*, IV.v.b.

had presented in his discourse. Nevertheless, Reid's opposition to the views expressed by the spokesmen for the landed interest is abundantly clear.

Three aspects of Reid's argument are of interest. First, Reid takes from earlier mercantilist writers their emphasis on the economic benefits of the 'carrying trade', that is, the import of goods to either a home or a foreign port that are subsequently exported to other markets. Among the writers that Reid cites on commerce, William Petty was the first to focus on the carrying trade as a means to enrich the nation. In his *Political Arithmetick*, he maintained that the prosperity of the Dutch was due to their success in the fishing and shipping sectors, which had turned them into 'the Factors, and Carriers for the whole World of Trade'. The dominance of the Dutch in shipping and trade had benefited the United Provinces because 'Husbandmen, Seamen, Soldiers, Artizans and Merchants, are the very Pillars of any Common-Wealth' and, in his view, every sailor is 'not only a Navigator, but a Merchant, and also a Soldier'. Consequently, the cultivation of trade, and especially the carrying trade, by the Dutch increased their power as well as their wealth, insofar as 'the Labour of Seamen, and Freight of Ships, is always of the nature of an Exported Commodity, the overplus whereof, above what is Imported, brings home mony, *&c*'.[223] The benefits of 'Trading and Huxtering from Port to Port' were similarly extolled in the mercantilist text *Britannia Languens*, said to be written by the Whig apologist William Petyt. Like Petty, the author of *Britannia Languens* pointed to the success of the Dutch in the carriage of goods and the 'Trade from *Port to Port*' as a model for the English to follow, and said of the carrying trade that it will 'cause a great *Navigation*, and also bring in very much *Treasure*, and therefore if it be added to the Trade of *Exportation*, must render a Nation the Miracle of Riches and Power'.[224]

The importance of the carrying trade was also highlighted in a work Reid recommended to his students, Matthew Decker's *An Essay on the Causes of the Decline of the Foreign Trade*. Decker was highly critical of Britain's complex system of taxes, duties and bounties in the *Essay*, and insisted that Britain needed to create free ports in which the removal of elaborate customs regulations would allow trade to flourish. Such ports would, he maintained, stimulate the growth of the carrying trade, which in turn would strengthen the nation by increasing the number of sailors and create more employment for those in jobs ancillary to

[223] Petty, *Political Arithmetick*, in Petty, *Economic Writings*, vol. I, pp. 258–60.

[224] [William Petyt], *Britannia Languens: Or, a Discourse of Trade* ... (1689), p. 34. Pages 34–46 of the text are taken up with a lengthy discussion of the carrying trade and how England would benefit from emulating the Dutch.

this branch of trade, like 'Watermen, Carmen, Porters, Coopers, Packers, *&c.*'[225] Significantly, Decker emphasised that Britain could expand its carrying trade by creating public warehouses for the import and export of corn. 'By encouraging our Navigation', he wrote, 'the more of the Carrying-Trade must we get [and] ... the Importation of Corn upon Speculation for better Markets, and its Re-exportation when the Markets are advanced, must give constant Employment to a vast number of Ships'.[226] Reid's enumeration of the advantages gained by the carrying trade in grain was thus rooted in mercantilist political economy and, even though he agreed with Adam Smith's positive assessment of the carrying trade in grain in the *Wealth of Nations*, he did so for reasons that differed from Smith's.[227]

Moreover, Reid's defence of the warehousing of grain for import and export is a variation on earlier mercantilist schemes for the creation of public granaries. Petty had briefly mentioned the economic advantages of 'publick store-houses' for corn and other commodities in his *Political Arithmetick*.[228] However, at the beginning of the eighteenth century John Law advanced a detailed plan for the establishment of a Council of Trade in Scotland that would oversee the economic improvement of the nation. As part of this plan, Law suggested that the Council be given the power 'to build and erect granarys for the well-keeping stores and quantities of corn in all such places of this kingdom, as they shall judge necessary'.[229] According to Law, the construction of public storehouses for grain would contribute to the economic well-being of Scotland because they would help to avoid fluctuations between the 'extream cheapness' of provisions and the 'extream dearth of grain'; they would also serve to raise the price of corn and thereby provide additional revenue for 'the owners of land, and raisers of corn'.[230] Because Scotland was 'more subject to uncertain seasons' than 'any [other] country in Christendom', he urged that such granaries be built, especially given 'the many and destructive famines this nation hath been exposed unto' in the past. The warehousing of corn would, he believed, put an end to the kind

[225] [Sir Matthew Decker], *An Essay on the Causes of the Decline of the Foreign Trade, Consequently of the Value of the Lands of Britain, and on the Means to Restore both*, second edition (1750), pp. 19, 107–8.

[226] [Decker], *An Essay*, p. 170.

[227] See pp. 112–13. Compare Smith, *Wealth of Nations*, IV.v.b.41–42. Smith's view of the carrying trade in general was more qualified than Reid's; see Smith, *Wealth of Nations*, II.v.30–35. In paragraph 35 Smith attacked the mercantilists for confusing cause and effect, writing that 'the carrying trade is the natural effect and symptom of great national wealth: but it does not seem to be the natural cause of it'.

[228] Petty, *Political Arithmetick*, in Petty, *Economic Writings*, vol. I, pp. 274–75.

[229] John Law, *Proposals and Reasons for Constituting a Council of Trade in Scotland* (1751), p. 24.

[230] Law, *Proposals and Reasons*, pp. 24, 61, 80–81.

of catastrophic food shortages that had afflicted Scotland in the 1690s and, in addition, would allow the Scots to establish a grain trade to rival that of the Dutch. Law proclaimed that once the warehouses were in operation, Scotland 'may be easily brought into a condition of being one of the greatest store-houses for grain of all the countrys in the northern-world' and promised that considerable wealth would be generated by the import and export of corn at advantageous prices.[231]

As mentioned above, another proposal for the creation of public granaries was floated by Matthew Decker. Decker maintained that Britain's trade would benefit by the removal of the bounties on the export of corn and the formation of companies in each county in order 'to erect Magazines of Corn'. The advantages of these storehouses would be five-fold. First, they would foster the growth of the grain trade in Britain. Decker viewed this branch of commerce as 'a solid Trade' that was profitable in and of itself, and one that had the added advantages of stimulating the growth of manufactures (by keeping subsistence and labour costs low) and of fuelling the growth of the shipping industry.[232] Secondly, by keeping the cost of labour down the granaries would ensure that the working poor were kept in more regular work, while the expansion of trade more generally would create more jobs. Thirdly, the provision of food in times of scarcity would prevent widespread mortality and thereby help to increase the population. Fourthly, as we have already seen, he claimed that a flourishing carrying trade in corn would generate considerable wealth. Lastly, he asserted that the four economic consequences of 'erecting Publick Magazines of Corn' he enumerated would in turn lead to an increase in the value of land, which would further benefit the nation.[233] The warehousing of grain was thus a vital element in Decker's plan to encourage the recovery of Britain's foreign trade, because he saw the county corn warehouses as an engine of economic prosperity.

Reid knew the details of Decker's plan and he was probably also acquainted with Sir James Steuart's proposal for the establishment of a privately operated 'Meal-bank' in Lanarkshire. Writing under the pseudonym of 'Robert Frame, Writer in Dalserf', Steuart broached the idea in his *Considerations on the Interest of the County of Lanark*, wherein he considered the economic state of Lanarkshire in relation to the rapid growth of trade and manufactures in Glasgow. His rationale for creating a storehouse for meal was rooted in his diagnosis of the problems associated with the way in which the Glasgow food markets were run, and especially with the manner in which the corporate privileges of groups such as the

[231] Law, *Proposals and Reasons*, pp. 81–88, 137–40.
[232] [Decker], *An Essay*, pp. 168–70.
[233] [Decker], *An Essay*, pp. 171–72.

'Butchers, Bakers, Poulterers, [and] Herb-merchants' in the city had limited the supply of food from the outlying countryside.[234] The one exception he noted was the provision of oatmeal, for there was already a market to which anyone from the country could bring their meal to sell. However, the existence of this 'free' market could not be turned to advantage because there were no large private granaries in the west of Scotland like there were in East Lothian and the north and, in addition, farmers were forced to feed their cattle with straw in the winter rather than hay, so that there was little or no corn available early in the season. Furthermore, he remarked that 'the commons who live in towns; and who are instructed, by example, to consider riot and disorder as very noble exertions of liberty; deter the merchant from embarking in the corn-trade'.[235] These factors, combined with the poor road system and the inclement weather in the region, led to periodic and unpredictable shortages which drove food prices up. In order to combat the wildly fluctuating prices of grain, Steuart proposed that a company be formed to operate a 'Meal-bank', which would ensure that prices would remain reasonably steady due to the fact that there would be a reliable and properly managed source of oatmeal.[236] That Reid likewise highlighted the problem of fluctuating grain prices and held that it was an economic and social phenomenon that ought 'by all means that human Wisdom can devise to be prevented or lessened as much as possible' attests to his indebtedness to the writings of Steuart, as well as to those of Law before him, and we can therefore see his defence of the warehousing provisions in the 1773 Corn Law as being rooted in the granary schemes of his predecessors (108). For Reid, maintaining the price of subsistence at a relatively uniform level through the use of grain stores was a key component of effective police.[237]

A third point relates to the question which Reid raises at the beginning and the very end of his paper but does not address directly: whether or not a lower average price for corn and oatmeal benefited the nation.[238] The pamphlet war over Sir Adam Fergusson's draft bill reflected the two sides of the debate, with the Glasgow merchants holding to the commonplace that lower subsistence costs

[234] [Sir James Steuart], *Considerations on the Interest of the County of Lanark* (1769), p. 60.

[235] [Steuart], *Considerations*, pp. 64–66.

[236] [Steuart], *Considerations*, pp. 65–72. Steuart suggested that if his proposal was found impractical, at the very least the Glasgow city fathers needed to collaborate with the landed interest in regulating the markets in Lanarkshire so that the supply of oat meal was as uniform as possible.

[237] It should be emphasised that Reid did not think that specific grain prices should be set by law, but rather that the fluctuations in price should be minimised. In his paper on usury, Reid states: 'There appears no reason therefore for fixing a Rate of Interest by Law which is to regulate the Money Market, any more than for fixing by Law the price of Beef or Grain or any other Commodity' (130). Reid was thus to some extent willing to let the market set food prices.

[238] See pp. 107, 117.

meant lower wages and hence more competitive prices for commodities. As the authors of the Glasgow *Memorial* put it, 'whenever provisions are plenty [*sic*] and cheap, manufactures flourish: Whenever they are scarce and dear, manufactures decay. And the true cause of the present flourishing state of manufactures, in every part of Britain, is the plenty and cheaper price of provisions, with which the kingdom has been blessed for these two last years'.[239] That is, they maintained that the 1773 Corn Law, and especially its provisions for the warehousing of grain, had had a positive impact on the British economy. On the other side, the landed interest contended that, in general, higher food prices would stimulate production in the agricultural sector and thereby ensure that there was enough corn and other grains to feed the population.[240] While agreeing that higher subsistence prices were not necessarily detrimental to the economic well-being of the nation, the anonymous author of *Corn-Bill Hints* justified his position in different terms, arguing that 'with regard to the flourishing of manufactures, provisions may be too cheap, as well as too dear. Low prices infallibly produce, among the inferior ranks of people, habits of idleness and debauchery; high prices as certainly promote the contrary ones of industry and temperance'.[241] Citing writings by Sir William Temple, David Hume and Arthur Young, the pamphleteer asserted that 'the rate of the prices of provisions, most favourable for a place of trade and manufactures, is one approaching rather towards what the workman will call dear, and not fluctuating, but accompanied with a considerable degree of uniformity'.[242]

The broad theoretical debate over food prices to which the author of *Corn-Bill Hints* alludes was also bound up with the dispute among political economists over the question of wages, which Reid had earlier addressed in the Aberdeen Philosophical Society and to which he returned in his paper on the 1773 Corn Law. On the one hand, there were those such as Decker who linked the cost of subsistence to wage levels and who believed that low prices for both food and labour were beneficial for the economy.[243] On the other, many mercantilist commentators followed Sir William Temple in insisting that wages should be kept low even if food prices were relatively high because this would promote

[239] See the version of the Glasgow *Memorial* in the *Scots Magazine* 39 (1777), p. 572.

[240] For this argument see especially the anonymous *Essay on the Corn Laws*, cited in note 217, especially pp. 22–24.

[241] Anon., *Corn-Bill Hints*, cited above note 217, p. 3.

[242] Anon., *Corn-Bill Hints*, p. 4. The author referred to Temple's *Observations upon the United Provinces of the Netherlands*, Hume's essay 'Of Taxes' and Young's tours of England and Wales.

[243] Decker, *An Essay*, p. 170. In the context of the debate over Fergusson's Corn Bill, the claim that the price of subsistence regulated wages was made in 'A Peep at the Corn Bill', p. 294 (see note 215).

industry and frugality among the labouring poor.[244] These arguments were, in turn, opposed by a minority of writers, such as Hume, Wallace and Smith, who suggested that high wages rather than want were a more effective spur to labour.[245] Reid occupied something of a middle ground between these last two positions, for while he agreed that 'there is no Spur to Labour equal to Necessity' and that 'the wages of Labour *ought* to be such as makes it necessary for the bulk of Labouring people to labour not for a few years onely but for Life', he also stated that 'it is most for the benefitc of the Country that the wages of meer Labour should never be below necessary Subsistence, & on the other hand that it should not be a great deal above it'.[246] Yet he was far more worried by wages that were below what he called 'necessary Subsistence' since they led to 'misery & depopulation', whereas 'High wages of Labour tends to promote population among the Labouring people, which multiplies the Labouring hands, and if the Number of Labouring hands be increased while the demand for Labour continues the same their Wages will soon fall to a Moderate Subsistence' (114). Moreover, he also echoed Steuart and Smith in denying that wages were invariably linked to the price of subsistence, and in doing so rejected the formulaic claim of Decker and many others that economic competitiveness rested on the interlocking pillars of low food prices and low wages.[247] Consequently, Reid believed that wages had to be managed so that they were neither too low to cause genuine hardship among the working poor nor too high to serve as an effective spur to labour. For Reid, then, effective police for the labouring poor had to minimise fluctuations in the price of grain and control wages in order to avoid the extremes of indigence and excess. He thus agreed with both the landed and commercial interests that some form of control over wages and the cost of food was necessary, and he rejected the radical argument put forward in Smith's *Wealth of Nations* that such controls ought to be removed from the marketplace on the ground that 'famine has never arisen from any other cause but the violence of government attempting, by improper means, to remedy the inconveniences of a dearth'.[248] Reid may have been willing to accept specific aspects of Smith's analysis of the Corn Laws but he by no means wholly endorsed Smith's trust in the market.

[244] Sir William Temple, *Observations upon the United Provinces of the Netherlands* (1673), p. 109.

[245] Hume, 'Of Commerce', in Hume, *Essays Moral, Political and Literary*, p. 265; Wallace, *A Dissertation*, p. 160; Smith, *Wealth of Nations*, I.viii.44–48. Hume was, however, not entirely consistent since he also believed that necessity is a spur to industry.

[246] See pp. 113, 114 (emphasis added).

[247] See p. 115; compare Steuart, *An Inquiry* (1767), vol. II, pp. 503, 509, and note 232 (p. lxxxix) above; Smith, *Wealth of Nations*, I.viii.29–34, 52–56.

[248] Smith, *Wealth of Nations*, IV.v.b.5. On Smith's view see Hont, *Jealousy of Trade*, pp. 412–19.

Not long after Reid read his paper on the warehousing of grain to the Glasgow Literary Society, he introduced a 'voluntary' question, 'Whether is it proper that the interest of money should be regulated by law in cases where the parties have contracted', at a meeting held on 20 March 1778.[249] Like his previous paper, Reid's text addressed legislation that had been brought before the House of Commons, namely a bill to regulate usury and the sale of annuities. The bill was given first and second readings in the Commons in May 1777, but was then abandoned. Eventually a revised bill dealing specifically with annuities passed into law in 1777 as 'An Act for Registering the Grants of Life Annuities; and for the Better Protection of Infants against such Grants'.[250] During the course of the eighteenth century, taking out a life annuity became a common stratagem used by those in debt to raise money. The Parliamentary committee initially struck to consider the question of usury and annuities recognised this widespread practice and stated that 'the Purchase of Annuities for the Life of the Grantor, being generally intended as a loan of Money, ought to be regulated' by the law governing interest rates.[251] Moreover, according to one pamphleteer, the trade in annuities in London had recently become the most profitable way to avoid the legal restrictions on the rate of interest charged on loans, which had been set at 5% in the reign of Queen Anne.[252] Given that life annuities involved a contract between a borrower and a lender typically involving an interest rate in excess of that specified by law, the common use of, and the lively trade in, annuities thus had a direct bearing on the general problem of usury as Reid would have understood it in 1777.

The most striking feature of Reid's paper is the lengthy preamble tracing the 'revolution' that had taken place in attitudes towards commerce in general and to money lending in particular. Reid had already pointed to the broad outlines of his historical narrative in his reflections on paper credit given to the Wise Club in 1761, wherein he suggested that 'Usury may very justly be prohibited by Law in a Nation that has no trade and as justly permitted in a Trading Nation'.[253] His preamble can thus be seen as giving voice to ideas that he had developed over the

[249] 'Laws of the Literary Society in Glasgow College', GUL, MS Murray 505, pp. 66–67.

[250] Hoppit, *Failed Legislation*, pp. 444–45 (reference 118.042); 17 George III c. 26, 'An Act for Registering the Grants of Life Annuities; and for the Better Protection of Infants against such Grants', in Ruffhead, *Statutes at Large*, vol. VIII, pp. 505–6.

[251] Anon., *Report from the Committee Appointed to Take into Consideration the Laws now in Being against Usury, and the Present Practice of Purchasing Annuities for the Life of the Grantor* (1777), p. 11.

[252] Anon., *Reflections on Usury: Containing an Account of those Usurious Contracts, Carried on under the Mode of Undervalued Annuities: To which is Added the Substance of the Bill now before the House to Prevent Them; with Cursory Observations on it* (1777), pp. 12–19.

[253] See pp. 82–83.

course of roughly twenty years and which grew out of his reading of Aristotle, the modern natural lawyers and the stadial historians of the eighteenth century. For his earlier comments on usury were rooted in Aristotle's distinction between the 'natural art of acquisition' found in the lives of shepherds and hunters, and the 'art of wealth-getting' associated with 'exchange and retail trade'. In the former art, 'industry springs up of itself' and exchanges for the necessities of life take place by barter, whereas in the latter art money is used to facilitate commercial transactions between individuals and nations for food and other commodities. Moreover, according to Aristotle the 'unnatural' art of wealth-getting gave rise to usury, which is 'the most hated sort' of exchange 'by which men gain from one another'.[254] The natural lawyers from Grotius onwards elaborated on Aristotle's depiction of the different 'modes of life' and 'modes of subsistence' in connection with their ideas of pre-political forms of life and their search for an account of property and of political obligation. These ideas were gradually transformed in the eighteenth century to theories of socio-economic stages of civilisation and, as we explain in connection with Reid's lectures (lv–lix), we may see him as one of the contributors to this considerable conversion of ideas from one purpose to another. It is very likely that Pufendorf was particularly on Reid's mind, as he was for so many other Scottish thinkers at the time. Despite his deep philosophical differences with Pufendorf, Reid organised his lectures on natural jurisprudence along lines laid down by the Saxon, and some of his key ideas in economics were formulated within this framework. In the present context, Reid would have been particularly interested to note Pufendorf's point that as society changed, the perception of the moral standing of money lending shifted. Of the Old Testament prohibition of lending money at interest among the Jews, Pufendorf claimed that the Jewish nation condemned usury because 'that Nation had then a more plain Way of Trading, which consisted in Pasture and Husbandry, or Manufactures; *Merchandise* was simple and moderate, the Secrets of Trade and Navigation being not known to them; and in such a State no one borrows, but when he is pressed with Necessity'. In such a pre-commercial society, usury was seen as oppressive and hence forbidden, even though the lending of money to other trading peoples was permitted. By contrast, in the modern commercial world of most European states, Pufendorf thought that 'Money is borrowed for other Ends', such as the accumulation of personal wealth, which meant that charging interest for a loan was entirely justifiable in moral terms.[255] Although the overall point of Pufendorf's own discussion was the question of the authority of natural law and positive law

[254] Aristotle, *Politics*, 1256a–1258b, in Aristotle, *The Complete Works*.
[255] See Pufendorf, *Law of Nature*, V.7.viii–xii (quotations from section ix).

in the matter of usury, he thus formulated an idea that was to interest Reid and other Enlightenment thinkers for their purposes, namely that changing economic circumstances had altered not only the uses to which money was put but also the moral perception of loans made at interest.

Reid wove together threads from the narrative created by Aristotle and Pufendorf in his brief history of attitudes towards usury. Following Pufendorf, he saw the advent of commerce in modern Europe as producing 'a great Revolution in the Sentiments of Men with regard to buying & Selling borrowing & lending' (124). Whereas Cicero and the ancient moralists had all condemned 'the Retailing bussiness … as vile & odious because … men cannot deal without lying and falsehood', Reid said that the commercial revolution in Europe had led to a rejection of the traditional view, with 'the Retailer' now seen as 'a very usefull and necessary member in the Commercial System', who 'may be as honest a Man as the Merchant or any other Citizen' (124). Similarly, the ancients and the moderns had opposing views of the legitimacy of charging interest on money loans. Echoing Pufendorf, Reid claimed that in societies without commerce, individuals borrowed money only out of necessity. Because there was little or no credit in such societies, loans were typically made on the basis of 'Friendship or Compassion' or the receipt of a 'pledge' as a guarantee. Charity was thus the norm, although Reid acknowledged that there were those who loaned money at interest and who thus had 'great opportunities of oppressing the poor'. And it was these money lenders who elicited condemnation for their practices and prompted the belief that interest charged on loans was morally reprehensible (123–24).

In commercial societies, on the other hand, money was regarded as a commodity like any other, and usury was no longer equated with the charging of interest. Rather, it was generally recognised that a 'reasonable' rate of interest on a loan was equivalent to 'the price paid for the Use of Money', whereas usury came to be understood as the demand for 'exorbitant & excessive' interest. Reid also maintained that borrowing in commercial societies was not solely a function of necessity, for the rise of commerce had spawned a multiplicity of uses for money and had removed the stigma attached to securing a loan. According to Reid, in commercial societies loans were thought to generate public and private benefits, on the grounds that they '[put] it in the Power of the borrower to enlarge his Traffick, to encourage industry, and give bread to the Poor, at the same time that he profits both the Lender and himself'.[256] Consequently, the 'lending money upon Interest' was no longer viewed as being intrinsically immoral among modern commercial nations, even though the practice had been closely associated with

[256] See p. 125.

'the oppression of the Poor' in the non-commercial societies of the past. But this apparent 'revolution' in our moral sentiments did not involve the replacement of one moral standard with another. He insisted that even in commercial societies pawnbrokers were condemned for their exploitation of the poor, which for him illustrated the uniformity of the principles of practical morality among humankind. Furthermore, he contended that our familiarity with commercial life had enabled us to draw the proper moral distinction between usury and interest that had previously been obscured among peoples whose non-commercial mode of living precluded their making this distinction. On Reid's reading of history, then, commerce had promoted the refinement rather than the fundamental transformation of our moral sentiments.[257]

As Reid himself indicated, his historical preamble might have struck his listeners as being tangential to the question of the legal regulation of interest rates (125). However, the distinction he drew in the preamble between usury and interest was central to the argument of the second part of his paper, which, in the context of contemporary discussions of these matters, was a radical one. For what Reid's historical analysis implied was that the law setting the maximum rate of interest passed in the reign of Queen Anne had its conceptual origin in a pre-commercial past and thus reflected the confusion of usury and interest characteristic of non-commercial societies (133). He maintained that the poor ought still to be protected from usurers such as pawnbrokers and, while he recognised the practical difficulties in formulating a distinction at law between those who borrowed out of necessity and those who did not, he suggested that impoverished individuals 'who borrow upon a Pledge' deserved the protection of legislation specifying the legal rate of interest. That is, usury was in his view immoral and should therefore be curbed by law (126–28). But when it came to transactions in a commercial society such as Britain between lenders and borrowers who were equals, he held that the market should be left to itself to set interest rates because the mechanism of the marketplace established the 'just' price for the use of money. Money, he emphasised, was a commodity and, as such, its price (interest) was a function of supply and demand.[258] Consequently, he argued that the law then in force governing the rate of interest was either unnecessary

[257] See p. 125. In a debate in the *Weekly Magazine, or Edinburgh Amusement* in the spring of 1772, George Hay had argued in very similar historical terms to distinguish usury from interest, but he suggested the exposure to risk and the loss of opportunity on the part of the lender as the justification for the taking of interest. Hay also supported having a legally fixed rate of interest. Hay collected the whole debate in his *Letters on Usury and Interest* (1774); cf. Mark Goldie, 'The Scottish Catholic Enlightenment'. We have found no indication that Reid was aware of Hay's work.

[258] See p. 130. Reid's view of interest was taken over from Locke.

or, more importantly, unjust because it favoured either the borrower or the lender (131–33). Reid's position regarding interest rates set by law was thus far more 'liberal' than that of Adam Smith, for example, who did not question the propriety of the legislative regulation of the rate of interest.[259]

A decade later, the radical nature of Reid's treatment of usury and interest was not lost on members of the Bentham circle in London. Following the publication of Jeremy Bentham's *Defence of Usury* in 1787, James Gregory forwarded a copy of Reid's paper to the barrister George Wilson, who in turn sent the manuscript on to his friend Bentham. Although the characteristic tone of metropolitan condescension colours Wilson's assessment of the paper, he grudgingly admitted that, for all of its faults, Reid's analysis of usury displayed 'a great effort of liberality & good sense'. For his part, Reid displayed greater generosity in his endorsement of Bentham's work. But he remained convinced that 'when the Buyers are the many, the Poor, & the Simple, [and] the Sellers few rich & cunning, the former may need the Aid of the Magistrate to prevent their being oppressed by the latter', and he also preferred his own account of the history of attitudes towards usury in his preamble to that found in Bentham's *Defence*.[260] Bentham was evidently aware of Reid's assessment of the *Defence*, for in an unpublished preface drafted for the second edition of the work, published in 1790, Bentham acknowledged Reid's criticisms and noted that 'the only ground on which he differs from me is that of the origination of the prejudice [against usury], of which his paper gives as might be expected an account more ecclesiastical than mine'. Nevertheless, the draft preface shows that he had hoped to publish either the complete text of Reid's discourse or excerpts from it, although his plan did not come to fruition, for reasons which remain unclear.[261] We see, then, that Bentham was not the only major thinker in late-eighteenth-century Britain to question the need for legal restrictions on interest rates, and our publication of Reid's paper thus brings to light a highly significant contribution to the early modern debate on usury that deserves to figure in future histories of the subject.

[259] Smith, *Wealth of Nations*, II.iv.14–17.

[260] George Wilson (quoting Reid) to Jeremy Bentham, [4 December 1788], in Reid, *Correspondence*, pp. 201–3. For Bentham's history of the concept of usury see letter 10 in Jeremy Bentham, *Defence of Usury; Shewing the Impolicy of the Present Legal Restraints on the Terms of Pecuniary Bargains* (1787), pp. 94–109. In his commonly used *Jeremy Bentham's Economic Writings*, the editor, Werner Stark, suggested that Reid's paper was not to be found (vol. I, p. 28n). In fact it came to light only in 1980 as a donation to Aberdeen University Library. A critical edition of Bentham's work is scheduled to appear in M. Quinn (ed.), *Writings on Political Economy: I* (Oxford, Clarendon Press).

[261] Jeremy Bentham, 'To Dr Smith' [1790], in *The Correspondence of Adam Smith*, p. 402.

Because the minutes of the Glasgow Literary Society covering the period November 1779 to May 1794 are no longer extant, we do not know if Reid formally discussed any political, social or economic topics in the Society during this time and there are no surviving manuscripts that suggest that he did so. However, one of his last contributions to the proceedings of the Society was his penultimate discourse, 'Some Thoughts on the Utopian System', which he read at the meeting held on 28 November 1794.[262]

'Some Thoughts on the Utopian System' is an intriguing document that can be read in several different lights, some of which we indicate here. As we have seen above (xxxiii–xxxvii), the paper was clearly meant as Reid's response to the British and especially the Scottish debate about the French Revolution and the way this debate had developed over the course of events until late 1794. At the same time, the paper drew on ideas that Reid had held as fundamental for most, probably all, of his life as a philosophical thinker, not only about politics but also about morals.[263] The paper is in that sense something of an intellectual testament. A closer look at the paper therefore serves to draw together leading themes not only in the papers of the present volume, but in the Reidian *oeuvre* as a whole.

The theme that structures the argument of the paper is the opposition between two societal models, the 'system of private property' and the 'utopian system'. In the latter there is no private property; everything is owned and administered by the state. Reid's critical analysis aims to show that (nearly) all moral and political corruption in actually existing societies, especially those of modern commercial society, arises from private ownership. And the suggested remedy is the imaginary Utopia that Reid goes on to elaborate in some detail. Private property is an expression of the 'Desire for Distinction and Preeminence', which, after the pursuit of subsistence, is the most basic of human desires. Private property rests on acquisitiveness and self-interest, which entails competition, inequality and dependence. This is the bane of the common good as a moral motive, and it makes people blind to the basic moral equality of all human beings. For these reasons private property also corrupts politics, for it leads people to pass off the interests of their particular section of society as the public interest and to use political power and the law as means to institutionalise this deception.

The key to the Utopian system is that it offers a replacement for private property as the means to satisfy the human need for distinction, and this replacement

[262] 'Minutes of the College Literary Society, 1790–99', GUL, MS Gen.4, p. 8; notwithstanding the title of the manuscript, this set of minutes begins on 7 November 1794. Reid's final discourse, which was on muscular motion, was given on 4 December 1795 (p. 34).

[263] For an earlier attempt by one of us to read the paper in the light of Reid's lectures on natural jurisprudence, see Haakonssen, *Natural Law and Moral Philosophy*, pp. 216–20.

is the possibility of moral pre-eminence in the community. Once private property is abolished and replaced by public ownership, people's productive capacity is in the service of the common wealth. This again means that individual effort is marked not by acquisitions but by the recognition offered by others, and Utopia organises this into a system of public honours that is undergirded by state allowances of the conveniences and luxuries of life: 'Servants, Horses, Chariots, Houses and Furniture' (147). Both in its psychology of mutual recognition and in its moderate embrace of the good things in life, Reid's Utopia is the exact opposite of Rousseau's primitivism, and Reid had in fact never been sparing in his criticism of the Genevan.[264] Reid had a vision of moral progress and suggested an arrangement that was meant to lead people into the practice of their other-regarding potential, but in order for this to work Utopia had to make sure that people appreciate that moral recognition is something worth having. This is achieved primarily by moral education aimed at the formation of good characters and the suppression of bad, self-interested tendencies. Such education has to be universal in the community, for moral abilities are neither hereditary nor preserved by social class. The implication is that moral achievement is a matter of personal effort, and Reid thought that such efforts were so varied that Utopia would have 'a much greater variety of Ranks than in any other' system (146–47). In other words, our natural equality is the basis for social inequality in Utopia as well as in the 'system of private property', but inequality in the former is both an expression of and a spur to moral betterment. Reid does, however, recognise that some individuals are beyond the reach of moral education and the social control of communal recognition. Such people are subject to punishment and forced labour for the public.[265] Making society into one coherent system requires supervision and the keeping of records for each individual's moral effort in contributing to the common weal. The result is,

> that in this System, the State is burthened with a load of Work, additional to the common cares of Government, too great to be well accomplished. The Education of all the Youth of both Sexes, The Oversight of all the labouring hands, The collecting, storing and dispensing the Produce of their Labour: The publick Registers that must be kept of the Merits & Demerits of every

[264] In his lectures on the culture of the mind, Reid treated his students to some severe criticism of Rousseau's *Discourse on Inequality* (1755); see Reid, *Logic, Rhetoric, and the Fine Arts*, pp. 42–45, 72, and 81; see also his *Inquiry*, pp. 201–2 and his *Practical Ethics*, p. 148. Cf. Peter Diamond, *Common Sense and Improvement*, pp. 354–55, and J. C. Stewart-Robertson, 'Reid's Anatomy of Culture: A Scottish Response to the Eloquent Jean-Jacques'.

[265] Cf. the apprehension about servants and manual labour debated in the Aberdeen Philosophical Society in 1762 and discussed by us on pp. lxvii–lxix.

> Individual, & of every Step of his advancement in Honour and Rank. The Regulations for confering Degrees with Justice & Impartiality, and the Management of the trading Stock of the Nation, these things, without doubt, will require much Attention & Fidelity, and many hands. (149)

In all three branches of government, however, the absence of private property, the abolition of domestic private business and the employment by all in the public service will mean a drastic reduction in the tasks that they currently have. Taxation, customs and excise will all disappear; so too will business regulations, property law and associated law suits; and much else.

If taken at face value, Reid's Utopia is a radical work within its genre in the eighteenth century; few others proposed the outright abolition of private property.[266] Reid himself signalled the radicalism, not only by his invocation of Thomas More's work as his guiding light, but also by his frank declaration that his sketch was purely speculative. In fact, already in his Aberdeen oration from 1762, he used More's *Utopia* and Harrington's *Oceana* as examples of the usage of the word 'idea' to refer 'to fruit of the human mind which … never existed in reality'.[267] It is on the same note that he concludes 'Some Thoughts'. However, pure speculation was of the greatest importance in Reid's eyes. In order properly to appreciate his intentions in writing and delivering his paper, it may be useful to relate it to some particular themes in his work in general.

Perhaps most fundamental is the idea of humanity's educability, both individually and collectively. It runs as a red thread through Reid's work that while the human mind has been naturally endowed with intellectual and active powers, these powers need to be cultivated through education; that this can be done more or less well; and that there are objective measures for the right or wrong exercise of the powers of the mind, namely the extent to which they rely upon the principles of reasoning – 'common notions', 'axioms' – that make up humanity's common sense. The education of the individual is a matter of social interaction, and there is therefore an interchange between individual and collective development, which Reid tended to see in perfectibilist terms, though ever so cautiously. In this regard, his Utopia is simply an extension of his common sense moral theory and the associated moral progressivism.

In this connection we may see the Utopian system as Reid's response to Harringtonian republicanism, as he understood it. Harrington is not mentioned in the Utopia paper, but Reid had concluded his lectures on Harrington with

[266] Cf. Gregory Claeys (ed.), *Utopias of the British Enlightenment*, p. xxv. For a thorough historical typology of ideal societies, see J. C. Davis, *Utopia and the Ideal Society*, ch. 1.

[267] Reid, *Philosophical Orations*, oration IV, para. 29.

two criticisms directly relevant to the argument in 'Some Thoughts'. First, Harrington was concerned only with the regulation of landed property, but in the commercial society that Britain in the meantime had become it was other forms of property that endangered 'that Equality among the Citizens which a Republick seems to require'. Secondly, Reid 'doubted whether there is in this Model sufficient provision for preserving that degree of Morals and publick Virtue which is necessary in a Commonwealth' (43, 44). By abolishing private property, replacing the market (the heart of a commercial society) with public provisioning and turning society into a school for virtue, Utopia prevented these problems. At the same time, Utopia's bureaucratic-administrative state – to use a later terminology – would seem to satisfy Reid's obsession with regulatory machinery in the same way that Harrington's labyrinthine Oceana obviously did, as we see in the lectures on politics (38–41). Read in the context of Reid's political economy in the lectures on police, the Utopian system is clearly mercantilism taken to its logical conclusion, where the concessions to the historical reality of the exchange of goods can be ignored because such exchange has been replaced by the exchange of moral goods.

Perhaps a greater conundrum is the relationship between Utopia and the thought of Montesquieu, 'the greatest political Writer that either ancient or modern times have produced', who was 'French by nationality' but nevertheless 'British by nature and enthusiasm' because of his appreciation of the modern British polity.[268] It is obvious, however, that in Utopia there is no political process, and certainly not of the British sort. Adversarial politics is premised upon the reality of human fallibility; in Utopia this has been replaced by administration of the sort that is implied by the possibility of moral objectivity. Reid himself of course always emphasised our fallibility, and even in Utopia there is some provision for human error. But for him the concept of being wrong implied the concept of being right, so to speak. The adversarial politics of uncertainty that he found institutionalised in Hanoverian Britain, and which Whig thinkers and Montesquieu had theorised as a system of balances, could be made morally intelligible only if one could specify what it would mean to say that a community *was* morally certain. Utopia was the place where such certainty was as great as might be humanly possible, and the idea of it served to put into perspective what actual politics was – or ought to be – about. It is here that Reid most fundamentally differs from Hume. For Hume, the fallibility of adversarial politics was not a matter of uncertainty about the right moral answers; it was a matter of living with each other without having to ask such questions. Accordingly, when Hume allowed himself a flight of utopian fantasy, it

[268] See p. 51; and Reid, *Philosophical Orations*, oration I, para. 11.

was inspired by Harrington and had the basic point of suggesting an institutional machinery that made the moral virtue of individuals as irrelevant as possible for the peaceful functioning of society.[269]

It is worth remembering these basic differences when considering the position of Reid's Utopia paper within his work as a whole. Hume and Reid may seem remarkably similar in their conception of a science of politics. According to both of them such a science is probabilistic and based upon very general features of humanity, something that Reid had stressed in his lectures and repeats at the end of 'Some Thoughts' as one of the reasons why a utopian scheme could not simply be introduced. One had to take into account the uncertainty of how actual people as a matter of fact behave in any given society at a particular time, and this was not a matter that politics as a science could explain with accuracy and politics as an art control with certainty. However, exactly for that reason the political theorist had to step outside of the science of politics in order to think with certainty, as Reid did in the Utopia paper. In this regard the paper is a piece of moral philosophy, or political jurisprudence as he would call it. But insofar as it provides common notions with which to think about actual political action, the paper is part of the science of politics that he presented to his students. The work is therefore at the core of Reid's approach to politics as an art and a science.

[269] See Hume, 'Idea of a Perfect Commonwealth', in *Essays, Moral, Political and Literary*, pp. 512–29.

THE MANUSCRIPTS

Part One: Reading

I

4/III/19, 1r Aug 27 1768

Read the Charter of Charles 2d to William Penn Proprietary & Governour of Pensilvania 4th March 1681*

The Subordination of this Government to the English Empire and to the Parliament of England is reserved in the clearest & most express terms. By Article 11 Goods and Merchandizes from Pensilvania are to be imported onely in to the Ports of England & not in to any other Countrey, there to be disposed of, or within a Year to be exported to any other country According to Law; Provided always that they pay such Customs & Impositions Subsidies and duties for the Same, to us our Heirs & Successors, as the rest of our Subjects of England for the time being shall be bound to pay, and to observe the Acts of Navigation and other Laws in that behalf made.

By Article 12 The said William Penn, shall admit and receive in and about all such Havens Ports Creeks & Keys (to be erected in Pensilvania) all Officers and their Deputies who shall from time to time be appointed by the farmers or Commissioners of our Customs for the time being.*

By Article 13 Saving to us our Heirs and Successors Such Impositions and customs, as by act of Parliament are & shall be imposed

Article 14. How the Said Government may be forfeited to the Crown*

Article 20 We covenant and grant to and with the said William Penn his Heirs and Assigns, that we shall at no time hereafter Set or make any Imposition custom, or other Taxation Rate or contribution upon the dwellers of the foresaid Province, for Lands tenements goods and Chattels within the said Province or upon goods and Merchandise within the said Province or to be laden or unladen within the Ports of the Same, unless the same be with the consent of the Proprietary, or chief Governour, or Assembly, or by Act of Parliament in England.*

Read The Frame of the Government of the Province of Pensilvania in America Together with certain Laws agreed upon in England by the Governour and divers freemen of the afforesaid Province; To be further explained and continued there by the first Provincial Council that shall be held if they see meet. 25 Aprile 1682*

The preface is admirably wrote Shewing from Scripture that Government is the Ordinance of God for these two Ends First to terrify evil doers Secondly to encourage and cherish those that do well. This gives to Government a Life beyond Corruption, & as durable as good men shall be.* As to Models of Government the Author thinks they may be variable as times and Circumstances require, and that it is not easy to frame any one that shall serve all places Alike. With regard to the Controversy between the several Admirers of Monarchy Aristocracy & Democracy; he onely lays down this Distinction as belonging to all three That any Government is free to the People under it (whatever be the frame) where the Laws Rule, and the People are a party to those Laws; and more than this is Tyranny Oligarchy or Confusion. He observes that
4/III/19,1v there is hardly any Government | so ill designed by its first founders, that in good hands will not do well enough; and the best in ill ones can do nothing that is great or good

Governments rather depend upon Men than Men upon Governments

Good Laws do well, but good Men do better: For good Laws may want good Men, & be abolished or evaded by ill men; but good Men will never want good Laws nor Suffer ill ones. That therefore which makes a good constitution must keep it viz Men of Wisdom and Virtue, Qualities that, because they descend not with worldly inheritances, must be carefully propagated by a Virtuous Education of Youth. – The Ends of Government to support Power in Reverence with the People, & to secure the People from the abuse of Power. Liberty without Obedience is confusion, & Obedience without Liberty is Slavery. To carry this Evenness is partly owing to the Constitution and Partly to the Magistracy. And where neither of these fail the Government is like to endure.*

This Frame of Government is perfectly Republican & Harringtonian consisting of a Council for deliberating and Preparing and a General Assembly for Enacting Laws. The Governour has three votes in the Council The Council to consist of 72 a third part of which to be changed by election every year and after the first seven years Incapable of being elected for a year

The Council divided into four Committees, viz 1 Of Plantations 2 A Committee of Justice & Safety 3 Of Trade & Treasury 4 Of Manners

Each Committee to consist of eighteen, six of every Region of the council Two for every County Magistracy to be chosen by the freemen in the county Courts, whereof one shall be preferred by the Governour, otherwise the first in the list to be the Magistrate. A list of two for the Provincial Magistracies to be made by the Council whereof the Governour to Choose one. All Elections and Determinations of Moment in the Council & Assembly to be by Ballot

The Assembly never to exceed five hundred*

An Excellent Body of Laws follows.*

II

4/III/21,1r Aug 1769

The History of King Henry 2d and of the Age in which he lived in 5 Books; to which is prefixed a History of the Revolutions of England from the Death of Edward the Confessor to the Birth of Henry 2d by George Lord Littleton. 3d Ed 8o Dodesly 1769.*

Read Vol 2 which contains onely the last part of Book 2d

Henrys interposition in favour of Pope Alexander, who had Fled to France and was Supported by France & England in opposition to Victor who was supported by the Emperor*

The Death of Theobald Arch bishop of Canterbury and the Election of Becket to that See. The Settlement of Some Commotions in ‹W›ales. Anno 1163 A Court held at Wood Stock where Malcom King of Scotland and the Princes of Wales attended his Summonds and payed their Homage both to him and his eldest Son as Heir to his Kingdom The Rest of the Book is taken up with the personal Character of Henry and the Manners Laws and State of the Nation.*

Characters of Saxons and Normans. from William of Malmsbury*

The Military Art in those Days*

The Construction of their Gallies for War & their Naval Battles.*

The Greek wild Fire which is said "with a pernicious Stench and livid flames to consume even flint and Iron; it cannot be extinguished by water; but by sprinkling Sand upon it the Violence of it may be abated, and vinegar poured upon it will put it out." Vide Montesquieu, Causes de la Grandeur &c* The Greek Emperors for some time kept the Secret of this Composition to themselves and it was of great Use in the Defence of the Empire. But in the twelfth Century it was known to many Nations*

The Attention given in those Days by several Princes to maritime Force. A Law of King Athelstan That a Merchant who has made three voyages beyond the British Channel or Narrow Seas shall be entitled to the Privilege of a Thane. The Trade and Wealth of England at that time very Considerable. Laws against pillaging wrecked Ships.*

England Divided into 243600 Hides or Plough Lands by Alfred or some preceeding King. According to this Division the Military and other Charges of the Kingdom were imposed.*

A Knights fee was two hides or two hides and a half.|

4/III/21,1v There are said to be in England at this Time 60215 knights fees of which Number 28115 belonged to the Church. A mesne tennant who had more than a single knights fee was called a Vavasor*

A Barony was Knight Service enlarged and Erected into a Barony Every Baron or Nobleman was obliged to serve the King in his Wars at home and Abroad with such a Number of Knights as answered to the knights fees of which his Barony was composed.*

Scutage or Escuage was a pecuniary Commutation for personal Service in forreign Wars. In the Ordinary Course the Military tenants were to serve forty days at their own Charge and if the Service continued longer it was to be at the Kings Charge. Two Shillings or three shillings a day were the Wages of a Knight or horseman. Out of this they were to maintain their Horses and their Esquires, servientes, or armigeri. who seem to have made the foot of the army and to have been Archers or Slingers.*

One kind of knights Service was Castleguard; and those who held by that tenure performed their Service within the Realm and without limitation to any certain Term.*

About the end of the eleventh or beginning of the twelfth Century, a new kind of Militia was established in France for the Security of the Principal Cities. The Communities by their Charters had a power to levy forces and a determined Number was to be enrolled in every parish and to march under the Banner of the Church they belonged to, in case of any attack upon the territory, and for the Suppressing of Seditions and outrages of all kinds within the limits thereof. This institution besides other motives, had perhaps a view to make the town forces a check upon those of the Barons, and was probably introduced into england with the Normans.*

Henry the 2d first introduced Scutage or Escuage: At first it was allowed to the Spiritual Barons and their military tenants in a War with the Welsh. But on the Occasion of Henrys Expedition against Toulouse it was extended to all the inferiour tenants in chief and to almost all the sub vassals who held by knights service. It was afterwards often allowed in wars against Scotland and Wales even to the greater vassals of the Crown, when they did not hold some Office of grand Sergeantry which required their attendance*

Before the Conquest the Hereditary Estates of the Anglo Saxon Nobility were Thane land, Boc land or Charter land; and were allodial and not Subject to Military Service. But both the Greater and lesser Thanes frequently had other lands holden by a feudal Tenure, yet not
4/III/21,2r like the | Norman feuds hereditary, but granted at will, or for a certain term of years or for life or lives; in which they resembled the lands of the vulgar called folk land. And such Grants were called Benefices.

These Benefices were made hereditary Fiefs under william the Conqueror, and most of the bocland was converted into the same kind of tenure.*

In the Infancy of the Feudal System when the lands were held at pleasure or for Life, the feudal laws were very Simple, & were all comprehended in the Service due by the tenant and the reciprocal protection due by the Superior. But when fiefs were made hereditary (a custom which was introduced by degrees) this gave occasion to a complex System of feudal Law.

From hence arose in the first place the payments made on the Death of the Vassal by the Heir which in the Law term were called Reliefs. The Relief of a Knights fee under Henry 2d was 100 shillings and of Lands held in Soccage, a years value by the custom of the kingdom. But with regard to Baronies and Serjeanties the relief was at the Kings Discretion.

2 The perpetuity of fiefs produced also the Right of wardship. by which the Superior had the Custody of the Lands while the Heir was a Minor, as well as the custody of the heir whether Male or Female. The male heir entered to the possession of his Land at 21. But the Female heir continued in the custody of the Superior till she was married. She being obliged to marry with his Consent, & he to provide her in a husband when she was 14 such as should not desparage her. As the Husband was to be the Vassal of the Superior it was reasonable that no person should be brought in to a Relation to him which was accounted nearer than that of Blood without his consent. On the other hand Female heirs were not obliged to marry at the will of the Superior, they might continue unmarried, or purchase by money the priviledge of marrying the man they liked.*

There were four kinds of Aid due from the Vassal to his Lord. 1 To assist him in paying the Relief he owed to the King or his Superior 2 to contribute towards his Expence of making his Eldest Son a Knight at
4/III/21,2v least if he was a Knight himself. 3 To assist him to portion his | eldest Daughter. 4 To contribute to the Ransom of their Lord if he was taken prisoner.*

It was usual for the King to commit to others the Custody of the lands and persons of his Wards, either under Account to him or without account as a beneficiary grant. And Inferior Lords did the same.*

The heir was obliged to do homage to his Lord as soon as he conveniently could. And Homage done to the King was called liege Homage. The Homage done to a Subject was made with a salvo of that which was due to the King*

Fiefs of all kinds reverted to the Lord if the tenant died without heirs and this extinction of the Original Grant of the fief was called an Escheat. The fief also returned to the Lord if the vassal refused to perform any of the duties required of him by his tenure, or would not acknowledge that tenure, or dismembered the Estate or greatly impaired it, or committed any grievous injury or offence against his Lord. A Conviction of Felony likewise forfeited the land to the Superior, even though he obtained the Kings pardon*

A Female heir by incontinence before Marriage forfeited her Land to the Lord.*

It seems wonderfull that free holders possessed of allodial Estates should be willing to convert them into fiefs subject to the services and burthens above mentioned. Yet there were reasons that induced men to desire this. The possessors of fiefs had several Priviledges A higher value was set upon their persons; the Compositions for injuries done them were greater; they were exempted from tallage and many other impositions which fell heavy upon the possessors of allodial Estates. The Protection of their Lord, or the near relation they stood in to the King by being his vassal was also a considerable inducement.*

The Number of Earls, Comites was regularly the same with that of the Counties. This was the highest order of Nobility known at that Time. The Earldom was properly an Office the Earl being the Supreme Judge of the County and having one third of the Amerciaments in the County Court due to the King as his perquisite. But every Earl had also a Barony. The Earl had also the command of the Military Force of the County. And
4/III/21,3r because this was often | inconsistent with the exercise of his Judicative

Capacity there was in every County a Vice comes or Sheriff, who was an officer put in by the Crown.*

Many of the Nobles and Gentry held lands of the Crown by the Service of Grand Serjeantry, that is, for doing some personal Service about the King. There was also a tenure by petit Serjeantry, which obliged the Vassal to yield yearly to the King a bow a Cutlas or dagger or other such small things belonging to War. This Service was but Soccage in effect.*

Follows a Dissertation on Chivalry or the Honour of Knight hood.*

By the Statute of 12 Charles 2 it is declared That all tenures by knights Service of the King, or of any other Service, and by knights service in Capite, and by soccage in capite of the King, and the fructs and consequences thereof shall be taken away or discharged; and that all tenures of any Honours Mannours Lands, tenements & Hereditaments; are turned into free and common Soccage*

The State of villeins or slaves, in this period in England Manumission in the Sheriff Court by giving a lance & a Sword*

The Counties were divided into hundreds & tythings which last was composed of ten freeholders with their families who were all pledges to the King for the good behaviour of each of them, and obliged if any man of the tything had committed a Crime to bring him to justice or purge themselves by oath of the chief man of the tything both of the guilt of the fact, and of being parties to the delinquents escape.*

In this period the Pandects were found by the Pisans at Amalplie when that City was taken by them in 1137. About forteen years after Gratian a Benedictin Monk at Bologna published his Decretum. In 1170 Gerardus Niger & Obertus de Odo two Senators of Milan published a Compilation of the feudal Laws. Towards the latter end of Henry 2 That Treatise of the laws and Customs of England commonly ascribed to Glanville was written. The Books of Scots Law called Regiam Majestatem are copied from Glanville*

A long Dissertation to shew that the Commons were represented in Parliament from the earliest times.*|

4/III/21,3v A Dissertation on the Royal Revenue in this Period*

State of Learning Universities. Increase of Religious houses*

Manner of Living.*

In this Age says Camden the Use of Silk made by Silk worms was brought out of Greece into Sicily and then into other parts of Christendom*

Book 3d Vol 4 This Volume continues the History of Henry from the Promotion of Becket to the See of Canterbury to the time of his Assassination that is from 1163 to 1170.* The far greatest part is employed in tracing through all their intricate mazes the maneouvres of Henry and Becket against each other. The Character of both as well as of Pope Alexander are strongly marked through the whole. The composition of the Work seems to me to be excellent; For there is nothing that leads one to reflect on the Author but upon the subject onely

---

September 1769 Read The History of the Reign of the Emperor Charles 5, with a view of the progress of Society in Europe from the Subversion of the Roman Empire to the beginning of the 16th Century in three Volumes by William Robertson DD &‹c› London 1769. Dedicated to the King*

Sect 1

The State of the European Nations before the Roman Conquests The Effect of those Conquests, in civilizing the conquered Nations, but at the same time destroying their Military Spirit.*

Causes of the Success of the Northern Nation‹s› in destroying the Roman Empire. The Ravages they Made from Anno 395 to 576.*

Introduction of the Feudal Policy & the Effects it produced to the End of the eleventh Century. Oppression of the Barons Ignorance Disunion and weakness of Kingdoms.*

Causes which cooperated after this Period to rouse the Minds of Men and to enlightten them in the principles of Knowledge & Liberty.

1 The Crusades. A Notion was universally spread about the beginning of the eleventh Century that the thousand years mentioned by St John Revelation 20. 2, 3, 4 were accomplished and that the End of the World was at Hand. This encouraged the Spirit of making pilgrimages to Jerusalem, and made People more ready to part with their property to defray that Expence. The Reports of Pilgrims concerning the dangers of this P‹i›lgrimage, the Oppressions suffered by Christians in those parts and the Cruelties of the Turks disposed the Minds of Men to that
4/III/21,4r Enthusiastick Zeal for Recovering the holy Land which | was enflamed to the Highest Pitch by the Preaching of Peter the Hermit by the Bulls of the Popes, & by the great Privileges and immunities granted to those who engaged in this Expedition.

The Effects of the Crusades in enlightening those who had been engaged in them, by what they might observe of the more improved

State of Italy and of its trading Cities Venice Genoa and Pisa especially of Constantinople The Turks more polished in those days than the European Christians The Crusades depressed the Nobility by inducing them to sell their Estates many of which were bought at a small price by Kings Communities & by the Church. The trading Cities of Italy were aggrandized by the Crusades and enabled to assert their Independance.*

2 The forming Cities into Communities Corporations or bodies Politick and granting them the priviledge of municipal Jurisdiction, contributed more than any other Cause to introduce regular Government Police and Arts and to diffuse them over Europe.*

3 Cities having obtained personal Freedom & municipal Jurisdiction soon obtained Political Power and were admitted by their Deputies into the Assemblies of the States*

4 Liberty being introduced into Cities by degrees diffused itself into the whole body of the people & Slavery even of the lowest orders was by degrees abolished.*

5 A more equal and Vigorous administration of Justice began to obtain. 1 By the prohibition of private War. Under this head in the Proofs there is a very curious Account of the methods taken to restrain
4/III/21,4v and at last to abolish private War| The Treuga Dei or Truce of God. the Brotherhood of God, the Treuga Regis Clause in an English Indictment
4/III/21,4r of assaulting one who was in the Peace of God and of the King. | & 2. of the form of trials by Combat whose history the Author gives 3 The Authorizing the Right of Appeal from the Courts of the barons to those of the King. The steps by which this was brought about delineated*

6 The Power of the Canon Law produced improvement in Jurisprudence*

7 The Revival of the Study and Knowledge of the Civil Law which gave rise to a Distinction of Professions, opened new paths to honour and Wealth, & gave new employment to the vigor of the human Mind, when formerly it had no object but the acquiring of military Skill & address.*

8 The Spirit of Chivalry introduced more liberal Sentiments and more generous manners.*

9 The progress of Science*

10 The progress of Commerce which was greatly aided by the invention of the Mariners Compass.*|

4/III/21,4v Sect 2

View of the Progress of Society with respect to the National Force requisite in forreign operations.

The loss of the English Territory in France an advantage to both Kingdoms. Charles 7 first establishing a Standing Army. The same was the first Monarch of France who by a Royal Edict without the Concurrence of the States General of the Kingdom levied an extraordinary Subsidy upon his people. Broke the Power of the Nobility. Corrupted the Assemblies of the States. Henry 7 of England his Measures to break the Power of the Nobility. The Union of the Kingdoms of Spain under Ferdinand and Isabella. The Union of the Houses of Austria & Burgundy by the Marriage of the Archduke of Austria Maximilian to Mary Daughter of Charles the Bold & heiress of the Dutchy of Burgundy.*

The Expedition of Charles 8 into Italy. The confederacy raised against him by the Italian Powers. The feudal Militia laid aside & standing Armies of hired troops substituted in their place. Taxes became necessary*

The League of Cambray against the Venetians. The League to expell the French from Italy.*

Sect 3

A View of the Political Constitution of the Principal States of Europe at the beginning of the 16 Century.

State of the Ecclesiastical Territory. State of Venice. Of Florence. Of Naples. Of Milan*

State of Spain. Privileges of the Aragonese Cortes, & Rights belonging to the Justiza. The Castilian Cortes. Reasons why the kingly power was more limited in Spain than in other kingdoms in Europe & the Power of the Cities and Nobles great. The Measures of Ferdinand and Isabella to enlarge their Prerogative The Masterships of the three military Orders of St Jago Calatarva, & Alcantara annexed to the Crown. The Holy Brotherhood.*

State of France. General Assembly of the States disused on Account of the Power and Independence of the Great Lords. The Kings by slow and Cautious Steps assumed Legislative Power. The Government of France under the first Race of its Kings Democratical under the 2d Aristocratical became under the third Monarchical.*

State of Germany and of the Turkish Empire*

III

3/I/5, 3r May 1773 I Read

The Principles of Money, applied to the present State of the Coin of Bengal, &c composed for the Use of the Hon. The East India Company

By Sir James Steuart Bart. 1772.*

Facts

The Standard of the Bengal Money has ever been Silver, though Gold has been occasionally coined. The most common Silver Coin is the Rupee of one Sicca or ten Massa Weight; of the fineness of 98/100. One Sicca is 16 Annas; & one Anna 12 Pice. These are the Names of Weight and one Sicca is 179 gr, & 5511 decimals of a grain troy weight*

The principal Rupees in Bengal, are those of Madrass, Bombay Surat and the Siccas of Bengal. The Standart Weight of all these is the Same and their fineness ought to be the same, but their denomination is different. The Coin carries upon it the year of the Kings Reign, and is called a Rupee of as many Suns as the King has reigned years. Thus the Rupees coined in 1770 are called Rupees of the eleventh Sun because the King began to reign in 1760. During the first years currency these Rupees are counted 16 per Cent better than Current Rupees; during the second years Currency they are counted 13 per Cent above Current; during the third years Currency and ever after they are counted 11 per Cent above Current, and are then called Sunat Rupees. There are however many Rupees as good as these Sunats, which are rated onely 10 per Cent above Current. So that the Sunats have an arbitrary Batta of one per Cent allowed them above their real Value The Rupees of the Second Sun a Batta of 12 per Cent, & those of the first Sun a Batta of 15 per Cent. The Current Rupee therefore is a Meer Denomination.*

There are various Mints established by ancient Custom, where the Regulations both as to the Weight & the fineness of the Coins, are different, though they are all called Rupees. From this & from punching holes, and filling up these holes with base metal, as well as diminishing the weight of the Coin, after coming from the Mint, the current value of Rupees of different Provinces is very different. This has introduced a general and insupportable abuse, called Shroffage.

The Shroffs are a Sort of Bankers or Money changers, whose |

3/I/5,3v business it is ‹is› to set a Value upon these different Currencies, according to every Circumstance either in their Favour, or to their Prejudice. When a Sum of Rupees is brought to a Shroff, he examines them piece by piece, ranges them according to their fineness, & then by their weight. Then he allows for the different legal Battas upon Siccas and Sunats; and this done, he values in gross, by the Rupee current, what the whole quantity is worth.*

Before the year 1766 Gold Coins called Mohurs had been coined at Dehli but without any Legal Value. They were of the same Weight and fineness with the Sicca Silver Rupees. Their value compared with the silver Rupees was not fixed by Law, but left to Convention, so that they circulated at the Rate of 12, 13, 14, & even sometimes 15 Silver Rupees.

In the year 1766 there being a Scarcity of Silver by the exportation to China and other places, & considerable quantities of Gold being in Bengal; it was thought proper to make a Coinage of Gold, in which Encouragement should be given to the bringing the Gold to the Mint. For this Purpose the Government of Bengal gave to their Gold Mohurs a legal Value of 17½ per Cent above their real Value in proportion to Silver. After the issuing of this Gold currency, no body would pay willingly in silver Rupees. By this Operation the Shroffs gained for once 17½ per Cent upon the Gold they bought up and brought to the Mint, but the Company lost annually 17½ of all that part of their Revenue which was payed in the Gold Coin.*

By a Regulation in 1771 The Siccas of the 11 Sun coined in 1770 are for the future to pass for the full legal Value they had at first coming from the Mint; and all the Siccas to be issued or coined in all Subsequent years are in like manner to retain their first denomination. The intent of this Regulation is, that in a few Years, all silver Rupees coined before the 1771 ‹Regulation› shall be recoined, & that the whole currency of Bengall shall have a Denomination 16 per Cent above its real Value. That is that 100 Rupees in Coin should be denominated & pass in all Payments under the Name of 116 Rupees current.*

One ounce of British Standart Silver sells now in England at 5 sh 8 ‹d› A Sicca Rupee of Silver 98/100 fine and of just weight is worth intrinsically 26,94 ‹pence› the Current Rupee by the new regulation of 1771 is worth onely 23,22 ‹pence›

The Current Rupee before the Regulation of 1771 was 10/11 parts of the sicca Rupee and in real Value 163,228 grains troy weight of the fineness of 98/100 and in english money at the above rate of 5.8 the oz Sterling Silver is worth 24,49 ‹pence›*|

3/I/5,4r The Regulations proposed for Remedying the abuses of the Coin are agreeable to the Authors Principles & to all sound Principles about Coinage*

There are onely two things of which I am not Satisfied.

1 The Author seems to lay a great Stress upon this That the Current Rupee which is in all time to come to be the Measure of Price in Bengal shall differ in its value from every Species of Money coined. The coined silver Rupee for instance is allways to be 11/10 parts of the Rupee current This makes the reckoning the price of things in current Money much more intricate, & I do not see the least advantage gained by it.*

2 The Author proposes that all Silver Bullion brought to the Mint should pay 2½ per Cent for Coinage & Gold one per Cent. I am doubtfull whether it is not better that nothing should be payed for Coinage as it is in England.*

3 I do not see a good reason why the aliquot parts of a Rupee should be made of a baser alloy than the Rupees, to wit 80/100 fine. Although indeed the Author gives them no legal value above their real intrinsick value; increasing their weight in the same proportion as he debases their fineness.*

Facts

In the Space of three Years the Company carried 720,000 £ Sterling to the China Market*|

The East India Company have imported, during the three last years, about 27 Millions of Pounds weight of Tea; in which Time have been Sold about 24½ Millions, of which 3½ millions have been exported; & Government has received for duties upon teas during the above period of Time about 2150,000 £ Sterling

The Q‹u›antity of forreign teas belonging to the French Dutch Swedes & Danes smuggled into Britain Ireland & America is estimated at four millions of pounds weight.*

The System of Paper Credit in the Colonies of North America is this The Paper is issued upon no other Security than the bare promise of the Colony to make it effectual, with an Obligation to receive it in paying their Taxes, but without providing any fund to pay upon Demand or even an Interest corresponding to the Sum during the delay of Payment. This

Scheme is so defective and liable to so many Objections, particularly that of gradually debasing their Money of Account, that it ought never to be imitated by any trading Nation.*

IV

4/III/23,1r 10 Jan 1776 Read The Constitution of England or an Account of the English Government by J. L. de Lolme Advocate Citizen of Geneva London 1775 8o Kearsley page 448*

The Ancient Government of England was, according to this Author, totally overturned by William the Conqueror. The Feudal System introduced at once, and the Lands divided among his friends and followers. He divided England into 60215 Military fiefs all held of the Crown; the possessors of which were, on pain of forfeiture, to take up arms & repair to his Standard on the first signal. He subjected the Barons as well as the Common people to all the rigours of the feudal Government. He even imposed upon them his tyrannical Forrest Laws. He assumed the power of imposing taxes, & the whole Executive power of Government. But what was of the greatest Consequence, he arrogated to himself the most extensive Judicial Power, in the Establishment of the Court called Aula Regis, a formidable Tribunal, which received Appeals from all the Courts of the Barons, and decided in the last resort on the Estates Honours & Lives of the Barons themselves; which being wholly composed of the great Officers of the Crown, removeable at the Kings pleasure, and having the King himself for President, held the first Nobleman in the Kingdom under the same controul as the meannest Subject.*

The English groaned under this Tyrranical Government 40 years after the Conquest till the Reign of Henry 1. who having ascended the throne to the exclusion of his elder Brother, to gain the affection of his Subjects, mitigated the Rigor of the feudal Laws both in favour of the Lords and their Vassals. Under Henry 2 Liberty took a farther stride. The Ancient Tryal by Jury, made again its appearance*

Under the weak and Despotick reign of King John Anno 1215 the whole Nation rising against the King compelled him to sign the Charta de Foresta and the famous Magna Charta

The Author thinks that the chief Cause of the Nation's joyning so unanimously, was their being all united in one Body by the Conquest and feeling the same Oppression.*

Edward the first from his numerous and prudent Laws has been called the English Justinian. Judge Hales affirms that there was more 4/III/23,1v improvement made in the Laws of England in the first 13 years | of Edward 1st than has been ever since. He first appointed the Sheriffs to invite the Towns & Boroughs to send Deputies to Parliament whence the Origin of the House of Commons. With much reluctance and after many evasions he confirmed Magna Charta no less than 11 times in the Course of his Reign. It was enacted that whatever was done contrary to it should be void and null. That it should be read twice a year in all Cathedrals; and that Excommunication should be denounced against any one who should presume to violate it.*

At length he converted into an established law a priviledge of which the English had hitherto onely a precarious Enjoyment Statute 24 Edward primi. Nullum tallagium vel auxilium, per nos, vel hæredes nostros, in regno nostro ponatur seu levetur sine voluntate & assensu Archiepiscoporum Episcoporum Comitum Baronum, Militum, Burgensium et aliorum liberorum hom' de nostro regno.*

Under Edward 2d the Commons began to annex Petitions to the Bills by which they granted Subsidies. This was the Dawn of their Legislative Authority Under Edward 3d They declared they would not in future acknowledge any Law to which they had not consented. Soon after this they impeached and procured to be condemned some of the first Ministers of State. Under Henry 4 they refused to grant Subsidies till an answer had been given their petitions.*

The House of Commons consists of 558 Deputies whereof 45 from Scotland. A Member for a County must have 600 £ of a Land Estate for a Town or Borough 300*

The commissions of the Judges do not cease at the Kings Death; they hold them Quamdiu se bene gesserint. But may be removed upon an Application from both Houses of Parliament.*

No amendment allowed to be made to a money Bill by the House of Lords*

V

4/III/13,1r October 1777 Read The Constitution of England.

By J. L. De Lolme, Advocate, Citizen of Geneva 1775*

Causes of the Liberty of the English Nation. 1 The great Power of the Crown under the first Norman Kings created an Union between the Nobility & the people. 2 It formed one undivided State 3 The Union of the Executive Power in one Person which makes it to be more easily resisted 4 The Division of the Legislative. ‹5› The privilege of Proposing Laws left to the People. ‹6› The Representative of the Commons.

A King in a Commonwealth, leaves no Room for the Nobles to engross the Power of the State or to overturn its Constitution

VI

4/III/12,1r Advantages of the british Constitution from Mr de Lolme*

1 The placing the Executive power in One & making it hereditary

1 This renders it sacred & inexpugnable. Checks the Ambition of such as in Republicks from engrossing power have become tyrants, & prevents any Citizen from ever rising to a dangerous greatness.*

Suppose a Man by the greatness of his abilities and publick Services to have got great Authority in the House of Commons. All he can hope for by this is to become the kings first Minister. He cannot be a Consul or a Dictator. There is still one above him, on whom he depends, & to whom he must be subject. If he is raised to the House of Peers his influence in the other house is lessened or lost. And while he is chief Minister he will allways have many rivals from Ambition or disappointment. a discontented party who watch his Motions. And he is placed in a Station which naturally creates envy and Jealusy in the body of the Nation.*

2 The Executive power by being placed in one is more easily confined*

2 The division of the Legislative power, necessary to the restraint of it no less than the union of the Executive to the restraint of it

Opposition & Contest in the Legislative power is Salutary but pernicious in the Executive. The former onely an Opposition of Opinions.*

3 That the King has no power to propose Laws but onely to assent to them except in Acts of Grace*

4 The people deligating their power to representatives*

The Qualification for voting for Members of Parliament ough‹t› to be higher. as it is in Scotland.

VII

4/III/20,1r From Cardinal Contareni de Republica & Magistratibus Venetorum 12o Venetiis 1592*

The Patrician Youth who have compleated their 20 Year come to one of the Magistrates called Advocatorii, with their Father, or Mother if the Father be dead, or nearest Kinsman if both Parents be dead: And by two witnesses of Reputation prove themselves to be the Sons of him whom they profess to be their father and to be born in Lawfull Marriage and of a Mother that is a Gentle woman: Then the Parent or nearest Kinsman takes an Oath that the Youth is past 20 years of Age; & he is inrolled by the Advocatory. Of those who are thus inrolled and who do not exceed twenty five years; one fifth Part is determined by lot on the 4 of December yearly to have a Seat in the great Council.

If a Mans Father and Grand father have not been inrolled he must have his claim judged by the College of Forty, & before his claim to be a Nobleman of Venice is judged he must deposit 500 Ducats which are forfeited to the treasury if he fails in making good his claim

Those who exceed 25 years of Age if not inrolled before must be inrolled in the same Manner as the Youth, with this difference that they are intitled to sit as Members of the great Council by their being enrolled whareas onely one fifth part of those who are inrolled and are under 25 sit in that Council.*

VIII

4/III/22,1r Taken from A Table of English silver Coins &‹c› by Martin Folkes Esq. pag 142.*

A Table shewing the several Adulterations that have been made in the Standard of our Money, from the Norman Conquest:

Years of the King's reign & AD		Fineness of the Silver		Weight of 20 Shillings Troy weight			Value in present money			Propor-tion	Fine Gold to fine Silver
		oz	dwts	oz	dwts	gr	£	s	d		
Conquest	1066	11	2	11†	5		2	18	1½	2.906	No Gold
28 Edward 1	1300			11	2	5	2	17	5	2.871	No Gold
18 Edward 3	1344			10	3		2	12	5¾	2.622	12.583
20 Ditto	1346			10			2	11	8	2.583	11.571
27 Ditto	1353			9			2	6	6	2.325	11.158
13 Henry 4	1412			7	10		1	18	9	1.937	
4 Edward 4	1464			6			1	11		1.055	10.331
18 Henry 8	1527			5	6	16	1	7	6¾	1.378	11.267
34 Ditto	1543	10		5			1	3	3¼	1.163	10.435
36 Ditto	1545	6		5				13	11½	0.698	6.818
37 Ditto	1546	4		5				9	3¾	0.466	5.
3 Edward 6	1549	6		3	6	16		9	3¾	0.466	5.151
5 Ditto	1551	3		3	6	16		4	7¾	0.232	2.011
6 Ditto	1552	11	1	4			1	0	6¾	1.028	11,005
1 Mary	1553	11		4			1	0	5¾	1.024	11,005
2 Elizabeth	1560	11	2	4			1	0	8	1.033	11.001
43 Ditto	1601	11	2	3	17	10	1			1	10.905

†NB The Saxon or Tower Pound which was then the common Weight & continued to be the Money Weight till the 18 of Henry 8 was but 11 oz 5 dwt troy so that 20 Shillings in Tale was then exactly a pound in weight.

IX

4/III/23b,1r Les Interests de la France mal entendus 3 Vol Amsterdam 1756*
The Author reckons that the kingdom of France with Lorrain contains 150,000000, of Arpents square measure and 17,000000 of Inhabitants*

Part Two: Lectures on Politics

4/III/1: Principles of Politics 1765*

4/III/1,2r* Heads of Lectures on Politicks

1 The Principles of Politicks in General Division.

2 The Constitution of a Despotick Government

3 The natural Consequences of Despotick Government with Reflexions

4 The Gothic Aristocracy Poland the Ancient Aristocracy Venice

5 Haringtons Oceana. Agrarian Rotation Suffrage. Parish Hundred & Tribe Elections.

6 Senate & popular Assemb‹l›y.

7 Musters of the Youth. Education. Censorial Power. Titles of honour

8 Provincial Government. Reflexions upon this Model of Government.

9 Other Commonwealths Ideal or Real

10 Pure Monarchy.

11, 12, 13. British Constitution with Reflexions

Police

1 Of Population

2 Of National Virtue

3 Of Learning

4 Of National Riches wherein they Consist how at first produced & acquired & kept

5 Of Commerce Natural Artificial the different periods of the Last

6 Of Money. As a Commodity & a Medium of Commerce Weighed or Coined.

7 Of false Maxims with regard to Money

8 Of Interest of Money, & Exchange with forreign Nations. Ballance of Trade

9 Of Banks & Paper Credit. Of Luxury

10 Of Premiums, imposts, Prohibitions Free Ports as they affect Traffick

11 Of Navigation & Colonies as they Affect Trade

12 Of The Effects of Trade on the Morals & Strength of a Nation

13 Arms Naval, & Land Forces. Hired Troops, Standing Armies Militia Forts

14 Revenue. Crown Lands. Customs, Excise, Land Tax. Taxes on the Necessaries of Life on Luxury. Poll Taxes Census. Lotteries National Debt. |

4/III/1,1r Politic‹s› is the Art of Modelling and Governing Societys of Men so as to answer the End proposed by them

The Principles of Political Reasoning must be the Active Principles ‹of› Human Nature‹,› the Principles according to which the Governed commonly Act not those according to which they ought to Act.* How the Politician differs from the Man of Address & Sagacity. & from the Cunning Man. The General Principles of Action among Men are Such as these*

1 Men will generally be just honest & true where they have no Temptation to be otherwise

2 Men have always a Strong Resentment of Injuries and will resist them where it is in their Power & have commonly some Gratitude for good Offices.

3 Tho a cool Desire of Happiness & a Regard to duty have some Influence on the Actions of All men yet it does not appear that either of these are the Prevailing Principles in Most Men

4 It may be therefore expected of the Generality of Men that they will do things contrary either to their real Interest or their Duty when they have Strong temptations. either knowingly or by imposing upon themselves

5 Few Men will do the most Atrocious Acts of Wickedness even upon a Strong Temptation till they have been long hardned by vicious habits

6 Men always esteem Virtue Wisdom & Power in others where they are not objects of Envy and desire to be possessed of them or to be thought to be possessed of them themselves

7 Mens private Affections are commonly Stronger then their publick ones

8. Mens Characters are formed mostly by Education Custom & Example

9. In a Great Number of Men taken without Distinction there will always be found a few that are far Superior to the Rest in Wisdom or Virtue Power or all these

10. People will not long receive Laws from Governors unless they have an opinion that the Governors have superior Power Superior Wisdom & Virtue or Right to Govern.

11 Like Effects may be expected from like Causes, and similar Conduct from persons of like Characters in like Circumstances.

12 In all great Bodies of Men who either meet together or can easily communicate their Sentiments to each other, the many will be led by a few, of Superior Parts, Superior Eloquence or Superior Character, & will imbibe their Sentiments Passions and Opinions.|

4/III/1,1v Definition of the 3 Simple Forms of political Government Despotism Pure Aristocracy pure Democracy.* All others Mixt

The Parts of Supreme Power‹:› Legislative Executive Judiciary.* The imposing of Taxes.*

1 Despotism Requires* 1 That the Grand Seignior should be possessed of the Greatest part or Whole of the Land as his property & that the Subjects should be his Tennants at Will and hold it by military Service.* 2 That no Honours or Offices be Hereditary. but depend on the will of the Prince* 3 That there be a Standing Army of Soldiers that have no interest in the Country sufficient to keep the people in Awe. 4 That there be no Standing Laws or very few.* 5 That the Provinces be governed by a Basha & his Deputies who have both the civil & Military Power 6 That these be often Changed. 7 That the punishment of crimes against the State be Severe & Sudden without formal trial 8 That the Apparent Sucessor to the Crown have no Access to corrupt the Army 9 The Reigning Family be believed to have a Divine Right. 10 That the Subjects be trained by Education and Instruction of their Priests to absolute & unlimited submission to the will of his Superiors as to the will of Heaven.

Maxims relating to Despotism

1 The Grand Seignior will commonly throw the whole care of the Government upon one Person called the Grand Vizir & be entirely Swallowed up in the Pleasures of his Seraglio. The Choise of the Vizir & other Officers of State will commonly depend on the Women and Eunuchs.* 2 The Grand Vizir must be Sacrifised when the Army is out of Humor or he must Sacrifice the Grand Seignior. 3 The Government of Families will be absolute as well as that of the State. 4 Commerce can never flourish in such a State 5 Learning will commonly be discouraged 6 Patience Contentment Resignation Contempt of Riches & a Contemplative Devotion Caution Secrecy & fair Dealing will be the Characteristic Virtues of the People 7 Such a Government under a good and Vigilant & peaceable Prince may be happy but such a one will be most likely to fall a Sacrifice to the Army. 8. A despotic Government in the Hands of Warli‹k›e Princes is fit for making Conquests & very difficult to be conquered. But if once conquered easily submitts to the Victor.

9 A good Turk ought to spend his vacant hours either with his wives or in the Exercises of his Religion 10 As the Grand Seignior derives his Authority in a Great Measure from the Religion of the Country so that that is the onely thing that sets any bounds to it. The power of the Clergy is therefore a blessing in Such a Government. The Grand Seignior can not impose a New Tax but this Occasions the Greater Oppression by his Bashaws

Turkey the most perfect Model of Despotism

4/III/3: Principles of Politics 1766

4/III/3,1r May 5*
1766

Politicks |

4/III/3,5r Politicks like most other Branches of Knowledge that relate to Practice may be considered either as an Art or as a Science. If we consider it as an Art it may be defined to be The Art of Modeling & governing a State so as to answer the End intended by it. The business of the politician is either to frame a Model of Government for a larger or lesser political Society. Or to preserve repair alter or amend a Government already formed. To discover the latent seeds of those diseases, which if not cured in time are destructive of the political Union, & bring it to dissolution at last, & to be able to find out and apply the proper Remedies |

4/III/3,1r It is very obvious that the end of Government ought to be the good and happiness of the Governed: And therefore every Model or Form of Government, if we judge of it by the moral Standard is to be more or less approved according as it tends more or less to promote this end. In this view the Destruction of a bad form of Government may be a mean to the Production of a better But there may be other ends of Government proposed, and as an expert Physician ought to understand the nature and Effects of Poisons as well as Medicines; so an able Politician ought to understand the nature & Effects of all kinds of Government the bad as 4/III/3,5r well as the good.| Many Ancient and Modern Authors have confounded Politicks with Morals, which ought carefully to be avoided. Machiavel & Harrington free from this Fault. There is a Branch of Jurisprudence which is very properly called political Jurisprudence. The Object of this Branch. The Rights & moral Obligations that arise from the political Union.*

The same Question may be considered either in a political or in a Moral Light‹.› Instance Tolleration of those who are not of the established Religion.*|

4/III/3,1r Politicks considered as a Science is the Knowledge of those principles by which we may Judge of the Constitution and Effects of Government‹.› Knowledge in Politicks enables us to Judge whether such a particular form of Government is properly fitted and adapted to promote the happiness & preserve the Rights of the Subjects: Or whether on the contrary from the nature and constitution of the Government the subjects will frequently be oppressed, injured, and tyrannically used? Whether the Political Body will be quiet & peacable or on the contrary tumultuous and Seditious. Whether it will be strong to defend itself against forreign Ennemies, or feeble & easily subdued in War.

Political Bodies as well as Natural Bodies of Man and Animals are liable both to internal Disorders and Diseases and to external hurts & injuries.* It is by political Knowledge that the Governours of States are enabled often to foresee those disorders that are incident to the political Body and to prevent them, or to discover their causes when they happen; & to apply proper remedies‹.› Politicks has a like Relation to States & to Government as the Science of Medicine has to the human Body, and the Politician is the State Physician. He knows wherein the Sound & healthfull Constitution of the State consists. When any disorder appears in it he can judge by the Symptoms what is the cause of that disorder and he knows what are the Remedies and can pre‹s›cribe for them with
4/III/3,5r great probability of Success. | The Nature of a Political Body compared
4/III/3,1r with the Natural | The Analogy between Prudence in an individual and Political Knowledge in the Government of a State‹.›* Prudence consists chiefly in chusing proper Means to accomplish the Ends we have in View. So does Political Knowledge‹.› The ends of a Private Man concern him self chiefly & his family & Friends. The ends of a Politician concern the State. Prudence distinguished from Craft in the Politician as in the Private Man. Prudence in the one as in the other grounded chiefly upon the Knowledge of Mankind‹.› Objection. No Government framed or changed by Art

Every Science must be grounded on certain principles & if Politicks can be at all reduced to a Science, as I doubt not but it may, there must be certain first Principles from which all our Reasonings in Politicks are
4/III/3,1v deduced | as there are certain first Principles or Axioms in Mathematicks upon which all our Reasonings in Mathematicks are built, and as there

are in Morals certain first Principles, as we have had occasion to shew, upon which our Reasoning in the Science of Morals are built.*

It is easy to shew that the first Principles of Politicks, upon which all Political Reasoning is grounded, must be taken from the Knowledge of Mankind. By the Knowledge of Mankind I mean not the Knowledge of the peculiar temper and talents of individuals but the Knowledge of the temper and Disposition, the Principles of Action and general tenor of Conduct that is common to the whole Species.

Every Political Body may be conceived as a vast Machine made up of a great Number of Parts.* The Motions of the Whole are made up of the Motions of the several Parts, and the motion of each Part must depend upon the powers that operate upon that part and put it in motion. So that it is impossible to know scientifically the Effects that will be produced by the whole Machine without knowing the parts of which it is compounded and the powers that actuate those parts, for the Effect of the whole is an aggregate or composition of the Effects of the several Parts. The parts of which a Commonwealth or State is made up are Men. Each of whom has his particular Principles of Activity in himself, his fears, his hopes his desires, his passions, his Reason, his Conscience. These principles in every individual influence him to a certain course of Action or operation. And the Operation of the Several Individuals makes up the Operation of the Whole Political Body. We cannot therefore know how Political Bodies will act, what Effects they will produce in given Circumstances, but by knowing how individuals of Mankind act in the various Circumstances in which they may be placed. But if on the other hand we know how human Creatures will Act when placed in the Circumstances in which the members of such a Political Society are placed; then we may know; the Effects with regard to the whole Body which will result from the United Operation of the Several Parts. Hence it is evident that the first Principles of Political Reasoning must in general be of this Kind, to wit, That such is the Nature of Mankind that Men placed in such Circumstances will generally act in such a Manner. If any Principles of this kind can be ascertained from our Knowledge of human Nature, or from Experience; Such Principles must be the foundation of all Political Reasoning. And the Conclusions that may justly be drawn from such Principles will make up the Science of Politicks. If on the other hand no Such principles can be discovered then there is no Such Science as Politicks.

Here a general Objection against all Political Knowledge may occur which we shall consider before we proceed farther.

It may be said that human Actions are free and do not necessarly follow upon motives.* We cannot therefore fortell how a man will act in any particular Situation even although we know all the principles and motives which influence him because he may yield to the force of those motives or he may resist them and act contrary to them. And if we cannot know how any one man will act in a particular case how shall we know
4/III/3,2r how a great many will act since the many are made up | of individuals. If men always acted according to the Strongest motive there is some foundation for human foresight of their Actions from the knowledge of their Situation and the Principles of their Nature. But if there is no Necessary connexion between Actions and the Motives of the Agent there is no foundation left for any human knowledge of the Actions of free Agents, how they will behave in given Situations‹,› consequently no foundation for any political Knowledge.

In answer to this objection I shall endeavour to prove these two things 1 That although the Objection seems onely to affect those who hold the Liberty of human Actions yet it will be found equally strong against those who hold them to be necessary 2 That against the reality of Political Knowledge even on the supposition of Liberty, this objection has no force.

1 This Objection if it had any force would leave no foundation for Political Knowledge to those who hold human Actions to be necessary any more than to those who hold them free. Because it must be acknowledged by those who hold the necessity of human Actions that the motives or Causes from which those Actions necessarly follow cannot be known to a Spectator, nay that they cannot be known to the Agent himself. It is evident from experience that the same Motives have not always the same Operation upon the same Man, and that different Men in like Circumstances as far as can be perceived act differently. A Fatalist will say that in these cases there were some causes unknown to us which produced this variety. Now the uncertainty of the Event to us will be the same when it proceeds from causes or motives that are unknown as when the motives do not necessarly produce the Action. Upon the Supposition of Necessity the Action necessarly depends upon the Strongest motive, but there are motives so hidden & obscure that we cannot perceive them nor have we any Standard by which we may judge of their Strength. For it must be acknowledged by those who hold the necessity of human Actions. That in human Actions sometimes passion prevails over our Reason sometimes Reason prevails over passion.

Sometimes the desire of fame prevails over the desire of riches or of pleasure and sometimes yields to them. A present good is sometimes preferred to a future and sometimes a future to a present nor can there be any certain rule asscertained by which we can judge when the one or when the other will be most prevalent. Now our Ignorance of the event will be the very same whether it proceed from ignorance of the causes of that Event or from, the want of a necessary connexion between those causes and the event which is supposed to be their Effect. From hence I think it appears evident that a Fatalist supposing his System to be true, has no better means of establishing any Principles of Politiks than the Assertor of the Liberty of human Actions. If the fatalist affirms that certain Rules may be pointed out according to which men generally Act, although sometimes from unknown Causes they may deviate from those Rules. This may be affirmed no less on the Supposition of our being free. And whether those deviations from the common Rules of Conduct be the Effect of Necessary but unknown Causes or whether they be the Effect of Caprice in men who act freely, they are equally unaccountable. And all that can be inferred from them is That Politicks is founded chiefly on Probability and not on Demonstration. This is undoubtedly true. |

4/III/3,2v 2 There is indeed no force in the objection that has been moved to prove that we may not know how men will commonly act in certain given circumstances notwithstanding the liberty of human Action. A wise man will act wisely though it be ever so much in his power to act otherwise. And a good man will act a good part although it be in his power to act a bad one. The Supreme being being perfectly wise and good always invariably acts according to perfect wisdom and goodness although he acts with perfect freedom. And in proportion as men are wise and good they will act wisely and well Human wisdom and goodness are both imperfect and therefore we cannot reckon upon it that they will always act the wisest and the best part. But there is some degree of Wisdom some degree of virtue even in Men. One that has no degree of wisdom or prudence is an Idiot or Changeling. Some Such there are of the human Species but a political Society could not be formed of Such. Men must be supposed to have common understanding in order to form a Commonwealth. Now there are many things with regard to the conduct of men of common Understanding which we may rely upon with great Security notwithstanding their being free Agents. Thus we may rely upon it that a man of common Understanding will take some Care of himself, both to avoid what is hurtfull and to procure what is agreable and usefull, that he will take some Care of his Children and have some Natural Affection to his Family Friends and Acquaintance We may reckon upon it, that he will have some sense of good offices done him, and some resentment of Injuries. That in proportion to his Strength and Courage he will defend himself & his Rights, and repell Injuries. The common principles of human Nature lead every Man good and bad to act such a part, in the common occurrences of Life. And a Man in whom these principles of Conduct did not exert their Force must be as great a prodigy as a Man born without hands or feet, which indeed has sometimes happned but is an Event so rare that in the course of human affairs we never think it deserves attention.

But farther it ought to be observed that we may form much more certain conclusions with regard to the conduct of a body of Men united in political Society than with respect to the conduct of an individual. For although the Many are made up of individuals, yet it is easier, in many cases to guess at the behaviour of the Many than at that of the individuals which compose it‹.› The jarring Passions Interests and Views of individuals when mingled together make a Compound whose Nature is more fixed and determined than that of the Ingredients of which it is made up. Wisdom and Folly, Reason and Passion Virtue and Vice blended together make a pretty Uniform Character in great Bodies of Men in all Ages and Nations; where there is not an uncommon Degree of general Corruption on the one hand or of Virtue on the Other‹.› It is from this Uniformity of Character in a Multitude of Men notwithstanding of the Diversity of the Individuals of which it is composed, that all General Principles in Politicks are derived

2 Objection.* The good or Bad Effects of Government depend entirely upon the Administration & not upon the form of the Government. See D. Humes Essay 3 Whether Politicks may be reduced to a Science‹.› The best Monarchy Hereditary. The best Aristocracy a Nobility without Vassals The best Democracy a people voting by their Representatives. Despotick Governments easily held when conquered.* |

4/III/3,5r Axiom 1.* To denominate a Man truly Virtuous it is necessary not onely that he should have the Principles of Virtue in his Constitution, which all men have in some degree, but that these, in the general Course of his Life, should be superior to the temptations to which he is exposed, so that his conduct be in the main agreable to his Duty. This degree of Virtue is not supposed in the Axiom laid down. But it may w‹e›ll be supposed that the generality of men will not do bad things without any temptation. This must be true of every man at least that is not corrupted in his principles and morals to the highest degree so as to have totally lost all sense of duty and even all regard to character. which it is to be hoped is the case of very few if any at all of mankind. And indeed if we should suppose that the generality of Men of any Nation were so abandoned as to have no degree of regard to Justice Honesty and truth, I think it is not possible that they could be kept together under any kind of Government but that of absolute Slavery. They behoved to be chained as wild beasts and have the dread of punishment constantly hanging over their heads to keep them from doing mischief.

If men were to be perfectly virtuous & proof against all temptations there would be no Need of Civil Government. Men would do their duty without being compelled by Laws and punishments. It is therefore very true which a sacred writer observes that the Law is not made for the just but for the unjust.* What is here said of Law which is a part of political Government may be applyed to the whole of it. |

4/III/3,5v The bulk of Men are neither so good as they ought to be nor so bad as they might be. Natural Affection, Gratitude, Compassion & other good Affections have commonly a considerable degree of force even in the vicious. A Regard to Character & dread of the Contempt and Indignation of Mankind are powerfull restraints even upon bad Men, Common Prudence & the desire of self preservation oblige them to abstain from open Violations of the rights of others. When individuals are found, who break through all these Restraints; the terror of legal Punishment and publick Disgrace, are a very proper Adminicle, to those Restraints that Nature hath provided against criminal Conduct. And when all these restraints lose their force a man is no longer fit for Society, he is justly cut off as a rotten member by capital Punishment for the terror of others. There is therefore a certain degree of profligacy that makes a Man fit onely for a prison, for the stocks or the Gibet. And if we should suppose all Men of this Character they would not be materials fit for Political Society.

In some States of Society the generality of men may live very innocently with a small degree of Virtue. This is the case of rude Nations. Small Property* In othe‹r› states there will be both greater exertions of Virtue in some individuals and greater corruption in other‹s›. Difference of Ranks‹,› great Trust‹,› Refinements of high living.

Axiom 2 Personal Injuries have often occasioned Revolutions in States One of the chief Advantages of civil Government is that it puts the determination of differences among men in the laws and Judicatures and thereby greatly weakens the fury of Resentment and Revenge

Axiom 3. It is good that Men be instructed in their Duty & Interest but this is not enough.

Axiom 4 The more a people are corrupted in their Morals the less they are capable of freedom. That degree of Liberty which men will abuse to their own hurt and that of others ought to be taken from them. Good Men ought to have liberty‹,› they are entitled to it and will make a good Use of it. But in proportion as Men are disposed to make a bad use of their Liberty it is for their own good & necessary for the safety of others that it should be taken from them. |

4/III/3,6v Axiom 9. When we consider the Nature of Political Government, there is something in it that may seem at first view strange and difficult to be accounted for. In all Governments a few govern the Many the greater part are led & there is perhaps not above one hundred part of the whole that can be said to direct and govern in matters that concern the whole Body, the Multitude are swayed by the Judgement of a few,

4/III/2: Principles of Politics 1766, *cont.*

4/III/2,1r* Having pointed out some of the Axioms or first Principles upon which reasoning in Politicks must be grounded, you will see by the Specimen I have given, for I do not pretend to a full enumeration, of what kind those axioms are. They are the rules according to which men generally Act. The Actions of Men are the Subject of all Political Reasoning. The design of it is to shew how great bodies of Men will act in the various Situations in which they are placed & how they may be placed in such Situations as to lead them or the greater part of them to act the part which it is intended they should act. We must therefore in this Science suppose Men endowed with that degree of Understanding which we actually perceive in the generality of Men that are come to maturity. Children that are under Age are not capable of political Government. They are under the restraint and discipline of parents until they come to be of Age to act for themselves. And as there are some few of the human race that are born ideots, and never acquire the Understanding of a Man, or to be capable of directing their own Conduct, they must likewise be entrusted to the care of others, who may guard them from doing hurt to themselves or others. And they do not properly make a part of the political Body‹.›

There can be no reasoning with regard to their Actions, nor do political Events depend upon them. Thus we see that when we reason in Politicks about the Actions of Men, we do not include Children or Ideots in the Number on account of their defect of Understanding.

It is farther to be observed that political Reasonings suppose not onely a certain degree of Understanding in Men but likewise a certain degree of Morals. Mankind with regard to their Morals may be comprehended under three Classes

1 There are some individuals of Mankind so very profligate and abandoned as to break through all the restraints which either their own interest or that of their families and friends or a regard to reputation lay upon them. There can be no Reasoning about the Actions of such profligates, nor any dependance upon them that they will act by the Rules of common prudence & decency. It is to be hoped that those of this
4/III/2,1v character are so few in comparison, that they may be altogether | overlooked in political Reasoning. A political Society could not be formed of such Men. It would have no cement or principle of Union & therefore would immediately fall to pieces and dissolve.

When such Characters appear in Society, they must either be confined as wild beasts for the common Safety, or they must be delivered over to publick Justice for the terror of other‹s› & cut off from the political Body as rotten members. The maxims of Politicks therefore do not extend to these

2 On the other hand it is to be hoped that in all great bodies of Men there are to be found some Persons of such perfect Virtue and Integrity that they have no need of the restraints of human laws and goverment. They discharge their Duty to the publick & to individuals from principle and inclination and would injure no man even tho they could do it with impunity.

If any Society of Men were so happy as to be made up of persons of this Character, it might be without Laws and Government, or all kinds of Government would be alike & have the same Effect. But the Number of Persons of such incorruptible Virtue is so small in any great Body of Men, that they also are overlooked in political reasonings and the Common maxims of Politicks do not apply to them.

3 There remains a third Class which comprehends the great bulk of Mankind and of every Political Society. And it is to them onely that the Maxims of Politicks can properly be applyed, because upon them and their Conduct all political Events must depend.

They are neither so abandoned as the first class, nor so much to be trusted as the second, they fill up all the interval between the two, and are such as we may reasonably expect men to be, of whose characters we have no particular knowledge

Political Prudence is grounded upon the very same Principles as the Prudence of a private Man in his transactions with other Men. Real Prudence in the conduct of Life requires that we should keep the proper mean between too much trust in those we deal with and to‹o› much distrust. If we go into the first extream, we expose ourselves to frequent danger & disappointment. If we go into the other extream we shall frequently lose the best opportunities of carrying on our business The prudent Man takes the just medium between these extreams, and by that means generally accomplishes his Ends. The political Reasoner in like Manner must form his judgment of the conduct of political Societies,
4/III/2,2r neither upon the Supposition that they are more vicious & | profligate than men generaly are nor upon the Supposition that they are more virtuous & upright. And you will easily perceive that the Axioms or Principles I have mentioned are applicable to persons of such a middle Character which will allways be found to make up the great body of every political Society

Having thus pointed out the first principles from which we must Reason in Politicks, I proceed to the first branch of that Science I proposed to handle, to wit the various Forms of Political Government with their Causes & Effects.

It is usual in treating of this Subject to consider the Causes of political Government in general

4/III/5: Despotic Government. Aristocracy

4/III/5,1r* April 17 1765

We have explained as briefly as we could the Nature of Despotick Government; the Principles, upon which alone it can stand firm; and the natural Consequences of it with regard to the Commerce‹,› learning‹,› Morals and happiness of a Nation that is thus governed.*

From the Nature of this Government it is evident that the Reason of State in such Governments is not the Good & happiness of the Governed but the gratification of the Monarch‹.› he is so far exalted above his slaves that he considers them as created onely to serve his ambition his lust & even his Caprice‹.› Thousands of his slaves must be buried in mines digging for Rubies and Diamonds to Adorn his Diadem and his Throne‹.› A vast Empire must be ransacked for fine Women who are shut up by hundreds in the Seraglio to serve his pleasures; great numbers of Eunuchs must be made and trained up to guard the Women and to do all the offices of the Seraglio. The Eunuchs & the Women are his onely Companions. And these are valued in proportion to their Address in inventing new pleasures & amusements; His Mind is enervated by sloth sensuality and Luxury. He sees not his Subjects nor do they see him Least they should conceive him to be but a man. His repose must not be disturbed by the groans and miseries of the wretched. Like the Gods of Epicurus he lives far removed from human affairs and deigns not to concern himself about beings so far below his Notice. He throws the Whole burthen of the Government upon his grand Vizier and neither knows nor desires to know what is doing in his vast dominion. If his subjects are oppressed and plundered and ravaged by cruel Bashas‹,› their cries cannot reach the throne. If the Seraglio be safe and in peace‹,› he hears of what happens beyond its precincts, if he hears of it at all, as we hear of a Revolution in China or Japan.

But after all what is this Mighty Monarch who is thus to be pampered at the expence of the labour and treasure and blood of Millions of the human Race? Why, by his birth he is a man of the same Nature with the meannest of his Slaves. By his Education and manner of Life he is sunk below humanity. He is neither endowed with that Knowledge that enlarges and elevates a human Mind, nor with those habits of Prudence Selfcommand temperance fortitude Justice and goodness which constitute real Worth and Merit. Yet with all this worthlessness
4/III/5,1v & real Meanness he conceives himself a God, or something of a | nature far superior to other Men. And every thing that is said or done to him‹,› every thing about him conspires to fix this vain conceit of his own Superiority.

Such Must be the Monarch in those Despotick Governments be for the most part. This is the natural Consequence of his training and manner of Life; and such we know from History the greater part of Such Monarchs are and have been.

The depression of the Subjects in such a Government must bear proportion to the Exaltation of the Soveraign. Those who on account of their poverty and meanness are unknown to the people in power have the best chance to escape oppression. Every man that is eminent in Riches in

Authority or in Parts and in Knowledge becomes a mark to the avarice or envy or jeaulosy of those who have him absolutely in their power. This state to men who are trained up with a sense of Liberty would be intollerable, they would rather in habit the wilds of America with the Hurons or Eskimaux than be the slaves of the Great Mogul. But man is a very tractable Animal and can be trained to bear the extremities of want poverty pain hunger cold and even Slavery itself with patience and resignation.

The ancient Greeks and Romans who enjoyed a happy Climate and a moderate temperature of Air thought it impossible for human Creatures to subsist either in the torrid or in the frigid Zone, but Experience has discovered their Error. A laplander or a Samoeid thinks his country the finest in the World which an Italian would conceive it the greatest Misery to be condemned to. An Eskimaux can Regale upon a meal of raw fish or Whale blubber which a person used to the delicacies of cookery could not swallow if he should starve. The meanest cottager in England who is an object of pity and Charity on account of his poverty, lives in a more delicate manner and has more real Riches and Accommodations in his house furniture apparel & table than a Canadian Prince at the head of his tribe. In like manner a Chinese or a Subject of the Great Mogul, thinks himself more happy in being the slave of a mighty Monarch, than the Subject of a free Government. Lord Molesworth in his Account of Denmark page 75 observes very justly that Slavery like a sickly constitution becomes in time habitual so as to be thought no burthen. It mortifies ambition Emulation and other troublesome as well as active qualities which the sense of Liberty produces.* And the Slave banishing all thought of the future and reflexion upon the past sings in his chains like a bird confined in a Cage and makes the best of the present Moment. |

4/III/5,2r There is not a more mortifying view of human Nature than we are presented with when we reflect that so great a part of the human Race have been for thousands of years held in this dreadfull Slavery of Despotick Government. But it would be still more Mortifying to conceive as the Ingenious Montesquieu does that those Climates which Nature has favoured most by a variety of natural Productions for the use of the human Species should by a kind of fatality be necessarily subjected to this kind of Government.*

This kind of Government‹,› the most simple and inartificial‹,› therefore has prevailed among the least enlightened Nations and must always keep those Nations in Ignorance of the Rights of Mankind and the principles of policy. This Government cannot continue long in a single City, but once Settled in a large Empire may last for many Ages

April 18

Oligarchy and Aristocracy sometimes confounded‹.› sometimes by ancient writers Oligarchy is considered as the corruption of Aristocracy as Despotism is by ‹them› accounted the corruption of Monarchy, and Anarchy the Corruption of Democracy.*

Aristocracy may either obtain in a Smal State like that of Venice where the Nobility can often Meet in council by living in one city‹,› or in a large State where the Nobility have large land Estates live in their Castles, surrounded by their Vassals and Dependants whom they can Arm in their own Defence; as in Poland. We may call the first the Ancient Aristocracie, the last the Gothic Aristocracy.*

Of the first the Venetian Government is the best Model. The Government consists of an Assembly of the whole Nobility A Senate and annual Magistrates. The Senate & Magistracy Chosen by the Assembly

Account of the Constitution of Venice

Account of the Constitution of Polland

Corrollary 1 In the Gothick Aristocracy every Noble man will be almost independant of the Laws and must be possessed of the civil & military power in his own territory. The King will be elective and have little or no Power. Every Nobleman will have a negative in the Diet, the people will be slaves to their several Lords

2 In the Ancient Aristocracy the Nobility will be in perfect Subjection to the Laws, the Whole body will be closely United and the people will not be subject to any particular Lord but to the Laws |

4/III/5,2v 3 In such a State the Army ought to consist of forreigners hired The city should be secured from the possibility of being attacked by them. The Nobility should be allowed to marry the Daughters of the commons. And should from time to time adopt commoners into their Body.

Democracy cannot Subsist but by delegating a part of their Power to Magistrates and a Senate & to representatives of the people. And therefore will coincide with that Mixed kind of Government called a Common Wealth. The Democracies of Athens And Sparta & other Ancient Cities Require a certain equality of Rank among the Citizens

Mixed forms of Government of these I shall mention three‹;› the Republican the Pure Monarchy and the limited Monarchy‹.› Of the

Republican form of Government the Oceana seems to be the most perfect Model. Which I shall therefore describe.

To these Mixed Forms add the Gothick. of which a proper Specimen may be the English Government about the Time of Henry 2 See Lord Littletons History of Henry 2 vol 3d*

4/III/7: Harrington's Oceana

4/III/7,1r* April 19

The Principles of a Commonwealth*

1 An Agrarian which is the foundation or bottom upon which this Grand Machine must be supported*

2 The Constituent parts of it consisting of a Senate proposing A Representative of the people resolving and A Magistracy Executing.*

3 The freedom of Voting and Rotation both which are secured by the Ballot.*

1 Division of the Citizens into free men and Servants. He that wasted his Patrimony incapable of Office or Suffrage in the Commonwealth*

2 Into horse and foot 100 £ per Annum a Horseman*

3 Into Elders and Youth. From 18 to 30 Youth, From 30 Elders*

The Territory in to Parishes Hundreds & Tribes*

The Ballot of the Parish A Proposer chosen by lot‹.› Every person proposed Balloted. until a fifth part be proposed and chosen by ballot. The 1 & 2 Overseers the 3 Constable the 4 & 5 Church Wardens the whole being a fifth part of the Elders are deputies of the parish for a Year.* Election of Ministers to vacant parishes* The Deputies the Militia of the Commonwealth*

April 22

Such a District as contains about 100 Deputies makes a Hundred.*

Election of the Hundred, Justice of the Peace, first Jury man, Captain of the Hundred, Ensign these of the horse‹.› Jury men Overseers of the Ballot*

Second jury man, high Constable, Coroner, of the foot

Ballot of the Hundred five Suits of Gold Balls Determined by lot which shall be used. Seven Gold balls put into the ‹urn› and the seven proposers chosen by lot. Three Competitors proposed for each office‹,› first one for each office by each of the proposers then a second &c, who must have a Majority of the proposers. The person of the three who has most above half is chosen*

Twenty Hundreds make a tribe*

Deputies of the Tribe Mustered into Troops & Companies*

Command of the Troops and companies allotted to the Captains and Ensigns by lot.*

Pavilions with the Urns for horse & foot.* |

4/III/7,1v Magistrates of the tribe chosen in the first days Election. Lord High Sheriff. 2 Lord Lieutenant 3 Lord Custos Rotulorum Muster Master 4 Conductor being Quarter Master General. 5 & 6 Two Censors‹.› Two lots for the suit of the balls one for the side Urns, Another for the Middle Urn. 24 Electors Chosen by Lot.

In the side Urns 60 Gold Balls divided in proportion to the Number of horse and foot with as many blanks as make up the whole number of horse and foot respectively. Those who draw goold balls at the Side Urns to proceed to the Middle Urn where there are 24 Gold & 36 silver balls. Those who draw the first six Gold balls are the first Order of Electors & so on. Four orders in all

The Order of the files Outward Inward Middle, in advancing to the Ballot determined by lot.

Four Competitors for each Office to be named by the four Orders of Electors. and he that has most above half is chosen*

The Functions of the Magistrates of the Tribes

These together with the 20 Justices & 40 Jury men are the Phylarch or Prerogative troop of the Tribe whose offices are 1 They are the Council of the Tribe, 2 Receive the Itinerant Judges 3 To hold the Quarter Sessions. 4 All Commissions ishued into the Tribe by the Parliament ‹or of› Chancery are directed to the Phylarch or some of that troop & executed by them 5 In Levys of Money the Parliament Taxes the Tribes, They the Hundreds and they the parishes, who shall levy it upon themselves. Ten children alive‹,› no taxes. Five‹,› half taxes. 25 Years & not married or married three years and no children‹,› double taxes*

No Debate in any popular Assembly. The pillar of Nilus.*

2d Day's Election in the Tribe 2 knights 3 Deputies out of the horse & 4 Deputies out of the foot. No Man to be thus chosen who has not been married*

Agrarian Law.*

April 23

Constitution of the senate

Six Magistrates annually Chosen viz Strategus‹,› Orator, two Censors‹,› a third Commissioner of the Seal & a third Commissioner of the Treasaury*

Four Councils‹;› State War Religion Trade. Election of Ambassadors in Ordinary‹.› Dictator‹.› Emergent Elections by Scrutiny*

Constitution of the Prerogative Tribe or Popular Assembly*

Triennial Magistrates one Captan & one Cornet of the third Region of the Horse & One Captain & one Ensign of the foot*

Annual Officers Two Tribune of the horse & two of the foot*

Provincial Knights and Deputies*

4/III/5: Harrington's Oceana, *cont.*

4/III/5,3r April 23*

The Essays of the Youth. 26 Order*

4/III/6: Reflections on Harrington. Other Commonwealths

4/III/6,3r* We have given an Account of the Parish Elections in the Commonwealth of Oceana. By ballot one fifth Part of the Elders of the Parish are chosen, who are called Deputies & who have not served in that office the year before. The two first are the Overseers of the Parish. They are Under Censors, & have the ordering of the Ballot at the next years Election. The third Deputy is Constable of the Parish the 4 & 5 Church Wardens. Officers already known in the Constitution of England

We have likewise described the Manner of the Election of Ministers in this Commonwealth, which is popular as in a Commonwealth it ought to be; And I conceive it is the best form for a Popular Election of Ministers that has ever been contrived

Those who contend so earnestly for popular Elections of Ministers among us are for allowing the people to chose upon having heard a Man preach two or three times, which is altogether an insufficient trial for enabling the people to make a true Judgment.* Harrington gives them a Years Trial wherein they have access to observe his abilities and diligence in every branch of his office & therefore may make a much more

Rational Choice. A Soldier will form a good Judgment of his Officer when he has served a Campaign under him. But if he was desired to form his Judgment onely by seing the behaviour of that officer at a Review, he would think you mocked him, and if he was a sensible man would not pretend to judge upon so insufficient a Trial. Two or three Sermons are as insufficient a trial of the Qualifications of a Minister of a Parish as the figure an Officer makes at a Review is of his military Abilities.

We gave account likewise of the Elections in the Commonwealth of Oceana at the Rendevous of the Hundred, where all the Deputies within that precinct meet annually on a day prefixed, & chuse by ballot out of their Number 1 Justice. 1 Jury man. 1 Captain 1 Ensign. of the Horse & 1 Jury man one high Constable and one Coroner of the foot. The Offices of Justices Jury men Constable & Coroner are well known already in the English Government. & The Captain & Ensign are to serve in their Offices in the Militia. These of the Horse. Jury men half horse half foot

The Parish Elections are annually upon the Monday next ensuing the last of December

The Elections of the Hundred upon the Monday next ensuing the last of January The elections of the Tribe come Next to be explained which are partly of annual Officers partly of triennial. First of the annual Officers of the Tribe. 1 Lord High Sheriff. 2 Lord Lieutenant 3 Lord Custos Rotulorum Muster Master General. 4 The Conductor 5 & 6 two Censors.

All the Deputies of the tribe‹,› in order to make this Election‹,› appear in Arms at the Rendevous of the Tribe upon the Monday next ensuing the last of Feb. where they are mustered into Troops of Horse and Companies of foot. By the Lord High Sheriff and Custos Rotulorum from the Lists transmitted to them by the high Constables of the Several Hundreds.

The Captains of the 1, 2, 3d, Troop and of the 1, 2, 3, &c Companies fixed by drawing gold balls for the horse & Silver for the foot out of an Urn |

4/III/6,1r

Of Haringtons Oceana*

Every part of this plan is admirable yet there are some things Necessary both to the Establishment and Duration of such a Government, that this excellent Political writer has not adverted to.

1 He lays to‹o› great Stress upon the Ballance of property as the onely Source of Dominion Such a Ballance of Property as he prescribes is not sufficient for the Establishment or Continuance of a Republick.

Three Sourses of Submission in the Governed 1 The opinion of Power 2 The Opinion of Right 3 The opinion of Wisdom and Virtue & Courage. Any one of these may preserve a Government long where it is not opposed by the others. And it is onely where all three concurr that the Government cannot be changed by the Governed.

The first Supported the Roman Emperors. The second supports most hereditary Monarchys. The third Oliver Cromwel

A People that believe that they have both the Power and Right in their hands may chuse to submit to Kingly or Monarchical nay even to Despotic Government. 1 From Ignorance of the Evils it tends to produce & want of Experience 2 In order to redress greater Evils 3 From the want of a Sense of Liberty 4 From ignorance of any other form of Government. The People of Israel chusing a King. English recalling the Banished Family. Harringtons prophecy Danes giving up their Liberties.*

The Difficulty of totally Changing the Form of a Government even from worse to Better.

It is not probable that O. Cromwell could have established Harringtons Commonwealth in England. because of the Attachment of the People to the Old Forms the Hereditary Nobility and the Opinion of the greatest Part of the Right of the Royal Family There

2 The duration of Such a Government as Harrington proposes. Requires the preservation of Morals. the Suppression of Luxury. The inspiring the people with a Spirit of Liberty‹,› of Zeal for the Government‹,› of Moderation in the Use of Riches‹,› of Respect to the Laws & Magistrates. Of the Virtues requ‹i›red in each kind of Government. |

4/III/6,1v Of Honour & Ignominy in a Republick
Of Respect to Magistrates & to Elders
Of Frugality & equal Expence in private persons & buildings.
Of Magnificence in Magistrates & in publick buildings
Of publick Education.
Of Industry. Law anent Bankrupts.
How Citizens are to be distinguished from Servants by a Census.* & Character How a Citizen may be degraded. by the Overseers or Censors for a Year. By a Hundred for life if he has never born Magistracy‹,› by a Tribe if he has born Magistracy in the tribe onely‹,› by the popular assembly whatever he is
Of Honours & Titles of Honour. & Precedency.
Precedency and Priviledges of Citizens above Servants

Titles of Honour Conferred onely by the People in the Hundred Tribe or Parliament, never to descend beyond the third Generation unless renewed.

Of Colonies Ancient Modern. The Trade of modern Colonies with the Natives in Cultivating Sugar Indigo Tobacco Pimento Tar Wood Logwood. Their Government Limitations of their Trade. Their Influence in the Government and in the House of Commons. The colonies and Great trading Companies have produced what is called the Moneyed Interest which seems to bear hard both upon the Landed Interest and the trading Interest.* Modern Colonies tend to Depopulation.*

The Utopia of Sir Thomas More. Paraguay

Population. Education Abbé de St Pierre's Political Colleg* National Riches. Trade & Commerce. Easy Conveyance Store houses Ballance of forreign Trade Exchange. Money, Banks, Land Bank. Publick Revenue. Customs Excise Pol Tax Sumptuary Laws |

4/III/6,2r If the Oceana of Mr Harrington is considered in itself onely, or if it were once established in a Nation sufficiently enlightned, & not prejudiced against this or in favours of another form of Government. I conceive it to be the best model of Republican Government that has ever been proposed. The Author was a Man of great Genius, he made Politicks his Sole Study and had examined the Constitution of Most States ancient and Modern with a view to discover the Principles of Political Government. He has united in one Uniform and consistent System the best things in all the Ancient Republicks, as well as in that of Venice. I confess I think it difficult to conceive how any part of it could be better contrived, for the time in which he lived either to prevent Sedition among the Subjects, or for defence against forreign Enemies. And I conceive most of those Authors who find fault with Harringtons model of a Commonwealth, not excepting Montesquieu himself,* have rather shewn an Inclination to find fault than supported their censures by good Reasons. I shall onely make two observations on this Plan considered in itself & then I shall make some Observation upon it as a plan for the Government of England at the time it was offered

1 It may be doubted whether even the Agrarian Law of Harington be a Sufficient Security against an undue Accumulation of wealth in the hands of one or a few, and a sufficient security for that Equality among the Citizens which a Republick seems to require. That the Ballance of Power in a State follows the Ballance of Land Property was indeed first observed by Harington and is certainly one of the most important

discoverys in the Science of Politicks, the honour of which is entirely due to him. But as Harrington acknowledges that there may be some Exceptions to this general rule, there may possibly be others which he did not discover There are some Species of Property now known in Britain which are not restrained by Harringtons Agrarian, whereby men may accumulate very great Estates unsuitable to the Nature of a Republican Government.

The publick funds amount to 130,000,000 £ Estates in the colonies |

4/III/6,2v 2 It may be doubted whether there is in this Model sufficient provision for preserving that degree of Morals and publick Virtue which is necessary in a Commonwealth.

4/III/14: Monarchy

4/III/14,1r* There is a certain Character and Temper in the Subjects that suits every Government This has been observed by Montesquieu and it is what he calls the principle of the Several Governments by which he seems to mean onely that the stability and duration of such a Plan of Government requires that the Subjects Should be chiefly actuated by such a Principle.

This Principle in Despotism he makes to be fear
in Monarchies Honour in Republicks Virtue*

Despotism suits best with the warm Climat‹e›s.* How little reason have we to envy the Asiatics the Temperature of their Air Their Rubies & Diamonds and Silk; Their Spiceries and all the other noble productions of the Climate

Let me rather be free if I should wander in the Wilds of America with the Canadians or Eskimaux and live upon Roots an‹d› game rather than be a Slave and wallow in all the Luxury of an Eastern Court.

Of Pure Monarchy

In this form of Government first described by Montesquieu* The Monarch has all the parts of the Supreme power in himself but Exercises it by fixed Laws & Subordinate Powers. It is therefore essential to this Government to have a Register of the Laws. The Parlements of France described Their Power to remonstrate against the Kings Edicts.

A Hereditary Nobility with Jurisdictions.*

A Standing Army of the Nobility Gentry and Peasants

The Law a separate Profession.

Ambition and the Love of Honour encouraged.*

The Glory of the Monarch substituted in place of the love of ones Country.* |

4/III/14,1v The Monarch must be hereditary and the Succession regulate‹d› by fundamental laws ‹He› must appear to his people. He must be gracious and affable to all about him. Keep A Splendid Court He must if possible add the Glory of a Conqueror to his other Titles Encourage the Nobility to live at Court to Spend their Fortunes in high living and to have a dependance by Places in the Army and Civil Government. He ought to be an encourager of Learning. Acts of Clemency should belong to him, but Acts of Severity or Justice be always left to his Courts.

Taxes ought to be farmed but not to the Nobility or Army.

Every man should depend upon the Court and expect to rise by its favour. and look upon disgrace at Court as the greatest of all Evils.

Such a Monarchy is apt to grow is very dangerous to its Neighbours. Difficult to Conquer. Learning and Arts may flourish in it but Commerce will never meet with great Encouragement.

It may degenerate into Despotism by crushing the Nobility and taking away their Jurisdictions 2 By taking away the priviledges of Parliaments. & their independency

The power of the Monarch may be diminished. 1 By the Subjects being more enlightned. By Unsuccessfull Wars or bad administration. By Minoritys By disputed Succession and Pretenders to the Throne

Reflexions on the French Monarchy

Its Power very great and all its Neighbours, we in particular‹,› ought to be jealous of it. Its power had been greater had it not been for the ambition of its Monarchs. Lewis 14. The Present King. The most pacific Kings lay the foundation of its Strength. Monastries and Nunneries weaken it |

4/III/14,2r What* Montesquieu has said with regard to the leading Principle of the different forms of Government needs Explication and I conceive when properly understood is of great Consequence in Politicks.* He Observes that in Despotick Government the Leading principle is fear, in Monarchy Honour, & in Democracy Virtue. For understanding this it is proper to observe that as every Government that is secure and lasting must be in some degree adapted to the principles by which human creatures are commonly influenced in their conduct, so there are some Governments that are more adapted to one principle of human Nature others to another. That Principle which is peculiarly adapted to the Nature of the Government will always be cherished by that and the natural tendency of the Government will be to mould Men into that Character and temper which agrees best with the Nature of the Government‹.› On the other hand the More that Principle, that temper and Character prevails which is suited to the Nature of the Government, the more smo‹o›thly & easily will the wheels of Government move.

Thus in a Republick the great End of the Government is the common good of the Whole and the Preservation of civil Liberty. That Spirit therefore in the Subjects which is best adapted to this form of Government is the Love ‹of› their Constitution and the love of Liberty and of the Laws‹;› this the true Spirit of a free Government and while this Spirit prevails the Government will be well administ‹e›red and powerfull against its Enemies. &c Sparta. Athens. Rome.

In a Despotick Government The Arbitrary Will of one Man Moves the whole Machine. And therefore the most abject & tame Submission to the Sovereign is the onely thing that can make such a Government go on smoothly. And Fear or Supers‹ti›tion are the onely principles that can produce such an Abject Submission in a great Empire to the arbitrary will of one. These therefore are the principles of a Despotic Government.

That* Principle of Honour which, According to Montesquieu, in a Monarchy supplies the want of Virtue, is nothing else but an Ambition to be distinguished and applauded, a strong desire to cut a figure in the
4/III/14,2v Eyes of men especially of those that are above us in Rank. | Here a Man is taught that his Virtues ought to be such as shew an elevation of Spirit his Morals ought not to be too strait or Stiff. That his behaviour should allways be frank and Polite. The Virtues which this Principle of Honour inspires are not th‹o›se which point out our duty to others but such as teach us what a man owes to him self. Not those that draw our affections towards our fellow creatures but those that may give us some distinction & preeminence above them. This Honour does not judge of Actions by their Justice or Utility but by their brilliancy and lustre. It aims not at real Worth but at Distinction and Fame. Sincerity Modesty Justice Temperance are to the Man of Honour plebeian Virtues, which have little connection with the Principle of Honour and ought not to stand in its way, when it aims at any thing that ‹is› spirited and Noble. The Man

of Honour to raise his fortune can Supplant the man that confides in him. He can boast of an amorous intrigue with a person of superior rank or of eminent Perfections, tho the wife of his Friend or benefactor. If he can gain a Post by servile adulation and flattery of one whom in his heart he despises, or by a dexterous piece of Craft & cunning, this is a laudable finesse in which he will glory. His honour requires that ‹he› should be open and speak the Truth, not from the love of Sincerity and Truth; By no Means. but because to speak the truth is a Sign of boldness and Courage.

This Principle of Honour always inspires Politeness and Good Breeding. Men of high Rank in all Countries distinguish themselves by Politeness to their inferiors, the desire of Respect naturally produces this. Every obliging thing which a great man says or does to us is taken as a great favour. It is a very cheap way of acquiring respect and bringing men under obligations. Politeness and good breeding is undoubtedly a most amiable accomplishment, an accomplishment which real Virtue and Humanity ought to inspire. As men are born to live together and mutually to promote each others Satisfaction comfort and happiness. And nothing tends more to promote peace harmony and good will in Society than a polite and obliging behaviour in men towards one another. But this amiable Quality does not always proceed from the principles of true Virtue & humanity‹;› it is often the offspring of Vanity and the desire of Esteem. In the Monarchical Government there is a Gradation of Rank from the Monarch down to the peasant and day labourer. This kind of Government encourages Ambition and every man as he aspires to a hi‹g›her Rank emulates the Manners of those that are above him.

4/III/11: The British Constitution

4/III/11,1r* Of Monarchy

1 The french Monarchy a Model of Pure Monarchy

Aristocracies

Poland. The United Provinces Venice.

Republick

Harringtons Oceana

Constitution of Brittain*
Distribution of the Supreme Power

Judiciary. Nomination of Judges Various Judicatories. Power of Juries their Nomination & Election. Office of the Judge. Subordination of Courts Supreme Judicature. Attainders.*

Legislative Power. 1 King* Hereditary preferable to Elective‹.› Rules of Succession. No reason for Excluding the Female Line. Popish heirs excluded & those who marry Papists‹.›* inconvenient to marry Subjects. The King can do no Wrong

Prerogative Revenue.

Peers. Hereditary except in Scotland.* Ought to have a Considerable Share of the Landed Interest. Are an Intermediate Power that Binds the King & Commons together. And therefore ought to have an Interest both in preserving the Liberties of the People & the Prerogative of the Crown. The Place of Extinct Families should be Supplied from Time to time from the Richest of the Commons. Nobles & Commons ought to Marry. And the Younger Sons of the Peers to be Commoners The King can make Peers but cannot unmake them

The Constitution of Electors of the House of Commons. ought to be such as to make them an Equal Representative. Some Inequalities arise 1 From the decay of Burroughs once great. 2 From the Improvement of Land Rents 3 From excluding th‹o›se that Hold of Subjects.* The Nature of Holdings and of the Feudal Law. The changes that have happned in it.* The inconvenience of having the Superiority divided from the Property among Subjects.*

The Constitution with regard to Elections. Enlisting of Barrons & Power of Head Courts. Power of the Sherifes.* Returns. Controverted Elections Removing of Military force from the place of Elections.*|

4/III/11,1v The Meetings of the Legislature.* The calling & prorogation of the Parliament belongs to the Crown. Because their Sitting Constantly is not Necessary. This prerogative checked by the Expence of the Government being provided from Year to year. Estimates for the Publick laid always before the House of Commons Money Bills must take their Rise there & not be altered or tacked else where. Liberty of Speech. & Liberty of Access to the King. Liberty to Impeach any Subject. The Lords ought to Judge in Impeachments. The Speaker of the House The Order of Passing Bills The first Second & third Reading Engrossing.* The Order of Debate & of Voting by the Committe‹e› of the Whole House. house Dividing Conference in the Painted Chamber.*

The Accounts of Public Expences & of the Public Debt. ly on the Table.*

The Habeas Corpus Act & its Suspension.* Liberty of the Press.* Tolleration. Papists

The Forms of Sitting & Proceeding in the House of Lords. Wool Sacks*

Acts of Pardon & Oblivion* take their Rise from the Crown & have one Reading in each House

By Laws of Corporations Justices of the Peace & Commissioners of Supply & the Limits of their Power & Jurisdiction.*

Executive Power. Kings Over the Army Legislative Raises & dissolves it.* The Nomination to all Military Offices. restrained to protestants.* Military Discipline regulated by the Mutiny Act.* Army has the same Interest as the Subjects in General.

Making War Treaties Naming Ambassadours. Naming Officers of the Excise & Customs. Justices of the Peace Commissioners of Supply. All the Judges Bishops. The Officers of the Navy Officers of the Crown

Of Political Parties in the British Constitution Natural Accidental

Religious Parties Their Association with Political Ones Natural & Accidental

Defects or Inconveniences in the British Constitution.

1* The preservation of it Depends on the Preserving a Ballance of King Lords & Commons who have or may Apprehend they have Different & Contrary Interests & various Accidents may alter this Ballance. Concessions made to a Good King may be abused by a Bad one. The House of Commons may be weakened by the Inequality of the Representative The Kings Power Increased by the Augmentation of the Revenue, the Multiplication of Places |

4/III/11,2r **1*** The British Constitution lays a foundation for the Division of the State in to 2 Parties who may be called the Court & Country Party*

There are 3 Interests in the State King Lords & Commons. The 2d is not so considerable as to form a third Party but divides in to the other two.

The Parties in the Roman State Patricians & Plebeians

Three things must occasion this Division in our Government 1 The different apprehensions of those who wish well to the Constitution. & act from publick principles.

2 The interested views of those that want to keep their places or to get into places

these two arise from the Nature of the Constitution

3 The designs of those that are Enemies to the Constitution or to the Administration

Neither the One nor the Other of these parties is always in the Wrong

Accidental Parties

Whig & Torry. The Jacobite & Revolutioner Church Man & Dissenter High & Low Church. Associations of Parties sometimes Natural sometimes Accidental Papist or High Church Arminian & Courtier. Puritan Calvinist & Republican or Country man. High Church & Torry Low Church Dissenter & Whig. Since the Revolution Torry & Jacobite & High Church. & Anticourtier, Whig Revolutioner Low Church or Dissenter

In Scotland Jacobite & Episcopalian. Revolutioner & Presbyterian

Jacobites a Faction Revolutioners Not so Distinction between a Party & Faction.*

See Rapin Dissertation on Whigs & Torries. Bullinbrokes Dissertation on Parties Cleghorn's Discourse*

2 The British Constitution lays a foundation for Corruption or undue Influence in Elections and Nominations which may be used by the Ministry or by the Candidates to Offices & to faction in those that would be in it. A place at Court often got by Opposition to the Administration rather than by serving the Nation. and kept by serving the Administration rather than serving the Public. The giving a Place to a Demagogue in our Constitution answers to the Ostracism of the Athenians

The Commons unequally represented*

3 The preservation of our Constitution depends on keeping the Ballance even between the three parts of the Legislature. Chiefly between the King & Commons which seems to be a ticklish thing.

1 What adds Weight to the Kings Scale. Personal Abilities. Long uninterrupted hereditary Succession. connexion with forreign Princes The Civil List the Number of Places & Pensions in his Disposal. besides the parts that are more fixed viz his Executive Power & his Part in the Legislative.

Trade brings an increase of Property to the Commons & to that Part of them that will always be most zealous for Liberty. The power of giving or withholding money their great Security

Whether the Crown could Stand without the Dependance that the Commons have on it.

Whether the Ballance of the British Government inclines more to Liberty or Despotism

See Hume Essay on the Independancy of Parliaments on the above Question*|

4/III/11,2v **4** The British Constitution has a tendency to a Corruption of Morals & seems to have no sufficient provision against that. The Corruption of Morals grows from the Influence of the Example of a Court. the Manner in which Elections & Nominations to offices are carried on The Number of Oaths the Profanation of the Sacrament in being made a Qualification to a place.* The Abuse of Liberty of Speech & of the Press. its degenerating into a Spirit of Libertinism The Contempt of Religion & of the Clergy. The Numbers that live a City Life The increase of Trade which makes every thing be bought & Sold How far it is in the Power of a King & Court to stop the Progress of Vice by their Example ‹&› Influence Strict Execution of the Laws against Immorality. By its Power in Universitys & the Church & in the Disposal of Places

The Censorial Power in Ancient Republicks how far capable of being revived. Whether a Proper Church Discipline might Supply its place & how far the Clergy might be entrusted with this Power. Of the Education Election & deprivation of Clergymen. The Constitution of the Churches both of Scotland & England has a tendency to Corruption of Morals among the Clergy. Which must be followd by Corruption among the people – The Encouragement of Rural Life & making it free and independ‹ent› tends to preserve the Morals of a People

5 A certain Degree of corruption of Morals Makes a people incapable of free Government. & therefore the br*

4/III/8: The British Constitution, *cont.*

4/III/8,1r April 28

We began to consider the Constitution of the Government of Great Brittain, which if we may rely upon the Judgment of Montesquieu the greatest political Writer that either ancient or modern times have produced, is more admirably fitted for preserving the liberty of the Subject than any other form of government that ever existed, or even any model that ever was proposed even the Oceana itself.

Harrington* says that Author has in his Oceana examined to how high a pitch political Liberty may possibly be carried, but one may say that while he searched for this Liberty in his Model of a Commonwealth he had it before his eyes in the real constitution of his Country, and that he built Chal‹ce›don in the Sight of Byzantium.* perhaps however Montesquieu did not consider that the British Constitution was not the same when Harrington wrote as it is now. I do not affirm says he that the extreme degree of liberty which is to be found in this constitution ought to mortifie those who enjoy Liberty onely in a moderate degree. An excess of the best things is not always desirable and human Nature suits itself better to a mediocrity than to the extremes even of things that are good.* Yet this admirable Plan of Government in which every british man glories, and for which the most enlightened of other nations do envy us; was never contrived by any Lawgiver, it is the work of time and Accidents The generosity and Courage of the British Nation impatient of tyrranny has always made them shake it off when they began to feel it and make such changes in their Political System as seemed most proper for preventing for the future the grievances they had already felt.

It is one of the advantages of this Government that we may freely philosophize about the principles of Policy and even of our own Government as well as about every other object of human knowledge. A happiness which is not enjoyed in an equal Degree under any other Government Montesquieu's L'Esprit des Loix was burnt in France & he as well as the other best political writers of that Nation do not chuse to own what they write.* In Brittain we see that the Subjects have not onely the Liberty to canvass the form of Government but to arraign the administration of it in a manner that never was permitted in any other Government under heaven. This liberty indeed has of late been much abused & it is to be wished that the abuse of it may not make it necessary to lay some restraint upon it. But there is no Restraint upon a calm and candid Philosophical Discussion of the Principles of our happy Constitution, nor even on pointing out the Defects and weak sides of it that those who have it in their Power may apply the proper Remedies |

4/III/8,2r Lords Spiritual 2 Archbishops 24 Bishops. & formerly 26 Abbots & 2 Priors

All these hold or are Supposed to hold certain ancient Barronies of the King in virtue of which they have their Seats in the House of Peers.

It is of no Consequence whether we make the Lords Spiritual & Temporal two Estates or one.

The Lords Temporal consist of all the Peers of the Realm for the Bishops although Lords of Parliament are not Peers. The Peers are distinguished by their different Titles of Nobility Dukes Marquises Earls Vicounts Barons.

A Hereditary Nobility is necessary in a Limited Monarchy. Equally inconsistent with Despotism & a Republick‹.› Necessary that they should be an independent and Separate Branch of the Legislature

1 Duke. Dux Originally signified the General or leader of an Army. Came to be made a Title of Honour first on the Continent & the fashion spread into Britain. From the time of the Norman Conquest till Edward 3 No Dukes in England probably because the Kings were Dukes of Normandy but when Edward 3 claimed to be King of France he made his Son Edward the Black Prince and this dignity was afterwards bestowed upon others chiefly of the Royal Family*

In the Reign of Queen Elizabeth no Dukes. Villiers Duke of Buckingham the first after that. 1620*

2 Marquess Marches. Originally a Lord of the Marches.

3 Earl. Ealdorman Comes. Sometime after the Conquest called Counts. Sherreff of a Shire In Writs Commissions and other formal Instruments any Peer of the Degree of an Earle is stiled by the King his trusty and well beloved Cousin. The Rise of this Custom from Henry 4*

4 Viscount or Vice Comes. originally the Deputy of the Earl in his Government of a Shire

5 Baron. Originally every Lord of a Mannor who had Jurisdiction in his Mannour or the priviledge of holding a Baron Court was a Baron. And all such Barons as held of the King had a right to sit in the great Council of the Nation. About the time of King John* it came to be in use that the King called onely the greater Barons in Person and the lesser Barons were Summoned by the Sherrif to sit by their Representatives in another House, which gave Rise to the Separation of the two houses of Parliament. By degrees the tittle of Baron came to be confined to those who were called by the Kings Writ to the upper House and in Richard the seconds time it was made a meer tittle of Honour by his conferring it on divers persons by his Letters patents*

The Right of Peerage originally territorial. Instance the Bishops. & in Henry 6 the Castle of Arundel was adjud‹g›ed to confer an Earldom on its Possessor.* But when alienations became frequent the dignity of Peerage became Personal.

Priviledges of the Nobility

1 In Criminal Cases a Nobleman must be tried by his Peers. Sitting in Judgment they give their Verdict not upon Oath but upon their Honour. But when called as Witnesses are Sworn Scandalum Magnatum.* Can

lose their Nobility onely by Death or Attainder. One instance of a Degradation by act of Parliament.*

Scotch Peers. 16 chosen by Ballot.* this a Temporary Expedient which ceases when the Number is reduced to 16.

House of Commons Their Priviledge to their Persons 40 days before and after the Session Money bills take their Rise there. Quali‹fi›cations of the Electors, of the Elected. Manner of election. |

4/III/8,2v By Statutes of 8. & 10 Henry 6.* The Knights of the Shires shall be chosen by the people dwelling in some Counties having freehold to the value of 40 shillings a year within the county which by subsequent Statutes must be free of all charges and deductions except Parliamentary and Parochial taxes. freehold i.e. for term of life at least.

40 shillings at that time equal at least to 20 £ now

The Estate must have been assessed to some land tax and at least 12 Months before

Elected Knights must have 600 £ per Annum free or copyhold Estate‹.›* Burgesses 300 £

Many Restrictions to lessen the Influence of the Crown in Elections.

Method of Elections.

Method of passing bills

Adjournment Prorogation and dissolution

Impeachments Attainders Suspension of the Habeas Corpus Act.

4/III/9: Population. National Virtue. National Riches

4/III/9,1r May 6 1765*

The primary Object of the Science of Politicks is the Constitution of a State, and the natural Effects and consequences of that Constitution and this capital part of the Political Science may be reduced to these two Problems. First a Constitution or form of Government being given to point out the Natural Effects and Consequences of that Constitution whether for Instance it will be lasting or of short duration, whether powerfull against forreign Enemies or weak and Easy to be conquered, whether internally quiet and pe‹a›ceable or turbulent and Seditious, whether the Subjects will be oppressed or enjoy the common Rights and Liberties which mankind are entitled to. The second Problem is‹,› having given the End for which a Constitution of Government is intended‹,› to point out that Constitution or Model of Government which will most effectually promote and secure this end. It is very obvious that the End of Government ought to be the good and happiness of the Governed. And therefore every Form or Model of Government if we judge of it by the moral Standart is to be more or less approved of according as it tends more or less to promote this end. |

4/III/9,2r The chief ends of Political Society Security from forreign Enemies and the maintenance of Peace and justice among the Subjects, these Ends are to be attained by a proper form and Model of Government. But there are also Subordinate ends of Political Society the attainment of which tho not necessary to the being or continuance of it may yet conduce greately to its well being and Prosperity. The proper means of Promoting these are likewise an object of the Science of Politicks. I cannot pretend to enumerate all these far less to insist upon them. The chief of them may I think be reduced to these heads. Population. Virtue, Learning, Riches & Opulence, Publick Revenue and Arms.

The Importance of Population. In some States it may be left to the Course of Nature. In Some States laws and Customs obtain to prevent it. Exposing of Children. One of a family marrying Persecution. Reasons of the defects in Population in Modern Governments.

Two methods of Population 1 By admitting and Naturalizing forreigners Effects of this in Holland. Of a Naturalization Bill in England.* Colonies made up in a great Measure of forreigners. disadvantages of forreigners both at home and in the Colonies

2 By encouraging marriage or rather removing the discouragements to it which arise from the improvements of Society.* High Living high Land Rent dearth of the necessaries of life high taxes upon the poor Leudness & prostitution The Rate of the Natural Increase of Mankind when these impediments are removed, is to double in 25 years*

1 Many ancient Nations found themselves too populous* The population of the Earth owing to this. The Reasons 1 The want of the Arts necessary for subsisting many upon the territory of the State 2 The want of traffick which brings men Subsistence from all the Corners of the Earth. 3 The small degree of industry or riches necessary to maintain a family before luxury took place made them propagate faster. And fewer live unmarried

2 Modern States find a great want of Population. Causes 1 They can maintain more people, & make their Numbers turn to account.* 2 Monastries Nunneries & Celibacy of Clergy 3 Luxury & high living which prevents many from marrying & makes Women less fruitfull.

4 The Waste of Men in Standing Armies Navies and long Voyages. 5 The great Number of horse kept for riding on horseback or in Wheel Carriages & for other Articles of Luxury. |

4/III/9,2v May 7 1765

We have considered the importance of Population in a State and the proper means of promoting it. And we are next to consider the importance of Virtue in a State and the Means by which it may be most effectually promoted. We do not here intend to consider the importance of Virtue in a moral or Religious but onely in a political Light. That Virtue is the highest Excellence of a Man that it contributes more than all other things put together to make a man usefull to others and happy in himself in the present Life and is the onely mean of securing happiness in the life to come; these are no doubt truths of the highest importance, but they do not belong to our present Argument which leads us onely to consider how far Virtue is necessary or conducive towards making men good citizens or good Members of a State. As far as it is so it deserves the Care and Attention of the Legislator and he neglects an important part of his province if he takes no Care of it.

It appears to be very certain that all wise Schemes of Political Government suppose men to be neither perfectly virtuous nor perfectly vicious & profligate‹.› if men were perfectly virtuous there would be little Use for political Government men would live very happily without it, they would onely need to know their duty in order to do it and would not need to be compelled to it by laws & sanctions. on the other hand if all the members of a state were as wicked and profligate as some individuals are‹,› no Scheme of Government would be sufficient to hold them together, the Society behoved to disband, every individual would be as a beast of prey to the rest and they would mutually destroy each other. All political Government therefore supposes human Nature to be in some middle State between these extreme degrees of Virtue and vice. And indeed it has always been so in the bulk of Mankind. and we have no reason to believe that there is any nation on the face of the Earth where the whole or the greater part are so extreamly wicked and so abandoned as some individuals in every nation may be found to be

But between the extremes of Virtue and vice which may ‹on the› one hand make Political Government unnecessary or on the other hand make it impossible there are a great many different degrees of Corruption of

Morals in the body of a State which may make the political Government more or less easy and more or less secure and quiet.

Montesquieu conceives that fear without Virtue is sufficient to support a Despotick Government, that a principle of honour without Virtue is sufficient to support a pure Monarchy such as that of France but he conceives that a Republick cannot Subsist without Virtue.* I agree with this Author that a greater degree of Virtue is necessary in a Republick or in any free Government than in a Despotick Government or pure Monarchy.*|

4/III/9,3r The means of promoting and preserving Virtue in a State

1 Good Education. Publick Schools properly endowed and provided.

2 Execution of the Laws against Vice and Immorality.

3 Zeal & Strictness of Life in the Ministers of Religion & Magistrates

4 Care of the Army and Navy. Learning and Arts*

---

1 What is to be called Riches in a Nation?

2 Food and Rayment, Houses Furniture Lands. How far Riches

3 The Riches of the Whole is the Sum of the Riches of Individuals

4 As every Mans Riches is the Ballance between his Goods & his Debt so it is in a Nation.

What things have influence on the Price of Commodities or of Labour & skill

4/III/15: National Riches. Commerce. Money. False Maxims

4/III/15,1r* Of National Riches

1 Def*‹:› By Riches I mean The Possession & Property of alienable things by which human life is Supported or its Pleasure or Happiness increased, either really or in the Common opinion.*

1 There are things which the Earth Spontaneously affords that come under the Denomination of Riches. Grottos Caves or Groves for Shelter. Wood for Various Uses Some fruits and animals for food Water for drink Skins of Beasts for Cloathing some Gold & other things which it is Needless to Ennumerate

2 But the far greatest part of what may be called Riches is produced by human Labour & Industry.* Food & Drink Weaving Houses Utensils Tame Animals Metals Wood Machines Vehicles Jewels &c. And the

Riches produced by Labour in every Civilized State do so far exceed the Spontaneous productions of the Earth that the latter may pass almost for Nothing Compared with the former‹.› The Earth affords the Materials but it is Labour & Industry that gives them form & the far greatest part of their worth

3 Yet some parts of the Earth aford greater variety of Materials or such as are brought to perfection with less labour. And in this Respect the Warm Climates are generally preferable to the Colder, which require more Labour & Industry in their Inhabitants

4 A great deal of the Riches produced by labour must be consumed by Use by time or Accidents.

5 The Whole Acquired Riches of the Human Race consists of the Overplus of what is produced by Labour above what is Consumed

6 A Man that in the Course of his Life produces more by his Labour than what he consumes makes the World Richer by the Overplus

2 Def‹:› N.B. I reckon a Mans consumption not onely what he consumes by use but what perishes in his custody by Time or accidents.

7 A Man that in the Course of his life consumes more than he produces by his Labour makes the World poorer by the Overplus

8 The Riches of the Human Race will allwise Rise or fall in the Compound proportion of the usefull Labour & Industry Directly and the Consumption Reciprocally. |

4/III/15,1v 9 Altho every thing that can be called Riches was originally produced by the Labour of some Body (excepting the Spontaneous productions of the Earth which are altogether Inconsiderable) Yet being by their Nature alienable they are frequently found, in the possession of those that never produced them

10 Riches may be alienate either Involuntarly by force or fraud or Voluntarly by gift bargain or Exchange.

3 Def‹:› Where Riches are given in Exchange for other Riches Supposed to be of equal Value Such a Transaction is called Commerse

What a Man produces by his Labour or purchases with a View to Employ it in Commerce is called a Commodity*

11 The Comparative Value of Different Commodities is influenced by so many Things that it is extreamly Difficult if not impossible to settle it by any General Rules.

12 If one Nation had the Sole property of any Necessary of Life that Nation might oblige all others to give what they pleased to demand‹,› that is to be their Servants

13 But when the Necessarys or Conveniencys of Life are in Many different hands that have Separate Interests. & cannot combine to fix a price upon their Commodities. Every one is divided betwixt the desire of a high price & the fear of having his Commodity ly on his hands while others vend theirs at a lower price. The Buyer is agitated by like hopes and fears as the Seller. however bargains will be Struck. Some at a higher price some at a lower till at last after vibrating for a while the price will Settle nearly at a Medium betwixt the highest and the lowest.*

14 The most Equal Value of Commodities is that which enables those that produce them by their Labour to purchase all the Conveniencies and Accommodations of Life which labourers of that kind are by the Customs & Opinions of the Countrey entitled to.

4 Def‹:› Altho the Value of Comodities as defined in the last Article be very Variable according to the Customs or Opinions of different nations or of the same Nation at different times Yet since we cannot find any more equal or Natural Standart of the Value of Commodities we shall call this their Natural Value*

15 When Commodities have once come to settle at their Natural price, That price cannot be afterwards increased (if we exclude Monopolies & Combinations of the Sellers or Buyers‹)› but by an Increase of the Demand or a Decrease of the Commodity. Or at least by a general Opinion of the Increase of the Demand or Decrease of the Commodity |
4/III/15,2r In either of these cases the fear of the Commodity lying on hand decreases in the Seller & makes him insist on a greater price. The buyer is prompted to offer a higher price lest the Commodity be all taken up by other buyers.

A General opinion of the Increase of the Demand or Decrease of the Commodity will have the same Effect for a Time. But Commonly. Such Opinions if ill founded do not last long in a Civilized Country people being very attentive to their Interest and not easily deceived in that Respect where their passions do not blind them.

16 The Decrease of the price of a Commodity must in like Manner be occasioned by an Increase of the Commodity or a Decrease of the Demand either Real or in opinion.

17 The Increase or Decrease of the price of Commodities is not alwise in the Simple proportion of the Causes above mentioned but Commonly as I apprehend in a Greater. Thus Suppose two Countries A & B have a Mutual Commerce in Corn & that Neither of them deals with any Other Country in that Commodity‹.› A commonly furnishes B with

10,000 Quarters of Wheat & has no more to Spare. In a Certain Year B has a demand for ten thousand Quarters as usual but A can onely Spare 7000. I apprehend that in this Case the price would rise more than in the proportion of 7 to 10. However it must be acknowledged that much would depend upon the possibility or easiness of Supplying the want of Corn by other provisions.

On the other hand if A has 15,000 Quarters to spare and has no other Market than with B this would probably sink the price more than in the proportion of 15 to 10. Yet this Depends much on Circumstances. If the Commodity be such as will not keep to another year or if the Sellers are in such Circumstances as that they cannot keep it. It must be sold at any Rate & the price will fall one half or perhaps more But if the Corn will keep to another Year & the Sellers in Opulent Circumstances & furnished with Conveniencies they will keep up the price nearly in proportion to the Natural Value. And this will be the More easy if the
4/III/15,2v Buyers have also ability & convenience | to buy & keep it for one or More Years

18 Hence it is obvious that Commodities that may be long kept do not rise or fall in their prices so much in proportion to the Causes abovementioned as these which cannot be long kept.

19 It is likewise Evident that the Opulence of the Buyers & Sellers & their Accommodations for Store is a Mean of preventing the fall or Rise of Commodities that may be kept.

20 Vice Versa A great Rise or fall of such Commodities as are Mentioned in the last article above or below their Natural Value is an Indication of Poverty or Bad Management in the Dealers that suffer by it.

21 There may be other Remote Causes besides these Mentioned Art 15 & 16 of the Rise & fall of Commodities but they seem onely to operate in proportion as they affect the plenty of the Commodity or the Demand for it. The Death of a Prince may raise the price of Black Cloath but it does this onely by increasing the Demand for it. Riches and Luxury increase the price of Commodities the same way.

22 To the Causes Mentioned Art 15, 16, We may add this as a third Immediate Cause of the Rise of prices viz where their Expence to the Manufacturer or Merchant is visibly & at once increased as by a Tax by the Rising of Insurance for Import And in this Case the Rise of the price is often Greater than ‹the› increase of the Sellers Expence. Thus the Tax on Glass raised the price of that Commodity more than the Amount of the Tax‹.›* In these Cases the buyer expects that the Commodity will

be raised as much as answers the tax. And the Sellers have of an opportunity of representing the tax as more heavy upon them then it really is. And as the Merchant foresees there will be less demand when the price is raised they are before hand in providing less plenty of thc Commodity.

23 When Commodities by any of the Causes Mentioned are raised above or brought below their Natural Value they have still a tendency to return to it in the Natural Course of things.

24 As the price of most Com‹m›odities is still rising and falling it is necessary where there is a Considerable Commerce to have some Commodity that may Serve for a Common Measure of the Value of others. This Common Measure must be something that ‹is› easily kept‹,› easily Conveyed‹,› not perishable and is not liable to sudden Risings and fallings in its own value. Gold and Silver by most civilized Nations 4/III/15,3r have been Made the | common Measure of the price of Commodities and are very fit for that Use. And to prevent the Necessity of alwise proofing and weighing those metals when we take them in Exchange for Commodities it has been found Convenient to Coin them in to pieces of different weight which have a Certain Figure & Stamp to ascertain their value*

25 Those that do not labour themselves must be supported by the Labour of Others. Those whose fortunes & Stations excempt them from bodily Labour‹:› their Servants & Attendants Lawiers Physicians Divines School Men Soldiers Excise & custom house Officers &c Sailors‹.› there are others whose Labour does not produce Riches but transferrs them from one hand to another or fits them for Consumption‹:› Merchants. Cooks Apothecaries Taylors. Others direct the Labourers‹:› Stewarts overseers bookke‹e›pers &c Besides many that are at times unable to labour through infancy old age Sickness bearing & Nursing Children. If we consider that all these are maintained by the Labour of Others & most of them consume several Times as much as most Labouring men‹,› we shall see that the Labour of less than one half of Men produces the Riches of the Whole

26. Hence the Riches of a Country are owing to the following Causes
1 When a great proportion of the Inhabitants are Industri‹o›us & frugal & few Idle or profuse
2 When the Labour is employed in a great measure upon things that are more permanent or not for immediate Consumption or‹,› if they are so‹,› are sent Abroad & not consumed at home. Or when it supplys the place of forreign Importations

3 The Invention of Usefull Machines or Methods by which the same work may be done by fewer hands or in Shorter Time

27. Yet a Dealer in Manufactures who employs many hands does cæteris paribus enrich the Country more than one who employs few because besides the profits of the dealer we are to take in the profits of the people that Labour for him

28 Nay a Manufacture that hurts the Dealer may yet profit the Nation tho this cannot often happen & rather by Accident than from the Natural Course of things. |

4/III/15,3v Of Domestic Commerce*

29 A Nation may be Rich & flourishing by the Industry of its inhabitants without any forreign trade

30 Without Forreign Trade A Nation can have no silver and Gold but from Mines in the Country.

31 It signifies little to a Nation whether silver and Gold be in plenty or Scarce without forreign Commerce

Of Forreign Commerse

‹32› The difference betwixt the Import & Export of a Nation is what it gains by forreign Commerce & is called the Ballance of Trade.

Of Commerce with our Collonies

The History of Commerce

The Other Effects of it with regard to the Manners of a people

Their Morals. Peace & War, the Arts & Sciences Liberty

See Montesquieu Hume Preceptor. Petty Davenant*

Characteristics of the present political State of Great Brittain Wallace*

The Querist. 5th Edition 1750 Bishop of Cloyne*

Essay on the Advantages and disadvantages which respectively attend France & Great Britain with regard to Trade &c by Mr Tucker of Bristol*

Sir Mathew Decker Enquiry into the Causes of the Decay of forreign Trade & the Remedies thereof*

Of the National Debt the consequences of it & the Schemes for paying it Hooke.* |

4/III/15,4r Gold and Silver a proper Measure of the Price of Commodities

1 Because they do not rise and fall much in value being durable and always esteemed

2 Because divisible into small parts

3 Because the Quantity and Fin‹e›ness on which the value depends may be exactly assertained.

4 Because easily conveyed 5 Because they keep without Waste

‹6› Facilitates Exchange

The price of things Measured by Oxen or sheep in homers time*

Gold and Silver at first Weighed. Inconveniences of this.

Afterwards coined by States. Coin authorised by Law as a lawfull tender of Payment.*

The Practices of Princes upon Coin.

The practices of false coiners Clippers washers Sweaters. &c

State of the Coin in King Williams Time Lockes Treatises*

Laws of the Mint. Penal Laws against melting the Coin against Coining against Exporting.*

False Notions concerning Money

1* That it receives its value from Edicts of Princes or States*

Silver & Gold must have ‹a› Value that depends not on the Will of Princes and States 1 Because it cannot be found out‹,› dug from the Mines and Refined without much Labour and Expence. 2 Because it has allways been in demand as a commodity and is usefull for Vessels for ornaments for Utensils It has therefore a Natural Price as other Commodities have. Gold and Silver must have a Natural Price compared with one another & with other Metals and other Commodities

2 It cannot have an unnatural Price fixed upon it by Princes and States without Injury to the Subjects and injury to trade. 1 If the price fixed upon it is too low it can Neither be dug if it is in the Country nor imported by trade but will be exported. 2 If too high‹,› labouring people will leave the Country. It will be counter fitted

3 It cannot be raised or lowered without bringing distress to the Country. Raising the Denomination enriches the Monied Man, at the Expence of others. Lowering the Denomination has the contrary Effect. |

4/III/15,4v It is not altering the Denomination that can produce any Effect on Commerce good or bad. But it is making the same quantity of Silver to be an eq‹u›ivalent to a greater or less quantity of other goods|

4/III/15,4r **2** That it is good policy to forbid the exportation of it.*

3 That the Riches of a Nation consists in the Quantity of Money yet it must consist chiefly in the Quantity of Commodities which are not perishable

4 That the price of other things must rise in a state in proportion to the plenty of Money.*

5 That base Money is more profitable to a Nation than that which is fine. Of the proportion between Gold and Silver‹.› The Nation ought to have onely one Standart viz Silver*

The difficulty of knowing the Ballance of Forreign Trade*

Ways in which the wealth of a Nation may be increased independent of the ballance of forreign Trade

1 Money spent by forreigners.

2 Natives who live Abroad

3 Subsidies

4 Naturalizing rich forreigners‹.› Emigrations of such

5 The alteration of the Coin by wearing or by any other Means. Why Bullion is dearer than Coin? Does not the loss of this fall upon the Bank?

6 That trade is hurtfull with a Nation which takes not of our Commodities an equal Value to what we take of theirs This Maxim False* |

4/III/15,4v **7** That Banks & Paper Credit is hurtfull to the Nation*

4/III/16: Banks. Paper Credit

4/III/16,1r Tho' Silver and Gold be the common Measure of the price of Commodities, yet it may be said that those Metals have not allways the same Value

Theire Value different in different Ages.

How it is to be estimated. The lowest value the Maintenance of those who dig & refine it. This varies according to the depth and fertility of Mines & the Improvements in the Art of refining.

Effects of Manufactures. 1 Trades & professions they produce. 1 Labourers in the various parts of the Manufacture who work either by days wages or by the piece The great advantage of this to the poor. It multiplys labouring hands, employs those usefully who would otherwise be idle.

2 The Merchant. Subordinate to him are porters carriers Waggoners Ships & Sailors. Carpenters Rope Sail

3 The Retailer.

Of Banks*

Bank Credit an Obligation upon the Bank to pay to the person that has it so much Money on demand.

Great Commerce requires much Money to carry it on

______________________________ *

The Armour of Diomed (says Homer‹)› cost 9 Oxen, that of Glaucus 100

Salt the Instrument of Commerce in Abyssinia

A Species of Shells in some parts of India

Dried Cod at Newfoundland

Tobacco in Virginia

Sugar in some of the West Indies

Iron among the ancient Spaniards. Copper among the Romans‹.› Servius Tullius first coined Copper Money‹;› the As or pondo was a pound of Copper. In the later times of the Republick it was onely half an ounce‹,› that is the 24th part of a pound,

The Romans began to coin Silver five years before the first punick War. but the‹y› always reckoned Money either by Asses which was a copper Coin or by Sestertij which was 2 ½ Asses. |

4/III/16,1v The Northern Nations who established themselves upon the Ruins of the Roman Empire seem to have used Silver money first & to have always reckoned by it. There was little Gold coined in England till the time of Edward 3 & no copper till James I of England

4/III/10: Banks. Paper Credit, *cont.* Morals. Arms Revenue

4/III/10,1r May 13 1765

We have divided the ends of Political Society into primary and Secondary or principal and Subordinate. The primary and Principal Ends are Defence against forreign Enemies and internal peace & Justice among the Citizens. These are Secured by a proper form Of Political Government of which we have discoursed. The secondary and Subordinate Ends of Political Society are whatever may render the Society more happy and flourishing. The chief things of this kind and of which I proposed to discourse Are the following 1 Population. 2 Virtue 3 Learning and Knowledge 4 Riches & Opulence 5 Publick Revenue, 6 Arms. We have dispatched what we intended to say of the three first and began to Discourse of the 4 which is indeed so copious a Subject and has been so little handled in a Systematical way that it is difficult to reduce it in to method. In order to prevent Embarrassment we have endeavoured to give a Distinct notion of what is understood by Riches. All alienable property which contributes to the convenience and accommodation of Life either Really or in the general opinion comes under the Denomination of Riches. We have endeavoured to shew that almost every thing we can call Riches is produced by human Labour and industry.* We have considered how the productions of human Labour come to be rated and what are the causes why things which require equal Labour in the production of them have notwithstanding very unequal Values or prices put upon them, And what it is that we may call the Natural Price of Commodities. We have endeavoured to shew the causes which raise the Market Price of Commodities above or sink it below their natural Value. We have considered the Use of Money as a common Measure of the Price of Commodities as a mean of facilitating the exchange of them and as a Commodity of intrinsick value. We have mentioned the advantages and disadvantages of coining and Stamping gold and Silver by which it is converted into what we call money and have given some Account of the practices of Princes and their Ministers in debasing the Coin & thereby defrauding their Subjects and Creditors. And last of all we endeavoured to refute several false Notions which have been entertained upon the Subject of Money Such as That it receives its value from Laws or Edicts of princes. That it may be kept in a Country by laws prohibiting the Exportation of it. That the Riches of a Nation Consist in the Quantity of Money that Circulates in it. That the price of Commodities will be doubled if the Quantity of Money in a Nation is doubld & raised or diminished in proportion to the Quantity of money L'Esprit des Loix, Livre 22 chapitre 8.* Lastly that the Money may be kept in a State by making it of a base Alloy. We proposed in the next place to consider the Nature of Credit. Which will lead us to the Consideration of Interest and of Banks and what is called Paper Money.

In order to Reason distinctly about Credit, the various kinds of it and their Effects. It is necessary to take a general View of what we call
4/III/10,1v Traffick | which we distinguished into Natural and artificial.* Natural Traffick is where a man buys things that he may use them, but Artificial Traffick is when a man buys things not for his own Use but that he may sell them again at an advanced price and make profit upon them. There can be no society wherein every man supplies all his own necessities

without any exchange of commodities with others. In natural Traffick there will be Credit. All bargains must be either for ready payment or upon Credit.

The most convenient time for buying will not always be the most convenient time for paying It is accidental if these two points of Time Coincide.

The Steps by which Artificial Traffick or the Profession of Merchants is introduced into Society. 1 Labour assorted into particular Trades and Arts which are made distinct Professions. As Shoe makers Weavers Taylors Blacksmiths farmers and the like‹.› The Advantage of this to Society‹.› 2 Markets or Fairs for the Sale of those several Commodities. 3 Merchants who buy at one Market and carry to another‹.› 4 Manufacturers who hire artificers to work for them. The last state most favourable to Commerce‹;› it multiplys professions, makes men more dexterous and Skillful in their several Professions more laborious and produces better commodities. Gives rise to the Invention of Machines, & the multiplication of them by which more work is done with the same Quantity of Labour

The effects of Traffick in making Money fruitfull and employing the whole Money in circulation. When this happens People fall upon ways to enlarge the circulation by credit. Paper Credit what

Of Interest of Money.*

May 14

2 Different meanings of the Word Credit.* It sometimes signifies money due to a man. and is opposed to Debt which signifies money or value due by him. But at other times it signifies the Esteem which Men have of a mans Riches and Integrity in his dealing which makes it safe to trust him with money. How Paper Credit differs from Common Credit? In this onely that it is easily transferred from one man to another without loss of time or Expence.

Wherein Paper Credit agrees with money or differs from it* 1 It answers the same purpose with money as a measure of the Value of Commodities 2 As a mean of facilitating the Exchange of Commodities In both these respects it not onely answers the purpose of Money but in some degree is preferable to Gold and Silver. For first it is more easily conveyed. 2 It is not liable to clipping or wearing 3 it is sooner Sold and 4 If it is lost there is no loss to the Nation.

We are next to consider wherein Paper Credit differs from money and the Essential Difference lies in this that it has no intrinsick value‹,› its value depends entirely upon things extrinsic to it. Let a man be ever so carefull of his banknotes yet if the bank fails and becomes insolvent his Notes are onely waste paper. If the bank is suspected no body will take its notes as payment. And in general the Circulation of those bank Notes must be limited to places where the bank is known and believed to stand upon a Solid foundation. It is not so with Money. The value of
4/III/10,2r Gold and Silver coin depends not upon any | thing extrinsic to it. If I am possessed of 100 £ Sterling in Gold or Silver what ever bank breaks or Stops my money loses none of its value. The value of it does not even depend upon its stamp and form for if it is melted down into a Mass it is still of the same value It is current in all civilized nations and loses nothing of its value by being carried beyond Seas.

2 We may observe that what ever the quantity of Paper Credit is which is in a Nation. That Nation is no richer upon that Account In this also it resembles Common Credit which always supposes as much debt and the one ballances the other.

May 15 1765

Whether Banks are a benefit to a trading nation or destructive

Of Luxury. How far it tends to Opulence*

Of Forreign trade‹;› the Ballance of Trade & Exchange

The Things that tend to enrich a Nation Industry, Frugality

The Cultivation of the Ground, & encouragement of Those that are employed in it. Invention of Machines Taste and Skill in productions that go to forreign Markets. Low price of Labour and increase of Labouring hands. Effects of Trade carried to the highest pitch

May 16 1765

It increases cities corrupts the Morals of a Nation. Makes every thing venal. Creates a moneyd Interest distinct from the Landed & trading interest.

Arms* Naval Strong Places Land Forces. Hired Standing Armies Militia

May 17 1765

Revenue Crown Lands Customs Excise Tax on Luxury Land Tax, Taxes on the necessarys of Life Poll Tax or Census. National Debt. Lotteries

4/III/11: Revenue, *cont.*

4/III/11,2v* Of the Manner of Raising the public Money by Excises & Customs. whether This is more suitable to a free Government than Poll Taxes or a Census. It increases the power of the Crown is more heavy upon the Subject. Yet perhaps a Census would be looked upon as more oppressive.

Of Farming the Revenue

Of Morgaging the Revenue & of the Public Debt.

This enlarges the Power of the Crown. Creates a Moneyd Interest. Where the Money is due to forreigners diminishes the Riches of the Nation increases the Number of Taxes. Whether the Multiplying Taxes does not increase Industry & how far see Hume.* It makes the burthen of War less Sensible

Of the National Debt of Brittain.

Of Banks and Paper Credit & its Consequences

Of National Riches Agriculture Trade The Price of Commodities. the Ballance of Trade Exchange. &c

Whether all Governments must have a period as Men have

APPENDIX TO THE LECTURES ON POLITICS

4/III/4: Value and Price

4/III/4,1v March 25*

Of the Price of Things.

That men may be enabled to make exchanges with one another in traffick it is necessary that some price or value should be put upon things which are the subjects of traffick. Traffick and Commerce when carried to a considerable pitch produces a wonderfull Change in many of our Notions, but in none of them does it produce a greater Change than in our notions of the Value of things which may be the Subjects of Traffick. If we suppose a man cut off from all traffick and exchange with other men. The several things which he accounts his property would return to their original Value pretty nearly, and be estimated by him pretty much in the same manner as they would be before traffick was begun In this case a man will value every thing according to the benefite, advantage or pleasure he receives by it. Land can be of no use to him but as far as he tills and plants it or feeds his cattle in it or hunts in it. If he is not straitned in these Articles any body may take the rest that pleases‹;› he does not think it worth occupation‹.› If he had a forrest of the finest Wood a very small part of it serves all the purposes he can have for wood. If he had full granaries he can consume but a very small part before the grain is corrupted and all that is over is of no more value to him than the clods of the field. If he had Gold and Jewels in aboundance they would probably be of no more value in his eye than a bed of tulips. He would not even find that pleasure in his riches which they borrow from the vanity of a man who enjoys them in civil Society because they could procure him no courtship or flattery.

Yet even in this unsocial State the man would put some comparative estimation upon the things that were usefull or agreable in proportion to their Use or agreableness. Thus if we should suppose his habitation to take fire and that it is not in his power to save everything: he would endeavour to save in the first place what he valued highest and other things, in proportion to the value he put upon them. However the comparative value he puts upon things in this State is measured onely by his own wants & Desires.

If we now shift the Scene and suppose him to have access to exchange his property with other men for what he had occasion for, his notion of the Value of things will by degrees be altered‹,› will become more complex and be subjected to a different Measure. For although he will at first be disposed to consider onely his own wants and desires in rating things, he will soon learn to take in the desires and wants of other
4/III/4,2r men into the Account. Thus we shall suppose him | very dexterous above others his neighbours at making bows and arrows and that he has a store of this kind by him of which he uses onely a few of the best. The rest are of no use to him and he could without any loss give them for a song. Others however who have not skill to make so good for themselves will desire to have them and find great benefite from what is altogether useless to him. They will therefore be willing to give him for one of

them something which he values. And now his superfluous bows acquire a value in his own Eye, for every thing is worth what it brings So that we see this value or Estimation is produced Solely by the wants and desires of others not by his own. He will in like manner learn to put a value upon all his Superfluities which may be usefull to others Nay he will learn to estimate his time his Labour and his Skill upon which before he could never have thought of putting a price‹;› now his labour for a day or a week may be valued according to the value of what is produced by it. Indeed in his former State we may account among his superfluities all the time which was not employed in providing his conveniences. But now this as well as other superfluities can be turned to account.

The State of Society not only gives a value to those things which the proprietor put no value upon before‹,› Such as all his superfluities that can be usefull to other people & even his superfluous time his skill and ingenuity: but it likewise greatly alters the value of things which men formerly put some value upon. Every part of my property is more or less valuable according to what I can have in exchange for it. And what was highly valuable to me in a solitary state because usefull and Scarce, may perhaps in the Social State be easily had from others who have more than they have use for. So that their plenty diminishes the value of my small pittance.

We may add that if there were no Exchanges among men no man would ever think of putting any value upon what was the property of another man because it is not attainable by him and therefore can be of no use to him. There may be fruitfull fields and rich materials in the Moon for what we know. We never think of valuing the commodities of that planet while we despair of having any traffick thither. But we put a value upon the lands and moveables of other men as well as upon our own because they are in commerce and are bought and Sold.* |

4/III/4,2v We have seen how men estimate things in a solitary or unsocial State and what a mighty change is made in the value they put upon them in a social & commercial State. But it may still be asked by what rule or measure must they be estimated in this last state or can any such rule be discovered.

It is difficult in this question to separate the Provinces of Morals and Politicks Though I have given such Definitions of these as make them very Distinct Sciences, & propose to handle them distinctly; yet in this particular Question and in some others they meet as it were together. In Politicks we do not enquire what is Right or wrong, but what are the Causes that produce such or such Events in Society; or on the other hand what are the Effects and consequences that follow from such or Such Constitutions. But in Morals of which Jurisprudence is a part we enquire what is right or wrong in human Conduct, what conduct in us is consistent with the rights of our fellow Men & what inconsistent.* When therefore we here enquire into the natural Measure of the Price of things in Society it is that we may be able to determine more justly the limits of right and wrong in those Contracts wherein a price or Value is put upon things. It can admit of no doubt, that a Man taking advantage of the Ignorance or Necessity of another may take an unreasonable or exorbitant Price and thereby Injure his Neighbor; even the civil Laws of all Nations suppose this and allow redress for such injuries. But it is impossible to determine when we injure others in this way without knowing upon what principles the Natural and Reasonable Price depends & how it is measured.

4/III/17: Value and Price, *cont.*

4/III/17,1r As the natural Use of Commodities which are the Object of Commerce, is to Supply Mens real or Imaginary Wants and to gratify their desires; their greater or less subserviency to this End, must be the Natural Measure of their Value. But this Value is by no means the measure of their Price. It is onely the utmost limit beyond which the price cannot go. A Man that sells his Birthright for a Mess of Pottage, shews that in his present distress he values the one more than the other.* Yet on ordinary occasions he would pay no more for his pottage than the Market price. When Bargains are made there is a kind of Conflict between the desires of the buyer and those of the Seller. The buyer desires to have the Commodity as cheap as he can have it. The seller desires to have as good a price as he can get. These contrary desires, after some bidding and coning, like lines that cross one another meet in a certain point, and there the bargain is struck. Since therefore the price of things having such dependance upon the wants of individuals real or imaginary their opinions whether wise or foolish their desires whether reasonable or unresonable; it may seem impossible to discover any fixed principles or Rules by which it is governed. The Price of things in Commerce is an Event that depends upon a vast Multitude of Contingencies which may seem beyond the reach of Human Prudence and foresight.

Indeed I apprehend it is so in some Measure and that the most skillful in Subjects of this Nature ought to be modest & even somewhat diffident in their Conclusions.

Yet as the Rules or Maxims that Regulate the price of things are a subject of Curious Speculation to a Philosopher, & as the knowledge of them, if they can be known, is of great importance in a Commercial State, Every Attempt to discover and ascertain such Maxims is laudable. Nor ought we to despair of being able to do something in this way that may be of Use‹.› Although the Many are made up of individuals, yet it is easier, in many cases relating both to Government & Commerce, to guess at the behaviour of the Many than at that of individuals taken Separately. The jarring passions interests & views of individuals when thrown together into one Body, make a compound whose nature is more fixed and determined than that of the Ingredients of which it is made up‹.› Wisdom and Folly Reason and Passion Virtue an‹d› Vice blended together make a pretty uniform Character in the Multitude of all Nations and in all Ages It is from this Uniformity of Character in a Multitude of Men, notwithstanding the diversity of the Individuals‹,› that all general Principles relating both to Government & Commerce must be derived

When a man brings his Goods to Market he deals with the Multitude of which some indeed would easily be imposed upon but there are others as quick sighted as he is himself. & he must deall equally by all otherwise he will soon lose his character. He must likewise consider that if he fixes his price too high other dealers in the same commodity may under sell him and draw all the business. Prudence therefore will lead him to sell at what is, in his own Estimation, a moderate Profit.

If one Man had the sole Property of any of the Necessaries of Life,
4/III/17,1v & power to defend that Property he might make all others | give him what he pleased to demand, that is he might make them his Servants. Thus Pharaoh by monopolizing the Corn of Egypt became proprietor of all Egypt.

But when the Necessaries or Conveniences of Life are in many hands who have separate interests, & cannot combine ‹&› have not such Confidence in each other to fix a price upon their Commodities, every ones desire of a high price is tempered by his fear of having his good‹s› lie on his hands while others sell theirs, at a reasonable rate.

As all goods that come to Market are produced by human Labour or Ingenuity, the price of them may be considered as the price of that Labour & skill which is employed in fitting them for the Market. This is the lowest price they can have for any considerable Time However there is not such an equality among men even ‹in› the State of Nature, far less in political Society but that a days Labour of one Man may bear a much higher price than a days Labour of another man. One mans Labour may require a Stock of expensive Tools, a Stock of Materials, or of Money, it may require an expensive apprenticeship or education; Fashion regulates the manner in which persons of particular occupations & professions must live and that must in a great degree regulate the price of their Labour or the profits of their profession. Some Occupations require uncommon talents or such a degree of study and Thought as the bulk of Mankind are incapable of, and where such uncommon Endowments are turned to supply the wants or gratify the desires of a few of the Rich or a great many of the Multitude they bear a high price. Such a Poet as John Milton might at this day make a Fortune in Brittain, tho an hundred years ago he could hardly make bread. I know no reason for this but that the productions of such Artists were much less in demand at that time than Now.

From these general Observations we may form some Notion of what we may call the Natural or Reasonable Price of a Commodity To Wit that it is such as enables those by whose Labour the Commodity is produced to live in the manner in which according to the Customs and Opinions of the Country, they are entitled to live. I cannot fix any other Standart of what is commonly called a Reasonable Price. Yet this very Standart must vary as Customs and Opinions vary in different Countrys, or change in the Same country in Succession of time.*

It may seem to be a necessary consequence of the Definition we have given of the natural price of Commodities, that when the Expence of living among all ranks even down to the lowest is increased by the spread of Luxury, the Price of the Commodities produced by their Labour should be increased nearly in the same proportion‹.› I think indeed this must be the case & I apprehend will be found to be the case where the Labourers are not more industrious, nor have discovered any methods of producing the same quantity of the Commodity in the same time by fewer hands; either by the help of Machines or by the division of the work into different professions or by some such Means. |

4/III/17,2r I believe it will be found that the wages of a Journey man Taylor Weaver watchmaker or of a journey man in any other profession is risen within a hundred years much in the same proportion as the expence of his living. yet the work produced by him may bear no greater price now than it would have done then. This may be the case when by greater skill & industry or by new Inventions or the division of Labour, when I say by any or all of these means his work turns out to as good account to the Master as it would have done in former times when the wages was less.

But when human Wit is at a stand in the invention of better ways of making any particular commodity then the price of it must rise as the expence of living of the people employed in it rises.*

It is a pretty strange Phenomenon that the ordinary price of grain is so little advanced for an hundred years back, notwithstanding that Rents are raised‹,› taxes increased and the expence of living to the farmer perhaps at least doubled. I can impute this onely to these causes that the Industry of Farmers is increased and the Art greatly improved. I speak onely of corn Farms, for with regard to grass farms the advance in the price of cattle seems adequate to the advance of the farmers Expence. But as to corn farms I think it is evident that a farmer that lived an hundred Years ago in the way that farmers then lived and that had all the industry and skill that farmers now have might have made twice as much of his farm then as he can do now. Yet I believe it is true that farmers in general are full as rich now as then. Therefore his additional Expence by the raising of his Rent by taxes and high living seems to be all ballanced by the increase of Industry and Skill in the farmer & his Servants and the improvement of the Art.

Another Phenomenon that deserves Attention is that the price of Beef Mutton fouls Eggs Butter and Cheese has increased so Much with in a Century when the price of Corn has advanced so little. The Causes of this I conjecture to be these 1 The demand for Corn is not much increased if at all, Luxury Manufactures Navigation do not increase the consumption of Corn for people at sea & in great towns consume less corn than those that live in the Countrey. The enlarging of inland trade and the multiplication of Draught horses by that means seems to be the onely thing that Could increase the consumption of corn for 100 years past. And I conceive this begins now to affect the price of Corn. 2. Luxury Navigation & Manufactures must greatly increase the Consumption of Butcher Meat Tallow Hides Poultry Butter and Cheese. Perhaps it may be objected to what I have said that it is easy for a farmer to turn his corn fields into Grass and that he will undoubtedly do so when he finds it his interest, so that the Phenomenon mentioned is not at all accounted for by what I have said. To this I answer That it is far from being an easy matter to turn a Corn farm into a Grass farm. Those who

4/III/17,2v have been accustomed to corn farming | have prejudices against turning their fields into grass which we see often get the better of their visible Interest. We know that in Scotland when a Gentleman would turn his Estate from Corn to Grass he must turn out his tenants and depopulate the Country bringing a great odium upon himself‹;› he must take the Estate in his own hand and while he is his own tennant he gets a very bad account of the Rent, he must employ a great many hands to ditch and drain to fence & divide his Grounds perhaps he must bring these hands from another part of the Country‹;› he must prepare & lay down his fields for Grass at a Great Expence‹;› he must buy cattle and turn Grasier himself till it appears how the Experiment Succeeds and after all he must get a set of New Tennants and tennants Servants‹;› he must build new houses & accommodations for them. And if he has money & skill Patience and spirit to go through this long operation in the course of twenty years he indemnifys himself and greatly improves his rent for the future. But is it to be expected that many should take this course? it is evident from the principles of human Nature and the condition of Land lords and tenants that this work can go on but very slowly among the Landlord‹s› and more slowly still among tennants. However this work has been going on in Scotland for some time past‹,› in England much longer. So that the advanced price of butcher Meat has very considerably increased the quantity of pasture. The reason why it has not diminished the Quantity of Corn I take to be that a great deal of barren ground has been taken in to Culture both in the Northern Counties of England & Wales and in Scotland. I shall onely add on this point that the bounty on the Exportation of Corn has encouraged the raising Corn & by that means helped to keep the price from rising‹,› and the opening our ports to the Importation of Irish Cattle will lessen the temptation of turning our ground into Pasture.*

It is a very important Question upon this Subject, whether a field employed in Corn or the same field employed in raising butcher Meat will feed most labouring people. I confess I am not able to answer this Question. If the butcher meat feeds more people than the Corn then the turning our fields into grass is a good thing for the Nation although the price of Corn should at last be thereby greatly increased. But if the Corn feeds more people; then the great Consumption of butcher Meat ought to be discouraged. I am apt indeed to think that the last is true‹;› at least it seems evident that a man can be maintained cheaper out of the market by Grain & vegetables than by butcher Meat notwithstanding the present high price of Grain. And from this it must follow either that Corn fields maintain more people than Grass fields or that the profits of the Grasier and Butcher are exorbitant compared with those of the corn farmer.|

4/III/17,3r What I have said amounts to this That in every Country there is a certain Price of Commodities that are in Commerce which is Natural Reasonable & Equitable. That this price depends chiefly upon the labour & Expence laid out by those who produce the Commodity, & the rank in life which those labourers are thought entitled to hold. With regard therefore to Corn and Flesh Meat which are produced by the Labour of the farmer & his Servants, every thing which increases the Expence of the Farmer and his Servants tends to increase the natural price of these Necessaries of Life. High Rents Taxes Luxury An Increase of the demand for flesh Meat has the same tendency; and tho' for a considerable time it may seam onely to raise the price of flesh meat yet in course of time it must also raise the price of Corn. The Multiplication of Draught horses increases the Demand both for grass and Corn. The bounty on Exportation of Corn tends to increase the Produce of Corn. But it is very doubtfull whether this advantage is not ballanced by its tendency to increase the price of flesh. I conceive that open ports both for Exportation & Importation of the Necessaries of Life are much more conducive to keep them at a moderate price than either Prohibitions or Encouragements. Yet I think the shutting up the ports in the present Emergenc‹y› when there was so great apprehension of a general Dearth abroad and some fear that we had nothing to spare at home was a good measure.* This measure may be considered as a heavy tax upon farmers and dealers in Corn for the common benefite of the Nation. It might be expected that such a Measure should put those in bad humor who feel the weight of it, and induce them to exert all their Art to raise the price at home. They ought to be indulged a little in this. It is equitable that when they are not allowed to carry their Goods to the best Market, they should on that account have the better price for them at home.

4/III/4: Value and Price, *cont.*

4/III/4,2r* Profits of those who sell may vary from other circumstances Such as that the commodity often lyes long on hand, is perishable, got or kept with danger‹,› much subject to variation in the price. Combinations to raise prices wrong. Monopolies in order to raise the price to an unreasonable height is no less so. The Utility and Necessity of a common Measure. The properties requisite in such a Measure. Universal Estimation & permanent Value. Durable easily conveyed. Divisible into Small parts. Silver & Gold fittest for this Purpose. They may either ‹be› weighed. Alloy to prevent wearing. or 2 Coined & Stamped. The intention of the Stamp to ascertain their Value. Gives no Value. The Practices of Princes and States in debasing the Coin or Raising its Nominal Value. These practices injurious to individuals because Money is not barely a Measure of the price of things but it is a commodity which has an intrinsick value according to its weight and fineness. Contrary to Equity. The counterfiting coining clipping or washing the Coin highly criminal or uttering false coin knowingly. Melting it down or exporting it made criminal in most nations.*

Part Three: Discourses, Discussions and Conversations

I

2/II/16,1r Whether Paper Credit be a Benefite or a Disadvantage to a Nation‹?›*

All Traffic or Bargaining among Men must be either upon Credit or for ready payment. It appears evident that trade can be carried but to a very Smal Extent upon ready payment, and that as long as there is any Faith or Honesty among Mankind bargains will be made upon Credit nor is it easy to conceive how Credit of itself can be hurtfull to a Nation unless the Debitor fails. On the Contrary Credit has a manifest tendency to increase both the Number of traders and the Stock imployed in trade and therefore if an extensive trade be beneficial to a Nation Great Credit must be so likewise; providing always that the Debitors are good and if they are not their credit must soon fail. There must be many moneyed people who cannot themselves employ it in trade. Such as Widows Minors Old Men and those who are tied down to a place or a profession which does not allow them the opportunity of trading as well as those who through natural incapacity or want of knowledge and Education cannot profitably employ themselves in this way. Now if there is no Credit the Money belonging to such people must be hoarded up lie dead and produce Nothing. But Credit makes it all active and Industrious. The Lender is supported by the interest of it, the Borrower enriched by the profit he makes of it and numbers of Manufacturers Sailors day Labourers and others live by the Circulation of it and are thereby induced to profitable Labour when otherwise they might be Idle. So that it would seem that as long as there are Idle hands in a Nation or labouring hands that might be more profitably employed, as long as there are heads capable of contriving and executing schemes of trade more extensive then their own proper fortunes without credit can enable them to carry on, As long as there is money lying dead and inactive. Credit is the proper Remedy of these Evils, bringing such heads and hands and Money together to cooperate for the publick Utility which before by being disunited were partly useless and partly burthensome to the publick. A Nation may be

a long time without Trade as it may be without many other usefull and Profitable Arts and the first beginnings of Trade in a Nation are often Casual. But when once it begins it is very apt to Spread and the Spirit of it becomes contagious. So that where it once begins it will commonly go on till the Demand for Money fixes a Reasonable price upon the Use of it. Then the Hoarded Stores are brought forth and all the money in the
2/II/16,1v Nation keeps a constant circulation.* Let us suppose that | there is still a Demand for more Money to be employed in trade after all the hoarded Money is brought forth. This demand must be supplyed or Trade must be at a Stand and make no farther progress. Nor does ther‹e› appear to be any other way of Supplying the Demand but by borrowing from abroad or by paper Credit. If Credit in general be beneficial and necessary to a Trading Nation. It is not easy to conceive that Paper Credit should be hurtfull. For what is Paper Credit, it is nothing else but Credit that is easily transferable from one hand to another. Thus if I lend Money to the Bank upon a bill or Bond this is common Credit against which there is no Objection Made But if I indorse this bill and give it to another for value and he to a third this is paper Credit which is thought ruinous & destructive.*

Those Arguments against Paper Credit which have been thought most unanswerable are founded upon two Maxims which have been commonly received among writers on this Subject but which seem to have no certain foundation in Reason or Experience.

1 It is said that the Money that circulates is the representative of all the Commodities of a Nation and is equal to them in value. So that if the money is doubled or trebled the Commodities continuing the Same the Price of every thing will be raised in the Same proportion.*

2 It is said that Paper Credit ‹has› the same Effect in raising the price of Commodities as real Specie And hence it is inferred that paper credit increases the price of Commodities in the same proportion as it increases the Current Money. And therefore must be prejudicial to Trade.*

There appears to be no Just foundation for either of these Maxims for First why Should the Money of a Nation be a representation of the whole Commodities. There is as much reason to estimate every mans Stock by his ready Cash which appears at first Sight ridiculous. If a Mans house is robed and all the Money in his possession carried of‹f› he does not lose perhaps the fiftieth part of what he is worth. And a forreign enemy Should invad us and not leave a farthing Money in Britain the loss perhaps would not be equal to one fiftieth part of the National Riches|

2/II/16,2r In like Manner if the Money in Brittain were doubled by the exportation of Commodities equal in value to the whole of our Money we should not be one farthing richer. Yet by the Maxim we are now speaking of the Expence of every thing should be doubled.

As a private mans Expence will commonly bear proportion to his Riches it may be very probably so in a Nation so that if we were twice as rich the Consumption of Commodities in the Nation would no doubt be about twice as great. But the doubling or trebling our money would onely be the adding one or two fiftieth parts to our Riches and it is inconceivable how this should make us double or triple our expence. Besides that the proportion of Money in a nation to its riches is extreamly variable. And as a private man may exhaust his money upon a project which will bring him ample returns after a Course of Years So likewise may a Nation. The settling a large Colony or carrying on a forreign war may exhaust even a trading Nation of Money and yet be profitable in the issue.*

2 But Supposing that the increase of real money did increase the riches of a Nation in the same Proportion. it does not follow that Paper Money will do so Because the creating of Paper Money creates as much Debt as Credit If the Bank issueth a hundred thousand pound in Notes They dont give these Notes away for Nothing. No Man gets twenty shillings worth of them but for value. No Man therefore is richer or thinks himself richer on account of these Notes. But perhaps the Bank is made richer? By no Means the Bank onely borrows 100000 £ and must repay it when these Notes return. So that the Bank must have this hundred thousand pound in the Debit as well as the Credit of its accounts and therefore it adds nothing either real or imaginary to its riches. Now if neither the Bank nor its Creditors imagine themselves richer by this Creation of paper Money why should they spend more upon that Account. Perhaps the Bank employs a part of this £ 10000‹0› in trade and makes profit of it and the Circulation of it makes a demand for Commodities and raises
2/II/16,2v their price. Thus indeed | the price of Commodities may gradually be raised but this is the necessary effect of an extended Trade and must tend more to the benefite of a Nation than its detriment.*

The Notion of the French Ministry in Laws time that the Paper Money in the Nation could not exceed in value the cash. And that therefore it behoved them either to raise the value of the Coin or Reduce that of the Paper. produced all the Confusion ruined & beggared Law and occasioned the ruin of thousands.*

The Policy of Nations in prohibiting the Exportation of Silver & Gold, of Coin & of Corn.*

In prohibiting the running down of the Coin*

The Prohibition of clipping debasing sweating false coining just and Necessary* |

2/II/16,3r Traffic and Bargaining in one Degree or Other is the necessary Consequence of Society. For there can be no Society among men where every individual can easily supply all his own wants by his own Labour onely without need of exchanging commodities or craving any assistance from the Labour of others And where there is common Honesty, Credit will naturally be introduced by Traffick.* For as every bargain is made either for ready payment or upon Credit; It must often happen that the most convenient time for buying is not the most convenient time for making payment. It is meerly accidental if these two points of time do coincide, even when Men buy onely for their own use and consumption. This is the first state of Traffic, and as it arises by necessary consequence from the Nature of human Society we may call it the Natural Traffic of Mankind. And we see that even in this Natural Traffic more bargains will be made upon Credit than for ready payment, where there is either common honesty in the Society or Laws to enforce the execution of Justice.*

When buying and Selling is made an Art and Profession to which men apply themselves in order to support their families and make ‹themselves› rich we may call this Artificial Trade and it is evident that where it is introduced into Society there will be much more occasion for Credit.*

A Nation may be a long Time without artificial Trade as they may be without other profitable Arts: And the first beginnings of it are often Accidental. But when it is once begun it is apt to spread fast and the Spirit becomes Contagious if there is nothing in the nature of the Government to check it |

2/II/16,3v The Spirit of Trade produces vast changes in a Nation which deserve the attentive consideration both of the Philosopher and Politician. And in some cases ‹it› seems to alter the very Nature of right and wrong. Thus where there is no artificial Trade Money is a barren Subject. And it is as much a common office of humanity for a Man to lend his money to a Neighbour without usury as to lend his plate or his Jewels. But where Trade prevails Money is a Subject no less fruitfull than Land and may be let at a reasonable rent. And therefore Usury may very justly be prohibited by Law in a Nation that has no trade and as justly permitted in a Trading Nation.*

Trade cannot be carried on without Money either of ones own or borrowed. The greater the Stock in trade is the greater commonly will be the profit. Therefore trade may be carried on to advantage till all the money in the Nation is employed in it. But it happens often that those who have Money cannot or will not employ it in this way themselves. This must

II

6/I/13,1r Question. What are the best Expedients for preventing an extravagant rise of Servants Wages, & for obliging them to bestow their labour when Agriculture and Manufactures require it‹?›*

The design of the present Enquiry will be answered if we can determine the general Causes which Influence the rise & fall of Servants Wages. The price of Labour like the price of all other things must rise as the demand for such Labour increases and the number of Servants is diminished; it must on the other hand fall when the demand for servants is lessened or their Number increased.*

The demand for house and farm Servants, to whom this Enquiry is confined,* seems to vary very little and the causes that influence it to operate but Slowly.

If we suppose the Number of householders & farmers now in the Nation to be the Same as it was an hundred years ago, the onely causes that can increase the demand for Servants are either when farmers turn their Lands into cropts that need more Labour as from Grass to Corn or from Corn to Garden Stuff. Or housholders living in a more luxurious way so as to need more Servants, either for State or for cleaning rooms and furniture or attending children.

It does not appear that either of these Causes have produced any considerable increase of demand for house or farm Servants in this Nation for an hundred years past. The farmers do not need more Servants now than before & the Increase of Luxury seems rather to have diminished the house Manufactures than increased the number of house Servants.

Supposing therefore the Demand for Servants to be nearly the Same as it has been for many Years. We may next consider whether there is as great Plenty to answer this Demand.

1 It is evident that the increase of Armies and fleets must occupy many of Servile condition.* The officers of A Battalion of 500 Men if they lived at home might be well served with 40 or fifty of their Men. The same may be said of the Crew of a Ship of War or even of a Merchants ship of burthen.

2 Whether our Colonies diminish the Number of Servants is not so 6/I/13,1v clear, and it depends upon this Whether Of our people | that go to the colonies there is a greater proportion of S‹er›vile Condition or not? which considering how much many of our Colonies are served by Blacks and other forreigners is perhaps not so easy to determine. Yet I am apt to think this Question is to be determined in the affirmative & that a greater proportion of Servants than of persons of higher rank settle in our colonies. And consequently that our colonies diminish the Number of home Servants.

3 But the chief Cause of the diminution of hands for Service is the great Increase of Manufactures. which now imploy a vastly greater proportion than formerly of those of Servile condition Luxury and Trade concur in producing this Effect. and it is hard to say whether our Manufactures for home Consumption or those for Exportation be most increased. Both in proportion to their Increase must diminish the number of hands for house or farm Service. It is to be observed that altho Manufactures are mostly confined to towns. & even to a few towns yet they drain all parts of the Nation of Servants, the demand for apprentices and journey men and other manufacturers makes a Scarcity of Servants first in the Neighbourhood but by degrees the high wages given in such places both to manufacturers & Servants draws them from all places of the Nation to such trading Towns. many of them ma‹d›e rich by their high Wages, get out of the servile condition and so to increase the demand for servants and lessen their Number at the same time

4 The application given for some time past to the Improvement of Ground by draining ditching fencing trenching &c must employ a greater proportion of Labouring hands than was employed in this way formerly and thereby diminish the Number of house & farm Servants

5 Cheapness of the Necessarys of Life makes many who use to serve chuse to live free as they can earn in two or three days what will maintain them seven, and thus they may live idle the other four or if they chuse to work may save money.* It seems indeed to be reasonable that when the maintenance of a Servant is cheaper his wages should be higher

It happens also that more Servants marry and become householders in cheap Years but tho this may diminish the Number at that period it produces greater plenty afterwards. On the contrary a long continued dearth altho' it makes servants more plenty at that time yet in the issue it depopulates the country of Servants by hindring the poor from marrying |

6/I/13,2r 6. Whenever the profits of other bodily Labour increase, the wages for instance of day Labourers or Manufacturers, the number of Servants must be diminished and their wages increased.* The state of Servitude is always against the grain, and every one will get out of it as soon as he can see another way of maintaining himself.

7 The plenty of Servants depends much upon the time they usually continue in service. Where married Servants are very little used, a greater number is necessary to supply the demand. The same Number of Servants serving twenty years a head will do twice as much work as if they served onely ten years a head.

If these are the general Causes that influence the price of Servants Labour, the natural and practicable remedies of high wages of Servants must in general be whatever tends to increase the number of persons of Servile Condition or to lessen the demand for them. The natural means of doing this seem to be.

1 The repressing of Luxury & high Living; which furnish employment to a great number of hands that would otherwise be servants. The conveniencies of one family of fashion employ more hands than those of five families did an hundred years ago. A country house and a town house with the furniture & appurtenances of both‹.› Policy, Improvements, wheel Carriages and other utensils. Apparel Jewels and Trinkets. Books Pictures prints and Statues. Forreign and domestic commodities for the table. What a number of hands must be employed in furnishing out all these articles.

2 The Army ought to be employed in countrey Labour as much as is consistent with their military duties. Perhaps it might be advantageous to the nation in many respects as well as for increasing the number of Servants if the Army were totally Disbanded in time of peace and a sufficient Number of Regiments for a Standing Army formed out of the Navy. By which our brave Sailors would have less temptation to enter into forreign Service and would be qualified either for Sea or Land Service as there was occasion for them.

3 The encouraging Marriage among those of Low condition, to which we may add the Suppressing begging and Idleness

4 The using married Servants as much as may be by which the same number of hands may go twice or thrice as far in supplying the Demand for Servants.

5 The invention and Use of Machines. whereby a great deal of work is done by few hands. & the Elements of Air Water or fire are pressed into the Service of Mankind* |

6/I/13,2v 6 It might be of Some Use if the usual Punishments of Criminals Such as Fines imprisonment Banishment corporal Punishments & even Death were turned into temporary or perpetual Servitude according to the nature & degree of the Crime.*

III

6/I/7,1r Whether it be better that every Verdict of a Jury should be unanimous as it is in England or that the Verdict should be by a Majority as it is in Scotland‹?›*

As the life of every british man who is tried for a capital crime depends upon the Verdict of his Jury; And the laws with regard to the Verdict of a Jury are different in South and north Brittain, the former requiring unanimity in every verdict the lat‹t›er onely a majority it seems to be an enquiry not onely of curiosity but of considerable importance which of these methods is equitable and most for the publick good.* I know not Whether my Judgment in this Question be in any degree influenced by an attachment to the Laws of my Country (which indeed seem to me to be inferior to no body of Laws in point of Equity and good Sense) however the method used in Scotch Juries appears to me more agreable to reason and Equity and to the publick good. I shall offer my reasons for thinking thus, which are these three. 1 That the Scot‹c›h method is more equitable and reasonable with regard to the Jury. 2 That it has a greater tendency to produce an equitable Verdict 3 That it is more favourable to the innocent tho perhaps not so favourable to the guilty.

With regard to the Jury the English Method seems to me to lay a very unreasonable hardship upon them. Twelve Men are sworn to give their judgment upon the indictment according to their Conscience, and if they were not sworn, their office lays them under the strongest obligation to give no opinion but what in their Conscience the‹y› believe to be right. Let us first suppose that after fully debating the matter among them selves they are all of one opinion and consciencíously agree in their Verdict.

In this case there is no hardship arises to the Jury either by the Scotch or English Method. But Secondly Suppose that after full reasoning and debate they differ in their Judgments what shall they do? they cannot give an unanimous verdict without violating their Consciences. Yet they must give an unanimous Verdict or Starve for they are inclosed and can neither have meat nor drink fire nor candle but at the pleasure of the Judge.* I acknowledge that hunger and thirst and other natural Necessities may at last produce unanimity or at least a profession of it. But if this is a reasonable or equitable way of producing unanimity why is it not extended to the bench as well as to the jury why not to every council and Assembly. Why not to both houses of Parliament, or to a general Council of the Church. If these bodies of Men met in council upon the weighty affairs of Church or State were to be used as an English Jury, it would probably have a very great Effect to produce Unanimity in their Determinations and we should as rarely hear of a Minority in the one as in the other. I know of no body of Men that have a right to judge and yet are obliged to be unanimous in their Judgment but an english Jury and a Polish Diet and the constitution of both in this respect savours strongly of the Gothick and barbarous Ages in which they were invented.* |

6/I/7,1v 2 Let us consider next whether the Scotch or English method gives most reason to expect a just and Equitable Verdict. That mankind actually have and ought to have more confidence in the wisdom and Equity of a Sentence given by a body of twelve men than in that which is given by one or two cannot be doubted. When a number of Men speak their Sentiments upon the cause freely and are heard with candor. The light and Reason of the Whole is communicate to every individual, and every one is better able to judge than he was before; as an Object is more illuminated by many lights than by one. And as we expect more Reason & Judgment in a body of Men than in a Single Man, so we expect less of Partiality or Prejudice A free debate upon a point wherein the prejudices and partialities of the disputants are on different Sides has a very strong tendency to remove prejudice on both sides to put partiality out of Countenance. That confidence therefore which mankind have in the judgment and decision of a Number of Men met together in council more than in a Single Man is evidently founded in Reason.* But what is it that we understand by the decision or judgment of a body of Men. In a point that must be determined this way or that way, Where for instance

the accused must be found guilty or not Guilty, It seems to be altogether incongruous to require an unanimous Judgment either for either side of the Question, that the prisoner be unanimously found guilty or unanimously found not guilty. If the law were that the judge should acquit the prisoner unless the jury unanimously find him guilty, this would be intelligible for as the prisoner must be condemned or acquit so the jury must be unanimous or not unanimous. and there is no medium in the one case more than in the other. As there is no medium between acquiting and condemning there ought to be no medium between the method by which a man is acquit and the method by which he is condemned. The weight of a Sentence passed by a body of Men must depend upon their debating the point freely and giving their opinion without for‹ce› or fear. This is the case when a jury are not compelled to unanimity. by starving but where they are compelled by any means the authority which their number gave to their Sentence is lost. Because it may be thought that they are not swayed by their Reason but by their fears. In Barbarous Ages as Reason is weak other Methods are laid hold of to determine controversies. The time was when privat‹e› combat or the trial Ordeal were thought proper when Reason could not decide* In like manner in English Juries unanimity being conceived necessary to give weight to the Verdict, when Reason cannot produce that Effect hunger and thirst are brought to its aid. Every one may see whether these are the proper Judges of Right and wrong. And whether it must not often be the case as has been alledged that wretches hang that Jury men may dine.* It will I conceive be allowed that a superior Strength of constitution of body or a Superior resolution in bearing hunger and thirst is not always a Sign of Superior Judgment and Equity. Now the last determination in an English Jury must be by the Qualities not of the Understanding of the heart but of the Stomach And I cannot help |
6/I/7,2r thinking that it were more equitable if the law were that when a ‹jury› cannot come to unanimity by reasoning that they should go to blows and that the Judgment of the victorious party should determine the fate of the Criminal.

IV

2/II/17,1r Whether By proper Laws the number of Births in every parish might not be doubled, or at least greatly increased?*

It is beyond doubt that the strength and Riches of a Country consists, in having the labour and Industry of a number of hands, properly directed. The number of hands fit for labour, and the right government and direction of these labouring hands, are the sources of all our National wealth & Strength We shall allow then that the right Government & wise administration of a State claims the first place as that which hath the hig‹h›est influence on National Strength & Riches, but the population of it is justly entitled to the second.*

If Men and Women could marry when they would, without great inconveniencies, they would all where sickness or some uncommon accident did not hinder ‹them› be married before twenty years of Age It is reasonable to think that in this case their number would be doubled at least in 25 years. This therefore we may consider, as the rate of the natural increase of Mankind, where impediments are removed.* And at this rate, one pair in five hundred years would increase to above two Million, & in 1000 years to above two million of millions, a greater number perhaps than is presently upon the face of the Earth. There seems therefore to be nothing wanting to increase the population of a state in time, to any degree desired, but to remove those impediments which check and restrain the natural inclination of mankind to pair, when they come to mature age.* The impediments to marriage in high Life, and in low Life are different, and require different Remedies.

Luxury, and the fashion of high Living create a thousand imaginary wants in men of fortune on which they can consume what they have, even in a Single life; they can cut a greater figure in this state, and gratify all their Appetites at an easier rate than by maintaining a wife suitably to their Rank and raising a Family.

These impediments might in a great measure be removed 1st by high taxes upon those that live unmarried. I mean so high as might disable
2/II/17,1v them from living with greater Eclat than those | who have families* 2ly By Excluding them from places of Honour and Profit.* 3dly By discouraging fornication in the most Effectual Manner. For fornication & marriage are like the scales in a ballance as the one rises the other must fall, & when the natural Passion can easily discharg it self the one way it will make but a feeble effort the other. I think it needs not be proved that population is much more effectually promoted by Marriage than by Fornication. This is as evident as it is that trees can be raised more successfully in an enclosure than in the common.

But it is not of very great consequence with regard to population whether the people of Fortune increase or not as they do not make the twentieth part of a State & they will always find Heirs to their Fortunes. It is the poor people who must beget labouring hands which are most wanted and which make 19/20 parts of the whole. It is therefore of the greatest consequence that marriage be encouraged among them or at least the discouragements to it removed.*

Now these discouragements are chiefly two. The want of present necessaries to take up a house & family, & the fear of starving or being beggars when they have got more children than they can maintain. To remove these Discouragements

1 Those who marry under the Age of 21 if they neither have of their own nor can have from their parents the necessary charges of taking up a house, ought to have a right in law to demand out of a publick fund appointed for this purpose what is necessary for providing them in the most frugal Manner, payable when the woman is about to ly in. For it is not absolutely necessary that she should have a house before & if she has no Children she ought to have no title. The Overseers of the Parish
2/II/17,2r or a Jury may judge | of the Supply that is necessary & certify the same to those who have the management of the fund.

2 A man who has more children than Can be maintained by his own & his wifes Industry. ought to have a right in Law to demand out of the said publick fund, what by the verdict of a Jury is necessary over & above the produce of their Industry to maintain them, untill they can put them off to service.

Now it may be observed Two Labouring people may commonly spend as much before they be twenty from vanity & extravagance as is necessary for taking up a house & if they were taxed every year after, while they remain unmarried this would induce them both to be frugal in their younger years and to marry early. So that they may by being less extravagant in their younger years than they commonly are be able to marry at twenty without any expence to the publick. And by proper laws they may be induced or compelled to be so Farther Two Labouring people can commonly maintain them selves & 4 Children. If they have 5 Children the eldest will commonly be eight or 9 years old and may be put out to work upon an indenture according to the laws & acts of parliament that are in force without any Expence to the publick.* Hence it appears that barring accidents of bad health, famine double or triple births and the like, the publick might not be put to any considerable Expence by all the regulations necessary for encouraging marriage among the Labouring people. & Whatever Expence were necessary this way might easily be furnished by a tax upon the unmarried. |

2/II/17,2v It would be endless to propose the particular laws that might encourage marriage among this Rank of People we shall onely mention one or two

1 That those who are unmarried & above 21 years of Age instead of being obliged to work six days in the year upon the highways should be obliged to work 30 days, 2 That those that have three children under such an age should be exempted from working on the highways and from being pressed into the land or Sea service, unless in a pressing necessity the Legislature should suspend this Law for a time.

It would be of use to have some standard by which we might Judge whether a State is upon the increase or decrease in population as the Egyptians judge of their future cropt by the rising of the river Nile Untill a better can be found out we offer the following.*

By Halley's tables of Mortality 30 persons of 1000 die in the year.* Taking this for granted; in a parish consisting of 1000 Souls, there must be 30 births in a year, to keep up the number without increase or decrease. But by Buffons tables of Mortality, of 1000 persons 40 die in a year, which would require 40 births to keep up the number.* Now I find by Calculation that if none were to die; in order to double the number of people in 25 years, 28,5 must be born every year, for every 1000 persons. Hence it follows that the greatest increase of people is when 58,5 or by Buffons principles 68,5 are born in a year for every 1000 And at this rate the people will double in 25 years. That to preserve an equallity 30 or by Buffons principles 40 must be born in a year for every 1000 And what is below this indicates decrease and Depopulation. |

2/II/17,3r There are but two ways in which Mankind can be propagated, by Lawfull Marriage or promiscuous lust

These two ways are mutual Discouragements to each other; They are different channels by which the same natural appetite is drained. and in proportion as the one is dammd up it will flow more plentifully by the Other. It follows from this that one mean of encouraging marriage is by discouraging fornication in the most effectual Manner.

It needs not be proved that population is more effectually promoted by marriage than by fornication. As trees are better raised in an enclosure than in the common The discouragements to marriage increase with the polish and luxury of Life. Luxury creates many wants even in the lower ranks of Men people in single life find a thousand temptations to

Spend what they can earn, even in that State, and are loath to live meaner in a married State.

If it were not for such Discouragements it may well be presumed that all or almost all men and women would marry young. It deserves therefore the consideration of the Legislature whether the discouragements might not be in a great measure removed.

I find by calculation that in order to double the number of people in 25 years it is necessary (although none were to die) that 28,5 be born every year for every thousand. Now by Halleys Tables 30 of a thousand die every year by Buffons 40 of a thousand therefore if the first are to be trusted 58,5 persons if the second 68,5 persons must be born of every thousand in the year in order to double the number in 25 years |

2/II/17,3v The immediate Causes of Multiplication and Population in Mankind as in other Animals are the Generative Faculty. The natural Affection of Men to their Ofspring and the Means of procuring the Necessaries of Life. For it is evident in the nature of the thing that in order to mens Multiplying & peopling the Earth they must be born and they must have food and the Necessaries of Life

The Provision the Author of Nature has made for the Multiplication of Mankind by the natural Appetites between the Sexes. The Passion of Love, the Proportion of Males & females. The Natural Affection of Parents and the fertility of the Earth natural and Artificial. As the Earth is limited in Extent so also in fertility. And therefore it can afford subsistence to a limited number onely. Therefore the Intention of Providence must be that Mankind should never exceed that limited Number.* The laws of Nature in that case bar all farther multiplication, & the Number that die in a year must equal the Number born. What has been said of the Earth in general must be true of any particular country or Island which cannot draw the Means of Subsistence from any other Country.

The Means of Subsistence depend on the Wants of Men and the productions of the Earth for the Supply of those Wants.

V

6/I/14,1r Feb 1763

Question Whether it is best that Courts of Law should be different from Courts of Equity, or that the same Courts whether subordinate or supreme should judge both according to Law and Equity‹?›*

There are three different senses in which a Court may be said to Judge according to Equity and not according to Law which are extreamly different from each other and I apprehend we may have a more distinct view of this question and be more of one opinion about it by distinguishing them.

1 A Court may Judge that to be equal and Just which is either 1 contrary to the meaning and intention of the Law or 2 which is not determined to be either just or unjust by the Law. So that Judgments of these two kind‹s› are either contrary to Law or without any foundation of Law and rest solely upon the Discernment of the court of what is just and equal in the case before them.

3 A Court may be said to judge according to Equity and not according to Law, when they interpret the Law accor‹d›ing to the Spirit and not according ‹to› the letter of it. In this Judgment the law is the Rule of Judging, and the case is determined according to what appears to the court to be the true meaning and intention of the Legislator, although not according to the letter of it.

1 In a free Government I do not see that any Court of Judicature which is not the Legislature it self ought even to be suffered to pass Sentences against the meaning and in‹t›endment of the Law although it should appear to the court that the law in the case in hand is not just and equitable. This is indeed judging of the Law & condemning the Law which is not the province of a Court even of Equity as I apprehend but is competent onely to the Legislature it self. If the Law is thought to be
6/I/14,1v unjust, proper remonstrances are to be made to the | Legislature to have it repealed or corrected but that the law should continue in force and that a Court of Equity should yet have power to Judge contrary to it would surely be a Solœcism in Government for it would thus be in force and not in force at the same Time.

2 As to Judgments which have no foundation in Law but in Equity onely. I see no reason why even in the freest Governments there may not be such, or why even inferior Courts should not have power to pass them.

The Actions of men are infinitely diversified and the same Action may have very different effects or consequences according to its circumstances. What is prohibited by no law may in particular cases molest hurt or disquiet our Neighbour. And it is reasonable that in such cases it should be hindered by Magistrates and Judges

Suppose I pray or Read the Scriptures in my Family with such noise and vociferation that my neighbours family separated from mine by a thin partition is molested his ‹family› sick perhaps really hurt and endangered. Now if I am so unreasonable as to persist in this practice after I am acquainted of the hurt and molestation arising from it to my neighbour may not a justice of the peace or a magistrate give him redress and provide for his quiet.

I conceive a main part of the office of Magistrates and Justices, is to provide remedies for things troublesome and hurtfull to society which are too minute to be specified by the legislature. The by Laws of Corporations and Societies are so many supplements to the Law of the Land which are expressly allowed by the Legislature. The forms of procedure in Courts are commonly determined by courts and are likewise to be considered as Supplements to the Law. |

6/I/14,2r 3 As to th‹o›se Judgments which are grounded upon the reason and intendment of the Law although not within or contrary to the letter of it. It seems to me necessary that all Courts should have power to make such interpretations where they appear to be well founded.*

All Laws are general Propositions Judgments of human Actions are particular propositions.* Now the Question here must be whether a Court is onely to consider what particular propositions are literally and grammatically contained under the general one or not contained under it. Or whether they are also to consider the meaning and intention of the legislator and what particular propositions are contained under it or not contained under it.

The imperfection of Language is such or perhaps the variety of human Actions rather is such that it is very doubtfull whether laws can be contrived and expressed so as the letter of them is precisely commensurate t‹o› the meaning‹.› the cases could not all be in the view of the lawgiver to which the reason and Intention of the Law extends. therefore it is to be expected that some of them may not be included in the letter of it. One human Action may be ‹so› very like to another in its appearances and description that it is hardly possible to describe the one in general words which do not include the other yet one may be innocent the other highly criminal. In all criminal Laws the malice or malus animus is essential to the crime yet this malus animus must be judged of by the common signs of human purposes and intentions. which cannot be reduced to rules.*

Take any speech or any writing in the World let a Grammarian sit down to interpret it from the words without any regard to the scope and intention of the Speaker or writer let a Sophist sit down to consider all
6/I/14,2v the literal | interpretations that can be drawn out of it. We shall soon be

satisfied that a Court has less power to pervert law which is obliged to interpret the laws by Equity than a court which is tied down onely to the letter of the law

A Court of Law which is not a court of Equity must naturally be a Court of Chicanery. Every letter and Syllable will be tortured a thousand meanings found out that were never intended. Cases that are perfectly similar in their Nature will have quite contrary decisions, and cases most widely different will receive the same determination. And of these things I apprehend the Courts of Law in a Neighbour nation furnish numberless examples. Juries will naturally be tempted to assume undue liberties in their verdicts, in order to correct the evils arising from the too literal an explication of the Law. which may be as dangerous as if that power had been in the court*

Perhaps it may be thought a proper Medium to oblige courts of Law among the different meanings which Laws are capable of to chuse that which is most agreable to Equity and to the Spirit of the Law but not to make any interpretation or application of the Law that falls not within the letter of it. But I think it very probable that the inconveniencies attending this are still greater than what arise from allowing Courts even to extend or restrain the letter of the Law when Equity and the reason of the Law requires it.

1 In some Cases the letter of one law may contradict the letter of another law. Here the court cannot determine at all but by the Spirit and intention of the Law

2 There may be cases plainly included in the reason of the Law which are not within the letter of It

3 There may be cases which fall within the letter of the Law but to which the reason of it is no ways applicable.

VI

4/III/23a,1v Dr Smith* informed me that many Years ago Mr Glasford* computed that in Glasgow there are 4000 Looms employed in Manufactures and 2000 in the Neighbourhood of Glasgow employed by Glasgow Merchant‹s› This year 1770 I have been informed that there are 2100 Looms in Paisley Mr Glasford reckoned the manufactures produced by each Loom at £ 50 a year which seems to be a Moderate computation as it makes all the cloath a man Works in a day to be onely about one shilling & five pence value* The trade of Glasgow according to the same Gentlemans Account may be reckoned at 900,000 or 1000,000 a year.*

The Tobacco imported from Virginia and Mary land into Brittain is about 90.000 Hogsheads of which Glasgow has 36.000*

VII

3061/4,1 What are the bad consequences of the Diminution of our Coin by wearing? and what the means of preventing those Consequences?*

The Invention of Money for the Purposes of Commerce, may for its Utility, its Antiquity, and universal Reception among all civilized Nations, be compared to the Invention of the Plough for the Purposes of Agriculture. The Use both of the one and of the other may serve to distinguish the civilized Tribes of Man kind from the Savage & barbarous*

They resemble each other in this Respect also, that, notwithstanding their being from the earliest ages Universally used, they seem not to be brought to the highest Perfection of which they are capable. There have been recent improvements made upon the Plough, nor are Men yet of one Mind about the best form & the best Manner of using it.* Money and Coin has been an object of attention to the most enlig‹h›tned Politicians in every Age. Yet Men still differ in many important Points, with regard to the manner of making it most usefull to Commerce.

It has been very generally agreed that the precious Metals Silver & Gold are the most proper Materials for Money. Their universal Estimation, the high Price they bear among all Nations compared with an equal Bulk or Weight of other Commodities. Their Divisibility, their Incorruptibility, Their being less subject to fluctuation in their plenty, or Scarcity, than most commodities; These Qualities, which will hardly be found united in any other Subject, seem to point out Silver and Gold, as intended by Nature for a Measure of the Price of all other commodities. And accordingly they have been used for this purpose by every Nation
3061/4,2 who has made any considerable progress in | Commerce*

But whether these Metals when used as Money, ought to be pure, or debased to a certain degree by the mixture of some baser Metal; whether they ought to be estimated by weight onely, or by tale* in pieces authorised by a publick Stamp, these are points wherein the Commercial World is not so generally agreed. The European Nations have long used Silver and Gold Coin authorised by the State, & debased with more or less alloy and have been chiefly in use of estimating it by tale, trusting to the publick Stamp to vouch both its fineness and its weight.

But the Chinese who are not looked upon as Children in matters of Commerce, use onely fine Silver & estimate it solely by weight.* Whether this Method be upon the whole best I will not take upon me to say. to determine this Question would require a knowledge of the advantages and disadvantages of both Methods which can onely be the fruit of long Experience & which can hardly be acquired in the shade of an Accademical Life. But there appear to be two very important good Effects of the Chinese Method 1 That thereby the Government is relieved of a very considerable & weighty burthen, that is, the care of the Publick Money. The Laws relating to the Mint & Coinage & to the counterfeiting & debasing the Melting or exporting the publick Money make no inconsiderable part of the Statutory Law in European Nations. Wheras I apprehend there is no occasion for any Laws of this kind in China. 2 Another obvious Effect of the Chinese method is, That Rapacious Princes and Ministers are deprived of one Mean of oppressing their Subjects. Having nothing to do with the Subjects Money any more than with their Cattle, they have no opportunity of playing tricks with it. In Europe the Subjects Money must pass through the Princes hands as often as he thinks proper. And he can by a kind of Legerdemain put one half in his treasury and yet give back the whole Sum he received. It is easy to see from Theory the Danger to the Subjects Property from this Operation;
3061/4,3 and | from fact we learn that in England two thirds of the Subjects Money hath been swallowed up by this Operation Since the beginning of the forteenth Century. In Scotland about thirty five thirty sixth parts, and in France about seventy one seventy two Parts. For about the time mentioned the English pound the Scotch pound & the French Livre were each of them a Pound of Silver. Now near three Pounds English, thirty six pounds Scotch, & seventy two Livers go to make a pound of Silver.*

Nay this prerogative of coining Money seems to put it in the Power of Princes not onely to pick the pockets of their Subjects, but even to put out their Eyes. For they have been able to make men believe, and many Nations do still believe that there needs no more to convert a penny to a shilling and a Shilling into twelve shillings than the Princes Proclamation although this be a Miracle almost equal to transubstantiation.* The Chinese I conceive by their Method of using money must be free from Oppressions & Impositions of this kind under which Europe has groaned for so many Centuries.

However as European States have followed the Mode of using coined Money, we shall confine our Speculations to that Subject. There are two Ends proposed by Coining both of great Importance to facilitate Commerce. 1 That the degree of finness may be ascertained by publick Authority. 2 That the weight may be ascertained by the same Authority. Now if both these Ends can be fully answered by Coining Money, it would indeed seem to me to be more fit for Commerce than weighed Silver*

The intrinsick value of a Piece of Money must depend upon its weight & fineness taken together; when both these are given the value
3061/4,4 is given. If every Crown every shilling | six pence & every other Silver coin have the same degree of finness, & a certain known weight; all pieces of the same Name having equal weight & pieces of different Names having a certain known proportion in weight. It is evident I say that upon this supposition coined money is a measure of the price of commodities no less just and adequate than fine Silver weighed. For in this Case a Sum of Money counted in pounds Shillings and pence is as precisely ascertained in its intrinsick value as fine Silver weighed. Add to this that the counting money by tale seems to be an easier Operation for the bulk of Mankind than it is to carry about a ballance & weights in ones pocket to weigh money.

I should therefore without hesitation judge that coined money received in tale is more fit for Commerce than fine Silver weighed; if the weight and fineness of every piece is fairly ascertained by the Coinage, & universally known

What then are the proper Means of ascertaining the finness and weight of coined Money so that every man may know its intrinsick value, by its being denominated in Pounds shillings and pence, as accurately as if he had weighed it in fine Silver?

It is evident in the first Place that the Coinage must be entirely taken into the hands of the State, & it must be made capital for any Subject to coin money without the Authority of the Government. All clipping or other ways debasing the publick Coin must be punished by the most severe Laws. I think all the European Nations have also prohibited under severe Penalties the melting it down or exporting it. The Mint must be under the strictest Regulations, and carried on by Persons of sufficient Skill, to give to every piece the precise degree ‹of› fineness and weight allowed by Authority; and of the most untainted faith & in‹t›egrity.* |

3061/4,5 The Fidelity of the Government itself ought to be as inviolable as that of the Persons it employs in the Mint For the Government must determine the degree of fineness of the Coin & the Weight of every Denomination.

The Reason that makes Silver with a certain Alloy preferable to fine Silver in Coin, is the very same as in other kinds of Silver Work, to wit, that fine Silver is too Soft & therefore more liable to wear. On the other hand too great an Alloy makes it brittle, spoils the colour makes it liable to rust & to be corroded by many Acid Substances.*

But the most essential Duty of the Government in this Matter is to take care that when the finness and Weight of the Coin has once been fixed in the manner most convenient for traffick, that it be never afterwards varied. Every Variation is accompanied with ‹the› most flagrant Injustice. Suppose for instance that by Prerogative or by Act of Parliament a Pound Sterling were made a fifth more than it is. That is that every piece of English Money were recoined one fifth heavier & of the same finness. The consequence of this would be that every Debtor would be loaded with a fifth part more of Debt than he truely owed; Every Creditor would be authorised to take a fifth part more than was due to him. And the Nation would be loaded with a fifth more of Publick Debt and the Taxes on every commodity would be increased in the same Proportion. Every One Sees that such a Revolution in property made by a kind of Legerdemain is wantonly oppressive in the highest degree. If on the other hand the value of a pound Sterling was diminished one fifth there would be the like revolution in property with this Difference that those who were the gainers in the first case would now be the losers & those who were losers by the first Variation would be gainers by the last.* |

3061/4,6 I believe there is no State in Europe that has not on some occasions been guilty of this gross inequity, sometimes perhaps from Ignorance, but more frequently from Avarice. It is much to the Honour of Great Brittain that since the 43 Eliz no such Variation has been practiced upon the British Coin either in its fineness or weight.* And it is to be hoped that a Nation so enlightned in matters of Commerce, will never permit any change in the Standard of the Coin for the future while it retains its Liberty.

But supposing a Government so wise so just and equitable as to fix upon a proper Standard of the Publick Coin and to stick to it invariably. There remain two inconveniences which attend coined Money, and make it a less perfect Measure of the price of commodities than pure

Silver weighed 1 The first is the Practice of counterfeiting or adulterating the Coin, which the British Government have never yet been able entirely to prevent. The 2d The wearing of Money*

Suppose our Coin to come from the Mint, as I believe it does from the British Mint, in Spotless Purity and Perfection, yet how difficult is it to guard against Counterfeits. Many wretches have been hanged for this Crime & probably many guilty of it have escaped. We have very frequent Advertisement in the publick Prints of Counterfit Coin both Gold & Silver by which innocent people have been cheated, & the marks of it are pointed out to prevent the spreading of the Imposture. I say nothing of the general Belief that three fourths of the Shillings that pass current are coined at Brimmingam, because I think Sir James Stewart in his *Political Œconomy* has said enough to discredit this vulgar Opinion.* However it certainly requires great Attention in the Government as well as caution in individuals to prevent Imposition by counterfit Coin.

3061/4,7 There are other practices of infamous Wretches that | diminish the Weight of the Lawfull Coin Such as clipping, filing, sweating, & others perhaps that have not yet found Names in the Language.

It has never been in the Power of Government to prevent such Practices, and so far as they prevail they defeat one end of coined Money, which as was before observed is to ascertain the weight of the Piece, with this additional Evil that if the adulteration is not manifest we are obliged to receive it in payment as if it was of full weight. It is well known that in King Williams Time the Shillings were so clipped that at an Average they wanted between a third part and a half of their Weight. The Nation was thought to be in no small danger of Ruin from the State of the Coin.* And it was a Matter of the most serious Deliberation how to remedy so destructive an Evil in the midst of an expensive war. Among the Different Schemes proposed, that of the worthy & ingenious Mr Locke was in the Main adop‹t›ed, to wit that the clipped Money Should all come in to the Exchequer be recoined of the old Standard and after a day prefixed should not be received in payment. This Operation of recoining the Money and making good the deficiency occasioned by clipping cost the Nation 1 200,000 £ Sterling*

The second Inconvenience I mentioned which accompanies the Estimating Money by Tale is the diminution of its weight by wearing. When the circulation is rapid, as it allways is where traffick is vigorous, it is impossible to prevent this Diminution. And we find from Experience |
3061/4,8 that it may be very considerable. A Sum in Shillings and sixpences of

our Current Coin will be found at an average to want at least five per Cent of its just Weight & consequently of the intrinsick Value which it ought to have.* So that we are in the Same State as the Chinese would be if the weights by which their Money is weighed had by long Use lost five per Cent of the Standard weight. The Consequences of this Diminution of the Weight of our Coin & the Remedies were proposed as the Subject of this Evenings Conversation. Perhaps the Length of the Preamble requires an Apology, but as the Principles laid down in it are not quite forreign to the Subject so they may yield a larger field for Speculation.

In order to trace the Consequences of this Reduction of the Weight of our Money I lay down this as a Principle, That Money is not onely a Measure of the Price of other Commodities but is really a Commodity itself and therefore has an Intrinsick Value or Price which will, like the price of all other Commodities, be Regulated by the Plenty of it and the Demand there is for it. As I think no body now denies this who knows any thing of this Subject I shall take it for granted.*

1 The first consequence of the Diminution of the Coin by wearing in the Degree above mentioned, is, That every Creditor is obliged by Law to abate 5 per Cent of what is due him and no Debtor can be obliged to pay more than 19 shillings of the pound of what he owes. Accordingly the National Debt is diminished five per Cent & the publick Revenue is diminished in the same Proportion. So likewise are all Money Rents and all Pensions and Offices whose Sallaries are payed in Money.

2 A Second Consequence is that the Price of all Commodities reckoned in the Current Denomination must be increased five per
3061/4,9 Cent. The wearing of the Coin can make no alteration | of the value of Corn compared with Silver. If a Bushel of Corn be worth an ounce of Silver, that is five shillings and two pence of heavy Money it will in its intrinsick Value be as well worth 5 shillings 5 pence of light money. And the same thing may be said of other Commodities

3 This Diminution of our Coin makes forreign Exchange to be in appearance 5 per Cent more against us than it really is. Supposing a french Livre to be in intrinsick value equal to 10½ pence of heavy british Coin it will be worth 11 pence of light coin. And whatever we may do at home we may be sure forreigners will value our Money according to its weight.

4 The Diminution of our Coin by wearing I conceive is the Cause of the great Price of Bullion beyond that of current Coin. The medium price of Sterling Silver Bullion Sir James Stewart says is 5 shillings 5

pence per Ounce.* I think by the Accounts in News Papers the medium price is rather higher since his book was wrote.* A pound of Silver Bullion coined makes just 62 Shillings by the Statute of 43 Elizabeth & consequently 5 shillings 2 pence as it comes from the Mint is just an ounce troy weight.* Why therefore should the price of Bullion be 5.5 at a Medium and sometimes 5.7?* I have asked this Question of many without receiving a Satisfying Answer. An Ounce of Silver is surely worth an ounce of Silver of the same fineness. And it is inconceiveable that having the kings Image impressed upon it should make it of less value that it was before Especially when by putting it in to a melting pot that image can be defaced and the Silver again reduced to bullion. It is true the Law forbids melting Coin under a Penalty But this Law can have little effect when it is so easy to break it without the possibility of detection or Proof |

3061/4,10 But the Diminution of our Coin by wearing Accounts for this Phenomenon which otherwise would appear so unaccountable. Although it be true that 5.2 of new silver Coin is an ounce and therefore worth an ounce of Silver Bullion, yet the current Coin is so much wore that it will take at least 5.5 of it to weigh an ounce and therefore an ounce of Sterling Bullion will be of intrinsick value equal to 5.5. of current light Coin.

5 Another Consequence of this Diminution of our Coin is that the Mint must be idle and the Nation in want of Coin for the purposes of Commerce.* This consequence is strictly connected with the last. Since Bullion is at 5.5 per ounce, the Mint cannot buy Bullion in order to coin it without losing 3 pence upon every ounce every Ounce of Silver that they Coin. How therefore shall the Mint be supplied ‹?›

When Merchants concerned in the Spanish Trade bring home great Quantities either in Barrs or in Spanish or portuguese Coin. May not this silver be coined? No doubt it may. And the Mint is open to receive it and to turn it into Coin weight for weight, without Charge. What more can be desired of the Mint. But alas! the Merchant finds that his Silver has lost of its value by being coined 3 pence upon every ounce as long therefore as he can get 5.5. for it in bullion he will not be such a fool as to send it to the Mint, & have its value brought down to 5.2. And I apprehend that were it not for the Bank of England the Mint must before now
3061/4,11 have had nothing to do. The Merchants the | Bankers, the Government itself depend for a Supply of Money in every Exigence upon the Bank of England. The Bank has nothing without itself upon which it can

depend. It must therefore depend upon its own Cash. But as that may be exhausted, by War by an unfavourable Ballance of Trade, by great Sums laid out in forreign Settlements it has allways been a part of the policy of the Bank of England to buy & keep by them great Quantities of Bullion, which in a Strait they send to the Tower to be coined. But as they must lose 3 pence on every ounce of Silver they Coin, we may be sure they will coin no more than is barely sufficient for keeping their Credit. And as the Bank of England are so great Sufferers by the diminution of the Coin, they will probably at last apply for a redress of this Evil.

6 The last Consequence I shall mention is that this Diminution, when it begins once to be sensible, and to operate the Effects already mentioned, has a tendency to go on with an accelerated Motion, like a Stone going down hill. It has been shewn already that the Lightness of the Coin makes the Mint go on heavily so that there is little supply of new Silver coin. 2 The new Silver Coin disappears almost as soon as Coined from various Causes 1 If there are still any hoarders of Money they will if they have any Sense hoard the heavy Money rather than the Light because it is of more real Value. 2 If Men have occasion to send abroad or carry abroad british money they find their interest in sending heavy money, because abroad it will pass according to its weight And
3061/4,12 3ly | All that work in Silver gain 3 or 4 pence an Ounce by melting down every new piece of Silver Coin that comes in to their hands. They have even a profit by picking out the heaviest pieces they find & melting them, though they be some what diminished by wearing. The Laws against melting down the Coin will have little Effect while men can make profit by it, and can easily prevent the possibility of Detection

These are the most obvious Consequences as it appears to me, of the diminution of our Coin by wearing, and they appear to be such as make it not unworthy of the Legislature to seek out a Remedy of this Evil. We are next to consider what may be the most effectual Remedy.

I apprehend that as the Law now stands our current money, diminished as it is by wearing, is still a lawfull tender of payment, and that no Creditor can refuse to take twenty shillings for a pound Sterling on account of their being worn providing they be not adulterate. If this be Law, as I take it to be the Remedy must be from a new Act of Parliament by which in all time to come no man shall be obliged to take money in payment that is deficient in weight. So that the Coinage shall be understood to ascertain the finness onely; but not at all to ascertain the weight of the Coin. We observed before that European States have

proposed two ends by coining one to ascertain by publick Authority the degree of fineness of the pieces coined another end is to ascertain their weight, and if both these ends could be effectually answered by Coinage it would without doubt facilitate traffick. Experience has taught us that the first of these Ends is tollerably answered by Coining in the
3061/4,13 british | Government since 43 Elizabeth. During that time the standard of fineness has never been varied, & it may be hoped will not be varied for the future. Individuals may sometimes be imposed upon by counterfeit Coin, but this will probably be soon detected and the Evil cannot spread very far.

Granting therefore that we may be sufficiently ascertained of the fineness of our Silver Coin by the Kings Stamp, so as to know that we do not receive base metal in payment, & that we may safely trust the faith of the Mint in this article It is next to be considered whether we can trust the Mint for the Weight of it. I make no doubt but the Mint in this Matter does its duty and that every 62 shillings when they come from the Mint weigh a Pound Troy. But can the Mint or the Government undertake that these 62 shillings shall have the same weight when they have been worn in the ordinary course of Circulation for 60 years?

This surely is impossible. So that no Coinage can possibly ascertain the weight of Coin that is worn, & consequently no Coinage can ascertain its real Value, for its value depends upon its weight. As therefore the Government cannot ascertain the Weight of worn Money, it ought not to attempt an impossibility. An Act of Parliament cannot make eleven ounces of Silver to be twelve ounces, nor can it make eleven ounces to be of equal Value with twelve ounces. And if it obliges me to accept of eleven ounces from the Man who owes me twelve Is not this establishing iniquity by a Law.

From what has been said it appears evident that the faith of Government ought never to have been interposed for the weight of the publick Coin, but onely for its fineness. It was men being obliged to receive the publick Coin by tale without regard to its weight that produced the Evil
3061/4,14 of clipping in King Williams Time. At that time | very little of the current Money was milled: & therefore clipping did not manifestly adulterate it, and a Man could not refuse a Shilling on account of its being clipt. Thus by clipping a little more and a little more the Money lost above a third of its value and the Nation was in danger of Ruin. As all our Money has been milled since that time, clipping would be a manifest adulteration, & I conceive no man is obliged to receive a shilling that is clipped. But

Now its diminution by wearing is an Evil of the same Nature though from a different Cause Both agree in diminishing the weight, & in the same proportion the real Value of the Coin; and both require the same Remedy.

It may be objected that it would be very troublesome to weigh Money in payments. To this I answer first That although it might be troublesome at first yet a little Practice would make it very easy, wherever it was necessary. No Man would think it necessary to weigh an unworn Shilling, and a little practice would enable a man to guess within half a farthing what a worn shilling wanted of its due weight. Weighing would hardly be necessary but in considerable Sums, and even in them, onely for a short time, because the light Money would all come into the Mint and be new coined.

I shall conclude with considering what the Natural Consequences would be of Such a Law.

1 It is evident that the price of Bullion would be brought down to 5.2 of weighed Money. Which would have these effects 1 that no man would lose by carrying either light Money or his Bullion to the Mint. and thus the Mint would be fully supplied and Money be in greater plenty and Still renewed as it began to wear. 2 That no Man would have any Interest in melting down Coin when he can have bullion as cheap. 3 No Man could have any Interest in filing or otherwise diminishing the weight of the Coin because he takes as much from the current value as he takes from the weight; or in carrying the Coin abroad when he can get bullion 4 No Man would have interest in hoarding heavy Money more than
3061/4,15 light.| ‹5› Our Money remaining invariably of the same fineness and the same weight would be a proper Measure of the price of things. As things go now, a Pound Stirling is no fixt value. It is for instance at least five per Cent worse than it was in the beginning of this Century, & if no Remedy is applied to the gradual Diminution of the Coin it will probably be 10 per Cent worse before the end of it. What confusion would be produced if the pound weight were as unfixed as the pound Sterling is! Yet surely the one ought to be as invariable as the other

Evils of such a Nature as that we have under consideration can not be cured without loss to Individuals or Expence to the publick. To remedy the clipped Money in 1695, cost the Nation 1200,000£ in the midst of an Expensive War. which was levied by a tax on houses & Windows.* and When we consider that this sum was received in loan by the Government in light Money, & that it behoved to be afterwards payed in heavy money with a high interest, the expence must have been above 1½ Millions. In 1694 The Bank of England lent the Government a Million in light Money which was repayed with an interest of 8 per Cent in heavy Money. By this the Government as Sir James Stewart reckons lost another Million.* Were we to examine particularly the State of the Publick funds in 1695 and in some preceeding and Subsequent Years; I believe it might be shewn that the diminution of the Money by clipping had a very considerable share in bring‹ing› upon the Nation that load of publick debt which we have never been able to shake off. The losses suffered by individuals probably were not less than those suffered by the Government. For all Debt contracted before 1695 and not payable till the new Coinage was over would be increased a third by the Reformation of the Money. It does not appear however that the Parliament made any provision for private losses of this kind

If such a Law as that I have mentioned was made. Every Debtor would after the Act takes place find his Debt increased 5 per Cent but what he loses the Creditor gains, and I conceive it would be equitable, that the Law should provide against such loss or gain. |

3061/4,16 Thus if I had borrowed 1000 £ before the Act Supposed and am bound to pay it after the Act takes place, I ought to pay onely 950 of full weight which is an equivalent for 1000 of light Money A Man who has 1000 in the Stocks ought to have his capital reduced to 950 when he is payed his capital or interest in heavy Money. By this Means every Mans Lent money would be reduced 5 per Cent in its Denomination but would not be in the least diminished in its real Value & the same thing may be said of every mans Debt. This is fair and equitable but if no provision of this kind were made, Every man would unjustly gain an addition of 5 per Cent to his lent Money while its denomination continued the Same and Every Man who had debt would be unjustly loaded with an addition to it of 5 per Cent although it was nominally no More than before.

VIII

3061/3,1 Question Whether the Storing or Warehousing of Grain or Meal for Reexportation be highly prejudicial to the Interest of this Country, & whether it ought to be prevented if possible?*

Every Member of this Society will easily perceive that this Question has a Relation to the Corn Bill for Scotland which is under Deliberation as an Amendment of the British Corn Law enacted the 13th of his present Majesty.* This Corn Bill has been under the Consideration of the Landed Interest in the several Counties in Scotland since last Session of Parliament, in order to frame such a Bill to be presented to Parliment this Session as when turned into a Law may regulate the Corn & Meal trade in Scotland in the most advantageous Manner for the good of the Country.*

Many Counties have met and published their Resolutions upon this Subject, which have given a great Alarm to the trading Interest, who apprehend that the Effect of the Law proposed by the Landed Men will be to raise the price of the Necessaries of Life so high, & consequently the Wages of Labour, & the price of our Manufactures that other Nations will undersell us in forreign Markets & our Manufactury must go to Ruin.* The Landed Interest on the Contrary think that the keeping up the price of grain tends to encourage Agriculture which is the greatest and most Important trade of every Country.*

Among the Resolutions which the Landed Men in several Counties have made this is One That the Warehousing of Grain for Reexportation is highly prejudicial to the Interest of this Country, & therefore ought not to be allowed, & the warehousing of Meal to be privented if possible.*

This Resolution seems to have a Reference to the Corn Law passed in the 13 of his present Majesty whereby it is permitted at all prices to import Corn duty free in order to be reexported; provided it is in the mean time lodged in the Kings Warehouse; and this Liberty is restricted to twenty five of the different Ports of G. B. perhaps because there are not proper Warehouses in the Others.* The Landed Gentlemen seem to think this part of that Law highly prejudicial to the Interest of this Country & therefore that it ought to be repealed, and as there is no
3061/3,2 Liberty given by the Law hitherto to warehouse Meal | at all Prices Duty free in Order to Reexportation they want that none should be given in time to come.*

We may with the more freedom Examine the Propriety of this Resolution of a Part of the Landed Interest in Scotland, as one Part of the Resolution, to wit, that which respects the Warehousing of Grain is directly contrary to the Wisdom of the British Nation declared by the Act of Parliament already mentioned, and as the other Part of the Resolution, to wit, that which respects the warehousing of Meal seems to be contrary to the principle of the Act which can propose no End by the Warehousing of Grain that will not be equally promoted by the

Warehousing of Meal. It is obvious that the End proposed by the Act is to open a Door for the carrying Trade in Grain to British Merchants

There seems to be no branch of traffick more just more innocent or less liable to objections of any kind than the carrying trade is in general. If I fetch Commodities from Russia Sweden Denmark, into a British Port, & have them locked up in the Kings Ware house untill I have an Opportunity of reexporting them to France or Spain. And if I bring back goods from france or Spain to be sent to Russia or Sweden; can any kind of traffick be more just or more innocent. I maintain by my Traffick british Sailors which are the strength of the Nation and can never be too much multiplied. And If I gain a fortune to my self it is so much added to the Riches of the Nation without detriment to any Man.*

But surely it is not the carrying Trade in general that offends the Landed Interest. It is onely the carrying Trade in Grain & Meal

It must be acknowledged that there are some things that distinguish the carrying Trade in Grain and Meal from other branches of that kind of Traffick. In other branches of this trade Merchants Store the Commodities of one Country in order to carry them to another. In the Corn and Meal Trade the Commodity is stored in cheap years in order to sell it out to the same Country or to any other in dearer years. In most other Commodities the produce may be proportioned to the demand by increasing or diminishing the Number of hands employed in
3061/3,3 producing the Commodity | and the Quantity produced is in proportion to the Number of hands employed. But in the production of Grain it is quite otherwise From the Variations of Seasons it happens in all parts of Europe & I believe over all the World that the same Field cultivated by the same Number of hands and with Equal Skill and Expence, shall produce twice as much grain in one year as in another. The fluctuation of the price arising from the fertility or barrenness of Seasons, is one of the greatest inconveniencies that afflicts the labouring poor, for if their Wages do not go much beyond the prices of their Subsistence in ordinary years they must fall below it in years of Dearth

That This fluctuation of the price of Grain, ought by all means that human Wisdom can devise to be prevented or lessened as much as possible, every Person acquainted with political Subjects acknowledges.* The great Difficulty in providing against this fluctuation arises from this that Corn is both a very bulky & a very perishable Commodity. It cannot be stored without considerable Expence and considerable Waste, & can be kept onely for very few years without corrupting & becoming unserviceable. So that the whole grain in a kingdom must consist chiefly of the product of the last cropt.

The Variations in the yearly produce of the Silver and Gold Mines are as great as the Variations of the Cropts of Corn or perhaps much greater. Yet this makes no such Fluctuation in the Value of those Metals, because the whole Quantity of them that is in Commerce is not what the Mines have produced in one or a few years last past, but what they have been gradually producing for fifty or an hundred years, in which the deficiency of one years produce bears no considerable proportion to the whole.

As it is not at all impossible but that human ingenuity may contrive better & more effectual Means of preserving Grain or Meal than have hitherto been in Use; so nothing seems to offer fairer for the discovery of such Means than Publick Warehouses for Grain or Meal, in which no Expence will be spared to make them as perfect as possible. It will become an Object to Chymists & Natural Philosophers to discover the Causes of the Corruption of Grain & Meal & if possible to discover the
3061/3,4 Remedies; a very im | portant branch of Philosophy, to which, I believe very little Attention has been given hitherto.*

When a Merchant imports Grain in order to Exportation, & puts it in the Kings Warehouse, it is to be understood that if the price at home comes to be so high as that grain may according to Law be imported for home consumption, in that Case this Merchant may sell out at home what he has already imported. And for the same Reason if Grain bought at home is Warehoused in Order to Exportation, it may be again sold at home if the Merchant finds his Account in that Method of disposing it rather than exporting it. By this Means the home Market may be supplied more readily with forreign grain when the price is high at home; or with our own grain when there is a better Market for it at home than abroad. as far as the savings of good Cropts can be kept in Store for supplying the Deficiencies of the bad.

1 The Effects which this Act for storing Grain in the Kings Warehouses has a Tendency to produce I think may be reduced to three, all of which, I think with Submission to the Landed Interest, are so far from being highly prejudicial to the Interest of this Country, that they are very beneficial to it. First it opens a New branch of Trade to our Merchants from which the Corn Laws before excluded them. I mean the Carrying Trade in Grain. The Dutch have monopolized this trade hitherto, and as they have from Choice carried it on for more than a hundred years we may safely judge that their Merchants find it a beneficial Trade

And that this trade is no less Beneficial to the Country than to the Merchants we may judge from this That although of all Countries in Europe Holland produces least Grain in proportion to the Demands of its inhabitants, yet of all the Countries in Europe it has least felt the Effects of Dearth. its Storehouses being in years of General Dearth the Granary of Europe. It needs no proof that in such years Grain may be had cheaper by the Dutch than by those Countries to which it is carried from Dutch Granaries.

2 A Second Effect which the Storing of Grain in Cheap years tends to produce is, to make the price of Grain more equal than it would otherwise be, & less subject to rise high above the Medium price at one
3061/3,5 time, | and to fall far below it at another time.

That this is the tendency of the Act mentioned is demonstrable from this acknowledged Axiom in Commerce that an increase of the Demand for any Commodity tends to raise the Price, & that an Increase of the Quantity that supplies the Demand tends to lower the price.* It needs not be proved that the time for storing any Commodity is when it is below the medium Price. And then the storing, by increasing the demand beyond what it would be if there was no storing, increases the price, & consequently brings it nearer to the Medium.

It is as evident on the contrary that the time for disposing what is stored is when the price is above the medium, and the supply of the Demand from opening the Stores must bring down the price & bring it nearer to the Medium price.

The Act of Parliament supposes the Medium price to be between 44 & 48 shillings the Quarter for wheat & in proportion for other grain. And it is evidently the intention of the Act to keep the price within those limits as far as can be done by prudent Regulations. For this purpose a high Premium is given for Exportation no less than 5 shillings per Quarter untill the price rises to 44. but no farther. When the price is above 44 shillings all Exportation is prohibited, & importation is loaded with a duty equal to a prohibition untill the price rise to 48 shillings namely a Duty of 8 shillings upon every Quarter. And when the price rises above 48 shillings then importation is allowed on paying a very triffling Duty. This shews evidently the Intention of the Act to prevent as far as can be done by human Means the price of Wheat from falling below 44 or from rising above 48. If it is below 44 we ought to export & by lessening the Quantity in the home Market to raise the price. If the price is above 48 Exportation is prohibited absolutely & importation though

not encouraged is allowed almost duty free. If the price is between |
3061/3,6 those two limits Exportation is absolutely forbid, & Importation is in Effect forbid by being loaded with a Duty of 8 shillings per Quarter.*

Thus I think it appears both that this warehousing Clause, has a tendency in its Nature to lessen the fluctuation of the price of Grain, and that the Legislature intended it for this Effect, as this is evidently the design of the whole Act of which it makes a part.

3 A third Effect which the Store housing Clause of the Act so often mentioned tends to produce is To bring the Medium price of Grain somewhat lower than it would be without this Expedient.

For the proof of this Let us observe that the demand for Grain may be supposed to be equal & constant when there is the same Number of persons to be fed with it. Whence it follows that if Store housing tends upon the whole to enlarge the Supply it must at the same time tend to lessen the medium price. And that it has this tendency a little Reflexion may satisfy us. For in the first Place it is a certain Maxim that the more a Commodity is under the usual price it will be the less frugally used and the more of it will be wasted. And therefore as Storehousing has a tendency to keep Grain from falling so far below the medium price as it would do other wise it will in some measure make it to be more frugally used and less of it to be wasted. What would be wasted on Account of its cheapness is led up in the Storehouses & kept till it becomes more precious, & thus helps to supply the future demand.

Secondly the cheaper Grain is the more of it will be applied to other purposes than to the feeding of Men, and by that Means the Supply for that purpose will on the whole be lessened.

When Grain is very cheap more of it is given to fouls to horses dogs Swine and other Animals, more is made in to Stearch Hair Powder and Batter, more of it is converted into Malt, or distilled into Spirits. And whatever cannot be Stored must be either wasted or converted into something which will not supply the future demand of Grain in the Market. Whereas if by storehousing, some part of the superfluity of cheap years is redeemed from such purposes, it comes afterwards to
3061/3,7 Market & supplies the | future demand. Thus I think it is proved that the Storehousing of Grain tends to make the Supply of the Market of Grain somewhat larger upon the whole than it could be without this Expedient. And if the Supply is increased while the Demand continues the same this must lessen somewhat the medium Price

Thus I have endeavoured to shew what are the Effects which the warehousing of Grain according to the fore mentioned Act of Parliament has a real Tendency from its Nature to produce.

It remains to be considered whether these Effects are highly prejudicial to the Country as several Counties of the landed Gentlemen have determined.

As to the first, the opening to Merchants the carrying trade in Grain and Meal, it cannot I think be supposed that this can give Offence to the Landed Interest, considered in it self. We may be certain that Merchants will employ their Stock in this trade no longer than they find it profitable. The profit of every British Merchant in this trade is so much clear gain to the Nation, and as they must employ british ships and Sailors, the wages of those Sailors & the value of the Ships employed is an addition to the National Riches. The carrying Trade has this particular advantage over other branches of Commerce that Nature has set no Limits to its Extent.

The Exportation of a Country is limited both from the Quantity of the Commodity that can be produced, the Quantity that can be spared and the Demand of other Countries for that Commodity. The trade of Importation must be limited to the Quantity of the imported Commodity which we can afford to consume The Domestick Trade of a Country is limited to what one Part of the Country demands & another part can spare. But the carrying Trade knows no such Limits. As long as there is any one Nation on the face of the Earth to whom the Merchant can carry with Profit the Commodities of any other Nation, he has still Room for extending his carrying Trade. Hence we find that those States who have made a figure in Commerce in Ancient or in Modern times, have allways sooner or later gone into this Trade and by that means have given an Extent to their Traffick which it could not possibly have attained in any other Branch |

3061/3,8 The History of Tyre and Carthage & Alexandria & Marseiles in ancient times of Venice Genoa the Hans Towns and Holland in Modern times are a Sufficient Proof of this.* The trade of Spain and Portugal with their Colonies is mostly a Carrying Trade as they Produce but a very small part of the Commodities they send out, & consume but a small part of what they bring home. Our Trade with our Colonies was in a Considerable degree a Carrying Trade, as we exported forreign Commodities to them. and brought back Commodities from them for the Use of many parts of Europe as well as for our own Use. The English and Dutch & Swedish East India Trade is chiefly a Carrying Trade. Those Nations Supply all Europe with East India Goods. And a great Part of their Riches flows from this Source.

The Carrying Trade in Corn is a great Trade in Holland.* It might be much greater with them and with other nations were it not for the absurd policy of Most Nations in Europe with regard to the Corn trade. The Corn Law of the 13th of his present Majesty shews more illumination on the Subject of the Corn Trade than any of the Laws we had before on that Subject, having placed that Article of Commerce in many Respects on a better footing than it was before; and the permission of storing Corn for Reexportation seems to be one of the most unexceptionable parts of it.* We conclude therefore that the Clause in Question for Warehousing Grain is beneficial to the Nation in this View that it opens a Door to the carrying trade in Grain to British Merchants, which before was very improperly shut against them by the british Corn Laws, & which I believe continues to be shut against the Merchants of most Countries in Europe except in Holland

2 Another remarkable Effect which we have shown the storing of Grain and Meal to have a tendency to produce, is to keep the price of those Commodities nearer to the Medium price, without so great Vibrations above or below it as would otherwise happen.* That this is a real Benefite to the publick & not in any respect prejudicial, has I think been very generally acknowledged on all sides We have shewn that the Corn Act under Consideration had this in View. The Utility of it may I think appear in a clear Light from the following Reflexions |

3061/3,9 In every civilized Nation the people may be divided into two Classes those that Labour and those who live by the labour of others. The first Class is by far the most numerous & it is by their Labour that not onely their own Subsistence but all the Opulence & Conveniences of the other Class & the Riches of the State are produced. There is no Spur to Labour equal to Necessity, and we see that in all Nations the labourers are those who are under a Necessity to labour for their Subsistence.* The great Ambition of Labouring people is to acquire a Competency that may exempt them from the Necessity of Labouring. Happy it is for mankind that this can happen onely to a few in Comparison, otherwise that Labour would be at a Stand, by which all the Necessarys all the Conveniencies and all the Luxury of Life are produced.

It seems to be a necessary Consequence of this that in a Country which draws no supplys of Labourers from foreign Countrys, the wages of Labour ought to be such as makes it necessary for the bulk of Labouring people to labour not for a few years onely but for Life.

I believe this is actually the case in all trading & industrious countrys that have been for some considerable time at a Stand with regard to population and with regard to the Demand for Labour. In such Countrys the price of meer Labour will be brought down to little more than the necessary Subsistence of the Labouring hands.

By the Necessary Subsistence of Labouring people I mean their Subsistence not onely when they labour but when by sickness by old age by holy-days or from other Causes they are necessarily hindred from Labour. and not onely the Sustenance of the Labourers but of their Wives & Children while they are incapable of Labour.

Having thus endeavoured to define the Notion of Necessary Subsistence of Labouring people as nearly as can be done I think it is evident that when a Country does not draw labouring hands from abroad it is most for the benefite of the Country that the wages of meer Labour should never be below necessary Subsistence, & on the other hand that
3061/3,10 it should | not be a great deal above it.*

If on the one hand the Wages of Labour should be below necessary Subsistence, the Labouring people must steal or beg or be unable to bring up children, & misery & depopulation will be the consequence. This ‹is› the most dreadfull Event that can befall a Nation.

If on the other hand the wages of Labour should be greatly above necessary Subsistence, one part of the Labouring people will become wanton & riotous & labour less. Another part by their frugality & industry will soon get out of the Rank of Labouring people, and thus the Quantity of Labour will upon the whole be diminished & the source of National Riches be thereby drained. The last of these Events however is by far less to be dreaded than the first. High wages of Labour tends to promote population among the Labouring people, which multiplies the Labouring hands, and if the Number of Labouring hands be increased while the demand for Labour continues the same their Wages will soon fall to a Moderate Subsistence.*

Since therefore the Prosperity of a Country in the Situation we have Supposed depends much upon a certain proportion between the price of Labour & the necessary Subsistence of the Labourers it is evident that this proportion may be broke two ways, either by the rise or fall of wages, or secondly by the rise or fall of the Expence of necessary Subsistence. The Rise and fall of Wages depends on the Demand for that kind of Labour for which the wages is given, & the Number of hands that are ready to supply that Demand. But the Expence of Necessary Subsistence depends more upon the price of Grain than upon any thing else, because

Grain is the chief part of the Subsistence of Labouring People. Hence it appears that if the price of Grain were allways the same the Expence of Necessary Subsistence would be nearly the Same, & the due proportion between the wages of Labour and the price of Subsistence could onely be varied by the Variations that happen in Wages. If the rise and fall of Grain kept pace with the rise and fall of wages, they might still keep the same proportion to each other notwithstanding their Variations. But they are so far from Corresponding in their risings & fallings so as to keep the same proportion to each other that they commonly move contrary ways For in those transient & temporary Variations when Subsistence is dearest Labour is commonly cheapest and when Subsistence is cheapest by the low price of Grain then the Wages of Labour will for a time rise, so that by these Variations taking contrary Directions the due proportion
3061/3,11 between the price | of Subsistence and the Wages of Labour is more disturbed than it would be by any one of them taken singly.*

As we have therefore Shewn that the Storing of Grain has a Tendency to lessen the Variations in the price of Grain from high to low, it must have a tendency likewise to preserve that proportion between the Expence of necessary Subsistence & the Wages of Labour which is of great Importance to the happiness & Prosperity of a Country.

3 The last Effect I mentioned which the Storing of Grain & Meal has a tendency to produce, though perhaps in a small Degree, is to bring down the Medium price of those Commodities. This I apprehend is the Effect of that Measure which the landed Gentlemen are chiefly afraid of, and which they wish to prevent as highly prejudicial to the Country. Let us therefore consider a little the Natural Consequence of bringing down the Medium price of Grain and Meal that we may judge whether it is an Event which ought to be dreaded as prejudicial to the Country

First With regard to the Landlord it is acknowledged that if the medium price of Grain fall his money Rent in as far as it arises from the production of Grain will be lessened when the current leases are run out. The more valuable the production of Land is the higher will be the Rent to the Landlord after deducing the Expence of Culture and the Profit of the Farmer

But We ought here to observe First that there are many Estates which do not produce Grain at all but Cattle, Butter, Cheese, Hay, Wood Copice Hopes, Saffron & numberless other Articles different from Grain The Cheapness of Grain must be a great advantage to all such as it enables the Cultivators to live Cheaper & consequently to pay a higher rent to the Landlord. Secondly that there ‹are› a great Many Landed Estates which produce no more Grain than is sufficient to feed the Cultivators. To these the cheapness of Grain brings neither advantage nor loss, as the same Quantity will feed the same Number of persons whether it be cheap or Dear. The onely Estates affected by the cheapness of Grain are those which produce Grain for a Market |

3061/3,12 If the whole Rent of the Estate arises from this kind of Production, the Money value of that Rent will fall in the same proportion as the price of grain falls. If half of the Rent arises from the production of Grain for a Market the Rent will be diminished one per Cent when the Medium price of Grain falls two per Cent & so ‹on› in proportion.

It may farther be observed that supposing such a fall in the medium price of Grain the loss will fall upon the tennant of the Estates last described and not upon the Landlord while his Lease continues.

We may therefore divide the Nation into two Classes one of which are immediate losers & the other immediate gainers by a fall in the medium price of Grain & Meal. The first Class comprehends the Landed Men whose Rents arise in whole or in part from the Sale of Grain produced upon their Estates. And in place of the Landlord we must substitute the tennant while his current Lease lasts. This is the losing Class

The gaining Class consists of all who purchase Grain or Meal for their own Consumption, and that of their familys & labouring Servants & all whose tennants do so

Whatever the first of these Classes loses the other gains. This I think is a fair Account of the immediate Consequences of a fall in the Medium price of Grain. And there does not appear in it any thing very much to be dreaded, But rather something to be desired if we prefer the Interest of the Many to that of the few.

If we consider the more remote Consequences of bringing down somewhat the medium price of Grain, they appear still more comfortable. When the Medium price of Grain is lessened the Expence of Necessary Subsistence to the labouring Part of the Nation is lessened Every kind of Labour may therefore be afforded cheaper & the wages of Labour may be lessened without hurt to the Labouring hands Every article of Export even Grain itself may be exported cheaper and with more advantage in Competition with other Nations.*

It ought to be considered that the Estates which produce Grain for a Market are much more benefited at the Expence of the Nation by the high premium upon Exportation & by the Prohibition of Importation,

than they can be hurt by the clause for warehousing; and that this clause as far as it can affect the Price of Grain is no more but an Expedient for using with frugality & with as little waste as possible what we have bought from them & payed. And the cloathing Counties might as
3061/3,13 reasonably | demand that no Man should be permitted to turn his Coat as the Landed Men that we should not be permitted to store Grain or Meal, in order that it may go farther to supply the Demand.

When I buy a Coat, I may make it last as long as I can, and it would appear very oppressive if the producers of Wool or Cloath should desire an Act of Parliament to restrain me from doing so. In like manner when the Merchant has bought Grain from those who produce it. and payed them the Market price for it. They say he must not be allowed to store it in order to make it serve farther & to prevent waste The sooner it is consumed he will come the sooner to Market there must therefore be no Storing. This I confess has to me the appearance of a cruel and oppressive Policy much worse than that of the Dutch in burning a part of their Spices when they have a great Cropt. For what they destroy of the Cropt is their own Property but the producers of Grain would by prohibiting Warehousing, destroy a part of the Cropt after they have sold it & been payed for it.

To conclude; the Effect which the Storing Grain or Meal would have in bring‹ing› down the Medium price would probably be so inconsiderable as hardly to deserve consideration in the present Question, unless some Art should be found out of keeping it longer without waste or corruption than we are presently possessed of. Therefore, whether it would be prejudicial to the Country or not, to bring down the Medium price of Grain & Meal, does not so properly belong to the Question now under the Consideration of the Society, although it is a political Question that may very well deserve to be discussed on some future Occasion.

IX

3061/5,1* To prevent Oppression, by exorbitant Interest for money borrowed, it seems to have been thought necessary by many States ancient and modern to fix by Law the highest Interest that may be taken for the loan of money, and to make it highly criminal to take any higher than the Law allows. But this legal Rate of Interest has been very different in different States & in the same State at different times. Thus in the time of Queen

Elizabeth & King James 1 the Legal Interest was 10 per Cent it is now 5 in Britain, but in some of our West India Islands it is 8 in others if I mistake not it is onely six.* To take an Interest beyond what the Law allows is the Crime of Usury, a Crime which in our Law is so heignous that for near 200 years before the time of Queen Anne, the punishment of it was confiscation of the Usurer's whole moveables. Since that time it has been mitigated to the forfeiture of thrice the Sum usuriously lent, which must still be acknowledged a heavy punishment.*

It is probably in Consequence of its being conceived to be a very heighnous Crime that our Law allows of methods for the Probation of it which are contrary to the general Maxims of common Law. If there is a written Bond in the hands of the Usurer, he may be forced to exhibit his own Bond in order to convict himself Contrary to the Common Maxim Nemo tenetur Edere instrumenta contra se.* Where the Crime cannot be proved otherwise it may be by the Usurers Oath, contrary to the common Maxim *Nemo tenetur jurare in suam turpitudinem.** I apprehend the
3061/5,2 Laws of most other | Nations in Europe will be found of the same Spirit.

Among the Ancient Greek States we read of Interest of Money from the tenth part of the principal yearly to the third part, that is, from ten per cent to thirty three & a third.*

The Romans Laws in early times allowed the Usuræ centesimes that is the hundred part of the principal Monthly or twelve per Cent in the Year, in later times it was reduced to the half or third of this that is to 6, & to four per Cent.*

From these instances we see that in the Ancient World the Interest of Money differed in different times and places at least as much as in the Modern. But the Sentiments of Men with regard to this method of making Money by lending at interest seem to have been very different in early & in later times. Aristotle in the 1st Book of his Politicks 10 chapter talking of the various ways of getting Money, considers Agriculture and the rearing of Cattle as honourable & natural, because the Earth itself and all Animals are by nature fruitfull. But to make gain from Money, which is naturally barren & unfruitfull is most justly accounted dishonourable and is had in detestation. it is a perversion of Money from its natural Use, to wit that of purchasing what we want.* Old Cato being asked what he thought of this way of getting Wealth. Answered. What do you think of robbing on the high way.* And David the King of Israel describing the Righteous Man says he putteth not out his Money to Usury nor taketh a Reward against the Innocent.* The Jews by the

Law of Moses were expressly forbid to take any Interest of Money lent to an Israelite because he was a Brother* The Christians in the primitive times conceiving the distinction between Jews and Gentiles taken away by the Christian Law and that they ought to look on all Men as Brethren inferred (partly perhaps from the prohibition given to the Jews, & partly from the general Sentiments respecting Usury) that it was against the Christian Law to take Usury from any Man.* There is no Crime against which the Fathers in their Homilies declaim with more vehemence.* The same Abhorrence of Usury of every kind appears in the Canon Law in so much that the penalty by that Law is Excommunication, nor is the Usurer allowed burial Untill he has made Restitution of what he had got by Usury, or Security was given that Restitution should be made after
3061/5,3 his Death.* About the Middle of last Century we shall find the | Divines of the Church of England very often preaching against all Interest of Money, even that which Law allowed, as a gross immorality.* And not much earlier I think it was the most General Opinion both of Divines & Lawiers, that although Law permitted a certain Rate of Interest, to prevent greater Evils and in compliance with the general Corruption of Men, as the Law of Moses permitted polygamy, & permitted divorce for slight Causes among the Jews, yet that the Rules of Morality did not justify the taking any Interest at all for Money, at least that it was a very dubious point whether they did.* It appears in the Debates of the house of Commons that this opinion was maintained by many of the Members who were Lawiers in the Debate upon a Bill brought in onely about forty years ago.*

So far however have the Sentiments of Men changed upon this point, that Now no Divine or Lawier pretends that it is immoral, No Man thinks it inconsistent with the Strictest Morals to take legal Interest from those debtors who are able to pay it. The Government pays four or five Million Sterling a year of Interest for borrowed Money.* One half of the trading Stock of Scotland & a great proportion of the trading Stock of England is borrowed Money for which many Millions of Interest is payed.* It is probable that the Interest payed for Money in Britain is more than the Land Rent of the Whole Island. Yet I never remember to have heard this mentioned from the Pulpit as one of the crying Sins of the Land.

So great a Revolution in the Sentiments of Men upon a point of Morality, I apprehend is a Phenomenon not very Common. An investigation of the Causes of this Phenomenon would be worth while upon its own Account. But I shall make some brief Reflexions upon it chiefly because I think it will give Light to the Question before us.

I apprehend that there is no Science or System of Principles in which Men of all Ages and Nations agree so much, as in the practical Principles of Morals.* Yet it cannot be denied that as Mens Interests and Passions are apt to byass their Judgments in particular Cases wherein
3061/5,4 they are interested, so even with | regard to general Rules, the bulk of Mankind have not the talent of making nice Distinctions, even where there is a real Difference; nor do they allways attend sufficiently to special Circumstances of Actions which may sometimes have a great influence upon their Morality or Immorality. It happens sometimes that the Right and the wrong when we consider them materially, if we may be allowed to use that scholastick term, differ onely in degree, and the precise degree where the right ends and the wrong begins is not easily determined* Thus to take four per Cent in the year for money lent & to take forty differ onely in degree, the first we account moderate & lawfull, the last oppressive & immoral. And it is hardly possible to fix accurately the limit between the moderate & the oppressive, supposing the Law of the Land to be silent upon the point.

In cases of this Kind where what is Honest & what is Dishonest differ onely in Degree, if that Species of Action never or very rarely occurs to our Observation in the Degree that is honest, but allways in that which is Dishonest; Men will be very apt to condemn the whole Species without making any Exception of Cases that are imaginary and never occur in real Life.

And in General in any Species of Action which in certain Circumstances is honest and Laudible, but in other Circumstances base; if the cases never occur in real Life in which it is honourable, the whole Species will be condemned & had in detestation; but if in some future period by the change of Manners, this Species of Action should often appear in those Circumstances that make it just and laudable, we correct our former Sentiments, we are led to distinguish cases in which there did not before appear a Difference.* The Odious Name which was formerly given to the whole Species, is now restrained to cases that are really base and dishonourable, and a Name is given to those Cases that are honest which implies no disapprobation.

Thus if mankind had never observed any Instance wherein Resistance to the Civil Government proceeded from any other Motive than private Ambition or other private Passions, all such Resistance would

be universally condemned. The odious name of Rebellion or some such Name that implys Disapprobation would be given to it in all cases without Exception. But when History or Experience furnishes us with
3061/5,5 many Examples of Tyrannical and Opressive civil Governments | not onely resisted but overturned & more equitable Governments substituted in their place, and all this plotted and carried on & executed from a regard to the publick good. We learn then to distinguish lawfull Resistance from Rebellion. and while we detest the last, we find Reason in some cases to honour the first as the Noblest Exertion of publick Spirit.*

Again let us suppose that in a Society the borrowers of Money are onely the Indigent the unfortunate the Stranger the fatherless and the Widow who have none to assist them; who borrow from hard Necessity, & therefore must borrow upon such terms as they can, however hard & oppressive. Let us suppose on the other hand that the Lenders on Interest are a very few avaritious persons who have no bowels, who are fed and enriched by the distresses of the miserable & are thereby hardened beyond all feeling of Compassion A publick Calamity which reduces many from Opulence to Indigence is their Harvest and rejoices their hearts. A Man who is pressed by Necessity either to supply the Wants of Nature or even to support the Rank he has held in Society, considers as a Blessing even a short Reprieve from the Destruction that stares him in the face. The Usurer affords him this Repreve, but it is in order to bring inevitable Destruction upon him when the day of payment comes. He pledges the smal inheritance which should preserve his children from beggary or servitude, he pledges the Garment that should cover him in hopes that some fortunate Event may bring him aid, but when the day of payment comes he finds himself unable to relieve his pledge. The hard hearted Usurer greedily seizes the forfeiture and adds it to his ill gotten Store, regardless of the misery it produces.

While the Usurer is viewed in this Light, must he not be odious and his trade odious to every Man that has Bowels. If this is the way to live by lending Money, will every honest Man say, let me beg my bread, or die in jail with a good Character and a good Conscience rather than make money in such an odious and disgracefull Manner. Is it any wonder that in a Christian Society the Usurer should be Excommunicated and denied the Rites of Burial. A good Man, from the Detestation of such a Charac-
3061/5,6 ter, will think it his Duty to keep at the greatest Distance not onely | from the Crime, but even from the least Suspicion of it, and he will hardly be able to do this in such a State of things, but by never lending Money upon

interest at all. So that in such a State of things it may with great propriety be a part of the Character of an Upright Man that he putteth not out his Money to Usury nor taketh a Reward against the Innocent.

Let us now consider whether the State of Society we have supposed be a meerly imaginary one which never had an existence among Mankind; or whether on the other hand it has not always been the State or very nearly the State of those Countrys and Times wherein all Interest taken for the loan of Money was odious & accounted immoral. I apprehend this must really be the State & has allways been the State of Countries where there is no Commerce.

We give the Name of Commerce, not to all buying & selling for that must have been among Mankind from the beginning; Nor do We give the Name of Commerce to that intercourse which arises from Man's being divided into different trades and Occupations, for that is to be found in every nation that is not Barbarous. There may be a great Variety of Trades in a Nation, yet if there is no such trade as that of the Merchant there is no Commerce. The Merchant Exports Imports Transports. Those Employments and others which they introduce as subservient to them make what we call Commerce*

The shoemaker who makes shoes for his village & neighbourhood, cannot be said to be employed in commerce. But if he can furnish a great Stock of leather and other Materials, employ a great Many hands, and keep in Store a large Assortment of Shoes till they are bought by the Merchant for Exportation or Transportation. He is not now a Shoemaker but a manufacturer of Shoes and is engaged in Commerce.

What Aristotle observes of Money is true that it is not naturally fruitfull as Land and flocks and Herds are. But Money may be made fruitfull by Art. And the Art which makes it fruitfull is Commerce* In Countries where there is no Commerce there will always be some poor and others rich. The Rich have no occasion to borrow. Necessity is the cause of Borrowing when nothing is to be made by it, for no Man borrows for pleasure.* And as a Man in easy circumstances will very rarely have any occasion to borrow where there is no commerce, so he will endeavour to conceal it when he does, because it is a Sign of Poverty and Necessity.
3061/5,7 We know that Many Men have Made themselves really poor | in order to avoid being thought poor. The borrower says Solomon is servant to the Lender.* So it must be when borrowing is a Sign of Poverty; but the Maxim is not at all applicable to our times, when the Rich as often borrow from the poor as the poor from the Rich.

Where there is little borrowing there will be little Credit. In commercial Nations the Credit of people in Commerce is mostly grounded either upon the perswasion that the Borrower is employing the Money he borrows in a gainfull traffick, or upon the Observation that he has long been in the course of borrowing and paying honestly.* Neither of these Causes of Credit can have a place where there is no Commerce. In such a Situation the Credit we give to a Man must be grounded on Friendship or Compassion or we must take a pledge. When a Man lends out of friendship or Compassion he will not think of taking Interest. And the man that makes a trade of lending to the necessitous without friendship or Compassion will make all the Advantage he can of the Necessity of the borrower. I think therefore we may conclude that in a Country where there is no Commerce, there will very rarely be any borrowing but by those who are in Necessity, that good Men will lend onely out of friendship or Charity, not for Profit, and that those who lend for profit will have great temptation & great opportunities of oppressing the poor, and will generally be so odious that no good man will follow the employment. It will indeed, except in very great cities, be a trade, which, without oppression, a man could not live by.*

I know of no trade in a commercial Country, that has any resemblance to that of a Usurer in a Country without Commerce, unless it be the Pawnbroker. The Pawnbroker's dealings are onely with the poor and the Necessitous. We see that it is an odious Employment, The few that follow it in London are often found to make rich but it is commonly conceived to be by the oppression of the poor. Yet Pawn brokers are restrained by very severe Laws not to take above legal Interest, & to expose to open sale the Pledges that are not redeemed within a certain time after the Money is due.* But not withstanding all the restraints that a wise Legislature can lay upon this trade in a Country of Liberty and Commerce a Pawn Broker is an odious Trade. A Charitable Corporation was established not very many years ago, with a view to prevent the Oppression of the poor by Pawnbrokers. Many Members of the House of Commons and others of Respectable Character were members of this Corporation some of them are still alive. In a little time this Corporation was corrupted by the trade they carried on; and the publick Cry against
3061/5,8 their | Oppression became so loud that the House of Commons found it necessary to make a parliamentary Enquiry into their Conduct, the Consequence of which was that several Members of the House who were members of that Corporation were expelled and the Corporation

was broke. So dangerous a thing it is even to men of Character to be exposed to great temptations of oppressing the poor.*

I think what has been said may Account for, what we find to have been a Fact, to wit that in Countrys which had not Commerce those who made a trade of lending Money upon interest were held in detestation as the cruel Oppressors of the Poor, and their whole traffick condemned as Criminal and Unlawfull.

We find in those times and places where this notion prevailed of the Unlawfullness of lending out Money upon Interest, there actually was not any thing that could be called Commerce. The Tyrians the Zidonians the Carthaginians The Egyptians were commercial States.* But what the State of borrowing and lending Money was among them, & what their Notions concerning it ‹were› we are left to conjecture having no Records to give us Light as far as I know. Athens and Rome began to be commercial so short ‹a› time before their Liberties were lost that Commerce could not be said to have taken Root in them or to have had time to rippen and produce its natural fruits

In the time of Pomponius Atticus the City of Athens was in debt and borrowed at a very high Interest. Atticus however though a Man of great frugality & Oeconomy lent large Sums to that City and to many of his friends both in Greece and Rome but took no Interest.*

In later times the Commerce of Europe was confined first to a few cities in Italy and Spain and afterwards by degrees spread to the Hanse towns.* These for Ages engrossed the trade of Europe & by that means alone grew up into consideration. Within two or three hundred years past Commerce has spread its wings and begins to be courted by all the Nations of Europe and has produced a great Revolution in the Sentiments of Men with regard to buying & Selling borrowing & lending. Cicero in his Books of Offices considering what Employments were honest, thinks that that Merchandise which dealt in Exportation & Importation might be exercised without Dishonour, But the Retailing bussiness he condemns as vile & odious because says he in this Employment men cannot deal without lying and falsehood.* But the Enlargement
3061/5,9 of Commerce has taught another | Lesson. We find the Retailer a very usefull and necessary member in the Commercial System, & that he may be as honest a Man as the Merchant or any other Citizen

In like manner the taking Interest for Money lent, which in Ancient times appeared to wise and good Men in the same light as Murder and Robbery, appears to us perfectly innocent They considered all lending upon Interest as precipitating to Misery and Destruction a person in Distress for a paultry gain to ourselves. We consider it, as putting it in the Power of the borrower to enlarge his Traffick, to encourage industry, and give bread to the Poor, at the same time that he profits both the Lender and himself.* They had not the Means to distinguish that Rate of Interest which was reasonable from that which was exorbitant & excessive, and therefore good Men thought the onely safe way was, to have nothing to do with it. The borrowers being Men in Necessity & the lenders upon Interest Men of no Conscience; the Usurer & the oppressor were synonimous Words. By the Extension of Commerce in Modern Times, the Use of Money has a certain Value which can be as well Ascertained as the value of Corn or Cattle. Every Commodity which is dayly bought and sold by great Numbers, where the buyers and Sellers are upon an equal footing, neither of them pressed by hard necessity, comes to have a Market price which is its real Value at that time and place, and so it is in all Commercial Countries with Interest, which is the price paid for the Use of Money.*

There appears therefore no change in mens moral Sentiments in Ancient and in modern times. A Mans enriching himself by the oppression of the Poor always was, & is, and will be immoral The lending money upon Interest was in ancient times used onely as a Mean to promote this detestable Purpose & therefore was justly had in Detestation by good Men. In Modern times by means of Commerce the same practice enriches the borrower as well as the lender, & at the same time promotes industry and gives bread to the Indigent. |

3061/5,10 I am sensible that all that has been said may seem forreign to the Question proposed, and though it should account for the change of mens Sentiments in modern times with regard to the lawfullness of taking interest for money lent, yet it may seem to have little connexion with the propriety of regulating the Rate of Interest by Law. I hope however the Observations that have been made will enable us to form a more accurate Judgment in that Matter.

And first I think it is manifestly proper that the Law should fix the Rate of interest in cases where there is no Contract.*

Such Cases may happen from many different Causes. For instance when a Sum of money becomes due the Right to it is litigated by the Debtor. The Litigation continues for years, the money in the meantime continuing in the hands of the Debtor. At last he is found to have had no good plea nor even what the Law calls a *probabilis causa litigandi.**

here it is just that he not onely pay the principal but the interest upon it while he unjustly detained it. But what interest he shall pay the Law must determine. Again suppose a Man is abroad when a sum falls due to him, & that he has no Attorney who has power to receive it. The Debtor keeps it in his hand & uses it for years. Here there is no Contract what interest it shall pay & therefore that defect should be supplied by Law to prevent Litigation. The Case of Tutors who have the administration of the Money of Minors is very similar. Factors on sequestrated Estates have often occasion to retain the Rents for years untill the claims upon them be adjusted; by our Law they are liable for legal Interest as well as the Sum they raise from a year after it becomes due.*

In these Cases and others of like Nature where there was not between the parties any Bargain what the Rate of Interest should be, it seems proper and Necessary that it should be determined by Law. Which may be done in either of two ways. First by a constant Rate fixed at once by the Legislature, to take place in all cases without regard to the casual
3061/5,11 variations of the Market Rate. Thus 5 per Cent has been fixed | by our Law ever since the reign of Queen Anne as the Rate which takes place in such Cases.* Or Secondly the Rate of Interest to take place in such Cases might be fixed annually by a Jury, as near to the Market Rate for the Time as can be done; In like Manner as the price of Victual, is fixed annually by a Jury in what is called the Fiars.*

Having considered the Cases where there is no Contract or bargain Let us next consider how far the Law ought to interpose in Cases where there is a Contract between the Parties. And here if the Law could distinguish between the poor and the Rich, between those who borrow from hard Necessity, to prevent going to Prison or having their goods carried off by legal Execution; and those who borrow to extend their trade and increase their profit; I say, if this distinction can be made by Law, I heartily agree that with regard to the first of those Cases, I mean those who borrow from Necessity, the Law should fix the highest Rate of Interest that can be taken, and that the Law should be enforced with the severest Penalties, such as our present Laws inflict upon Usurers.* Nothing surely calls more loudly for the Attention of Legislators than the Protection of the Poor against those who would take advantage of their Necessity. God in Heaven hears their Cry, & his Vicegerents on Earth ought never to shut their Ears against it. The Crime is so heighnous, & so odious, that where it can be discovered it ought to meet with a most exemplary Punishment. And I make no doubt but that those severe laws which we shall find in our own and other Nations against Usury; And those declamations against it which we find in the Writings of Divines and Moralists have allways had this crime in their Eye. The taking Interest for Money, & the taking advantage of the Necessitys of the Poor, were so conjoyned in the practice of the times and in the Imagination of Men that they were not able to separate the one from the other.

It is very difficult however to distinguish by a Law the poor from the Rich; those who borrow from Necessity from those who borrow in order to increase their Wealth. There are many in real Necessity who would rather forego such a Priviledge of Poverty than plead it so as to expose their Necessity to the World.

3061/5,12 I submit it, whether it would not answer the purpose of distin | guishing those who borrow from Necessity to hold all to be of this Description who borrow upon a Pledge.*

A Man does not borrow in this way who can give good personal Security and he who cannot give good personal Security for what he must borrow may be considered as in Necessity. It seems reasonable therefore that such severe Laws as those we at present have should take place against Pawn brokers. And it is the more reasonable as the pawn broker has absolute security from his Debtor, having a pledge in his hand.*

In a great City like London I apprehend the trade of a Pawnbroker however odious or suspicious ought to be tollerated. In such places there are vast multitudes who have no friend to aid them in Distress who live from day to day, or from week to week, without realizing any stock for a time of Distress. When such a Man falls sick, the whole Revenue of a poor family is totally stopt at once. A physician must be called which brings a new Charge. If he would borrow, his personal security depends on his recovery and his being able by his future industry to pay the debt by degrees at the same time that he has his family to maintain. A Man out of Charity may lend him on this Security, but perhaps he has no person of whom he can expect so great a favour. His onely resourse is to sell some part of his furniture or to pledge it with a pawn broker. This Trade lays a Man under so great temptation to deal hardly with the poor, & the oppressive Exercise of it is so highly criminal, that very strict Laws and very severe penalties such as those of our Laws against Usury seem here to be necessary & proper. On the other hand the Pawnbroker is justly entitled not onely to a reasonable Interest for his Money but to the Expence of Warehouses for preserving goods that are pledged & of insuring them against fire & thieves.* And what rate of Interest this may require, the Law I think ought to determine, nor does there appear any difficulty in determining this by Law. A young Man of Fortune Under the Power of Parents or Tutors, who has spent more Money than he dare avow, on gaming or other pleasures, may likewise be considered as in great Danger of being overreached by those who lend him, if therefore the Law sees it meet to regulate Transactions between him and his Creditors. I have no objection to this interposition of Law.

The onely Case that remains to be considered is where the parties have not onely made a bargain about the Rate of Interest to be paid but are upon such an equal footing that the borrower cannot be said to be pressed by any Necessity. He borrows that he make profit by borrowing and increase his gain. The Question here is whether the Law ought to leave this borrower to take care of his own Interest as it does in other bargains he makes. Or whether it ought to prohibit him to give above such a rate however much it might be for his advantage to give more. |

3061/5,13 We observed before that in a Country where there is no Commerce there will be hardly any borowing of Money but in Cases of Poverty and Necessity. And when borrowing becomes a Sign of Necessity and is understood to be so, it will be avoided by those who are in Easy Circumstances on this very Account. For we see that men are generally as averse from being thought in Necessity as from being really so.

But in a Country such as Great Britain where Commerce has taken Root, & grown up to such a Size as to spread its branches over the Land, the Money borrowed from Poverty and Necessity bears a very small Proportion to that which is borrowed for the Purpose of Commerce & for the purposes of Government. One half of the trade of Scotland and a Great proportion of that of England, including not onely what is employed directly in Export or Import but the Manufactories subservient to it & the Improvement of uncultivated Land & of Fisheries, is carried on by Borrowed Money.* Besides what is borrowed by Mercantile Companies or Individuals for carrying on of Commerce; Every Bank Note is a Debt of the Bank to the person who holds it.* Besides private Debt we know the publick Debt must by this time be 150 Millions.* In a word it appears reasonable to extimate the Debts owing in Great Britain at many hundred Millions. And I think it is not probable, that one Million of this Debt falls under the Description of Money borrowed by the poor from Distress and Necessity.

If we look back into the State of Britain 100 years ago or even a great deal less; we find two Interests onely that made any figure, to wit the Trading Interest and the Landed Interest, & these two were thought to comprehend the whole Interest of the Nation. But insensibly in the Memory of Persons yet alive there has sprang up a third Interest which is become too considerable to be over looked, and that is the Monied Interest. consisting of those who live upon their money either by puting it in the publick funds or lending it to private hands either on personal Security or Morgage. The heighth to which this monied Interest is grown up gives us another View of the prodigious Enlargement of the intercourse of borrowing and lending of Debt and Credit in a Commercial Country. While trade flourishes and the Nation prospers (which God grant may be long) this monied Interest will grow. But if Trade decays and publick Credit fails, this monied interest, the youngest Child of Commerce, will remove to some other Country*

This immense Difference in the intercourse of borrowing & lending between a Country where there is no Commerce and a Commercial Country, seems at first Glance to point out, that the Laws which regulate this intercourse should not be the same in both. Perhaps in such a Country as Judea which had no Commerce nor any sea Coast it might be most for the publick good to prohibit alltogether the taking interest from Jews as the most effectual way to prevent the oppression of the poor.* While at the same time they were allowed to lend at interest to their commercial Neighbours, the Tyreans & Zidonians. Perhaps while Commerce is in its infancy and those who borrow for the sake of Commerce are few compared with those who borrow from Necessity, the interest of a small Number of the Subjects should yield to that of a great Number, and the laws restricting interest of money to a certain Rate with very heavy penalties upon those who go beyond it, may be beneficial upon the whole. But when by the extension of Commerce the Money borrowed for the sake of Commerce is to that which is borrowed from Necessity as many hundred millions to one it ought to be considered whether the restraints proper to be laid upon the lenders of the one
3061/5,14 Million | ought to be extended to the lenders of the many hundreds who are in a very different Situation.

In a Commercial Country thousands of transactions of borrowing and lending pass every week or every day, and that not in a secret way but in the Eye of the World. Suppose then that the Law allowed every man to take and to give any rate of Interest which the borrower & Lender agree upon, as I am told it is in Holland.* What would be the consequence? Is it not obvious that there would be a Market rate at all times as much fixed, & as much known to the dealers in Money as the Market price of Beef or Mutton is known to those who go to the flesh Market? If the Market for Money is as extensive as the Market for Beef. The market Price of the one may be as easily ascertained as the market price of the other. When the demand is increased or the Quantity which supplies that demand is diminished then the Market price rises. On the other hand when the demand is lessened or the Quantity brought to the Market increased then the price falls. Thus an open Market fixes a price upon every thing that is bought and sold in it without any interposition of Law. And when the seller is as desirous to sell as the buyer is to buy; When both buyers and sellers are too numerous to combine; there will be such a Competition of Buyers against Buyers, and Sellers against Sellers as will bring the Price to what is equitable.*

Nor is it possible for Legislature or for private Judgment to judge of the Natural and reasonable price of Commodities by any other mean so accurately as by observing their Market price in such a Market as we have supposed.

The Use of Money is a Commodity in a Commercial Nation, no less than the property of Money: and Interest is the price payd for the Use of it. This price therefore, that is, the Rate of Interest will be fixed by the Market according to the Demand for the Use of Money, & the Quantity brought into the Money Market to supply that Demand. And the Market Rate, that is, the Natural and reasonable Rate will vary from time to time according as the Demand and the Supply varies.*

In this view of things, which I think is a just view in a Mercantile Country, it be may be asked what has the Law to do with regard to the Rate of interest any more than with the price of Beef. And I think the answer is, Nothing at all.* If the butcher taking advantage of the Ignorance or weakness or Necessity of his Customer takes a shilling for the
3061/5,15 pound of his beef when the Market price is three pence, the | Law ought to punish him and I suppose would. In the same Manner if the Lender taking advantage of the Ignorance or weakness or Necessity of a borrower takes 20 per Cent with good Security when the Market Rate is 5 per Cent he ought to be punished. There appears no reason therefore for fixing a Rate of Interest by Law which is to regulate the Money Market, any more than for fixing by Law the price of Beef or Grain or any other Commodity.

But let us Suppose that the Law fixes, as it really has done, the maximum rate of interest; so that every lender that takes more forfeits thrice the sum lent.*

First we may be permitted to ask why the Law has not likewise fixed the minimum with as severe a penalty upon the man who borrows at a lower Rate. This seems as reasonable as the other. The borrower and lender are equally intitled to favour as both are supposed capable of understanding their own interest. The one has the same interest in lending as the other in borrowing. And there is nothing that should give one an advantage over the other in making the bargain. It seems evident that the Legislatur‹e› goes upon the Idea of those times when the borrowers were the poor & the Necessitous who being liable to great oppression by the Rich Usurer are intitled to special Favour but the lenders now are as poor & necessitous as the borrowers, in commercial countrys they are indeed more so. Because they comprehend the Widow the Orphan the Aged and in firm all who live upon the interest of a small Stock.* In this case then the Law guards the Rich against the oppression of the poor, when it intends onely to guard the poor against the oppression of the Rich.

But let us consider the consequences of fixing the highest rate of Interest as our Law does. This Legal Rate is either equal to the Market Rate or it is below it or above it

1 Suppose it equal to the Market rate which is the most favourable Supposition, the Consequence is that those who can give good security borrow neither cheaper nor dearer than they would do if there was no Law. In this case therefore the Law has no Effect and is perfectly useless. But as the Market rate of Interest varies according to the Demand for Money & the Supply, it can hardly be supposed that the Legal Rate will allways be equal to the Market Rate unless that Legal Rate be fixed anew every year, as the Fiars of Grain and Meal are. |

3061/5,16 Let us suppose in the second place that the Legal Rate of interest is below the Market Rate. That the Legal Rate for instance is five per Cent and that the market Rate which we have shewn to be the natural and Reasonable Rate is six per Cent.

1 If this Law could be executed it would in reality amount to this. The Law takes out of the pockets of the monied Interest one sixth part of their yearly income and puts it in the pockets of the trading Interest Those two great interests ought to be equally under the protection of Law. The very intention of Law is to secure every Man in his own Property. The Law indeed may require a part of my property for the publick Service. And even in this case Justice requires that ‹p›ublick burthens should be laid as equally as possible upon all the Subjects. But to take by law

the property of one part of the Subjects in order to enrich another part already as rich as they, is evidently contrary to the very end of Government, and is a very improper Exercise of Legislation*

2 It will be impossible to execute such a Law in Most Cases. Probably the Widow the Orphan, & other needy and unskillfull people must submit to it, & be reduced one sixth part of their living. But the opulent & artfull of the Monied Interest will find means of evading it. The terms of lending and borrowing may be concealed from every body but the parties themselves and when they find their mutual interest in making a bargain contrary to Law, it is the interest of both parties to conceal them. There will be no way of discovering the transgression of the Law but by the Oath of Parties & by this means the honest man will be ensnared & ruined & the wicked will Escape and be rewarded for his perjury. This is the Natural Effect with regard to the Monied Man, the Lender. As to the Mercantile Man or borrower If he respects the Law he must give up one half of his trade and thereby one half of his Revenue. But if he follows the Example of others he must be accessory to all the trick Chicane & Perjury which follows upon it. There are no Laws more improper, or that ought with more care to be avoided by a wise Legislature, than those which tend to corrupt the Morals of the Subjects, by laying them under a Strong temptation to trick, cozenage, and Perjury.*

Let us Suppose in the last place that the Legal Interest is higher than the natural or Market Rate. The Law in this case will have very little
3061/5,17 Effect, no Man will give more for the loan of Money | than he thinks it worth as the Market goes. With regard to the knowing dealers in Money therefore this Law produces no Effect good nor bad. The knowing Moneyed Man finds he must lend as the Market goes or not at all. And the knowing Merchant will never give more for Money than he can make by it. But if the borrower be simple and the lender Artfull, the borrower is in danger of being imposed upon by the Law and made to give for what he borrows A higher interest than it is really worth. Such a Law would prove too strong a temptation to those who borrow Money for Widows Orphans & Minors to defraud them by charging them with legal Interest while they really borrow at the market Rate. The Law too would fall very heavy upon those who have other peoples Money in their hands, when it was impossible to make any bargain about the Interest. They would be obliged by Law to pay more than they could make of it.

I have onely one observation more to make, and that relates to the penalty for taking a higher Interest than the legal this is the forfeiture of three times the Sum lent. This very heavy penalty must suppose something very criminal in the lender, but there is no penalty imposed for an equal Crime of the same kind in the borrower. Suppose a Man worth 3000 £ lends to a weak Man of equal fortune 1000 £ and by imposing upon his Ignorance or weakness makes him agree to pay for it six per Cent, that is defrauds his weak neighbour of 10 £. What says the Law in this Case? why it determines that for this fraud he shall not onely make restitution but moreover shall forfeit 3000 £ that is all that he has, and the forfeiture would have been the same if the fraud had onely been of ten pence Suppose now the borrower to be the cunning Man, and that he perswades the weak or ignorant lender to lend the 1000 £ at 4 per Cent when he might have five. His Crime appears to be perfectly equal to the crime we first supposed in the lender, and it is impossible for the nicest casuist to discern a grain of guilt in the one that is not in the other. Yet in the one Case the Law pronounces absolute Ruin against the fraudelent Lender in the other Case the Law is very mercifull to the fradulent Borrower, it would perhaps reduce the fradulent bargain, & even this is dubious, but it certainly would do no more

3061/5,18 Here it is evident that the Law favours the Borrower | but is extreamly Rigorous towards the Lender. Yet in a Commercial Country, there appears no Reason for this Partiality; since in such Countrys the borrower is for the most part the Richer Man of the two and least in danger of being oppressed or circumvented.

The Law therefore which fixes the highest Rate of Interest without Exception, even when there is a fair Bargain between parties that are upon an equal footing, and much more the grievous penalty annexed to that Law, seems to be dictated by the Spirit of other times than the present, by the Spirit of Times in which Commerce is not begun or is yet in its infancy, and not of Times in which it is grown to such strength as it is at present in Great Britain.

It is the happiness of British Subjects that they may speak their Sentiments concerning Laws made or to be made with freedom & even in a more publick manner than I now do. Every good Subject ought to use this freedom with Modesty and Diffidence, as I desire to do. Justice requires us to observe that since the present Rate of Interest was fixed by Law, the Market Rate seems never to have been considerably above or below it, by which Means the inconveniencies arising from the Law have been the less felt. And as to the penalty I believe criminal Prosecutions for Usury have been rare and the Instances much more rare where any honest Man has incurred the penalty through Ignorance or Inattention. Although I have heard of one or two such Instances.

X

3061/6,1 Some Thoughts on the Utopian System*

There are two Questions in Politicks which are perfectly distinct, & which ought never to be confounded. The first is, What is that Form or Order of political Society which, abstractly considered, tends most to the Improvement and Happiness of Man?

The second Question is, How a Form of Government which actually exists and has been long established may be changed, and reduced to a Form which we think more eligible?

The second Question is difficult in Speculation and very dangerous in Practice: Dangerous, not onely to those who attempt it but to the Society in General.

Every Change of Government is either Sudden and Violent; or it ‹is› gradual pe‹a›ceable and legal.

A violent Change of Government, considering the Means that must be used to effect it, & the uncertainty of the Issue, must be an Object of Dread to every wise, & every humane Man.

It is to wrest Power from the hands of those who are possessed of it, in the uncertain hope of our being able, and the more uncertain hope that, after a violent Convulsion, it shall fall into hands more to our Mind.

The Means of effecting such a change are Plots, Conspiracies, Sedition, Rebellion, Civil War, Bloodshed & Massacre in which the innocent and the Guilty promiscuously suffer.

If we should even Suppose that a total & sudden Change of Government could be produced without those violent Means: That by a Miracle
3061/6,2 those in Power and Office should voluntarily lay | down their Authority, and leave a Nation to chuse a new form of Government. Suppose also that, by another Miracle, foreign Enemies should not take the advantage of this State of Anarchy. What would be the Consequence?

A very small State, like an ancient Greek City, when they banished their Tyrant, might meet & consult for the common good.

The issue of this Consultation commonly was, to chuse a Wise and disinterested Man, who was superior to themselves in political knowledge, & to give him Power to Model a Government for them. And this was perhaps the wisest Method they could take. For a good Model of Government can never, all at once, be invented by a Multitude, of which the greater part is ignorant, & of the knowing, the greater part is led by Interest or by Ambition.*

A great Nation however cannot meet together to consult. They must therefore have Deputies chosen by different Districts. But previous to this, the Number and Limits of the Districtes, the Qualifications of the Electors and Candidates, & the Form & Method of Election must be ascertained. How these preliminaries are to be fixed when all Authority is dissolved & the Nation in a State of Anarchy, is a Question I am not able to resolve.

Supposing however this difficult point to be happily settled, and the Electors of a District, met to chuse a Deputy. Is it to be supposed that all or the greater part of those Electors are to be determined by a pure and disinterested regard to the good of the Nation? He surely knows little of human Nature who would admit such a Supposition. We know from long Experience how such Elections proceed. The poor Electors must have their Bellies or their purses filled, their burthens lessened or their Superiors mollified. The Rich must have their private Attachments & Friendships gratified, or good Deeds done, or promised or expected. There may no doubt be Electors who are both knowing and perfectly
3061/6,3 disinterested, but the proportion they | bear to the whole, I am afraid is too small to be brought into Estimation.

Such being the Electors, who are to be Candidates? It were to be wished that they should be the wisest & the best Men of the District. But this is rather to be wished than expected. It is evident they must be Men who have it in their power and in their inclination to offer the Inducements by which a Majority may be gained. Without this their pretensions would be laughed at.

To pass over these things, Suppose an Assembly of Deputies met, & a Constitution of Government determined, unanimously, or by a majority. Whether this Constitution is to be imposed upon the Nation, by a Despotick Authority of the Deputies, or to be again submitted to the choice of the People, I cannot pretend to determine; nor shall I enumerate the Dangers that may arise from the one of these ways or the other. After all the favourable Suppositions I have made, it seems to me that to bring such a Government to a f‹i›rm and settled Condition must be the work of a Century.

For we may observe that the Stability of a Government, if it be at all tollerable depends greatly upon its Antiquity. Customs & Manners by which we & our Forefathers for many Generations have been governed, acquire an Authority and a Sanctity independent upon their Reasonableness or Utility. To this Disposition of human Nature, I think it is owing, rather than to Climate or to any peculiarity in the Genius of the People, that very imperfect forms of Government, when by a mild Administration they have continued for many Generations, & acquired the Authority of Antiquity, continue to subsist after they become very tryrannical. When intollerable Grievances are felt that produce Sedition, they are imputed, not to the Form of Government, but to the fault of those who administer it. Thus in Turkey, a Sedition is quelled by the Sacrifice of a Vizier, a Mufti, or sometimes of a Sultan, without any Attempt
3061/6,4 to alter the form of Government. | Into this Reverence for the Ancient Form of Government I think we must likewise resolve that Maxim, admitted by all Political Writers, That when an ancient Government is over turned, either by Conquest or by internal Disorder, the safest way to establish a new one, is to keep as much as possible to the old Forms of Procedure, and the old Names of Offices.*

What I have said hitherto relates to violent & sudden Changes of the Form of Government, and the Conclusion from the whole is, That such Changes are so dangerous in the Attempt, so uncertain in the Issue, and so dismal and destructive in the means by which they are brought about, that it must be a very bad form of Government indeed, with circumstances very favourable to a Change concurring, that will justify a Wise and good Man in putting a hand to them. It is not with an Old Government as with an old House, from which the Inhabitant, who desires a new one, may remove with his Family and Goods till it be pulled down and rebuilt. If we pull down the old Government, it must be pulled down about our Ears, and we must submit to the Danger of having the New built over our Heads.

But there may be changes that are not sudden & violent, but gradual peaceable and legal. New Laws and Ordinances wisely contrived may remedy the Defects of a Constitution, remove grievances, and promote general happiness.

This must be granted; Yet so limited is the Wisdom of Man, so short his Foresight, that new Laws, even when made with the best intention, do not always produce the Effect intended and expected from them, or they bring unforseen inconveniences that do more than counter ballance their good Effects. For this Reason even such Changes ought not to be rashly made, but with good Advice & for weighty Causes.

Surely every Man who has the skill and ability to mend the Constitution by such peaceable Means merits the Blessings of a Nation. And
3061/6,5 every Constitution, in proportion as it gives Scope | for such Amendments, by allowing due Liberty of printing and petitioning, & by giving the people a share in the Legislature, is in the way, of having its defects supplied & its Errors corrected.

We have the Comfort to think that in this Respect as in many others the British Constitution excells all others we know

The Change made at the Revolution in 1688 was violent indeed but necessary. It affected onely one branch of the Legislature, & by the good Providence of God was brought about with fewer of the Evils that commonly attend such Revolutions than could have reasonably been expected. Since that time, we have had no Revolution, but such gradual and peaceable changes, by new Laws, as have improved the Constitution and greatly promoted the Prosperity of the Nation; and it is to be hoped we may long continue to have such.

Having said so much with regard to changes in Governments which actually exist, whether violent or peaceable I proceed to what I chiefly intended in this Discourse; To consider abstractly that Form of political Society which seems to be best adapted to the Improvement and Happiness of Man.

This is a point merely Speculative. For it may be that the Form which in Speculation seems best fitted to the end proposed may be impracticable in a particular Nation, or even in any Nation that exists

Man, who is the Subject of all political Discussion whether Speculative or Practical, may be considered in two Views. In the first he is the Subject of Speculative Politicks in the second of Practical

First he may be considered *in puris naturalibus** as the Schoolmen speak, that is, such as Nature has formed him; a Being who brings into the World with him the Seeds of Reason and Conscience, along with various Appetites and Passions, by which he is often miss led into
3061/6,6 Error, and seduced into wrong Conduct by Temptations | that arise from within, or from external circumstances: At the same time capable of a high Degree of Improvement in Knowledge & Virtue, by right Education and good Government; and on the other hand, of great Degeneracy, to Barbarity & even to Brutality, by the Want or the Corruption of these Means. This is the Man of Nature, the Sub‹jec›t of Speculative

Politicks, & the Subje‹c›t of what is to be said in this Discourse. The practical Politician, who is to Model or to direct the Government of a Nation actually existing, has to do with Men who are not in the State of Nature, but who by Education & by the State of Society in which they live have acquired Habits & Dispositions, which it is not in his Power to eradicate, and which may be called a second Nature. To this second Nature as well as to the first his Principles of Government must be adapted.*

If it be asked, to what purpose it is to turn our Attention to points merely Speculative and visionary? I answer that Speculative points ought not to be excluded from the Circle of human Knowledge. They tend to enlarge our Conceptions & to strengthen our Faculties. Speculation has a like Effect with regard to our intellectual powers as bodily Exercises have, with regard to the health strength and agility of the Body. Besides, when political Discussions have come to be so much in fashion among all Ranks, it may perhaps be as profitable to most men, to employ their thoughts upon what is merely speculative, as upon what may influence their practice.*

It were to be wished that the Conduct of Men in Society was directed uniformly by the Principles of Religion & Virtue; but this is not to be expected, & if it were, there would be no need of civil Government. The materials of the Political Fabrick are Men, not such as they ought to be, but such as they are, made up of Reason & Passion of Virtue and Vice. The state of human Nature is such that to produce happiness and Comfort in human Society, the Principles of Virtue & Religion need the Aid and Cooperation of other Principles of an inferior Order, which
3061/6,7 shall have sufficient Influence to restrain Men from | wrong Conduct, & induce them to do what is Right*

Wrong Conduct is always owing, either to Error of Judgment, or some Temptation which leads Men to do what they know to be wrong If there be any so very corrupt as to do mischief for mischiefs sake without any temptation, they are not fit to be members of Society, and can onely be Objects of Restraint and Punishment.

From this it follows that in an enlightned Society, Crimes will bear proportion to the Number and Greatness of Temptations, and that the least of ill conduct will be found in a Society in which, the Minds of the Citizens are p‹r›operly enlightned in their Duty, and have at the same time the least temptation to do ill.

But to the happiness of Society it is not sufficient that Men do no ill; they must do good; and by their Industry and Activity promote the common Stock of Happiness.

To aid the Principles of Virtue and Religion in exciting Men to that Industry and Activity which the happiness of Society requires, the Love of publick Esteem Honour & Rank seems, of all the inferior principles of human Nature, to be the best adapted. It is by far a more generous and Noble Principle than the Love of Money or of private Interest. It is also more allied to Virtue. A Man may acquire Riches by means Honest or Dishonest, but to acquire Esteem his Conduct must be accounted Honest and Laudable. Esteem is the natural Reward of Merit, and so strong is the natural desire of it in all Men, that if every Mans Merit or Demerit were publickly known, & if he were to carry about with him through Life & to leave at his Death, a degree of publick Este‹e›m or Contempt proportioned to it, we can hardly conceive a Man so degenerate, as not to be moved to Industry and Activity in his Station by so powerfull an incitement.

From what has been said I think we may in general conclude that the best Form of political Society is that in which these three things
3061/6,8 concur. First that the most effectual Means be used | to strengthen in the Minds of the Citizens the Principles of Virtue and true Religion & to enlighten them in what is right & wrong, honourable and dishonourable. Secondly That the Temptations to wrong and criminal Conduct be as few as possible. and Thirdly, That publick Esteem, Honour and Rank be proportioned as exactly as possible to real Merit.*

If this be so, Political Knowledge as far as it is Speculative, must be the Knowledge of the means by which these three Ends may be most effectually accomplished.

As to the first, the Means of enlightening the people in what is right and wrong & strength‹en›ing in their Minds the Principles of true Religion and Virtue, though I conceive it to be a point of very high Importance with regard to political Government, yet it has been so often treated of, with regard to a higher End, to wit the Happiness of Men in another World, that I shall pass over it altogether, lest I should seem to degrade Religion by considering it as an Engine of State.*

I proceed therefore to consider in what State or Order of Society there is least temptation to ill Conduct, and I confess that to me the Utopian System of Sir Thomas More seems to have the advantage of all others in this respect.*

In that System, it is well known there is no private Property. All that which we call *Property* is under the Administration of the State for the common benefit of the whole political Family.*

This Government indeed very much resembles that of a single Family, which is the onely Government that can be said to be purely the Institution of Nature, all others that exist being artificial & the Contrivance of Men.*

It is the appointment of Nature, that Man should subsist by Labour, and to the comfortable Subsistance of a Nation, a certain Quantity and Kind of Labour is necessary. By this Labour, almost all that which we call Property is produced;* and there are two ways in which this Labour
3061/6,9 may be regulated. Either every Man | labours for himself & his Family, as his Necessity & Desire prompt him, & is proprietor of the produce of his own Labour; Or, every Man labours for the whole Nation, the produce of his Labour being put to the common Stock from which every Citizen is supplied according to his Wants.

The first we may call *the System of private Property*, which is exemplified in all Nations. The second is *the Utopian System*, which as far as we know has not been followed by any great Nation. It has been practised in different ages by Societies of Conobites and Monks who have lived sequestered from the World, by the labour of their own hands. It was practised by our Saviour and his twelve Apostles who had a common Purse during his Ministry on Earth; and after his Ascension, the first Christians had all things in common, they that had Lands or Houses sold them and laid the price at the Apostles feet, and distribution was made to every Man as he had need. After the Christians amounted to a Multitude consisting of several thousands, the seven Deacons were chosen to manage and distribute this common Stock. And it was probably, their dispersion into different Countries, by the persecution of the Jews, that put an end to this Community of Property among Christians.*

This System was also established by some Jesuites, over a large tract of Country in Paraguay, which by good Deeds & without Force they brought from a savage State under their Despotick Authority. The Jesuites who governed this Country with a mild but despotick Authority, carried on a large Traffic to different parts of South America, & paid a piastre to the king of Spain for each of their Subjects, amounting about the middle of this Century as it is said to above four hundred thousand. But the Subjects had neither Money nor Property nor Traffick. This Government of the Jesuites in Paraguay lasted about a hundred and fifty years, & ended onely by the entire Destruction of the Society of Jesuites.*

In the Utopian System, the People are fed, cloathed, & have their 3061/6,10 Wants supplied by the Publick, the Labour of the | People must therefore be directed by the Publick, in such manner that the produce of it may be sufficient in Kind & Quantity for this purpose. The Labourers in every Profession must be trained, directed and overseen, and the produce of their Labour received and stored by proper Officers.

The means by which this is to be done will be a Subsequent Consideration, but first we ought to consider, whether the End be of importance to the Happiness of Society.

Suppose then a Nation of which the individuals have all their wants supplied by the Publick, the Produce of their Labour being to be put to a publick Stock for the common benefit. I would endeavour to prove that in such a Nation the Temptations to wrong or criminal Conduct would be small, compared with those which must happen in any System of private Property.

It is a Proverb of the highest authority that the Love of Money is the Root of all Evil.* Like other Proverbs it must be understood to admit of Exceptions. But the truth of it, (which no Christian will deny) requires, that the Exceptions should be few compared with the instances in which it holds good. There may, no doubt, be Crimes which have no Relation to the Love of Money. But by far the greater part of those we find in human Society, spring either immediately or more remotely from this Root. Nor will this appear strange if we consider how this Root, when once admitted, spreds & infects the whole Society. Let it be observed, by the way, that the Words, *Property*, *Money*, & *Riches*, may be used in this Subject Promiscuously as equivalent Terms; because Money is the Measure of all Property & all Property may ‹be› bought or sold for its Value in Money. Riches signify onely a superfluity of Property either in Money or in other kinds.

Next to the Desire of Life and of the necesary means of Life, the Desire of Distinction and Preeminence among his fellow men is one of 3061/6,11 the strongest natural Desires of Man; And when his | whole Activity is not necessarily employed in providing the means of Subsistence, is the strongest, the most general, & lasting spring of Activity and Exertion.* Now Riches, in all civilized Societies, seem to have advantages above all other Qualifications for gratifying this Desire. For,

First, in all such Societies, Riches are more looked up to than Wisdom or Virtue or Learning or Art, or any other Qualification by which one Man excells another.

Secondly, Riches are the Means of gratifying almost every desire. They are a Species of Power, which is a Natural object of Desire to all Men. They may be equally subservient to the best Purposes & to the worst, to the Happiness or Misery of the Possessor & of many others. In bad Men they feed Pride, Vanity, Luxury, and Voluptuousness; they invite to Oppression & Revenge & furnish the Means of gratif‹y›ing every bad Passion. In Good Men they may be the Means of doing much good.

Thirdly Riches & Hereditary Rank which commonly arises from Riches and accompanies them are the onely Advantages which a Man can transmit to his Posterity or Family.

Fourthly we may observe that the Acquisition of Riches requires neither Talents nor Virtue; so that this Road to Distinction invites all Men, even those who may despair of attain‹in›g it by other means.

I add in the last place, that though many of our Passions may be satiated by their Objects, & even surfeited; the Love of Money is never satiated. It grows in old Age when other Passions fade.

These particulars have been mentioned to shew the Reason why when private Property is once admitted, the Desire and the pursuit of it, & consequently all the Evils that spring from that Root should be so universal, and so prevalent in Society.

Indeed when we take a general View of Society, What is it else but a Scramble for Money? In a few perhaps, who have inherited fortunes, it
3061/6,12 is a Competition who shall make the most brilliant Exhibition | of Riches by Shew and Magnificence. Such is become the serious bussiness of Mankind, in consequence of the System of private Property!*

The Utopian System may be figured, by a Sum of Money prudently distributed to a great Multitude according to their Wants and their Merits. The System of private Property, to a like Sum, thrown promiscuously among the same Multitude leaving them to scramble for it.

Private Property has always been, & must necessarily be very unequally divided. Time, & the Progress of Society, naturally tend to increase this inequality, till at last the greater part of a Nation, by their Poverty are depressed & dependant upon the few that are rich; They must Labour, like Beasts of Burthen, to feed the Pride & Luxury of the Rich, & to earn a small Pittance for their own necessary Subsistence. By this Means both are equally corrupted; the greater Part being debased into a State of Servility, which tends to stiffle every generous Sentiment, & to produce Envy & Discontent in all, Adulation and cunning in the more timorous, & in the more daring, Theft, Robbery, Murder, Sedition & Rebellion.

On the other hand the Rich, being as much elevated above the natural Condition of Man, as the poor are sunk below it, & that commonly without Regard to Virtue or Merit, are as much corrupted by their Riches as the poor by their poverty. It is unnecessary to ennumerate the Vices to which Riches tempt the unprincipled; they are obvious to Reason & well known by Experience.

Nor is it less evident that the Distinction attending upon Riches very much diminishes the Inducement which such Persons would otherwise feel, to distinguish themselves by more valuable Qualities.

For, among the Evils which may justly be imputed to the System of private Property, this is not the least, That the strong Desire which all
3061/6,13 Men have of Distinction and Eminence, which naturally | excites them to honourable and usefull Conduct in Society, & is implanted in us by the Supreme Being for that purpose, is perverted to the Love of Money, as the easiest and surest road to Distinction.

In the System of private Property every Man has his private Interest, distinct, not onely from the Publick interest, but from the Interest of every Individual with whom he has any connection or intercourse. There is an Interest of every Individual & and an Interest of the whole political Body. These different Interests must in innumerable cases interfere, and cross one another. And the publick Interest crosses that of every individual, because the publick must be supported at the Expence of the Individuals.

From this opposition of Interests arise Dissafection to the publick, Discontent, Contentions, Parties, and Law Pleas, by which all the bad Passions of Men are stirred, and fed. And in the same propor‹tion› publick Spirit and all the natural benevolent Affections are checked opposed and born down.

In the Utopian System there are no private Interests opposed to that of the Publick. A regard to the Publick acts without an Antagonist; nor is there any clashing of private Interests to produce Quarrels and Law suits. The benevolent Affections have no interested Motives to obstruct their Operation.

I know of no Temptations to bad Conduct that are peculiar to the Utopian System; deducing therefore those that are common to both Systems the ballance against that of private Property consists of all the Temptations which occur, in an enlightned & flouris‹h›ing Nation, in the acquisition of property, in guarding it from the incroachments of other Men, & in spending & laying it out. The Temptations from poverty in the greater Part, from the greedy desire of gain in some, and from Superfluity of Riches in others.

3061/6,14 I grant, that notwithstanding the Temptations mentioned | Men guided by the Principles of Virtue and Piety may a‹c›quire Property by fair and honest means, and without hurt to the Publick may guard it prudently & peaceably, & lay it out temperately and charitably. But in all political reasoning we must consider, not what Men may do, or what they ought to do, but what it may be expected they will do in the present weak and corrupted State of human Nature. We see in our dayly Experience that Temptations of Interest overcome, not onely, the Sense of Duty, but the natural good Affections to Neighbours, to Friends, to the nearest Relations & even to the Publick.

From what has been said I think it appears that the Utopian System is that in which there are fewest Temptations to bad Conduct. I proceed therefore to consider whether in this System, Men may not have sufficient Inducement to all the Labour and Exertion necessary to the Subsistence and Happiness of the Society; by degrees of publick Esteem, Honour & Rank proportioned to their Merit.

With a View to this, it is absolutely necessary, that the right Education of all the Subjects, should be attended to by the State, as one of its principal Concerns; & should be under the Direction of Persons qualified for that Office, & having a Degree of Rank & publick Esteem, suited to the Dignity and Importance of their Charge.

It is Education generally that makes a Man to be what he is; not onely knowing or ignorant, but good or bad. For this we have the Authority of another Proverb. Train up a Child the way he should go, and when he is old he will not depart from it.*

What more can be desired in order to the greatest happiness of Society, than that its Members, in their several Departments, should go on to old Age in the Way they ought to go? The mean to attain this End,
3061/6,15 in the Judgment of the wisest of Men | is to train them properly. Till this be done, it is in vain to expect from any System of Government, that Perfection and Happiness of Society which every good Man desires. The Materials of the Political Fabrick must be formed to fit the places for which they are destined. Without this there can neither be beauty nor Stability in the Building.

It seems to be a natural Consequence of the System of private property, that the Education of the Youth in all Nations (if we except what is said of one or two very ancient ones) has been left to the Judgment and Affection of the Parents. And as the far greatest part of Parents in every Nation, is poor and ignorant, it is a necessary consequence, that the Education of the far greatest part of the Citizens must be very different from what it ought to be; and that this most efficacious mean of their acting a proper part in Society, has been wanting.

In a Utopian Government, as the Labour and Exertion of the Citizens is all for the publick Emolument, it must be one of the most important concerns of the Publick to train them properly for that Purpose.*

So much has been wrote upon Education in ancient and modern times, that I shall not touch on that Subject. I would onely observe, that to teach Men to read & write, the use of Numbers, & the various Exercises that contribute to the health strength & agility of the Body, and even to teach Latin Greek Mathematicks and the various branches of Philosophy, & to instruct them in the principles of any particular Science or Art usefull in Society; all this, however skillfully performed, is but the Body of right Education. These Attainments are all of an ambiguous Nature, and may be used either to the Good or to the Hurt of Society, according to
3061/6,16 the Character of him who possesses them. And therefore, to form | the Character to good Habits and good Dispositions, & to check those that are vicious; this is the Soul and Spirit of right Education. To accomplish this as far as can be done by human Means, requires great Knowledge of human Nature, constant Attention, great Temper, Patience and Assiduity. The Diseases of the Mind while it is pliable and docile as well as those of the Body may, by prudent Means, be cured or alleviated.

Those who superintend Education in an Utopian Society, ought to be Men who by their Merit have attained publick Respect and Honour; which may give Authority to their Admonitions, & make them Examples worthy to be imitated by those under their Care. And, as Nature has not made the Talents of Body or Mind that are usefull in Society, hereditary, or peculiar to any Rank; the Symptoms of such Talents in whatever Rank ought to be carefully observed & cultivated, that they may in due time be put to their proper Use.

There is an Education that ought to be common to all the Citizens; such as may enlighten their Minds in the duties of Life, & dispose them to the practice of them. Another Education must follow this, suited to the different Employments for which the young Citizens are destined, according to their various Talents of Body and Mind, and as the publick exigency requires.

As the Labour in every Employment is for the Publick, it must be overseen by Officers appointed by the Publick, who shall at stated times make a Report to superior Officers of the Industry, Skill and moral behaviour of every Individual under their Charge.

It is a capital Defect in the System of private Property that the different Professions and Employments are not honoured & esteemed in proportion to their real Utility, & the Talents required for the discharge of them. The most usefull and necessary Employments are held in no Esteem. Nor indeed do they deserve it; because they are undertaken onely for the sake of private Interest. Their Utility to the publick is
3061/6,17 accidental, & not in the View of those who practise them. | It is otherwise in a Utopian State where every Man labours in his Calling, not for his own, but for the publick benefit. He is therefore justly intitled to publick Esteem in proportion to the Utility the public receives from his labour, and the Difficulty to performing it.

In such a Society, there must be a Scale of Honour, in which all the different Professions and Employments have a Rank assigned them, proportioned to their Utility and the Talents necessary for discharging them. There must likewis‹e› be Distinctive ba‹d›ges or habits, by which every Mans Rank & the Respect due to him may be known, and observed in all cases of Precedency. And, as in every Profession and Employment there will be different degrees of Eminence & Proficiency, these ought, in a Utopian System, to be used as a Spur to Emulation and Exertion. If in the Literary Professions the Degrees of Undergraduate, Batchelor, Licentiat & Doctor by found usefull to excite to Industry in those Professions, why may not like Degrees for every Employment be appointed. In a Utopian Society this ought by no means to be omitted. As in that Form of Society, next to the Principle of Virtue, the Desire of publick Esteem and Honour is the grand Spring which gives Motion to the whole Machine of the Commonwealth, it is proper that there should ‹be› many Roads to publick Honours, that every Man in his Station may be prompted to exert himself for the publick Good.

For this cause besides the Kinds & Degre‹e›s of publick Honours I have mentioned, there ought to be an Order of Merit for those who have remarkably benefited the Commonwealth in any way not comprehended in these I have mentioned, which also will have various Degrees. If we add to this the Honours & Dignities arising from Offices of Trust and Authority in the State, which must be many, and of different Degrees;
3061/6,18 it will appear, that in such a | State there will be a much greater variety

of Ranks than in any other; and these distinguished, not by Riches or Hereditary Descent, which are Distinctions not founded in Nature but on human Institution; but distinguished in a more natural way, by their Talents natural & acq‹u›ired, by their Exertions for the publick Good, and by the Authority & Trust they have merited of their fellow Citizens.

Luxury and Intemperance in eating and drinking are pernicious in every State, and in a System of private property can hardly if at all be prevented. How they are prevented in a Utopian State is so obvious that it need not be mentioned. The Subsistence of all ought to be such as tends to health & strength, & therefore most liberal to those whose Labour requires it. Nature seems to point to no other difference among Citizens in this Article.

But there is a Splendor and Magnificence, in having Servants, Horses, Chariots, Houses and Furniture, which does not appear to me to be incompatible with the Utopian State, though Sir Thomas More seems to be of another Mind.*

When such Splendor is bestowed by the State, as the Reward of Merit, either in a Mans Life or at his Death; it is the most Substantial Reward such a State can give, and proves an incentive to Merit in others, as well as creates Respect in the lower Orders.

On the other hand, when Splendor & Magnificence is produced merely by Riches without Regard to Merit, it feeds Pride & Insolence in the Possessor, inflames the Love of Money in those who can acquire it, & produces Envy and Malignity in those who cannot.

When I speak of *Servants* in the Utopian State, the word seems to convey a degrading Idea of Dependance, unsuitable to the Dignity of a Citizen of Utopia, and therefore we should rather call them Attendants or Retainers. When a Utopian of Rank is allowed more or fewer Attend-
3061/6,19 ants either for Honour or for | usefull Purposes, they are the Servants of the State as he likewise is, though of a higher Rank. They depend not upon the person whom they attend, but upon the State & upon their own Merit for their Subsistence and for their Reward, & he has the same Dependance. They have all the Privileges that belong to Citizens of Utopia, and therefore are not degraded by such Attendance.

What I have said is intended to shew, That every Citizen of Utopia, being properly educated, may, without the Motive of private Interest, have sufficient Inducement to exert himself in his Station for the publick good, by being secured in liberal Subsistence, and in such degrees of publick Esteem Honour and Rank as are propo‹r›tioned to his Merit.

But if after all some Persons should be found so degenerate, as that either their Laziness and Indolence, or other vitious Inclinations, are not to be overcome by these Inducements; the Utopian State has a mean in reserve for such Persons; and that is Dishonour & Disgrace; of which a Man may be made to carry about with him the Marks, as others do of their Dignity and Honour.*

Supposing the Nature of some so very bad, that neither the Motives of Honour, nor of Disgrace, are sufficient to make them act their part in Society, penal Laws and Punishment, as in other States, are still in reserve for them, and in the Utopian State ought to be applied to them onely. Such Persons have the Temper of Slaves, and ought to be degraded into that state, being altogether unworthy and incapable of being Citizens of Utopia.*

It is ob‹v›ious that in a Utopian State the Subjects can have no Traffick either with one another or with Foreigners; but the State may be Commercial. It may be so with great advantage; having the whole Stock of the Nation in its disposal. And it ought to be so, that what, in the produce of the Nations Industry is over and above its Consumption,
3061/6,20 may be disposed of to other | Nations or Individuals for its Value, & that the Utopians may be supplied with such forreign Commodities as are necessary or convenient.*

A Utopian State ought, by frugal Management of the publick Stock, and by proper Incitements to the Industry and Labour of the Subjects, to be always provided in ample Stores & a rich Treasury, by which not onely the annual Consumption of the Citizens may be supplied, but an Accumulating Fund may be reserved for foreign Traffic, for the Expence of defensive Wars, for accidental Losses by unfruitfull Seasons, Inundations, Earthquakes or Tempests, and by unforeseen Variations in Commercial Affairs.

When the loss of Property occasioned by such Evils falls onely upon a Publick Stock which is able to bear it, & affects no Individual, every Man may imagine what a Comfort it must be to a Nation, to be free from the fears & from the Sufferings produced in other Nations by such Calamities. A Utopian has every thing that pertains to his Subsistence, and to his Rank in the Society, insured upon the Stock and Credit of the Nation, against all Accidents, excepting that of his own Misbehaviour. He fears no loss of Fortune or of Consideration by Fire or Water or any other Element, by Insolvency of Debtors or of Tenants, or by Depredations of Enemies Foreign or Domestick.

It may seem, that in this System, the State is burthened with a load of Work, additional to the common cares of Government, too great to be well accomplished. The Education of all the Youth of both Sexes, The Oversight of all the labouring hands, The collecting, storing and dispensing the Produce of their Labour: The publick Registers that must be kept of the Merits & Demerits of every Individual, & of every Step of his advancement in Honour and Rank. The Regulations for confering Degrees with Justice & Impartiality, and the Management of the trading
3061/6,21 Stock of the Nation, these things, without doubt, | will require much Attention & Fidelity, and many hands

To form an equitable Judgment of a Utopian Government in this Respect, it would be necessary to ballance these additional burthens that are laid upon it, with those of which it is relieved; and likewise with those of which the Subjects are relieved; For as Government and Subjects are one Whole, having one common interest, what is taken from one Part & laid upon another Part, does not increase the burthen of the Whole.

In this System, Government is relieved of all the Care and Trouble of imposing and levying Taxes of Customs Excise and all others, affecting either moveable or immoveable Property, and of all the hands employed for that purpose, & for preventing and discovering the Frauds which Citizens are tempted to by private Interest and Avarice, in opposition to the publick Interest.

In a System of private Property Taxes of all Kinds though necessary for the Support of Government, are attended with this Inconvenience, that they set the Interest of the Whole in Opposition to the Interest of the Individuals, which is apt to produce Disaffection to the Publick, Sedition & Rebellion, and will always be attended with Smugling, Frauds, & Concealments which corrupt the Morals of the Citizens & produce innumerable Law pleas

To manage the whole Traffick of a Nation is, no doubt, a business of great Labour, and must require the Employment of many hands in its various subordinate Departments. But it is to be considered whether one great Mercantile Stock, may not be managed better, and more profitably for the Nation, than when it is divided into thousands of different Stocks, of Companies and Individuals, whose private Interests must in innumerable cases cross one another, & that of the Publick. |

3061/6,22 The right Education of the Youth is a matter of such high Importance in a Utopian State, that if it should require more or abler hands than are commonly employed in it, this will be more than compensated by its Effects on the Manners and Morals of the Citizens.

The Regulations for conferring, with Justice & Impartiality, Degrees of Honour and Rank, fall within the Rules of common Prudence, as Cases of this kind must happen more or less in every Society. Onely it may be observed that in Utopia interested Motives to Partiality have no Place. And that the Character and Behaviour of Candidates, their Skill Exertion and Merit, must be perfectly known, from the particular Inspection they are under.

The Registers kept in Utopia of the Reports of Overseers, & of the Degrees of Honour and Advancement conferred on every Citizen, furnish the Government with a Fund of Statistical knowledge of great Importance, which could not otherways be had. From these are known the Strength or Weakness, the Defects and Redundancies of the whole political Body, and of every part of it. If there be a Deficiency of any Article of Life in the whole, or in any part from unfruitfull Seasons or any other Accident, it will be k‹n›own in time to provide a Supply. If a Redundancy it will be stored or exported to a Market. A Defect or Redundance of Hands in any Employment may be corrected. Any usefull Invention or Improvement is not kept a Secret by the Inventer for his private Interest, or confined to the knowledge of a small Neighbourhood, but is immediately made known to the whole Nation. The Persons fit for offices of Trust & Government will be known, and such Offices filled, not by Intrigue or Connection with great Men, as is common, but according to the publick Judgment of their Capacity and Merit

It may farther be observed that if a Utopian Government be burdened
3061/6,23 with much work in its Executive branch it is relieved of a | great deal in its Legislative and Judiciary branches

1st The Laws relating to Customs Excise & other internal Taxes; the Judicatures Superior & Subordinate which are appointed to put those Laws in Execution, & all the Pleas between Government and Subjects to which they give occasion, have no place in Utopia.

2ly All the Laws and Judicatures for determining pleas of Interest between Subject and Sub‹j›ect, or between the Subjects and Foreigners, are likewise excluded in this System.

How great a Body of Law is required to regulate the Acquisition, the Conveyance, and the Succession to Landed Property, its Limits, its priviledges, Servitudes, & variety of Holdings? And what a World of business does it occasion to Judicatures higher & lower? How many the Laws required to determine Disputes about moveable property?*

The variety of Transactions which Property gives rise to, is boundless and in an ancient and flourishing Nation, is still accumulating, by new Inventions, new Trades, & new Fashions, which give rise to new Frauds and Injuries, & require new Laws. Thus the Body of Laws, which the Regulation of Property, and the Redress of Wrongs in Matters of Property, require, is still accumulating, till it becomes too great a Study for a Life, and must be divided & subdivided into various Professions and Departments, & besides Judicatures and Judges, employs an Host of Counsellors, Advocates, Sergeants Sollicitors Conveyancers, Clerks, Registers, who are supported by what some of them have been pleased to call, the glorious Uncertainty of Law.*

3dly We may observe, that as Property is the chief bone of Contention among Mankind, by which the Passions of Anger & ill will are stirred and by which Men are tempted to hurt one another in their Person Reputation as well as Property; in the Utopian System, all contention about Property being removed, and the feuel that feeds evil & malevolent Passions being withdrawn; the Evils which they produce in Society will very rarely appear.

3061/6,24 So that to compensate the Labour laid upon the Executive | Branch of an Utopian Government & the Hands employed for that purpose, we ought to put in the other Scale, the Savings of Labour and of Hands in the Legislative and Judicative Branches.

In the Legislative Branch is saved the Labour of contriving and imposing the Taxes of every kind necessary for the Support of Government. and the greater Labour of making the Laws for the Regulation of Property Real & Personal in the Infinite variety of Transactions civil & commercial that take place in Society.

In the Judicative Branch is saved the Labour of Judging and determining in all claims and pleas to be decided by those Laws.

The saving of Hands is likewise great in the Utopian System, first to the Government, of the Hands necessary for the Labour above mentioned in Lawmaking & in Judging; & secondly to the Subjects of Counsellors, Pleaders, Conveyancers, and all their Retainers whatsoever who are employed in the Execution of the laws about Property.

A third Saving to the Subjects, which is the greatest of all, is, that they are relieved of all the bitter Fruits which Spring, either immediately, or more remotely, from Contentions and Lawsuits about Property.

One who considers these things can hardly forbear to conclude, that in a Utopian State the Code of Law will be reduced to such a diminutive Size, that it will hardly be thought worthy to be made a distinct Profession. The Law may be understood by every Man come to years of Discr‹e›tion, & perhaps may be all contained in the Almanack.

What I have said of the Utopian System may be summed up in these three particulars First That the Temptations to wrong and criminal Conduct are by this System greatly diminished beyond what they must be in every System of private Property

Secondly that by proper Education, and by D‹e›grees of Honour |
3061/6,25 and Rank conferred according to Merit, the Citizens of Utopia may have sufficient Inducement to all the Labour and Industry which is necessary to the comfortable Subsistence of the Nation. and Thirdly That the Labour required in the Executive Branch of an Utopian Government, is compensated, by the Labour of which it is relieved in its Legislative and Judicative Branches; and much more by the Subjects being relieved of all the bad passions, Quarrels, Contentions & Lawsuits arising from Differences about Property.

The view I have hitherto taken of the Utopian System presents its fairest side: To form an equitable Judgement of it, it ought likewis‹e› to be contemplated on its darker Side

First it may be observed that political Reasoning is not of the Demonstrative but of the probable kind.* The Heart of Man is a Labrinth, too intricate to be fully traced by his Understanding, and we oft'en see, not onely Individuals, but great Bodies of Men act a part very different from that which by the common principles of human Nature we would have expected. And therefore political Writers are wont to borrow Aid to their reasoning from Examples of what has been done or has happened in similar Cases. In the present Subject, we are totally deprived of this Adminicle to our Reasoning, & therefore it must have the less Force. We cannot borrow Examples from Utopian Governments, because no Nation was ever so governed.

Secondly As the present State of Man is a State of Trial and Improvement; Temptation is necessarily implyed in it. It is by Temptation that Virtue is tried, exercised, and Streng‹t›hned. That Innocence, which is the Effect of having never met with Temptation, is, no doubt, a very amiable thing. But tried Virtue which has encountered strong Temptations, and has come off Victorious, is an Object of much higher Esteem, both with God and Man. Man even in the State of Innocence was not exempted from Temptation. Some have more or greater than others, but to what Degree Temptation may be proper for the present State of Man, is not for us to kno‹w›, it can onely be known by him who made us, and who will judge us. |

3061/6,26 Thirdly it may be observed, That as the Utopian System greatly lessens Temptations to bad Conduct, so it deprives Men of the Opportunity of exercising some very eminent Virtues, to which the different Conditions of Poverty and Riches give occasion. The Man depressed by Poverty, who not onely resists the Temptations of that State and discharges the duties of it, but is contented, & thankfull for his Lot as that which his Father in Heaven sees to be the best for him, who looks with indifference upon the Splendor of Riches without a covetous Eye, without Envy or Malignity; Such a Man under all his Depression carries a noble Soul. His Poverty exalts him, & makes his Virtue more Eminent. The Temptations that arise from Riches and high Estate, are perhaps more difficult to be overcome than those which spring from poverty this is granted; & therefore, they require a greater degree of Virtue to conquer them. If such a Man thinks of himself no more highly than he ought to think, condescends to those of Low Degree, spreads Happiness and alleviates Misery as far as his power reaches, he is a kind of God upon Earth his Riches are a Blessing to himself and to all around him.

The Utopian System leaves no room for these noble Virtues. The Utopian may have the Disposition but he wants the Opportunity of exercising them.

I add in the fourth place, That the Desire of publick Esteem Honour and Rank, which must be encouraged in the Utopian System, as the chief Aid to Virtue for exciting Men to do their Duty in Society, may be carried too far; so as to supplant the Virtue which it ought onely to Aid. When this is the Case the Utopian indeed does his Duty, but he does it, to be seen of Men, when he ought to have higher Motives. And perhaps the constant pursuit of Honour & of the Esteem of Men, may produce an undue Elation of Mind, unfriendly, & unsuitable to that Humility, and that Sense of our Dependence and Demerit, which Religion requires.|

3061/6,27 To conclude, Since we neither live, nor does it seem to be the design of Providence that we shall ever live, in a Utopian Society, but among Men surrounded with Temptations, and whose Interests interfere & cross on‹e› another in innumerable Instances let us not expect Perfection, in Individuals, in Societies, or in Governments.

We are conscious of many Imperfections in ourselves. Those who hold the Reins of Government are Men of like Passions, & have greater Temptations.

The Relation between a Government and its Subjects, like that of Marriage, or of Parent and Child, is strong & important. It is a Relation instituted by the Author of Nature, as without Government Men must be Savages. To preserve and strengthen this sacred Tie, concerns the honour and the Interest of both Parties. The Duties are reciprocal. Protection and the Benefite of Laws on one hand. Respect, Submission, & Defence in Time of Danger on the other. Whatever is excellent in the Constitution, ought to be the Boast & the Glory of the Subject, as we Glory in the Virtues of our near Relations. If we see, or think we see, Imperfections in the Constitution or in the Government, we ought to consider, that there never was a perfect human Government on Earth; We ought to view such Defects, not with a Censorious and Malignant Eye, but with that Candor and Indulgence with which we perceive the Defects of our dearest Friends. It is onely Atrocious Conduct that can dissolve the Sacred Tie. While that is not the Case, every prudent and gentle mean should be used to strengthen and confirm it. As He is a good Friend or Neighbour with whom we can live in Peace, Amity and the Exchange of good Offices; So it is a good Government under which we can lead quiet and peaceable lives in all Godliness & Honesty.*

Editorial Notes

Part One: Reading

4/III/19: Pennsylvania Charter

3/3 Various published versions of this charter appeared in the eighteenth century. The fact that Reid refers to numbered sections in the charter makes it likely that he read the text included in *Votes and Proceedings of the House of Representatives of the Province of Pennsylvania. Beginning the Fourth Day of December, 1682*. 3 vols (Philadelphia, 1752–54), vol. I, pp. xviii–xxiv.

3/17 *Votes and Proceedings*, vol. I, p. xxi.

3/20 *Votes and Proceedings*, vol. I, p. xxii.

3/28 *Votes and Proceedings*, vol. I, p. xxiii.

4/2 [William Penn], *The Frame of the Government of the Province of Pennsilvania in America: Together with Certain Laws Agreed upon in England by the Governour and Divers Free-Men of the aforesaid Province. To be further Explained and Confirmed there by the First Provincial Council and General Assembly that Shall Be Held, if they See Meet* (1682). The date Reid has noted is not that of the publication of the pamphlet but rather the date upon which Penn signed the proposed constitution for Pennsylvania.

4/7 Reid transcribes Penn's wording in *Frame of the Government*, A2r. In the preface Penn quotes Galatians 3:19, 1 Timothy 1:9–10 and Romans 13:1–5.

4/29 [Penn], *Frame of the Government*, A2r–v.

5/6 [Penn], *Frame of the Government*, pp. 1–4.

5/7 [Penn], *Frame of the Government*, pp. 7–11.

4/III/21: Lyttelton, *History of Henry II*; Robertson, *History of Charles V*

5/12 George Lord Lyttelton, *The History of the Life of King Henry the Second, and of the Age in which He Lived, in Five Books: To which is Prefixed, a History of the Revolutions of England from the Death of Edward the Confessor to the Birth of Henry the Second*, third edition, 4 vols (London, 1769–71). Reid's notes are in fact taken from vol. III, not vol. II as stated.

5/16 Lyttelton, *History*, vol. III, pp. 1–16.
5/23 Lyttelton, *History*, vol. III, pp. 18–46.
5/24 Lyttelton, *History*, vol. III, pp. 46–50.
5/25 Lyttelton, *History*, vol. III, pp. 50–61.
5/26 Lyttelton, *History*, vol. III, pp. 61–63.
5/31 Montesquieu, *Considerations on the Causes of the Greatness of the Romans and their Decline* [1734], pp. 213–14.
5/33 Lyttelton, *History*, vol. III, p. 62.
6/3 Lyttelton, *History*, vol. III, pp. 63–81.
6/6 Lyttelton, *History*, vol. III, p. 82.
6/10 Lyttelton, *History*, vol. III, pp. 83–84.
6/14 Lyttelton, *History*, vol. III, pp. 84–85.
6/22 Lyttelton, *History*, vol. III, pp. 85–90.
6/25 Lyttelton, *History*, vol. III, pp. 90–91.
6/35 Lyttelton, *History*, vol. III, pp. 91–93.
7/4 Lyttelton, *History*, vol. III, p. 93.
7/14 Lyttelton, *History*, vol. III, p. 97.
7/39 Lyttelton, *History*, vol. III, pp. 100–7.
8/6 Lyttelton, *History*, vol. III, pp. 107–8.
8/9 Lyttelton, *History*, vol. III, pp. 109–10.
8/13 Lyttelton, *History*, vol. III, pp. 110–15.
8/21 Lyttelton, *History*, vol. III, pp. 117–18.
8/23 Lyttelton, *History*, vol. III, pp. 118–19.
8/32 Lyttelton, *History*, vol. III, p. 128.
9/2 Lyttelton, *History*, vol. III, pp. 134–42.
9/8 Lyttelton, *History*, vol. III, pp. 155–57.
9/9 Lyttelton, *History*, vol. III, pp. 158–82.
9/15 Lyttelton, *History*, vol. III, pp. 187–88.
9/17 Lyttelton, *History*, vol. III, pp. 188–96.
9/23 Lyttelton, *History*, vol. III, p. 196.
9/31 Lyttelton, *History*, vol. III, pp. 198–99, 202, 207–10. The relationship between Ranulf de Glanville's *Tractatus de legibus et consuetudinibus regni Angliae* (*c*. 1188) and the Scottish compilation of Roman and canon law known as the *Regiam majestatem* was a controversial topic in eighteenth-century Scotland; see Colin Kidd, *Subverting Scotland's Past: Scottish Whig Historians and the Creation of an Anglo-British Identity, 1689–*c.*1830*, pp. 149–50, and the references cited there.

9/33 Lyttelton, *History*, vol. III, pp. 216–34.
9/34 Lyttelton, *History*, vol. III, pp. 237–68.
9/35 Lyttelton, *History*, vol. III, pp. 282–99.
9/36 Lyttelton, *History*, vol. III, pp. 299–304.
9/39 Lyttelton, *History*, vol. III, p. 484.
10/3 The whole of book III of Lyttelton's five 'books' is taken up with the conflict between King Henry II and the Archbishop of Canterbury, Thomas Becket.
10/13 William Robertson, *The History of the Reign of the Emperor Charles V. With a View of the Progress of Society in Europe, from the Subversion of the Roman Empire, to the Beginning of the Sixteenth Century*, 3 vols (London, 1769).
10/17 Robertson, *History*, vol. III, pp. 1–3.
10/19 Robertson, *History*, vol. III, pp. 3–11.
10/22 Robertson, *History*, vol. III, pp. 11–21.
11/6 Robertson, *History*, vol. III, pp. 21–30.
11/10 Robertson, *History*, vol. III, pp. 30–36.
11/13 Robertson, *History*, vol. III, pp. 36–39.
11/16 Robertson, *History*, vol. III, pp. 39–42.
11/25 Robertson, *History*, vol. III, pp. 42–62.
11/27 Robertson, *History*, vol. III, pp. 62–65.
11/32 Robertson, *History*, vol. III, pp. 65–69.
11/34 Robertson, *History*, vol. III, pp. 69–72.
11/35 Robertson, *History*, vol. III, pp. 72–76.
11/37 Robertson, *History*, vol. III, pp. 76–82.
12/14 Robertson, *History*, vol. III, pp. 91–107.
12/18 Robertson, *History*, vol. III, pp. 107–17.
12/20 Robertson, *History*, vol. III, pp. 117–20.
12/25 Robertson, *History*, vol. III, pp. 124–43.
12/32 Robertson, *History*, vol. III, pp. 144–65.
12/37 Robertson, *History*, vol. III, pp. 165–72.
12/38 Robertson, *History*, vol. III, pp. 172–92.

3/I/5: Steuart, *Principles of Money*

13/5 Sir James Steuart, *The Principles of Money Applied to the Present State of the Coin of Bengal: Being an Inquiry into the Methods to be Used for Correcting the Defects of the Present Currency; for Stopping the Drains which Carry Off the Coin; and for Extending Circulation by the*

	Means of Paper-Credit. Composed for the Use of the Honourable the East-India Company ([London], 1772).
13/11	Steuart, *Principles*, pp. 14–15.
13/27	Steuart, *Principles*, pp. 15–16.
14/7	Steuart, *Principles*, p. 17.
14/24	Steuart, *Principles*, pp. 25–29.
14/33	Steuart, *Principles*, pp. 34–35.
15/2	Steuart, *Principles*, p. 40.
15/5	Steuart, *Principles*, pp. 46–56.
15/12	Steuart, *Principles*, pp. 46–47.
15/16	Steuart, *Principles*, pp. 45, 50, 52.
15/21	Steuart, *Principles*, p. 49.
15/24	Steuart, *Principles*, p. 57.
15/32	Steuart, *Principles*, p. 65.
16/3	Steuart, *Principles*, p. 76.

4/III/23: De Lolme, *Constitution of England*

16/6	Jean Louis De Lolme, *The Constitution of England, or an Account of the English Government; in which it is Compared with the Republican Form of Government, and Occasionally with the other Monarchies in Europe* (London, 1775).
16/23	De Lolme, *Constitution*, p. 8–16.
16/29	De Lolme, *Constitution*, pp. 26–28.
16/35	De Lolme, *Constitution*, pp. 28–30.
17/11	De Lolme, *Constitution*, pp. 34–38.
17/17	De Lolme, *Constitution*, p. 38. 'No tallage or aid shall be taken or levied by us or our heirs in our realm, without the good will and assent of archbishops, bishops, earls, barons, knights, burgesses, and other freemen of the land.' The translation is from the modern edition: Jean Louis De Lolme, *The Constitution of England; or, An Account of the English Government*, ed. D. Lieberman, p. 40, note b.
17/24	De Lolme, *Constitution*, pp. 49–50.
17/27	De Lolme, *Constitution*, p. 70.
17/30	De Lolme, *Constitution*, p. 90 note (a). Concerning the Latin statement, see De Lolme, *Constitution of England*, ed. Lieberman, pp. 67–68, note a: 'For so long as they shall well conduct themselves.'
17/32	De Lolme, *Constitution*, pp. 96–97.

4/III/13: De Lolme, *Constitution of England*

18/2 The topics enumerated by Reid in this set of notes are covered from a historical perspective in book I, chapters 1–4, and, from a constitutional perspective, in book II, chapters 1–8, of De Lolme's *The Constitution of England.*

4/III/12: De Lolme, *Constitution of England*

18/11 Reid's notes are taken from book II, chs 1–4 and 6–8 of De Lolme's *The Constitution of England.*
18/15 De Lolme, *Constitution*, pp. 170–81.
18/24 De Lolme, *Constitution*, pp. 181–89.
18/25 De Lolme, *Constitution*, pp. 191–94.
18/29 De Lolme, *Constitution*, pp. 195–99.
18/31 De Lolme, *Constitution*, pp. 210–16.
18/32 De Lolme, *Constitution*, pp. 238–54.

4/III/20: Contareni, *De magistratibus*

19/2 Gasparo Contareni, *De magistratibus & republica Venetorum libri quinque* (Venice, 1592).
19/21 Contareni, *De magistratibus*, pp. 10b–11a.

4/III/22: Folkes, *Table of Coins*

20/2 Martin Folkes, *A Table of English Silver Coins from the Norman Conquest to the Present Time. With their Weights, Intrinsic Values, and some Remarks upon the Several Pieces* (London, 1745).

4/III/23b: Goudar, *Les intérêts*

21/1 [Ange Goudar], *Les intérêts de la France mal entendus, dans les branches de l'agriculture, de la population, des finances, de commerce, de la marine, & de l'industrie*, 3 vols (Amsterdam, 1756).
21/3 [Goudar], *Les intérêts*, vol. I, pp. 9–10.

Part Two: Lectures on Politics

4/III/1: Principles of Politics 1765

22/0 We believe that this manuscript was the opening lecture on politics in 1765. If so, it would have been delivered on Tuesday 16 April, by which point in his course Reid was pressed for time, and this seems to account for the brevity of the opening remarks and the abrupt transition to the specific topic of despotism. For the timing, see the evidence in Reid, *Practical Ethics*, pp. 244–45, note 9. The discussion is considerably elaborated in the dated opening lecture from the following year, which we print after the present manuscript.

22/1 In the manuscript as it has been preserved, this is the third page. However, whether or not Reid presented the heads of his lectures on politics to the class, or whether the list was only for his own use, the page clearly provides a 'table of contents' that serves its purpose best when put first. What is more, if the folding of the sheet has been reversed over time, the 'heads' would in fact have come on the first page.

23/8 Cf. Reid, *Active Powers*, p. 179: 'The science of politics borrows its principles from what we know by experience of the character and conduct of man. We consider not what he ought to be, but what he is, and thence conclude what part he will act in different situations and circumstances. From such principles we reason concerning the causes and effects of different forms of government, laws, customs, and manners. If man were either more perfect or more imperfect, a better or worse creature than he is, politics would be a different science from what it is.'

23/11 The fullest explanation of the role of axioms or first principles in the structure of knowledge in general is given in Reid, *Intellectual Powers*, essay VI, ch. 4, pp. 452–67. The earliest account is in Reid, *Philosophical Orations*, in the conclusion of oration II (reproduced in Reid, *University*). Reid details the nature and function of first principles in moral reasoning in *Active Powers*, essay III, part iii, ch. 6, pp. 176–80, and essay V, ch. 1, pp. 270–78. See the latter work, pp. 271–72, note 1, for axiomatic usage in a variety of Reid's manuscripts. Concerning reasoning in politics, see also *Intellectual Powers*, pp. 488–89 and 558–59; and in political economy, below, pp. 57–62. For natural philosophy, see Reid, *Animate Creation*, p. 201. The list of first principles in this lecture should be compared with the one on pp. 30–32.

24/6 Montesquieu, *The Spirit of the Laws* (1748), book II, ch. 1: 'There are three kinds of government: REPUBLICAN, MONARCHICAL, and DESPOTIC. To discover the nature of each, the idea of them held by the least educated of men is sufficient. I assume three definitions, or rather, three facts: one *republican government is that in which the people as a body, or only a part of the people, have sovereign power; monarchical government is that in which one alone governs, but by fixed and established laws; whereas, in despotic government, one alone, without law and without rule, draws everything along by his will and caprices*' (p. 10).

24/7 Montesquieu, *The Spirit of the Laws*, book XI, ch. 6: 'In each state there are three sorts of powers: legislative power, executive power over the things depending on the right of nations, and executive power over the things depending on civil right' (p. 156). Reid presumably also had in mind Locke's separation of legislative, executive and federative powers read in light of Montesquieu; cf. Locke, *Two Treatises of Government* (1690), second treatise, chs 12–14.

24/8 Montesquieu's discussion of taxes is in *The Spirit of the Laws*, book XIII. Cf. also Reid, *Practical Ethics*, p. 159.

24/9 Reid's portrait of despotism is a somewhat free compilation with the following parts of *The Spirit of the Laws* as the main sources: book II, ch. 4 (final paragraph); book III, chs. 8–10; book V, chs. 14–16; book VI, ch. 1; book X, chs. 16–17. It is likely that Reid here and elsewhere in the lectures made use also of Paul Rycaut, *The History of the Present State of the Ottoman Empire containing the Maxims of the Turkish Polity, the most Material Points of the Mahometan Religion, their Sects and Heresies, their Convents and Religious Votaries, their Military Discipline, with an Exact computation of their Forces by Land and Sea* (1666), a work upon which Montesquieu drew.

24/11 See Montesquieu, *The Spirit of the Laws*, book V, ch. 14; book VI, ch. 1.

24/13 See Montesquieu, *The Spirit of the Laws*, book III, ch. 8; book VI, ch. 1.

24/15 See Montesquieu, *The Spirit of the Laws*, book V, ch. 14; book VI, ch. 1.

24/29 See Montesquieu, *The Spirit of the Laws*, book II, ch. 5.

4/III/3: Principles of Politics 1766

25/9 Both the heading and the content show that this was the opening lecture on politics in Reid's second year of lecturing at Glasgow. It is therefore a longer and more detailed version of the preceding lecture.

25/35 Concerning the relationship between political jurisprudence and politics, see the Introduction, pp. lx–lxiii.

26/3 Reid alludes to the common experience in a religiously divided Europe that toleration might be seen as a right to freedom of religion or as a prudent political means of promoting civic peace. His specific reference has been to the provision for a degree of toleration of Dissenters after the Revolution of 1688–89.

26/16 The organic analogy for society and the medical analogy for politics were common and often adopted by Reid. For example, the following is found in a fragmentary manuscript of his (MS 2131/7/VII/9, 1r. Cf. also Reid, *Active Powers*, pp. 148–49):

> A human Society has an obvious Resemblance to a human Body. The one consists of Many Members as well as the other. The Members have their different functions. As in the Natural Body there is a head to contrive and direct, hands to Execute, a Stomach to digest, bones to support and Strenthen, and Sinews to move the various parts. All these are made to cooperate for the good of the whole body‹.› Their Natural Function and Office is … to serve the Body in their several ways, and they are then in their most natural and perfect state when best fitted and disposed to serve the common interest. The same may easily be applied to the political Body. Whose Members have various offices assigned them for the common Good. The Resemblance between the Natural and the Political Body is so obvious and Striking that it has been observed in all Nations and in the rudest ages. The Fable of Menenius Agrippa recorded in the Second book of Livy is a sufficient Evidence of this.

26/27 Cf. Reid, *Intellectual Powers*, p. 53: 'In politics, we reason, for the most part, from analogy.'

27/2 Cf. note 23/11, p. 160.

27/10 Like Adam Smith and many others in the Enlightenment, Reid switched without hesitation between organic and mechanical analogies for political phenomena.

28/2 Reid devotes the fourth essay of his *Active Powers* to the question 'Of the Liberty of Moral Agents', with the key chapter for the present discussion being chapter 4, 'Of the Influence of Motives'.

30/27 The first objection against the possibility of a science of politics was the argument from the freedom of will; see page 28, lines 1–14. Here Reid considers the objection discussed by Hume in 'That politics may be reduced to a science', namely that politics is so dependent upon the particular characters of those who govern ('administer') that general principles cannot be found. Reid seems to have countered the objection with Hume's arguments, showing regularities according to the constitutional form of governance, for his formulation is close to that of Hume. Reid's reference to Hume's essay as 'No. 3' indicates that he was using the first edition in which that essay was so numbered, the recent *Essays and Treatises on Several Subject* (1764).

30/32 Folio 3r in the manuscript contains a small note on commerce. Although Reid indicated that his discussion of despotism would include its effect on commerce, there is no indication that this note was part of such a discussion. The note is most likely an isolated passage out of sequence (AUL, MS 2131/4/III/3, 3r):

> Commerce has of Late been made a Subject of Philosophical Disquisition; and as it must be acknowledged to be both a curious and interesting Subject, it has been pursued by many able Writers with much ingenuity, and with considerable Success.
>
> It has been made abundantly evident that very gross mistakes in the Political Eoconomy of States have been committed and are still committed through Ignorance of the Principles of Commerce. Future ages must reap benefit from every discovery of this kind, and may on the other hand be greatly hurt by false Notions upon this Subject.

30/33 The following sequence of numbered 'axioms' should be compared with the 'General Principles of Action' in the introductory lecture of 1765, pp. 23–24, and with the 'principles' mentioned just above in the present manuscript, pp. 26–27. In the list here, axioms 5–8 have not been preserved.

31/15 1 Timothy 1:9.

31/35 A central theme of Reid's essay 'Some Thoughts on the Utopian System' was that private property tends to corrupt the morals of people. See pp. 139–40.

4/III/2: Principles of Politics 1766, *cont.*

32/18 This manuscript is undated and may be from either the second or a subsequent year of lecturing at Glasgow.

4/III/5: Despotic Government. Aristocracy

34/27 As shown by the date, we here resume the sequence of Reid's lectures in 1765. Cf. note to 25/9.

34/31 The following discussion is clearly deeply informed by the analysis of despotism that runs through Montesquieu's *The Spirit of the Laws*. However, Reid's comments are not taken directly from specific passages in Montesquieu.

36/26 'Slavery, like a sickly Constitution, grows in time so habitual, that it seems no Burden nor Disease; it creates a kind of laziness, and idle despondency, which puts Men beyond hopes and fears: it mortifies Ambition, Emulation, and other troublesome, as well as active qualities, which Liberty and Freedom beget.' Robert Molesworth, *An Account of Denmark as it was in the Year 1692*, p. 75.

36/37 See Montesquieu, *The Spirit of the Laws*, book III, ch. 17.

37/8 Reid is referring to Aristotle's *Politics*, III.7.

37/14 The terminology and the analysis that follow stand squarely in the tradition of Harringtonian republicanism that Reid explicitly invokes. The points that Reid makes are themes throughout *Oceana* (1656) and will be taken up in detail below. In this tradition, 'Gothic' aristocracy generally meant feudalism.

38/5 Reid took extensive notes from vol. II of George Lyttelton, first Baron Lyttelton, *The History of the Life of King Henry the Second, and of the Age in which He Lived*. We print these notes at pp. 5–10.

4/III/7: Harrington's Oceana

38/6 This one-page manuscript seems to have been dislocated from its original place in the sequence, which is clearly indicated by the dates, and we place it accordingly within 4/III/5.

38/7 Harrington sets out his principles of a true republic, or 'ancient prudence', in the first part of 'The Preliminaries' in *Oceana* (in James Harrington, *The Political Works*, pp. 161–87), while the 'modern prudence', that is, post-classical, especially 'Gothic', corruption of proper government, is explained in the second part. This sets the stage for 'Oceana', Harrington's republican projection of England as the revived and purified ancient prudence that will rescue Europe from the bankruptcy that was feudalism. Reid picks up three key principles from 'The Preliminaries' and then proceeds to the main work.

38/9 According to Harrington, the only natural (as distinct from violent) foundation of 'domestic empire' is property, of which land is the only truly stable form. *Oceana*, p. 163. The ideal arrangement, namely that of Oceana, is a distribution of landed property that is sufficiently equal to secure a perpetual 'balance of dominion', so that 'no one man or number of men within the compass of the few or aristocracy can come to overpower the whole people by their possessions in lands'. *Oceana*, p. 181.

38/11 See *Oceana*, p. 181.

38/13 Ibid.

38/15 The main section of Harrington's *Oceana* is 'The Model of the Commonwealth of Oceana' (pp. 210–340), in which one of his main devices of composition was the detailing of thirty 'orders' that organise the imaginary society. Starting from 'the materials' for the 'building of a commonwealth', namely the people, Harrington began with orders that 'distribute' the people according to various basic criteria. Reid picks up a number of these orders, the first one being the distribution into free citizens and servants (p. 212), where the criterion is whether or not the person has the means of living independently of service for others. Civic status in Oceana was thus not hereditary but could be lost as well as acquired through the loss or acquisition of its material foundation (pp. 213, 216, 261–62).

38/16 Here is one of several indications that Reid was so immersed in Harrington's work that he felt free to use it from memory. He has reversed the order of the second and third orders in *Oceana*, giving first the distribution of the people according to property. Showing the close link in this form of republican thought between property, arms and civic status, the order creates an upper 'class' of those 'who have one hundred pounds a year in lands, goods or monies' and hence are 'of the horse', while those who have less are 'of the foot'. The former are the basis for the Senate; the latter are the popular assembly (*Oceana*, p. 213).

38/17 This is Harrington's second order (cf. the previous note). The distribution according to age is also of matter of military concern: 'the youth shall be the marching armies, and the elders the standing garrisons of this nation' (*Oceana*, p. 213).

38/18 'The fourth order distributeth the people, according unto the places of their habitation, unto parishes, hundreds and tribes. – For except the people be methodically distributed, they cannot be methodically collected, but the being of a commonwealth consisteth in the methodical collection of the people' (*Oceana*, pp. 213–14). This distribution is central to Oceana: 'the whole territory of Oceana, consisting of about ten thousand parishes, came to be cast into one thousand hundreds, and into fifty tribes' (p. 220). The parishes are organised by orders 1–6; the hundreds by order 7; the tribes by orders 8–12.

38/23 This summarises the fifth order, concerning the election of officers of the parishes (*Oceana*, pp. 214–15).

38/23 This is organised in detail in *Oceana*'s sixth order (*Oceana*, pp. 216–17).

38/24 Presumably the final two points were looking forward to the next lecture.

38/26 '*The seventh order*, requiring that … the deputies of every parish annually assemble in arms at the rendezvous of the hundred, and there elect out of their number one justice of the peace, one juryman, one captain, one ensign of their troop or century, each of these out of the horse, and one juryman, one crowner, one high constable, out of the foot' (*Oceana*, p. 218).

38/29 'Jury men Overseers of the Ballot' is a later addition. This is a point that Harrington makes after he has listed the officers elected out of the horse and out of the foot (*Oceana*, p. 218).

39/2 The details of the ballot make up the rest the seventh order (*Oceana*, pp. 218–20).

39/3 *Oceana*, p. 220.

39/4 *Oceana*, p. 221.

39/6 This is the eighth order (*Oceana*, pp. 221–22).

39/7 For a description of the pavilions, where the urns for balloting were kept and the officers of elections were seated, see *Oceana*, p. 220. The elaborate arrangements for the ballot are given in order 9 (p. 222).

39/22 Reid has made a valiant effort at summarising the labyrinthine election of officers of the tribes set out in order 10 (*Oceana*, pp. 223–24), where the deputies are ordered into 'middle, outward and inward' files and their turn at drawing balls from their respective urns is determined by lot. The drawing of gold balls, as described by Reid, determines the four orders, each consisting of six electors, who will, order by order, vote in secret for six 'competitors' for each of the magistracies mentioned.

39/32 This paragraph summarises the eleventh order, setting out 'the duties and functions of the magistrates' (*Oceana*, pp. 225–26).

39/33 'the lists of the tribes, youth and elders … give the whole number of people bearing arms. This account, being annually recorded by the master of the rolls, is called the Pillar of Nilus, because the people, being the riches of the Commonwealth, as they are found to rise or fall by the degrees of this pillar, like that river [the Nile], give account of the public harvest' (*Oceana*, p. 226). Reid makes use of this comparison in his discussion paper, 'Whether By proper Laws the number of Births in every parish might not be doubled, or at least greatly increased?' See p. 91.

39/36 The two knights elected by each tribe become senators for three years, sitting in 'the Pantheon or palace of justice'; the seven deputies of each tribe sit in the 'Emporium' as representatives of the people for three years and are known as 'the prerogative tribe' or 'the people'. This is the twelfth order (*Oceana*, pp. 226–27).

39/37 For Harrington, 'empire or sovereign power' is 'the natural product' of 'dominion' (property); consequently, the extent of the power of the people depends on its property. The agrarian law is aimed at curbing individual wealth to avoid concentration of power and at securing a distribution of it that ensures a wide popular basis for the exercise of political-cum-military power. In *Oceana* the thirteenth order decrees laws of inheritance that over time will achieve maximum wealth, yielding around £2,000 per annum and a high degree of equality also for those below this level. A key feature in this is the abolition of primogeniture. The regulations for the neighbouring 'Marpesia' (Scotland) are more restrictive (*Oceana*, p. 231).

40/5 The constitution of the Senate is set out in the fifteenth order (*Oceana*, pp. 247–48).

40/7 The four councils are set up by the sixteenth order, and the ambassadors (to France, Spain, Venice and Constantinople) are elected according to the seventeenth order. By the eighteenth order, election of officers on 'emergent occasions' happens through a procedure of scrutiny, except for the office of a dictator, which is determined in the following order.

40/8 Reid skipped the very detailed orders 19 and 20 for the actual operation of the councils (*Oceana*, pp. 250–53 and 255–57) and turned to the discussion of the popular assembly (*Oceana*, p. 266).

40/10 This is by the twenty-first order (*Oceana*, p. 267).

40/11 See order 22 (*Oceana*, p. 267). Reid does not refer to order 23, 'showing the power, function, and manner of proceeding of the prerogative tribe' (*Oceana*, p. 281), i.e. the legislative and judicial powers.

40/12 The twenty-fourth order provides for knights and deputies from the 'provinces' of Marpesia (Scotland) and Pamopea (Ireland) (*Oceana*, pp. 286–87).

4/III/5: Harrington's Oceana, cont.

40/13 It is unclear why Reid repeats the date. The disorder of the manuscripts (see note 38/6) may have begun with himself.

40/14 Reid ignores the twenty-fifth order, which concerns the fiscal arrangements of Oceana. The twenty-sixth order organises the 'youth', that is, the men of eighteen to thirty years of age, as the 'marching' army of Oceana. There are three steps by which the men are listed for military trials, and Harrington uses the word 'essay' for the list itself, for those on the list and for the trials they are to perform (*Oceana*, pp. 300–2).

4/III/6: Reflections on Harrington. Other Commonwealths

40/15 Although this single folio has been preserved as the end-sheet of 4/III/6, its content follows upon 4/III/5. It is partly a retrospect, partly an elaboration of the preceding overview of Harrington's system, whereas the material that appears first in 4/III/6 (as the manuscript has been preserved) presents Reid's assessment of that system, partly on its own terms, partly according to its relevance to current British politics. We print the paper in the sequence demanded by this reading, but cf. also note 40/13.

40/29 Here Reid enters forcefully into one of the most hotly disputed issues in eighteenth-century Scotland, namely who had the right to elect ministers in the Kirk: patrons from the nobility, or elders, or the congregation more generally? The Presbyterian form of church government had been re-established in Scotland in 1690, but the Patronage Act of 1712 opened the way for local magnates, heritors and leading elders to determine the election of ministers. Nevertheless, when such leaders did not act, the way was open for popular election by people whom the intellectuals of the Enlightenment, such as Francis Hutcheson, considered too uneducated and too vulnerable to the influence of fundamentalist preachers to be entrusted with ministerial elections. It is noteworthy that Reid's concern is somewhat different, namely the insufficient time available for ministerial candidates to make their mark. He may have been speaking from personal experience of his rocky start as a young minister at New Machar.

41/31 This folio has the character of what Reid lists in the 'Heads' of his lectures as 'Reflexions upon this [Harrington's] Model of Government' (p. 22), yet he has not covered every 'Head' so far. However, on the reverse of the page he gives brief notes that seem intended to cover 'Titles of honour' and 'Provincial Governments'.

42/15 The four historical examples illustrate the four causes of popularly induced despotism. First, the transition of ancient Israel from a theocratic republic to a monarchy with the election of Saul is a recurring theme in Harrington's *Oceana* (e.g. p. 175). Secondly, the Restoration of Charles II in 1660 was by Parliament. Thirdly, following Cromwell's death and the ensuing political uncertainty, Harrington feared that one of the great dangers for the creation of an 'equal' Commonwealth was that the religious fundamentalists and self-declared saints backed by the army would take power in a nation that by then had had only sporadic experience of even an unequal Commonwealth for half a generation. As a consequence Harrington issued this prophecy in *A Discourse upon this Saying: The Spirit of the Nation is not yet to be trusted with Liberty; lest it introduce Monarchy, or invade the Liberty of Conscience* (1669), reproduced in Harrington, *The Political Works*, pp. 735–45, at pp. 744–45:

> We hope ye are saints: but if you be men, look with all your might, with all your prudence, above all with the fervent imploration of God's gracious assistance … unto the well-ordering of your commonwealth. In the manner consists the main matter. Detest the base itch of narrow oligarchy. If your commonwealth be rightly instituted, seven years will not pass ere our clusters of parties, civil and religious, vanish, not through any force, as when the cold weather kills flies, but by the rising of greater light, as when the sun puts out candles. These in the reason of the thing are demonstrable, but suit better with the spirit of the present times, by way of prophecy. England shall raise her head to ancient glory, the heavens shall be of the old metal, the earth no longer lead, nor shall the sounding air eternally renounce the trumpet of fame.

Fourthly, the introduction of absolutism in Denmark in 1660 was a standard feature of the Whig image of that form of monarchy, shaped in particular by Molesworth's *An Account of Denmark*; cf. note 36/26.

42/33 The distribution happens not through a census, but through the first of the many 'orders' by means of which Oceana is structured (*Oceana*, p. 212); cf. note 38/15.

43/10 For Reid's understanding of the three 'interests' making up modern commercial society, see his paper on the storing or warehousing of grain, pp. 107–9; and his paper on interest, pp. 128–29, where he also outlines the emergence of the new 'interest', that of money; cf. pp. lvi–lvii.

43/10 The remaining notes on this folio are a later addition. Their topic is what in the 'Heads' of the lectures is billed as 'Other Commonwealths Ideal or Real', which is listed as following upon Reid's 'Reflexions' on Harrington, but he had already begun on other commonwealths earlier (pp. 37–38) and more follows in the remaining part of the present manuscript.

43/12 See Saint-Pierre's dream of an institution devoted to the cultivation of the science of politics, in his *Ouvrajes de politique, Vol. III: Projet pour perfectioner le gouvernement des etats* (1733), Premier partie: 'Sur la grande utilité d'une academie politique'.

43/29 See p. 51 and notes 51/30 and 51/34.

4/III/14: Monarchy

44/12 The text on 1r–v of this manuscript is in the same ink and writing style as the preceding and subsequent dated manuscripts from 1765. We therefore conjecture that it has been used during the otherwise undocumented period 23–28 April 1765. This is consistent with the content's general fit with topics 9 and 10 in the 'Heads' of lectures. In the margin of 1r Reid has indicated 'Add A'. This refers to 2r–v, where he has added material, in different ink, to elaborate on the original text. One part of the addition elaborates on Montesquieu's general principles, while the other is a more detailed discussion of the kind of honour that pertains to monarchy. However, Reid has not written the additional material so that it forms continuous prose with particular formulations in the original text, and it is not possible to insert it without causing confusion. Accordingly we print the two parts of the addition separately after the original text. In the original material, 1r–v, Reid is using Montesquieu to make his points, but he is not providing a systematic or sequential presentation of the relevant discussions in *The Spirit of the Laws*, and so it is somewhat arbitrary which points in the latter work we draw attention to. In contrast, the added material gives a fairly specific exposition of points in Montesquieu.

44/19 Montesquieu distinguished between the nature and the principle of the various forms of government; a government's 'nature is that which makes it what it is, and its principle, that which makes it act. The one is its particular structure, and the other is the human passions that set it in motion'; Montesquieu, *The Spirit of the Laws*, book III, ch. 1. The rest of book III sets out the principles mentioned by Reid.

44/20 See especially Montesquieu, *The Spirit of the Laws*, book III, ch. 17.

44/28 The basic outlines of the nature and principle of monarchy are in Montesquieu, *The Spirit of the Laws*, book II, ch. 4, and book III, chs 5–8.

44/33 Montesquieu, *The Spirit of the Laws*, book V, ch. 9.

45/2 Montesquieu, *The Spirit of the Laws*, book IV, ch. 2.

45/4 Montesquieu, *The Spirit of the Laws*, book III, ch. 5.

45/31 Here begins the first part of the additional material. See note 44/12.

45/34 Cf. note 44/19.

46/23 Here begins the second part of the additional material. See note 44/12.

4/III/11: The British Constitution

47/26 This manuscript is undated. It overlaps with both the preceding and, especially, the following manuscript, and it may be a later supplement to the latter.

47/32 To some extent influenced by Montesquieu's analysis in *The Spirit of the Laws*, book XI, ch. 6, and drawing on his knowledge of British constitutional history, Reid has combined different lines of analysis. In the background lies the ancient idea of the mixed constitution of democratic, aristocratic and monarchical elements. But his main division is into the separate functions of the three constituent parts of the sovereign power: the judicial, the legislative and the executive. Within this arrangement, he deals with the balance of powers between Crown and subjects and with the changing balance among the latter between nobility and commons, and within the commons the emergence of a new factor, that of the financial sector. All of this then leads up to his analysis of the changing system of parties and factions.

48/3 'Attainder' in criminal law was the complete loss of civil rights as a consequence of being sentenced to death; this included the 'corruption of the blood', that is, the disruption of lines of inheritance. However, attainder was also used as a political weapon. In earlier history it was used mainly by the Crown, whereas after the Revolution of 1688–89 it was used mainly by Parliament as a threat to control ministers of the Crown. It took the form of an Act of Attainder against a particular individual and was a prosecution without the requirement of common legal procedures before both Houses of Parliament in its capacity as the 'supreme judicature'. Cf. Blackstone, *Commentaries*, vol. IV, pp. 256 and 373ff.

48/4 The best contemporary account of the constitutional status of the monarchy is Blackstone, *Commentaries*, vol. I, chs 3–8. Volume I of the *Commentaries* was published only in 1765 and may not have been available to Reid when he first shaped his politics lectures for his course in Glasgow. But the shorter precursor of Blackstone's main work, his *An Analysis of the Laws of England*, had appeared in 1756 and had reached its fifth edition by 1762.

48/6 This refers to the 1701 Act of Settlement, which was occasioned by the death of Queen Anne's son, the Duke of Gloucester, in 1700. The Act settled – among other things – that only Protestant heirs to the throne of England were eligible and singled out one such heir, namely Princess Sophia, Electress of Hanover and granddaughter of James I. When both she and Queen Anne died in 1714, Sophia's son succeeded to the throne as George I. The principle of Protestant-only succession was a central part of the Revolution settlement in 1689, and the Act was incorporated into the Act of Union that created the new state of Great Britain in 1707. As Reid indicates, the Act provides for succession to the crown by means of the principles of succession to real estate at common law.

48/9 Reid has in mind the right to sit in the House of Lords, where the Scottish peers had to elect sixteen representatives, as provided for by the Treaty of Union of 1707.

48/20 In England the qualification for voting in the shires was restricted to freeholders with land to the value of forty shillings per annum, while in the boroughs it varied considerably, some voting corporately, others giving the vote to freemen. See Blackstone, *Commentaries*, vol. I, pp. 165–69. For Scotland after the Union, see note 48/23.

48/22 Reid's attention to feudalism is evident both from his reading of Lyttelton's *History of Henry the Second* (see pp. 3–10), from his deep interest in the Harringtonian interpretation of English history (see pp. 38–44) and in Montesquieu, who provided the European background in books 30–31 of *The Spirit of the Laws*. An authoritative history of feudal law had been published a few years before Reid's lectures in Glasgow, namely John Dalrymple, *An Essay Towards a General History of Feudal Property in Great Britain* (1757). He would undoubtedly also have been aware of Henry Home (later Lord Kames), *Essays upon Several Subjects concerning British Antiquities*, essay I, *Introduction of the Feudal Law into Scotland* (1747) and Kames's *Historical Law-Tracts* (1758), especially tracts III and V. As far as changes to feudal law are concerned, Reid may have had in mind the gradual dissolution in England of feudal laws and practices in tune with the rise of the Commons and the growth of commerce, and especially the dismantling by English courts of feudal property law, especially entails and primogeniture, so as to open up land for commerce. He would certainly have been aware of the campaign by Scottish reformers, led by Kames, to follow the English example and get rid of the feudal laws of property in Scottish law. This cause had been aired forcefully in Reid's lecture hall by his predecessor immediately before his arrival; see Smith, *Lectures on Jurisprudence*, (A) i.115–ii.1 and (B) 159–69; cf. Haakonssen, *The Science of a Legislator*, pp. 165–71.

48/23 In continuation of feudal law, Scots law maintained superiority and vassalage. However, the prerogative that only the superior of a given area could vote, whereas those who had the right to occupy, possess and use the land had no vote, had been revised by the Scottish Parliament in 1681. As a result, those who held land of the Crown worth £400 Scots (a little over £30 sterling) were entitled to the vote. This was maintained after the Union along with the forty-shilling freehold rule (see note 48/20). See *An abridgment of the public statutes in force and use relative to Scotland, from the union, in the fifth year of Queen Anne, to the twenty-seventh year of his present Majesty King George II, inclusive* (1755), vol. II, s.v. 'Parliament', section LXXVIII–LXXIX and XC.

48/25 In Scotland the sheriff was commonly in charge of such things as collecting claims to changes to the electoral roll and the presentation of this material to the Michaelmas meeting of the sheriff's head court, which was the meeting of heritors at which the electoral roll was revised. The sheriff also executed writs for elections to Parliament, fixed the date for the head court and called the meeting. See *An abridgment of the public statutes in force and use relative to Scotland*, s.v. 'Parliament', *passim*.

48/26 All soldiers had to remove at least two miles from any place of election at the latest the day before the election and were not to approach such a place until the day after the election.

48/27 For a contemporary account of the following, see the brief overview in Blackstone, *Commentaries*, vol. I, pp. 174–82. For a modern scholarly account of the workings of the House of Commons, see Thomas, *The House of Commons in the Eighteenth Century*.

48/35 Preparation in fair hand of legal documents, here when they passed between the two Houses of Parliament.

48/37 Part of the old Palace of Westminster that was destroyed by fire in 1834. The room was used for state ceremonies, including joint sittings of the two Houses of Parliament.

48/39 That is, the table of the House of Commons.

49/1 The habeas corpus act was suspended during the Jacobite insurrections of 1715 and 1745.

49/1 By contemporary standards Great Britain had a high degree of press freedom in the eighteenth century. Pre-publication censorship of print had ended in 1695, when Parliament did not renew the Licensing Act from 1662. Thereafter the main weapon to control publication was prosecution for libel, often supported by general warrants for arrest of unnamed persons and for search and seizure of unspecified papers and other property. This came to an end with the case of John Wilkes' onslaught, in his periodical the *North Briton*, on the King's speech to open Parliament in 1763. Despite Wilkes' notoriety, Parliament made general warrants illegal in 1766. In other words, the issue was topical when Reid gave his lectures. Other restrictions on the press were Parliament's ban on reporting of its proceedings, which was given up in 1771, and the enforcement of stamp duty, which was introduced in 1715.

49/4 A reference to the woolsack on which the Lord Chancellor sat as Speaker of the House of Lords.

49/5 Acts of amnesty that erase the crime itself.

49/8 In England the role of the Justices of the Peace (JPs) had grown steadily since their introduction early in the fourteenth century, to encompass not only judicial and policing tasks but also public works and other public services. In Scotland this development was both later and slower. Here the office was introduced by a statute of 1587, but only with the abolition of the Scottish Privy Council in 1708 and of the heritable local jurisdictions in 1747 did Scottish JPs acquire significance. Commissioners of Supply were introduced on a shire basis in Scotland by an act of 1667 in order to settle the value of estates as the basis for the cess (land tax), but gradually, from the late seventeenth century until local government reforms in the late nineteenth century, their functions were extended and became more and more those of county councils, and they were thus supplementing the work of the JPs. The commissioners were the privy councillors (until the abolition of the Council), senators (judges) of the College of Justice (the body encompassing the supreme civil and criminal courts of Scotland) who had property in the shire, and appointed landowners.

49/10 That is, the monarch calls and dissolves Parliament.

49/11 By the Test Acts of 1673 and 1678 (modified by the Bill of Rights of 1689) both civil and military officers under the Crown had to take the oaths of supremacy and of allegiance, make a declaration denying transubstantiation in the sacrament of the Lord's Supper and receive that sacrament in the Anglican Church.

49/11 The maintenance of an armed force within the realm required an annual act of Parliament in order to comply with the Bill of Rights of 1689. These acts provided for the discipline of the military, hence the name.

49/20 The enumeration begun here does not seem to be continued.

49/27 The sequence of five points beginning here is indicated by the size and position of the numerals in the margin of the manuscript. In order to avoid confusion with the numbers of the sub-sequence, we print the former numbers in bold.

49/28 In his discussion of the role of parties, Reid was taking up one of the key factors in English and British politics of the preceding century, and he was clearly particularly interested in a line of authors who not only wrote about but contributed to the political process. As a member of William of Orange's invasion army, the Huguenot historian Paul de Rapin de Thoyras was a participant observer of the Revolution of 1688–89, who subsequently wrote highly influential Whiggish accounts of the party division that had led up to and then been transformed by the Revolution. His work was therefore useful to Lord Bolingbroke, when in the 1730s the latter tried to cement a 'country' interest into a new party. He saw it as a fusion of dissident, more or less radical and republican Whigs and renegade Tories who, like himself, would subscribe to Revolution principles, ancient constitutionalism, (quasi-Harringtonian) ideals of land ownership, political authority and so on. But first of all they shared sharp opposition to the 'Court' interest, that is, the establishment Whigs in government, who were seen to stand for the 'corruption' that was deficit financing of large government, including military adventures overseas, the dominance of the 'monied interest', and the crown's control over Parliament through the disposal of offices. Part of this political rhetoric was the opposition between 'party' and 'faction', the former being defined by the pursuit of the 'common good', the latter by that of sectional interests. However, part of Bolingbroke's story was that most parties had been transient formations to meet particular political crises, and only factionalism had given them life beyond this. This was the case with Tories and Whigs, who were now irrelevant. The drift of this argument was that a party that had a grip on the truly common good was a party of the whole country and thus not really a party, except to the extent that it was resisted by a cabal of 'court' interests, that is, by a faction. This was the point of the pamphlet by the Edinburgh Professor of Moral Philosophy [William Cleghorn], *The Spirit and Principles of the Whigs and Jacobites Compared. Being the Substance of a Discourse delivered to an Audience of Gentlemen at Edinburgh 22 December 1745* (London, 1746). Cleghorn's discourse was an attempt to settle the ideological score between Whigs and Jacobites, before the military score had been finally settled. Cleghorn had enrolled in the University company of volunteers to defend the city against the Jacobite forces earlier in the year. Cleghorn made the point that a party that has the universal common good of the community as its aim is a party to end all parties, and he maintained that the Whigs were precisely such a party. But of course they were now defined by having the Jacobites as their opposition and were, in that sense, the established Whigs. By invoking Cleghorn, Reid thus added yet another complication to the politics of party, and, as one of his notes indicates, it was a 'Scottish' complication. In Scotland it was Whig versus Jacobite, not Whig versus Tory, that was the important division and, as Reid also indicated, this was again closely connected with associations of political and religious 'parties' that were different from those in England. Finally, it should be remembered that it was into this debate that Hume entered with his analysis of party politics in a number of his essays, especially 'Of Parties in General' (1741), 'Of the Parties of Great Britain' (1741) and 'Of the Coalition of Parties' (1758). One of Hume's central points was a rejection of Bolingbroke's whole idea of a politics beyond parties. Like it or not, parties were integral to the British political system, but many of their unfortunate qualities could be ameliorated by an understanding of why they came about and how they functioned. To this end Hume had made a general distinction between 'personal' and 'real' parties, and the latter he again divided into parties based on interest, principle and affection. These three categories have similarities with Reid's a few lines below, except that Hume's third category is of positive affections, Reid's of hostile affections.

50/12 Concerning the concepts of party and faction, see our Introduction, pp. l–li and note 49/28.

50/14 Paul de Rapin de Thoyras, *Dissertation sur les Whigs et les Torys; or, an Historical Dissertation upon Whig and Tory* (1717); Henry St

John, Viscount Bolingbroke, *Dissertation upon Parties* (1734); [William Cleghorn], *The Spirit and Principles of the Whigs and Jacobites Compared.* Cf. note 49/28.

50/22 It is unclear whether this inserted line belongs to the preceding or the following text.

50/39 David Hume, 'Of the Independency of Parliament', in *Essays Moral, Political and Literary*, pp. 42–46.

51/6 Although the oaths imposed by the Test Act of 1673 were ameliorated by the 1689 Toleration Act and subsequent legislation, it was still the case during the eighteenth century that holders of any office under the crown, MPs, all teachers and preachers, and others, had to swear elaborate oaths of allegiance to and affirming the supremacy of the existing royal house, to abjure all other claimants – specifically those of the house of Stuart – to make a declaration against the doctrine of transubstantiation and, in England, receive communion in the Church of England at least once a year. These requirements were central to the complaints and political campaigns of Dissenters from the Church of England, who generally found wide sympathy in Scotland. In view of the pervasiveness of oaths in public life, it is not surprising that the topic was a standard one also in moral philosophy and jurisprudence, and we find evidence of Reid's treatment of it from this angle in his lectures on jurisprudence. See Reid, *Practical Ethics*, pp. 58–59, with the explanatory notes pp. 221–24.

51/22 There is no continuation of Reid's account, and since it ends in the middle of a sentence (itself an addition) in the middle of the page, it remains uncertain whether he himself broke off, or whether some pages have been lost. One thing speaks for the former, namely that the second half of the folio has been used for an entirely different topic and that this has been added at a later time. This addition corresponds with the topics for the very end of the lectures on politics, and we print it accordingly; see p. 69 and note 69/5.

4/III/8: The British Constitution, *cont.*

51/30 This is clearly a slip of the pen. It is Montesquieu who says the following about Harrington.

51/34 Montesquieu, *The Spirit of the Laws*, book XI, ch. 6. Reid's formulation may be an echo of the contemporary translation by Thomas Nugent:

'Harrington in his *Oceana*, has also inquired into the highest point of liberty to which the constitution of a state may be carried. But of him indeed it may be said, that for want of knowing the nature of real liberty, he busied himself in pursuit of an imaginary one, and that he built a Chalcedon tho' he had a Byzantium before his eyes.' See Montesquieu, *Spirit of Laws* (trans. [Thomas Nugent]), pp. 230–31.

52/6 Montesquieu, *The Spirit of the Laws*, book XI, ch. 6.

52/20 All of Montesquieu's works were published anonymously. *The Spirit of the Laws* was put on the Index of Prohibited Books in 1751 and was the subject of much clerical criticism, but it is not clear what Reid refers to in saying that the work was burned.

53/10 Edward III, King of England 1327–77; Edward, Prince of Wales , since the sixteenth century known as 'the Black Prince', the reasons for this being disputed.

53/12 George Villiers was created Duke of Buckingham in 1623.

53/17 Henry IV, King of England 1399–1413.

53/23 John, King of England 1199–1216.

53/30 Richard II, King of England 1377–99.

53/33 Henry VI, King of England 1422–71.

53/38 Literally scandal or libel of magnates, introduced in England by a statute of 1275. For the eighteenth-century understanding of it, see Blackstone, *Commentaries*, vol. III, pp. 123–24.

54/2 Francis Mitchell, who was stripped of his knighthood in 1621. Concerning 'attainder', see note 48/3.

54/3 The Act of Union between England and Scotland of 1707 provided in para. 22 for the election of sixteen representative peers from among the Scottish nobility to sit in the new Parliament of Great Britain, and it stipulated that the Scottish Parliament should settle the method of election. The Parliament did this by an act of 5 February 1707.

54/8 8 Henry VI c. 7, Electors of the Knights of the Shires Act, 1429; 10 Henry VI c. 2, Electors of the Knights of the Shires Act, 1432.

54/17 Copyhold of land was by unfree men (originally villeins) who owed services to the manor, the nature of which depended on the local customs and were recorded in the manorial courts. Tenants held copies of these records, hence the name. See Blackstone, *Commentaries*, vol. II, pp. 90–98.

4/III/9: Population. National Virtue. National Riches

54/23 Here begins the second section of Reid's lectures on politics, that concerned with 'police', the meaning of which he lays down in his opening remarks. Cf. Adam Smith's concept of 'police', in Smith, *Lectures on Jurisprudence*, (A) vi.1 – 8 (pp. 331–34) and (B) 203ff (pp. 486ff).

55/21 Reid undoubtedly had in mind the 'Bill for Naturalizing Foreign Protestants' that Robert Nugent introduced into Parliament in 1747–48 and again in 1751. Parliament rejected it on both occasions. This generated a considerable public debate in the press (especially in the *London Magazine* of January, August and September 1747, and October 1748) and in many pamphlets, of which Josiah Tucker's *Reflections on the Expediency of a Law for the Naturalization of Foreign Protestants* was the most substantial; part I – *Containing Historical Remarks on the Disposition and Behaviour of the Natives of this Island, in regard to Foreigners* (1751) — set the debate into the historical context of Whig notions of liberty and, not least, into the toleration debate; and part II – *Containing Important Queries relating to Commerce, The Employment of the Poor, The Landed and National Interest, Taxes of all Kinds, particularly the Poor Tax, The Real Interest of Tradesmen, Reformation of Morals, Constitution both in Church and State, the Duties of Humanity, and the Principles of the Christian Religion* (1752) – considered the kind of socio-economic (as well as ethical) issues that were Reid's concern in the present context. Tucker also set the debate in a European context, and Reid's mention of the Dutch experience may refer to a tract by the 'late Prince of Orange', presumably William IV, which Tucker quotes as suggesting that the Dutch policy of toleration had helped people the Republic, and that the immigrants had settled and brought not only their funds but also 'established many Trades, Fabricks, Manufactures, Arts and Sciences' (Tucker, *Reflections*, part II, p. 20, note).

55/25 Reid expands upon this issue in one of his discussion questions 'Whether By proper Laws the number of Births in every parish might not be doubled, or at least greatly increased?', where he explains each of the points mentioned in the lecture notes. We print this paper at pp. 88–92. In his discourse on the Utopian system, he puts his ideas on family policy into a wider theoretical context. See pp. 144–45.

55/28 See [Benjamin Franklin], *The Interest of Great Britain Considered with Regard to her Colonies and the Acquisitions of Canada and Guadaloupe. To which are Added, Observations Concerning the Increase of Mankind, Peopling of Countries, &c.* (1760), pp. 23, 56.

55/29 The background to Reid's remarks on population was an intense debate about the matter. Many of the issues had been canvassed in Montesquieu's *Persian Letters* (1721) (letters 112–22), but the most immediate context was a lively discussion in Scotland. The most common standpoint, namely that the world's population had been larger in ancient times and had declined in modern Europe, was articulated with sophistication by the Edinburgh minister Robert Wallace, especially in *A Dissertation on the Numbers of Mankind in Antient and Modern Times. In which the Superior Populousness of Antiquity is maintained* (1753). This had been read in manuscript by David Hume, who responded by developing the opposite standpoint in his essay 'Of the Populousness of Antient Nations', published in *Political Discourses* (1752), and Wallace continued the debate by criticizing Hume in an extensive Appendix to *A Dissertation*. Reid's brief remarks indicate that he was largely in agreement with Wallace's central argument, that the world had always been able to maintain a larger population than it did at any given time, but that physical and moral causes prevented this. The task was to understand these changing causes so that their effect could be remedied. While early societies had failed to live up to their full demographic potential for the kind of reasons that Reid indicates, they had still been far more highly populated than modern societies, in which a plethora of moral causes combined to create a serious population deficit. Reid's points are largely consonant with Wallace's extensive analysis of moral causes, which is summarised in *A Dissertation* (pp. 83–84).

55/37 It is unclear what Reid intended here.

57/6 Cf. pp. xlvii–xlviii.

57/9 Montesquieu, *The Spirit of the Laws*, book III, ch. 3.

57/14 The third topic under 'police' was 'learning', but beyond the present reminder no further notes seem to have survived for it. The words 'Learning and Arts' and the points made below the horizontal line are later additions to the manuscript. The points about riches are developed in the following lecture.

4/III/15: National Riches. Commerce. Money. False Maxims

57/23 This manuscript is undated, but its 'axiomatic' form may indicate that it stems from Reid's teaching in Aberdeen, when he was particularly keen on this method of presentation. At the same time, it agrees closely with his recapitulation on 13 May 1765 of his preceding lectures (see pp.

65–66), and it fills the gap of three teaching days between the previously dated lecture, 7 May, and the summary on 13 May. The material in this manuscript overlaps considerably with one that migrated between the lectures on jurisprudence and the lectures on politics, 4/III/4 with 4/III/17. As it is impossible to insert the latter manuscript without seriously disrupting the order of Reid's presentation, we print it as an appendix to the lectures, pp. 69–78. It provides considerable additions to several parts of the present manuscript.

57/24 For the sake of clarity we print the numbered definitions in bold.

57/26 For Reid's wide concept of 'riches', see also his discussion paper 'Whether Paper Credit be a Benefite or a Disadvantage to a Nation', pp. 79–83.

57/33 Cf. 'Whether By proper Laws the number of Births in every parish might not be doubled, or at least greatly increased?', p. 89.

58/33 The place for this marginal addition has not been indicated by Reid, but it has the character of an additional definition, which, for the sake of the preexisting numbering, Reid may have wanted to insert as an extension of definition 3.

59/8 Reid also uses the concept of vibration in connection with prices in the paper on the storing or warehousing of grain, p. 113. As this earlier manuscript shows, Reid used this terminology *before* the publication of Sir James Steuart's *An Inquiry into the Principles of Political Oeconomy* in 1767.

59/17 Reid explains what he means by natural value in an extended lecture on price; see pp. 73–75.

60/39 Reid is referring to the glass tax of 1746 (19 Geo II c. 12)

61/19 For a further discussion see 'What are the bad consequences of the Diminution of our Coin by wearing? …', pp. 96–106.

62/10 In connection with the following three points, see also 'Some Thoughts on the Utopian System', p. 148.

62/24 It is impossible to tell whether Reid intended these references to apply to the specific matter of colonial trade or the more general issue of the moral effects of commerce. Some of the references are obvious: Montesquieu, *The Spirit of the Laws*, books XX and XXI; David Hume, *Political Discourses*; anon., 'On Trade and Commerce', in [Robert Dodsley], *The Preceptor: Containing a General Course of Education* (1748), part X. It is more uncertain which items in the extensive output of William Petty and Charles Davenant he had in mind, but their main works are, respectively, *Political Arithmetick* (1690) and *An Essay upon the Probable Methods of Making a People Gainers in the Ballance of Trade* (1699).

62/25 [Robert Wallace], *Characteristics of the Present Political State of Great Britain*, second edition (1758).

62/26 [George Berkeley], *The Querist, containing several Queries proposed to the Consideration of the Public* (1735–37). Reid has presumably used one of the editions published in London, Dublin and Glasgow in 1750–51. It is presently available in *The Works of George Berkeley, Bishop of Cloyne*, vol. VI, pp. 103–81.

62/29 Josiah Tucker, *A Brief Essay on the Advantages and Disadvantages which Respectively Attend France and Great Britain, with Regard to Trade* (1749).

62/31 [Matthew Decker], *An Essay on the Causes of the Decline of the Foreign Trade, Consequently of the Value of the Lands of Britain, and on the Means to Restore both* (1744).

62/33 Andrew Hooke, *An Essay on the National Debt, and National Capital: Or, the Account Truly Stated, Debtor and Creditor. Wherein is shewn, that the former is but a diminutive part of the latter; and a practicable scheme exhibited, where-by the whole may, with great facility, be paid off, at once, exclusive of the aid of the sinking fund, and without any diminution of the present revenues of the Crown, or annual expences of the people* (1750) (second edition 1751).

63/6 Homer, *Iliad*, VI.234–36.

63/9 On coinage, see 'What are the bad consequences of the Diminution of our Coin by wearing? …', pp. 96–106.

63/12 A large amount of bullion was sent abroad to finance the Nine Years' War (1688–97) and this led to a considerable increase in the illegal extraction of gold and silver from the stamped coin through clipping, 'sweating' (rubbing) and washing. John Locke was deeply involved in advising the government about recoinage as a solution to this and associated problems, as well as about the regulation of interest, leading to the publication of three pamphlets over the course of 1692–95 that are collected in *Several Papers relating to Money, Interest and Trade* (1696). We think this is Reid's reference, although only one of the pamphlets was published as a 'treatise' (and that not until 1718), namely *A Treatise of Raising our Coin* (1718). However, Reid might also, or in addition, be referring to *Two Treatises of Government*, of which the second treatise, in ch. 5, 'Of Property', gives Locke's general reflections on the origins and nature of money.

63/14 Through indentures with the Mint, the government controlled the coinage (quality of metal contents, weight of coins, etc.). Concerning the penal legislation to protect the currency Reid is likely to have had in mind the acts that progressively made interference treason, beginning with 25 Edward III, c. 5 (counterfeiting English coins; importing foreign counterfeit money) and extended by, among others, 3 Hen. V, c. 6; 5 Eliz., c. 11; 8 and 9 W. III, c. 26; and 15 Geo. II, c. 28, to include a wide variety of ways to corrupt coin. In addition, there were a large number of statutes making felonies and misdemeanours of other forms of manipulation. For an analysis of such legislation that is nearly contemporary with Reid's lectures, see Blackstone, *Commentaries*, book IV, chs 6 and 7, pp. 88–90 (high treason) and pp. 98–100 (felonies).

63/16 In the manuscripts, the sequence of five points beginning here is indicated by the position of the numerals in the margin. In order to avoid confusion with the numbers of the sub-sequences, we print the former numbers in bold.

63/16 Reid's discussion of this first false notion should presumably be set in the following context. Pufendorf had argued that while the function of certain materials, such as gold and silver, as money depends on people's agreement in the sense of acceptance, this does not entail that the value of the money can be fixed by fiat (convention does not entail arbitrariness). This point was developed by Barbeyrac in his commentary, where he defended Locke against real and imagined criticism for making such an inference. See Pufendorf, *Law of Nature* V.1.xii–xvi; Barbeyrac's notes in ibid., pp. 466–67, note 6; Locke, *Some Considerations of the Consequences of the Lowering of Interest, and Raising the Value of Money* (1692, second edition 1696), in *Locke on Money*, ed. Patrick Hyde Kelley, 1991, vol. I, pp. 233–35.

63/35 See the discussion paper 'Whether Paper Credit be a Benefite or a Disadvantage to a Nation', at p. 82.

64/2 In his 'Whether Paper Credit be a Benefite or a Disadvantage to a Nation', pp. 80–81, Reid did not seem to distinguish entirely clearly between this topic (number 4), the quantity theory of money, and the preceding topic (number 3), the mercantilist equation of money and wealth. See note 80/27, and our discussion in the Introduction, pp. lxii, lxvi. His likely targets for the criticism include Locke, *Some Considerations*, in *Locke on Money*, vol. I, pp. 264–66, Hume, 'Of Money' (1752), in *Essays Moral, Political and Literary*, and Montesquieu, *The Spirit of the Laws*, book XXII, ch. 2. A similar critique was about to be published by Sir James Steuart, *An Inquiry*, vol. I, pp. 394–413. See 'Whether Paper Credit be a Benefite or a Disadvantage to a Nation', p. 80/20–39.

64/5 See Locke, *Further Considerations concerning Raising the Value of Money* (1695), in *Locke on Money*, vol. II, pp. 422–23, and [Joseph Harris], *An Essay upon Money and Coins* (1757–58), vol. I, pp. 58–64. Harris more or less paraphrases a part of Locke's text (p. 422).

64/6 Reid's keenness on political arithmetic (see pp. xxviii–xxx) would have made him sympathetic to Joshua Gee's concern with the problem of establishing precise figures regarding the balance of trade; see Joshua Gee, *The Trade and Navigation of Great-Britain Considered* ..., fifth edition (1750), pp. 127–28. A similar point had already been made earlier by Josiah Child, *A New Discourse of Trade*, fifth edition (1751), pp. 114–19.

64/17 The *locus classicus* for this view is Thomas Mun, *England's Treasure by Foreign Trade. Or, the Balance of our Foreign Trade is the Rule of our Treasure* (1750). Mun's work was first published in 1664.

64/18 For Reid's discussion of this topic, see 'Whether Paper Credit be a Benefite or a Disadvantage to a Nation', pp. 80–82.

4/III/16: Banks. Paper Credit

65/1 In addition to the discussion in the lectures here and pp. 68–69, see 'Whether Paper Credit be a Benefite or a Disadvantage to a Nation', pp. 80–81; 'What are the bad consequences of the Diminution of our Coin by wearing? ...', pp. 96–106; and the paper on interest, pp. 117–34.

65/5 Reid drew a line across the page and below it he entered notes from Adam Smith's *Wealth of Nations*, book I, ch. 5. Although it is far from clear, we think that the notes were meant for Reid's lectures. In his actual reading notes, he usually indicated details of the book in question; see the manuscripts in Part One of the present edition. We quote the relevant passages from the *Wealth of Nations*:

> I.v.3: 'The armour of Diomede, says Homer, cost only nine oxen; but that of Glaucus cost an hundred oxen. Salt is said to be the common instrument of commerce and exchanges in Abyssinia; a species of shells in some parts of the coast of India, dried cod at Newfoundland, tobacco in Virginia; sugar in some of our West India colonies....'

I.v.5: 'Iron was the common instrument of commerce among the antient Spartans; copper among the antient Romans'. Reid's 'Spaniards' is a slip of the pen.

I.v.10: 'In the time of Servius Tullius, who first coined money at Rome, the Roman As or Pondo contained a Roman pound of good copper.... The Roman As, in the latter ages of the Republick, was reduced to the twenty-fourth part of its original value, and, instead of weighing a pound, came to weigh only half an ounce.'

I.v.24: 'The Romans are said to have had nothing but copper money till within five years of the first Punic war, when they first began to coin silver. Copper, therefore, appears to have continued always the measure of value in that republick.... The *As* was always the denomination of a copper coin. The word *Sestertius* signifies two *Asses* and a half. Though the *Sestertius*, therefore, was originally a silver coin, its value was estimated in copper.'

I.v.25: 'The northern nations who established themselves upon the ruins of the Roman empire, seem to have had silver money from the first beginning of their settlements, and not to have known either gold or copper coins for several ages thereafter. There were silver coins in England in the time of the Saxons, but there was little gold coined till the time of Edward III. nor any copper till that of James I. of Great Britain.'

4/III/10: Banks. Paper Credit, *cont.*, Revenue

66/8 See 'Of National Riches', pp. 57–62, and 'Whether the Storing or Warehousing of Grain or Meal for Reexportation be highly prejudicial to the Interest of this Country, & whether it ought to be prevented if possible?', pp. 113–15.

66/28 See Montesquieu, *The Spirit of the Laws*, book XXII, ch. 8.

66/35 For the roots of this distinction, see Aristotle, *Politics*, 1256b40–1257b23; see also 'Whether Paper Credit be a Benefite or a Disadvantage to a Nation', p. 81.

67/22 See Reid's detailed analysis in his discourse on usury, pp. 125–34.

67/24 For the following, see 'Whether Paper Credit be a Benefite or a Disadvantage to a Nation or not', pp. 79–80.

67/31 For Reid's analysis of gold and silver money, see 'What are the bad consequences of the Diminution of our Coin by wearing? ...', pp. 96–99.

68/21 See 'Whether By proper Laws the number of Births in every parish might not be doubled, or at least greatly increased?', pp. 83–85, and 'Some Thoughts on the Utopian System', pp. 141–42.

68/32 The word 'Arms' is a later addition, written in larger and bolder ink. It was meant as a heading for one of the final topics in Reid's lecture programme, hence we print it in bold. We know very little of Reid's views on the military. In the lectures on jurisprudence the surviving notes show that he discussed the standard topics in the law of war and peace, strongly influenced by Emer de Vattel's recent work *Le Droit des gens* (1758) from the English translation of which (1759) Reid took extensive notes; see Reid, *Practical Ethics*, pp. 81–82 and 153–75. His division between jurisprudence and politics would have led him in the present context to focus on the practical role of the military, and his brief key words indicate that he would have taken up the comparison of a standing army versus a citizen militia. The re-establishment of a militia in England in 1757 and the fears of a French invasion of the poorly defended Scottish coast during the crises of the Seven Years' War led to a strong revival of agitation for the establishment of a Scottish militia to support or supplement the weak army presence in the country. One of the high points in these campaigns was in 1759–62, and the issue would have been alive for Reid and his class a few years later. The argument in favour of a militia was dominated by the clerical 'Moderates', whose neo-republican ideals Reid largely shared, and we get an indication of his own argument in his discussion paper 'What are the best Expedients for preventing an extravagant rise of Servants Wages' (see p. 85). Cf. the Introduction, pp. lv, lxix.

4/III/11, 2v: Revenue, *cont.*

69/5 For the placement of this, the final material in 4/III/11, see note 51/22. The topics mentioned here correspond largely with the 'Heads' for the final section of Reid's course, to which he appears to have added the kind of retrospective considerations that we meet elsewhere in the lectures. For his ideas on the controversial issue of the national debt, see his discussion paper 'What are the bad consequences of the Diminution of our Coin by wearing? ...', pp. 105–6, and the paper on interest, pp. 128–29. For an indication of the jurisprudential justification of taxation, see Reid, *Practical Ethics*, pp. 158–59, and notes. For an influential contemporary discussion of the varieties of taxation, with which Reid was well familiar, see Hume, 'Of Taxes', in *Essays Moral, Political and Literary*, pp. 342–48. Lotteries abounded in Britain in the eighteenth century, and Reid had clearly touched upon the theoretical aspects of lotteries as part of the treatment of contract in the lectures on jurisprudence; see Reid, *Practical Ethics*, pp. 65 and 229, note 120.

69/14 Hume, 'Of Taxes'.

Appendix to the Lectures on Politics

4/III/4: Value and Price

69/22 As shown by the date, 25 March, this manuscript formed part of Reid's lectures on jurisprudence, where it covered price as an aspect of the theory of contract. This was a standard topic in the modern systems of natural law, which Reid followed in those lectures. However, in the margin of 2r Reid directs 'insert A', which is a manuscript that is part of the lectures on political economy, included under 'police' (4/III/17). The problem is that the amalgamation of the two manuscripts is incomplete: whichever of the two we take as the principal item will lead to an unallocated part of the other. What is more, we have no hard evidence of how Reid used the combined text; he may have used it in one version for the jurisprudence lecture, in the other for political economy. There is indirect evidence that he lifted the lecture of 25 March out of its sequence, and this may indicate that he reused it in some way in the later part of his course, on political economy; see Reid, *Practical Ethics*, pp. 326–27, for further details. At the same time, the topics dealt with in this amalgamated paper overlap considerably with those in his consecutively dated notes on political economy from 1765, which makes it impossible to insert the present text meaningfully in those notes; cf. note 57/23. As Reid himself explains when introducing insertion A on 4/III/4, 2r, the topics of value and price lay on the borderline between jurisprudence and political economy, as he conceived these disciplines, and accordingly we feel obliged to print the amalgamated text as an appendix to the lectures on 'police', even though it was already published in Reid, *Practical Ethics* (pp. 59–65). For our analysis of this important lecture, see the Introduction pp. lvii, lix.

Reid's tripartite division of the subject into the nature of value, the measure of value, and the nature of money is in accordance with the natural-law texts that he tended to use: Francis Hutcheson, *A Short Introduction to Moral Philosophy* (1742/47); citations below are from Hutcheson, *Philosophiae moralis institutio compendiaria with A Short Introduction to Moral Philosophy*, ed. Luigi Turco, pp. 209–13; Francis Hutcheson, *A System of Moral Philosophy* (1755), vol. II, pp. 53–64; Pufendorf, *Law of Nature*, V.1; Gershom Carmichael's notes to Pufendorf, *De officio*, 247–54, in *Natural Rights on the Threshold of the Scottish Enlightenment*, ed. James Moore and Michael Silverthorne, 2002, pp. 106–7.

71/29 The distinction between value in use and value in exchange was common in ancient and medieval authors, but Reid seems mainly to be in line with Pufendorf, *Law of Nature*, V.1.vi, and more particularly Hutcheson, *Short Introduction*, pp. 209–10, and Hutcheson, *System of Moral Philosophy*, vol. II, pp. 53–55. The subject is elaborated in a brief note in another fragmentary manuscript, 7/VII/6, 1r (see Reid, *Practical Ethics*, p. 225, note 105, for a description of the manuscript and its other contents):

> 1769 Mar 26 Exchanges have always been and must be where there is Society. To make Exchanges Equitably Things must be valued & estimated. In a Solitary State things may have a greater or less Value but have not properly a price for a price supposes Exchanges. In a Solitary State we value things which we have in property according as they are necessary usefull or agreable to ourselves. In Society we consider how far they may be usefull or agreable to others, with whom we may Exchange them. Things that cannot be appreciate 1 Such Ether Sun Moon as come not into property nor can be subjects of Commerce 1 Things Common 2 Things Sacred. 2 Things for which there can be no Competition either first because of no Value to any man or Secondly because they are inexhaustible and in every mans power to obtain. Or thirdly Where they are onely conveyed as appendages to other things. Such as a Wholesom Air fine prospect.

The distinction between 'necessary usefull or agreable' is formulated in the English translation of Pufendorf *Law of Nature* (V.1.iii), but it is less clear in the Latin original. The following points in the fragment ('Things that cannot be appreciate', including the spelling 'Wholesom') are in accordance with Pufendof, *Law of Nature*, V.1.v, and *Whole Duty of Man*, I.14.iii, where 'Things Common' are 'the Air, the Sky, the heavenly Bodies, and the vast Ocean', and 'Things Sacred' are religious places and offices. Things 'of no Value to any man' means of no value to any *other* man because they are not transferable, Pufendorf's example being personal freedom. Things inexhaustible are light and shade, wind, air and so on. But though not subject to price, such things can yet be associated with things that are subject to price so that they influence the latter's price (a block of land with 'Wholesom Air' and a 'fine prospect').

72/5 See pp. xxxix–xlii.

4/III/17: Value and Price, *cont.*

72/22 Cf. Genesis 25:29–34.

74/25 Reid's combination of a traditional subjective analysis of the concept of value with a labour concept of the measure of value, or price, may be compared with Adam Smith's controversial attempt in the same direction; see Smith, *Wealth of Nations*, I.iv.13 and I.v–vii; and cf. Smith, *Lectures on Jurisprudence* (A) vi.7–16 and 58–126, and (B) 205–9 and 223–44.

75/7 For Reid's analysis of the relationship between wages and prices, see 'Whether the Storing or Warehousing of Grain or Meal for Reexportation be highly prejudicial to the Interest of this Country, & whether it ought to be prevented if possible?', especially pp. 113–15. In the margin of the manuscript Reid wrote, 'A Ends'. However, 4/III/17 carries on for more than two densely written pages, while the manuscript into which 'A' was inserted, 4/III/4, is continued for another paragraph. Not only size but, more importantly, thematic continuity lead us to give priority to the former, while we print the latter separately after the completion of 4/III/17.

76/29 The bounty on the export of corn was introduced by 1 William and Mary, c. 12 (1688). Ireland was exempted from the general ban on the importation of live cattle by 32 George II, c. 11 (1758) and 5 George III, c. 10 (1765).

77/25 Reid is likely to refer to a ban on the export of wheat that followed a disastrous harvest in 1766, not only in Britain but in continental Europe. Faced with riots, the government imposed the ban through an order in Council instead of a bill in Parliament, and this made the measure a point of heated constitutional debate, hence, perhaps, the tone of Reid's opinion.

4/III/4: Value and Price, *cont.*

77/32 This is the final paragraph of 4/III/4, which was interrupted by the insertion of 4/III/17; see note 69/22. The sharply abbreviated presentation indicates that these points were meant to round off the topic of 'price' when it was discussed within the lectures on jurisprudence.

78/13 See 'What are the bad consequences of the Diminution of our Coin by wearing? …', pp. 96–106.

Part Three: Discourses, Discussions and Conversations

2/II/16: Paper Credit

79/1 This paper originates in a discussion in the Aberdeen Philosophical Society on 24 February 1761. The question 'Whether Paper Credit be beneficial to a Nation or not' was originally proposed by David Skene, but Skene was absent from the meeting at which it was discussed. Reid was asked to draw up an abstract of the discussion, which was entered into the Society's records on 23 June 1761. Another version of this manuscript survives among the papers of David Skene; see David Skene, 'Notes of Discourses in the Philosophical Society of Aberdeen', AUL, MS 540, fols 28r–29r. For an analysis of the context and argument of the manuscript, see our 'Introduction', pp. lxiii–lxvii.

80/7 On the economic benefits of credit that Reid mentions here compare, for example, Daniel Defoe, *The Complete English Tradesman, in Familiar Letters: Directing him in All the Several Parts and Progressions of Trade*, second edition (1727), pp. 337–43; Berkeley, *The Querist*, in *Works*, vol. VI, p. 124 (query 232); and Wallace, *Characteristics*, p. 27.

80/19 On paper credit as a stimulus to commerce see, for example, Berkeley, *The Querist*, in *Works*, vol. VI, pp. 129–30 (query 296); Wallace, *Characteristics*, pp. 27–29.

80/27 Montesquieu, *The Spirit of the Laws*, book IV, ch. 22 (p. 399); Wallace, *Characteristics*, p. 17; [Harris], *An Essay upon Money and Coins*, vol. I, pp. 67–68. Reid's formulation is not entirely clear, for it seems to make the quantity theory of money (that there is a direct relationship between the quantity of money and the prices of commodities) a corollary of the mercantilist idea that wealth equals money. Compare Reid's lectures on politics, pp. 63–64.

80/31 Hume, 'Of Money', in *Essays Moral, Political and Literary*, pp. 284–85. Hume's argument is quoted and elaborated upon in anon., *Essays. I, On the Public Debt. II, On Paper-Money, Banking, &c. III, On Frugality* (1755), pp. 21–25. On this pamphlet, see our Introduction, p. lxv.

81/16 Reid undoubtedly had England in mind as a trading nation that had benefited over the long term from a war that in the short term created serious economic problems. The Nine Years' War (1688–97) disrupted trade, dramatically increased the national debt, undermined the use of silver coin and caused a crisis in public credit in 1696–97. The deteriorating economic situation brought about by the War prompted the creation of the Bank of England in 1694 and the Great Recoinage of 1696. England's economy flourished in the eighteenth century, partly because of the establishment of the Bank and the efforts to improve the money supply.

81/34 Compare Wallace, *Characteristics*, pp. 26–31, for a similar argument.

81/39 The Scot John Law settled in Paris in 1714 and in 1715 tried unsuccessfully to persuade Louis XIV and the Controller-General of Finances, Nicolas Desmarets, to establish a bank that, in Law's view, would help to resolve the crisis that was then affecting the French economy. After the death of the King in September 1715, Law was caught up in the power struggle between the Regent, Phillipe, duc d'Orléans and the Parlement of Paris. Because the Regent supported Law's fiscal policies and his schemes for a bank (the General Bank, established in May 1716, which became the Royal Bank in December 1718) and for a trading company modelled on those in Britain (the Company of the West, launched in 1717, which was brought under the umbrella of the Mississippi Company in 1719), Law encountered fierce opposition from the Paris Parlement. The initial success of Law's schemes paved the way for his appointment as the Controller-General of Finances in January 1720, but with the collapse of the Mississippi System that year, he was forced out of office and went into exile. We cannot determine what Reid had in mind when he refers to the financial policy of the 'French Ministry' or the source(s) upon which he based his assessment of Law's predicament. Law's political and financial rise and fall in France is charted in Murphy, *John Law: Economic Theorist and Policy-Maker*.

82/2 On this point see query 561 of Berkeley's *The Querist*, in *Works*, vol. VI, p. 151. See also Reid's discussion in his politics lectures, pp. 63, 66.

82/3 See pp. 100–1.

82/5 See pp. 63, 78, 98, 100.

82/11 Reid's claim that commerce is a necessary consequence of society echoes Aristotle, *Nicomachean Ethics*, 1132b–33b, and *Politics*, 1257a–b. Compare also Jean Barbeyrac's assertion that 'in the State that things now are, Commerce, as well as Property, is necessary among Men in the Condition they are'. Barbeyrac was here countering the view of Thomasius that commerce was a function of the corrupted manners of humankind due to vice and fallen reason; see Barbeyrac's note to Pufendorf, *Law of Nature*, p. 459 (note 1). Moreover, Reid's claim reflects his general indebtedness to Pufendorf in his understanding of the historical development of human society; see the analysis in our Introduction, pp. lvii–lix.

82/21 Compare queries 46 and 47 of Berkeley's *The Querist*, in *Works*, vol. VI, p. 108–9.

82/26 Reid's distinction between 'Natural Traffic' and 'Artificial Trade' echoes Aristotle's distinction between two forms of property acquisition in *Politics*, 1256a–57b. For this distinction see also his lectures on politics, pp. 66–67.

83/2 For an extended discussion of this point, see pp. 117–25.

6/I/13: Servants' Wages

83/11 This paper originates in an occasional question discussed by the Aberdeen Philosophical Society on 12 January 1762. Reid was asked to prepare an abstract of the discussion, which he subsequently read to the Society on 9 February 1762. It is unclear whether this paper is the abstract drawn up by Reid or whether it is a text he drafted to present at the January meeting. For our analysis of the context and argument of this paper, see our Introduction, pp. lxvii–lxix.

83/17 For Reid on price see pp. 58–61 and 69–78, as well as Reid, *Practical Ethics*, pp. 59–64.

83/19 This limitation is not indicated by the question as it was formulated at the meeting of the Wise Club on 24 November 1761; see Ulman (ed.), *Minutes of the Aberdeen Philosophical Society, 1758–1773*, p. 106.

84/2 Britain was in an almost constant state of war throughout the eighteenth century. But in the early 1760s the country was engaged in two major conflicts, the Seven Years' War (1756–63) and, on the Indian sub-continent, the Third Carnatic War (1757–63).

84/38 Reid's wording echoes the formulation of this point in Sir William Temple, *Observations upon the United Provinces of the Netherlands*

(1673), pp. 109–10. The passage in Temple is quoted in Hume, 'Of Taxes', in *Essays Moral, Political and Literary*, p. 344.

85/8 The wages of labourers rose sharply in the period 1757 to 1760; see the figures in W. Hamish Fraser, *Conflict and Class: Scottish Workers, 1700–1838*, p. 36.

86/6 The use of machines had earlier been discussed in a meeting of the Wise Club held on 24 February 1761 in response to the question posed by Robert Traill, 'Whether the substituting of machines instead of mens labour, in order to lessen the expence of labour, contributes to the populousness of a country?'; see Ulman (ed.), *Minutes of the Aberdeen Philosophical Society*, p. 192.

86/10 The use of penal servitude had already been mentioned briefly at the meeting of the Wise Club held on 24 November 1761; see Thomas Gordon's abstract of the discussion in AUL, MS 3107/2/4. Cf. also Reid, 'Some Thoughts on the Utopian System', p. 148.

6/I/7: Jury Verdict

86/13 The question 'Whether the determination by unanimity or a majority in Juries is most equitable?' was proposed by David Skene and discussed in the Aberdeen Philosophical Society on 9 March 1762. For our analysis of this manuscript, see our Introduction, pp. lxxvii–lxxviii.

86/20 In England, juries comprised twelve members and were used in both civil and criminal cases. The decision of a jury had to be unanimous. In the Scottish legal system, juries were made up of fifteen men and were used only in criminal cases. As Reid indicates, cases were decided in terms of a simple majority.

87/9 Reid's wording alludes to a famous English judicial decision known as 'Bushell's case'. In September 1670 William Penn and his fellow Quaker William Mead were tried at the Old Bailey for causing a public disturbance by preaching in Gracechurch Street in the City of London on 14 August of that year. After two fractious days of proceedings, the bench instructed the jury to consider whether Penn and Mead were guilty of unlawful assembly. The jury initially found that Penn was 'guilty of Speaking or Preaching to an Assembly', whereas Mead was found not guilty. The bench refused to accept the verdict and blamed the juryman Edward Bushell for persuading his fellow jurors not to follow the instruction of the court. The members of the jury were then told that 'you shall not be dismiss'd till we have a Verdict that the Court will accept; and you shall be lockt up, without Meat, Drink, Fire, and Tobacco; you shall not think thus to abuse the Court; we will have a Verdict, by the help of God, or you shall starve for it'. The jury were kept overnight without 'a Chamber-pot, tho desired' and the court reconvened the following morning. When the jury returned the same verdict, they were threatened by the bench and were kept sequestered for a second night. The next day the jury found both Penn and Mead not guilty, much to the consternation of the bench. The members of the jury were then fined and imprisoned in Newgate. Bushell refused to pay his fine and had his case heard in the Court of Common Pleas. The Chief Justice of the Court, Sir John Vaughan, eventually found in Bushell's favour, arguing that it was juries rather than judges who decided questions of fact. For a contemporary account of the trial of Penn and Mead see 'The Peoples Antient and Just Liberties asserted, in the Tryal of William Penn and William Mead, at the Sessions held at the Old-Baily in London, the first, third, fourth and fifth of Sept. 1670. against the most Arbitrary Procedure of that Court', in [John Dunton], *A Collection of Choice, Scarce and Valuable Tracts, Being Taken from Manuscripts and Printed Books, Very Uncommon, and not To Be Found but in the Libraries of the Curious* (1721), pp. 304–49 (the quotations above appear on pp. 316–17). Vaughan's judgement is found in Edward Vaughan, *The Reports and Arguments of that Learned Judge, Sir John Vaughan, Kt. Late Lord Chief Justice of the Court of Common-Pleas, Being all of them Special Cases*, second edition (1706), pp. 135–58, and [Dunton], *Collection*, pp. 407–29. Vaughan's decision was seen as strengthening the independence of juries, and thereby making the jury system a bulwark of English liberty. For example, in a widely read account of the English jury system Giles Duncombe said of Bushell's case that 'the *Fining and Imprisoning of Jurors for giving their Verdicts*, hath several Times been declared in Parliament an Illegal and Arbitrary Innovation, and of dangerous Consequence to the Government, [and] the Lives and Liberties of the People'; Giles Duncombe, *Trials per Pais: Or, the Law of England concerning Juries by Nisi Prius, &c.* (1739), p. 243.

87/21 In the eighteenth century, it was generally thought that the origins of the English jury system dated back to the Saxons; see, for example, Duncombe, *Trials per Pais*, pp. 2–3. During the period of the Polish–Lithuanian Republic (1569–1795), the affairs of state were controlled by the *Sejm* or *diet*, which consisted of a chamber of 'envoys' drawn from the ruling nobility, and a senate comprised of the elected 'King', bishops and state officials. All decisions of the *Sejm* had to meet with unanimous assent. But beginning in the 1650s, each individual envoy had the power to block proposed legislation or resolutions under discussion by exercising what was known as their *Liberum Veto*. A single negative voice was sufficient to defeat any proposal. Consequently, the Republic suffered from political and legislative paralysis. Possible sources for Reid's knowledge of the Polish Diet were Samuel Pufendorf, *An Introduction to the History of the Principal Kingdoms and States of Europe* ... (trans. Joseph Sayer, 1748), vol. II, pp. 323–24 (this work was first published in 1682); and John Campbell's popular *The Present State of Europe* ..., sixth edition (1761), ch. 6.

87/37 For a slightly different formulation of this point, see Home, *Historical Law-Tracts*, vol. I, pp. 410–11.

88/19 Under the Normans, criminal cases were decided by duels and ordeals in both England and Scotland. In a duel, the accused and accuser fought, with the loser deemed the guilty party. Ordeals were of two kinds, involving either heated iron or water. In the former, a suspect was forced to hold on to a piece of iron that had been heated in a fire. Their hands were then bandaged. If the burns healed the suspect was declared innocent, but if they did not the suspect was found guilty. In an ordeal by water, a suspect was immersed in water. If they floated they were innocent. If they sank, they were deemed guilty. The outcomes of duels and ordeals were thought to reflect God's judgement on the suspect or accused. On the use of duels and ordeals in Scotland, and on the Scottish jury system more generally, see Ian Douglas Willock, *The Origins and Development of the Jury in Scotland*, especially pp. 8–9.

88/25 'The hungry Judges soon the sentence sign,/And wretches hang that jury-men may dine'; Alexander Pope, *The Rape of the Lock* (1717), canto III, lines 21–22.

2/II/17: Population Growth

88/35 The question 'Whether by the encouragement of proper laws the number of births in Great Britain might not be nearly doubled, or at least greatly increased?' was proposed by Reid and discussed in the Aberdeen Philosophical Society on 8 June 1762. Reid was asked to prepare an abstract of the discussion, which he read to the Society on 9 November 1762.

His abstract was formally entered into the Society's records on 23 November 1762. For our analysis of the context and argument of this manuscript, see our Introduction, pp. lxix–lxxvii.

89/8 The prioritisation of topics mentioned here was the one that structured the lectures on politics. In the late seventeenth and eighteenth centuries it was a commonplace, and especially in the writings of mercantilists, that the power and wealth of a nation were linked to the size of its population. See, for example, [William Petyt], *Britannia Languens: Or, a Discourse of Trade* (1689), pp. 16–17; Child, *A New Discourse of Trade*, pp. 134, 136; Charles Davenant, *An Essay upon Ways and Means of Supplying the War* (1695), in *The Political and Commercial Works of the Celebrated Writer Charles D'Avenant* (1771), vol. I, pp. 73–74; Berkeley, *The Querist*, in *Works*, vol. VI, p. 110 (query 62), p. 112 (query 87), p. 116 (query 130), p. 123 (query 217); Hume, 'Of the Populousness of Ancient Nations', in *Essays Moral, Political and Literary*, p. 382; Josiah Tucker, *The Elements of Commerce, and Theory of Taxes* ([1755]), pp. 11–13; [William Temple], *A Vindication of Commerce and the Arts; Proving that they are the Source of the Greatness, Power, Riches and Populousness of a State* (1758), p. [1].

89/14 For his claim that the human population doubles naturally in twenty-five years Reid was indebted to [Franklin], *The Interest of Great Britain Considered*, pp. 23, 56. Thomas Malthus subsequently adopted this figure in *An Essay on the Principle of Population, as it Affects the Future Improvement of Society* (1798).

89/21 Reid's terminology of 'checks' and 'restraints' on procreation and population growth derived from the writings of Sir Matthew Hale and Hume; see Sir Matthew Hale, *The Primitive Origination of Mankind, Considered and Examined according to the Light of Nature* (1677), p. 203, and Hume, 'Of the Populousness of Ancient Nations', in *Essays Moral, Political and Literary*, pp. 381, 404 and 420. The notion that there are 'checks' on population growth was, of course, given broader currency later in the eighteenth century by Malthus.

89/30 Compare Josiah Tucker, *A Brief Essay*, pp. 127–32.

89/31 Compare Tucker, *Elements of Commerce*, p. 17.

90/6 For another formulation of this point, see Wallace, *Characteristics*, p. 121.

90/36 Poor Law legislation in Scotland empowered JPs to enter children of the poor into apprenticeships; see Rosalind Mitchison, 'The Making of the Old Scottish Poor Law', p. 64.

91/15 The image of the Nile derives from Harrington's *Oceana*, as we see in the lectures on politics (p. 39).

91/16 Edmond Halley, 'An Estimate of the Degrees of the Mortality of Mankind, Drawn from the Curious Tables of the Births and Funerals at the City of Breslaw; with an Attempt to Ascertain the Price of Annuities upon Lives' (1693) and 'Some Further Considerations on the Breslaw Bills of Mortality' (1693).

91/20 See the section 'De la vieillesse & de la mort' in Georges Louis Leclerc, Comte de Buffon, *Histoire naturelle, générale et particulière, avec la description du cabinet du roi*, fifth edition (1752–66), vol. IV, pp. 336–424.

92/25 That the checks on population growth and the ratio between males and females in human populations reflect God's providential plan for humankind was elaborated at length in the lectures on 'oeconomical jurisprudence', where Reid set the issue in the context of the demographic literature: William Derham, *Physico-Theology: Or, a Demonstration of the Being and Attributes of God, from his Works of Creation*, eighth edition (1732), pp. 168–79; Engelbert Kaempfer, *Histoire naturelle, civile, et ecclesiastique du Japon* (1732); and Montesquieu, *The Spirit of the Laws*, book XVI, ch. 4. See Reid, *Practical Ethics*, section XVI, esp. pp. 116–31 and notes. The point had earlier been argued also in: Hale, *Primitive Origination of Mankind*, pp. 204, 226–27; John Arbuthnot, 'An Argument for Divine Providence, Taken from the Constant Regularity Observ'd in the Births of Both Sexes', (1710–12); [Robert Wallace], *Various Prospects of Mankind, Nature and Providence* (1761), pp. 114–23.

6/I/14: Courts of Equity

92/35 The question 'Whether it be best that Courts of Law and Courts of Equity were different, or that the same court had the power of determining either according to law or equity as circumstances require?' was proposed by Alexander Gerard and discussed by the Aberdeen Philosophical Society on 25 January, 8 February and 22 February 1763. For our analysis of this paper, see our Introduction, pp. lxxviii–lxxx.

94/16 On the interpretation of laws, compare Reid, *Practical Ethics*, pp. 114–15.

94/18 In this and the following paragraph, compare Reid's argument to that in Aristotle, *Nicomachean Ethics*, 1137b.

94/35 *Animus malus* can be translated as 'evil intention'.

95/13 Presumably Reid believed that because the Court of Session was both a court of equity and a court of law, Scottish juries were invariably governed by the principles of equity whereas their English counterparts were not. For this view of the Court of Session see Henry Home, Lord Kames, *Principles of Equity* (1760), pp. viii, xiii–xvi.

4/III/23a: Glasgow Trade

95/29 Adam Smith was given an honorary Doctor of Laws degree by the University of Glasgow in October 1762. This memorandum is the only evidence we have of direct personal contact between Reid and Smith.

95/29 John Glassford was one of the three most wealthy and powerful tobacco merchants in Glasgow prior to the collapse of the tobacco trade with the American colonies caused by the War of Independence (1775–83). He reportedly began his business career in textiles, and was a founding partner in the Glasgow Arms Bank (1750–93) and the Thistle Bank (established in 1761). In addition, he owned a number of other businesses in Glasgow and its environs. Like Adam Smith, he was a member of the Political Economy Club founded by the Glasgow tobacco merchant and Provost Andrew Cochrane.

96/1 During the second half of the eighteenth century Paisley became one of the most important centres for the manufacture of textiles in Britain. In the process Paisley grew in population from 6,799 inhabitants in 1755 to approximately 31,000 in 1801. According to Glassford's reckoning, the value of textile production in Paisley should have been around £105,000 in 1770. The recorded value of linens produced in Paisley in that year was £64,547.19.6, although the overall figure for the production of linens, silk and other textiles may have brought the total closer to Glassford's estimate. As Reid suggests, Glassford's number of £50 per annum for the value of the production of a loom was a conservative one, insofar as one contemporary writer estimated that in 1784 the average value of the production of a silk loom was £70; see Andrew Brown, *History of Glasgow; and of Paisley, Greenock and Port Glasgow; Comprehending the Ecclesiastical and Civil History of these Places, from the Earliest Accounts to the Present Time: And Including an Account of their Population, Commerce, Manufactures, Arts and Agriculture* (1795–97), vol. II, pp. 341, 343.

96/2 We have been unable to determine the accuracy of this estimate.

96/4 Reid's figures seem to be reasonably accurate. One of the late-eighteenth-century historians of Glasgow, James Denholm, records that in 1772 Britain imported 90,000 hogsheads of tobacco, of which Glasgow accounted for 49,000; James Denholm, *The History of Glasgow and Suburbs. To which is Added, a Sketch of a Tour to the Principal Scotch and English Lakes*, third edition (1804), p. 407 note. In 1777, the Glasgow merchant John Gibson recorded that in 1771 tobacco imports from Maryland amounted to 11,313,278 pounds of tobacco and from Virginia a further 33,986,403 pounds. The total amount of tobacco imported through Glasgow, Greenock and Port Glasgow that year was 46,055,139 pounds; John Gibson, *The History of Glasgow, from the Earliest Accounts to the Present Time; with an Account of the Rise, Progress and Present State, of the Different Branches of Commerce and Manufactures now Carried On in the City of Glasgow* (1777), pp. 219, 222. In the years 1768–71 the Glasgow ports accounted for roughly half of the tobacco imported into Britain; see Jacob M. Price, 'The Rise of Glasgow in the Chesapeake Tobacco Trade, 1707–1775', p. 181. Price's statistics (derived from customs records) correspond to those found in Denholm and Gibson.

3061/4: Diminution of Coin

96/6 We do not know for certain when Reid discussed the question 'What are the bad consequences of the Diminution of our Coin by wearing? and what the means of preventing those Consequences?', in the Glasgow Literary Society. For our analysis of the context and argument of Reid's paper and a suggested dating, see the Introduction, pp. lxxxi–lxxxiv.

96/11 Quoting Aristotle, Pufendorf saw the use of money as a central feature of a civilised state of society; Pufendorf, *Law of Nature*, pp. 466–67, and *Whole Duty of Man*, pp. 143–44. See also, for example, Montesquieu, *The Spirit of the Laws*, book XVIII, ch. 15, and book XXII, ch. 1; Hume, 'Of Money', in *Essays Moral, Political and Literary*, p. 291; and Hutcheson, *System of Moral Philosophy*, vol. II, pp. 55–56. Stadial historians of the eighteenth century typically associated the rise of agriculture with the advent of 'civilised' society, that is, the invention of the arts and sciences, the creation of legal systems that included laws governing private property in land, and the establishment of stable governments; for a discussion of the relevant texts of the period, see especially Ronald L. Meek, *Social Science and the Ignoble Savage*. But none of these writers used the plough specifically as a symbol of civilisation as Reid suggests.

96/16 The design of ploughs was a much-debated topic among agricultural improvers in eighteenth-century Scotland and elsewhere. Reid would have been familiar with discussions of the subject through his own reading, his membership of the Gordon's Mill Farming Club, and his friendships with leading improvers like Sir Archibald Grant of Monymusk and Lord Kames. See, for example, [Henry Home, Lord Kames], *The Gentleman Farmer: Being an Attempt to Improve Agriculture, by Subjecting it to the Test of Rational Principles* (1776), pp. 1–13; and, with good contemporary illustrations, the *Encyclopædia Britannica* (1771), vol. I, pp. 54ff.

96/29 Compare, *inter alia*, Aristotle, *Politics*, 1257a; Pufendorf, *Law of Nature*, pp. 467–68, and *Whole Duty of Man*, p. 144; Locke, *Some Considerations*, in *Locke on Money*, vol. I, p. 233; Montesquieu, *The Spirit of the Laws*, book XXII, ch. 2; Philip Cantillon, *The Analysis of Trade, Commerce, Coin, Bullion, Banks and Foreign Exchanges* (1759), pp. 34–35, 97; and [Harris], *An Essay upon Money and Coins*, vol. I, pp. 43–48.

96/32 That is, counting out a sum of money in terms of the face value of the individual coins.

97/4 On the use of silver by the Chinese see anon., 'On Trade and Commerce', in *The Preceptor*, vol. II, p. 387.

97/30 Reid may have derived these figures from [Harris], *An Essay upon Money and Coins*, vol. I, p. 52 note.

97/36 Compare Reid's politics lectures, pp. 63, 66. See also Steuart, *An Inquiry*, vol. I, p. 541, who likewise emphasises this point. Reid had addressed the topic of money and coinage in the lectures on jurisprudence in the context of price and value, the whole being part of the discussion of contractual relations; see Reid, *Practical Ethics*, pp. 64–65 with notes.

98/8 Compare Locke, *Some Considerations*, in *Locke on Money* vol. I, p. 312; and Hutcheson, *System of Moral Philosophy*, vol. II, p. 57.

98/39 For relevant English legislation governing coinage, see: 3 Henry V c. 6, 'It shall be Treason to clip, wash, or file Money', in Owen Ruffhead, *Statutes at Large*, vol. I, p. 454; 5 Elizabeth I c. 11, 'An Act against the Clipping, Washing, Rounding and Filing of Coins', in Ruffhead,

Statutes at Large, vol. II, p. 544; 14 Elizabeth I c. 3, 'An Act against the Forging and Counterfeiting of Foreign Coin being not current within this Realm', in Ruffhead, *Statutes at Large*, vol. II, pp. 594–95; 18 Elizabeth I c. 1, 'An Act against the diminishing and impairing of the Queen's Majesty's Coin, and other Coins current within this Realm', in Ruffhead, *Statutes at Large*, vol. II, pp. 600–1; 6 and 7 William III c. 17, 'An Act to prevent counterfeiting and clipping the Coin of this Kingdom', in Ruffhead, *Statutes at Large*, vol. III, pp. 560–62; 8 and 9 William III c. 26, 'An Act for the better preventing the counterfeiting the current Coin of this Kingdom', in Ruffhead, *Statutes at Large*, vol. III, pp. 644–46; 9 and 10 William III c. 21, 'An Act for the better preventing the counterfeiting, clipping, and other diminishing the Coin of this Kingdom', in Ruffhead, *Statutes at Large*, vol. III, pp. 672–73; 15 George II c. 28, 'An Act for the more effectual preventing the counterfeiting of the current Coin of this Kingdom, and the uttering and paying false or counterfeit Coin', in Ruffhead, *Statutes at Large*, vol. VI, pp. 185–86.

99/9 [Harris], *Essay upon Money and Coins*, vol. I, p. 57. Reid will have known about the problems associated with the use of too much alloy through his study of chemistry.

99/27 Reid here echoes Locke, *Some Considerations*, in *Locke on Money*, vol. I, pp. 309–11; Locke, *Further Considerations*, in *Locke on Money*, vol. II, pp. 415–16; Hutcheson, *System of Moral Philosophy*, vol. II, pp. 58–62; and Steuart, *An Inquiry*, vol. I, pp. 553–57.

99/32 In the period known as the Great Debasement (1542–51), Henry VIII and Edward VI both reduced the weight of gold and silver coins in order to raise revenue for the crown. Elizabeth I undertook a recoinage in 1560–61 and largely succeeded in removing the debased coinage from circulation. In 1601 (the forty-third year of Elizabeth's reign) the weight of silver coin was slightly reduced, with sixty-two rather than sixty shillings now taken from a pound of sterling silver. This weight for silver coin set in 1601 remained the standard until 1816. Reid took his information on English coinage from, *inter alia*, Locke, *Further Considerations*, in *Locke on Money*, vol. II, p. 459, and Martin Folkes' *A Table of English Silver Coins* (see p. 20 for Reid's reading note from this work).

100/3 Compare Steuart, *An Inquiry*, vol. I, pp. 540–41.

100/13 Steuart, *An Inquiry*, vol. II, p. 99, note.

100/27 On this point see, for example, Jean Barbeyrac's annotation to Pufendorf's *Law of Nature*, pp. 468–69, note 4, and Steuart, *An Inquiry*, vol. I, p. 605.

100/34 In addition to his *Some Considerations*, Locke published two tracts in 1695 that addressed the debate over recoinage: *Short Observations on a Printed Paper, Intitled, For encouraging the Coining Silver Money in England, and after for keeping it here*, and the work already referred to above, *Further Considerations Concerning Raising the Value of Money*. These tracts are published in Locke, *Locke on Money*, vol. II, pp. 346–59 and pp. 402–81. Locke's involvement in the framing of Parliament's plan for the recoinage is discussed in Patrick Kelley's editorial introduction to *Locke on Money*, vol. I, pp. 12–35. The specific details of the recoinage are set out in 7 and 8 William III c. 1, 'An Act for remedying the Ill State of the Coin of the Kingdome', in John Raithby (ed.), *The Statutes of the Realm*, vol. VII, pp. 1–4.

101/3 Shillings and six pence pieces were made of silver. Reid's estimate of the weight of the silver coin in circulation is less extreme than that found in the anonymous pamphlet *A Letter to the Members in Parliament, on the Present State of the Coinage: With Proposals for the Better Regulation thereof* (1771), p. 6, where the author claims that 'Three-fourths of the Shillings that are now current are base and counterfeit' and that 'Our Six-pences are wore so very much, that their Weight in common is from Three-pence to Five-pence; few weigh more; and if any weigh their full Weight, they are melted down'. Reid may have derived his figure of 5% from [George Whatley], *Reflections on Coin in General; on the Coins of Gold and Silver in Great-Britain in Particular; on those Metals as Merchandize; and also on Paper Passing as Money* (1762), pp. 11–12, or from Steuart, *An Inquiry*, vol. I, p. 598.

101/16 See, for example, Pufendorf, *Law of Nature*, pp. 470–71; Locke, *Some Considerations*, in *Locke on Money*, vol. I, pp. 214, 248–49; Hutcheson, *System of Moral Philosophy*, vol. II, pp. 57–58; and [Whatley], *Reflections on Coin in General*.

102/1 Steuart, *An Inquiry*, vol. I, p. 563. Steuart began writing *An Inquiry* after he settled in Tubingen in 1757, and by mid-1759 he had completed the first two books of the work. After his return to Britain in 1763 he continued writing and finished *An Inquiry* in October 1766.

102/2 In September 1772, the *Scots Magazine* included a report taken from London newspapers that the price of silver bullion varied between five shillings five pence and five shillings six pence per ounce; *Scots Magazine* 34 (1772), p. 484.

102/5 An indenture of July 1601 between the Crown and the Mint specified that a pound weight of silver bullion was to be divided into sixty-two shillings. Sixty-two shillings divided by twelve (1 lb = 12 ounces, in the troy system for precious metals) yields five shillings and two pence, which was the Mint price for an ounce of silver.

102/6 Compare Smith, *Wealth of Nations*, I.v.33.

102/24 Reid's assessment of the state of the Mint in the eighteenth century is an accurate one; compare Sir John Craig, *The Mint: A History of the London Mint from A.D. 287 to 1948*, pp. 239–50.

105/38 7 and 8 William III c. 18, 'An Act for granting His Majesty severall Rates or Duties upon Houses for making good the Deficiency of the clipped Money', in Raithby (ed.), *Statutes of the Realm*, vol. VII, pp. 86–94. Sections xxx–xxxi of the Act stated that the taxes levied were to be used to secure a loan of £ 1,200,000 to the Crown (pp. 92–93).

106/5 Steuart, *An Inquiry*, vol. I, p. 630, although Steuart does not here indicate that the English government lost an additional million pounds in paying off the loan from the Bank of England.

3061/3: Warehousing Grain

106/33 Reid opened the discussion of this question in the Glasgow Literary Society when he read this paper on 30 January 1778; for our analysis of the context and argument of Reid's paper, see the Introduction, pp. lxxxiv–xcii. The wording of Reid's question echoes that of a resolution adopted at a meeting of members of the landed interest held in Edinburgh in late November 1777: 'That the warehousing of either grain or meal for re-exportation is highly prejudicial to the true interest of this country, and to the exportation of native produce: That as the warehousing of oatmeal never hath been allowed, it ought not to be agreed to; and the warehousing of other grain ought to be prevented if possible' (*Scots Magazine* 40 (1778), p. 8).

107/2 13 George III c. 43, 'An Act to Regulate the Importation and Exportation of Corn', in Ruffhead, *Statutes at Large*, vol. VIII, pp. 222–28.

107/7 'A Bill to Amend and render more effectual so much of Two Acts, made in the Thirteenth and Fourteenth Years of the Reign of His present Majesty, as relates to the regulating the Importation and Exportation of Corn, in that Part of *Great Britain* called *Scotland*', in Sheila Lambert (ed.), *House of Commons Sessional Papers of the Eighteenth Century*, vol. XXVIII, pp. 88–101. The bill was intended to replace 13 George III c. 43 as it applied to Scotland. The proposed corn bill was formally presented to the House of Commons by the Scottish MP for Ayrshire, Sir Adam Fergusson, on 16 April 1777, near the end of the third session of the fourteenth Parliament. Discussion of the bill was postponed to the following session, which began on 18 November 1777 and lasted until 3 June 1778. The bill did not pass into law.

107/14 The view of the mercantile interest was forcefully stated in the *Memorial for the Merchants, Traders and Manufacturers of Glasgow* (1777), which was reprinted in the *Scots Magazine* 39 (1777), pp. 569–73. See also the issue for 3 July 1777 of the *Weekly Magazine, or Edinburgh Amusement* 37 (1777), pp. 1–5.

107/16 See, for example, anon., *Corn-Bill Hints, in Answer to the Memorial for the Merchants, Traders and Manufacturers of the City of Glasgow* (1777), pp. 3–12, and anon., *Essay on the Corn Laws; to Evince, on the Most Indubitable Ground, in Opposition to the Inflammatory Memorial for the Merchants, Traders and Manufacturers of Glasgow, the Equity and Expediency of Prohibiting the Importation of Oats or Oat-Meal, unless the Price of the Latter Shall Be at, or above, Sixteen Shillings per Boll* (1777), pp. 22–26.

107/20 For an example of these resolutions see the report of the county meeting in Banff held on 1 November 1777 in the *Aberdeen Journal; and North-British Magazine*, no. 1557, Monday 10 November 1777. The meeting resolved that 'the allowing Foreign Grain to be imported, and warehoused, and afterwards exported without Duty, will be highly prejudicial to the Agriculture of Great Britain'. The report of this meeting was subsequently published in the *Scots Magazine* 40 (1778), pp. 6–7.

107/26 'An Act to Regulate the Importation and Exportation of Corn', in Ruffhead, *Statutes at Large*, vol. VIII, p. 223. The Act names the ports of Ayr, Leith, Port Glasgow, Aberdeen and Kirkwall in Scotland.

107/31 For the position of the landed interest, see the *Scots Magazine* 40 (1778), p. 8; compare the Glasgow *Memorial* as printed in the *Scots Magazine* 39 (1777), pp. 571, 573.

108/12 On the carrying trade, see, for example, Sir William Petty, *Political Arithmetick*, in Petty, *Economic Writings*, vol. I, pp. 258–60; [Petyt], *Britannia languens*, pp. 21, 34–44; [Decker], *Essay*, pp. 19, 107–8, 170.

108/35 On the importance of the uniformity of grain prices, compare anon., *Corn-Bill Hints*, p. 4, and anon., *Essay on the Corn Laws*, pp. 24–25.

This point had earlier been insisted upon by Sir James Steuart; see Steuart, *An Inquiry*, vol. I, pp. 215–16, and vol. II, pp. 509–10; [Sir James Steuart], *Considerations on the Interest of the County of Lanark* (1769), p. 67.

109/18 Reid's comments reflect his Baconian view that natural knowledge ought to be applied to the solution of practical problems for the benefit of humankind; see especially Reid, *Philosophical Orations*, oration II (reproduced in Reid, *University*). His comments also register his belief that chemistry was an independent science that could not be reduced to the principles of natural philosophy because chemical phenomena such as elective affinities could not be explained in terms of the mechanical laws of Newtonian physics. This conception of the autonomy of chemistry was first articulated by William Cullen in his lectures at the University of Glasgow, and was subsequently taken up by Joseph Black and other men of science such as Reid working in Glasgow during the second half of the eighteenth century; see A. L. Donovan, *Philosophical Chemistry in the Scottish Enlightenment*, pp. 98–102.

110/16 On the relationship between price and demand, compare Reid's politics lectures, pp. 59–60. For this 'axiom', see, for example, [John Law], *Money and Trade Considered, with a Proposal for Supplying the Nation with Money* (1705), pp. 4–5; Hutcheson, *System of Moral Philosophy*, vol. II, pp. 53–55; and, applied to the price of subsistence, [Steuart], *Considerations on the Interest of the County of Lanark*, pp. 11–12. Reid viewed such axioms or 'principles' as being the foundation for reasoning in all the sciences, including politics, as we have seen, pp. 23–24 and 30–32.

111/3 'An Act to Regulate the Importation and Exportation of Corn', in Ruffhead, *Statutes at Large*, vol. VIII, pp. 223, 224, 226.

112/30 Reid's examples suggest that he was familiar with Cantillon's *Analysis of Trade*, pp. vii–xiii.

113/1 See, for example, [Decker], *Essay*, p. 169; Steuart, *An Inquiry*, vol. I, pp. 214–15.

113/9 Compare Smith's qualified praise for the 1772 Corn Law in *Wealth of Nations*, IV.v.b.46–53.

113/18 In *An Inquiry* Sir James Steuart variously applied the concept of the vibration of a balance to describe fluctuations in the relationships between, *inter alia*, trade and industry, and demand and prices. Such usage was known earlier, and Reid himself used it in the politics lectures (see p. 59).

113/29 On necessity as the spur to labour see especially Bernard Mandeville, *The Fable of the Bees: Or, Private Vices, Publick Benefits*, vol. I, pp. 192–94. Reid's echoes Mandeville's comment that 'When Men shew such an extraordinary proclivity to Idleness and Pleasure, what reason have we to think that they would ever work, unless they were oblig'd to it by immediate Necessity' (p. 192). For somewhat different formulations of the point, see Temple, *Observations upon the United Provinces of the Netherlands*, pp. 109–10; Hume, 'Of Commerce', in *Essays Moral, Political and Literary*, p. 267 (whose language Reid also echoes); [Steuart], *Considerations*, pp. 27–28; and, for a religious statement by an English divine Reid admired, Richard Baxter, *A Christian Directory: Or, a Summ of Practical Theologie, and Cases of Conscience* (1673), p. 454, where Baxter observes that 'Necessity is a constant spur to the poor'.

114/15 Reid here adopts the standard mercantilist line regarding the wages of the labouring poor.

114/30 On the relationship between high wages and the birth rate of the labouring poor, see, for example, Smith, *Wealth of Nations*, I.viii.39–42.

115/15 Compare Smith, *Wealth of Nations*, I.viii.29–35, and Steuart, *An Inquiry*, vol. II, p. 509. Steuart also made this point privately in a letter of 14 October 1777; see Sir James Steuart, *An Inquiry into the Principles of Political Oeconomy* (1767), vol. II, p. 738.

116/36 See, for example, [Decker], *Essay*, p. 170.

3061/5: Usury

117/30 When the Glasgow Literary Society met on 13 March 1778 Reid proposed the voluntary question 'Whether is it proper that the interest of money should be regulated by law in cases where the parties have contracted[?]' The next meeting, held on 20 March 1778, was entirely given over to Reid's paper and the responses to it. For our analysis of the context and argument of Reid's paper, see the Introduction, pp. xciii–xcvii.

118/3 The legal interest rate under Elizabeth I was 10% and under James I the rate was set at 8% in 1623; see 13 Elizabeth c. 8, 'An Act against Usury', in Ruffhead, *Statutes at Large*, vol. II, p. 582, and 21 James I c. 17, 'An Act against Usury', in Ruffhead, *Statutes at Large*, vol. III, p. 100. The legal rate of interest was lowered to 6% under Charles II and further reduced to 5% in the reign of Queen Anne; see 12 Charles

II c. 13, 'An Act for the restraining the taking of excessive Usury', in Ruffhead, *Statutes at Large*, vol. III, p. 164, and 12 Anne c. 16, 'An Act to reduce the Rate of Interest, without any Prejudice to Parliamentary Securities', in Ruffhead, *Statutes at Large*, vol. IV, p. 623.

Interest rates in the British West Indies varied. In Montserrat the rate was set at 8%, whereas in the Barbados, Jamaica and Antigua the rate was 6%; see Frank Wesley Pitman, *The Development of the British West Indies, 1700–1763*, p. 135. In 1773 foreign lenders were guaranteed 5% interest; see 13 George III c. 14, 'An Act to encourage the Subjects of Foreign States to lend Money upon the Security of Freehold or Leasehold Estates, in any of his Majesty's Colonies in the *West Indies*; and to render the Securities granted to such Aliens effectual for recovering Payment of the Money so to be lent, by Sale of Such Freehold or Leasehold Estates', in Ruffhead, *Statutes at Large*, vol. VIII, pp. 210–12. Given the strong trading links between the British West Indies and Glasgow, Reid may well have obtained his information about interest rates anecdotally from his friends and associates in the Glasgow merchant community. Printed sources available to him include: Richard Hall, *Acts, Passed in the Island of Barbados. From 1643, to 1762, Inclusive* (1764); anon., *Acts of Assembly, Passed in the Island of Jamaica; from the Year 1681, to the Year 1769, Inclusive* (1769–71); and [Edward Long], *The History of Jamaica* (1774), vol. I, pp. 555–61.

118/8 Reid is mistaken. The act passed in 1570 specified that the usurer would forfeit any interest taken above the legal rate of 10%. Under James I, the penalty for usury was changed to the forfeiture of three times the sum of money lent. This penalty was adopted in the usury legislation passed in the reigns of Charles II and Queen Anne. See 13 Elizabeth c. 8, in Ruffhead, *Statutes at Large*, vol. II, p. 582; 21 James I c. 17, in Ruffhead, *Statutes at Large*, vol. III, p. 101; 12 Charles II c. 13, in Ruffhead, *Statutes at Large*, vol. III, p. 164; and 12 Anne c. 16, in Ruffhead, *Statutes at Large*, vol. III, p. 623.

118/14 'No one is bound to produce writings against himself'.

118/16 'No one is bound to swear to his own guilt'. On these two legal maxims in relation to the crime of usury, compare Sir George Mackenzie, *The Laws and Customs of Scotland, in Matters Criminal: Wherein is to be seen how the Civil Law, and the Laws and Customs of other Nations do agree with, and supply ours* ([1678] second edition 1699), in *The Works of that Eminent and Learned Lawyer, Sir George Mackenzie of*

Rosehaugh, Advocate to King Charles II and King James VII (1716–22), vol. II, pp. 146–47.

118/20 Reid has taken his figures from Aristotle, *Rhetoric*, 1411a. Interest rates varied widely in ancient Greece. A rate of 10% was charged, for example, at the temple of Apollo on Delos. A rate of 30% or more would typically have been charged for a maritime loan, that is, a sum lent to finance the voyage of a trading ship; see Paul Millett, *Lending and Borrowing in Ancient Athens*, especially ch. 4.

118/24 Sources for this information available to Reid include: Tacitus, *The Annals* (VI.16) (see *Tacitus: The Histories and the Annals*, trans. Clifford H. Moore and John Jackson, 1925–37, vol. III, pp. 179–81); Justinian, *The Digest* (XXII.1.1–49) (see *The Digest of Justinian*, trans. Alan Watson, ed. Theodore Mommsen and Paul Kruger, 1985, vol. II, pp. 634–43); Montesquieu, *The Spirit of the Laws*, book XXII, ch. 22; and Hume, 'Of Interest', in Hume, *Essays Moral, Political and Literary*, pp. 305–6.

118/35 Aristotle, *Politics*, 1258a–b.

118/37 Cicero, *On Duties* (II.89): 'Someone asked [the Elder Cato] what was the most profitable activity for a family estate. He replied, "To graze herds well." … Then, when the questioner asked, "What about money-lending?", Cato's reply was "What about killing someone?"' (Cicero, *On Duties*, ed. M. T. Griffin and E. M. Atkins, 1991, p. 100).

118/39 Psalms 15:5: '*He that* putteth not out his money to usury, nor taketh reward against the innocent'.

119/2 Exodus 22:25, Leviticus 25:35–37, and, especially, Deuteronomy 23:19–20.

119/7 As Reid indicates, the prohibition 'Thou shalt not lend upon usury to thy brother' in Deuteronomy 23:19 was initially taken to apply only among the Jews. But in the writings of St Jerome and St Ambrose of Milan, the term 'brother' was interpreted as applying to all Christians. Hence usury came to be proscribed more generally in the early Christian church. For the classic study of this shift, see Benjamin Nelson, *The Idea of Usury: From Tribal Brotherhood to Universal Otherhood*, ch. 1.

119/8 See, for example: St Chrysostom's homilies V and LVI on the Gospel of Matthew in St Chrysostom, *A Select Library of the Nicene and Post-Nicene Fathers of the Christian Church, Volume X: Saint Chrysostom: Homilies on the Gospel of Saint Matthew* (ed. Philip Schaff, 1991, pp. 35–36 and, especially, 350–51); and St Basil, homily XII on Psalm 14, 'A Psalm of David against Usurers' (see *Exegetic Homilies*, trans. Agnes

Clare Way, in *The Fathers of the Church: A New Translation*, 1963, vol. XLVI, pp. 181–91).

119/13 These penalties for usury were laid down in 850 by the Synod of Pavia. See also the canons established at the second and third Lateran Councils held in 1139 and 1179, and the second Council of Lyon in 1274; Norman P. Tanner (ed.), *Decrees of the Ecumenical Councils*, vol. I, pp. 200, 223, and 328–30.

119/15 See, for example, the fourth of Robert Sanderson's sermons *ad populum* (see *The Works of Robert Sanderson*, ed. William Jacobson, 1854, vol. III, pp. 121–23), where Sanderson grants that usury may be lawful but is nevertheless reprehensible because it is harmful to individuals and to society more generally; see also the sixth of Sanderson's *Seventeen Sermons ad aulam*, in which he condemns enriching oneself by means of 'bribery or forgery, by usury and extortion, by sacrilegiously detaining or invading the Church's patrimony, by griping and wringing excessive fees from poor men, by delays of justice, by racking of rents to unreasonable proportion, by false weights and measures, and lies, and oaths' (vol. I, p. 156). Reid's copy of Sanderson's *XXXVI Sermons. Viz. XVII ad aulam, VI ad clerum, VI ad magistratum, VIII ad populum, with a Large Preface*, eighth edition (1689), survives in Special Collections in Glasgow University Library.

119/22 It is unclear which specific writers on usury Reid has in mind. One author whose work circulated widely in the seventeenth century and was reprinted in the early eighteenth century was Sir Thomas Culpeper; see *Sir Thomas Colepeper's Tracts concerning Usury Reprinted. Shewing Its Biting Quality on the Private and Publick. With Some Animadversions on the Writings of Dr. Lock, on that Subject* (1708). Culpeper's *A Tract against Usurie* was first published in London in 1621. Other notable discussions of usury include: Thomas Wilson, *A Discourse upon Usury: By way of Dialogue and Orations, for the Better Variety and More Delight of all those that Shall Read this Treatise* (1572); and Roger Fenton, *A Treatise of Usurie, Divided into Three Bookes: The First Defineth what is Usurie. The Second Determineth that To Be Unlawfull. The Third Removeth such Motives as Perswade Men in this Age that it May Be Lawfull* (1611). Fenton's tract prompted Sir Robert Filmer to respond in *Quæstio quodlibetica, or a Discourse, Whether it May Bee Lawfull to Take Use for Money* (1653). Reid's characterisation of the common attitude towards usury in England at the turn of the seventeenth century echoes details in Filmer's text and Reid may well have drawn on Filmer's historical survey of religious attitudes towards usury. Usury was also a standard topic in natural law, and Reid had discussed it in that part of his lectures; see Reid, *Practical Ethics*, p. 65, and for the relevant sources p. 229, note 118.

119/25 We have been unable to identify the specific debate in the Commons that Reid had in mind.

119/30 The amount of interest paid on the national debt by the government was said to be £4.3 million in John Dalrymple, Earl of Stair, *The State of the National Debt, the National Income and the National Expenditure* (1776), p. [2].

119/33 We have found no source for the plausibility of this and the following claim.

120/5 Cf. Reid, *Active Powers*, p. 290: 'there is no branch of human knowledge, in which there is so general agreement among ancients and moderns, learned and unlearned, as in the practical rules of morals'. See also Reid, *Practical Ethics*, pp. 10–11.

120/15 Cf. Reid, *Active Powers*, pp. 298–99: 'In the scholastic ages, an action good in itself was said to be *materially* good, and an action done with a right intention was called *formally* good. This last way of expressing the distinction is still familiar among Theologians.' The scholastic distinction was commonly accepted in reformed theology and in Scottish moral philosophy; see for example Carmichael, *Natural Rights on the Threshold of the Scottish Enlightenment*, p. 25; Hutcheson, *Short Introduction*, p. 116; Hutcheson, *System of Moral Philosophy*, vol. I, pp. 252–53; David Fordyce, *The Elements of Moral Philosophy* (1754), pp. 55–56.

120/33 Reid's patron and friend Lord Kames viewed the history of the law in similar terms; see Home, *Principles of Equity*, pp. iv–vi.

121/9 On this distinction see Reid, *Practical Ethics*, pp. 151–52, and the references cited there.

122/19 Compare this paragraph to Steuart, *An Inquiry*, vol. I, pp. 166, 175–81.

122/28 Aristotle, *Politics*, 1258a–b.

122/32 On this point compare Pufendorf, *Law of Nature*, p. 515, and Locke, *Some Considerations*, in *Locke on Money*, vol. I, p. 211.

122/37 Proverbs 22:7: 'The rich ruleth over the poor, and the borrower *is* servant to the lender'.

123/5 Reid blends together two different but related literatures in his comment on the grounds for credit in trade. In writings on usury it was common to justify interest on loans if the money being borrowed was used to increase the borrower's own wealth; see, for example, Pufendorf, *Law of Nature*, pp. 514–16. In writings on credit, it was typically said that credit was based on the regular payment of debts; see, for instance, [Daniel Defoe], *An Essay upon Publick Credit: Being an Enquiry how the Publick Credit Comes to Depend upon the Change of the Ministry, or the Dissolutions of Parliament; or whether it Does so or no*, third edition (1710), p. 9; and Defoe, *Complete English Tradesman*, pp. 419–23.

123/19 Reid's characterisation of money lending in non-commercial societies elaborates on Pufendorf, *Law of Nature*, p. 515.

123/28 By the 1770s pawnbrokers were regulated by a number of acts, including those dealing with usury, and what was the most important piece of legislation, 30 George II c. 24, 'An Act for the More Effectual Punishment of Persons Who Shall Attain, or Attempt to Attain, Possession of Goods or Money, by False or Untrue Pretences; for Preventing the Unlawful Pawning of Goods; for the Easy Redemption of Goods Pawned; and for Preventing Gaming in Publick Houses by Journeymen, Labourers, Servants and Apprentices', in Ruffhead, *Statutes at Large*, vol. VII, pp. 164–71. Paragraph xi of 30 George II c.24 specified that if a pawned item had not been claimed after two years, the pawnbroker could offer it for sale (pp. 166–67).

124/2 The Charitable Corporation for Relief of Industrious Poor, by Assisting them with Small Sums upon Pledges at Legal Interest, was established by a royal charter from Queen Anne in 1707. Modelled on similar bodies on the continent, the Corporation offered loans to the poor or those in somewhat better circumstances upon receipt of a 'pledge', that is, a piece of clothing, jewellery or a household item. The loans could be interest free or set at or above the legal rate of interest depending on the perceived social status of the person seeking assistance. Reid's patron, Sir Archibald Grant of Monymusk, became a member of the Committee that managed the Corporation in October 1725. Grant and his fellow Committee members, along with the employees of the Corporation, subsequently engaged in a variety of questionable or illicit financial activities which came to light after complaints to Parliament prompted an investigation of the Corporation's affairs in 1731–32. Some of those involved in the scandal fled the country, but the Parliamentary Committee struck to examine the affairs of the Corporation scrutinised the accounts and questioned Grant and most of his associates. In May 1732 the Parliamentary Committee concluded that the managers and employees of the Corporation were guilty of various misdemeanours and that Grant in particular was 'guilty of having been concerned in Copartnerships, in which the Cash of the said Corporation has been employed, and great Sums lost and embezzled; and of having been principally concerned in promoting, abetting, and carrying on many other indirect and fraudulent Practices in the Management of the Affairs of the Said Corporation'. Grant, who had been sitting as the MP for Aberdeenshire since 1722, was expelled from the House of Commons and retired in disgrace to his estates in the north-east of Scotland. Grant was still alive when Reid read his paper on usury to the Glasgow Literary Society, although he died shortly after, on 17 September 1778. See anon., *Mons pietatis Londinensis: A Narrative or Account of the Charitable Corporation, for Relief of Industrious Poor, by Assisting them with Small Sums upon Pledges, at Legal Interest* (1719), and anon., *The Several Reports, with the Appendix, which Is to one of them, from the Committee of the House of Commons, to whom the Petition of the Proprietors of the Charitable Corporation for Relief of Industrious Poor by Assisting them with Small Sums upon Pledges at Legal Interest, Assembled in their General Court, was Referred; and the Proceedings of the said House thereupon* (1732), p. 196.

124/11 One source for Reid's view of the early history of commerce was the preface to Cantillon's *Analysis of Trade*, pp. vii–xi; see also anon., 'On Trade and Commerce', in *The Preceptor*, vol. II, pp. 391–99. He would have known about the commercial activities of the Zidonians through the Old Testament; see, for example, Isaiah 23:2 on the merchants of Zidon.

124/21 See the life of Titus Pomponius Atticus in Cornelius Nepos (2.3–6) (see *Cornelius Nepos*, trans. John C. Rolfe, 1994, especially pp. 289–91).

124/24 Compare Cantillon, *Analysis of Trade*, pp. xii–xiii, and anon., 'On Trade and Commerce', in *The Preceptor*, vol. II, pp. 399–409.

124/33 Cicero, *On Duties*, I.150 (p. 58).

125/5 In addition to the views of Aristotle, Cato the Elder and Cicero cited above see also, for example, Plutarch, 'That We Ought Not to Borrow' (see *Plutarch's Moralia*, trans. F. C. Babbitt et al., 1927–76, vol. X, pp. 317–39). Examples of the 'modern' attitude towards usury can readily be found in the natural-law tradition; see Hugo Grotius, *The Rights of War and Peace* (1625) (ed. Richard Tuck, 2005, vol. II, pp. 753–60); Pufendorf, *Law of Nature*, pp. 509–20, and *Whole Duty of Man*, p. 153; Hutcheson, *System of Moral Philosophy*, vol. II, pp. 71–74.

125/17 Compare Hutcheson, *System of Moral Philosophy*, vol. II, pp. 71–72.
125/34 Cf. Hutcheson, *System of Moral Philosophy*, vol. II, pp. 73–74.
125/39 'A probable ground for action'.
126/11 On the laws governing tutors and factors on sequestered estates see James Dalrymple, Viscount Stair, *The Institutions of the Law of Scotland, Deduced from its Originals, and Collated with the Civil, and Feudal-Laws, and with the Customs of Neighbouring Nations*, third edition (1759), pp. 49–51 and 767–78.
126/19 See 12 Anne c. 16.
126/22 In Scotland, grain prices were set annually in February by the sheriffs and deputy sheriffs of each shire in consultation with a jury consisting of heritors and others familiar with the state of the previous year's crop. The price was known as the 'Fiar price', and the meeting at which the price was set the 'Sheriff-fiars' or 'fiars court'; see an 'Act Declaring and Appointing the Manner of Striking the Sheriff-fiars', dated 21 December 1723, in anon., *The Acts of Sederunt of the Lords of Council and Session, from the 1628 to 1740, Copied from the Books of Sederunt* (1740–53), vol. I, pp. 253–55.
126/33 As noted above, 12 Anne c. 16 stipulated that the convicted usurer had to pay a penalty of three times the amount of money of lent.
127/14 'A Pledge or Pawn is where Goods and Chattels are delivered in Security for Money lent'; introduction to anon., *The Law concerning Pawn-Brokers and Usurers: Containing all the Statutes and Cases in Law and Equity Extant, which Relate to Pawns and Usury, Disposed under Proper Heads* (1745), p. [i]. Drawing mainly upon Hutcheson, Reid had dealt with the idea of pledge in natural law earlier in his course; see Reid, *Practical Ethics*, pp. 52 and 110 with the commentary at pp. 210–11.
127/20 That is, the pawnbroker has in his possession the goods pawned for the money lent.
127/39 Reid echoes defences of pawn broking. See, for example, the anonymous pamphlet *An Apology for the Business of Pawn-Broking* (1744), and R. Campbell *The London Tradesman*, third edition (1757), pp. 296–97.
128/30 For these figures see, note 119/33.
128/32 Scottish bank notes were (and still are) issued with a promise by the bank in question to pay the bearer the value stated on the note. Notes were issued first by the Bank of Scotland (founded in 1695) and subsequently by the Royal Bank of Scotland (founded in 1727) as well as smaller, private banks. The use of paper currency was more common in Scotland than elsewhere.

128/33 Estimates of the size of the national debt varied. In 1772 Richard Price suggested that the national debt was 'a few millions less' than £148 million, but in 1778 he calculated that the debt was just over £140 million; Richard Price, *Observations on Reversionary Payments; on Schemes for Providing Annuities for Widows, and for Persons in Old Age; on the Method of Calculating the Values of Assurances on Lives; and on the National Debt*, second edition (1772), p. 136, and Price, *Two Tracts on Civil Liberty, the War with America, and the Debts and Finances of the Kingdom: With a General Introduction and Supplement* (1778), p.124. Price's lower estimate was in line with the calculations of John Dalrymple, the Earl of Stair, in *The State of the National Debt*, p. [2], where Stair stated that the debt was just over £139 million. Reid's figure of £150 million is also found in the pamphlet by 'a Wellwisher to the Prosperity of Britain', anon., *A Scheme whereby the Whole National Debt may be Paid in about Thirty Years, without any Additional Tax upon the Nation, or any Injury Done, either to Government, or its Creditors* (1778), pp. 19, 22. The official government figure for the debt was £143.1 million; see B. R. Mitchell, *British Historical Statistics*, p. 601.

129/13 The emergence of the 'monied interest' at the turn of the eighteenth century was a function of the financial revolution set in motion by England's wars with the French following the Glorious Revolution of 1688–89 (Geoffrey Holmes, *British Politics in the Age of Anne*, ch. 5). The social and political influence of the new 'monied men' became the subject of intense debate during the latter part of the reign of Queen Anne (1702–14). On this debate, see especially J. G. A. Pocock, *The Machiavellian Moment: Florentine Political Thought and the Atlantic Republican Tradition*, ch. 13.

129/21 On Judea, compare Pufendorf, *Law of Nature*, p. 514.

129/38 We have not been able to confirm this statement. As the authors of the standard economic history of the Dutch Republic in the early modern period note: 'a tangle of debt and credit linked the Republic's households, but we know very little about how this financial market functioned' (Jan De Vries and Ad van der Woude, *The First Modern Economy: Success, Failure and Perseverance of the Dutch Economy, 1500–1815*, p. 139). Reid's probable source for his information was a member of the branch of the Gregory family who were merchants in Campvere during the eighteenth century. Reid was in touch with his relations based on the continent and occasionally met with them in Scotland; see Reid to John

Bell, 27 June 1785, and Reid to James Gregory, 24 August 1787, in Reid, *Correspondence*, pp. 178, 190.

130/13 Reid's elision of the market price with the equitable or just price reflects his reading of Pufendorf, *Law of Nature*, p. 465.

130/24 Although Reid uses the language of a 'natural' rate of interest inherited from Locke and others, his account of the cause of fluctuations in interest rates in terms of demand and the quantity of money is rather less sophisticated than the analyses offered by earlier writers such as Locke and Hume. Compare Locke, *Some Considerations*, in *Locke on Money*, vol. I, pp. 216–18, and Hume, 'Of Interest', in *Essays Moral, Political and Literary*, pp. 295–307.

130/28 Reid thus follows Locke in arguing that interest rates should not be legally regulated; see Locke, *Some Considerations*, in *Locke on Money*, vol. I, pp. 211–19.

130/39 12 Anne c. 16.

131/13 Locke makes a similar point in *Some Considerations*, in *Locke on Money*, vol. I, pp. 212, 219–20.

132/3 Compare Locke, *Some Considerations*, in *Locke on Money*, vol. I, pp. 220–21.

132/21 This paragraph echoes Locke, *Some Considerations*, in *Locke on Money*, vol. I, pp. 212–14.

3061/6: The Utopian System

134/3 Reid read his discourse, 'Some Thoughts on the Utopian System' at a meeting of the Glasgow Literary Society held on 28 November 1794. For the context of this discourse and our interpretation of it, see the Introduction, pp. xcviii–cii. The paper should be read in conjunction with Reid's lectures on politics printed above, especially pp. 50–51, and with his lectures on political jurisprudence. For the latter see Reid, *Practical Ethics*, pp. 72–80 and 144–52.

135/5 In this and the following four paragraphs, Harringtonian–Machiavellian notions are particularly evident. For Reid's use of Harrington, see pp. 38–42, 43–44.

136/19 For the maxim of politics see, for example, Niccolò Machiavelli, *Discourses on the First Decade of Titus Livius* (I.25) (see *Machiavelli: The Chief Works and Others*, trans. Allan Gilbert, 1965, vol. I, pp. 252–53). Reid's engagement with Montesquieu in this paragraph attests to the intimate acquaintance with *The Spirit of the Laws* displayed in his lectures on politics; see pp. xlvii–l, 44–47, 51–52.

137/30 'The pure state of nature'.

138/8 On the distinction between 'political jurisprudence' and 'politics' see pp. 25–26, and Reid, *Practical Ethics*, pp. 14–16.

138/18 Compare Hume, 'Idea of a Perfect Commonwealth', in *Essays Moral, Political and Literary*, pp. 512–14, and Adam Smith, *The Theory of Moral Sentiments*, IV.1.11 and VI.ii.2.18.

138/28 Reid elaborated upon this theme in his lectures on politics. See pp. 30–34.

139/24 To the extent that one emphasises the first of these points – the perfectibility of moral character – as Reid does elsewhere (see the Introduction, p. xlvii), his scheme approaches what has been called the 'perfect moral commonwealth'. To the extent that the two latter points are seen to predominate, the model is properly utopian; see J. C. Davis, *Utopia and the Ideal Society: A Study of English Utopian Writing, 1516–1700*, ch. 1. Reid's distinction between 'the Man of Nature' and our 'second Nature' shaped by education and society echoes the writings of Mandeville and Rousseau.

139/34 Reid thus differentiates himself from those writers who followed in the footsteps of Machiavelli and emphasised the political uses of religion; see, for example, Machiavelli, *Discourses on the First Decade of Titus Livius* (I.11–15) (see *Machiavelli: The Chief Works and Others*, trans. Allan Gilbert, 1965, vol. I, pp. 223–34), and Jean-Jacques Rousseau, *Of the Social Contract or Principles of Political Right* (see *The Social Contract and Other Later Political Writings*, trans. and ed. Victor Gourevitch, 1997, pp. 142–51).

139/38 Sir Thomas More coined the word 'utopia' in the title of his famous work published in 1516, which marked the renewal of utopian speculation in Western thought. The reception of More in the eighteenth century is too complex to be indicated here but, for a start, see Frank E. Manuel and Fritzie P. Manuel, *Utopian Thought in the Western World*, chs 16, 17, 22 and 23. We have no hard evidence about how Reid came to read More's *Utopia* which would allow us any non-interpretative shortcuts. It should, however, be noted that there are a number of similarities between Reid's utopian sketch in this discourse and 'the model of a perfect government' constructed by the Scottish minister Robert Wallace in his *Various Prospects of Mankind, Nature and Providence*, prospects II–IV, and that both Reid and Wallace are implicitly critical of Hume's 'Idea of a

Perfect Commonwealth' in pitting adaptations of More against Hume's redeployment of Harrington. We do not know which edition of *Utopia* Reid used, but apart from numerous Latin editions, Ralph Robinson's (1551) and Gilbert Burnet's (1684) English translations were reprinted throughout the eighteenth century. Burnet's translation was published in 1743 and 1762 in Glasgow by the Foulis brothers, who also printed a Latin edition in 1750; see Philip Gaskell, *A Bibliography of the Foulis Press*, pp. 43, 149, 248.

140/2 Sir Thomas More, *The Best State of a Commonwealth and the New Island of Utopia* (see *The Yale Edition of the Complete Works of St Thomas More*, ed. R. S. Sylvester et al., 1963–97, vol. IV, pp. 103–5).

140/6 More, *Utopia*, p. 149.

140/10 See pp. lv–lvi and 57, and cf. Reid, *Practical Ethics*, pp. 204–12, for the details of Reid's theory of property.

140/29 See Acts 4:32–7 and 2:44–5. See More, *Utopia,* p. 219 (where Coenobites are referred to) and 243. In Gibbon's famous thirty-seventh chapter on, *inter alia*, the 'Origin, Progress and Effects of Monastic Life', he explains that the 'monks were divided into two classes: the *Cœnobites*, who lived under a common, and regular, discipline; and the *Anachorets*, who indulged their unsocial, independent fanaticism'; see Edward Gibbon, *The History of the Decline and Fall of the Roman Empire* (ed. David Wormersley, 1994, vol. II, p. 426). For the seven deacons, see Acts 6:1–6.

140/39 In the third quarter of the eighteenth century, the Society of Jesus and (not least) its activities in South America provided exciting news for all of Europe. Founded by Loyola in 1534 and recognised by Pope Paul III in 1540, the Society played a significant role in the Spanish settlements in America in the second half of the sixteenth century, Paraguay – a much more extensive area than the modern state – being established as a Jesuit province in 1604. By the middle of the eighteenth century, the Society of Jesus had become a hated and feared obstacle to the emerging enlightened absolutism in Spain and Portugal. Owing allegiance only to the General of the order and to the Pope, the Jesuits enjoyed an independence that in the colonies enabled them to be, or to run, a virtual state within the state. Thus, the independent trading activities of the Jesuits' Indian missions, especially with the British, flew in the face of the new centralist mercantilism of the two Iberian crowns. In 1750 there was an attempt to solve the long-standing conflict over the Spanish–Portuguese borders in South America. A treaty that involved the clearance of seven Jesuit reductions (settlements wherein converted indigenous peoples lived and worked) and the takeover of their land by the Portuguese was made. This led to armed uprisings by the Indians of the reductions, in which the exact role of the Jesuits is still a matter of dispute; for a recent account of these uprisings see Barbara Ganson, *The Guaraní under Spanish Rule in the Río de la Plata*. By the mid-1750s, however, the sensational news in Europe was that Jesuits were in arms against monarchs, and even that they had made one of their own king of Paraguay, the spurious Nicholas I. In addition, Jesuits were accused of being behind an assassination attempt on Joseph I of Portugal and as a consequence were expelled from all Portuguese territories in 1759. In 1764 the order was thrown out of France because of allegations of financial impropriety and, in 1767, it was banned from all of Spain for alleged subversive activity. Finally, in 1773 the Pope was prevailed upon by the Bourbon monarchs to dissolve the Society of Jesus. All this led to an intense war of words, and among the many Jesuit defences is one of the century's most significant histories of Paraguay, Pierre Charlevoix's *Histoire du Paraguay* (1756). Reid may have derived his information about the Jesuits from this work, but we are more inclined to think that he got it indirectly from Voltaire's *Essais sur les moeurs*, ch. cliv, which is largely derivative from Charlevoix and contains the specific points mentioned by Reid here (see *Oeuvres Complètes de Voltaire*, ed. A. J. O. Beuchot, 1829–40, vol. XVII, pp. 461–70). Reid would presumably also have been aware of Voltaire's use of the Paraguayan Jesuits in *Candide*, chs 14–15. Reid's attitude was undoubtedly influenced by Montesquieu's enthusiastic description of the Paraguayan experiment in *The Spirit of the Laws*, book IV, ch. 6, and only lightly tempered by the controversy over the Jesuits that broke out a few years after Montesquieu wrote, and by the less than rosy account of the reductions he found in Louis de Bougainville, *A Voyage round the World. Performed by Order of His Most Christian Majesty, in the Years 1766, 1767, 1768 and 1769* (1772), ch. 7 (which also mentions the payment of a piaster per Indian, p. 98, and describes the eviction of the Jesuits). The actual influence of More's and other utopian writings has been a matter of much dispute; for an assessment, see Magnus Mörner, *The Political and Economic Activities of the Jesuits in the La Plata Region*. Useful contemporary summaries are to be found in the *L'Encyclopédie* articles on the Jesuits and on Paraguay, which Reid may or may not have consulted.

141/17 1 Timothy 6:10. On greed and riches, see also More, *Utopia*, pp. 139, 241–43.

141/34 More, *Utopia*, pp. 139, 243–45.

142/26 Reid's criticism of existing property relations was bound to have been influenced by that of his friend and successor at King's College, William Ogilvie, in Ogilvie's anonymously published *An Essay on the Right of Property in Land, with Respect to its Foundation in the Law of Nature; its Present Establishment by the Municipal Laws of Europe; and the Regulations by which it Might Be Rendered more Beneficial to the Lower Ranks of Mankind* ([1781]), I.iii. See the Introduction above, p. xcviii. The appropriate scale on which to measure the degree of radicalism concerning property in Reid's utopian scheme is provided by, on the one hand, Thomas Spence's extreme redistributive plan in *The Rights of Man* (1793) and, on the other, the moderate proposals of Ogilvie, in *Essay*, part II, or Paine in part II of *Rights of Man* (1792) and in *Agrarian Justice* (1796). Compare also Reid's vision of a utopia with those articulated in the writings collected in *Utopias of the British Enlightenment*, edited by Gregory Claeys.

144/28 Proverbs 22:6.

145/9 More, *Utopia*, pp. 125, 159, 229.

147/16 For example, More, *Utopia*, pp. 69–71, 133–35.

148/6 More, *Utopia*, p. 153.

148/13 More, *Utopia*, p. 191.

148/21 More, *Utopia*, pp. 147–51.

151/2 For the traditional utopian dislike of law, lawyers and lawsuits, see More, *Utopia*, pp. 105, 195. If Reid read William Godwin's *Political Justice* (1793), which was published two years before this paper was presented, he would have found much to agree with on this point (see William Godwin, *Enquiry concerning Political Justice, and its Influence on Morals and Happiness*, ed. Isaac Kramnick, 1985, especially pp. 544–45, 684–95).

151/13 Reid alludes to the Irish actor and playwright Charles Macklin's farce, *Love à la Mode*, which was first performed in 1759. The character Sir Archy MacSarcasm observes that 'the law is a sort of hocus-pocus science, that smiles in yeer face while it pecks yeer pocket: and the glorious uncertainty of it is of mair use till the professors than the justice of it' (*Four Comedies by Charles Macklin*, ed. J. O. Bartley, 1968, p. 72). For an example of the attention paid by Scots to the play's portrait of a Scotsman in London, see, for example, the anonymous pamphlet *A Scotchman's Remark on the Farce of Love à la Mode* (1760).

152/23 For Reid's detailed analysis of demonstrative versus probable reasoning, see *Intellectual Powers*, essay VII, chs 1–3 (pp. 442–62). For his account of how to explain collective human activity, see the lectures on politics, pp. 29–30, 72–73.

154/22 1 Timothy 2:2.

Textual Notes

Part One: Reading

4/III/19: Pennsylvania Charter

3/1	Aug 27 1768 *written in the top left margin.*
3/19	are & *inserted.*

4/III/21: Lyttelton, *History of Henry II*; Robertson, *History of Charles V*

5/8	Aug 1769 *written in the top left margin.*
5/19	Anno 1163 *written in the left margin.*
8/37	due to the King *inserted.*
10/14	Sect 1 *written in the right margin.*
11/18	1 *added.*
11/18–22	Under this head … of the King. *marked as note* 'A' *to the text and written after the summary of Section 1 of Robertson's* History.
11/22	& 2 *added.*
12/1	Sect 2 *written in the right margin.*
12/21	Sect 3 *written in the right margin.*

3/I/5: Steuart, *Principles of Money*

14/9	Value] Denomination
14/26	*Reid has written over the line* 'continues to' *but it is not clear how he intended to revise his wording.*
15/19–21	no legal value … debases their fineness.] no more than their real intrinsick value.

4/III/13: De Lolme, *Constitution of England*

Along the left margin of the page Reid has written: History of the Colonization of the free States of Antiquity Cadel 1777 4to. *He refers to William Barron,* History of the Colonization of the Free States of Antiquity, applied to the Present Contest between

Great Britain and her American Colonies. With Reflections concerning the future Settlement of these Colonies *(London, 1777). Barron was a Church of Scotland minister who became the Professor of Logic, Rhetoric and Metaphysics at the University of St Andrews in 1778.*

4/III/12: De Lolme, *Constitution of England*

18/18–19 He cannot be a Consul or a Dictator.] He cannot be a Dictator or a Consul.

4/III/20: Contareni, *De magistratibus*

19/6 him] those
19/7 father] parents

Part Two: Lectures on Politics

4/III/1: Principles of Politics 1765

23/4 Modelling & Governing Societys of Men] Forming & Governing Political Societys
23/6–7 The Principles of Political Reasoning must be the Active Principles ‹of› Human Nature‹,› the Principles] The Principles of Politics must be drawn from Human Nature & be the Principles
23/8–10 How the Politician … Cunning Man *added.*
23/25–26 where they are not objects of Envy *inserted.*
23/32–33 Wisdom or Virtue Power or all these] Wisdom or Virtue or Both.
24/5 political *inserted.*
24/11 and hold it by military Service *inserted.*
24/12 or Offices *inserted.*
24/27–28 The Choise of the Vizir & other Officers of State] The Choise of whom
24/30 3 That the Grand Seignior be Heir to those who hold offices in the Government *written in the left margin. Reid may have intended to insert this point here.*
24/34 Caution Secrecy *added.*
24/36 & peaceable *inserted.*
25/5–8 The Grand Seignior … Model of Despotism *added.*

4/III/3: Principles of Politics 1766

This manuscript is made up out of two separate sheets of paper with different water marks that have been folded in half twice to yield four leaves in each quire. Folios 3v, 4r–v, 6r, 7r–v and 8r–v are blank.

25/9 May 5 1766 *written in the top left margin.*

25/12–20 Politicks like most other Branches … and apply the proper Remedies *inserted from folio 5r. The insertion is marked* A *in the left margin of folio 5r. In the left margin of folio 1r Reid has written* Substitute A *and drawn a line to indicate the passage to be substituted. The insertion is written in a different ink from that used on folio 1r. The substituted passage reads*: Politicks like most branches of Knowledge that relate to practice may be conceived either as an Art or as a Science. If we consider it as an Art it may be defined to be The Art of Modelling and Governing a State so as to answer the Ends proposed by it. And this Art I conceive may be reduced to these two Problems First A Constitution or Form of Government being given, to shew what are the natural Effects and Consequences of that Constitution, Whether for Instance it will be lasting or of short Duration, whether powerfull against forreign Enemies or weak and easily Subdued, whether it will be internally quiet and peaceable, or turbulent and seditious, whether the Subjects will be oppressed, or enjoy the common Rights & Liberties of Men.

The second Problem is, Having given the end for which a Constitution is intended, to shew that Constitution & model which will most effectually promote and Secure this end.

25/24–26 In this view the Destruction of a b‹ad› ‹f›orm of Government may be a mean to the Production of a better *added in a different ink.*

25/30–26/3 Many Ancient and Modern Authors … the established Religion. *inserted from folio 5r, where the passage is marked* B *in the left margin. Reid has written* add B *after the sentence ending* as well as the good. *The insertion is written in a different ink from that used on folio 1r.*

25/30 Ancient and Modern *inserted.*

25/31–32 Machiavel & Harrington free from this Fault. *added.*

26/10 frequently *inserted.*

26/25–26	The Nature … the Natural *inserted from folio 5r, where the passage is marked* C *in the left margin. Reid has written a corresponding* C *in the left margin of folio 1r. The insertion is written in a different ink from that used on folio 1r.*
26/26–33	The Analogy … the Knowledge of Mankind *inserted from the left margin of folio 1r. The insertion is written in a different ink.*
26/33–34	Objection … by Art *added in a different ink.*
26/35	certain] just
27/12	operate upon] move
27/13	scientifically *inserted.*
28/18–20	2 That against the reality … no force.] 2 That in reality this objection has no force on the supposition of Liberty, against the reality of Political Knowledge.
28/25	the motives or Causes from which those Actions necessarily follow] the motives from which those Actions follow
28/32	or motives *inserted.*
29/8–19	From hence I think … This is undoubtedly true. *added in a different ink.*
29/12	Rules] principles
29/35–30/32	Now there are … Conquered *added in different ink.*
30/33–34	not onely *inserted.*
31/2	totally *inserted.*
31/21–22	bad Men, Common Prudence] bad Men. And even common Prudence
31/23	the rights of *inserted.*
31/28	as a rotten member *inserted.*
31/30	prison, for the stocks or the Gibet.] prison, or for the Gallows.
31/36	individuals *inserted.*
32/13	something in it] something in the Nature of it

4/III/2: Principles of Politics 1766, cont.

32/18	some of *inserted.*
32/31	few *added.*
32/35–33/1	political Body‹.› There can be no reasoning] political Body, nor can there be any reasoning
33/13	that *inserted.*
34/3–4	be, of whose characters we have no particular knowledge] be with whom we have no particular acquaintance

4/III/5: Despotic Government. Aristocracy

34/27	April 17 1765 *written in the top left margin.*
34/31	Morals *inserted.*
35/1	even *inserted.*
35/1–3	Thousands of his slaves … and his Throne *inserted from the left margin.*
35/3	ransacked] searched
35/10	Least they should conceive him to be but a man *inserted.*
36/3	with] in
36/20	Chinese] turk
36/21	more *inserted.*
36/21–22	of a mighty Monarch] of such a mighty Monarch
36/23	page 75 *is written in the left margin.*
36/28	like a bird confined to a Cage *inserted in different ink.*
36/35–36	the human Species] human Creatures
37/2–3	This Government … for many Ages *added.*
37/4	April 18 *written in the left margin.*
37/17	& Magistracy *added.*
37/33	& to representatives of the people *inserted in different ink.*
37/35–36	The Democracies … among the Citizens *added in different ink.*
38/3–6	To these Mixed Forms … Ld Littletons Hist of Hen 2 vol 3d *added in different ink.*

4/III/7: Harrington's Oceana

	This one-page manuscript appears to have been dislocated from 4/III/5.
38/6	April 19 *written in the top left margin.*
38/8	bottom] Ground
38/10	2 An Assembly in whom is the result or whole legislative and part of the Judiciary power. Magistrates & A Senate Chosen by the people Accountable to them & going out by a Rotation *cancelled.*
38/10	Constituent parts of it] Superstructure
38/14–15	He that wasted … in the Commonwealth *added in different ink.*
38/16	100 £ per Annum a Horseman *added in different ink.*
38/17	From 18 to 30 Youth, From 30 Elders *added in different ink.*
38/20	untill a fifth part be proposed & chosen by ballot *added in different ink.*
38/23	Elections of Ministers to vacant parishes *written in the left margin.*

38/23–24	The Deputies the Militia of the Commonwealth *added in different ink.*
38/25	April 22 *written in the left margin.*
38/28–29	Jury Men Overseers of the Ballot *added in different ink.*
38/34	first one for each office by each of the proposers then a second &c *inserted in different ink.*
39/37	Agrarian Law. *added in different ink.*
40/1	April 23 *written in the left margin.*
40/6–7	Election of Ambassadors in Ordinary *inserted.*
40/7	Emergent Elections by Scrutiny *added in different ink.*

4/III/5 (3r): Harrington's Oceana, *cont.*

40/13	April 23 *written in the left margin.*

4/III/6: Reflections on Harrington. Other Commonwealths

See editorial note 40/15 for an explanation of the order in which this manuscript is printed.

40/15–41/30	We have given … out of an Urn *written in different ink and on paper bearing a different water mark than that found on the sheet used for folios 1r–2v.*
41/2	desired *inserted.*
41/13	Jury men *inserted.*
42/2–3	& Courage *inserted.*
42/14	Harringtons prophecy *inserted.*
42/18–19	Harringtons Commonwealth] a lasting commonwealth
42/33–34	& Character *inserted.*
43/12	Abbé de St Pierre's Political Colleg *inserted.*
43/13	Easy Conveyance Store houses *added.*
43/27	among the Subjects *added.*
43/38	in a State follows] in a State that has an extensive land Territory follows
44/9	in this Model *inserted.*

4/III/14: Monarchy

44/24	be free if I should *inserted.*
45/6–7	must be hereditary and the Succession regulate‹d› by fundamental laws *inserted.*

45/7–8 He must if possible add the Glory of a Conqueror to his other Titles *added.*
45/32–47/25 What Montesquieu has said … that are above him *inserted. Reid has marked the insertion point* 'Add A' *in the left margin and the inserted material with an* 'A'. *The inserted material is written in a different ink.*
46/8 & easily *inserted.*
46/13–14 and of the Laws *inserted.*
46/18 & tame *inserted.*
46/20 or Supers‹ti›tion *inserted.*
46/24–27 That Principle …above us in Rank. *This sentence is written at the top of folio 2r above the inserted material.*
46/26 strong *inserted.*
46/29 ought *inserted.*
46/30 be frank and Polite.] be attended with a certain Politeness.
46/37 to the Man of Honour] ‹?›
46/38 little] no
46/38 and ought not to] nor ought to
46/39 spirited] grand
47/6 he will glory] he glories
47/6–7 be open and *inserted.*
47/8 boldness and *inserted.*
47/12–13 taken as a great favour.] taken as a great favour by us.

4/III/11: The British Constitution

48/5 Rules of Succession *inserted.*
48/8 Prerogative Revenue. *inserted.*
48/32 & not be altered or tacked else where *added.*
48/36 & of Voting by the *inserted.*
48/36–37 house Dividing *added.*
49/9–10 Kings Legislative Raises & dissolves it *added.*
49/11–12 Army has the same Interest as the Subjects in General *added.*
49/16 Political *inserted.*
49/19 or Inconveniencies *inserted.*
49/34 publick] good
49/37 these two arise from the Nature of the Constitution *added.*
50/1 Neither the One nor the Other of these parties is always in the Wrong *added.*

50/5	or High Church *inserted.*
50/13–14	See Rapin Dissertation on Whigs & Torries. Bullinbroke Dissertation on Parties Cleghorn's Discourse *added.*
50/16–17	which may be used by the Ministry or by the Candidates *inserted.*
50/22	The Commons unequally represented *added.*
50/27	connexion with forreign Princes *added.*
51/7	it degeneration into a Spirit of Libertinism *added.*
51/21–22	5 A certain Degree … & therefore the br *added.*

4/III/8: The British Constitution, *cont.*

51/23	April 28 *written in the top left margin. 1v is blank.*
51/28	other *inserted.*
51/28–29	model that ever was proposed] form that ever was delineated
51/34–52/1	perhaps however … as it is now. *inserted from the left margin.*
52/25–28	But there is … the proper Remedies *added in different ink.*
53/1	Hereditary *inserted.*
53/4	Dux *inserted.*

4/III/9: Population. National Virtue. National Riches

54/23	May 6 1765 *written in the top left margin.*
55/5	*Reid has drawn a line in the margin alongside the following passage in the manuscript*:

A despotick Monarch may have many Ends that are no wise connected with the good of his people nay that are directly contrary to them. An Aristocracy may also have ends which are contrary to the good and happiness of their Subjects, and to agrandize themselves may grievously oppress the lower ranks of Men. It is onely a representative of the people who can have no interest inconsistent with the happiness of the whole political Society. Therefore I apprehend that we may safely affirm that no form of Government can be reconciled ‹with› the principles of sound Morals in which the people or such a representative of the people as cannot have a different Interest from the whole have not the Legislative power or such a share of it as that they may not be subjected to laws that are grievous to them without their consent.

There are two things essential to every Government which we can approve of as consistent with the rights of Mankind and the ends of

Government First that it be a Government of Laws and not of Men. Without this no man can know what is his own or what he has a right to expect from others. I had rather be left in the State of Nature to vindicate my Rights by the vigor of my arm and the assistance of my friends, than in a State of Society have my Rights depend upon the will of a Man, who is tied down by no law in his Judgment. The will of a Man is liable to be influenced by various motives bad as well as good by lust avarice ambition and revenge, and partial favour as well as by Justice equity and Mercy. A Man is a being compounded of Reason and Passion, and in most men the last principle is often prevalent over the first. But the Law is Reason without Passion. Its determinations are always the same in like cases and it favours the plaintiff no more than the defendant. A man may trust his rights with
1v a Judge who is | obliged to pass Sentence according to law & is liable to severe punishment if he does otherwise, for the same reason as a man will trust his money with a man whom he can compell to restore it if he should have a mind to keep it. A man who has no reason to doubt of the integrity of his Debitor, yet when he lends him A Sum of Money takes a Security by which he has it in his power to compell the debitor or his heirs to make just Restitution. And no Debitor however honest takes it ill that men who entrust him with their Money should take such a Security. In like a Man who is to judge of my Life and fortune ought to give some Security for his Judging equitably. And there can be no such security if there be no Law according to which he is obliged to Judge. There can therefore be no equitable Government without Laws. And all Despotick Government is in its very Constitution injurious to the Rights of Mankind because it assumes the power of Judging of Mens lives and Fortunes without giving any Security of its Judging according to Equity. But Secondly there is another thing Essential to every Government which is consistent with the Rights of Mankind and that is that the Laws be framed and directed with a view to the good & happiness of the Subject. If the Laws are not directed to this End Iniquity may be established by a law, the laws themselves may be iniqu‹it›ous and unjust and contrary to the rights of Mankind. It is possible that lawgivers may mistake the publick good even when they intend it. But such mistakes are commonly discovered by Experience and if the Law is very grievous the grievance will be felt and may be remedied. But where the publick good is not intended there is no remedy to be expected. And such

Government is iniq‹uit›ous and contrary to the rights of Mankind. Even that Dominion which we assume over the Brute Animals which serve us such as sheep oxen horses & dogs could hardly be reconciled to the principles of Morality, if their life was upon the whole made more unhappy by that Dominion. Far less can any Government of a few over the rest of the human Species be justified if it is not directed to the good and happiness of the Governed. For there is in human Government no Superiority of Nature in the Governors, as there is in mankind over the brutes. Every Government therefore which is not directed to promote the good of the Governed is a Usurpation without Right nor can any Length of Time give it a just Titlle. The people may be subject through fear or through ignorance. But if they are sufficiently enlightned to understand the Rights that belong to them as men, And if at the same time they have it in their power to shake it off and to establish a better and more equitable Government, I have no doubt but they have as good Right to do it as a man has to defend himself against a highway man. They need not search into ancient Records or Usages to prove their Right to be free and happy. Every man is born with this Right and if all his ancestors from Adam
2r had agreed to deprive him of this Right, this cannot | weaken it, altho it may put him in such circumstances as that it is not in his power to assert and vindicate his Right. *He has then written*: All that is marked in the Margin in the two preceding pages by a line drawn from top to bottom belongs to Political Jurisprudence.

55/9–10 the attainment of *added.*
55/18 Persecution *inserted.*
55/29–30 The population of the Earth owing to this *inserted.*
55/34 before luxury took place *inserted.*
56/4 May 7 1765 *written in the top left corner.*
57/2 easy and] difficult or
57/14 Learning and Arts *added in different ink.*
57/16–22 1 What is to be called Riches … Labour & skill *added in different ink.*

4/III/15: National Riches. Commerce. Money. False Maxims

Reid has numbered his definitions and propositions in the left margins of his pages.

57/29 Wood for Various Uses *inserted in a different ink.*

57/32	produced] got
58/8–9	which require more Labour & Industry in their Inhabitants *added in a different ink.*
58/10–11	consumed by Use by time or Accidents.] consumed by Use or Perish by time or Accidents.
58/12	Acquired *inserted.*
58/32–33	What a man produces … is called a Commodity *added from the left margin.*
58/37	If one Nation] If one Man or Nation
59/1	or Conveniencys *inserted.*
59/8	nearly *inserted.*
59/18–19	have once come to settle at their Natural price] have once a Settled price
59/34	or in opinion] or in the General opinion
60/1	Quarters of Wheat] Bolls
60/2	Quarters] Bolls
60/7	Quarters] bolls
60/14	nearly *added.*
60/19	so much in proportion to *inserted.*
60/22	& their Accomodations for Store *inserted.*
61/3	the Merchant forsees] the Merchant or Manufacturer forsee
61/4	providing] Making
61/5–6	are raised above or brought below] rise above or fall below
61/8	most *added.*
61/11–12	not perishable *inserted.*
61/18	ascertain] limit
61/22	their Servants & Attendants *inserted.*
61/23	Soldiers *added.*
61/23	Excise & custom house Officers &c Sailors *added.*
61/26–27	Others direct the Labourers‹:› Stewarts overseers bookke‹e›pers &c *added.*
61/28	infancy *added.*
61/28–29	bearing & Nursing Children *added.*
62/16	32 The Spirit of Commerce in a Nation is favourable to some Virtues and unfavourable to others. *cancelled.*
63/5	Facilitates Exchange *added.*
63/9	Hence the Notion of its Receiving its Value from Statute *cancelled.*
63/14	Exporting] transporting

63/17–34	Silver & Gold … of other goods *inserted. Reid has marked the insertion point* 'see A below' *and the inserted passage with an* 'A'. *The inserted material is written in a different ink.*
63/17	Silver & Gold] Money
63/27	but will be exported *added.*
63/27–28	If too high labouring people … be counter fitted] If too high it will be exported.
63/36	consists in] bears proportion to
63/36–38	yet it must consist chiefly in the Quantity of Commodities which are not perishable *added.*
64/4–5	The Nation ought to have onely one Standart viz Silver *added in a different ink.*
64/6–18	The difficulty of knowing … to the Nation *added in a different ink.*

4/III/16: Banks. Paper Credit

This set of notes is written on a sheet of paper whose size is strikingly different from the sheets that Reid normally used. Typically, Reid started with a large sheet of paper (the sheet used in MS 2131/4/III/13, for example, is 32.6 cm wide × 41.2 cm high). He then folded his sheet in half and then in half again to produce a quire of four leaves. This manuscript is written on a single piece of paper measuring 10.2 cm wide × 16.5 cm high.

4/III/10: Banks. Paper Credit, *cont.* Revenue

65/24	May 13 1765 *written in the top left margin.*
65/27	Defence against] Security from
66/3	notion] Idea
66/17	and disadvantages *inserted.*
66/28	L'Esprit des Loix Livre 22 chapitre 8 *written in the left margin.*
67/13	Manufacturers] Merchants *The rewording is in a different ink.*
67/22	Of Interest of Money. *is written in the left margin.*
67/23	May 14 *written in the left margin.*
68/10	in Gold or Silver *inserted.*
68/15	Credit] money
68/19	May 15 1765 *written in the left margin.*
68/28	May 16 1765 *written in the left margin.*
68/32	Strong Places *inserted.*

69/1 May 17 1765 *written in the left margin.*
69/2–3 Land Tax, Taxes on the necessaries of Life *added in a different ink.*

4/III/11, 2v: Revenue, *cont.*

69/6–7 or Census *added in a different ink.*
69/18 Agriculture *inserted.*

Appendix to the Lectures on Politics

4/III/4: Value and Price

Folio 1r of this manuscript contains material related to Reid's lectures on jurisprudence. See Reid, Practical Ethics, *pp. 58–59.*

69/21 March 25 *written in the top left margin.*
70/6 advantage *inserted.*
70/8 tills and *inserted.*
70/21 habitation] house
70/29–30 will become more complex *inserted.*
71/3 or Estimation *added.*
71/9 among his superfluities *inserted.*
71/23 was the property of] belonged to
71/26 We never think of valuing] but we never think of valuing
71/32 a social & commercial State.] a commercial and Social State.
71/35–72/15 It is difficult … & how it is measured. *This and the remaining part of 4/III/4, which we print below pp. 77–78, were added in different ink.*
72/4 in us *added.*
72/6 natural *inserted.*
72/9 It can admit of no doubt,] There can be no doubt,

4/III/17: Value and Price, *cont.*

Concerning the place of this manuscript inside 4/III/4, see editorial note 69/22, pp. 187–88.

72/16–75/7 As the natural Use … employed in it rises. *marked in the left margin* 'A' *at the beginning and* 'A Ends' *at the end of the addition.*

72/17	real or Imaginary *inserted.*
72/26	to have *inserted.*
72/27	desires to *added.*
72/28	after some bidding and coning *inserted.*
72/29	Since therefore the price] It might seem therefore that the price
73/7	such Maxims] them
73/9	up *inserted.*
73/17–19	It is from … must be derived *inserted from the left margin.*
73/22	quick sighted] sharp
73/23	otherwise he will soon lose his character *inserted.*
73/26	what is, in his own Estimation, a moderate Profit.] what in his own Estimation, is a moderate Profit.
73/33–34	have not such Confidence in each other *inserted.*
73/39–74/1	This is … considerable Time *added from the left margin.*
74/1	However] But
74/7	particular] certain
74/8	professions must live] professions of Life must live
74/28–29	by the spread of Luxury *inserted.*
75/8	ordinary *inserted.*
75/30	by that means *inserted.*
76/5	bringing a great odium upon himself *inserted.*
76/9	prepare & *inserted.*
76/13–14	he has money & skill Patience and spirit] he has spirit and Patience & money & skill
76/15	greatly improves] doubles
76/23	barren] New
76/39	& vegetables *inserted.*
77/11	natural *inserted.*
77/12	High Rents Taxes Luxury *added.*

4/III/4: Value and Price, *cont.*

77/32–78/13	Profits of those … criminal in most nations. *added in different ink, cf. textual note 71/35–72/15 above.*
78/8	These practices injurious … weight and fineness. *inserted from the bottom of the page.*
78/12	or uttering false coin knowingly *inserted.*

Part Three: Discourses, Discussions and Conversations

2/II/16: Paper Credit

79/4	upon ready payment] without Credit
79/17	lie dead *inserted.*
79/23	labouring *inserted.*
79/29–30	were partly useless and partly burthensome] were all useless or burthensome
81/17	the increase of real *inserted.*
81/35–82/5	The Notion … just and Necessary *These notes are written in a different coloured ink (black as opposed to brown) from the preceding text and were presumably jotted down at a later date. Reid has also added the following – written vertically – at the bottom of f 2v:* The proverbs of Solomon contain a very great variety of matter Not onely moral precepts and Instruction but various observations on the tempers the virtues and vices of men on the causes of their happines‹s› & Misery on the ways of attaining riches honour quiet & contentment of mind. of Making friends and preserving them and in a word every thing that relates to life and Manners. It must be no smal advantage to us if we will improve it aright to have upon Subjects of So great and general Concern the Observations of a person of So great Wisdom & so great Experience as Solomon was and one who was also guided by the holy Spirit in the composition of this Book. But it happens through the Nature of proverbial writing as well as from other Concurring Causes that many of his proverbs have a good deal of Obscurity in them. It is easy indeed to put a meaning upon a Single short detailed Sentence but where a Sentence is capable of two or three different meanings we cannot always be sure whether we hit upon the right one. Indeed if the Proverbs of any neighbouring nation should be translated into our language many of them would look very Strange and uncouth many of them very obscure to us we should stand in need not onely to know the language the rites customs and government of the Country in order to the understanding of them. Nay perhaps after all many of them would still be unintelligible to us till we knew in what manner or to what subjects they were commonly applyed. It may therefore be expected to be much more so with the proverbs of a people so distant in time and place and so

different from us in Language customs Manners Government and almost every thing wherein one man can differ from another.

82/6 one] some

82/8–9 supply all his own wants by his own Labour onely] supply his wants by his own Labour

82/19 either *inserted.*

82/39 therefore *inserted.*

6/I/13: Servants' Wages

This manuscript is largely transcribed in Walter Robson Humphries, 'The First Aberdeen Philosophical Society', Transactions of the Aberdeen Philosophical Society *5 (1938): 203–38, at pp. 229–32.*

83/9–11 *The text of the question addressed is written in a different ink.*

83/14 Labour] Servants Labour

83/24–25 or from Corn to Garden Stuff *added.*

84/2 The officers of *inserted.*

84/4 the Crew of *inserted.*

84/12 a greater proportion … persons of higher rank] more of Servile Condition than of higher rank

84/13 consequently *inserted.*

84/15 Service] Servants

84/22 Manufactures] Luxury and Trade

84/28–30 and so to increase … at the same time] and so both increase … their Number.

85/24–25 A country house and a town house] A country and town house

86/10 *Reid has added the following passage related to the discussion question*: To reduce the Wages of Servants by Laws or Acts of Justices of peace seems to be of all Methods the most unfit for the end proposed by it having a direct tendency to diminish the number of Servants. It will readily be allowed and experience proves it that when the wages that Manufacturers give are reduced. the number of Servants is increased. And if the manufacturers wages are increased the number of Servants is thereby diminished. By parity of Reason if you bring down servants wages, they will go away from the farmer to the manufacturer, and their number being diminished their wages must increase in spite of all Laws.

A general Naturalization would probably bring more rich people than poor into the Kingdom which would increase the Evil.

Below this passage, Reid has added the following: Dr Skene Whether the Verdict of a Jury should be unani‹m›ous or by a majority. Dr Campbel How far human Laws can justly make alterations in what seems to be founded on the Law of Nature. Mr Stewart Whether Human Laws be binding on the Consciences of Men Mr Reid Whether by proper Laws the number of births in Great Brittain might not be doubled or at least greatly increased. Mr Tho Gordon Whether the Current Coin of the Nation ought to be debased by alloy or raised in its value so as there shall be no profit made by exporting it Dr Gerard Whether it is better that Courts of Law & Courts of Equity be different or that the same Courts determine either according to Law or Equity as Circumstances require. Mr Farquhar. Whether Justice is most Effectually promoted in Civil & Criminal Courts where the Judges are Numerous or where few. Mr Beattie What are the Advantages & disadvantages of an Extensive Commerce

6/I/7: Jury Verdict

86/12 it is *inserted.*
86/16–17 the former requiring … onely a majority *added.*
86/18 an enquiry] a point
86/20 I know not *added.*
87/17–18 in the one as in the other.] in them as in an English Jury.
87/25 Equity] impartiality
87/25 given] pronounced
88/30 more] full as

2/II/17: Population Growth

Folios 1r–3r of this manuscript are transcribed in Humphries, 'First Aberdeen Philosophical Society', pp. 233–36.

88/34–35 *Written in the left margin.*
89/6–7 as that which hath … Strength & Riches *added.*
89/10–11 they would all … before twenty years of Age] they would all be married before twenty years of Age where sickness or some uncommon accident did not hinder

89/15 pair] man

89/15 two Million] a Million. *Over the line Reid has written, and then cancelled,* viz 1,048,616, *replacing the number with a revised figure of* 2,081,152.

89/16 above two million of millions] above a million of millions. *Over the line Reid has written the figure* 20,09900,0000000. *In the left margin he has cancelled* 1 500,000 : : 250,000,000000 *and written* 2:2081152:2,165596,823552 ≒

89/21 in high Life, and in low Life] in high and low Life

89/23 imaginary *inserted.*

89/24 on which they can consume] by which they can spend

89/25 even *added.*

89/28 1st *added.*

89/31 By *inserted.*

89/34 Passion] Appetite

89/34 discharg it self] be satisfied

90/1 the people of Fortune increase] such people marry

90/2 & they will always find Heirs to their Fortunes *added.*

90/8 take up] set up

90/8–9 or being beggars *inserted.*

90/12 nor can have from their parents] nor their parents can afford them

90/13 a] some

90/20 own *inserted.*

90/23–24 untill they can put them off to service.] untill they be ‹*blank*› years of age.

90/25 Now it may be observed *added.*

90/26 from vanity & extravagance *inserted.*

90/28 while] that

90/28 would] will

91/3 the particular laws] particular laws

91/8 2 That those] & those

91/14 judge of their] judge their

91/18 28 *cancelled over the line.*

91/22 28,5] 30

91/24 58,5] 60

91/24 68,5] 70

92/8 28,5] 30

92/11 58,5] 60

92/11	68,5] 70
92/13–31	The immediate Causes … the Supply of those Wants. *written in a different ink (black) from the rest of the manuscript (brown).*

6/I/14: Courts of Equity

92/32	*written in the top left margin.*
93/2	and not according to Law *inserted.*
93/6	1 *added.*
93/7	2 *added.*
93/26–27	but that the law should continue in force and that a Court of Equity should yet have power] but to suppose that the law is to continue in force and that a Court of Equity has power
94/3	from it *added.*
95/11–12	to correct the evils arising from the too literal] to supply the too literal
95/14	to oblige courts of Law] to permit courts of Judicature

4/III/23a: Glasgow Trade

95/33	manufactures] wool

3061/4: Diminution of Coin

96/16	form] form of a Plough
96/22	among all Nations *inserted.*
96/24–25	their plenty, or Scarcity,] plenty, or Scarcity,
97/2	its *inserted.*
97/6–9	to determine … Accademical Life.] It would require an acquaintance of the advantages and disadvantages of both Methods which can onely be the fruit of long Experience to determine this Question.
97/12	the Mint] Money
97/29	near *added.*
97/33	able to make men] made to
98/4	degree of *inserted.*
98/6	Now if both these Ends can be] Now supposing these Ends to be
98/7	indeed *inserted.*
98/12	known *inserted.*
98/37	precise degree *inserted.*

99/5	The Reason] The sole Reason
99/18	than he truely owed *added.*
99/18	Every Creditor] and Every Creditor
99/23	wantonly *inserted.*
100/30	in the Main *added.*
100/30–32	to wit … received in payment] to wit that after a day prefixed the clipt Coin should pass onely according to its weight that it Should all come in to the Mint be recoined without charge and of the old Standard.
100/32–34	This Operation … 1200,000 £ Sterling *added from the left margin. After the addition Reid has cancelled the following*: This was the Remedy adopted. and this put an immediate Stop to the Evil. It was no longer any Mans interest to clip the Money. It was every mans Interest to bring to the Mint all the clipt Money in his possession, and to receive an equal Weight of new Coin in place of it It was no longer the Interest of any Man to hoard the money that remained unclipped, so that all the hoarded Stores came into circulation. Thus a temporary Recourse to the Chinese Method of weighing money saved the Nation, when Money in tale had brought it to the brink of Destruction.
101/1	at least *inserted.*
101/8	quite *inserted.*
101/11	Money] Silver coined or uncoined
101/13–14	will, like the price of all other Commodities, be Regulated] will be like the price of all other Commodities Regulated
101/32	against us *inserted.*
101/38–39	medium price] price
103/8	are so great] are by this Means great
103/18	because it is of more real Value *inserted.*
103/34	their being worn providing they] its being worn providing it
103/37–38	shall be understood] be understood
103/38	onely *inserted.*
104/6	*Note in right margin*: Suppose one gets heavy Gold for light Silver he pays £46 14 6 for a pound of Guineas when the Guineas are Melted down into an Ingot he may carry them to Market and get £2.6 for his trouble NB an Ounce of Gold in Coin is worth £3 17 10½ whatever Gold Bullion sells for beyond this is so much clear gain to him that Melts down our heavy Guineas, or sends them abroad.

104/31–32	It was men being obliged … that produced] It was this that produced
104/39–105/1	But Now] But
105/1	though] springing indeed
105/2	Both] But both
105/19–20	and Still renewed as it began to wear *inserted.*
105/21	bullion as cheap.] bullion as cheap & when he takes as much from the current Value as he takes from the Weight.
105/23–24	because he takes … from the weight *inserted.*
105/26	invariably] allways
105/28	value] thing
105/28–31	It is … before the end of it.] It was for instance at least five per Cent better in the beginning of this Century than it is now, & if no Remedy is applied … before the end of this Century than it was at the beginning of it.
105/33	as the other] as the other is.
105/38	and *inserted.*
106/24	Lent money] stock

3061/3: Warehousing Grain

107/3–4	Session of Parliament,] Session of Parliament when the Bill was presented,
107/29–30	Duty free *inserted.*
107/36	as *inserted.*
107/38–108/2	can propose … British Merchants] evidently appears to be intended to open a door for the Carrying Trade in Grain in G. B.
108/12	to any Man.] to any Man. The Dutch have long been in the possession of the carrying trade their laws favour while the laws of most other Nations are unfavourable to it excepting in the East India Trade. They understand their Interest as well as any Nation in Europe. And we may judge that they find their Account in it by their Continuing it for more than a Century. Why should the Landed Gentlemen desire to exclude our Merchants from so honest & so usefull a branch of Traffick?
108/23	is in proportion] is very nearly in proportion
108/26	Field] Extent of Land
108/30	labouring *inserted.*
108/31–32	in ordinary years *inserted.*

108/33–35	That this fluctuation … acknowledges.] This fluctuation of the price of Grain, every Person acquainted with political Subjects acknowledges, ought by all means that human Wisdom can devise to be prevented or lessened as much as possible.
109/3–4	The Variations … much greater.] The Variations in the produce of the Silver and Gold Mines are as great or perhaps much greater than the Variations of the Cropts of Corn.
109/7	last past *inserted.*
109/19	Grain] Grain or Meal
109/21	grain] grain or Meal
109/21	according to Law *inserted.*
109/33	I think *inserted.*
110/5	years of *inserted.*
110/9–10	Effect which … to make] Effect of the Storing of Grain in Cheap years is, that it tends to make
111/14	upon the whole *inserted.*
111/16–18	that the more … more of it] that when a Commodity is greatly below the usual price it will be less frugally used and more of it
111/27–29	When Grain … is converted into Malt] When Grain is very cheap the more of it is given to fouls to horses dogs Swine and other Animals, the more is made in to Stearch and Batter, the more of it is converted into Malt
111/31	will] does
112/11	and as they must employ] and if they employ
112/19–20	The Domestick Trade … can spare *inserted from the left margin.*
112/22–23	carry with Profit … he has still] carry the Commodities of any other Nation, with Profit, he has still
112/28	& Marseiles *inserted.*
112/37	& Swedish *inserted.*
113/2	with them and with other nations *inserted.*
113/36	Labourers] Labour
113/39	trading & industrious *inserted.*
114/6–7	by old age *inserted.*
114/19	This ‹is› … a Nation. *added.*
114/25–30	The last of … Moderate Subsistance. *inserted from the right margin.*
114/35	secondly *added.*
114/37	is given *inserted.*
115/5–7	If the rise … their Variations *inserted from the right margin,*

replacing a deleted sentence which reads: And these Variations in most kinds of Labour are far less than the Variations that happen in the price of Grain.

115/7–8 But they are] The Variations in the Wages of Labour and in the Price of Subsistence

115/8 in their risings & fallings *inserted.*

115/9 to each other *inserted.*

115/10 For in those transient & temporary Variations] so that

115/11 commonly *inserted.*

115/12 Labour will for a time rise] Labour rise highest

115/13 due *inserted.*

115/19 Expence] Price

115/21 & Meal *inserted.*

115/23 those Commodities] Grain

115/35 But *added.*

115/35 First *inserted.*

116/9–10 for a Market *inserted.*

116/13–14 of the Estates last described *inserted.*

116/23 & all whose tennants do so *added.*

117/3–4 what we have bought from them & payed *inserted.*

117/11 has bought] buys

3061/5: Usury

117/30 Quest. Whether it be proper to fix by Law the highest lawfull Rate of Interest, so as to make it Penal, in any case, to take a higher Interest for the loan of Money. *cancelled.*

117/30 To prevent Oppression, by exorbitant Interest for money borrowed,] In order to prevent the Oppression of those who are obliged to borrow money, by the exaction of exorbitant Interest,

117/33 higher than] higher price for the loan than

118/2 some of] some parts of

118/13–14 Contrary to … contra se *inserted.*

118/17 most *inserted.*

118/19 ten] five

118/25 in the Ancient World *inserted.*

118/38 out] forth

118/39 Innocent] Righteous

119/2 because he was a Brother *inserted.*

119/5	partly perhaps] very probably
119/5	partly] partly perhaps
119/19	permitted divorce] divorce
119/25	forty] forty or fifty
119/27	Now *inserted.*
119/35	crying Sins] Sins
120/2	before us] before us Whether it be necessary or Expedient in the present State of Society among us to fix by a Law a Rate of Interest which, no Man can go beyond without being guilty of the Crime of Usury. Whether it be … Crime of Usury *cancelled.*
120/4	practical *inserted.*
120/8	even *added.*
120/18	moderate & the oppressive] lawfull & the unlawfull
120/37–38	Resistance to] Rebellion against
121/6	& executed *inserted.*
121/20–21	as a Blessing even *inserted.*
121/22	Repreve, *inserted.*
121/26	fortunate Event] good fortune
121/32	let me beg] let me rather beg
121/33–34	rather than make … disgracefull Manner *inserted.*
121/37	not onely] both
121/38	least *inserted.*
122/17	there is no Commerce.] they are not commercial.
123/23–24	The few … but it is commonly] and although the few that follow it in London are often found to make rich, it is commonly
123/28	But] Yet
123/30	a Pawn Broker is an odious Trade. *inserted.*
124/4	to wit *inserted.*
124/8	We find] Now
124/11	The Egyptians *inserted.*
124/15	their Liberties] their full Liberties
124/23	and Spain *inserted.*
124/23	by degrees *inserted.*
124/25	alone] onely
124/35	usefull and *inserted.*
125/6	was reasonable] is reasonable
125/14	of them *inserted.*
125/15	is its real Value] may be its real Value
125/16	in all Commercial Countries *inserted.*

125/35 many different] a variety of
125/39 what the Law calls *inserted.*
126/12 these]such
126/21–22 the price of Victual, is fixed annually by a Jury in what is called the Fiars.] the price of Victual to take place in similar cases, is fixed by a Jury annually in what is called the Fiars.
126/28 extend] enlarge
127/4–5 the Imagination of Men] their Imagination
127/18 severe Laws] Laws
127/28 and his being able] and being able
128/2–7 A young Man … interposition of Law. *inserted from the right margin.*
128/26–27 and a Great proportion of that of England *inserted.*
128/32 of] upon
128/38–129/13 If we look … some other Country *inserted from the left margin.*
129/14 in the intercourse] between the state
129/17 in both.] in both Countrys.
129/20 from Jews *inserted.*
129/30 hundred millions] hundreds
129/31 proper to be laid *inserted.*
130/12–13 of Buyers against Buyers, and Sellers against Sellers] among them
131/10 now *inserted.*
131/12 indeed *inserted.*
131/13 all *inserted.*
131/13 a small Stock] their small Stocks
131/15 onely *added.*
131/22 they would do *inserted.*
131/37 indeed *inserted.*
132/1 part] set
132/2 already as rich as they *added.*
132/4 in most Cases *inserted.*
132/9–10 when they find their mutual interest in making a bargain] as far as they are
132/28 the knowing Merchant] the Merchant
132/30 by the Law *inserted.*
133/3 of the same kind *inserted.*
133/4 of equal fortune *inserted.*
133/16 Lender] person

133/16–17 is very mercifull to the fradulent Borrower, it *inserted.*
133/24 The Law therefore which] It seems therefore to me that the Law which
133/28 in which] wherein
133/32–33 Sentiments concerning Laws made or to be made with freedom & even in a more publick manner than I now do.] Sentiments with freedom & even in a more publick manner than I now do concerning Laws made or to be made.

3061/6: The Utopian System

The opening pages, 134/4 to 137/17, and the final paragraph, 154/4 to 154/22, of 'Some Thoughts on the Utopian System' were published in the Glasgow Courier *on 18 December 1794 under the title 'Danger of Political Innovation' (hereafter referred to as GC). They were then reprinted in [Robert Cleghorn],* Sketch of the Character of the Late Thomas Reid, D.D. Professor of Moral Philosophy in the University of Glasgow; with Observations on the Danger of Political Innovation, from a Discourse Delivered on 28th. Nov. 1794 by *Dr. Reid*, before the Literary Society in Glasgow College *(Glasgow, 1796), pp. 9–16 (hereafter referred to as S), and in Appendix II of Archibald Arthur*, Discourses on Theological and Literary Subjects *(Glasgow, 1803), pp. 518–23, under the heading 'Observations on the Danger of Political Innovation, from a Discourse delivered on the 28th November 1794, before the Literary Society in Glasgow College, by DR. REID, and published by his consent' (hereafter referred to as A). There are minor differences in accidentals and wording in the three published versions. The manuscript has been collated with these published versions. We have recorded differences in wording, but we have not noted variations in accidentals or the organisation of paragraphs. An earlier transcription of the complete text was published in Reid,* Practical Ethics, *pp. 277–99. A version in which Reid's prose has been transformed into modern English and some elisions made is to be found in Shinichi Nagao (ed.),* Politics and Society in Scottish Thought *(Exeter, 2007), pp. 179–200.*

134/8 Question *omitted in GC, S and A.*
135/15 those Electors] the electors *in GC, S and A.*

135/22 who are both knowing] both knowing *in GC, S and A.*

135/26 & the best Men] and best men *in GC, S and A.*

135/36 from the one] from one *in GC, S and A.*

135/38 f‹i›rm. *The most likely reading of this word in the manuscript is 'form', but we have followed the reading given in GC, S and A.*

136/2 upon] on *in GC, S and A.*

136/5 Reasonableness or Utility] reasonableness and utility *in GC, S and A.*

136/19 Offices] officers *in S and A.*

136/25 with] which *in S.*

136/25 very *inserted.*

136/38 intended and *omitted in GC, S and A.*

137/17 Nation;] nation— *in GC, S and A. The text in GC, S and A then jumps to 154/4. The exclusion of material from the manuscript is indicated in the printed texts by the use of long dashes.*

138/5 live *inserted.*

138/30 Men] them

138/37 Citizens are p‹r›operly enlightned in their Duty, and have] Citizens being p‹r›operly enlightned in their Duty, they have

139/20–21 & to enlighten them in what is right & wrong, honourable and dishonourable *inserted.*

140/16 we may call] is

140/27 this common Stock] the common Stock

140/32 from a savage State *inserted.*

140/36 as it is said *inserted.*

140/38 of the Jesuites in Paraguay *inserted.*

141/12 would endeavour to prove] conceive

141/14 any] the

142/22 but] than

142/25 become *inserted.*

142/26 consequence of *inserted.*

142/36 own *inserted.*

142/39 Envy & Discontent in all] Envy Discontent

144/2 Part *inserted.*

144/10 present *inserted.*

144/12–13 to Neighbours, to Friends, to the nearest Relations] to Neighbours, Friends, the nearest Relations

144/31 The mean] The proper mean

146/20 and observed *added.*

147/13	having *inserted.*
147/18	Substantial] proper
148/33	such] these
151/11	Sollicitors *inserted.*
151/17	as well as Property *inserted.*
151/27	the Laws] Laws
152/19	hitherto *inserted.*
152/26	that which by the common principles of human Nature *inserted.*
152/34–39	It is by Temptation … God and Man. *inserted from the left margin.*
153/3	is not for us to kno‹w›, it *inserted.*
153/4	who *inserted.*
153/9–10	and discharges the duties of it *inserted.*
153/13	; Such a Man *added.*
153/17	poverty this is granted; & therefore, they require] poverty & therefore require
153/23	leaves no room for] gives no opportunity to the Exercise of
153/28	Aid to Virtue] Aid to the Principle of Virtue
153/30	When this is the Case the Utopian indeed does his Duty] In this Case the Utopian indeed may do his Duty
153/33	undue *inserted.*
153/37–38	and whose Interests interfere & cross on‹e› another in innumerable Instances *inserted.*
154/5	Child] Children
154/5–7	It is a Relation … must be Savages. *inserted from the left margin.*
154/19	As He is] He is
154/21	So it is] And it is
154/21	So it is] so is it *in GC, S and A.*
154/22	lead … Honesty.] “lead … honesty.” *in GC, S and A.*

Bibliography

Manuscript Sources

Aberdeen University Library (AUL)

Gordon, Thomas. 'Questions Discussed by the Aberdeen Philosophical Society'. MSS 3107/2/1–8.

'Minutes of the Rectorial Elections, Marischal College, 1723–1860'. MS M 104.

Reid, Thomas. Birkwood Collection. MSS 2131/1–8.

—— 'Original Papers of Thomas Reid, 1710–1796'. MSS 30061/1–26.

Skene, David. 'Literary Essays'. MS 475.

—— 'Notes of Discourses in the Philosophical Society of Aberdeen'. MS 540.

Glasgow University Library (GUL)

Jack, Robert. 'Dr. Reid's Lectures, 1774–1776'. MSS Gen. 116–18.

'Laws of the Literary Society in Glasgow College'. MS Murray 505.

'Minutes of the College Literary Society, 1790–99'. MS Gen. 4.

'Professors Receipt Book, 1770–[1789]'. Spec. Coll. MS Lib. (uncatalogued).

Mitchell Library, Glasgow

Baird, George. 'Notes from the Lectures of Dr. Thomas Reid, 1779–1780'. MS A104929.

Newspapers and Journals

Aberdeen Journal; and North-British Magazine

Edinburgh Evening Courant

Edinburgh Magazine

Glasgow Courier

London Magazine

Scots Magazine

Weekly Magazine, or Edinburgh Amusement

Primary Sources

Anon. *An abridgment of the public statutes in force and use relative to Scotland, from the union, in the fifth year of Queen Anne, to the twenty-seventh year of his present Majesty King George II, inclusive.* 2 vols. Edinburgh, 1755.

—— *Abstract of Some Statutes and Orders of King's College in Old Aberdeen. M.DCC.LIII. With Additions M.DCC.LIV.* [Aberdeen], [1754].

—— *Acts of Assembly, Passed in the Island of Jamaica; from the Year 1681, to the Year 1769, Inclusive.* 2 vols. Saint Jago de la Vega, 1769–71.

—— *The Acts of Sederunt of the Lords of Council and Session, from the 1628 to 1740, Copied from the Books of Sederunt.* 2 vols. Edinburgh, 1740–53.

—— *An Apology for the Business of Pawn-Broking.* London, 1744.

—— *Asmodeus; or, Strictures on the Glasgow Democrats. In a Series of Letters, Several of which were Lately Published in the Glasgow Courier.* Glasgow, 1793.

—— *Considerations on our Corn-Laws and the Bill Proposed to Amend them.* Aberdeen and Edinburgh, 1777.

—— *Corn-Bill Hints, in Answer to the Memorial for the Merchants, Traders and Manufacturers of the City of Glasgow.* Glasgow, 1777.

—— *Essays. I, On the Public Debt. II, On Paper-Money, Banking, &c. III, On Frugality.* London, 1755.

—— *Essay on the Corn Laws; to Evince, on the Most Indubitable Ground, in Opposition to the Inflammatory Memorial for the Merchants, Traders and Manufacturers of Glasgow, the Equity and Expediency of Prohibiting the Importation of Oats or Oat-Meal, unless the Price of the Latter Shall Be at, or above, Sixteen Shillings per Boll.* Edinburgh, 1777.

—— *The Law concerning Pawn-Brokers and Usurers: Containing all the Statutes and Cases in Law and Equity Extant, which Relate to Pawns and Usury, Disposed under Proper Heads.* [London], 1745.

—— *A Letter to the Members in Parliament, on the Present State of the Coinage: With Proposals for the Better Regulation thereof.* London, 1771.

—— *Memorial for the Merchants, Traders and Manufacturers of Glasgow.* Glasgow, 1777.

—— *Mons pietatis Londinensis: A Narrative or Account of the Charitable Corporation, for Relief of Industrious Poor, by Assisting them with Small Sums upon Pledges, at Legal Interest.* London, 1719.

—— 'On Trade and Commerce'. In [Robert Dodsley], *The Preceptor: Containing a General Course of Education.* 2 vols. London, 1748. Vol. II: 383–464.

—— *Reflections on Usury: Containing an Account of those Usurious Contracts, Carried on under the Mode of Undervalued Annuities: To which is Added the*

Substance of the Bill now before the House to Prevent them; with Cursory Observations on it. London, 1777.

—— *Report from the Committee Appointed to Take into Consideration the Laws now in Being against Usury, and the Present Practice of Purchasing Annuities for the Life of the Grantor*. [London], 1777.

—— *A Scheme whereby the Whole National Debt may be Paid in about Thirty Years, without any Additional Tax upon the Nation, or any Injury Done, either to Government, or its Creditors*. [London], 1778.

—— *A Scotchman's Remark on the Farce of Love à la Mode*. London, 1760.

—— *The Several Reports, with the Appendix, which Is to one of them, from the Committee of the House of Commons, to whom the Petition of the Proprietors of the Charitable Corporation for Relief of Industrious Poor by Assisting them with Small Sums upon Pledges at Legal Interest, Assembled in their General Court, was Referred; and the Proceedings of the said House thereupon*. London, 1732.

—— *Votes and Proceedings of the House of Representatives of the Province of Pennsylvania. Beginning the Fourth Day of December, 1682*. 3 vols. Philadelphia, PA, 1752–54.

Arbuthnot, John. 'An Argument for Divine Providence, Taken from the Constant Regularity Observ'd in the Births of Both Sexes'. *Philosophical Transactions* 27 (1710–12): 186–90.

Aristotle. *The Complete Works of Aristotle: The Revised Oxford Translation*. Edited by Jonathan Barnes. 2 vols. Princeton, NJ, 1984.

Arthur, Archibald. *Discourses on Theological and Literary Subjects*. Glasgow, 1803.

Bacon, Sir Francis. *The Philosophical Works of Francis Bacon, Baron of Verulam, Viscount St. Albans, and Lord High Chancellor of England.* Edited by John M. Robertson. London, 1905.

Barron, William. *History of the Colonization of the Free States of Antiquity, applied to the Present Contest between Great Britain and her American Colonies*. London, 1777.

Baxter, Richard. *A Christian Directory: Or, a Summ of Practical Theologie, and Cases of Conscience*. London, 1673.

Beattie, James. *The Correspondence of James Beattie*. Edited by Roger J. Robinson. 4 vols. Bristol, 2004.

[Beldam, William]. *Considerations on Money, Bullion and Foreign Exchanges; Being an Enquiry into the Present State of the British Coinage; Particularly with Regard to the Scarcity of Silver Money. With a View to Point Out the Most Probable Means of Making it More Plentiful* [1771]. London, 1772.

Bentham, Jeremy. *Defence of Usury; Shewing the Impolicy of the Present Legal Restraints on the Terms of Pecuniary Bargains*. London, 1787.

—— *Jeremy Bentham's Economic Writings: [A] Critical Edition Based on his Printed Works and Unprinted Manuscripts*. Edited by Werner Stark. 3 vols. London, 1952–54.

Berkeley, George. *The Querist, containing several Queries proposed to the Consideration of the Public* (1735–37). In *The Works of George Berkeley, Bishop of Cloyne*. Edited by A. A. Luce and T. E. Jessop. 9 vols. London, 1948–57, vol. VI, pp. 103–81.

Blackstone, Sir William. *An Analysis of the Laws of England*. London, 1756.

—— *Commentaries on the Laws of England*. 4 vols. Oxford, 1765–69.

Bolingbroke, Henry St John, first Viscount. *Dissertation upon Parties*. 1734.

Bougainville, Louis-Antoine, Comte de. *A Voyage round the World. Performed by Order of his Most Christian Majesty, in the Years 1766, 1767, 1768 and 1769* [1771]. Translated by Johann Reinhold Forster. London, 1772.

Brown, Andrew. *History of Glasgow; and of Paisley, Greenock and Port Glasgow; Comprehending the Ecclesiastical and Civil History of these Places, from the Earliest Accounts to the Present Time: And Including an Account of their Population, Commerce, Manufactures, Arts and Agriculture*. 2 vols. Edinburgh, 1795–97.

Buffon, Georges Louis Leclerc, Comte de. *Histoire naturelle, générale et particulière, avec la description du cabinet du roi*. 27 vols. Fifth edition. Paris, 1752–66.

Campbell, John. *The Present State of Europe; Explaining the Interests, Connections, Political and Commercial Views of its Several Powers, Comprehending also a Clear and Concise History of each Country, so far as To Shew the Nature of their Present Constitutions* [1750]. Sixth edition. London, 1761.

Campbell, R. *The London Tradesman* [1747]. Third edition. London, 1757.

Cantillon, Philip. *The Analysis of Trade, Commerce, Coin, Bullion, Banks and Foreign Exchanges* [1730?; 1755]. London, 1759.

Carmichael, Gershom. *Natural Rights on the Threshold of the Scottish Enlightenment. The Writings of Gershom Carmichael*. Edited by James Moore and Michael Silverthorne. Indianapolis, IN, 2002.

Carte, Thomas. *A General History of England*. 4 vols. London, 1747–55.

Charlevoix, Pierre-François-Xavier de. *Histoire du Paraguay*. 3 vols. Paris, 1756.

Child, Sir Josiah. *A New Discourse of Trade* [1690]. Fifth edition. Glasgow, 1751.

Cicero, Marcus Tullius. *On Duties*. Edited by M. T. Griffin and E. M. Atkins. Cambridge, 1991.

Claeys, Gregory (ed.). *Utopias of the British Enlightenment*. Cambridge, 1994.

[Cleghorn, Robert]. *Sketch of the Late Thomas Reid, D.D. Professor of Moral Philosophy in the University of Glasgow; with Observations on the Danger of Political Innovation, from a Discourse Delivered on 28th Nov. 1794 by Dr. Reid, before the Literary Society in Glasgow College*. Glasgow, 1796.

[Cleghorn, William], *The Spirit and Principles of the Whigs and Jacobites Compared. Being the Substance of a Discourse delivered to an Audience of Gentlemen at Edinburgh 22 December 1745*. London, 1746.

Cobbett, William, and T. C. Hansard. *Cobbett's Parliamentary History of England, from the Earliest Period to the Year 1803. From which Last-Mentioned Epoch it is Continued Downwards in the Work Entitled, 'The Parliamentary Debates'*. 36 vols. London, 1806–20; reprinted New York, NY, 1966.

Contareni, Gasparo. *De magistratibus & republica Venetorum libri quinque*. Venice, 1592.

Craig, John. 'Account of the Life and Writings of John Millar, Esq'. In John Millar. *The Origin and Distinction of Ranks: Or, an Inquiry into the Circumstances which Give Rise to Influence and Authority, in the Different Members of Society*. Edited by John Craig. Fourth edition. Edinburgh, 1806.

Culpeper, Sir Thomas. *Sir Thomas Colepeper's Tracts concerning Usury Reprinted. Shewing its Biting Quality on the Private and Publick. With some Animadversions on the Writings of Dr. Lock, on that Subject*. London, 1708.

Dalrymple, James, first Viscount Stair. *The Institutions of the Law of Scotland, Deduced from its Originals, and Collated with the Civil, and Feudal-Laws, and with the Customs of Neighbouring Nations* [1681]. Third edition. Edinburgh, 1759.

Dalrymple, John, of Cousland, 4th Baronet. *An Essay Towards a General History of Feudal Property in Great Britain*. London, 1757.

Dalrymple, John, fifth Earl of Stair. *The State of the National Debt, the National Income and the National Expenditure* [1776]. Fourth edition. London, 1776.

Davenant, Charles. *An Essay upon the Probable Methods of Making a People Gainers in the Ballance of Trade*. London, 1699.

—— *The Political and Commercial Works of the Celebrated Writer Charles D'Avenant, LL.D. Relating to the Trade and Revenue of England, the Plantation Trade, the East-India Trade and African Trade*. Edited by Sir Charles Whitworth. 5 vols. London, 1771.

[Decker, Sir Matthew]. *An Essay on the Causes of the Decline of the Foreign Trade, Consequently of the Value of the Lands of Britain, and on the Means to Restore both* [1744]. Second edition. London, 1750.

Defoe, Daniel. *An Essay upon Publick Credit: Being an Enquiry how the Publick Credit Comes to Depend upon the Change of the Ministry, or the Dissolutions of Parliament; or whether it Does so or no* [1710]. Third edition. London, 1710.

—— *The Complete English Tradesman, in Familiar Letters: Directing him in All the Several Parts and Progressions of Trade* [1726]. Second edition. London, 1727.

De Lolme, Jean Louis. *The Constitution of England, or an Account of the English Government; in which it is Compared with the Republican Form of Government, and Occasionally with the other Monarchies in Europe* [1771]. London, 1775.

—— *The Constitution of England; or, an Account of the English Government.* Edited by David Lieberman. Indianapolis, IN, 2007.

Denholm, James. *The History of Glasgow and Suburbs. To which is Added, a Sketch of a Tour to the Principal Scotch and English Lakes* [1797]. Third edition. Glasgow, 1804.

Derham, William. *Physico-Theology: Or, a Demonstration of the Being and Attributes of God, from his Works of Creation* [1713]. Eighth edition. London, 1732.

[Dodsley, Robert]. *The Preceptor: Containing a General Course of Education.* 2 vols. London, 1748.

Duncombe, Giles. *Trials per Pais: Or, the Law of England concerning Juries by Nisi Prius, &c.* [London], 1739.

[Dunton, John]. *A Collection of Choice, Scarce and Valuable Tracts, Being Taken from Manuscripts and Printed Books, Very Uncommon, and not To Be Found but in the Libraries of the Curious*. London, 1721.

Encyclopædia Britannica. 3 vols. Edinburgh, 1771.

Fenton, Roger. *A Treatise of Usurie, Divided into Three Bookes: The First Defineth what Is Usurie. The Second Determineth that To Be Unlawfull. The Third Removeth such Motives as Perswade Men in this Age that it May Be Lawfull*. London, 1611.

[Filmer, Sir Robert]. *Quæstio quodlibetica, or, a Discourse, Whether it May Bee Lawfull to Take Use for Money*. London, 1653.

Folkes, Martin. *A Table of English Silver Coins from the Norman Conquest to the Present Time. With their Weights, Intrinsic Values and some Remarks upon the Several Pieces*. London, 1745.

Fordyce, David. *The Elements of Moral Philosophy* [1754]. Edited by T. D. Kennedy. Indianapolis, IN, 2003.

[Franklin, Benjamin]. *The Interest of Great Britain Considered with Regard to her Colonies and the Acquisitions of Canada and Guadaloupe. To which are Added, Observations Concerning the Increase of Mankind, Peopling of Countries, &c.* London, 1760.

Gee, Joshua. *The Trade and Navigation of Great-Britain Considered....* [1729] Fifth edition, Glasgow, 1750.

Gerard, Alexander. *Liberty the Cloke of Maliciousness, both in the American Rebellion and in the Manners of the Times*. Aberdeen, 1778.

Gibbon, Edward. *The History of the Decline and Fall of the Roman Empire* [1776–88]. Edited by David Wormersley. 3 vols. London, 1994.

Gibson, John. *The History of Glasgow, from the Earliest Accounts to the Present Time; with an Account of the Rise, Progress and Present State, of the Different Branches of Commerce and Manufactures now Carried On in the City of Glasgow*. Glasgow, 1777.

Godwin, William. *Enquiry concerning Political Justice, and its Influence on Morals and Happiness* [1793]. Edited by Isaac Kramnick. Harmondsworth, 1985.

[Goudar, Ange]. *Les intérêts de la France mal entendus, dans les branches de l'agriculture, de la population, des finances, de commerce, de la marine, & de l'industrie*. 3 vols. Amsterdam, 1756.

Graunt, John. *Natural and Political Observations ... upon the Bills of Mortality* [1662]. In Sir William Petty. *The Economic Writings of Sir William Petty. Together with the Observations upon the Bills of Mortality* (vol. II, pp. 314–435). Edited by C. H. Hull. 2 vols. Cambridge, 1899. Reprinted New York, 1963.

Grotius, Hugo. *The Rights of War and Peace* [1625]. Edited by Richard Tuck. 3 vols. Indianapolis, IN, 2005.

Hale, Sir Matthew. *The Primitive Origination of Mankind, Considered and Examined according to the Light of Nature*. London, 1677.

Hall, Richard. *Acts, Passed in the Island of Barbados. From 1643, to 1762, Inclusive*. London, 1764.

Halley, Edmond. 'An Estimate of the Degrees of the Mortality of Mankind, Drawn from the Curious Tables of the Births and Funerals at the City of Breslaw; with an Attempt to Ascertain the Price of Annuities upon Lives'. *Philosophical Transactions* 17 (1693): 596–610.

—— 'Some Further Considerations on the Breslaw Bills of Mortality'. *Philosophical Transactions* 17 (1693): 654–56.

Harrington, James. *The Political Works of James Harrington*. Edited by J. G. A. Pocock. Cambridge, 1977.

[Harris, Joseph]. *An Essay upon Money and Coins*. 2 vols. London, 1757–58.

[Hay, George]. *Letters on Usury and Interest; Shewing the Advantage of Loans for the Support of Trade and Commerce*. London, 1774.

Heineccius, Johann Gottlieb. *A Methodical System of Universal Law: Or, the Laws of Nature and Nations Deduced from Certain Principles, and Applied to*

Proper Cases [1738]. Translated by George Turnbull and edited by Thomas Ahnert and Peter Schröder. Indianapolis, IN, 2008.

Home, Henry, Lord Kames. *Essays on the Principles of Morality and Natural Religion* [1751; third edition 1779]. Edited by Mary Catherine Moran. Indianapolis, IN, 2005.

—— *Essays upon Several Subjects concerning British Antiquities; Viz. I, Introduction of the Feudal Law into Scotland. II, Constitution of Parliament. III, Honour. Dignity. IV, Succession or Descent. With an Appendix, upon Hereditary and Indefeasible Right*. Edinburgh, 1747.

—— *The Gentleman Farmer: Being an Attempt to Improve Agriculture, by Subjecting it to the Test of Rational Principles*. Edinburgh, 1776.

—— *Historical Law-Tracts*. 2 vols. Edinburgh, 1758.

—— *Principles of Equity*. Edinburgh, 1760.

Hooke, Andrew. *An Essay on the National Debt, and National Capital: Or, the Account Truly Stated, Debtor and Creditor. Wherein is shewn, that the former is but a diminutive part of the latter; and a practicable scheme exhibited, whereby the whole may, with great facility, be paid off, at once, exclusive of the aid of the sinking fund, and without any diminution of the present revenues of the Crown, or annual expences of the people* [1750]. Second edition. London, 1751.

Hume, David. *Essays Moral, Political and Literary*. Edited by Eugene F. Miller. Revised edition. Indianapolis, IN, 1987.

—— *Essays and Treatises on Several Subjects*. 2 vols. London, 1764.

—— *Political Discourses*. Edinburgh, 1752.

Hutcheson, Francis. *Philosophiae moralis institutio compendiaria with A Short Introduction to Moral Philosophy* [1742; 1747]. Edited by Luigi Turco. Indianapolis, IN, 2007.

—— *A System of Moral Philosophy, in Three Books*. 2 vols. London, 1755.

Justinian. *The Digest of Justinian*. Translated by Alan Watson and edited by Theodore Mommsen and Paul Kruger. 4 vols. Philadelphia, PA, 1985.

Kaempfer, Engelbert. *Histoire naturelle, civile, et ecclesiastique du Japon ...* Composée en Allemand, traduite en François sur la version Angloise de Jean-Gaspar Scheuchzer [by J. Neaulme]. 3 vols. The Hague, 1732.

Kames, Henry Home (Lord). See Home, Henry, Lord Kames.

Lambert, Sheila (ed.). *House of Commons Sessional Papers of the Eighteenth Century*. 147 vols. Wilmington, DE, 1975.

[Law, John]. *Money and Trade Considered, with a Proposal for Supplying the Nation with Money*. Edinburgh, 1705.

—— *Proposals and Reasons for Constituting a Council of Trade in Scotland.* Glasgow, 1751.

Locke, John. *Locke on Money*. Edited by Patrick Hyde Kelley. 2 vols. Oxford, 1991.

—— *Several Papers relating to Money, Interest and Trade*. London, 1696.

—— *A Treatise of Raising our Coin*. London, 1718.

—— *Two Treatises of Government* [1690]. Edited by Peter Laslett. Cambridge, 1960.

[Long, Edward]. *The History of Jamaica*. 3 vols. London, 1774.

Lyttelton, George, first Baron Lyttelton. *The History of the Life of King Henry the Second, and of the Age in which He Lived, in Five Books: To which is Prefixed, a History of the Revolutions of England from the Death of Edward the Confessor to the Birth of Henry the Second* [1767–71]. Third edition. 4 vols. London, 1769–71.

McDouall, Andrew. *An Institute of the Laws of Scotland in Civil Rights: With Observations upon the Agreement or Diversity between them and the Laws of England*. 2 vols. Edinburgh, 1751–52.

Machiavelli, Niccolò. *Machiavelli: The Chief Works and Others*. Translated by Allan Gilbert. 3 vols. Durham, NC, 1965.

Mackenzie, Sir George. *The Works of that Eminent and Learned Lawyer, Sir George Mackenzie of Rosehaugh, Advocate to King Charles II and King James VII*. 2 vols. Edinburgh, 1716–22.

Mackintosh, James. *Vindiciae Gallicae and other Writings on the French Revolution*. Edited by D. Winch. Indianapolis, IN, 2006.

—— *Memoirs of the Life of the Right Honourable Sir James Mackintosh* [1835]. Edited by Robert James Mackintosh. Second edition. 2 vols. Boston, MA, 1853.

Macklin, Charles. *Four Comedies by Charles Macklin*. Edited by J. O. Bartley. London and Hamden, CT, 1968.

Mandeville, Bernard. *The Fable of the Bees: Or, Private Vices, Publick Benefits* [1714]. Edited by F. B. Kaye. 2 vols. Oxford, 1957.

Malthus, Thomas. *An Essay on the Principle of Population, as it Affects the Future Improvement of Society*. London, 1798.

Millar, John. *The Origin of the Distinction of Ranks: Or, an Inquiry into the Circumstances which Give Rise to Influence and Authority, in the Different Members of Society* [1771]. Edited by John Craig. Fourth edition. Edinburgh, 1806.

—— *An Historical View of the English Government. From the Settlement of the Saxons in Britain to the Revolution in 1688* [1787; second edition 1803]. Edited by Mark Salber Phillips and Dale R. Smith. Indianapolis, IN, 2006.

Molesworth, Robert. *An Account of Denmark as it was in the Year 1692*. London, 1694.

Montesquieu, Charles-Louis de Secondat, Baron de. *Considerations on the Causes of the Greatness of the Romans and their Decline* [1734]. Translated by David Lowenthal. Indianapolis, IN, and Cambridge, 1999.

—— *Persian Letters* [1721]. Translated by Margaret Mauldon. Oxford, 2008.

—— *The Spirit of the Laws* [1748]. Translated and edited by Anne M. Cohler, Basia Carolyn Miller and Harold Samuel Stone. Cambridge, 1989.

—— *The Spirit of Laws* [1748]. Translated by [Thomas Nugent]. 2 vols. London, 1750.

More, Thomas. *The Best State of a Commonwealth and the New Island of Utopia*. In *The Complete Works of St Thomas More*. Edited by R. S. Sylvester et al. 15 vols. New Haven, CT, 1963–97. Vol. IV.

Mun, Thomas. *England's Treasure by Foreign Trade. Or, the Balance of our Foreign Trade is the Rule of our Treasure* [1664]. Glasgow, 1750.

Murray, Patrick, fifth Lord Elibank. *Thoughts on Money, Circulation and Paper Currency*. Edinburgh, 1758.

Nagao, Shinichi (ed.). *Politics and Society in Scottish Thought*. Exeter, 2007.

Nepos, Cornelius. *Cornelius Nepos*. Translated by John C. Rolfe. Cambridge, MA, 1994.

Nieuwentyt, Bernard. *The Religious Philosopher: Or, the Right Use of Contemplating the Works of the Creator* [1715]. Translated by John Chamberlayne. 3 vols. London, 1718–19.

[Ogilvie, William]. *An Essay on the Right of Property in Land, with Respect to its Foundation in the Law of Nature; its Present Establishment by the Municipal Laws of Europe; and the Regulations by which it Might Be Rendered more Beneficial to the Lower Ranks of Mankind*. London, 1781.

Paine, Thomas. *Agrarian Justice, opposed to Agrarian Law, and to Agrarian Monopoly*. London, 1797.

—— *Rights of Man. Part the Second. Combining Principle and Practice*. London, 1792.

[Penn, William]. *The Frame of the Government of the Province of Pennsilvania in America: Together with Certain Laws Agreed upon in England by the Governour and Divers Free-Men of the aforesaid Province. To be further Explained and Confirmed there by the First Provincial Council and General Assembly that Shall Be Held, if they See Meet*. [Place of publication not stated], 1682.

Petty, Sir William. *The Economic Writings of Sir William Petty. Together with the Observations upon the Bills of Mortality*. Edited by C. H. Hull. 2 vols. Cambridge, 1899. Reprinted New York, 1963.

—— *Political Arithmetick*. London, 1690.

[Petyt, William]. *Britannia Languens: Or, a Discourse of Trade, Shewing, that the Present Management of Trade in England, is the True Reason of the Decay of our Manufactures, and the Late Great Fall of Land-Rents; and that the Increase of Trade, in the Method it Now Stands in, Must Proportionably Decay England* [1680]. London, 1689.

Plutarch. *Plutarch's Moralia.* Translated by F. C. Babbitt et al. 15 vols. London, 1927–76.

Pope, Alexander. *Poetical Works.* Edited by Herbert Davis with an introduction by Pat Rogers. Oxford and New York, NY, 1985.

Price, Richard. *The Correspondence of Richard Price.* Edited by W. Bernard Peach and D. O. Thomas. 3 vols. Cardiff, 1983–94.

—— *Observations on Reversionary Payments; on Schemes for Providing Annuities for Widows, and for Persons in Old Age; on the Method of Calculating the Values of Assurances on Lives; and on the National Debt* [1771]. Second edition. London, 1772.

—— *Political Writings.* Edited by D. O. Thomas. Cambridge, 1991.

—— *A Review of the Principal Questions in Morals* [1758]. Edited by D. D. Raphael. Oxford, 1948.

—— *Two Tracts on Civil Liberty, the War with America, and the Debts and Finances of the Kingdom: With a General Introduction and Supplement.* London, 1778.

Pufendorf, Samuel. *An Introduction to the History of the Principal Kingdoms and States of Europe ... Enlarged and Continued down to the Year 1743, by M. Martiniere* [1682]. Translated by Joseph Sayer. 2 vols. London, 1748.

—— *The Law of Nature and Nations: Or, a General System of the Most Important Principles of Morality, Jurisprudence and Politics* [1672]. Translated by Basil Kennet. Fifth edition. London, 1749.

—— *The Whole Duty of Man, According to the Law of Nature* [1673]. Edited by Ian Hunter and David Saunders. Indianapolis, IN, 2003.

Raithby, John (ed.). *The Statutes of the Realm.* 11 vols. [London], 1810–28.

Rapin de Thoyras, Paul de. *Dissertation sur les Whigs et les Torys; or, an Historical Dissertation upon Whig and Tory.* London, 1717.

Reid, Thomas. *The Correspondence of Thomas Reid.* Edited by Paul Wood. Edinburgh, 2002.

—— 'An Essay on Quantity; Occasioned by Reading a Treatise, in which Simple and Compound Ratio's Are Applied to Virtue and Merit'. *Philosophical Transactions* 45 (1748): 505–20.

—— *Essays on the Active Powers of Man* [1788]. Edited by Knud Haakonssen and James Harris. Edinburgh, 2010.

—— *Essays on the Intellectual Powers of Man* [1785]. Edited by Derek R. Brookes and Knud Haakonssen. Edinburgh, 2002.

—— *An Inquiry into the Human Mind on the Principles of Common Sense* [1764]. Edited by Derek R. Brookes. Edinburgh, 1997.

—— *The Philosophical Orations of Thomas Reid Delivered at Graduation Ceremonies in King's College, Aberdeen, 1753, 1756, 1759, 1762*; reproduced in Reid, *University*.

—— *Thomas Reid on the Animate Creation: Papers Relating to the Life Sciences*. Edited by Paul Wood. Edinburgh, 1995.

—— *Thomas Reid on Logic, Rhetoric and the Fine Arts. Papers on the Culture of the Mind*. Edited by Alexander Broadie. Edinburgh, 2005.

—— *Thomas Reid on Mathematics and Natural Philosophy*. Edited by Paul Wood. Edinburgh, forthcoming.

—— *Thomas Reid on Practical Ethics: Lectures and Papers on Natural Religion, Self-Government, Natural Jurisprudence and the Law of Nations*. Edited by Knud Haakonssen. Edinburgh, 2007.

—— *Thomas Reid and the University*. Edited by Alexander Broadie and Paul Wood. Edinburgh, forthcoming.

Richardson, William. 'An Account of some Particulars in the Life and Character of the Author'. In Archibald Arthur. *Discourses on Theological and Literary Subjects* (pp. 493–517). Glasgow, 1803.

Robertson, William. *The History of the Reign of the Emperor Charles V. With a View of the Progress of Society in Europe, from the Subversion of the Roman Empire, to the Beginning of the Sixteenth Century*. 3 vols. London, 1769.

Rousseau, Jean-Jacques. *The Social Contract and other Later Political Writings*. Translated and edited by Victor Gourevitch. Cambridge, 1997.

Ruffhead, Owen. *The Statutes at Large, from Magna Charta, to the Twenty-Fifth Year of the Reign of King George the Third, Inclusive*. New edition, revised and corrected by Charles Runnington. 14 vols. London, 1786.

Rycaut, Paul. *The History of the Present State of the Ottoman Empire containing the Maxims of the Turkish Polity, the most Material Points of the Mahometan Religion, their Sects and Heresies, their Convents and Religious Votaries, their Military Discipline, with an Exact computation of their Forces by Land and Sea* [1666]. London, 1667.

St Basil. *Exegetic Homilies*. Translated by Sister Agnes Clare Way. In *The Fathers of the Church: A New Translation*. Vol. XLVI. Washington, DC, 1963.

St Chrysostom. *A Select Library of the Nicene and Post-Nicene Fathers of the Christian Church, Vol. X: Saint Chrysostom: Homilies on the Gospel of Saint Matthew*. Edited by Philip Schaff. Edinburgh, 1991.

Saint-Pierre, Charles-Irénée Castel, abbé de. *Projet pour perfectioner le gouvernement des etats, Vol. III: Ouvrajes de politique*. Rotterdam, 1733.

Sanderson, Robert. *The Works of Robert Sanderson, D.D., Sometime Bishop of Lincoln*. Edited by William Jacobson. 6 vols. Oxford, 1854.

Smith, Adam. 'The Anderson Notes', in R. L. Meek, 'New Light on Adam Smith's Glasgow Lectures on Jurisprudence', *History of Political Economy* 8 (1976): 439–77, at pp. 467–77.

—— *The Correspondence of Adam Smith*. Edited by Ernest Campbell Mossner and Ian Simpson Ross. Second edition. Oxford, 1987.

—— *An Inquiry into the Nature and Causes of the Wealth of Nations* [1776]. Edited by R. H. Campbell, A. S. Skinner and W. B. Todd. 2 vols. Oxford, 1979.

—— *Lectures on Jurisprudence*. Edited by R. L. Meek, D. D. Rapahel and P. G. Stein. Oxford, 1978.

—— *The Theory of Moral Sentiments* [1759]. Edited by D. D. Raphael and A. L. Macfie. Oxford, 1976.

Spence, Thomas. *The Rights of Man, as Exhibited in a Lecture, Read at the Philosophical Society, in Newcastle, to which Is now First Added, an Interesting Conversation, between a Gentleman and the Author, on the Subject of his Scheme*. Fourth edition. London, 1793.

[Steuart, Sir James]. *Considerations on the Interest of the County of Lanark*. Glasgow, 1769.

Steuart, Sir James. *An Inquiry into the Principles of Political Oeconomy: Being an Essay on the Science of Domestic Policy in Free Nations*. 2 vols. London, 1767.

—— *An Inquiry into the Principles of Political Oeconomy* [1767]. Edited by Andrew S. Skinner. 2 vols. Edinburgh and London, 1966

—— *The Principles of Money Applied to the Present State of the Coin of Bengal: Being an Inquiry into the Methods to be Used for Correcting the Defects of the Present Currency; for Stopping the Drains which Carry Off the Coin; and for Extending Circulation by the Means of Paper-Credit. Composed for the Use of the Honourable the East-India Company*. [London], 1772.

Stewart, Dugald. *Account of the Life and Writings of Thomas Reid, D.D. F.R.S. Edin. Late Professor of Moral Philosophy in the University of Glasgow*. Edinburgh, 1803.

Stiles, Ezra. *Discourse on the Christian Union*. Boston, MA, 1761.

Tacitus, Cornelius. *The Histories and the Annals*. Translated by Clifford H. Moore and John Jackson. 4 vols. London, 1925–37.

Tanner, Norman P. (ed.). *Decrees of the Ecumenical Councils*. 2 vols. London, 1990.

[Temple, William]. *A Vindication of Commerce and the Arts; Proving that they are the Source of the Greatness, Power, Riches and Populousness of a State*. London, 1758.

Temple, Sir William. *Observations upon the United Provinces of the Netherlands* [1673]. Edited by Sir George Clark. Oxford, 1972.

Tucker, Josiah. *A Brief Essay on the Advantages and Disadvantages which Respectively Attend France and Great Britain, with Regard to Trade*. [1749]. Third edition. London, 1753.

—— *The Elements of Commerce, and Theory of Taxes*. [Bristol], [1755].

—— *Reflections on the Expediency of a Law for the Naturalization of Foreign Protestants*. Part I, *Containing Historical Remarks on the Disposition and Behaviour of the Natives of this Island, in regard to Foreigners*. London, 1751. Part II, *Containing Important Queries relating to Commerce, The Employment of the Poor, The Landed and National Interest, Taxes of all Kinds, particularly the Poor Tax, The Real Interest of Tradesmen, Reformation of Morals, Constitution both in Church and State, the Duties of Humanity, and the Principles of the Christian Religion*. London, 1752.

Turnbull, George. *Education for Life: Correspondence and Writings on Religion and Practical Philosophy*. Edited by M. A. Stewart and Paul Wood. Indianapolis, IN, 2014.

—— *The Principles of Moral and Christian Philosophy* [1740]. Edited by Alexander Broadie. 2 vols. Indianapolis, IN, 2005.

Ulman, H. Lewis (ed.). *Minutes of the Aberdeen Philosophical Society, 1758–1773*. Aberdeen, 1990.

Vattel, Emer de. *Le Droit des gens. Ou principes de la loi naturelle, appliqués à la conduite et aux affaires des nations et des souverains*. London, 1758.

—— *The Law of Nations, or Principles of the Law of Nature applied to the Conduct and Affairs of Nations and Sovereigns*. 2 vols. London, 1759.

Vaughan, Edward. *The Reports and Arguments of that Learned Judge, Sir John Vaughan, Kt. Late Lord Chief Justice of the Court of Common-Pleas, Being all of them Special Cases* [1677]. Second edition. London, 1706.

Voltaire, François-Marie Arouet de. *Oeuvres Complètes de Voltaire*. Edited by A. J. O. Beuchot. 72 vols. Paris, 1829–40.

[Wallace, Robert]. *Characteristics of the Present Political State of Great Britain* [1758]. Second edition. London, 1758.

—— *A Dissertation on the Numbers of Mankind in Antient and Modern Times. In which the Superior Populousness of Antiquity is maintained* Edinburgh, 1753.

—— *Various Prospects of Mankind, Nature and Providence*. London, 1761.

'W.C.'.'A Peep at the Corn Bill'. *Weekly Magazine, or Edinburgh Amusement* 36 (1777): 293–94.

[Whatley, George]. *Reflections on Coin in General; on the Coins of Gold and Silver in Great-Britain in Particular; on those Metals as Merchandize; and also on Paper Passing as Money*. London, 1762.

Wilson, Thomas. *A Discourse upon Usury: By Way of Dialogue and Orations, for the Better Variety and More Delight of all those that Shall Read this Treatise* [1572]. With an introduction by R. H. Tawney. London, 1925. Reprinted London, 1962.

Secondary Sources

Aitken, George A. *The Life and Works of John Arbuthnot M.D., Fellow of the Royal College of Physicians*. Oxford, 1892.

Bonar, James. *Theories of Population from Raleigh to Arthur Young*. London, 1931. Reprinted London, 1966.

Buchanan, Moses Steven. *History of the Glasgow Royal Infirmary, from its Commencement in 1787, to the Present Time*. Glasgow, 1832.

Clelland, Martin J. *Historical Sketch of the Glasgow Society of the Sons of Ministers of the Church of Scotland, Instituted Anno 1790*. Fifth edition. Glasgow, 1910.

Coats, A. W. 'Changing Attitudes to Labour in the Mid-Eighteenth Century'. *Economic History Review*, new series 11 (1958): 35–51.

Craig, Sir John. *The Mint: A History of the London Mint from A.D. 287 to 1948*. Cambridge, 1953.

Davis, J. C. *Utopia and the Ideal Society: A Study of English Utopian Writing, 1516–1700*. Cambridge, 1981.

De Vries, Jan, and Ad van der Woude. *The First Modern Economy: Success, Failure and Perseverance of the Dutch Economy, 1500–1815*. Cambridge, 1997.

Diamond, Peter J. *Common Sense and Improvement: Thomas Reid as Social Theorist*. Frankfurt a. M., 1998.

Donnachie, Ian, and George Hewitt. *Historic New Lanark: The Dale and Owen Industrial Community since 1785*. Edinburgh, 1993.

Donovan, A. L. *Philosophical Chemistry in the Scottish Enlightenment: The Doctrines and Discoveries of William Cullen and Joseph Black*. Edinburgh, 1975.

Donovan, Robert Kent. 'Evangelical Civic Humanism in Glasgow: The American War Sermons of William Thom'. In *The Glasgow Enlightenment* (pp. 227–45). Edited by Andrew Hook and Richard B. Sher. East Linton, 1995.

—— 'The Popular Party of the Church of Scotland and the American Revolution'.

In *Scotland and America in the Age of Enlightenment* (pp. 81–99). Edited by Richard B. Sher and Jeffrey R. Smitten. Edinburgh, 1990.

Drummond, Andrew L., and James Bulloch. *The Scottish Church, 1688–1843: The Age of the Moderates*. Edinburgh, 1973.

Emerson, Roger L. *Professors, Patronage and Politics: The Aberdeen Universities in the Eighteenth Century*. Aberdeen, 1992.

Feavearyear, Sir Albert. *The Pound Sterling: A History of English Money*. Second edition. Revised by E. Victor Morgan. Oxford, 1963.

Finn, Margot C. *The Character of Credit: Personal Debt in English Culture, 1740–1914*. Cambridge, 2003.

Firth, Ann. 'Moral Supervision and Autonomous Social Order: Wages and Consumption in Eighteenth-Century Economic Thought'. *History of the Human Sciences* 15 (2002): 39–57.

Forbes, Duncan. *Hume's Philosophical Politics*. Cambridge, 1975.

Forbes, Margaret. *Beattie and His Friends*. Westminster, 1904.

Frängsmyr, Tore, J. L. Heilbron and Robin E. Rider (eds). *The Quantifying Spirit in the Eighteenth Century*. Berkeley, CA, Los Angeles, CA, and Oxford, 1990.

Fraser, W. Hamish. *Conflict and Class: Scottish Workers, 1700–1838*. Edinburgh, 1988.

Ganson, Barbara Anne. *The Guaraní under Spanish Rule in the Río de la Plata*. Stanford, CA, 2003.

Gaskell, Philip. *A Bibliography of the Foulis Press*. Second edition. Winchester, 1986.

German, Kieran. 'Jacobite Politics in Aberdeen and the '15'. In *Loyalty and Identity: Jacobites at Home and Abroad* (pp. 82–97). Edited by Paul Monod, Murray Pittock and Daniel Szechi. Basingstoke and New York, NY, 2010.

Gibson, A. J. S., and T. C. Smout. *Prices, Food and Wages in Scotland, 1550–1780*. Cambridge, 1995.

Glass, D. V. *Numbering the People: The Eighteenth-Century Population Controversy and the Development of Census and Vital Statistics in Britain*. Farnborough, 1973.

—— *The Population Controversy*. Farnborough, 1973.

Goldie, Mark. 'The Scottish Catholic Enlightenment'. *Journal of British Studies* 30 (1991): 20–62.

Gordon, Barry. 'Lending at Interest: Some Jewish, Greek and Christian Approaches, 800 BC–AD 100'. *History of Political Economy* 14 (1982): 406–26.

Grabner, Judith V. 'Maclaurin and Newton: The Newtonian Style and the Authority of Mathematics'. In *Science and Medicine in the Scottish Enlightenment* (pp. 143–71). Edited by Charles W. J. Withers and Paul Wood. East Linton, 2002.

Grandi, Giovanni B. 'Hume and Reid on Political Economy'. *Eighteenth-Century Thought* 5 (2014): forthcoming.

Gray, Malcolm. 'The Social Impact of Agrarian Change in the Rural Lowlands'. In *People and Society in Scotland, Vol. I: 1760–1830* (pp. 53–69). Edited by T. M. Devine and Rosalind Mitchison. Edinburgh, 1988.

Haakonssen, Knud. 'Enlightenment and the Ubiquity of Natural Law'. In *Time in the Age of Enlightenment* (13th International Congress for Eighteenth-Century Studies) (pp. 45–57). Edited by Wolfgang Schmale. Bochum, 2012.

—— 'Natural Jurisprudence and the Identity of the Scottish Enlightenment'. In *Religion and Philosophy in Enlightenment Britain* (pp. 258–277). Edited by Ruth Savage. Oxford, 2012.

—— 'Natural Jurisprudence and the Theory of Justice'. In *The Cambridge Companion to the Scottish Enlightenment* (pp. 205–21). Edited by Alexander Broadie. Cambridge, 2003.

—— *Natural Law and Moral Philosophy: From Grotius to the Scottish Enlightenment*. Cambridge, 1996.

—— 'Natural Law and Personhood: Samuel Pufendorf on Social Explanation'. Max Weber Lecture, European University Institution, 2010. Available at http://cadmus.eui.eu/handle/1814/14934 (accessed April 2014).

—— *The Science of a Legislator: The Natural Jurisprudence of David Hume and Adam Smith*. Cambridge, 1981

Harris, Bob. 'Parliamentary Legislation, Lobbying and the Press in Eighteenth-Century Scotland'. *Parliamentary History* 26 (2007): 76–95.

—— *The Scottish People and the French Revolution*. London, 2008.

Hegeland, Hugo. *The Quantity Theory of Money: A Critical Study of Its Historical Development and Interpretation and a Restatement*. Götoborg, 1951. Reprinted New York, NY, 1969.

Holcomb, Kathleen. 'Thomas Reid in the Glasgow Literary Society'. In *The Glasgow Enlightenment* (pp. 95–110). Edited by Andrew Hook and Richard B. Sher. East Linton, 1995.

Holmes, Geoffrey. *British Politics in the Age of Anne*. Revised edition. London, 1987.

Hont, Istvan. *Jealousy of Trade: International Competition and the Nation-State in Historical Perspective*. Cambridge, MA, and London, 2005.

Hoppit, Julian. 'Attitudes to Credit in Britain, 1680–1790'. *Historical Journal* 33 (1990): 305–22.

—— (ed.). *Failed Legislation, 1660–1800: Extracted from the Commons and Lords Journals*. With an introduction by Julian Hoppit and Joanna Innes. London and Rio Grande, OH, 1997.

—— 'Financial Crises in Eighteenth-Century England'. *Economic History Review*, second series 39 (1986): 39–58.

—— 'Political Arithmetic in Eighteenth-Century England'. *Economic History Review*, new series 49 (1996): 516–40.

—— *Risk and Failure in English Business, 1700–1800*. Cambridge, 1987.

Hume, L. J. *Bentham and Bureaucracy*. Cambridge, 1981.

Humphries, Walter Robson. 'The First Aberdeen Philosophical Society'. *Transactions of the Aberdeen Philosophical Society* 5 (1938): 203–38.

Hunter, Ian. *Rival Enlightenments: Civil and Metaphysical Philosophy in Early Modern Germany*. Cambridge, 2001.

Hutchison, Terence. *Before Adam Smith: The Emergence of Political Economy, 1662–1776*. Oxford and Cambridge, MA, 1990.

Innes, Joanna. *Inferior Politics: Social Problems and Social Policies in Eighteenth-Century Britain*. Oxford, 2009.

Jones, Norman. *God and the Moneylenders: Usury and Law in Early Modern England*. Oxford and Cambridge, MA, 1989.

Kidd, Colin. 'North Britishness and the Nature of Eighteenth-Century British Patriotisms'. *Historical Journal* 39 (1996): 361–82.

—— *Subverting Scotland's Past: Scottish Whig Historians and the Creation of an Anglo-British Identity, 1689–c.1830*. Cambridge, 1993.

—— *Union and Unionisms: Political Thought in Scotland 1500–2000*. Cambridge, 2008.

Kitagawa, Kurtis G. 'Not Without the Highest Justice: The Origins and Development of Thomas Reid's Political Thought'. PhD Thesis, University of Edinburgh, 1994.

Kyd, James Gray (ed.). *Scottish Population Statistics: Including Webster's Analysis of Population, 1755*. Edinburgh, 1975.

Li, Ming-Hsun. *The Great Recoinage of 1696 to 1699*. London, 1963.

Maas, Harro. 'Where Mechanism Ends. Thomas Reid on the Moral and the Animal Oeconomy'. *History of Political Economy* 35 (2003): 338–60.

Manuel, Frank E., and Fritzie P. Manuel. *Utopian Thought in the Western World*. Cambridge, MA, 1979.

Marshall, M. G. 'Scottish Economic Thought and the High Wage Economy: Hume, Smith and McCullogh on Wages and Work Motivation'. *Scottish Journal of Political Economy* 45 (1998): 309–28.

Meek, Ronald L. *Social Science and the Ignoble Savage*. Cambridge, 1976.

—— (ed.). *Turgot on Progress, Sociology and Economics*. Cambridge, 1973.

Meikle, Henry W. *Scotland and the French Revolution*. Glasgow, 1912.

Millett, Paul. *Lending and Borrowing in Ancient Athens*. Cambridge, 1991.

Mitchell, B. R. *British Historical Statistics*. Cambridge, 1988.

Mitchison, Rosalind. 'The Making of the Old Scottish Poor Law'. *Past and Present* 63 (1974): 58–93.

—— 'The Movements of Scottish Corn Prices in the Seventeenth and Eighteenth Centuries'. *Economic History Review*, new series 18 (1965): 278–91.

—— *The Old Poor Law in Scotland: The Experience of Poverty, 1574–1845*. Edinburgh, 2000.

Mokyr, Joel. *The Enlightened Economy: An Economic History of Britain, 1700–1850*. New Haven, CT, and London, 2009.

Monod, Paul Kléber. 'Thomas Carte, the Druids and British National Identity'. In *Loyalty and Identity: Jacobites at Home and Abroad* (pp. 132–48). Edited by Paul Monod, Murray Pittock and Daniel Szechi. Basingstoke and New York, NY, 2010.

Mörner, Magnus. *The Political and Economic Activities of the Jesuits in the La Plata Region: The Hapsburg Era*. Stockholm, 1953.

Muldrew, Craig. *The Economy of Obligation: The Culture of Credit and Social Relations in Early Modern England*. Basingstoke and London, 1998.

Murphy, Antoin E. *John Law: Economic Theorist and Policy-Maker*. Oxford, 1997.

Nagao, Shinichi. 'The Political Economy of Thomas Reid'. *Journal of Scottish Philosophy* 1 (2003): 21–33.

Nelson, Benjamin. *The Idea of Usury: From Tribal Brotherhood to Universal Otherhood*. Second edition, enlarged. Chicago, IL, and London, 1969.

Noonan, John T., Jr. *The Scholastic Analysis of Usury*. Cambridge, MA, 1957.

Palladini, Fiammetta. 'Pufendorf Disciple of Hobbes. The Nature of Man and the State of Nature: The Doctrine of *socialitas*'. *History of European Ideas* 34 (2008): 26–60.

Pitman, Frank Wesley. *The Development of the British West Indies, 1700–1763*. New Haven, CT, 1917. Reprinted [New York, NY], 1967.

Pocock, J. G. A. *The Machiavellian Moment: Florentine Political Thought and the Atlantic Republican Tradition*. Princeton, NJ, and London, 1975.

Price, Jacob M. 'The Rise of Glasgow in the Chesapeake Tobacco Trade, 1707–1775'. *William and Mary Quarterly*, third series 11 (1954): 179–99.

Robbins, Caroline. *The Eighteenth-Century Commonwealthman: Studies in the Transition, Development, and Circumstance of English Liberal Thought from the Restoration of Charles II until the War with the Thirteen Colonies*. Cambridge, MA, 1959.

Ross, Ian Simpson. *Lord Kames and the Scotland of his Day*. Oxford, 1972.

Rusnock, Andrea A. 'Biopolitics: Political Arithmetic in the Enlightenment'. In

The Sciences in Enlightened Europe (pp. 49–68). Edited by William Clark, Jan Golinski and Simon Schaffer. Chicago, IL, and London, 1999.

—— *Vital Accounts: Quantifying Health and Population in Eighteenth-Century England and France*. Cambridge, 2002.

Sargent, Thomas J. and François R. Velde. *The Big Problem of Small Change*. Princeton, NJ, and Oxford, 2002.

Schneewind, J. B. 'The Divine Corporation and the History of Ethics'. In *Essays on the History of Moral Philosophy* (pp. 149–69). By J. B. Schneewind. Cambridge, 2010.

Scott, Hew, and John Alexander Lamb. *Fasti Ecclesiae Scoticanae: The Succession of Ministers in the Church of Scotland from the Reformation*. Revised and enlarged edition. 9 vols. Edinburgh, 1915–61.

Selgin, George. *Good Money: Birmingham Button Makers, the Royal Mint, and the Beginnings of Modern Coinage, 1775–1821*. Ann Arbor, MI, 2008.

Shelton, George. *Dean Tucker and Eighteenth-Century Economic and Political Thought*. London and Basingstoke, 1981.

Sher, Richard B. *Church and University in the Scottish Enlightenment: The Moderate Literati of Edinburgh*. Edinburgh, 1985.

—— 'Commerce, Religion and the Enlightenment in Eighteenth-Century Glasgow'. In *Glasgow. Vol. I: Beginnings to 1830* (pp. 312–59). Edited by T. M. Devine and Gordon Jackson. Manchester and New York, NY, 1995.

Skinner, Andrew S. 'Money and Prices: A Critique of the Quantity Theory'. *Scottish Journal of Political Economy* 14 (1967): 275–90.

Smith, J. H. *The Gordon's Mill Farming Club, 1758–1764*. Edinburgh and London, 1962.

Stangeland, Charles Emil. *Pre-Malthusian Doctrines of Population: A Study in the History of Economic Theory*. New York, 1904. Reprinted New York, NY, 1966.

Stewart-Robertson, J. C. 'Reid's Anatomy of Culture: A Scottish Response to the Eloquent Jean-Jacques'. *Studies on Voltaire and the Eighteenth Century* 205 (1982): 141–63.

Szechi, Daniel. *1715: The Great Jacobite Rebellion*. New Haven, CT, and London, 2006.

Tayler, Alistair, and Henrietta Tayler. *1715: The Story of the Rising*. London, 1936.

Thomas, P. D. G. *The House of Commons in the Eighteenth Century*. Oxford, 1971.

Tomaselli, Sylvana. 'Moral Philosophy and Population Questions in Eighteenth-Century Europe'. In *Population and Resources in Western Intellectual*

Traditions (pp. 7–29). Edited by Michael S. Teitelbaum and Jay M. Winter. New York, NY, 1988.

Walker, David M. 'Equity in Scots Law'. *Juridical Review* 66 (1954): 103–47.

Wennerlind, Carl. *Casualties of Credit: The English Financial Revolution, 1620–1720*. Cambridge, MA, and London, 2011.

Whatley, Christopher A. *Scottish Society, 1707–1830: Beyond Jacobitism, Towards Industrialisation*. Manchester and New York, NY, 2000.

Whelan, F. G. 'Population and Ideology in the Enlightenment'. *History of Political Thought* 12 (1991): 35–72.

Wiles, Richard C. 'The Theory of Wages in Later English Mercantilism'. *Economic History Review*, new series 21 (1968): 113–26.

Willock, Ian Douglas. *The Origins and Development of the Jury in Scotland*. Edinburgh, 1966.

Winsor, Mary Pickard. 'Robert Wallace: Predecessor of Malthus and Pioneering Actuary'. In *From Ancient Omens to Statistical Mechanics: Essays on the Exact Sciences Presented to Asger Aaboe* (pp. 215–24). Edited by J. L. Berggren and B. R. Goldstein. Copenhagen, 1987.

Wood, Paul. *The Aberdeen Enlightenment: The Arts Curriculum in the Eighteenth Century*. Aberdeen, 1993.

—— 'Aberdeen Philosophical Society'. In *Oxford Dictionary of National Biography*. Online edition.

—— '"The Fittest Man in the Kingdom": Thomas Reid and the Glasgow Chair of Moral Philosophy'. *Hume Studies* 23 (1997): 277–313.

—— 'The Hagiography of Common Sense: Dugald Stewart's *Account of the Life and Writings of Thomas Reid*'. In *Philosophy, Its History and Historiography* (pp. 305–22). Edited by A. J. Holland. Dordrecht, 1985.

—— *The Life of Thomas Reid: The Culture of the Mind*. Edinburgh, forthcoming.

—— 'Thomas Reid and the Culture of Science'. In *The Cambridge Companion to Thomas Reid* (pp. 53–76). Edited by Terence Cuneo and René van Woudenberg. Cambridge, 2004.

—— 'Thomas Reid, Natural Philosopher: A Study of Science and Philosophy in the Scottish Enlightenment'. PhD thesis, University of Leeds, 1984.

—— 'A Virtuoso Reader: Thomas Reid and the Practices of Reading in Eighteenth-Century Scotland'. *Journal of Scottish Thought* 4 (2011): 33–74.

Yeager, Jonathan M. *Enlightened Evangelicalism: The Life and Thought of John Erskine*. New York, NY, 2011.

Index of Persons and Titles

General Index

Fermentation Processes: Modeling, Optimization and Control

Fermentation Processes: Modeling, Optimization and Control

Ricardo Aguilar-López

MDPI

Basel • Beijing • Wuhan • Barcelona • Belgrade • Novi Sad • Cluj • Manchester

Editor
Ricardo Aguilar-López
Biotechnology and Bioengineering
Centro de Investigación y
de Estudios Avanzados
México City
Mexico

Editorial Office
MDPI AG
Grosspeteranlage 5
4052 Basel, Switzerland

This is a reprint of articles from the Special Issue published online in the open access journal *Fermentation* (ISSN 2311-5637) (available at: www.mdpi.com/journal/fermentation/special_issues/025W010HK9).

For citation purposes, cite each article independently as indicated on the article page online and as indicated below:

Lastname, A.A.; Lastname, B.B. Article Title. *Journal Name* **Year**, *Volume Number*, Page Range.

ISBN 978-3-7258-2542-4 (Hbk)
ISBN 978-3-7258-2541-7 (PDF)
doi.org/10.3390/books978-3-7258-2541-7

Contents

Preface

Fermentation plays an important role in the food, pharmaceutical, biofuels, metabolite industries, etc. As a result, the demand for high-quality products with low energy consumption and operational safety is increasing; these can operate within very complex biological systems. However, this has made processing difficult, leading to the development of intensive engineering strategies to achieve these performance objectives. Therefore, modeling and simulation tasks for optimization and the control purposes of fermentation equipment are incredibly important.

The main goal of this Special Issue is to include the latest developments and advancements in process fermentation technology and bioprocessing to achieve progress in these key industrial sectors. Special attention will be given to certain research topics, such as highly predictive modeling techniques, the detailed simulations to characterize realizable operating conditions, the application of multiobjective optimization with the newest mathematical techniques, the design of online estimation procedures for process monitoring purposes and new controller designs, and improvements for the closed-loop operation performance.

Overall, the aim of this Special Issue is to support the development of sustainability assessment tools to measure the socioeconomic and environmental performances of innovative technical advances for fermentation processes.

Ricardo Aguilar-López
Editor

fermentation

Article

Enhanced Succinic Acid Production and Electronic Utilization Efficiency by *Actinobacillus succinogenes* 130Z in an ORP-Controlled Microbial Electrolysis Cell System

Jieyi Peng [1,2,3], Shuo Zhao [1,2,3], Ying Li [1,2,3], Zhen Wang [1,2,3,*] and Li Chen [1,2,3]

1 Jiangsu Key Laboratory of Marine Bioresources and Environment, Jiangsu Ocean University, Lianyungang 222005, China; liying8722@126.com (Y.L.)
2 Co-Innovation Center of Jiangsu Marine Bio-Industry Technology, Jiangsu Ocean University, Lianyungang 222005, China
3 Jiangsu Institute of Marine Resources Development, Lianyungang 222005, China
* Correspondence: zhenwang@jou.edu.cn; Tel.: +86-181-216-27717

Abstract: Microbial electrochemical systems have shown great value as a means of enhancing the efficiency of fermentation reactions, but at present, there is no reliable means to balance the extracellular electron supply and corresponding intracellular demands in these systems. The current work describes the unique use of an oxidation–reduction-potential (ORP)-level-controlled microbial electrolysis cell (MEC) system to successfully balance the extracellular electron supply and succinic acid fermentation via *A. succinogenes* (130Z). The ORP-controlled MEC system with neutral red (NR) yielded a significant increase in succinic acid production (17.21%). The utilization of NR in this MEC system improved the ORP regulatory sensitivity. The optimal approach to the ORP level control was the use of a −400 mV high-voltage electric pulse-based strategy, which increased the yield of succinic acid by 13.08% compared to the control group, and reduced the energy consumption to 52.29% compared to the potentiostatic method. When compared to the −1 V constant potential MEC system, the high-voltage electric pulse-based ORP strategy for the MEC system control provided sufficient electrons to this system while using less electricity (11.96%) and producing 12.48% (74.43 g/L) more succinic acid during fed-batch fermentation. The electronic utilization efficiency of the ORP-controlled MEC system was 192.02%, which was 15.19 times that of the potentiostatic system. The electronic utilization efficiency is significantly increased in the ORP-controlled MEC system. Succinic acid production is ensured by a high-voltage electric pulse-based method, while the influence on cell growth and power consumption are minimized. Fed-batch fermentation with the high voltage electric pulse-based ORP strategy for MEC system control is noted to be ideal to achieve a further increase in succinic acid concentration and electronic utilization efficiency.

Keywords: ORP-controlled MEC system; *Actinobacillus succinogenes*; microbial electrolysis cells; succinic acid; fed-batch fermentation

Citation: Peng, J.; Zhao, S.; Li, Y.; Wang, Z.; Chen, L. Enhanced Succinic Acid Production and Electronic Utilization Efficiency by *Actinobacillus succinogenes* 130Z in an ORP-Controlled Microbial Electrolysis Cell System. *Fermentation* **2024**, *10*, 109. https://doi.org/10.3390/fermentation10020109

Academic Editor: Ricardo Aguilar-López

Received: 9 January 2024
Revised: 13 February 2024
Accepted: 14 February 2024
Published: 17 February 2024

1. Introduction

In recent years, microbial electrochemical systems (MESs) have shown increasing promise in a number of biotechnological applications, including waste treatment, chemical generation, and the production of renewable energy [1–4]. Microbial electrolysis cells (MECs) are a form of MESs that can utilize electrons within a cathode chamber in order to yield specific chemical compounds through the activity of specific electrochemically active microbes [3]. Such MECs have been used to produce a range of chemical products, including alcohol, butanol, butyric acid, and succinic acid. In one study, researchers were able to achieve a 34% increase in *Clostridium tyrobutyricum* BAS7-mediated butyric acid production by applying a −1.5 V cathodic potential to their MEC system while using neutral red (NR) as an electron carrier [5]. Methyl viologen has been utilized in such

MEC systems as well, being used to promote the reduction of acetate at a −0.55 V applied cathodic potential, leading to a 6-fold acceleration of ethanol production [6]. When an MEC was subjected to a constant −1.8 V potential during a 60 h fermentation reaction, this was sufficient to yield 18 g/L succinic acid [7]. While the increase in the product concentration was obvious, the electron utilization was inefficient due to the complex culture conditions and potentiostatic method. This meant that the extracellular electronic supplement using the potentiostatic method far exceeded the intracellular electronic requirements. As such, there is an urgent need to develop reliable methods suited to controlling MECs.

Redox reactions are essential mediators of a wide range of essential biological processes [8]. The redox potential of a system is determined based upon factors including the pH equilibrium constant, concentrations of dissolved oxygen, and the amounts of particular compounds dissolved in a given medium [9]. ORP measurements have been an increasing subject of focus. Liu et al., for example, found succinic acid yields from *Escherichia coli* LL016 at a −400 mV ORP level to be 39% higher than at a −200 mV ORP level [10]. Similarly, in a mixed-acid anaerobic *Corynebacterium crenatum* fermentation system, a culture potential of −300 mV led to a 0.31 g/g succinic acid yield, which was 72% higher than when this ORP value was instead −40 mV [11].

For ORP-controlled fermentation reactions, appropriately lower ORP levels lead to higher intracellular NADH levels and/or $NADH/NAD^+$ ratios [10]. Intracellular NADH and NAD^+ are essential for many biological reactions, and as such, the use of ORP-controlled fermentation reactions that modulate this $NADH/NAD^+$ ratio and yield higher NADH concentrations lead to increased enzymatic activity and ATP synthesis, along with reductive metabolite production [11,12]. In MECs, the intracellular NADH levels have also been shown to be increased upon the application of an appropriate potential to the cathode [13]. In these MECs, it is possible for electrons to be transferred to a given mediator and then to microbes, thereby compensating for any shortage in reducing power [5]. As such, in MECs, these higher intracellular NADH levels are linked to increased enzymatic activity and ATP synthesis, along with reductive metabolite production [7]. As such, modulating the ORP represents an attractive means of controlling MEC processes.

The redox potential of the extracellular environment plays a pivotal role in the regulation of cellular metabolism, as it influences metabolic flux, intracellular enzymatic activities, and the balance of redox cofactors, such as the $NADH/NAD^+$ ratio, which are essential for various metabolic pathways [14–16]. As such, many different approaches have been employed to regulate the extracellular redox potential. For example, Liu et al. controlled the redox potential during succinic acid production by engineered *Escherichia coli* through the use of dithiothreitol (DTT) and potassium ferricyanide ($K_3Fe(CN)_6$) as respective reducing and oxidizing agents [10]. Additionally, the selection of carbon sources with varying oxidation states has been demonstrated to be a viable method for redox control. This strategy was effectively applied in the fermentation process of *A. succinogenes* NJ113 to produce succinic acid, showcasing the versatility of redox management in bio-production systems [12].

In the present investigation, we sought to implement a robust feedback control mechanism in MECs to augment the yield of succinic acid as well as to elevate the electron utilization efficiency. This encompassed the strategic selection of regulatory parameters, the meticulous design and refinement of the feedback control system, and the elucidation of the feedback regulation mechanism.

Therefore, in this study, we have explored the practicability of leveraging the ORP as a feedback regulatory parameter within MECs. In tandem, we examined the effects of NR, serving as an electron mediator within the MECs, on the efficacy of the control system. Furthermore, we refined the electron provisioning strategy by manipulating the applied electrical potentials, thereby elevating the regulatory system's efficiency. This study also explores the use of a fed-batch fermentation approach, which could potentially enhance succinic acid production by providing a steady supply of substrates and maintaining optimal growth conditions throughout the fermentation process. The results from such research could have significant implications for industrial biotechnology. By demonstrating the feasibility of ORP manipulation to improve biochemical synthesis in a bioelectrochemical system, this work contributes to the development of more efficient and sustainable methods for producing valuable chemicals like succinic acid.

2. Results and Discussion

2.1. ORP-Controlled MEC System Development

In our previous research, within microbial electrolysis cells (MECs) operating without feedback control, a succinic acid concentration of 18.09 g/L was achieved using corn stover hydrolysate as the carbon source, while the utilization of molasses as the carbon source resulted in a succinic acid concentration of 83.67 g/L [7,17]. Existing research indicates that optimizing the startup cathode potentials, operating potential, and even polarity reversal has a significant impact on the electrosynthesis process, yet it does not result in effective feedback regulation [7,18,19]. In the present study, an ORP-controlled MEC system was utilized to explore the impact on the extracellular redox potential, cell growth, and succinic acid production. The relative cell growth, succinic acid production, and ORP variability for *A. succinogenes* in non-electric and ORP-controlled MEC systems are shown in Figure 1.

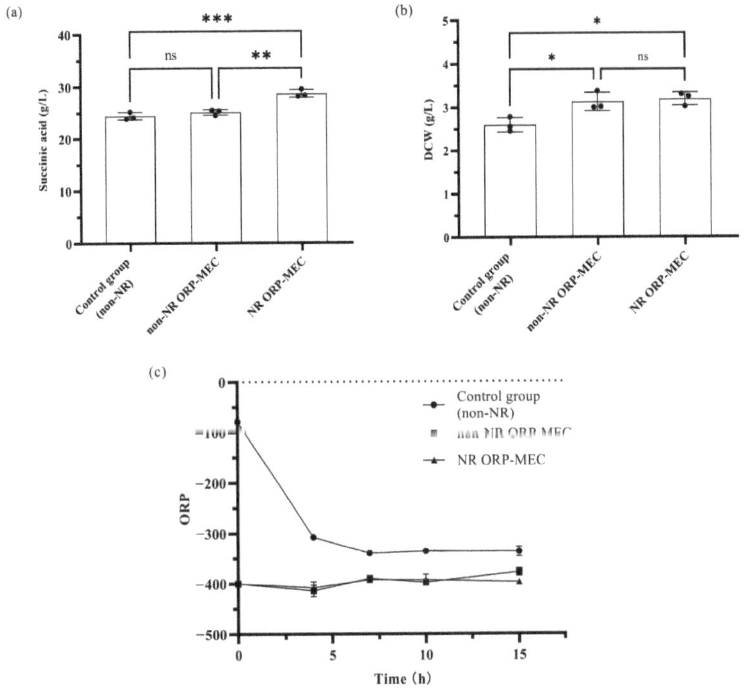

Figure 1. Effects of an ORP-controlled MEC system on succinic acid production. (**a**): Succinic acid; (**b**): biomass; (**c**): ORP value. The cells were cultured for 15 h with an initial sugar concentration of 50 g/L. Each value is the average of three parallel replicates and is represented as mean ± standard deviation. * $p < 0.05$ between two relevant treatments, ** $p < 0.01$, *** $p < 0.001$, ns: not significant.

The use of NR as an electronic mediator or electronophore was investigated in an effort to improve *A. succinogenes* succinic acid production. The ORP-controlled MEC system with NR yielded a 17.21% increase in succinic acid production relative to the non-electric MEC system (non-NR) (Figure 1a). When NR was added to a reaction mixture, the electricity delivered by the cathode could be used by *A. succinogenes* to boost succinic acid production.

After 15 h of fermentation, there was a 20.44% increase in the cell growth for the electric MEC system when ORP was maintained at a constant −400 mV relative to the non-electric system (Figure 1b). After 7 h of fermentation, the ORP in the non-electric MEC system decreased and remained stable at −350 mV (Figure 1c). These results suggested that the use of a cathode to apply a potential was effective as a means of controlling the extracellular ORP values and that maintaining an appropriate ORP value led to improved *A. succinogenes* growth in this MEC system.

In addition, the relatively low ORP regulatory sensitivity and the high applied voltage (≥−1.3 V) have the potential to limit the utility of this ORP-controlled MEC system, while a high ORP regulatory sensitivity and a relatively low applied voltage (−0.8 V) were obtained when NR was added to the ORP-controlled MEC system. With anaerobic conditions and pH control, the ORP of a system is determined based upon the amounts of particular compounds dissolved in the medium. As an electronic mediator, NR can effortlessly accept and release electrons. Therefore, when NR was added to the medium, a high ORP regulatory sensitivity and low applied voltage were obtained.

2.2. *The Impact of Different Potential Applications on Succinic Acid Production*

The exploration of various methodologies for the enhancement of fermentation reactions through the application of potential has yielded noteworthy findings. This study systematically evaluated the efficacy of different electrical strategies in augmenting the utility of MECs in producing valuable chemical compounds.

In the context of this research, the introduction of NR as a mediator in the MEC systems was a pivotal variable. NR's role was to facilitate electron transfer, thus influencing the ORP within the system. By maintaining the ORP at a targeted level of −400 mV, two distinct approaches were employed: one involved the application of a continuous low potential, while the other involved intermittent high-voltage electric pulses. These strategies were compared against a baseline non-electric MEC system, serving as a control within the experimental design.

Both the continuous low-potential and the high-voltage pulse methods significantly outperformed the control in terms of the succinic acid production. Specifically, the continuous low-potential approach resulted in a 10.12% increase, achieving a concentration of 28.62 g/L, while the high-voltage pulse method saw a 13.08% increase, culminating in a concentration of 29.39 g/L of succinic acid after a 15 h fermentation period. These results were visually corroborated by Figure 2a, which graphically represents the enhanced production levels.

Moreover, the impact of these electrical interventions on the metabolic directionality of the microbial consortia was profound. This was evidenced by the increased ratios of succinic to acetic acid, which were 33.34% and 8.14% higher in the continuous low-potential and high-voltage pulse systems, respectively, compared to the control. The peak ratios, occurring at the 10 h mark, were 2.44 for the continuous low-potential system and 1.98 for the high-voltage pulse system, indicating a more efficient biosynthetic conversion to succinic acid in the ORP-controlled environments.

Interestingly, despite the differences in electrical strategies, there was no discernible variance in the cell growth between the two systems at the 15 h mark, as illustrated in Figure 2b. This suggests that the application of electrical potential, in this case, did not negatively impact the microbial proliferation.

This study also delved into the energy efficiency of the two systems. It was noted that the total electric charge applied in the high-voltage pulse system was 562.88 Coulombs, which was substantially less—only 82.28%—of that used in the continuous low-potential system. This parameter was crucial in determining the overall sustainability and practicality of the electrical enhancement strategies.

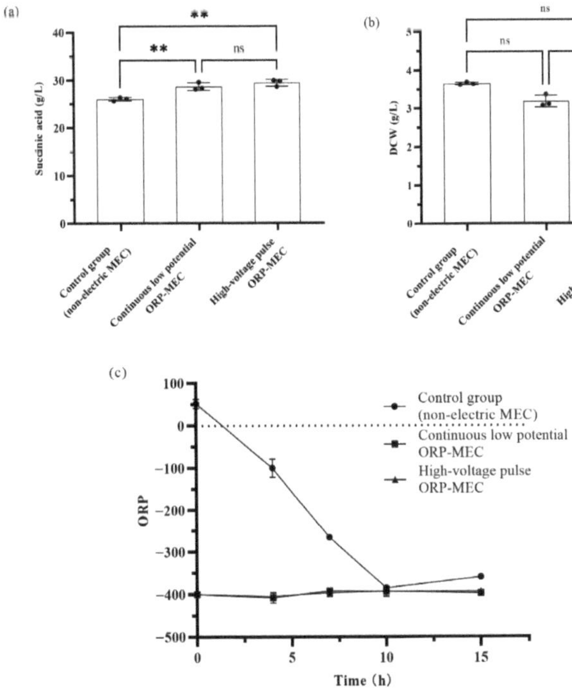

Figure 2. Effects of the voltage applied methods on succinic acid production in an ORP-controlled MEC system. (**a**): Succinic acid; (**b**): biomass; (**c**): ORP value. NR was added to the three MEC systems. The cells were cultured for 15 h with an initial sugar concentration of 50 g/L. ** $p < 0.01$ between two relevant treatments, ns: not significant.

Given the superior succinic acid yields, favorable metabolic shifts, and lower energy input, the high-voltage electric pulse-based ORP-controlled MEC system (HPORP) emerged as the more advantageous approach. Consequently, it was selected for further experimentation, with the aim of refining the process and potentially scaling it for industrial applications.

2.3. Different ORP Value Impacts Succinic Acid Production

The extracellular ORP levels are recognized for their influential role in modulating organic acid fermentation processes. In light of this, our research delved into the correlation between the ORP levels and the biosynthesis of succinic acid within an ORP-regulated MEC framework.

Our study revealed that the optimized succinic acid concentration peaked at 29.39 g/L when the ORP was meticulously controlled at −400 mV, as delineated in Table 1. This ORP level not only facilitated the highest yield of succinic acid but also delivered a remarkable electronic utilization efficiency of 177.58%. In contrast, the application of a potentiostatic method that maintained a constant potential of −1 V (referred to as CPMEC) did not yield a significant enhancement in succinic acid production when juxtaposed with the aforementioned −400 mV ORP level. This was a pivotal observation, especially considering that the CPMEC method resulted in a substantially higher energy consumption, tallying at 91.23% more than the −400 mV strategy.

Table 1. Effects of ORP optimization in ORP-controlled MEC system.

ORP Level	Succinic Acid (g/L)	Succinic Acid/ Acetic Acid (10 h)	Acetic Acid (g/L) (10 h)	Electric Charge (C)	Electronic Utilization Efficiency
Control	25.99 ± 0.33 [c]	1.83	6.85 ± 0.25 [c]	/	/
CPMEC	29.03 ± 1.17 [a]	1.94	9.28 ± 0.98 [ab]	1076.42 ± 91.22 [a]	83.04%
−350 mV (HPORP)	27.32 ± 0.43 [b]	2.03	8.39 ± 0.14 [b]	288.26 ± 35.36 [c]	135.64%
−400 mV (HPORP)	29.39 ± 0.14 [a]	1.98	10.05 ± 0.25 [a]	562.88 ± 16.02 [b]	177.58%
−450 mV (HPORP)	28.62 ± 0.67 [ab]	1.94	8.40 ± 0.16 [b]	1123.98 ± 96.82 [a]	68.80%

[abc] denotes significant ($p < 0.05$) differences between groups.

The implications of these findings underscore the importance of the extracellular ORP as a critical parameter in fermentation reactions. By sustaining an optimal ORP level, the yields of succinic acid were markedly improved within the ORP-controlled MEC system. Notably, the electronic utilization efficiency of this system was found to be 113.85% higher than that of the conventional potentiostatic approach. It is particularly noteworthy that the electron utilization efficiency exceeded 100%, which suggests that the ORP-controlled MEC system might not only provide a sufficient supply of extracellular electrons but could also potentially enhance the enzymatic activity within the fermentation pathway under suitable ORP conditions.

This enhanced enzymatic activity could be attributed to the more favorable redox conditions created by the ORP-controlled environment, which may lead to a more efficient electron transfer process and thereby stimulate the metabolic pathways involved in succinic acid production. Consequently, the ORP-controlled MEC system emerges as a highly viable and energy-efficient alternative to traditional potentiostatic methods, paving the way for more sustainable and cost-effective biotechnological applications in organic acid production.

2.4. The Impact of Fed-Batch Fermentation on the ORP-Controlled MEC System

The fed-batch fermentation strategy is a widely acknowledged technique for achieving elevated concentrations of target metabolites in various bioprocesses. In our current study, we integrated the fed-batch methodology with an ORP-controlled MEC system to enhance the production of succinic acid.

During the course of our 48 h fermentation period, the implementation of fed-batch fermentation in the ORP-controlled MEC system resulted in a substantial increase in the succinic acid concentration, reaching an impressive 74.43 g/L, as depicted in Figure 3. This represents an increase of 10.81% and 12.44% over the succinic acid yields obtained from the non-electric and potentiostatic (constant −1 V) MEC systems, respectively. Notably, the application of a cathode-mediated potential in the ORP-controlled MEC system was correlated with accelerated microbial growth rates, whereas the continuous exposure to the potential was observed to have a detrimental effect on cell proliferation.

Further analysis, as illustrated in Figure 3c, revealed that the ORP-controlled MEC system achieved a higher rate of succinic acid productivity, quantified at 0.735 $g\ L^{-1}\ h^{-1}\ g^{-1}{}_{DCW}$, when compared to the control setup. This enhanced productivity can be attributed to the optimized extracellular conditions provided by the ORP control, which are conducive to microbial activity and succinic acid biosynthesis.

Comparative studies indicated that the potentiostatic (constant −1 V) system, which subjects the microbial culture to a sustained high voltage, led to lower succinic acid concentrations due to the inhibitory effects of prolonged high-voltage application on cell growth. Such conditions can negatively impact the bacterial cells, undermining their viability and metabolic capacity for succinic acid production [7].

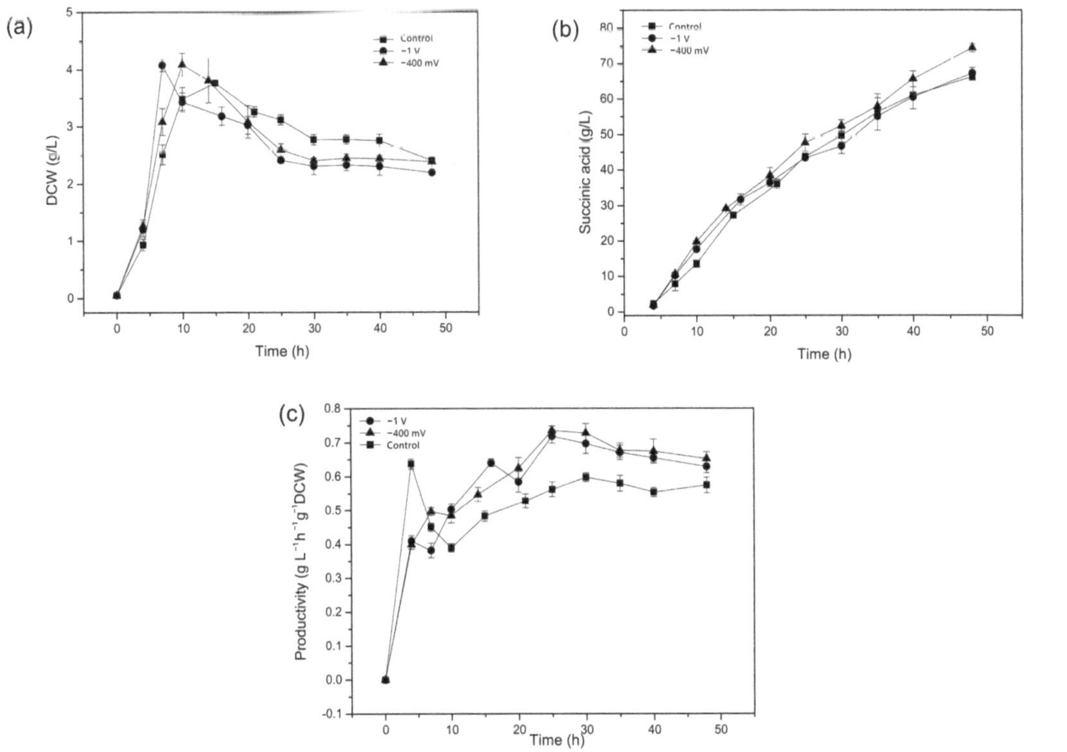

Figure 3. Effects of fed-batch fermentation in an ORP-controlled MEC system. (**a**): Succinic acid concentration; (**b**): dry cell weight; (**c**): succinic acid productivity. Control: non-electric fed-batch fermentation; −1 V: potentiostatic (constant −1 V) MEC systems with fed-batch fermentation; −400 mV: ORP-controlled (−400 mV) MEC systems with fed-batch fermentation.

The superior performance of the fed-batch ORP-controlled MEC system was further substantiated by its energy consumption and electronic utilization efficiency. The system utilized 1748.62 coulombs of electricity, which was only 55.30% of the energy consumed by the potentiostatic system. Moreover, the electronic utilization efficiency of the ORP-controlled system reached 192.02%, a staggering 15.19-fold increase over the potentiostatic system.

In conclusion, our study demonstrates that the high-voltage pulse-based ORP-controlled MEC system is not only more effective in providing the necessary electrons for microbial metabolism but also does so with a greater energy efficiency, significantly boosting succinic acid production. These compelling findings highlight the practical applicability and advantages of an ORP-controlled MEC system in industrial-scale fermentation processes, offering a promising avenue for sustainable and cost-effective organic acid production.

3. Materials and Methods

3.1. Strain and Growth Media

A. succinogenes (130Z) was obtained from MBI International (Plaistow, NH, USA). Chemicals utilized in this study were from Aladdin (Shanghai, China), Fluka Chemical (Buchs, Switzerland), Oxoid Ltd. (Cambridge, UK), and Sinochem (Shanghai, China), and were of reagent-grade purity or higher. Carbon dioxide was obtained from the Nanjing Special Gases Factory (Nanjing, China). The media used for cellular growth were prepared as follows (per L): glucose, 10 g; yeast extract (YE), 5 g; $NaH_2PO_4 \cdot 2H_2O$, 9.6 g; $K_2HPO_4 \cdot 3H_2O$, 15.5 g; $NaHCO_3$, 10 g; NaCl, 1 g; and corn steep liquor, 2.5 g. This culture media underwent a 15 min sterilization step at 121 °C. Sugars were separately sterilized and then added to the media following this autoclaving.

3.2. MEC System and Fed-Batch Fermentation

The Chemistry Department of Michigan State University (East Lansing, MI, USA) provided the MEC system used in this study, which contained anode and cathode compartments kept separate through the use of a cation-selective membrane (Nafion, NY, USA). Fine carbon felt was used for both anodes and cathodes, which were 70 mm × 50 mm × 5 mm, with 10.6 cm^2/g total surface area. A 1 mm, 1.0 Ω/cm platinum wire (Sigma–Aldrich, St. Louis, MO, USA) was used to connect the anode and cathode. A power supply (PMC 1000/DC, AMETEK, Santiago, MN, USA) was used to provide potential to this MEC system. The volume in both the anode and cathode compartments was 280 mL. Inoculations before experimental fermentation were controlled at a 5% ratio in the cathode compartment. *A. succinogenes* cells and catholyte were added into the cathode compartment, with CO_2 added at a rate of 25 mL/min. The catholyte was composed of (per L): glucose, 50 g; $NaHPO_4 \cdot 12H_2O$, 31.5 g; $NaHCO_3$, 10.0 g; $NaH_2PO_4 \cdot 2H_2O$, 8.5 g; and YE, 5.0 g. The anolyte was composed of (per L) 5.8 g NaCl, 15.6 g $NaH_2PO_4 \cdot 2H_2O$, and 35.8 g $NaHPO_4 \cdot 12H_2O$. In addition, the catholyte was supplemented with 0.0288 g/L NR (determined by experiment) that had been subjected to 0.22 nm syringe filtration, and the anolyte was supplemented with 0.02% dithiothreitol that had been subjected to 0.22 nm syringe filtration. Prior to sterilization, 10 M NaOH was used to adjust the catholyte pH to 7.0. Once the fermentation reaction began, 1% alkaline magnesium carbonate was added to the catholyte in order to maintain pH balance. As a reference electrode, an Ag/AgCl electrode was used. The potential between the reference electrode and the cathode electrode was defined as a constant potential. No potential was supplied to the control non-electric MEC system, in which the open circuit voltage was monitored.

During fed-batch MEC, the catholyte initially contained the following (per L): $NaHPO_4 \cdot 12H_2O$, 31.5 g; $NaHCO_3$, 10.0 g; $NaH_2PO_4 \cdot 2H_2O$, 8.5 g; YE, 15.0 g; and NR, 0.0288 g. The initial glucose concentration was 50 g/L, and when the glucose concentration fell to <5 g/L, 50 g/L glucose was added, while alkaline magnesium carbonate served to maintain pH for the 48 h fermentation duration.

3.3. ORP-Controlled MEC System

A redox potential electrode (METTLER P14805-SC-DPAS-K8S/225, Zurich, Switzerland) was used to measure ORP, which was regulated via power supply (PMC 1000/DC, AMETEK). For the continuous low-potential strategy (LPORP), the potential was maintained from −0.4 V to −0.6 V. When the ORP levels rose above the set point, additional reductive potential was applied, whereas when these levels fell below the set point, additional oxidative potential was applied. For the high-voltage electric pulse strategy (HPORP), a 1-s periodic potential was employed, with a −1 V potential applied for 0.5 s and no potential applied for the remaining 0.5 s. Whenever ORP levels rose above the set point, a periodic potential was applied. No potential was applied when ORP levels fell below the set point, with open-circuit voltage instead being monitored. The −1 V constant potential MEC system (CPMEC) had a −1 V and was constantly applied throughout the 48 h fermentation reaction period (Table 2).

Table 2. ORP-controlled MEC system.

MEC System	Potential (V)	Frequency (s/s)	ORP-Controlled
CPMEC	−1	1	No
LPORP	−0.4~−0.6	1	Yes
HPORP	−1	0.5	Yes

3.4. Analytical Methods

High-performance liquid chromatography (Agilent 1290; Agilent Technologies, Santa Clara, CA, USA) was used to measure glucose and organic acid concentrations using an HPX-87H column (300 × 7.8 mm, Bio-Rad, Santa Clara, CA, USA). For detection, the column was warmed to 55 °C, with detection at 215 nm, a 20 μL injection volume, and a mobile phase composed of 8 mM sulfuric acid with a 0.6 mL/min flow rate. Succinic acid yields were defined based on the amount of succinic acid generated per gram of glucose.

3.5. Equation

Electronic utilization efficiency refers to the ratio of the theoretical charge required for the target metabolic product to the actual charge consumed by the MEC system.

$$\text{Electronic utilization efficiency (\%)} = (\Delta M_S \times NA \times q \times 2)/Q \times 100$$

ΔM_S: The molar quantity of succinic acid increased by MEC compared with non-electric MEC. NA: Avogadro's constant. q: The charge of an electron. 2: The synthesis of 1 mol NADH requires 2 mol electrons. Q: The charges consumed by MEC.

4. Conclusions

The research undertaken in this study has provided a comprehensive analysis of the parameters that govern the efficiency of succinic acid production in an ORP-controlled MEC system, particularly focusing on the role of neutral red as an electron mediator, the application of voltage, and the optimization of ORP and fed-batch culture conditions.

The incorporation of NR into the MEC system has been a pivotal step in enhancing the production of succinic acid. NR, as an electron mediator, has improved the sensitivity of the system to ORP regulation. This heightened sensitivity allows for more precise control over the redox environment within the MEC, which is crucial for the metabolic processes of the microorganisms involved, particularly *A. succinogenes* (130Z).

This study found that the optimal approach to ORP level control was the use of a −400 mV high-voltage electric pulse-based strategy. This strategy not only provided the necessary extracellular electrons for the microbial metabolic processes but also seemed to stimulate enzyme activity related to succinic acid production. The result was an electronic utilization efficiency of 192.02%, an impressive figure that indicates the system's ability to exceed the theoretical electron transfer efficiency. This could suggest that the ORP-controlled MEC system is capable of redirecting electron flow to enhance enzymatic pathways that are beneficial for succinic acid synthesis.

The efficiency over 100% indicates that the system may be capturing and utilizing electrons more effectively than anticipated, which could be due to several factors such as enhanced mediator performance, improved microbial metabolism, or more effective electron transfer mechanisms. This exceptional utilization efficiency also implies that the system can sustain a long-term fermentation process, providing a consistent and enhanced yield of succinic acid.

This research validates ORP control as a method to enhance succinic acid production in MEC systems, offering a pathway to more efficient and economical industrial fermentation with potential for commercial scaling, contingent on maintaining system performance. Future work in this area may focus on further refining the electron mediator system, perhaps by identifying new compounds that can perform better than NR, or by engineering microorganisms to more effectively interact with the existing mediators. Additionally, exploring the integration of this technology with other renewable energy sources or waste-to-energy systems could further improve the sustainability and economic viability of the process.

In summary, this research has not only provided insights into the effective management of the ORP in MEC systems but has also showcased the potential for these systems to revolutionize the production of valuable biochemicals like succinic acid, aligning with the principles of green chemistry and sustainable industrial processes.

Author Contributions: Methodology, J.P. and S.Z.; formal analysis, J.P., S.Z. and Y.L.; resources, Z.W.; writing—original draft preparation, J.P.; writing—review and editing, Z.W.; supervision, Z.W. and L.C. All authors have read and agreed to the published version of the manuscript.

Funding: This research was supported by the the National Nature Science Foundation of China [grant no. 21576134, 21390200]; 863 program of China [grant no. 2014AA021703]; Jiangsu Postdoctoral Research Funding [grant no. 2021K348C]; Lianyungang Postdoctoral Research Funding [grant no. LYG20210004] and Lianyungang "521 High-level Talent Cultivation Project" [grant no. LYG06521202342].

Institutional Review Board Statement: Not applicable.

Informed Consent Statement: Not applicable.

Data Availability Statement: All data are included in the manuscript.

Acknowledgments: This work was supported by the Priority Academic Program Development of Jiangsu Higher Education Institutions.

Conflicts of Interest: The authors declare no conflicts of interest.

References

1. Kumar, G.; Bakonyi, P.; Zhen, G.; Sivagurunathan, P.; Kook, L.; Kim, S.H.; Toth, G.; Nemestothy, N.; Belafi-Bako, K. Microbial electrochemical systems for sustainable biohydrogen production: Surveying the experiences from a start-up viewpoint. *Renew. Sustain. Energy Rev.* **2017**, *70*, 589–597. [CrossRef]
2. Wang, H.; Luo, H.; Fallgren, P.H.; Jin, S.; Ren, Z.J. Bioelectrochemical system platform for sustainable environmental remediation and energy generation. *Biotechnol. Adv.* **2015**, *33*, 317–334. [CrossRef] [PubMed]
3. Wang, H.; Ren, Z.J. A comprehensive review of microbial electrochemical systems as a platform technology. *Biotechnol. Adv. Int. Rev. J.* **2013**, *31*, 1796–1807. [CrossRef] [PubMed]
4. Dai, S.; Korth, B.; Schwab, L.; Aulenta, F.; Vogt, C.; Harnisch, F. Deciphering the fate of sulfate in one- and two-chamber bioelectrochemical systems. *Electrochim. Acta* **2022**, *408*, 139942. [CrossRef]
5. Park, D.H.; Laivenieks, M.; Guettler, M.V.; Jain, M.K.; Zeikus, J.G. Microbial utilization of electrically reduced neutral red as the sole electron donor for growth and metabolite production. *Appl. Environ. Microbiol.* **1999**, *65*, 2912–2917. [CrossRef]
6. Steinbusch, K.J.J.; Hamelers, H.V.M.; Schaap, J.D.; Kampman, C.; Buisman, C.J. Bioelectrochemical ethanol production through mediated acetate reduction by mixed cultures. *Environ. Sci. Technol.* **2010**, *44*, 513–517. [CrossRef] [PubMed]
7. Zhao, Y.; Cao, W.; Wang, Z.; Zhang, B.; Chen, K.; Ouyang, P. Enhanced succinic acid production from corncob hydrolysate by microbial electrolysis cells. *Bioresour. Technol.* **2016**, *202*, 152–157. [CrossRef] [PubMed]
8. Berovič, M.; Rošelj, M.; Wondra, M. Possibilities of redox potential regulation in submerged citric acid bioprocessing on beet molasses substrate. *Food Technol. Biotechnol.* **2000**, *38*, 193–201.
9. Li, J.A.; Jiang, M.; Chen, K.Q.; Ye, Q.; Shang, L.A.; Wei, P.; Ying, H.J.; Chang, H.N. Effect of redox potential regulation on succinic acid production by *Actinobacillus succinogenes*. *Bioprocess Biosyst. Eng.* **2010**, *33*, 911–920. [CrossRef] [PubMed]
10. Liu, R.; Liang, L.; Min, J.; Ma, J.; Chen, K.; Jia, H.; Ping, W.; Ouyang, P. Effects of redox potential control on succinic acid production by engineered *Escherichia coli* under anaerobic conditions. *Process Biochem.* **2014**, *49*, 740–744. [CrossRef]
11. Chen, X.J.; Jiang, S.T.; Zheng, Z.; Pan, L.J.; Luo, S.Z. Effects of culture redox potential on succinic acid production by *Corynebacterium crenatum* under anaerobic conditions. *Process Biochem.* **2012**, *47*, 1250–1255. [CrossRef]
12. Li, J.; Jiang, M.; Chen, K.; Shang, L.; Wei, P.; Ying, H. Enhanced production of succinic acid by *Actinobacillus succinogenes* with reductive carbon source. *Process Biochem.* **2010**, *45*, 980–985. [CrossRef]
13. Rabaey, K.; Rozendal, R.A. Microbial electrosynthesis—Revisiting the electrical route for microbial production. *Nat. Rev. Microbiol.* **2010**, *8*, 706–716. [CrossRef] [PubMed]
14. Bai, F.; Fink, B.D.; Yu, L.; Sivitz, W.I. Voltage-dependent regulation of complex II energized mitochondrial oxygen flux. *PLoS ONE* **2016**, *11*, e0154982. [CrossRef] [PubMed]
15. Wu, Y.; Lin, Y.H. Fermentation redox potential control on the 1,3-propanediol production by *Lactobacillus panis* PM1. *Process Biochem.* **2022**, *114*, 139–146. [CrossRef]
16. Zheng, T.; Xu, B.; Ji, Y.; Zhang, W.; Xin, F.; Dong, W.; Wei, P.; Ma, J.; Jiang, M. A staged representation electrochemical stimulated strategy to regulate intracellular reducing power for improving succinate production by *Escherichia coli* AFP111. *Pediatr. Obes.* **2021**, *16*, 2000415. [CrossRef] [PubMed]
17. Wang, Z.; Li, H.; Feng, J.; Zhang, A.; Ying, H.; He, X.; Jiang, M.; Chen, K.; Ouyang, P. Enhanced succinic acid production from polyacrylamide-pretreated cane molasses in microbial electrolysis cells. *J. Chem. Technol. Biotechnol.* **2017**, *93*, 855–860. [CrossRef]

18. Li, J.; Li, Z.; Xiao, S.; Fu, Q.; Kobayashi, H.; Zhang, L.; Liao, Q.; Zhu, X. Startup cathode potentials determine electron transfer behaviours of biocathodes catalysing CO_2 reduction to CH_4 in microbial electrosynthesis. *J. CO_2 Util.* **2020**, *35*, 169–175. [CrossRef]
19. Li, Z.; Fu, Q.; Kobayashi, H.; Xiao, S.; Li, J.; Zhang, L.; Liao, Q.; Zhu, X. Polarity reversal facilitates the development of biocathodes in microbial electrosynthesis systems for biogas production. *Int. J. Hydrogen Energy* **2019**, *44*, 26226–26236. [CrossRef]

fermentation

MDPI

Article

Comparative Study of the Extracellular Holocellulolytic Activity of *Fusarium solani* and *Aspergillus* sp. in Corn Stover

Mariana Alvarez-Navarrete [1], Katia L. Alonso-Hurtado [2], Alberto Flores-García [2], Josué Altamirano-Hernández [2], Mauro M. Martínez-Pacheco [2,*] and Crisanto Velázquez-Becerra [3]

1 Tecnológico Nacional de México, Instituto Tecnológico de Morelia, Morelia 58120, Michoacán, Mexico; maralvnav@yahoo.com.mx

2 Instituto de Investigaciones Químico Biológicas, Universidad Michoacana de San Nicolás de Hidalgo, Morelia 58040, Michoacán, Mexico; 1316242f@umich.mx (K.L.A.-H.); aflores@umich.mx (A.F.-G.); josue.altamirano@umich.mx (J.A.-H.)

3 Facultad de Ingeniería en Tecnología de la Madera, Universidad Michoacana de San Nicolás de Hidalgo, Morelia 58120, Michoacán, Mexico

* Correspondence: mauro.martinez.pacheco@umich.mx

Abstract: Fungal holocellulases are interesting for their possible applications in the bioconversion of corn crop residues into molecules with technological significance. Holocellulase (xylanases and cellulases) production from *Fusarium solani* and *Aspergillus* sp. with corn stover as a carbon source was compared using a Box–Wilson design. The fungal holocellulase production was different in both fungi. For *F. solani*, the maximum endoxylanase and β-xylosidase activities were 14.15 U/mg and 0.75 U/mg at 84 h of fermentation on 350 g/L corn stover, while *Aspergillus* sp. was 5.90 U/mg and 0.03 U/mg, respectively, at 156 h and 1000 g/L corn stover. The production of holocellulases in both fungi was reduced with increasing carbon sources. The nitrogen source induced the holocellulases in *Aspergillus* sp., but not in *F. solani*. Interestingly, when verifying the optimal culture conditions, the production of endoxylanases by *F. solani* was higher when compared to the predicted value. With regard to the endoxylanase and β-xylosidase activities of *Aspergillus* sp., these were close to the predicted values. Based on the optimization model, *F. solani* and *Aspergillus* sp. produce an interesting holocellulolytic activity in a growth medium with corn stover as the only carbon source. The fermentation time and the amount of corn stover required to obtain maximum holocellulase production are possible advantages for *Fusarium solani* and *Aspergillus* sp., respectively.

Keywords: endoxylanase; β-xylosidase; endocellulase; holocellulases; *Fusarium solani*; *Aspergillus* sp.

Citation: Alvarez-Navarrete, M.; Alonso-Hurtado, K.L.; Flores-García, A.; Altamirano-Hernández, J.; Martínez-Pacheco, M.M.; Velázquez-Becerra, C. Comparative Study of the Extracellular Holocellulolytic Activity of *Fusarium solani* and *Aspergillus* sp. in Corn Stover. *Fermentation* **2024**, *10*, 84. https://doi.org/10.3390/fermentation10020084

Academic Editor: Gunnar Lidén

Received: 4 January 2024
Revised: 21 January 2024
Accepted: 25 January 2024
Published: 30 January 2024

1. Introduction

Agricultural and agroindustrial activities give rise to a significant amount of solid waste that generates pollution. The amount of corn stubble and cob generated in Mexico is 17.5 million tons of corn stubble per year [1]. Both materials are mainly made up of lignocellulosic biomass, where cellulose (45%) and hemicellulose (35%) are present in greater quantities [2,3]. Holocellulose is the sum of the cellulose and hemicellulose fractions. Hemicellulose is mainly composed of xylan (28–35% dry basis), which can be used to obtain microbial xylanases on a large scale. Xylanases are produced by bacteria, fungi, and actinomycetes [4,5]. Filamentous fungi are especially interesting since they secrete these enzymes into the medium and their level of activity is notable compared to yeasts and bacteria [6]. *Aspergillus* and *Trichoderma* species are widely used for the commercial production of xylanases [7,8]. The enzyme preparations obtained from these fungal species are very specific for certain applications. Xylanases have various industrial uses, such as in livestock, food, paper and cellulose pulp, textiles, and the manufacturing of chemical products such as xylitol and ethanol [9], as well as in the exploitation of lignocellulosic materials from agricultural, agro-industrial, and municipal waste to obtain molecules with important technological value [10], such as in the production of biofuels [11].

The cost of enzymes accounts for 50% of the total cost of the hydrolysis processes of lignocellulosic materials, so research efforts have been directed to reducing the cost of the production of enzymes. The exploration of organisms with new enzymes, the genetic improvement of organisms used in industry and enzyme engineering, and the study of factors related to enzyme production are the strategies to achieve this objective [12,13].

Regarding the first strategy, a large number of fungal species still exist without being studied in the great microbial diversity of our planet. *Fusarium solani* is a candidate for the production of extracellular xylanases. There have been few reports on the efficient production of xylanases and exploratory studies about its xylanolytic activity [14] and optimization of enzyme production [15,16]. In a previous study, *Fusarium solani* was isolated from bean crops, identified, and selected from a group of one hundred and three fungal isolates for its notable ability to produce extracellular xylanases [17]. Based on the third strategy to reduce the cost of enzymes, corn stover is a potentially profitable source for the fermentative production of fungal xylanases. Several factors have been studied to determine their effect on the production of holocellulases in filamentous fungi, such as the type and concentration of carbon source and nitrogen source, pH, temperature, and time of incubation. In relation to the concentration of the carbon source, studies have been carried out using lignocellulosic residues with different moisture levels to evaluate the production of xylanases. Due to its high demonstrated xylanolytic activity, *F. solani* is a fungus with biotechnological potential for the production of these enzymes with wide industrial application. An organism considered as a standard in the production of industrial xylanases, as well as other metabolites, such as *Aspergillus* sp., for a comparative study of enzymatic production can be used as a reference to determine the potential of *F. solani* in the production of extracellular holocellulases; this species has not been exploited as extensively in the industrial sector as the species of the genus *Aspergillus*. The aim of this work was to compare the holocellulolytic activity of *Aspergillus* sp. and *Fusarium solani* in corn stover as a carbon source under different growing conditions.

2. Materials and Methods

2.1. Biological Material

Fusarium solani (accession number KP137441, GenBank (NCBI)) was isolated from horticultural field crops (22°35′00″ N, 102°15′00″ W) [17]. The *Aspergillus* sp. strain was isolated from a bean field crop (23°29′0″ N, 103°53′0″ W). It was previously selected for its ability to produce extracellular holocellulases and was identified using molecular tools in the Laboratory of Cellular Physiology at the Institute of Chemical Biological Research of the Universidad Michoacana de San Nicolás de Hidalgo. The fungi isolates were inoculated in a PDA medium for their maintenance and propagation.

2.2. Fungus Molecular Identification

Genomic DNA extraction was carried out using the modified method of Lin [18]. The oligonucleotide pair internal transcribed spacers (ITS5 and ITS4), which were specific to the selected fungal isolates, were used in the PCR assays. Forward primer (ITS5): GGAAGTAAAAGTCGTAACAAGG and reverse primer (ITS4): TCCTCCGCTTATTGATATGC. The reaction mixture was prepared in a total volume of 25 μL, with a final concentration of 2 mM $MgCl_2$, 200 mM Tris-HCl, pH 8.4, 500 mM KCl, and 0.2 mM each dNTP. For each reaction, 0.04 U/μL *Taq* 5U polymerase (Invitrogen, Carlsbad, CA, USA), 0.2 μM each primer, and 1 μL fungal template DNA were used. The reaction was performed in a Techne C-512 PCR system thermal cycler (Barloworld Scientific, Staffordshire, UK) using the following PCR conditions: denaturation at 95 °C for 8 min; 35 cycles of denaturation at 95 °C for 15 s, annealing at 50 °C for 20 s, and extension at 72 °C for 1 min; final extension at 72 °C for 5 min; and cooling at 4 °C until recovery of the samples [19]. Amplification products were visualized on 1.0% agarose gel (*w*/*v*) stained with ethidium bromide in a Transiluminator

3UV^{TM} model LMS-20E UVP and analyzed using the program Quantity One 4.2.1, see Supplementary Material (SM) (Bio-Rad, Hercules, CA, USA). After amplification, the products were directly sequenced using a sequencer 3730xI (Applied Biosystems, Foster City, CA, USA). All sequencing products were edited and analyzed using the software BioEdit 7.1.3.0. Then, the sequences were used as a query to search for similarities using the BLAST network services on the NCBI database.

2.3. Experimental Design

Different culture conditions were studied to optimize fungal xylanase production via fermentation. Five factors were studied: fermentation time, and concentrations of carbon source, yeast extract, ammonium sulfate, and urea. The concentrations of the carbon source were stablished in such a way that the moisture or water availability in the culture medium was different in each experiment. Solid, semi-solid, and liquid culture media were generated (Table 1). Washed, dried, and milled corn stover was used as a carbon source (CS). A Box–Wilson (BW) rotatable composite experimental design was used as a fractional factorial design 2^{k-1} with sixteen factorial experiments, ten axial experiments, and one central experiment. Twenty-seven different experiments were generated and replicated three times (Table 1). The BW design has the advantage of reducing runs compared with other experimental designs and can estimate the curvature effects of factors, i.e., when it is suspected that the effect of the factors on the dependent variable is nonlinear [20]. The experiments were randomized to avoid biased results in the application of the design. In Table 2, the decoded levels of each factor are shown. Response variables measured were the activities of endo-β-1,4-xylanase, exo-β-1,4-xylosidase, and endocellulase (collectively referred to as *holocellulases* or *holocellulolytic activity*).

Table 1. Experiment generated from the rotatable composite Box–Wilson design (S: solid, Ss: semi-solid, L: liquid).

Experiment Number	Coded Factors					State of Aggregation (Type of Culture Medium)
	x_1	x_2	x_3	x_4	x_5	
1	−1	−1	−1	−1	+1	Ss
2	−1	−1	−1	+1	−1	Ss
3	−1	−1	+1	−1	−1	Ss
4	−1	−1	+1	+1	+1	Ss
5	−1	+1	−1	−1	−1	Ss
6	−1	+1	−1	+1	+1	Ss
7	−1	+1	+1	−1	+1	Ss
8	−1	+1	+1	+1	−1	Ss
9	+1	−1	−1	−1	−1	S
10	+1	−1	−1	+1	+1	S
11	+1	−1	+1	−1	+1	S
12	+1	−1	+1	+1	−1	S
13	+1	+1	−1	−1	+1	S
14	+1	+1	−1	+1	−1	S
15	+1	+1	+1	−1	−1	S
16	+1	+1	+1	+1	+1	S
17	−2	0	0	0	0	L
18	+2	0	0	0	0	S
19	0	−2	0	0	0	S
20	0	+2	0	0	0	S
21	0	0	−2	0	0	S
22	0	0	+2	0	0	S
23	0	0	0	−2	0	S
24	0	0	0	+2	0	S
25	0	0	0	0	−2	S
26	0	0	0	0	+2	S
27	0	0	0	0	0	S

Table 2. Decoded factors and their corresponding values to the coded levels.

Variable (g/L or h)	Decoded Factor				
	−2	−1	0	+1	+2
x_1 Carbon source	25	350	675	1000	1325
x_2 Yeast extract	1	3	5	7	9
x_3 Ammonium sulfate	0.5	1	1.5	2	2.5
x_4 Urea	5	35	65	95	125
x_5 Time	48	84	120	156	192

2.4. Inoculum Preparation

Separately, spore suspensions of *Aspergillus* sp. and *F. solani* were obtained from PDA plates previously seeded with both fungi. After the addition of sterile deionized water, the surface of the solid culture media was gently scraped, and the spores were extracted using a micropipette. The spore suspension was deposited in glass test tubes. The spore suspension was centrifuged at 3500 rpm for 10 min. The supernatant was discarded, and the spores were resuspended in sterilized deionized water. This procedure was repeated four times. The spore concentration was quantified by account in a Neubauer chamber. Fermentation flasks from the experimental design were inoculated with 1×10^6 fungal spores/mL.

2.5. Xylanase Production by Fermentation

Based on the experiments listed in Table 1, the required amounts of CS and the three nitrogen sources were combined. A trace element and vitamin dissolution was added (100 µL per milliliter of culture medium) (MEM Vitamin solution 1000×, Sigma Cell Culture), composed per liter of deionized water as follows: 2.0 g KH_2PO_4, 0.3 g $MgSO_4 \cdot 7H_2O$; 0.3 g $CaCl_2$, 5.0 mg $FeSO_4 \cdot 7H_2O$, 1.56 mg $MnSO_4 \cdot H_2O$, 2.0 mg $CoCl_2$, 1.4 mg $ZnSO_4 \cdot 7H_2O$. Culture media were autoclaved at 121 °C for 15 min. Twenty-seven different fermentation flasks, with their respective replicates (n = 3), were inoculated with 1×10^6 fungal spores/mL of *F. solani*. The above procedure was repeated with *Aspergillus* sp. The inoculated flasks were incubated for the stated time in the BW design at 150 rpm and at room temperature.

2.6. Extraction of Holocellulolytic Enzyme

The flasks were removed from incubation, and then 10 mL of 50 mM sodium citrate buffer at pH 5.0 was added to wash the solids. The supernatant was filtered from the solids through filter paper and centrifugated at 10,000 rpm for 4 min, and was used to quantify the holocellulolytic activity and extracellular protein.

2.7. Holocellulolytic Enzyme Assays

2.7.1. Endo-β-1,4-Xylanase, Endocellulase, and β-1,4-Xylosidase Activities Assays

Endo-β-1,4-xylanase, endocellulase, and β-1,4-xylosidase activities were measured using the modified methods of Bailey [21], Ghose [22], and Kristufek [23], respectively. The substrates were 1% (*w*/*v*) CMC, 1% (*w*/*v*) birchwood xylan, and 10 mM PNPX (Sigma Naucalpan Estado de México), respectively. The reducing sugars were quantified using the method of Miller by adding 1 mL of DNS reagent [24]. One unit (U) of enzyme activity is defined as the amount of enzyme that releases 1 µmol of reducing sugars per minute under assay conditions. Each assay was performed in duplicate.

2.7.2. Extracellular Protein Quantification

The extracellular protein was quantified using the method of Lowry [25] with BSA as standard. Each assay was performed in duplicate.

2.8. Optimization of Fermentation Conditions for Xylanase Production

A general second-order model was adjusted to the experimental results of the BW design to estimate the effects of the factors on the response variables. The main effects as well as the interactions and quadratic effects were included in the model used, which is shown by Equation (1).

$$y_n = \beta_0 + \sum_{i=1}^{k} \beta_i x_i + \sum_{i=1}^{k} \beta_{ii} x_i^2 + \sum_{j}^{k} \sum_{i=1}^{k} \beta_{ik} x_i x_j + \varepsilon_i \quad (1)$$

where y_n is any of the response variables, x_i and x_j are the $k = 5$ factors, and the β coefficients are the regression parameters.

The parameters of Equation (1) were obtained using multiple linear regression using the least squares method and the significance of the effects was evaluated at $\alpha = 0.5$. To find the optimal conditions for holocellulase production, the desirability profile method was used as described by Derringer and Suich [26].

For each response, a desirability function was assigned a number between 0 and 1 to the possible response values, with 0 representing a completely undesirable value of response and 1 representing a completely desirable or ideal response value. Depending on whether a particular response is to be maximized, minimized, or assigned a target value, different desirability functions can be used. The 0 and 1 values of desirability were assigned to the minimum and maximum endoxylanase and β-xylosidase activities obtained from the BW design experiments, respectively. Conversely, for endocellulase activity, 0 and 1 values were assigned to maximum and minimum enzymatic activity, respectively. One of the objetives of this study was to achieve maximum endoxylanase and β-xylanase activities with minimal endocellulase activity.

3. Results

3.1. Holocellulolytic Activity of *F. solani* and *Aspergillus* sp. in BW Experiments

The endoxylanase activity from *Aspergillus* sp. was higher than that of *F. solani* (Figure 1a) in most experiments, but the maximum endoxylanase activity was observed in experiment 2 (350 g/L, 3.0 g/L, 1.0 g/L, and 95 g/L of CS, yeast extract, ammonium sulfate, and urea) with *F. solani* in contrast with *Aspergillus* sp., whose maximum activity was achieved in experiment 11 (1000 g/L, 3 g/L, 2 g/L, and 35 g/L, CS, ammonium sulfate, yeast extract, and urea, respectively) (Table 3). Regarding β-xylosidase activity, *F. solani* showed more activity than *Aspergillus* sp. in thirteen of twenty-seven experiments (Figure 1b). The maximum β-xylosidase activity was achieved with *F. solani* in experiment 2 (0.75 U/mg), which represented more than double the maximum activity achieved by *Aspergillus* sp. in experiment 22 (0.28 U/mg) (Table 3). *F. solani* showed slightly higher cellulolytic activity than *Aspergillus* sp. in most of the experiments performed (Figure 1c). *Aspergillus* sp. exhibited the maximum cellulase activity in experiment 20, whereas *F. solani* had the highest activity in experiment 2 (Table 3).

Table 3. Comparison of the maximum experimental holocellulolytic activity of *F. solani* and *Aspergillus* sp.

Fungal Isolate	Holocellulolytic Activity	Maximum Enzymatic Activity (U/mg)	Experiment Number/Type of Culture Medium
Apergillus sp.	Endoxylanase	5.90	11/S
	β-xylosidase	0.28	22/S
	Endocellulase	1.80	20/S
F. solani	Endoxylanase	14.15	2/Ss
	β-xylosidase	0.75	2/Ss
	Endocellulase	2.00	2/Ss

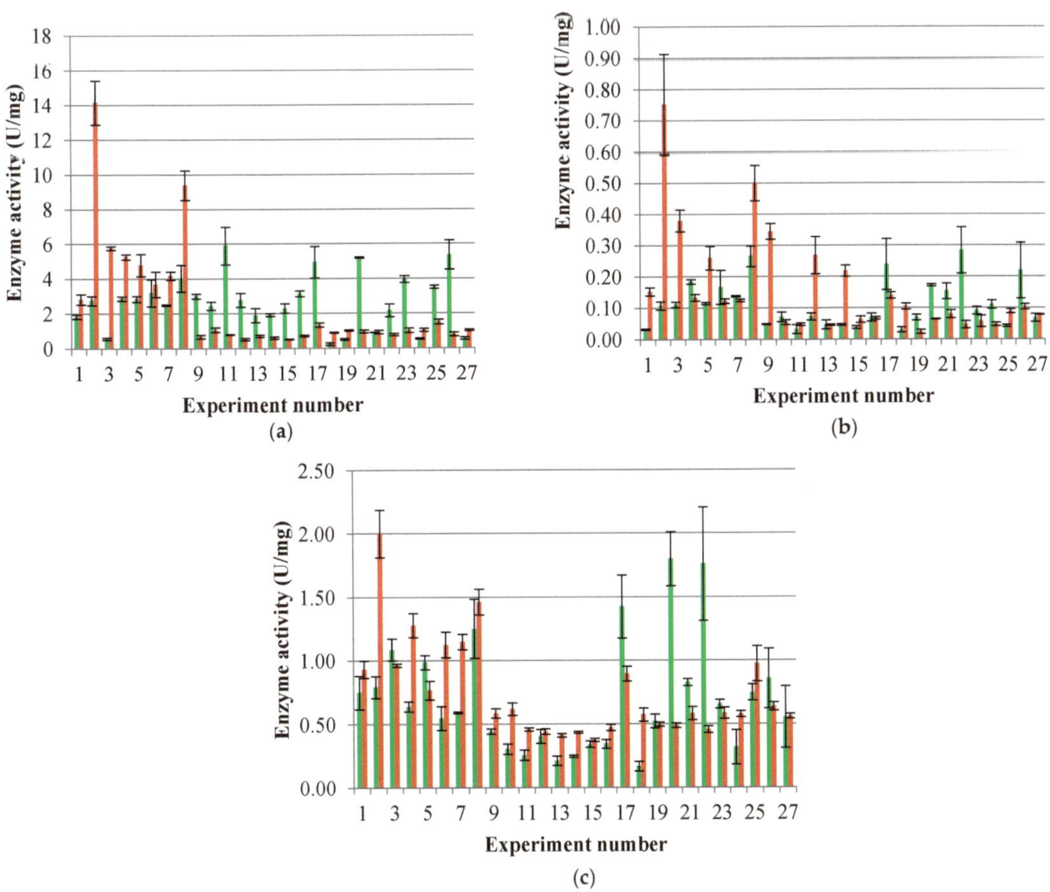

Figure 1. Holocellulolytic activity of *F. solani* (red) and *Aspergillus* sp. (green). (**a**) Endoxylanases; (**b**) β-xylosidases; (**c**) endocellulase. Values represent the $\overline{X}$ ± standard error, n = 3.

3.2. Predicted and Experimental Data

The holocellulolytic activity results were statistically analyzed to evaluate whether second-order polynomial models predict holocellulase production in both fungi. Based on the statistical analysis of the data, the residual plots were obtained (Figure 2). The ANOVA for the quadratic models is shown in Tables 4 and 5. The R^2 coefficient values indicated that the fit was acceptable for endoxylanases and endocellulases with *F. solani*, but not for β-xylosidases with *F. solani* (Table 4). As for *Aspergillus* sp., the adjustment was lower for the three enzymatic activities (Table 5). According to the F test, the models were predictive in all cases, since the calculated values of F were greater than the tabulated values. The small p-values also indicated the significance of the models, since these were less than the value of $\alpha = 0.05$.

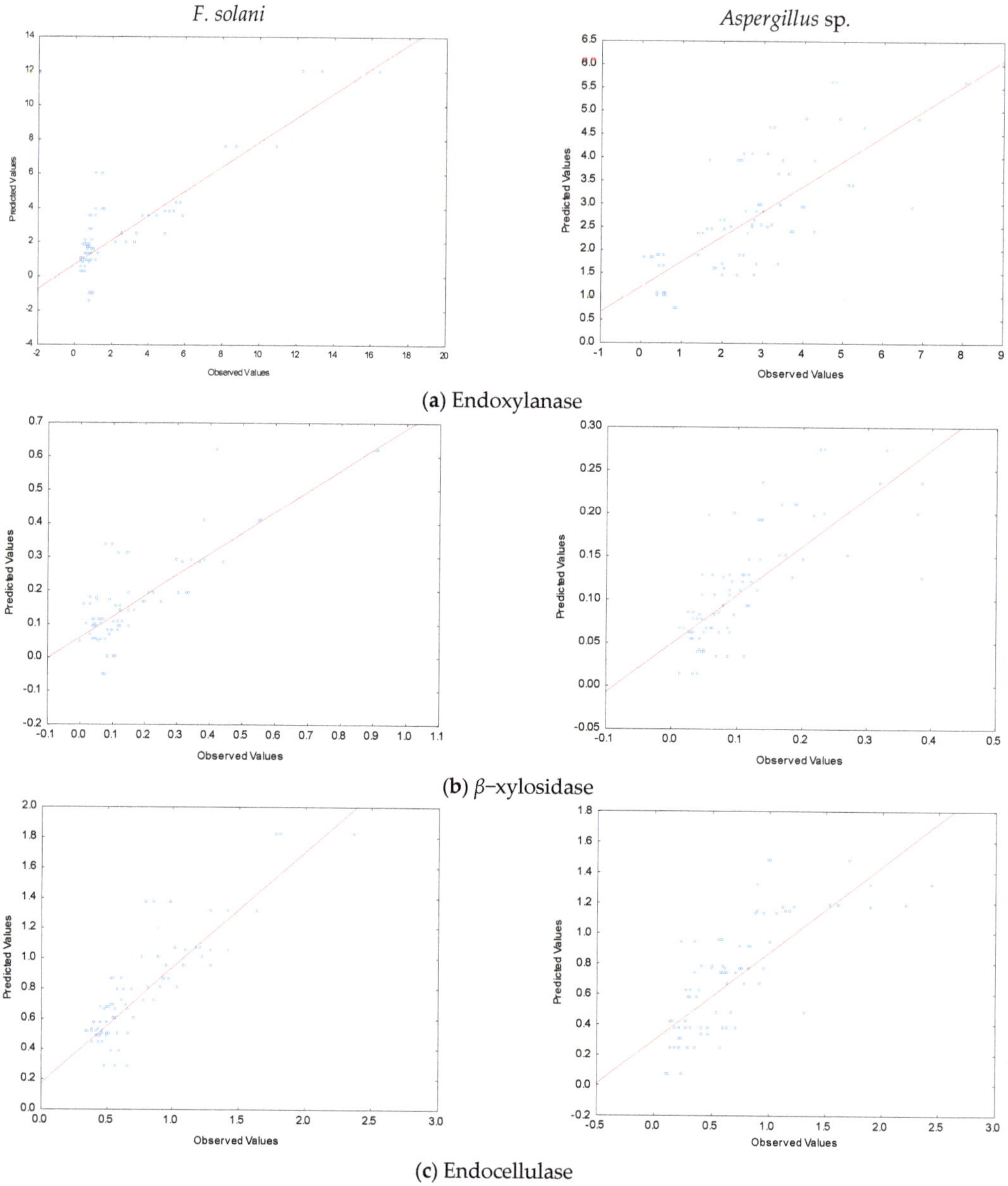

Figure 2. Correlation between the values predicted by the Box–Wilson design (Y-axis) and the experimental values of enzyme activity (X-axis). (**a**) Endoxylanase, (**b**) β-xylosidase, (**c**) endocellulose.

Table 4. ANOVA for the second-order polynomial model, *F. solani* (test of SS whole model vs. SS residual).

Holocellulolytic Activity	Multiple R	Multiple R^2	Adjusted R^2	Residual df	Residual SS	Residual MS	F	p
Endoxylanase	0.846260	0.716156	0.621541	60	228.9577	3.815961	7.569184	0.000000
β-xylosidase	0.789536	0.623367	0.497823	60	0.9051	0.015085	4.965312	0.000001
Endocellulase	0.875081	0.765767	0.687689	60	2.8643	0.047739	9.807753	0.000000

Table 5. ANOVA for the second-order polynomial model, *Aspergillus* sp. (test of SS whole model vs. SS residual).

Holocellulolytic Activity	Multiple R	Multiple R^2	Adjusted R^2	Residual *df*	Residual *SS*	Residual *MS*	F	p
Endoxylanase	0.736937	0.543076	0.390768	60	100.1864	1.669773	3.565639	0.000071
β-xylosidase	0.751477	0.564718	0.419624	60	0.2708	0.004513	3.892084	0.000023
Endocellulase	0.756309	0.572003	0.429337	60	8.0694	0.134490	4.009392	0.000015

3.3. *Effect of Factors on Holocellulase Production*

The identification of the nutritional factors that affect the fungal production of the holocellulolytic activity was carried out using an ANOVA. Figure 3 shows that the individual nutritional factors, interactions, and quadratic values had an effect on the production of holocellulases by *F. solani*, while the holocellulolytic activity production in *Aspergillus* sp. was influenced by a smaller number of nutritional factors.

The production of holocellulases in *F. solani* decreased with increasing CS concentration because of the lower moisture content of the culture media. *Aspergillus* sp. behaved in a similar way, since the increase in CS concentration caused a lower production of β-xylosidases and endocellulases, but did not affect endoxylanase production.

The nitrogen source, yeast extract, and ammonium sulfate had no effect on holocellulase production by *F. solani*, but urea did. In *Aspergillus* sp., the increase in the concentration of yeast extract favored the production of holocellulases. In particular, the production of β-xylosidases depended on an adequate supply of the three nitrogen sources assayed, since it was affected positively by these. The fermentation time was not a factor that affected holocellulase production in *Aspergillus* sp., whereas in *F. solani*, an increase in the culture time caused lower holocellulolytic activity.

3.4. *Optimization of Holocellulase Production*

The goodness degree of the fermentation process for the production of holocellulolytic enzymes, which is represented by the *desirability* function, was investigated to optimize the fermentation conditions. The minimum and maximum values of the holocellulolytic activities were obtained from the results of the BW design. The minimum and maximum limits for optimization were set and transformed to encoded desirability values, 0 and 1, respectively, to explore the best holocellulase production conditions.

The optimization was carried out jointly based on the desirability values specified for the three enzymatic activities. For both fungi, the combination of the best conditions was obtained, which maximizes the endoxylanase and β-xylosidase activities while minimizing the endocellulase activity (Table 6). The maximum production of holocellulases by *F. solani* was achieved after 48 h of fermentation, with an initial concentration of 25 g/L, 1.0 g/L, 2.5 g/L, and 0.7 g/L of CS, yeast extract, ammonium sulfate, and urea, respectively. The optimal conditions were similar for *Aspergillus* sp., although its demand for a nitrogen source was greater, with yeast extract and urea values of 9.0 g/L and 1.3 g/L, respectively. Furthermore, the fermentation time was four times longer (192 h) and its holocellulase production lower than for *F. solani*.

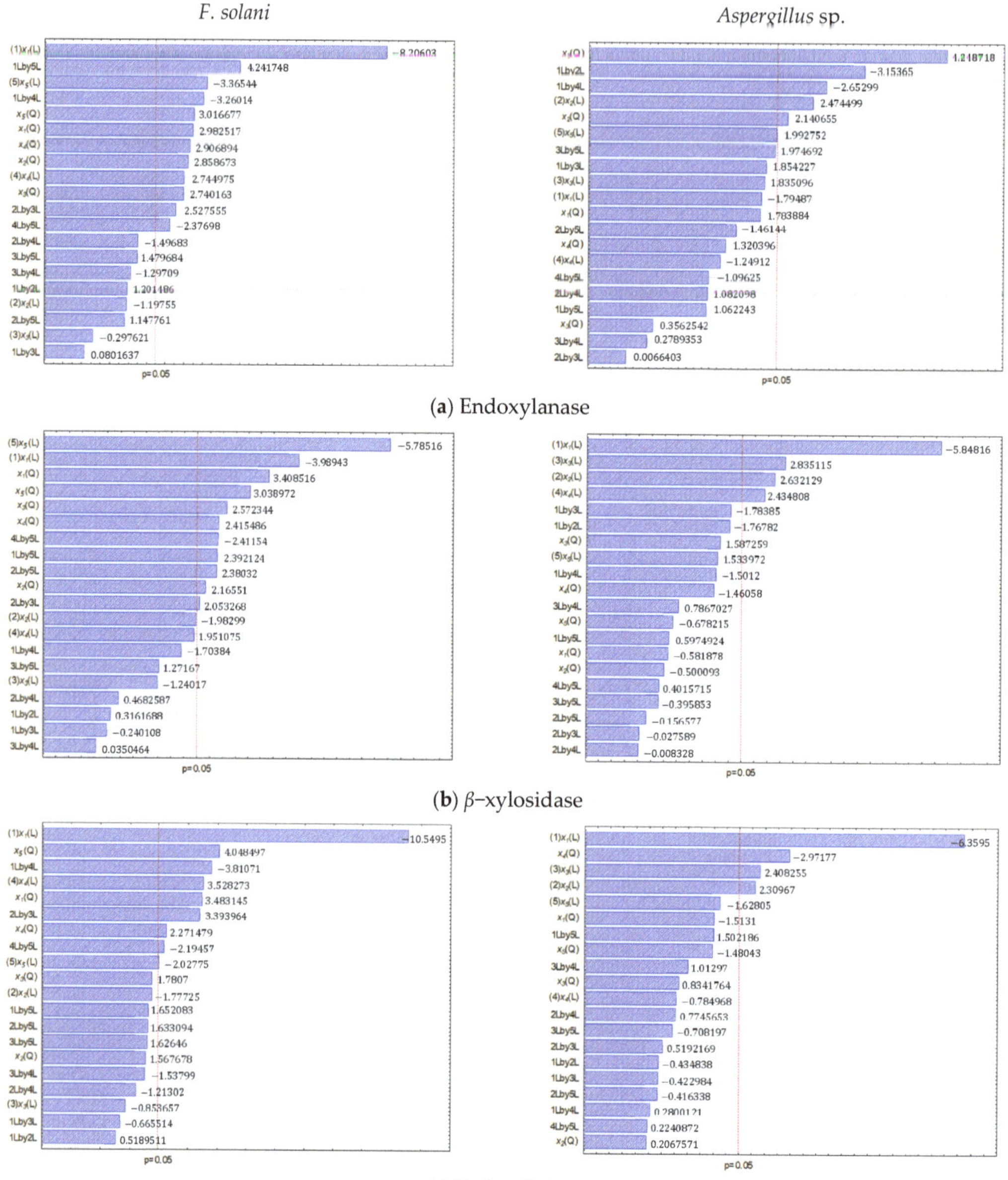

(**a**) Endoxylanase

(**b**) β−xylosidase

(**c**) Endocellulase

Figure 3. Effect of factors on response variables: (**a**) endoxylanase; (**b**) β-xylosidase; (**c**) endocellulase. (L) Linear effect of the factor, (Q) quadratic effect of the factor, (x_iLbyx_jL) effect of interaction of linear factors x_i and x_j. The bars that cross the dotted red line correspond to the factors that have a significant effect on the production of holocellulases in their linear, quadratic forms or in interaction with other factors.

Table 6. Comparison of the theoretical optimal conditions to produce holocellulases by *F. solani* and *Aspergillus* sp.

Fungus	Fermentation Time (h)	Optimal Nutritional Condition (g/L)				Holocellulolytic Activity (U/mg)		
		CS	Yeast Extract	$(NH_4)_2SO_4$	Urea	Endoxy-Lanase	β-xylosidase	Endocellulase
F. solani	48	25	1.0	2.5	0.7	20.48	1.19	2.38
Aspergillus sp.	192	25	9.0	2.5	1.3	13.20	0.50	0.74

3.5. Verification of Optimal Conditions to Produce of Holocellulases

Based on the optimal conditions found for the production of holocellulases by *F. solani* and *Aspergillus* sp., the activity values predicted by the model were verified through fermentation experiments based on the optimal combination of the nutritional factors studied. Table 7 shows the holocellulolytic activity predicted by the model and that obtained experimentally from the optimal values of the factors. The production of endoxylanases by *F. solani* was higher when compared to the predicted activity values. The β-xylosidase activity was close to the predicted value, while cellulolytic activity was not detected under these optimal conditions. Regarding *Aspergillus* sp., the endoxylanase and β-xylosidase activities were lower, but close to the predicted values, and the observed cellulolytic activity exceeded the predicted value.

Table 7. Verification of optimal culture conditions to produce fungal holocellulases. Experimental values represent the $\overline{X} \pm$ standard error, n = 3.

Holocellulolytic Activity (U/mg)	*F. solani*		*Aspergillus* sp.	
	Theoretical	Experimental	Theoretical	Experimental
Endoxylanase	20.48	25.0 ± 0.19	13.20	9.03 ± 0.64
β-xylosidase	1.19	1.01 ± 0.01	0.50	0.29 ± 0.01
Endocellulase	2.38	0	0.74	2.25 ± 0.06

4. Discussion

Filamentous fungi are suitable for developing bioconversion processes through solid-state fermentation (SSF) due to their ability to grow on low-water-content substrates [27]. Although filamentous fungi adapt easily to environments with reduced humidity, in this study, critical humidity levels restricted the production of holocellulases by both fungi, since the increase in the concentration of CS causes a reduction in the amount of water available. In the case of *Aspergillus* sp., the effect was smaller than in *F. solani*. It was observed that the levels of enzymatic activity was influenced by the culture conditions and the nature of the fungus [28–31]. The maximum holocellulolytic activity of *F. solani* was present in semi-solid culture, while for in *Aspergillus* sp., it was observed in solid culture.

Aspergillus sp. are distinguished by their significant xylanolytic activity. Various reports exist on the production of xylanases in liquid culture from *A. awamori* [32], *A. oryzae* NRRL 3485, *A. phoenicis* ATCC 13157, *A. foetidus* ATCC 14916 [33], *A. niger* [34], and *Aspergillus* sp. [35], although studies on *Aspergillus* sp. for xylanase production in solid culture are more numerous [36–42].

Aspergillus sp. is recognized as a filamentous fungus that produces large amounts of extracellular xylanases. However, in this work, the maximum holocellulolytic activity was achieved by *F. solani*. Interestingly, in all semi-solid culture media, the endoxylanase activity of *F. solani* was superior to that of *Aspergillus* sp.

F. solani is a phytopathogenic fungus that causes wilt diseases in a wide variety of plants such as pumpkin, pea, soybean, bean, potato, alfalfa, blueberry, peanut, and tomato crops [28,43]. *F. solani* was previously isolated from bean crops. The hemicellulose content of bean straw is 14.5% [44]. The great xylanolytic activity exhibited by this fungus could be related to its virulence and the significant hemicellulose content of this crop.

In contrast, in this work, the maximum endoxylanase activity was obtained in a semi-solid culture media (experiment 2). Martínez-Pacheco et al. [5] optimized the production of xylanases with low cellulases in *Fusarium solani* by means of a solid-state fermentation with beechwood xylan as a model carbon source. They found that the major production of endoxylases (12 U/mg) and *β*-xylosidases (0.53 U/mg) was observed in solid and liquid cultures, respectively. However, for larger-scale production, the use of this carbon source would not be economically profitable. In contrast, Moctezuma-Zárate et al. [45] obtained maximum xylanolytic activity (47.5 ng xylose/min·mg protein) from *F. solani* through a fermentation liquid medium supplemented with xylan (Sigma) as inductor.

Moisture content, which is inversely proportional to the carbon source concentration, was an important variable for the production of holocellulases by *F. solani* because it showed lower activity in culture media with low moisture (high concentration of carbon source). Bakri et al. [46] observed the same effect of moisture level: the xylanase production by *F. solani* on wheat bran was optimum (1593 U/g substrate) using an intermediate level of moisture (75%), with respect to the values explored, since a lower moisture ratio leads to the reduced solubility of the nutrients of the solid substrate, lower degree of swelling, and higher water tension.

In terms of the concentration and type of nitrogen source, yeast extract and ammonium sulfate had no effect on holocellulase production by *F. solani*, but urea did on xylanase production. Urea caused the maximum production of xylanase by *F. solani* in a fermentation liquid medium supplemented with xylan (Sigma).

In this work, the increase in the concentration of yeast extract favored the production of holocellulases by *Aspergillus* sp. In particular, the production of *β*-xylosidases depended on the adequate supply of the three nitrogen sources studied. This factor demonstrates that microorganisms, specifically filamentous fungi, have very specific nutrient requirements. In particular, the source of nitrogen required may be different from one fungus to another. Ellatif et al. [47] concluded that malt extract was the most suitable nitrogen source for producing xylanase by *Trichoderma harzianum* kj831197.1, as it offered the maximal enzyme activity. The optimal conditions for xylanase production by *T. harzianum* included the addition of ammonium sulphate [48].

F. solani produced more holocellulases in a short time, and as it increased, its holocellulolytic activity was reduced compared to *Aspergillus* sp., which required a long incubation time to increase its enzymatic activity. The production of primary metabolites by microorganisms, as enzymes, is highly influenced by their growth, which is determined by the availability of the nutrients in the substrates. Therefore, the time of fermentation could be affected by moisture content, which determines this availability. This means that there is a close relationship between the fermentation time and the moisture content of the culture medium. The optimal conditions for holocellulose production vary widely from one fungal isolate to another, especially the time of peak xylanase activity: *F. solani* on xylan (Sigma), 13 days [49]; *Fusarium graminearum* on wheat bran, 6.4 days [50]; *Fusarium* sp. XPF5 on xylan, 4 days [51]; *Fusarium solani* on beechwood xylan, 5 days [5]; *T. harzianum* on wheat bran, 6 days [48]; *Aspergillus fumigatus* SD5A (SmF), 7 days, and *A. fumigatus* L1. (SSF), 5 days, both grown on corn cob [52].

Aspergillus sp. exhibited a greater capacity to adapt to different culture conditions due to its significant level of holocellulolytic activity and its abundant growth in the different experiments. In addition to its great xylanolytic activity, *Aspergillus* sp. is recognized as a good producer of commercial cellulases [53], though, interestingly, *F. solani* showed the highest holocellulolytic activity in one part of the experiments carried out. Specifically, like *Aspergillus* sp., this indicates its adaptability to a wide variety of culture conditions, making this fungus a potential source of cellulases. *F. solani* showed greater sensitivity to various culture conditions since it was more demanding in its nutritional requirements compared to *Aspergillus* sp., and was able to grow on corn stover as the only carbon source and exhibit holocellulolytic activity. Some species of the genus *Fusarium* stand out for their great ability to adapt to extreme environmental conditions. This is the case for *Fusarium* sp. XPF-5, which is considered a thermo-alkaliphile, making it a potential candidate for large-scale xylanase production and use in biotechnological processes [50].

Various studies have shown that filamentous fungi grow better on solid substrates and the production of extracellular enzymes increases. However, fermentation in liquid culture has the advantage of providing homogeneous media, with fewer pH and temperature gradients and with greater availability of nutrients and oxygen. The best theoretical conditions for the production of holocellulases by both fungi were liquid cultures. The maximum predicted values for endoxylanase and β-xylosidase activities with *F. solani* were higher than those observed before optimization. As for *Aspergillus* sp., these predicted values were lower after optimization, since the objective was to reduce cellulolytic activity.

Interestingly, after experimentally verifying the optimal conditions, the endoxylanase activity of *F. solani* was higher than the values predicted by the model. The predicted values are the result of an idealization of the fermentation process for the production of holocellulases, based on the conditions explored, so the response is not always close or equal to the predicted value. On the other hand, although it was observed that cellulolytic activity was closely related to xylanolytic activity in both fungi, in the case of *F. solani*, it was possible to reduce it without affecting xylanolytic activity. SSF presents several advantages in comparison with submerged fermentation (SmF), such as fewer energy requirements and higher productivity, although several operational aspects must be considered, since there remains no effective technical solution (e.g., aeration and gradients of concentration), so only a few compounds are industrially implemented.

5. Conclusions

The present study reveals that *F. solani* is a fungal isolate with high potential for use in the industrial production of enzymes due its high holocellulolytic activity compared with *Aspergillus* sp. The maximum holocellulolytic activity of *F. solani* was obtained in semi-solid media, whereas with the wild strain of *Aspergillus* sp., this was achieved in a solid medium, which is related to their high adaptability in a wide variety of culture conditions. For years, *Aspergillus* sp. has been industrially exploited for enzyme production, but these findings make *F. solani* a potential source of holocellulases. Based on the optimization model, *F. solani* and *Aspergillus* sp. produce interesting holocellulolytic activity in a growth medium with corn stover as the only carbon source. This is a potential alternative means of valorizing agricultural waste such as corn stover through the fermentation and holocellulase production of *Fusarium solani*. The fermentation time and the amount of corn stover required to obtain maximum holocellulase is a possible advantage for *Fusarium solani* and *Aspergillus* sp., respectively.

Supplementary Materials: The following supporting information can be downloaded at: https://www.mdpi.com/article/10.3390/fermentation10020084/s1.

Author Contributions: Conceptualization, M.A.-N. and K.L.A.-H.; methodology, M.A.-N., K.L.A.-H. and A.F.-G.; validation, C.V.-B. and J.A.-H.; formal analysis, M.M.M.-P.; investigation, M.A.-N. and K.L.A.-H.; resources, M.M.M.-P.; writing—original draft preparation, M.A.-N. and K.L.A.-H.; writing—review and editing, C.V.-B. and M.M.M.-P.; supervision and funding acquisition, M.M.M.-P. All authors have read and agreed to the published version of the manuscript.

Funding: This research was funded by Universidad Michoacana de San Nicolás de Hidalgo, grant number 2.1 mmmp, and the APC was funded by the M3P Foundation.

Institutional Review Board Statement: Not applicable.

Informed Consent Statement: Not applicable.

Data Availability Statement: Data are contained within the article and supplementary materials.

Acknowledgments: The authors thank the M3P Foundation. K.L.A.-H. has a scholarship from CONAHCYT.

Conflicts of Interest: The authors declare no conflicts of interest.

References

1. Barrera-Guzmán, L.A.; Cadena-Iñiguez, J.; Ramírez-Ojeda, G. Implementation of stubble in agricultural production: A review. *Agro-Prod.* **2022**, *IX*, 185–193. [CrossRef]
2. Kwiatkowski, C.A.; Harasim, E.; Haliniarz, M.; Gawęda, D.; Misztal-Majewska, B.; Chojnacka, S. Chemical composition of stubble crop biomass depending on a crop plant species and tillage system. *J. Elem.* **2019**, *24*, 1371–1381. [CrossRef]
3. Morales-Máximo, C.N.; López-Sosa, L.B.; Rutiaga-Quiñones, J.G.; Corral-Huacuz, J.C.; Aguilera Mandujano, A.; Pintor-Ibarra, L.F.; López-Miranda, A.; Delgado Domínguez, S.N.; Rodríguez Magallón, M.d.C.; Morales-Máximo, M. Characterization of agricultural residues of *Zea mays* for their application as solid biofuel: Case study in San Francisco Pichátaro, Michoacán, México. *Energies* **2022**, *15*, 6870. [CrossRef]
4. Garg, G.; Mahajan, R.; Kaur, A.; Sharma, J. Xylanase production using agro-residue in solid-state fermentation from *Bacillus pumilus* ASH for biodelignification of wheat straw pulp. *Biodegradation* **2011**, *22*, 1143–1154. [CrossRef]
5. Martínez-Pacheco, M.M.; Flores-García, A.; Zamudio-Jaramillo, M.A.; Chávez-Parga, M.C.; Alvarez-Navarrete, M. Production of extracellular xylanase from a wild isolate of *Fusarium solani*. *Rev. Argent. Microbiol.* **2020**, *52*, 328–337. [CrossRef]
6. Liu, W.; Shi, P.; Chen, Q.; Yang, P.; Wang, G.; Wang, Y.; Luo, H.; Yao, B. Gene cloning, overexpression, and characterization of a xylanase from *Penicillium* sp. CGMCC 1669. *Appl. Biochem. Biotechnol.* **2010**, *162*, 1–12. [CrossRef]
7. Andrade-Hoyos, P.; Rivera-Jiménez, M.N.; Landero-Valenzuela, N.; Silva-Rojas, H.V.; Martínez-Salgado, S.J.; Romero-Arenas, O. Ecological and biological benefits of the cosmopolitan fungus *Trichoderma* spp. in agriculture: A perspective in the Mexican countryside. *Rev. Argent. Microbiol.* **2023**, *55*, 366–377. [CrossRef]
8. Kumar, R.; Verma, D.; Sharma, S.; Satyanarayana, T. Applicability of fungal xylanases in food biotechnology. In *Fungi and Fungal Products in Human Welfare and Biotechnology*; Satyanarayana, T., Deshmukh, S.K., Eds.; Springer: Singapore, 2023. [CrossRef]
9. Saldarriaga-Hernández, S.; Velasco-Ayala, C.; Leal-Isla Flores, P.; Rostro-Alanis, M.J.; Parra-Saldivar, R.; Iqbal, H.M.N.; Carrillo-Nieves, D. Biotransformation of lignocellulosic biomass into industrially relevant products with the aid of fungi-derived lignocellulolytic enzymes. *Int. J. Biol. Macromol.* **2020**, *161*, 1099–1116. [CrossRef] [PubMed]
10. Carrillo-Nieves, D.; Saldarriaga-Hernández, S.; Gutiérrez-Soto, G.; Rostro-Alanis, M.; Hernández-Luna, C.; Alvarez, A.J.; Iqbal, H.M.N.; Parra-Saldívar, R. Biotransformation of agro-industrial waste to produce lignocellulolytic enzymes and bioethanol with a zero waste. *Biomass Convers. Biorefin* **2022**, *12*, 253–264. [CrossRef]
11. Astorga-Trejo, R.; Fonseca-Peralta, H.M.; Beltrán-Arredondo, L.I.; Castro-Martínez, C. Use of corn stover for the production of 2G bioethanol, enzymes and xylitol under a biorefinery concept. *World Acad. Sci. Eng. Technol.* **2022**, *16*, 9. Available online: https://publications.waset.org/pdf/10012662. (accessed on 13 June 2023).
12. Howard, R.L.; Abotsi, E.; Jansen van Rensburg, E.L.; Howard, S. Lignocellulose biotechnology: Issues of bioconversion and enzyme production. *Afr. J. Biotechnol.* **2003**, *2*, 602–619. [CrossRef]
13. Narayanan Narayanan, M.; Sameh Samir, A.; El-Sheekh, M. A comprehensive review on the potential of microbial enzymes in multipollutant bioremediation: Mechanisms, challenges, and future prospects. *J. Environ. Manag.* **2023**, *334*, 117532. [CrossRef]
14. Marinho, G.O.; Nogueira, E.A.; Machado Pasin, T.; Brito de Oliveira, T.; Bretas Roa, J.P.; Nelson, D.L.; Benassi, V.M. An environmentally safe production of xylanases by *Fusarium* sp. EA 1.3.1 using agroindustrial residues: Biochemical characterization and potential applications. *Asian J. Biochem. Gen. Mol. Biol.* **2023**, *14*, 11–26. [CrossRef]
15. Kaur, D.; Joshi, A.; Sharma, V.; Batra, N.; Sharma, A.K. An insight into microbial sources, classification, and industrial applications of xylanases: A rapid review. *Biotechnol. Appl. Biochem.* **2023**, *70*, 1489–1503. [CrossRef]
16. Zhao, X.; Chai, J.; Wang, F.; Jia, Y. Optimization of submerged culture parameters of the aphid pathogenic fungus *Fusarium equiseti* based on sporulation and mycelial biomass. *Microorganisms* **2023**, *11*, 190. [CrossRef]
17. Alvarez-Navarrete, M.; Reyna López, G.E.; Flores García, A.; López Gómez, R.; Martínez-Pacheco, M.M. Selection and molecular identification of fungal isolates that produce xylanolytic enzymes. *Genet. Mol. Res.* **2015**, *14*, 8100–8116. [CrossRef]
18. Lin, R.C.; Ding, Z.S.; Li, L.B.; Kuang, T.Y. A rapid and efficient DNA minipreparation suitable for screening transgenic plants. *Plant Mol. Biol. Report.* **2001**, *19*, 379. Available online: https://link.springer.com/content/pdf/10.1007/BF02772839.pdf. (accessed on 1 September 2023). [CrossRef]
19. Carbone, I.; Kohn, L.M. A method for designing primer sets for speciation studies in filamentous ascomycetes. *Mycologia* **1999**, *91*, 553–556. [CrossRef]
20. Montgomery, D.C.; Runger, G.C. *Applied Statistics and Probability for Engineers*; John Wiley & Sons: New York, NY, USA, 1996.
21. Bailey, M.J.; Biely, P.; Poutanen, K. Interlaboratory testing of methods for assay of xylanase activity. *J. Biotechnol.* **1992**, *23*, 257–271. [CrossRef]
22. Ghose, T.K. Measurement of cellulase activities. *Pure Appl. Chem.* **1987**, *59*, 257–268. [CrossRef]
23. Kristufek, D.; Zeilinger, S.; Kubicek, C.P. Regulation of β-xylosidase formation by xylose in *Trichoderma reesei*. *Appl. Microbiol. Biotechnol.* **1995**, *42*, 713–717. [CrossRef]
24. Miller, G.L. Use of DNS for determination of reducing sugar. *Anal. Chem.* **1959**, *31*, 426–428. [CrossRef]
25. Lowry, O.H.; Rosenbrough, N.J.; Farr, A.L.; Randall, R.J. Protein measurement with the Folin phenol reagent. *J. Bio. Chem.* **1951**, *193*, 265–275. [CrossRef]
26. Derringer, G.; Suich, R. Simultaneous optimization of several response variables. *J. Qual. Technol.* **1980**, *12*, 214–219. [CrossRef]
27. Cebrián, M.; Ibarruri, J. Filamentous fungi processing by solid-state fermentation. In *Current Developments in Biotechnology and Bioengineering*; Filamentous Fungi Biorefinery; Elsevier: Amsterdam, The Netherlands, 2023; pp. 251–292. [CrossRef]

28. Gupta, V.K.; Gaur, R.; Yadava, S.K.; Darmwal, N.S. Optimization of xylanase production from free and immobilized cells of *Fusarium solani* F7. *Bioresources* **2009**, *4*, 932–945. Available online: https://bioresources.cnr.ncsu.edu/BioRes_04/BioRes_04_3_0932_Gupta_GYD_Opt_Xylanase_Prodn_Fee_Immob_Cells_434.pdf (accessed on 7 April 2023). [CrossRef]
29. Obruca, S.; Marova, I.; Matouskova, P.; Haronikova, A.; Lichnova, A. Production of lignocellulose-degrading enzymes employing *Fusarium solani* F-552. *Folia Microbiol.* **2012**, *57*, 221–227. [CrossRef]
30. Bakri, Y.; Jawhar, M.; Arabi, M.I.E. Molecular and xylanolytic variation identified among isolates of *Fusarium* species. *J. Plant Biol. Res.* **2012**, *1*, 51–56. Available online: http://www.inast.otg/jpbr.html (accessed on 7 April 2023).
31. Agustini, L.; Efiyanti, L.; Faulina, S.A.; Santoso, E. Isolation and characterization of cellulase- and xylanase-producing microbes isolated from tropical forests in Java and Sumatra. *Int. J. Environ. Bioener.* **2012**, *3*, 154–167. Available online: https://modernscientificpress.com/Journals/ViewArticle.aspx?gkN1Z6Pb60HNQPymfPQlZM2QzBATUXAyEhQZJVFyB5jxACLp2DSn8X3BE2yz4Gxm (accessed on 7 April 2023).
32. Lemos, J.L.S.; Fontes, M.C.A.; Pereira, N., Jr. Xylanase production by Aspergillus awamori in solid-state fermentation and influence of different nitrogen sources. *Appl. Biochem. Biotechnol.* **2001**, *91–93*, 681–690. [CrossRef]
33. Chipeta, Z.A.; du Preez, J.C.; Szakacs, G.; Christopher, L. Xylanase production by fungal strains on spent sulfite liquor. *Appl. Microbiol. Biotechnol.* **2005**, *69*, 71–78. [CrossRef] [PubMed]
34. Padmavathi, T.; Kavya, V. Isolation, identification and optimization of xylanase enzyme produced by *Aspergillus niger* under submerged fermentation. *J. Microbiol. Biotechnol. Res.* **2011**, *1*, 137–147. Available online: http://scholarsresearchlibrary.com/archive.html (accessed on 8 April 2023).
35. Sridevi, B.; Charya, M.A.S. Isolation, identification, and screening of potential cellulase-free xylanase producing fungi. *Afr. J. Biotechnol.* **2011**, *10*, 4624–4630.
36. Kheng, P.P.; Ibrahim, C.O. Xylanase production by a local fungal isolate, *Aspergillus niger* USM AI 1 via solid state fermentation using palm kernel cake (PKC) as substrate. *Songklanakarin J. Sci. Technol.* **2005**, *27*, 325–336. Available online: https://www.thaiscience.info/Journals/Article/SONG/10462555.pdf (accessed on 8 April 2023).
37. Shah, A.R.; Madamwar, D. Xylanase production under solid-state fermentation and its characterization by an isolated strain of *Aspergillus foetidus* in India. *World J. Microbiol. Biotechnol.* **2005**, *21*, 233–243. [CrossRef]
38. Xu, Y.-X.; Li, Y.-L.; Xu, S.-C.; Liu, Y.; Wang, X.; Tang, J.-W. Improvement of xylanase production by *Aspergillus niger* XY-1 using response surface methodology for optimizing the medium composition. *J. Zhejiang Univ. Sci. B* **2008**, *9*, 558–566. [CrossRef]
39. Liu, C.; Sun, Z.-T.; Du, J.-H.; Wang, J. Response surface optimization of fermentation conditions for producing xylanase by *Aspergillus niger* SL-05. *J. Ind. Microbiol. Biotechnol.* **2008**, *35*, 703–711. [CrossRef]
40. Maciel, G.M.; Vandenberghe, L.P.S.; Haminiuk, C.W.I.; Fendrich, R.C.; Bianca, B.E.D.; Brandalize, T.Q.S.; Pandey, A.; Soccol, C.R. Xylanase production by *Aspergillus niger* LPB 326 in solid-state fermentation using statistical experimental design. *Food Technol. Biotechnol.* **2008**, *46*, 183–189. Available online: https://ftb.com.hr/images/pdfarticles/2008/April-June/46-183.pdf (accessed on 8 April 2023).
41. Kavya, V.; Padmavathi, T. Optimization of growth conditions for xylanase production by *Aspergillus niger* in solid state fermentation. *Pol. J. Microbiol.* **2009**, *58*, 125–130. Available online: http://www.pjmonline.org/wp-content/uploads/archive/vol5822009125.pdf (accessed on 16 April 2023). [PubMed]
42. Regalado, C.; Vázquez-Obregón, I.; García-Almendárez, B.E.; Domínguez-Domínguez, J.; Aguilera-Barreyro, A.; Amaro-Reyes, A. Xylanolytic enzymes production by *Aspergillus niger* GS1 from solid state fermentation on corn stover and their effect on ruminal digestibility. *Electronic J. Biotechnol.* **2011**, *14*, 9. [CrossRef]
43. Silvestro, L.B.; Stenglein, S.A.; Forjan, H.; Dinolfo, M.I.; Arambarri, A.M.; Manso, L.; Moreno, M.V. Occurrence and distribution of soil *Fusarium* species under wheat crop in zero tillage. *Span. J. Agric. Res.* **2013**, *11*, 72–79. [CrossRef]
44. González-Rentería, S.M.; Soto-Cruz, N.O.; Rutiaga-Quiñones, O.M.; Medrano-Roldán, H.; Rutiaga-Quiñones, J.G.; López-Miranda, J. Optimización del proceso de hidrólisis enzimática de una mezcla de pajas de frijol de cuatro variedades (Pinto villa, Pinto saltillo, Pinto mestizo y Flor de mayo). *Rev. Mex. Ing. Quim.* **2011**, *10*, 17–28.
45. Moctezuma-Zárate, M.; Vargas-Morales, J.; Cárdenas-González, J.; Martínez-Juárez, V.; Acosta-Rodríguez, I. Induction of extracellular lytic enzymes by *Fusarium solani*. *Adv. Microbiol.* **2013**, *3*, 24–30. Available online: https://www.scielo.org.mx/pdf/rmiq/v10n1/v10n1a3.pdf (accessed on 16 April 2023). [CrossRef]
46. Bakri, Y.; Jawhar, M.; Arabi, M.I.E. Xylanase production by *Fusarium solani* in solid state fermentation. *Res. Biotechnol.* **2013**, *4*, 31–37.
47. Ellatif, S.A.; Abdel Razik, E.S.; Al-Surhanee, A.A.; Al-Sarraj, F.; Daigham, G.E.; Mahfouz, A.Y. Enhanced production, cloning, and expression of a xylanase gene from endophytic fungal strain *Trichoderma harzianum* kj831197.1: Unveiling the *in vitro* anti-fungal activity against phytopathogenic fungi. *J. Fungi* **2022**, *25*, 447. [CrossRef] [PubMed]
48. Dhaver, P.; Pletschke, B.; Sithole, B.; Govinden, R. Optimization, purification, and characterization of xylanase production by a newly isolated *Trichoderma harzianum* strain by a two-step statistical experimental design strategy. *Sci. Rep.* **2022**, *12*, 17791. [CrossRef] [PubMed]
49. Cruz-Davila, J.; Vargas Perez, J.; Sosa del Castillo, D.; Diez, N. *Fusarium graminearum* as a producer of xylanases with low cellulases when grown on wheat bran. *Biotechnol. Rep.* **2022**, *35*, e00738. [CrossRef] [PubMed]
50. Sharma, P.; Kaushik, N.; Sharma, S.; Kumar, V. Isolation, screening, characterization and optimization of xylanase production from thermostable alkalophillic *Fusarium* sp. XPF5. *J. Biochem. Tech.* **2016**, *7*, 1089–1092.

51. Elegbede, J.A.; Lateef, A. Valorization of corn-cob by fungal isolates for production of xylanase in submerged and solid state fermentation media and potential biotechnological applications. *Waste Biomass Valorization* **2018**, *9*, 1273–1287. [CrossRef]
52. Sakthi, S.S.; Saranraj, P.; Rajasekar, M. OOOptimization for cellulase production by *Aspergillus niger* using paddy straw as substrates. *Int. J. Adv. Sci. Tech. Res.* **2011**, *1*, 69–85. Available online: http://www.rspublication.com/ijst/index.html (accessed on 16 April 2023).
53. Rodríguez Couto, S.R.; Sanromán, M.Á. Application of solid-state fermentation to food industry—A review. *J. Food Eng.* **2006**, *76*, 291–302. [CrossRef]

fermentation

Communication

Bioprocess Intensification of a Continuous-Flow Enzymatic Bioreactor via Productivity Dynamic Optimization under Modeling Uncertainty

Ricardo Femat [1], Ricardo Aguilar-López [2,*] and Juan L. Mata-Machuca [3,*]

1 División de Control and Sistemas Dinámicos, Instituto Potosino de Investigación Científica y Tecnológica A.C. (IPICyT), San Luis Potosí 78216, Mexico; rfemat@ipicyt.edu.mx
2 Department of Biotechnology and Bioengineering, CINVESTAV-IPN, Mexico City 07360, Mexico
3 Department of Advanced Technologies, Instituto Politécnico Nacional, UPIITA, Mexico City 07340, Mexico
* Correspondence: raguilar@cinvestav.mx (R.A.-L.); jmatam@ipn.mx (J.L.M.-M.)

Abstract: In this contribution, a class of observer-based optimal feedback control is designed. The proposed feedback control is based on the Euler–Lagrange theoretical framework, and it is motivated by the productivity intensification from the chemical reactors, which is optimally increased. A Lagrangian is computed by employing the corresponding mass balance equation of a specifically selected biochemical compound. The resulting optimal controller is coupled with a novel uncertainty estimator with bounded feedback to derive an accurate estimation of the unknown terms and functions, mostly related to the reaction rate. Via Lyapunov analysis, it was shown that the proposed observer is asymptotically stable. The estimation of the unknown terms and functions is used by the proposed controller. The proposed methodology is applied to a generic model of an enzymatic biochemical continuous reactor with complex oscillatory dynamic behavior described by mass balance equations, so, in general, the proposed controller may be applied to any continuous stirred tank bioreactor; that is, the controller is independent of the specific kinetic functions. Numerical simulations show a satisfactory performance of the proposed control strategy.

Keywords: optimal feedback control; productivity intensification; enzymatic biochemical bioreactor; continuous stirred tank reactor

Citation: Femat, R.; Aguilar-López, R.; Mata-Machuca, J.L. Bioprocess Intensification of a Continuous-Flow Enzymatic Bioreactor via Productivity Dynamic Optimization under Modeling Uncertainty. *Fermentation* **2024**, *10*, 11. https://doi.org/10.3390/fermentation10010011

Academic Editor: Liang Yu

Received: 16 November 2023
Revised: 17 December 2023
Accepted: 19 December 2023
Published: 21 December 2023

1. Introduction

The continuous stirred tank bioreactor (CSTB) is a classical benchmark because it is one of the most popular types of equipment employed in the chemical and biochemical industries. This type of operation is flexible for production and ensures a suitable mixing operation in which the concentrations of chemical products and reactive products are adequately uniform throughout the bioreaction volume and within the outlet product stream. Despite such advantages, under an actual operation at an industrial-scale bioreactor, the operation is often far from idealized lab-scale bioreaction design because the influence of non-ideal flow, mass, and heat transport phenomena must be compensated for or attenuated toward the bioprocess intensification. The term 'process intensification' was introduced in the early 2000s. In the first years, the intensification concept was related to the optimal dimension design of the process equipment under predetermined operating conditions; however, industrial plants were required to provide a flexible and wide operational policy to respond to the high and changing demand of the market and the strict environmental legislation, along with process sustainability related to safe operation, high-quality products, energy saving, etc. Here, a new multidisciplinary conceptualization of industrial plants in design and operation is needed, so high predictive process modeling, multi-objective optimization, on-line monitoring, and control processes under the above-mentioned restrictions must be performed simultaneously.

Moreover, the bioprocess intensification via feedback is relevant because of the unpredictability caused by the strong influence of the highly nonlinear behavior on the chemical kinetics, which can induce dynamic complexity such as steady-state multiplicity, operational instability, or even more, oscillatory dynamic behavior [1,2].

Bioprocess intensification is a relatively recent concept that consists of searching for increased efficiency. Intensification combines optimization of capital, energy, environmental, and safety benefits with a radical reduction in a plant-scale fashion. Although the process intensification can be addressed via the reactor configuration strategies (see, for instance, ref. [3] for the photocatalytic case), a suitable alternative for the bioprocess intensification is to exploit the feedback control approaches to promote efficiency at the bioreaction yield, which allows users to overcome stable operation. In this sense, distinct problems can be formulated from the perspective of feedback control, such as, for example, the stabilization of the chemostat under maximum production concerns [4] or extremum seeking via robust sliding-mode control [5], which introduces an extremum-seeking control scheme using sliding mode techniques to guarantee the dynamic optimization of methane outflow rate in anaerobic digestion processes. The proposed control method includes an observer-based uncertain estimator that computes the unknown terms related to the growth kinetics and the inlet composition. Moreover, self-optimizing control of dynamical processes and extremum-seeking control are two techniques to handle these kinds of dynamic optimization problems [6–8]. The main goal of extremum-seeking methods is to determine the operating set-points, such that a performance function reaches its extremum values. That is, a feedback control step is a valuable tool to achieve secure and intensified operation while maintaining adequate bioreactor conditions and enhancing the system dynamics at previously selected set-points via a closed-loop operation under regulatory tasks. In this sense, an appropriate problem formulation and its solution can derive from intensification politics. Such an operational policy can be reached via lineal proportional–integral–derivative (PID), adaptive, predictive, and linearizing, among several other controllers [9–18], with certain success. Nevertheless, a different approach lies in the framework of optimal control, where the control engineers have tuned controller parameters through cost function optimization. There are several error cost functions, like integrated time-weighted absolute error (ITAE), integrated squared error (ISE), integrated exponential time squared error (IETSE), integrated squared time cubed error (ISTCE), and integrated time exponential time squared error (ITETSE), that are employed for obtaining optimal controller parameters [19,20]. Also, iterative methods such as numerical optimization, fminsearch subroutine, and soft computing-based optimization methods, which include artificial bee colony (ABC) optimization, particle swarm optimization (PSO), genetic algorithm, cuckoo optimization, and quasi-opposition-based equilibrium optimizer, are used to minimize the cost functions [21–25].

As mentioned above, the intensification of the practical operation of continuous bioreactors remains an important challenge for process engineers in the design, analysis, optimization, and control stages. This contribution addresses bioprocess intensification from the perspective of optimal feedback control. The underlying idea is to tackle the necessity of increasing the quality of the reactor operation under an optimal operational policy that includes optimal cost and maximum productivity. The underlying idea is to solve the tracking trajectory problem. The proposed intensification scheme is such that it accounts for the structured uncertainties and output-bounded disturbances, including uncertain initial and ambient conditions, variations in feed quality, and uncertainty in the process description [26]. This makes sense because the optimal design may lead to deviation from the optimal and potentially high-risk solution if the uncertainties are not considered. Therefore, the need to incorporate methodologies for uncertainty compensation in chemical processes is essential to achieving a robust process operation.

This manuscript is organized as follows. Section 2 describes the mathematical model of the CSTB. The proposed optimal control and the uncertainty observers are given in Section 3, together with their main technical characteristics. Section 4 contains a description of the main results obtained, and, finally, the concluding remarks of this work are provided in Section 5.

2. Bioreactor Modeling

In traditional model-based optimization techniques, the accuracy of the mathematical models of the processes is especially important. Particularly, the kinetic modeling in chemical reactors contains a wide set of model parameters that are subject to uncertainty in their thermodynamic and/or kinetic parameters, determined from experiments [27]. Besides the uncertainty and fluctuations present in the process, operations affect the reliability of model-based optimization, among others pressure, feed composition, or temperature. Such sensitivity might cause a violation of safety constraints and, hence, result in an infeasible process design. In general, system optimization under uncertainty is an important and active research issue. Diverse approaches that consider uncertainties have been reported for the optimization of chemical processes [28–31].

Let us consider a class of continuous-flow bioreactors where enzymatic reactions take place. As is well known, enzymatic reactions can present complex dynamic behaviors, such as sustained oscillations or, even more, chaotic behavior. This work has taken an enzymatic kinetics model under continuous operation, which can even exhibit chaotic oscillations [32]. The considered mathematical model is based on the classical mass conservation principle by considering a four-state variable dynamical system. For the considered bioreactor model, some assumptions are established: (a) the chemical reactions are performed in perfect homogeneous conditions in a well-stirred tank reactor under isothermal operation; (b) first-order kinetics are supposed for the reactions from C_4 to C_1 and C_2 and C_1 to C_2; (c) the reactive C_1 catalyzes the production of the compound C_3; both reactions from C_1 are catalyzed by C_2 and C_3, and the reaction from C_4 is also catalyzed by C_3; and (d) all the chemical species are involved in autocatalytic reactions and their kinetics are governed by the Michaelis–Menten structures.

The general chemical kinetic pathway is as follows [32]:

$$C_1 \rightarrow C_1^* \rightarrow C_2 + C_3$$

$$C_1 \leftrightarrow C_4 \rightarrow C_2$$

$$C_2 \rightarrow 2C_2^* \rightarrow \textit{Product}$$

$$C_3 \rightarrow 2C_3^* \rightarrow \textit{Product}$$

$$C_4 \rightarrow 2C_4^* \rightarrow C_3 + \textit{Product}$$

where C_i^* for i = 1, 2, 3, 4 are the corresponding activate chemical complexes, which are considered, as usual, in a pseudo-steady state.

The above kinetic model is extended to continuous reactor operation, showing complex oscillations. The mathematical model is defined by a set of four nonlinear ordinary differential equations, and it represents the mass balances for each one of the chemical compounds at the corresponding mass concentrations.

Mass balancing:

$$\dot{c}_1 = d_0 + k_8 c_4 - k_1 \frac{c_1 c_2}{c_1 + K} - k_2 \frac{c_1 c_3}{c_1 + K} + (c_{1,in} - c_1)u \quad (1)$$

$$\dot{c}_2 = k_3 c_1 + k_4 c_2 + k_9 c_4 - k_5 \frac{c_2}{c_2 + K} + (c_{2,in} - c_2)u \quad (2)$$

$$\dot{c}_3 = d_1 + k_6 c_1 c_3 - k_7 c_3 + (c_{3,in} - c_3)u \quad (3)$$

$$\dot{c}_4 = (k_{10} - k_8 - k_9)c_4 - k_{11}\frac{c_3 c_4}{c_1 + K} + (c_{4,in} - c_4)u \tag{4}$$

Here, $C = [c_1\ c_2\ c_3\ c_4]^T$ is the vector of mass concentrations. The inlet concentrations to the reactor have the following nominal values: $c_{1,in} = 150$ and $c_{2,in} = c_{3,in} = c_{4,in} = 0$, whereas the nominal value of the control input is given by $u = 0.015$. As usual, for these processes, let us consider that the control input is defined as $u = Q/V$, where Q is the volumetric inlet flow and V is the volume of the reactor, which is assumed as constant, as usual for these systems. As reported in [32], the set of kinetic parameters is given as follows: $k_1 = 1.0$, $k_2 = 1.0$, $k_3 = 1.0$, $k_4 = 0.25$, $k_5 = 152.5$, $k_6 = 1.0$, $k_7 = 130$, $k_8 = 0.001$, $k_9 = 1.0$, $k_{10} = 1.051$, $k_{11} = 0.5$, and $K = 0.001$. The corresponding initial conditions are arbitrarily assumed to be $c_{10} = 129.1$, $c_{20} = 76.06$, $c_{30} = 0.5895$, and $c_{40} = 21.38$. Here, $d_0 = 90$ and $d_1 = 2.2$ are constant load disturbances, which are included to simulate realistic process operation.

Killory's model [32] is selected for its capacity to generate complex oscillatory dynamic behavior; this is an important drawback for the operation of (bio)chemical reactors.

3. Controller Design

Generally, the theoretical framework of the optimal control is related to the calculus of variations, which concerns trajectory optimization tasks, where a functional $\mathfrak{J}(\mathcal{L}(\cdot)) := \mathbb{R}^q \to \mathbb{R}$ is a scalar called performance index, cost function, or cost index, which is for maximizing or minimizing, accordingly with the corresponding objectives to be reached by solving the Euler–Lagrange equation [33]. That is,

$$\frac{\partial \mathcal{L}}{\partial x_1} - \frac{d}{dx_2}\left(\frac{\partial \mathcal{L}}{\partial \dot{x}_1}\right) = 0 \tag{5}$$

The term $\mathcal{L}$ is named as the Lagrangian of the system under study.

In the most common case, the performance index $\mathfrak{J}$ can be represented by the following integral functional form as:

$$\mathfrak{J} = \int_{t_0}^{t_f} \mathcal{L}(t, x, u)dt + \mathcal{H}\left(x_f, t_f\right) \tag{6}$$

where $\mathcal{H}\left(x_f, t_f\right)$ is an algebraic term to be minimized (or maximized) at final conditions, subject to the following terminal constraints:

$$\mathcal{H}\left(x_f, t_f\right) = 0 \tag{7}$$

As the state equation, a class of nonlinear systems is considered as follows:

$$\dot{x} = f(x) + g(x)u \tag{8}$$

Its initial conditions are as follows:

$$x(t_0) = x_0 \tag{9}$$

As usual, $f(x) = [f_1(x)\ f_2(x)\ f_3(x) \ldots f_n(x)]^T$; then, $f(x) : \mathbb{R}^n \to \mathbb{R}^n$ is a nonlinear and bounded smooth vector field, and $g^{-1}(x)$ exists as the inverse of $g(x)$. Also, $x = [x_1,\ x_2,\ x_3,\ \ldots\ x_n]^T$; here, $x \in \mathbb{R}^n$ is the vector of state variables, such that $x \subset \mathcal{W}$; $\mathcal{W} = \{x_i,\ i = 1, 2, \ldots, n / x_i \in [0\ x_{i,max}]\}$, where $\mathcal{W}$ is a compact set, i.e., $\mathcal{W}$ is bounded and closed under the vector field operations.

Now, the following functional form [31] is considered:

$$\mathcal{P}(x, \dot{x}, u) = \int_0^T \mathcal{L}(x, \dot{x}, u)dt \tag{10}$$

Minimizing the functional (10) is required, therefore,

$$\delta\mathcal{P}(x,\dot{x},u) = \int_0^T \delta\mathcal{L}(x,\dot{x},u)dt \tag{11}$$

Here, the differential form of the Lagrangian $\mathcal{L}$ is given as

$$\delta\mathcal{L}(x,\dot{x},u) = \frac{\partial\mathcal{L}}{\partial x}\delta x + \frac{\partial\mathcal{L}}{\partial\dot{x}}\delta\dot{x} + \frac{\partial\mathcal{L}}{\partial u}\delta u = 0 \tag{12}$$

Now, to construct the corresponding Lagrangian for our purposes, let us consider the following alternative system representation based on Equation (8):

$$\dot{x} = f(x) + \alpha u + p(x,u) \tag{13}$$

From Equation (13):

$$p(\dot{x},x,u) = \dot{x} - f(x) - \alpha u \tag{14}$$

Therefore, from Equation (14), the corresponding Lagrangian for the performance index is proposed as

$$\mathcal{L}(x,\dot{x},u) \equiv \dot{x} - f(x) - \alpha u \tag{15}$$

From Equations (10) and (15), the functional that represents the performance index is

$$\mathcal{P}(x,\dot{x},u) = \int_0^T (\dot{x} - f(x) - \alpha u)\ dt \tag{16}$$

Here, the differential form of Equation (16) is

$$\delta\mathcal{P}(x,\dot{x},u) = \int_0^T \delta(\dot{x} - f(x) - \alpha u)dt \tag{17}$$

Applying Equation (12), the following differential equation for the control input u is performed:

$$\alpha u' + f' = 0 \tag{18}$$

By solving Equation (18), with $f(x_0) = 0$, we have that

$$u = -\alpha^{-1}\int_{x_0}^{x} f'(z)dz + u_0 \tag{19}$$

or

$$u = -\alpha^{-1}f(x) - u_0 \tag{20}$$

As can be observed, the control law (20) is realizable as feedback control only if the nonlinear term $f(x)$ is available. However, as is well known, the nonlinear terms are hard to model accurately, being an important source of parametric and/or structured uncertainties.

From the above, an alternative form of the controller (20) must be considered to avoid the above-mentioned drawbacks. Indeed, as non-ideal conditions and uncertain terms are present, the control approach given by Equation (20) is not realizable. So, a strategy must be proposed to compensate for the uncertain terms and reach a realizable control design. For this purpose, an uncertainty observer-based controller must be considered.

Uncertainty Observer-Based Estimator Design

Let us consider system (13), where the nonlinear term $f(x)$ is unknown, which is now considered a new unknown state variable, and the term $h(x)$ is the uncertain nonlinear dynamic behavior of $f(x)$, constituting an extended dynamical system as

$$\dot{x} = f(x) + a_1 u + p(x,u) \tag{21}$$

$$\dot{f} = h(x) \tag{22}$$

Coupled with a linearly measured output, $y = Cx$.

To analyze the convergence of the proposed observer, the following assumptions are introduced.

Assumption 1. *h(x) is a bounded unknown nonlinear vector field, i.e.,*

$$\|h(x)\| \leq \mathrm{M} < \infty$$

Assumption 2. $\left\|f(x) - \hat{f}(\hat{x})\right\| \leq \mathrm{K} < \infty$. *Here, f(x) is a nonlinear and unknown term of system (21) with uncertain dynamic h(x) and* $\hat{f}(\hat{x})$ *is the corresponding estimation of f(x).*

Now, the design of the uncertainty observer is established.

Proposition 1. *The following nonlinear system (23)–(24) is an asymptotic observer of the system (21)–(22):*

$$\dot{\hat{x}} = \hat{f}(x,u) + \alpha u + p(x,u) + g_1 sin(e_1) \tag{23}$$

$$\dot{\hat{f}} = g_2 sin(e_1) \tag{24}$$

where g_1 and g_2 are the observer gains and $e_1 = y - \hat{y} = Cx - C\hat{x}$, with C = [1 0] and $e_2 = f - \hat{f}$ being the observation errors.

Proof of Proposition 1. Let us define the observation error vector as:

$$\varepsilon = [e_1\ e_2]^T$$

Let us consider the observation error dynamic from Equations (21)–(22) and (23)–(24):

$$\frac{d\varepsilon}{dt} \equiv \dot{\varepsilon} = \begin{bmatrix} \dot{e}_1 \\ \dot{e}_2 \end{bmatrix} = \begin{bmatrix} f(x) - \hat{f}(\hat{x}) - g_1 sin(e_1) \\ h(x) - g_2 sin(e_1) \end{bmatrix} \tag{25}$$

Now, Assumptions 1 and 2 and the Cauchy–Schwartz inequality are applied to Equation (25):

$$\|\dot{\varepsilon}\| \leq \begin{bmatrix} K \\ M \end{bmatrix} - \begin{bmatrix} |g_1| \\ |g_2| \end{bmatrix} sin(e_1) \tag{26}$$

Note that

$$\|sin(e_1)\| \leq 1 \tag{27}$$

Then,

$$\|\dot{\varepsilon}\| \leq \wp - G \tag{28}$$

$$\text{Here: } \wp = \begin{bmatrix} K \\ M \end{bmatrix} \text{ and } G = \begin{bmatrix} |g_1| \\ |g_2| \end{bmatrix} \tag{29}$$

Let us propose the following quadratic form of a Lyapunov function:

$$V = \varepsilon^T \varepsilon \tag{30}$$

Note that this scalar function is a positive definite function.

The time derivative of the scalar function V is defined as

$$\dot{V} = \dot{\varepsilon}^T \varepsilon + \varepsilon^T \dot{\varepsilon} \tag{31}$$

Now, considering Equations (26)–(27):

$$\dot{V} \leq (\wp - G)^T \|\varepsilon\| + \|\varepsilon\|^T (\wp - G) \tag{32}$$

By adequately selecting the observer gains of the vector G:

$$\wp - G = -Q \tag{33}$$

Finally:

$$\dot{V} \leq -Q^T \|\varepsilon\| - \|\varepsilon\|^T Q \leq 0 \tag{34}$$

As can be observed, Equation (34) satisfies the stability condition of the Lyapunov criteria; therefore, it can be concluded that the proposed observer is asymptotically stable.

Note that an asymptotic observer, by definition, can lead the named estimation or observation error to zero at a large enough time, i.e., $\lim_{t\to\infty} e = 0$. The conclusion of this point is that the estimated terms converge to the *real* ones. □

Finally, under the proposal of the above uncertainty observer design, the realizable controller can be defined as

$$u = -\alpha^{-1}\hat{f} - u_0 \tag{35}$$

4. Results and Discussion

Numerical experiments were conducted to explore the reliability and performance of the proposed methodology. The experiments were performed on a PC with an Intel® Core™ i7 processor, employing MATLAB (v. 2022a) and the 23s library to solve ordinary differential equations under the initial conditions previously mentioned in Section 2.

From the bioreactor model, the selected productivity of the chemical compound corresponds to C_1, where $f(x) = d_0 + k_8 c_4 - k_1 \frac{c_1 c_2}{c_1 + K} - k_2 \frac{c_1 c_3}{c_1 + K}$ is the reaction rate term, which, as usual, is the most difficult term to be known, so it is considered the uncertain term, which is a realistic assumption. The considered control input corresponds to the input flow u. Considering that the application example shows complex and nonlinear oscillatory dynamic behavior, there are generally no rules for the tuning of the control's parameters. Therefore, via numerical simulations (not shown), we realize some experiments to calculate, via trial and error, the best selection of the corresponding parameters. As usual, in the control process for nonlinear systems, the parameters of the proposed optimal control are assumed to be α = 1 and u_0 = 0.015, yielding the following control structure: $u = 1 \times \hat{f} - 0.015$.

The uncertainty observer (23)–(24), coupled with the proposed controller (35), considers that C_1 is available as measured system output and as parameters g_1 = 10 and g_2 = 100, under the following initial conditions: $C_{10} = 1$ and $\hat{f}_0 = 1$. The proposed control strategy is turned on at t = 50 time units.

Now, Figure 1 shows the open-loop performance of C_1 concentration and the oscillatory dynamics of the bioreactor from the operation start-up until the controller start-up. When the proposed controller acts, the C_1 concentration responds immediately, eliminating the oscillatory behavior and increasing the C_1 concentration to a constant value of C_1 = 150, which is the first satisfactory response of the bioreactor.

Figure 2 is related to a phase portrait, where the uncontrolled concentrations, C_2, C_3, and C_4, are presented. Note that the oscillatory behavior is also eliminated, leading the bioreactor to a fixed closed-loop steady state. Now, it can be observed in Figure 3 that the performance of the uncertainty observer varies from the oscillatory open-loop operation to the closed-loop operation. The estimation methodology has satisfactory performance, as when the controller is active, the estimator again reaches the real reaction rate f without a large setting time (only 5 time units) and without large overshoots.

Figure 4 is related to the corresponding control effort; as can be seen, an important increase in the input flow is caused by the control law (35). This is a second important characteristic of the proposed methodology, considering that the bioreactor productivity

p, in a continuous operation, is directly proportional to the output concentration and the corresponding flow. From the above and because of the previous results, the open-loop and closed-loop bioreactor productivity is presented in Figure 5. The closed-loop productivity is stable and has increased by around 12.5%.

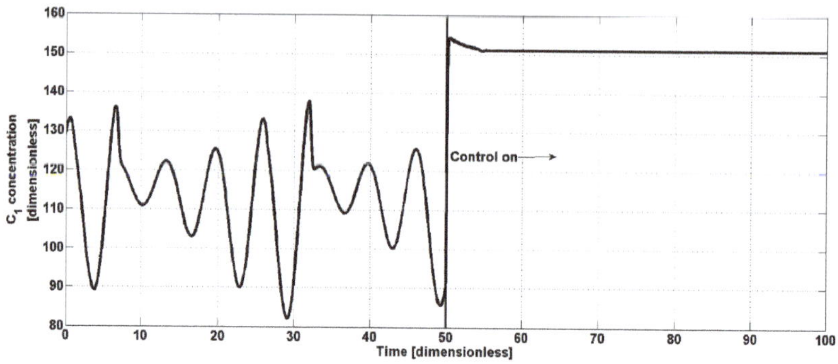

Figure 1. Open−loop and closed−loop dynamic behavior of C_1 concentration.

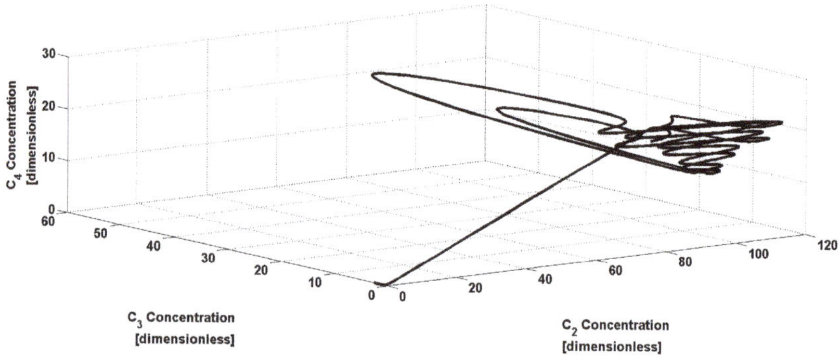

Figure 2. Open−loop and closed−loop behavior of uncontrolled concentrations.

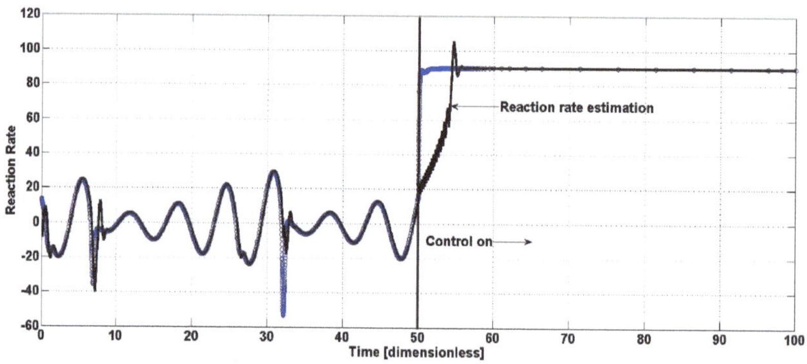

Figure 3. Open−loop and closed−loop performance of the uncertainty observer.

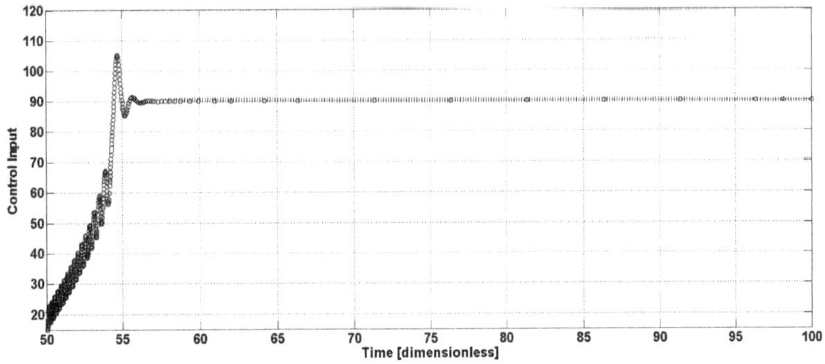

Figure 4. Dynamic behavior of the control effort u.

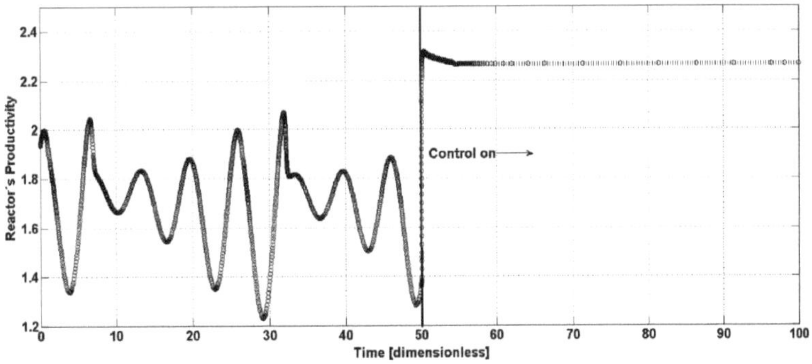

Figure 5. Open–loop and closed–loop dynamic behavior of the bioreactor productivity is referred to as C_1 concentration.

The intensification of biochemical processes is still an open and challenging problem. This is mainly because distinct approaches can be addressed towards biochemical process intensification. Among others, high productivity with a lower possible process scale, economical or yielding costs, or an increment in bioprocess efficiency aim for intensification. Meanwhile, feedback control strategies accompany most of the intensification goals. Robust and optimization properties of the feedback control are open problems whose solutions support biochemical process intensification.

5. Conclusions

This work presents a class of observer-based optimal controllers whose task is to maximize productivity in a continuous stirred tank bioreactor under the framework of Euler–Lagrange theory and the intensification concept. The proposed controller requires online information on the reaction rate for the selected chemical compound, so a novel uncertainty observer is presented with success to develop the proposed optimal control strategy. The observer has asymptotic convergence under the Lyapunov theoretical framework. The proposed controller is applied to a highly nonlinear bioreactor model, where the maximum bioreactor productivity is reached in a stable closed-loop steady-state operation by suppressing the open-loop oscillations of the mass concentrations in the bioreactor. The closed-loop productivity is also stable and is increased by around 12.5% in comparison with the highest open-loop productivity reached.

Author Contributions: Conceptualization and methodology, R.F. and R.A.-L.; software, R.A.-L. and J.L.M.-M.; validation, R.F., R.A.-L. and J.L.M.-M.; formal analysis, R.F., R.A.-L. and J.L.M.-M.; resources, J.L.M.-M.; writing—original draft preparation, R.F. and R.A.-L.; writing—review and editing, R.A.-L. and J.L.M.-M. All authors provided critical feedback and helped shape the research, analysis, and manuscript. All authors have read and agreed to the published version of the manuscript.

Funding: The research for this manuscript was funded by the Secretaria de Investigacion y Posgrado of the Instituto Politecnico Nacional (SIP-IPN) under the research grant SIP20231539.

Institutional Review Board Statement: Not applicable.

Informed Consent Statement: Not applicable.

Data Availability Statement: The data presented in this study are available on reasonable request from the corresponding authors (R.A.-L. and J.L.M.-M).

Conflicts of Interest: The authors declare no conflicts of interest.

References

1. Boodhoo, K.V.K.; Flickinger, M.C.; Woodley, J.M.; Emanuelsson, E.A.C. Bioprocess intensification: A route to efficient and sustainable biocatalytic transformations for the future. *Chem. Eng. Process. Process Intensif.* **2022**, *172*, 108793. [CrossRef]
2. Skupin, P.; Łaszczyk, P.; Goud, E.C.; Vooradi, R.; Ambati, S.R. Robust nonlinear model predictive control of cascade of fermenters with recycle for efficient bioethanol production. *Comput. Chem. Eng.* **2022**, *160*, 107735. [CrossRef]
3. Constantino, D.S.; Dias, M.M.; Silva, A.M.; Faria, J.L.; Silva, C.G. Intensification strategies for improving the performance of photocatalytic processes: A review. *J. Clean. Prod.* **2022**, *340*, 130800. [CrossRef]
4. Calderón-Soto, L.F.; Herrera-López, E.J.; Lara-Cisneros, G.; Femat, R. On unified stability for a class of chemostat model with generic growth rate functions: Maximum yield as control goal. *J. Process Control* **2019**, *77*, 61–75. [CrossRef]
5. Lara-Cisneros, G.; Aguilar-López, R.; Femat, R. On the dynamic optimization of methane production in anaerobic digestion via extremum-seeking control approach. *Comput. Chem. Eng.* **2015**, *75*, 49–59. [CrossRef]
6. Ariyur, K.B.; Krstic, M. *Real-Time Optimization by Extremum-Seeking Control*; Wiley: Hoboken, NJ, USA, 2003.
7. Dochain, D.; Perrier, M.; Guay, M. Extremum seeking control and its application to process and reaction systems: A survey. *Math. Comput. Simul.* **2011**, *82*, 369–380. [CrossRef]
8. Simeonov, I.; Noykova, N.; Gyllenberg, M. Identification and extremum seeking control of the anaerobic digestion of organic wastes. *Cybern Inf. Technol.* **2007**, *7*, 73–84.
9. Alvarez-Ramirez, J. Robust PI stabilization of a class of continuously stirred-tank reactors. *AIChE J.* **1999**, *45*, 1992–2000. [CrossRef]
10. Nema, S.; Padhy, P.K. Identification and cuckoo PI-PD controller design for stable and unstable processes. *Trans. Inst. Meas. Control* **2015**, *37*, 708–720. [CrossRef]
11. Lloyds Raja, G.; Ali, A. New PI-PD Controller Design Strategy for Industrial Unstable and Integrating Processes with Dead Time and Inverse Response. *J. Control Autom. Electr. Syst.* **2021**, *32*, 266–280. [CrossRef]
12. Onat, C. A new design method for PI–PD control of unstable processes with dead time. *ISA Trans.* **2019**, *84*, 69–81. [CrossRef] [PubMed]
13. Kosgey, K.; Zungu, P.V.; Kumari, S.; Bux, F. Critical review of process control strategies in anammox-mediated nitrogen removal systems. *J. Environ. Chem. Eng.* **2022**, *10*, 108068. [CrossRef]
14. Labutin, A.N.; Vaško, M.; Kuric, I.; Nevinitsyn, V.Y.; Sága, M.; Zagarinskaya, Y.N.; Volkova, G.V. Analytical Synthesis of Non-Linear Control Algorithms of a Chemical Reactor Thermal Mode. *Processes* **2021**, *9*, 644. [CrossRef]
15. Pipino, H.A.; Cappelletti, C.A.; Eduardo, J.; Adam, J. Adaptive multi-model predictive control applied to continuous stirred tank reactor. *Comput. Chem. Eng.* **2021**, *145*, 107195. [CrossRef]
16. Xavier, J.; Patnaik, S.K.; Panda, R.C. Process Modeling, Identification Methods, and Control Schemes for Nonlinear Physical Systems—A Comprehensive Review. *Chem. Biol. Eng. Rev.* **2021**, *8*, 392–412. [CrossRef]
17. Mukherjee, D.; Raja, G.L.; Kundu, P.; Ghosh, A. Improved fractional augmented control strategies for continuously stirred tank reactors. *Asian J. Control* **2022**, *25*, 2165–2182. [CrossRef]
18. Dubljevic, S. Quo Vadis advanced chemical process control. *Can. J. Chem. Eng.* **2022**, *100*, 2135–2139. [CrossRef]
19. Mousakazemi, S.M.H. Comparison of the error-integral performance indexes in a GA-tuned PID controlling system of a PWR-type nuclear reactor point-kinetics model. *Prog. Nucl. Energy* **2021**, *132*, 103604. [CrossRef]
20. Domański, P.D. Step Response Indexes. In *Control Performance Assessment: Theoretical Analyses and Industrial Practice*; Studies in Systems, Decision and Control; Springer: Cham, Switzerland, 2020; Volume 245, pp. 27–36.
21. Khanduja, N.; Bhushan, B.; Mishra, S. Control of CSTR using firefly and hybrid-firefly biogeography based optimization (BBFFO) algorithm. *J. Inf. Optim. Sci.* **2020**, *41*, 1443–1452. [CrossRef]
22. Alhazmi, K.; Albalawi, F.; Sarathy, S.M. A reinforcement learning-based economic model predictive control framework for autonomous operation of chemical reactors. *Chem. Eng. J.* **2022**, *428*, 130993. [CrossRef]

23. Zhang, G.; Tian, B.; Zhang, W.; Zhang, X. Optimized robust control for industrial unstable process via the mirror mapping method. *ISA Trans.* **2019**, *86*, 9–17. [CrossRef] [PubMed]
24. Mînzu, V.; Arama, I. Optimal Control Systems Using Evolutionary Algorithm-Control Input Range Estimation. *Automation* **2022**, *3*, 95–115. [CrossRef]
25. Andrés-Martínez, O.; Palma-Flores, O.; Ricardez-Sandoval, L.A. Optimal control and the Pontryagin's principle in chemical engineering: History, theory, and challenges. *AIChE J.* **2022**, *68*, e17777. [CrossRef]
26. Leyffer, S.; Menickelly, M.; Munson, T.; Vanaret, C.; Wild, S.M. A survey of nonlinear robust optimization. *Inf. Syst. Oper. Res.* **2020**, *58*, 342–373. [CrossRef]
27. Luo, Y.; Kurian, V.; Ogunnaike, B.A. Bioprocess systems analysis, modeling, estimation, and control. *Curr. Opin. Chem. Eng.* **2021**, *33*, 100705. [CrossRef]
28. Liang, E.; Yuan, Z. Robust dynamic optimization for nonlinear chemical processes under measurable and unmeasurable uncertainties. *AIChE J.* **2022**, *68*, e17733. [CrossRef]
29. Zhang, Q.; Feng, W. A unified framework for adjustable robust optimization with endogenous uncertainty. *AIChE J.* **2020**, *66*, e17047. [CrossRef]
30. Liang, E.; Yuan, Z. Adjustable robust optimal control for industrial 2-Mercaptobenzothiazole production processes under uncertainty. *Optim. Eng.* **2022**, *23*, 1987–2024. [CrossRef]
31. Wang, Y.; Biegler, L.T.; Patel, M.; Wassick, J. Robust optimization of solid–liquid batch reactors under parameter uncertainty. *Chem. Eng. Sci.* **2020**, *212*, 115170. [CrossRef]
32. Killory, H.; Rössler, O.E.; Hudson, J.L. Higher chaos in a four-variable chemical reaction model. *Phys. Lett. A* **1987**, *122*, 341–345. [CrossRef]
33. Aguilar-López, R. Chaos Suppression via Euler-Lagrange Control Design for a Class of Chemical Reacting System. *Math. Probl. Eng.* **2018**, *2018*, 3802801. [CrossRef]

fermentation

MDPI

Article

Optimization of a Bacterial Cultivation Medium via a Design-of-Experiment Approach in a Sartorius Ambr® 15 Fermentation Microbioreactor System

Antonio Baccante [1,*], Pasquale Petruccelli [1], Giovanni Saudino [1], Elena Ragnoni [1], Erik Johansson [2,*], Vito Di Cioccio [1] and Kleanthis Mazarakis [3,*]

[1] AchilleS Vaccines Srl, Via Fiorentina, 1, 53100 Siena, Italy; p.petruccelli@achillesvaccines.com (P.P.); g.saudino@achillesvaccines.com (G.S.); v.dicioccio@achillesvaccines.com (V.D.C.)
[2] Sartorius Stedim Data Analytics AB, Östra Strandgatan 24, 903 33 Umeå, Sweden
[3] Sartorius Stedim UK Ltd., Epsom KT19 9QQ, UK
* Correspondence: a.baccante@achillesvaccines.com (A.B.); erik.johansson@sartorius.com (E.J.); kleanthis.mazarakis@sartorius.com (K.M.)

Abstract: In the evolving landscape of sustainable biopharmaceutical process development, the utilization of bacteria in the production of various compounds via fermentation has attracted extensive attention from scientists. A successful fermentation process and the release of its associated products hinge on the synergy between an efficient bacterial strain and the formulation of a suitable growth medium. Balancing all nutrient levels of a growth medium to maximize microbial growth and the product quality is quite an intricate task. In this context, significant advancements have been achieved via the strategic implementation of design-of-experiment (DOE) methodologies and the utilization of parallel microbioreactor systems. This work presents a case study of the fermentation growth medium optimization of a Gram-negative bacterium of the Neisseriaceae family that releases outer membrane vesicles (OMVs), which represent a potential vaccine platform. To achieve this, the ability of Sartorius MODDE®13 DOE software to explore multiple variables and their interactions was combined with the functionality of a Sartorius Ambr® 15F parallel microbioreactor system. The findings reported in this study have led to the design of a well-suited fermentation medium for a Gram-negative bacterium and an improvement in the quality of the OMVs produced from it.

Keywords: high throughput; biotechnological process; OMVs; small-scale microbiological cultures; experimental design; multiple linear regression modeling

Citation: Baccante, A.; Petruccelli, P.; Saudino, G.; Ragnoni, E.; Johansson, E.; Di Cioccio, V.; Mazarakis, K. Optimization of a Bacterial Cultivation Medium via a Design-of-Experiment Approach in a Sartorius Ambr® 15 Fermentation Microbioreactor System. *Fermentation* **2023**, *9*, 1002. https://doi.org/10.3390/fermentation9121002

Academic Editor: Ricardo Aguilar-López

Received: 19 October 2023
Revised: 15 November 2023
Accepted: 21 November 2023
Published: 27 November 2023

1. Introduction

Currently, the biopharmaceutical industry is committed to enhancing the speed of process development and reducing the time and the operational costs of testing biological substances in the clinic. A key strategy in meeting these challenges is the application of high-throughput process development (HTPD) tools. HTPD methodologies significantly reduce the time needed for the execution of a large number of experiments in parallel through the application of quality-by-design (QbD) tools, such as the factorial design of experiments (DOEs), which represents an essential instrument that is fully adopted in modern process development and manufacturing organizations [1–3].

Among biological substances, vaccines represent one of the most successful treatments against infectious diseases, with unequivocal evidence of them decreasing morbidity and mortality in the global population [4].

A promising and attractive technology for vaccine development platforms is based on the use of outer membrane vesicles (OMVs). These are biological vesicular structures with a mean size ranging from 20 to 200 nm, and they are released spontaneously during the growth of Gram-negative bacteria. OMVs have been shown to play an important role in bacterial virulence, as well as in intercellular communication and nutrient acquisition. They are formed via a process that involves the bulging and pinching of the outer membrane This process can be spontaneous or induced by environmental factors, such as changes in pH or temperature [5].

As OMVs originate from the bacterial wall via blebbing into the extracellular environment, they consist of double-layer membranes and include bacterial outer membrane components and periplasmic space substances, such as membrane proteins, lipopolysaccharides (LPSs), transporters, toxicity factors, DNA, RNA, and enzymes [6–9].

Numerous studies have demonstrated that naturally released OMVs show remarkable biological characteristics, including immunogenicity and adjuvant activity. Furthermore, due to their optimal size, they can be easily taken up by immune cells. Since native OMVs resemble the outer membrane of the bacteria from which they originate, containing the same surface antigens present in the bacterial cell, they have gained attention in the development of new potential vaccines against specific bacterial diseases [8].

The process of producing OMVs involves a microbial cell culture, grown in a stirred-tank bioreactor (STR), which releases the vesicles during growth. Afterwards, the biomass is removed via centrifugation or tangential flow microfiltration, obtaining bacteria-free crude OMVs. These are ready to be further polished via tangential flow ultrafiltration to remove undesired smaller, soluble components.

Among researchers' aims is the optimization of the microbial culture medium and its operative conditions in order to maximize the OMV production yield. Alongside this, unwanted impurities, such as the soluble proteins and nucleic acids released during microbial growth, need to be maintained at the lowest levels. Medium optimization includes the identification of the most suitable nutrients and their appropriate concentrations, resulting in the highest levels of biomass and correlated OMV production [10].

The conventional methods employed to develop and optimize a cell culture medium rely on biochemical studies or a one-dimensional search approach, with individual nutritional factors examined separately. The one-factor approach is inefficient when applied to multiple medium components and may overlook crucial interactions between them, leading to the development of a non-optimal medium [10]. Also, this method entails performing numerous experiments in combination, both in shake flasks and in small-scale stirred-tank bioreactors (STRs), to evaluate the effects of varying the medium composition reagents. With this approach, standard medium development and process definition and optimization require months of intensive and expensive work. Furthermore, bench bioreactors need to be cleaned, prepared, and autoclaved prior to and after each run. To obviate this, substantially shorten the time required, and reduce the overall costs, an alternative method may be used. One such route is via the statistical design of experiment (DOE) associated with a parallel microbioreactor system, such as the Sartorius Ambr® 15F system (Advanced Microscale Bioreactor) [11–13].

A DOE provides a reliable basis for decision making, offering a framework for systematically changing all the important factors but only requiring a limited number of experiments. Such a set of DOE-based experiments does not usually involve more than 10–20 runs, but this number can be further optimized to meet specific requirements. Since the experiments are distributed in a quadratic experimental space, it is possible to identify a design space that will produce a better result. An analysis of the data acquired from the performed experiments will identify the optimal conditions and reveal which key factors influence the results.

Prior to conducting any experiments, the experimenter must specify the experimental objective, the number of responses to some input conditions, and the number of factors and their respective ranges of variation. The experimental design can then be created, and the designated experiments may be conducted either in parallel or sequentially. Each experiment provides some results, i.e., numerical values for the response variables. Once collected, these data are investigated using a regression analysis. This provides a model relating the changes in the factors to the changes in the responses. The model will indicate which factors are important, explaining how they combine to influence the responses. The modeling results may also be converted into response contour plots, so-called maps, which are used to clarify where the best operating conditions are to be expected [14].

The way this is carried out depends on the problem and the conditions under consideration, meaning that the shape and complexity of the experimental design may vary considerably. A common approach in DOE is to define a standard reference experiment of interest and perform new experiments that are laid out in a symmetrical fashion around the standard reference experiment. Hence, the standard reference experiment is usually called the center point.

The Ambr® 15F system is an automated mini-bioreactor system capable of running 24 disposable microbioreactors of 15 mL volume capacity, lodged in two culture stations (CS-1 and CS-2) containing 12 microbioreactors each. Each culture station has independent stirring speed control, allowing for 12 microbioreactors of the same stir speed at the same time. Each microbioreactor includes a miniature internal impeller and two optical sensors needed to monitor the pH and optical density (OD). A closed-loop control of dissolved oxygen, pH, and gas supply is present in all microbioreactors. The Ambr® 15F is installed in a bio-safety cabinet to ensure a sterile environment for automated inoculation, sampling, and feeding operations. The culture preparation and inoculation, feed and base addition, and culture sampling can be scheduled by programming the system through the associated software [12,13,15].

This study aims to show how to optimize a semi-defined culture medium utilized for a fastidious Gram-negative bacterium of the Neisseriaceae family and consequently improve the quality and yield of the released OMVs using the Sartorius Ambr® 15F system in combination with a DOE approach study managed using Sartorius MODDE®13 software.

2. Materials and Methods

2.1. Strain, Medium, and Inoculum

Recombinant Gram-negative bacteria of the Neisseriaceae family and OMV release were used for all studies reported in this publication. Bacterial growth was supported by employing a semi-defined medium free of animal components and containing essentially a phosphate buffer, lactic acid (carbon source), yeast extract and casamino acids, salts, trace elements, vitamins, and iron elements.

Although the bacterial strain and the medium components cannot be fully disclosed due to company restrictions related to intellectual property safeguards, the focus of this study was to demonstrate how to simplify a semi-defined medium. The medium in question initially contained high amounts of yeast extract (20 g/L) and casamino acids (10 g/L), employed for the growth of a fastidious Gram-negative microorganism of the Neisseriaceae family and to produce OMVs. We proved that, with the identification of essential key amino acids and the optimal concentrations of trace elements, vitamins, and iron citrate needed to grow this bacterium, it was possible to significantly reduce the quantity of yeast extract used, despite reaching the same level of growth obtained with a high yeast extract concentration. Due to this optimization, the analysis showed an increased quantity of produced OMVs and a noticeable reduction in unwanted contaminants, such as soluble proteins and nucleic acids, in the final purified OMV product.

All reagents used for this study were purchased from Merck, except for the yeast extract and casamino acids, which were bought from Becton Dickinson (BD).

For the inoculum cultivation media and the Ambr® 15F experiments, in addition to the undisclosed reagents, 7.5 g/L of lactic acid, 5 g/L of yeast extract, and 10 g/L of casamino acids without supplements (trace elements, vitamins, and iron citrate) were used. The media were sterilized using a 0.22 μm cut-off filter, Sartorius Sartolab® (Sartorius Biohit Liquid Handling Oy, Helsinki, Finland).

The 200-fold-concentrated trace element stock solutions contained the following substances: $CuSO_4 \times 4H_2O$ at 0.20 g/L, $ZnSO_4 \times 7H_2O$ at 0.15 g/L, H_3BO_3 at 0.5 g/L, and $MnCl_2 \times 4H_2O$ at 0.15 g/L.

The 100-fold-concentrated vitamin stock solutions consisted of 0.3 g/L thiamine chloride hydrochloride, 0.05 g/L nicotinic acid, 0.05 g/L pyridoxine hydrochloride, 0.2 g/L calcium pantothenate, and 0.2 g/L vitamin B12.

The 100-fold-concentrated iron citrate stock solution consisted of 4 g/L of $C_6H_5FeO_7$.

For each amino acid, a 100 g/L concentrated stock solution was prepared.

The above concentrated solutions were sterilized using the 0.22 μm cut off filter Sartorius Sartolab®.

Prior to this optimization study, the medium used for the 2 L benchtop bioreactor included a yeast extract (20 g/L) with a concentration higher than that of the inoculum, as well as 10 g/L of casamino acids. The medium was sterilized in an autoclave for 30 min at 121 °C. After being processed using the autoclave, the medium was supplemented with 7.5 g/L of lactic acid (carbon source), 5 g/L of the trace element stock solution, 10 g/L of the vitamin stock solution, and 1 g/L of the iron citrate stock solution.

The 24 different fermentation media used for the Ambr® 15F experiments were completed with trace element, vitamin, iron citrate, and amino acid stock solutions in accordance with the concentrations calculated using DOE software. The media were prepared using the Ambr® 15F's liquid handler by programming the associated software.

At the end of this study, the optimized medium used was composed of 5 g/L of yeast extract and 10 g/L of casamino acids. Additionally, it was supplemented with 5 g/L of the trace element stock solution, 10 g/L of the vitamin stock solution, and 10 g/L of the iron citrate stock solution. Furthermore, the media were enriched with the following amino acids: arginine at 0.40 g/L, glutamate at 10.6 g/L, histidine at 0.58 g/L, proline at 3.49 g/L, and glutamine at 0.12 g/L.

The inoculum culture process started with the thawing of one frozen stock research cell bank (RCB) of the strain (1 mL of culture with 20% glycerol stored at −80 °C). The stock was used to inoculate 200 mL of medium (containing only 5 g/L of yeast extract and sterilized via 0.22 μm orthogonal filtration) in a 1000 mL baffled polycarbonate Erlenmeyer flask with a vent cap. The flask was incubated at 37 °C ± 1 on a rotary shaker (orbital diameter 25 mm) at 150 rpm for 8 h. At the end of growth, the culture was placed in an exponential phase and showed a final optical density (OD_{600nm}) of 2.5, as measured using a photometer in 1 cm light path plastic cuvettes at 600 nm. The described inoculum procedure was used to initiate both the 2 L lab-scale benchtop bioreactor and the Ambr® 15F microbioreactors.

2.2. *Cultivation in the Bioreactor Systems (Ambr® 15F and 2 L)*

The fermentation runs reported in this article were performed using the Sartorius Ambr® 15F and the 2 L benchtop bioreactors (Sartorius UniVessel® Glass 2L, Biostat® B-DCU II MO. Sartorius Stedim Systems GmbH, Guxhagen, Germany). In both cases, the fermentations were conducted in batch mode.

The Ambr® 15F with 24 single-use microbioreactors was operated with an 8 mL working volume for the experiments in this study. The Ambr® 15F was set with an initial volume of 8 mL, and each microbioreactor was filled with the medium and additional solutions using the liquid handler according to the DOE conditions. To prevent foam formation, the medium contained polypropylene glycol 2000 (PPG) at a final concentration of 0.02% (v/v). The inoculum flask content was transferred to a 24-well plate to allow the Ambr® 15F liquid handler to initiate the inoculation phase for all microbioreactors, which were inoculated to an initial OD_{600nm} of 0.2. The pH was measured online via the sensor's patches embedded in each microbioreactor, and it was held at 7.20 using NaOH 1M or H3PO4 1M. Acid was added using the liquid handler, while the base was pumped into the microbioreactors via pumped liquid delivery. The offline pH reading was monitored using the analysis module (AM), which recalibrates the in-process pH sensor.

Dissolved oxygen (DO) was measured online using the sensor's patches embedded in each microbioreactor, and it was set at 30%. To maintain this value, a cascade (air–oxygen–

stirrer) was set as follows: air flow rate from 8 to 30 mL/min; oxygen enrichment flow rate from 0 to 30 mL/min; and stirrer from 750 to 3000 rpm.

The growth temperature of each bioreactor was set and maintained at 37 °C. Cell growth was monitored online using the Ambr® 15F's sensor technology, consisting of cell scattering and an analysis of reflectance-associated signals. By applying user calibration (performed earlier with the same microorganism employed in this study), the reflectance value was converted into a measure of optical density (OD_{600nm}). For the offline OD measurements at 600 nm, an external photometer in 1 cm light path plastic cuvettes was used.

The cultures were run in batch mode and ended when the growth stationary phase was reached. This was recognized when the online OD measurement graphical trend either remained constant or decreased.

The 2 L bioreactor contained 1.5 L of sterile medium, and it was assembled with baffles and two Rushton six-blade disc turbines (φ = 5.5 cm) used for mixing, one located 3.5 cm from the bioreactor bottom and the other 7 cm from the first turbine. The bioreactor operating conditions were as follows: temperature at 37.0 °C; dissolved oxygen (DO) at 30%; air flow rate from 1.5 to 3 L/min (1 to 2 vvm); and a stirrer from 200 to 1000 rpm. Air flow and agitation were set in cascade to maintain the DO value.

The pH was set at 7.2 and measured using an online sterilizable electrode (HAMILTON EasyFerm BIO HB Arc 225. Hamilton, Bonaduz, Switzerland). NaOH at 2M and H_3PO_4 at 1M solutions were used to maintain the pH setpoint. The DO concentration was detected using an online optical electrode (HAMILTON VISIFERM DO ECS 225 H0. Hamilton, Bonaduz, Switzerland). The 100% point was calibrated before the bioreactor inoculation with the same operative conditions.

The inoculum flask contents were used to inoculate the benchtop bioreactors. The volume of inoculum required for use was calculated to have an initial OD_{600nm} of 0.2 units in the bioreactor. Foam was controlled by adding PPG in the sterile medium to a final concentration of 0.02% (*v*/*v*). The bioreactors were run in batch mode, and the OD of the cultures was monitored during growth using the photometer at 600 nm in 1 cm light path plastic cuvettes.

During the batch fermentation, microbial biomass and OMVs were formed. The fermentation ended when the growth stationary phase was reached. The culture stationary phase was recognized when the OD_{600nm}, measured each hour, was equal to (or lower than) the previous measure. Furthermore, a DO spike associated with a stirrer drop and a reduction in the acid addition confirmed the stationary phase and the end of fermentation.

2.3. *Purification of OMVs*

OMVs were purified from the fermentation broth through a purification process that is extensively described in a number of articles [16,17]. At the end of fermentation, 1 L of culture was collected in 20 × 50 mL Falcon tubes and centrifuged at 4120× *g* for 30 min at +4 °C. The biomass was discarded, and the supernatant containing OMVs was filtered using a 0.22 µm filter (Sartorius Sartolab® RF 1000 PES) in order to reduce the bioburden. The obtained material was ultrafiltrated via tangential flow filtration (TFF) on a Sartoflow® Smart system from Sartorius (Sartorius Stedim Systems GmbH, Guxhagen, Germany), equipped with two Sartocon® Slice 200 Hydrosart® Cassettes (Sartorius Stedim Biotech GmbH, Goettingen, Germany) at a 300 kDa molecular weight cut-off (MWCO). The OMVs were repeatedly ultrafiltered using Tris and PBS buffers to remove all the residual small contaminants [18].

2.4. *Analytical Methods: OMV and DNA Quantification*

The OMV concentration was calculated as the total protein content through a Lowry protein assay [19], purchased from Bio-Rad (DC™ Protein Assay Kit II. Bio-Rad Laboratories Inc., Hercules, CA, USA), in accordance with the kit procedure. The protein concentration was estimated in comparison to a reference curve obtained using bovine serum albumin, as previously described in the literature [20].

Nucleic acid impurities were detected and estimated via a Picogreen assay, purchased from Thermo Fisher (Quant-iT™ PicoGreen™ dsDNA Assay Kits. Life Technologies Corporation, Eugene, OR, USA), according to the manufacturer's instructions [21]. The DNA concentration was estimated in comparison to a reference curve obtained with the calf thymus DNA standard provided with the kit.

2.5. Sartorius MODDE®13 Software

Sartorius MODDE®13 (MODeling and DEsign) is a Windows program for the generation and evaluation of statistical experimental designs, being part of the Umetrics® Suite of Data Analytics Solutions. MODDE®13 converts the experiments into information using a graphical data representation.

2.6. Statistical Analysis

The Lowry and the Picogreen assays were conducted in triplicate, and the data were averaged and are presented as the mean ± standard deviation. The statistical parts related to the DOE experiments are reported in the Supplementary Materials (Tables S2 and S3).

3. Results

Most fastidious microorganisms rely on a variety of trace elements, vitamins, and amino acids, which are typically not present in standard mineral media. Therefore, chemically undefined media containing complex components derived from natural sources are frequently used. Some examples of the complex nutrients frequently used are yeast extract, peptone, meat extract, and hydrolysates derived from either casein or soybeans. One of the most used complex supplements is yeast extract, particularly due to its rich composition of carbohydrates, amino acids, peptides, vitamins, trace elements, and diverse oligomeric compounds [16].

Initially, the bacterial strain was cultivated in a 2 L benchtop bioreactor with a semi-defined medium containing only 5 g/L of yeast extract. With this condition, it was possible to reach a final OD_{600nm} of the culture equivalent to 5 units. To increase the final OD_{600nm} value to an average value of 10 and, thus, increase the OMV production yield, the yeast extract concentration was raised up to 20 g/L. In this way, protein concentrations (corresponding predominantly to the OMVs' protein concentrations) were obtained after ultra-tangential flow filtration (TFF) equal to 0.23 mg/mL (fermentation run A) and 0.30 mg/mL (fermentation run B).

A possible approach to preventing the use of such a high yeast extract concentration and the consequences of the foregoing statement involved identifying the unknown auxotrophies of the bacteria, with the aim of obtaining a simplified and tailor-made medium. This, in turn, led to a reduction in medium expenses and prevented excessive nutrient residues at the end of the fermentation process.

The rapid time- and labor-saving identification of the essential nutrients is based on the application of the DOE associated with the 24-microbioreactor Sartorius Ambr® 15F system.

The first DOE experiment was based on the auxotrophy identification of various elements, including all amino acid, trace element, vitamin, and iron citrate solutions.

Essential amino acids can be divided into five distinct groups according to metabolic pathways [22–24]. The synthesis of amino acids commences with the intermediates derived from glycolysis, the citric acid cycle, or the pentose phosphate pathway.

The glutamate family includes the amino acids proline, glutamate, glutamine, and arginine, which are derived from α-ketoglutarate. As histidine can also be broken down into glutamate and enters the citric acid cycle through α-ketoglutarate, it is placed in this family. Serine is synthesized from 3-phosphoglycerate and can be converted into glycine and cysteine, making them part of the serine family. Pyruvate, which is the end product of glycolysis, can be converted into alanine, leucine, lysine, and valine, which fall into the pyruvate family. Oxaloacetate, an intermediate in the citric acid cycle, serves as a precursor for aspartate. Methionine, isoleucine, asparagine, and threonine can be produced from aspartate, categorizing them in the aspartate family. Finally, aromatic amino acids, including tryptophan, tyrosine, and phenylalanine, are synthesized from phosphoenolpyruvate and erythrose-4-phosphate, constituting the aromatic family [24].

Using a classification based on the intermediates or their precursors, which had no more than four groups of amino acids for the purpose of this study, a grouping scheme was devised as outlined in Table 1 (including the corresponding concentrations). For each amino acid, the related concentration was equivalent to the sum of the quantity contained in 20 g/L of yeast extract and in 10 g/L of casamino acids, as reported in the supplier technical manual [25]. These amino acid concentrations were established before this study to perform experiments aiming to completely remove the yeast extract and the casamino acids. These investigations demonstrated that our bacterial strain was unable to grow in the total absence of yeast extract and/or casamino acids but that it needed a minimal concentration of both. The minimal concentration of yeast extract was 5 g/L, while that of the casamino acids was 10 g/L. These concentrations ensured a minimal growth of the bacterial strain equal to 4 OD_{600nm} units.

Table 1. Classification and concentration of amino acids in four groups (g/L).

Group 1 [1]	**Group 2** [1]	**Group 3** [1]	**Group 4** [1]
Arginine (0.77)	Serine (0.55)	Aspartate (1.32)	Lysine (1.44)
Glutamine (0.06)	Glycine (0.72)	Asparagine (0.24)	Alanine (1.38)
Histidine (0.32)	Valine (1.38)	Threonine (0.47)	Tryptophan (0.1)
Proline (1.18)	Leucine (1.44)	Methionine (0.3)	Phenylalanine (1.08)
Glutamate (3.6)	Cysteine (0.05)	Isoleucine (1.16)	Tyrosine (0.2)

[1] Group 1: glutamate family; group 2: serine family and part of pyruvate family; group 3: aspartate family; group 4: aromatic family and part of the pyruvate family.

3.1. First DOE Experiment

In the initial medium, which contained 20 g/L of yeast extract and 10 g/L of casamino acids, the strain revealed a growth up to an average value of 10 OD_{600nm} units. As mentioned earlier, the first DOE experiment was based on the identification of strain auxotrophies for all amino acids and the effects of the trace element, vitamin, and iron citrate solution concentrations. The aim was to determine the optimal growth conditions that would enable the bacterial strain to maintain the minimum concentrations of yeast extract (5 g/L) and (10 g/L) casamino acids.

Following the amino acid group division reported in Table 1, four medium mixes were identified as being among the factors of this DOE, in addition to the trace elements, vitamins, and iron citrate solution. Each medium mix included the base medium (composed of a phosphate buffer, salts, lactic acid at 7.5 g/L, yeast extract at 5 g/L, and casamino acids at 10 g/L) and the five amino acids shown in Table 1; i.e., Mix 1 contained group 1 amino acids, Mix 2 contained group 2 amino acids, etc. Furthermore, minimum and maximum concentrations were established for each additional solution (trace elements, vitamins, and iron citrate). In this case, the value "1" corresponded to the minimum concentration and "20" to the maximum concentration of each solution (Table 2).

The concentrations of each amino acid are reported in Table 1.

The first design had three quantitative factors, illustrated as a cube with eight corners. There were also four formulation (mixture) factors, illustrated as a pyramid in each corner and in the center of the cube (see Figure 1). From the 160 potential experiments, 24 were chosen using a D-optimal algorithm integrated into MODDE software. The D-optimal design was only constrained by the number of experiments and the settings of the factors (see Table S2, Supplementary Materials).

Table 2. Factor settings of the first DOE.

Name	Abbreviation	Units	Type	Settings
Trace elements	Trace	mg/kg	Quantitative	1 to 20
Vitamins	Vitam	mg/kg	Quantitative	1 to 10
Iron citrate	Iron	mg/kg	Quantitative	1 to 10
Mix 2	Mix 2	g/kg	Formulation	0 to 1
Mix 3	Mix 3	g/kg	Formulation	0 to 1
Mix 4	Mix 4	g/kg	Formulation	0 to 1
Mix 1	Mix 1	g/kg	Formulation	0 to 1

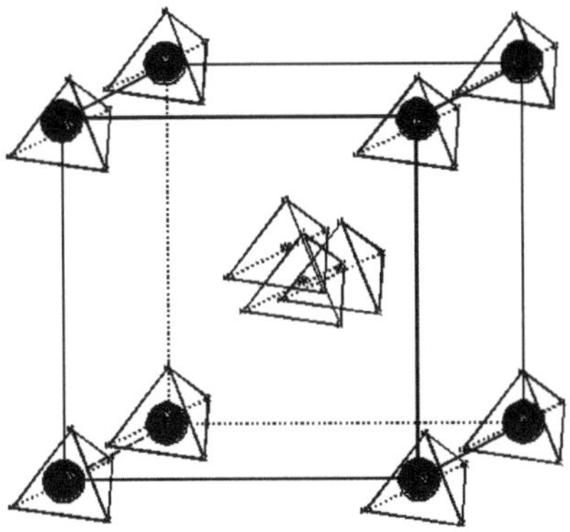

Figure 1. First DOE design, which was established as pyramids in each corner and in the center of a cube design. Each pyramid indicates the mixture (Mix 1, Mix 2 Mix 3, and Mix 4).

As a result of this DOE, we established the need to consider the maximum OD_{600nm} and the minimal value of doubling time (Td) among the 24 bioreactors (Table 3).

Table 3. Response settings of the first DoE.

Name	Abbreviation	Units	Condition	Objective	Min	Target
OD	OD	-	Required	Maximize	4	10
Duplication time	Td	h	Required	Minimize	-	1

The microbioreactor OD values were recorded by the Ambr® 15F system every 1 min and exported to an Excel sheet.

Td is defined as the time needed for the bacterial cells to divide, and it is expressed in hours. A high doubling time value indicates slow growth, while a short doubling time is equivalent to quick growth. Td is related to the bacterial growth rate as shown in the following equation [26]:

$$Td = Ln(2)/\mu, \tag{1}$$

where μ is the specific growth rate of the bacteria culture.

The Td value for each microbioreactor culture was calculated mathematically using Excel. We drew a semi-log plot of several collected points of OD_{600nm} vs. time, in which the y axis (OD) was scaled logarithmically. The Td value was computed by considering only the values included in the exponential phase and fitting them in the exponential mode. Specifically, we first obtained the following exponential function:

$$Y = Ae^{Bx}, \tag{2}$$

where Y represents the OD_{600nm} of bacteria at a given time $\times$ during the exponential growth phase; constant A represents the initial bacteria OD_{600nm} at the start of the exponential growth phase; e is Euler's number; and constant B determines the growth rate of the bacteria during the exponential phase.

In Functions (1) and (2), as B is equivalent to the specific growth rate (μ) of the bacterial population, Td was obtained as follows:

$$Td = Ln(2)/B \tag{3}$$

where Ln(2) is equal to 0.693.

Figure 2d shows the exponential growth curve related to culture station 2—bioreactor 2 (N14 experiment) and the related Td calculation.

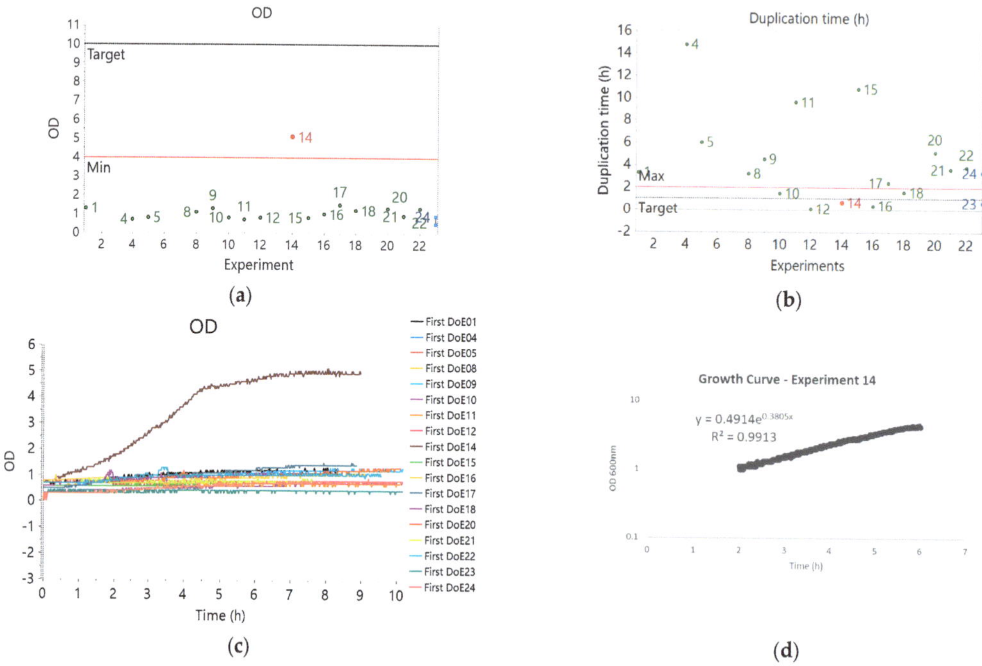

Figure 2. Results analysis: (**a**) OD_{600nm} results of first DOE, where experiment 14 shows the highest OD_{600nm} value; (**b**) duplication time results of first DOE, where experiment 14 shows low Td; (**c**) measured OD_{600nm} chart from Ambr® 15F software. In gold is the N14 experiment that reached the highest OD_{600nm} value and the lowest Td value. Some of the bioreactors are missing, as they did not reach the minimum threshold value for the OD_{600nm} reading. (**d**) Example of Td calculation: culture station 2—bioreactor 2 (N14 experiment).

MODDE®13 software was used to obtain the model fit and to perform an analysis of the results. As shown in the screenshots below (Figure 2), experiment 14 (including only Mix 1) showed higher OD_{600nm} values and a lower duplication time.

The results of the first DOE clearly showed that experiment 14 was by far the best experiment for OD_{600nm}. The model that was obtained with those results was not reliable enough due to the large number of experiments where the minimum OD_{600nm} was not reached. As such, we decided to focus only on experiment 14 and investigate this region further.

Experiment 14 included Mix 1 (composed of arginine, glutamine, histidine, proline, and glutamate), the minimal concentrations of trace elements (5 g/L of the 200-fold stock solution) and vitamins (10 g/L of 100-fold stock solution), and the maximum concentration of the iron citrate solution (10 g/L of 100-fold stock solution).

At this point, a second DOE was set to further optimize the process. We decided to focus on the composition of Mix 1's amino acids and to evaluate their optimal concentrations in a separate DOE.

3.2. Second DOE Experiment

The aim of the second DOE was to explore the different concentrations of the five amino acids included in Mix 1. For each of the five amino acids, we set the following minimum and maximum concentrations: arginine (from 0.4 to 2.3 g/L); glutamate (from 1.8 to 10.7 g/L); histidine (from 0.16 to 1 g/L); proline (from 0.6 to 3.5 g/L); and glutamine (from 0.03 to 0.2 g/L) (Table 4). The trace elements, vitamins, and iron citrate solutions concentrations were kept at the same values, defined in the previous N14 experiment, as well as lactic acid at 7.5 g/L, yeast extract at 5 g/L, and casamino acids at 10 g/L.

Table 4. Factor settings of the second DOE.

Name	Abbreviation	Units	Type	Settings
Arginine	Arg	g/L	Quantitative	0.4 to 2.3
Glutamate	Glu	g/L	Quantitative	1.8 to 10.7
Histidine	His	g/L	Quantitative	0.16 to 1
Proline	Pro	g/L	Quantitative	0.6 to 3.5
Glutamine	Gln	g/L	Quantitative	0.03 to 0.2

The maximum OD_{600nm} and the minimum duplication time (Td) values were considered as the results of this second DOE.

MODDE®13 software was used to generate the second DOE (Table 5) using an optimization design with five factors and two responses. The optimization design was primarily based on a fractional factorial design with 16 experiments, shown in rows 1–16 in Table 5. This was equivalent to half of the black corners in the graph. In addition, there were ten axial star points (rows 17–26 in the Worksheet). Half of the axial points in red were excluded in order to bring down the number of experiments to 21. Axial experiments with the highest factor setting for each factor were excluded. There were also three center points (see rows 27 to 29 in Table 5) (see Figure 3).

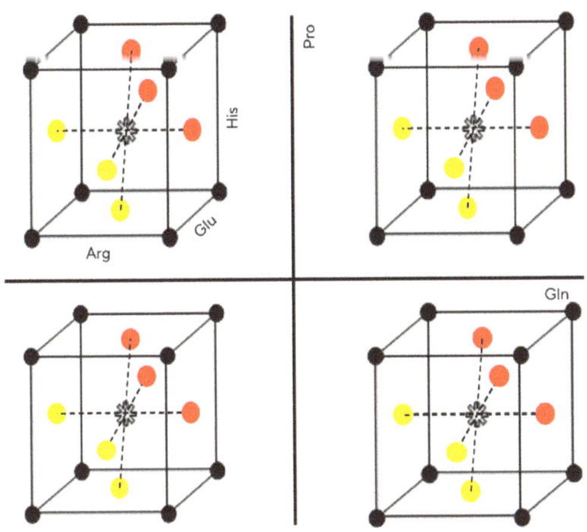

Figure 3. Second DOE design illustrated as cubes of 3 factors (Arg, Glu, His) in the high and low levels of the other 2 factors (Gln and Pro).

Table 5. Worksheet of experiment settings together with the results of the experiments of the second DOE. The conditions that were not run are displayed in red.

Exp No.	Exp Name	Run Order	Incl/Excl	Arg	Glu	His	Pro	Gln	OD	Td
1	N1	21	Incl	0.4	1.8	0.16	0.6	0.2	4	2.13
2	N2	23	Incl	2.3	1.8	0.16	0.6	0.03	3.2	2.36
3	N3	24	Incl	0.4	10.7	0.16	0.6	0.03	3.1	1.91
4	N4	7	Incl	2.3	10.7	0.16	0.6	0.2	3.1	2.58
5	N5	20	Incl	0.4	1.8	1	0.6	0.03	2.5	1.80
6	N6	13	Incl	2.3	1.8	1	0.6	0.2	2.3	2.60
7	N7	12	Incl	0.4	10.7	1	0.6	0.2	3	1.91
8	N8	14	Incl	2.3	10.7	1	0.6	0.03	3.2	3.04
9	N9	9	Incl	0.4	1.8	0.16	3.5	0.03	3.6	2.95
10	N10	8	Incl	2.3	1.8	0.16	3.5	0.2	3.6	2.05
11	N11	10	Incl	0.4	10.7	0.16	3.5	0.2	4	2.20
12	N12	3	Incl	2.3	10.7	0.16	3.5	0.03	2.3	2.11
13	N13	5	Incl	0.4	1.8	1	3.5	0.2	3.1	2.11
14	N14	15	Incl	2.3	1.8	1	3.5	0.03	2.8	1.80
15	N15	1	Incl	0.4	10.7	1	3.5	0.03	4.2	1.84
16	N16	26	Incl	2.3	10.7	1	3.5	0.2	3	1.92
17	N17	28	Incl	0.4	6.25	0.58	2.05	0.115	5.5	1.80
18	N18	18	Excl	2.3	6.25	0.58	2.05	0.115	-	-
19	N19	6	Incl	1.35	1.8	0.58	2.05	0.115	3.3	2.60
20	N20	25	Excl	1.35	10.7	0.58	2.05	0.115	-	-
21	N21	27	Incl	1.35	6.25	0.16	2.05	0.115	2.1	2.69
22	N22	16	Excl	1.35	6.25	1	2.05	0.115	-	-
23	N23	29	Incl	1.35	6.25	0.58	0.6	0.115	4.1	1.91
24	N24	11	Excl	1.35	6.25	0.58	3.5	0.115	-	-
25	N25	4	Incl	1.35	6.25	0.58	2.05	0.03	2.7	2.84
26	N26	22	Excl	1.35	6.25	0.58	2.05	0.2	-	-
27	N27	2	Incl	1.35	6.25	0.58	2.05	0.115	2.6	2.67
28	N28	19	Incl	1.35	6.25	0.58	2.05	0.115	2.4	2.24
29	N29	17	Incl	1.35	6.25	0.58	2.05	0.115	3.7	1.65

The condition numbers (quality) of the two models were 7.5 for the OD model and 10.3 for the Td model [27].

MODDE®13 software was used to analyze the model fit and the results. A multiple linear regression model was fitted and optimized for each response, which resulted in the coefficient models shown in Figure 4 (see Table S3, Supplementary Materials).

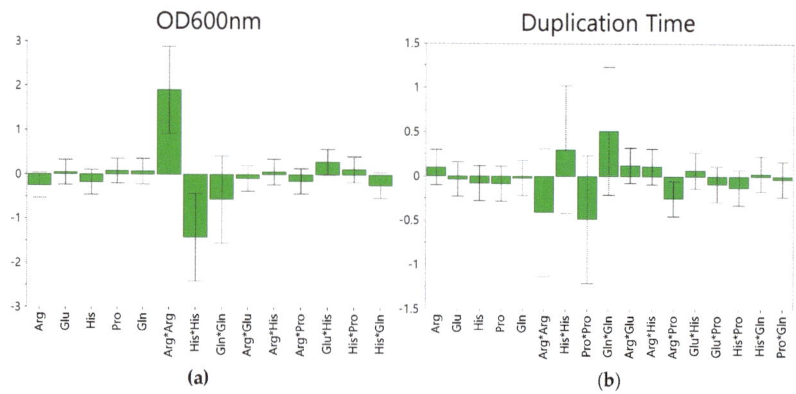

Figure 4. (**a**) Refined coefficient plot of OD_{600nm}; (**b**) refined coefficient plot of duplication time.

By inspecting the contour plots below, it was determined that using a lower amount of arginine can lead to better results, in terms of both maximizing OD_{600nm} and minimizing the duplication time, while keeping the concentration of the other amino acids around their average value settings.

3.3. Fermentation at 2 L Scale

After identifying the ideal amino acid concentrations based on the response contour plot (Figure 5) and to further confirm the data produced by the Ambr® 15F, two fermentations were run at the 2 L scale (runs C and D) using a Sartorius UniVessel Glass 2L BioSTAT B-DCU II MO with the operative conditions delineated earlier in Section 2. Briefly, there was 1.5 L of medium; a temperature of 37.0 °C; a DO of 30%; a pH of 7.2; an air flow rate from 1.5 to 3 L/min (1 to 2 vvm); and a stirrer with a range from 200 to 1000 rpm. Air flow and agitation were set in cascade to maintain the DO value.

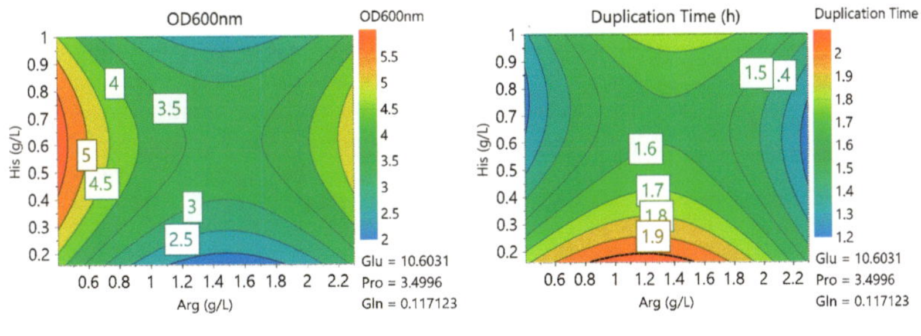

Figure 5. (**a**) Contour plot of OD_{600nm}; (**b**) contour plot of duplication time. The color in both plots goes from blue (low) to red (high). As OD should be maximized and duplication time minimized, it is shown in both plots that better results can be achieved by decreasing the concentration of Arg.

The medium consisted of a phosphate buffer, lactic acid at 7.5 g/L, salts, yeast extract at 5 g/L, and casamino acids at 10 g/L, as well as the following five amino acids: arginine at 0.40 g/L, glutamate at 10.6 g/L, histidine at 0.58 g/L, proline at 3.49 g/L, and glutamine at 0.12 g/L.

With the optimized media, cultures C and D reached final OD_{600nm} values of 10 units (Td = 1.27 h) and 10.2 units (Td = 1.10 h), respectively. The final OD_{600nm} values at the 2 L scale were higher than the OD units recorded in the Ambr® 15F under the same conditions. The higher OD values were mainly expected due to the better operative conditions that prevailed in the 2 L bioreactor, promoting the growth of bacterial cells.

The OMVs were recovered after fermentation and further purified as detailed in the Section 2.

3.4. OMV Characterization

To more accurately assess and define the beneficial effects of the optimized media on bacterial growth and, subsequently, on OMV production, a panel of analytical assays was carried out. The fundamental characteristics of OMVs suitable for vaccine development include low-impurity concentrations in terms of nucleic acids and soluble proteins, and a high OMV yield. For this reason, purified OMVs were characterized using colorimetric assays such as Picogreen [28] for DNA quantification and a Lowry protein assay to estimate the protein concentration and, thus, the OMV yield [20,29]. The procedure used to separate the analyzed OMVs from the fermentation broth, which entails centrifugation and ultrafiltration steps, is described in Section 2. Comparing the DNA and protein content produced during the fermentation process using the two distinct media (the initial standard medium pre-optimization and the optimized medium), the starting material (SM, hereinafter), which was the material before the ultrafiltration step, was examined first. The results reported in Figure 6 demonstrate that the SM obtained using the optimized medium showed a lower DNA concentration than the SM produced using the standard medium (Figure 6A, first four columns). Additionally, the SM comprising the optimized material had a protein content that was still lower than that of the other SM (Figure 6B, first four columns). By combining these two findings, it was evident that the bacteria grown in the optimized medium caused the release of considerably lower quantities of contaminants, making OMV purification easier and improving its suitability for vaccine production. Additionally, the final OMV product (FP, hereinafter) was characterized to evaluate the impact of the bacterial medium used on the OMV yield and contaminant concentration. Because the DNA concentration in the SM was lower than that of the optimized media, the DNA concentration in the FP was also lower than it was in the FP from the standard media (Figure 6A, second four columns). A reduction in the SM contaminant concentration allowed for a more efficient ultrafiltration step, which resulted in a significantly larger reduction in impurities in the FP. The Lowry test, which is routinely used to assess OMV yield, showed that the OMV concentration in the FP purified from the bacteria grown in the optimized medium was higher than that of the FP from the standard medium, as reported in the second four columns of Figure 6B. This shows that, by using the optimized medium, it is possible to reach a higher OMV yield, which is an essential parameter for a vaccine candidate. In conclusion, growing bacteria on an optimized medium significantly reduces the concentrations of contaminants while also significantly increasing the OMV yield.

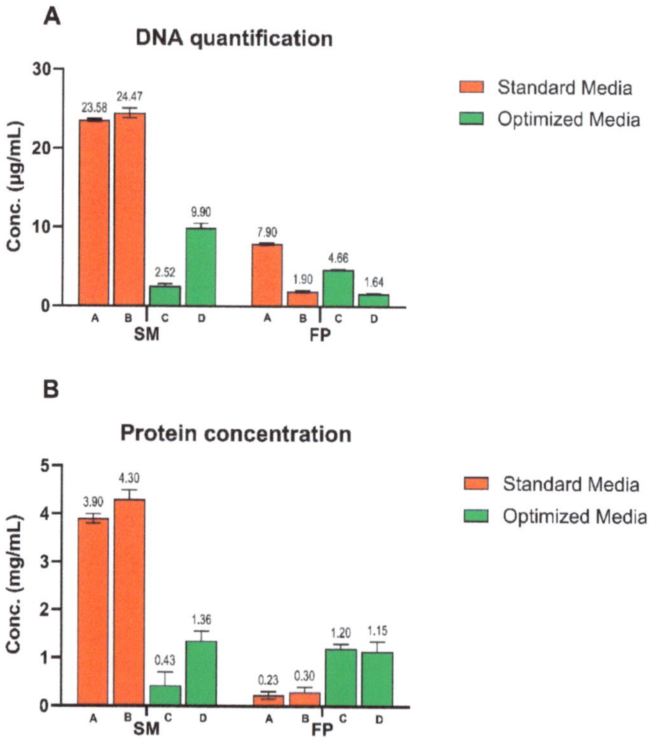

Figure 6. Colorimetric assays for the (**A**) DNA and (**B**) protein quantification of the starting material (SM) and final product (FP). Green bars are related to material produced from fermentation (runs C and D) in the optimized media, while red bars are related to material produced from fermentation in the standard media (runs **A**,**B**).

4. Discussion

In this study, the results show the suitability of the DOE approach in terms of optimizing a standard bacterial culture medium for the growth of a Gram-negative bacterium and consequently improving the yield and quality of the released OMVs. The OMVs need to meet the compendial standards for key quality attributes after the upstream and downstream production phases in terms of the presence of residual impurities, such as soluble proteins and nucleic acids [16,17].

The cultivation of the fastidious microorganism in question, before this optimization work, was carried out in a semi-defined medium with high concentrations of yeast extract (20 g/L) and casamino acids (10 g/L). Both of these complex compounds are particularly important, as they are the main nitrogen sources for bacterial growth and allow the cultivation to reach an average OD_{600nm} of around 10 units. However, the use of high concentrations of yeast extract results in the presence of elevated numbers of soluble proteins and nucleic acids after fermentation, as well as in the final product after the downstream steps.

At first, a preliminary study based on the classical one-factor-at-a-time (OFAT) optimization method was carried out by varying one medium component (factor) at a time while maintaining the other factors at a constant level [30]. The removal, the supplementation, and the replacement (data not reported) of some components (i.e., yeast extract, casamino acids, trace elements, vitamins, and iron citrate) were tested by running several experiments at flask scale and by using benchtop bioreactors. The main outcome of these tests was to determine the condition that ensured the minimal growth of the bacterium, which included the presence of at least one of the two complex components (yeast extract and casamino acids). Additionally, when only the two compounds were employed together, it was possible to achieve moderate growth. The drawback of running these tests in shake flasks and a benchtop bioreactor was the amount of time required to run a large number of experiments and the high costs in terms of the raw materials and work time needed. Furthermore, the OFAT method utilized could not be used to examine the interactions among the medium components of these studies.

To better identify a suitable medium composition, a statistical experimental method approach was employed. By knowing the most critical nutrients (factors) needed for the growth of the microorganism and entering them into the DOE software Sartorius MODDE®13, it was possible to delineate the experimental design space [14]. The execution of the experiments defined using the software was carried out on the microbioreactor system Sartorius Ambr® 15F, which allowed us to run 24 microbioreactors in parallel. Research of the key nutrients and their related concentrations for the optimization of the medium was performed by executing a first DOE based on a design constructed in MODDE®13 using the D-optimal algorithm, which resulted in 24 experiments (see Table S1 in Supplementary Materials). D-optimal designs are computer-generated designs, tailor-made for a specific problem. As detailed in Section 3, seven different factors were examined in the software in this DOE, and 24 conditions were run on the Sartorius Ambr® 15F. A significant number of experiments did not reach the minimal value of OD. Hence, the model was not reliable, and it was decided to explore the region of condition 14 (see Figure 2, Section 3), which showed the best results in terms of OD and Td. Experiment N14 included Mix 1 (composed of arginine, glutamine, histidine, proline, and glutamate), trace elements and vitamins at their minimum concentrations (5 g/L and 10 g/L, respectively), and the iron citrate solution at its maximum concentration (10 g/L). To further optimize the media and determine the correct concentration of each amino acid in Mix 1, a second DOE was set (see more details in Table 4 and Figure 3, Section 3) based on a central composite face-centered (CCF) optimization design with five factors. This allowed us to perform 29 experiments derived from MODDE®13. CCF designs are composed of a full or fractional factorial design and axial points placed on the faces of the factor range sides. As described in Section 3, 5 of the 10 axial points were excluded from the design to bring down the total number of experiments to 24. This second cluster of 24 conditions was tested on the Ambr® 15F. In this case, the results of the contour plots showed that the best medium conditions, resulting in a maximum OD and minimal Td values, included a lower amount of arginine and average concentrations of the other amino acids.

The process was tested on a bench-scale 2 L bioreactor, using the selected medium composition to confirm the results obtained using the Ambr® 15F. The starting material recovered after the fermentations and the final product obtained after the ultra-TFF were analyzed using a Lowry protein assay and Picogreen tests. The results clearly showed (see Figure 6) an improvement in the final optimized media compared with the standard media. The analytical data confirmed the optimization of this process, which led to a relevant improvement in the key quality attributes of the OMVs produced while maintaining a consistent bacterial biomass growth.

The DOE approach, in the context of fermentation medium optimization and the possibility to run all tests in parallel using a multi-microbioreactor system, allowed us to considerably shorten the time compared to the use of shake flasks. Furthermore, the Sartorius Ambr® 15F enabled better control of the physical culture parameters, such as pH and DO, than the shake flasks.

5. Conclusions

Currently, in the research and development of many promising pharmaceutical products like OMV-based vaccines, fermentation medium optimization represents a crucial step in terms of maximizing production yield and meeting key quality attribute standards, hence lowering the final manufacturing costs.

In this work, the suitability of the use of DOE software, such as Sartorius MODDE®13, coupled with a microbioreactor system like the Sartorius Ambr® 15F, is demonstrated in terms of optimizing the fermentation medium for the growth of a Gram-negative bacterium of the Neisseriaceae family. This capacity significantly increases the final product quality of OMV-based vaccines when applied to either the starting material post-fermentation or the final product post-purification.

As demonstrated via a quantitative analysis and compared to a traditional medium employed for the same microorganism, the yield and purity of the OMVs considerably increased. However, additional DOE and experiments are planned to further assess the microorganism cultivation and the associated OMV characteristics. This will ensure that the OMV production process has sufficient robustness to be fully scaled-up in an industrial manufacturing environment for large-scale production while also maintaining its high-quality features.

The DOE approach, combined with a multi-microbioreactor system, allowed us to considerably shorten the production time compared to the use of shake flasks. In fact, with the Sartorius Ambr® 15F, four days of work were needed to perform all the conditions defined with the DoE method. Given that, if all experiment conditions from the two DoEs were to be carried out using 125 mL or 250 mL shake flasks, considering the required time to prepare all the different medium combinations (which, in the Sartorius Ambr® 15F, is performed by the liquid handler autonomously), it would have taken at least two full weeks of work.

It is also important to highlight the fact that the DOE approach employed in this work contributed to our company's sustainability efforts by reducing resource consumption and waste generation.

Supplementary Materials: The following supporting information can be downloaded at https://www.mdpi.com/article/10.3390/fermentation9121002/s1, Table S1: Worksheet of experiment settings together with the results of the experiments of the first DOE; Table S2: ANOVA table of the two responses of the first DoE; Table S3: ANOVA table of the two responses of the second DoE.

Author Contributions: Conceptualization, A.B., K.M., E.J. and V.D.C.; methodology, A.B., K.M. and E.J.; software, K.M. and E.J.; validation, A.B. and K.M.; formal analysis, K.M. and E.J.; investigation, A.B., G.S., E.R. and P.P.; resources, V.D.C.; data curation, A.B. and K.M.; writing—original draft preparation, A.B., K.M., G.S. and P.P.; writing—review and editing, A.B.; visualization, A.B. and K.M.; supervision, V.D.C. and E.J.; project administration, A.B.; funding acquisition, V.D.C. All authors have read and agreed to the published version of the manuscript.

Funding: This research was funded by EMF EU Malaria Fund Berlin GmbH & Co. KG.

Institutional Review Board Statement: Not applicable.

Informed Consent Statement: Not applicable.

Data Availability Statement: Data are contained within this article or Supplementary Materials.

Acknowledgments: The authors would like to thank Corso Carboncini for his technical assistance in equipment and software installation.

Conflicts of Interest: The authors declare no conflict of interest. The work reported in this scientific publication was conducted by AchilleS Vaccines Srl in collaboration with Sartorius Stedim Data Analytics AB and Sartorius Stedim UK Ltd., which participated in this study by providing support in designing the experiments and analyzing the results using the DOE software Sartorius MODDE®13. The interaction with the two external Sartorius companies did not compromise the research's impartiality, and the authors upheld the principles of scientific independence. We affirm that there are no commercial or financial conflicts of interest associated with the reported research or its findings.

Abbreviations

AM	analysis module
Ambr®	advanced microscale bioreactor
CCF	central composite face
CS	culture station
DNA	deoxyribonucleic acid
DOE	design of experiment
DO	dissolved oxygen
FP	final product
HTPD	high-throughput process development
LPS	lipopolysaccharide
MODDE	modeling and design
MWCO	molecular weight cut-off
OD600nm	optical density at 600nm
OFAT	one factor at a time
OMVs	outer membrane vesicles
PPG	polypropylene glycol
QbD	quality by design
RCB	research cell bank
RNA	ribonucleic acid
rpm	rotation per minute
SM	starting material
STR	stirred tank bioreactor
Td	doubling time
TFF	tangential flow filtration
vvm	vessel volume per minute

References

1. Wales, R.; Lewis, G. Novel Automated Micro-Scale Bioreactor Technology: A Qualitative and Quantitative Mimic for Early Process Development. *BioProcess. J.* **2010**, *9*, 22–25. [CrossRef]
2. Delouvroy, F.; Le Reverend, G.; Fessler, B.; Mathy, G.; Harmsen, M.; Kochanowski, N.; Malphettes, L. Evaluation of the advanced micro-scale bioreactor (ambrTM) as a highthroughput tool for cell culture process development. *BMC Proc.* **2013**, *7*, P73. [CrossRef]
3. Rafiq, Q.A.; Hanga, M.P.; Heathman, T.R.J.; Coopman, K.; Nienow, A.W.; Williams, D.J.; Hewitt, C.J. Process development of human multipotent stromal cell microcarrier culture using an automated high-throughput microbioreactor. *Biotechnol. Bioeng.* **2017**, *114*, 2253–2266. [CrossRef]
4. Vázquez, M.E.; Mesías, A.C.; Acuña, L.; Spangler, J.; Zabala, B.; Parodi, C.; Thakur, M.; Oh, E.; Walper, S.A.; Brandán, C.P. Exploring the performance of *Escherichia coli* outer membrane vesicles as a tool for vaccine development against Chagas disease. *Mem. Inst. Oswaldo Cruz* **2023**, *118*, e220263. [CrossRef] [PubMed]

5. Kulp, A.; Kuehn, M.J. Biological functions and biogenesis of secreted bacterial outer membrane vesicles. *Annu. Rev. Microbiol.* **2010**, *64*, 163–184. [CrossRef] [PubMed]
6. van der Pol, L.; Stork, M.; van der Ley, P. Outer membrane vesicles as platform vaccine technology. *Biotechnol. J.* **2015**, *10*, 1689–1706. [CrossRef] [PubMed]
7. Balhuizen, M.D.; Veldhuizen, E.J.A.; Haagsman, H.P. Outer membrane vesicle induction and isolation for vaccine development. *Front. Microbiol.* **2021**, *12*, 629090. [CrossRef] [PubMed]
8. Kashyap, D.; Panda, M.; Baral, B.; Varshney, N.R.S.; Bhandari, V.; Parmar, H.S.; Prasad, A.; Jha, H.C. Outer membrane vesicles: An emerging vaccine platform. *Vaccines* **2022**, *10*, 1578. [CrossRef] [PubMed]
9. Wang, S.; Guo, J.; Bai, Y.; Sun, C.; Wu, Y.; Liu, Z.; Liu, X.; Wang, Y.; Wang, Z.; Zhang, Y.; et al. Bacterial outer membrane vesicles as a candidate tumor vaccine platform. *Front. Immunol.* **2022**, *13*, 987419. [CrossRef]
10. Zhang, G.; Mills, D.A.; Block, D.E. Development of chemically defined media supporting high-cell-density growth of lactococci, enterococci, and streptococci. *Appl. Environ. Microbiol.* **2009**, *75*, 1080–1087. [CrossRef]
11. Rameez, S.; Mostafa, S.S.; Miller, C.; Shukla, A.A. High-throughput miniaturized bioreactors for cell culture process development: Reproducibility, scalability, and control. *Biotechnol. Prog.* **2014**, *30*, 718–727. [CrossRef] [PubMed]
12. Moses, S.; Manahan, M.; Ambrogelly, A.; Ling, W.L.W. Assessment of AMBRTM as a model for high-throughput cell culture process development strategy. *Adv. Biosci. Biotechnol.* **2012**, *3*, 918–927. [CrossRef]
13. Fink, M.; Cserjan-Puschmann, M.; Reinisch, D.; Striedner, G. High-throughput microbioreactor provides a capable tool for early stage bioprocess development. *Sci. Rep.* **2021**, *11*, 2056. [CrossRef] [PubMed]
14. Eriksson, L.; Johansson, E.; Kettaneh-Wold, N.; Wikström, C.; Wold, S. *Preface—Design of Experiments—Principles and Applications*, 3rd ed.; Umetrics: Umea, Sweden, 2008; pp. 1–6. Available online: www.umetrics.com (accessed on 24 July 2023).
15. Velez-Suberbie, M.L.; Betts, J.P.J.; Walker, K.L.; Robinson, C.; Zoro, B.; Keshavarz-Moore, E. High throughput automated microbial bioreactor system used for clone selection and rapid scale-down process optimization. *Biotechnol. Prog.* **2018**, *34*, 58–68. [CrossRef] [PubMed]
16. Chutkan, H.; Macdonald, I.; Manning, A.; Kuehn, M.J. Quantitative and qualitative preparations of bacterial outer membrane vesicles. *Methods Mol. Biol.* **2013**, *966*, 259–272. [CrossRef] [PubMed]
17. Klimentová, J.; Stulík, J. Methods of isolation and purification of outer membrane vesicles from gram-negative bacteria. *Microbiol. Res.* **2015**, *170*, 1–9. [CrossRef] [PubMed]
18. Gerritzen, M.J.H.; Salverda, M.L.M.; Martens, D.E.; Wijffels, R.H.; Stork, M. Spontaneously released *Neisseria meningitidis* outer membrane vesicles as vaccine platform: Production and purification. *Vaccine* **2019**, *37*, 6978–6986. [CrossRef] [PubMed]
19. Lowry, O.H.; Rosebrough, N.J.; Farr, A.L.; Randall, R.J. Protein measurement with the Folin phenol reagent. *J. Biol. Chem.* **1951**, *193*, 265–275. [CrossRef] [PubMed]
20. Bauman, S.J.; Kuehn, M.J. Purification of outer membrane vesicles from *Pseudomonas aeruginosa* and their activation of an IL-8 response. *Microbes Infect.* **2006**, *8*, 2400–2408. [CrossRef]
21. Grande, R.; Di Marcantonio, M.C.; Robuffo, I.; Pompilio, A.; Celia, C.; Di Marzio, L.; Paolino, D.; Codagnone, M.; Muraro, R.; Stoodley, P.; et al. *Helicobacter pylori* ATCC 43629/NCTC 11639 Outer Membrane Vesicles (OMVs) from Biofilm and Planktonic Phase Associated with Extracellular DNA (eDNA). *Front. Microbiol.* **2015**, *6*, 1369. [CrossRef]
22. Akashi, H.; Gojobori, T. Metabolic efficiency and amino acid composition in the proteomes of *Escherichia coli* and *Bacillus subtilis*. *Proc. Natl. Acad. Sci. USA* **2002**, *99*, 3695–3700. [CrossRef]
23. Sparviero, S.; Dicke, M.D.; Rosch, T.M.; Castillo, T.; Salgado-Lugo, H.; Galindo, E.; Peña, C.; Büchs, J. Yeast extracts from different manufacturers and supplementation of amino acids and micro elements reveal a remarkable impact on alginate production by *A. vinelandii* ATCC9046. *Microb. Cell Fact.* **2023**, *22*, 99. [CrossRef]
24. Müller, J.; Beckers, M.; Mußmann, N.; Bongaerts, J.; Büchs, J. Elucidation of auxotrophic deficiencies of *Bacillus pumilus* DSM 18097 to develop a defined minimal medium. *Microb. Cell Fact.* **2018**, *17*, 106. [CrossRef] [PubMed]
25. Becton-Dickinson. *BD Bionutrients Technical Manual Advanced Bioprocessing*, 3rd ed.; BD: Sparks, MD, USA, 2006; Volume 52, pp. 28–29.
26. Yeoman, K.; Fahnert, B.; Lea-Smith, D.; Clarke, T. *Microbial Biotechnology*, 1st ed.; Oxford Biology Primers, Oxford University: Oxford, UK, 2021; p. 272.
27. Belsley, D.A.; Kuh, E.; Welsch, R.E. The Condition Number. In *Regression Diagnostics: Identifying Influential Data and Sources of Collinearity*, 1st ed.; John Wiley & Sons: New York, NY, USA, 1980; pp. 100–104.
28. Bitto, N.J.; Chapman, R.; Pidot, S.; Costin, A.; Lo, C.; Choi, J.; D'Cruze, T.; Reynolds, E.C.; Dashper, S.G.; Turnbull, L.; et al. Bacterial membrane vesicles transport their DNA cargo into host cells. *Sci. Rep.* **2017**, *7*, 7072. [CrossRef]
29. Shi, R.; Dong, Z.; Ma, C.; Wu, R.; Lv, R.; Liu, S.; Ren, Y.; Liu, Z.; van der Mei, H.C.; Busscher, H.J.; et al. High-Yield, Magnetic Harvesting of Extracellular Outer-Membrane Vesicles from *Escherichia coli*. *Small* **2022**, *18*, 2204350. [CrossRef] [PubMed]
30. Czitrom, V. One-Factor-at-a-Time versus Designed Experiments. *Am. Stat.* **1999**, *53*, 126–131. [CrossRef]

fermentation

MDPI

Article

Monitoring β-Fructofuranosidase Activity through *Kluyveromyces marxianus* in Bioreactor Using a Lab-Made Sequential Analysis System

Edwin J. Barbosa-Hernández [1], Jorge E. Pliego-Sandoval [2], Anne Gschaedler-Mathis [1], Javier Arrizon-Gaviño [1], Alejandro Arana-Sánchez [3], Ricardo Femat [4] and Enrique J. Herrera-López [1,*,†]

1 Biotecnología Industrial, Centro de Investigación y Asistencia en Tecnología y Diseño del Estado de Jalisco A.C., Camino Arenero 1227, Col. El Bajío del Arenal., Zapopan C.P. 45019, Mexico; edbarbosa_al@ciatej.edu.mx (E.J.B.-H.); agschaedler@ciatej.mx (A.G.-M.); jparrizon@ciatej.mx (J.A.-G.)

2 Centro Universitario del Sur, Departamento de Ciencias Computacionales e Innovación Tecnológica, Universidad de Guadalajara, Av. Enrique Arreola Silva No. 883, Cólon., Cd. Guzman C.P. 49000, Mexico; jorge.pliego@cusur.udg.mx

3 Departamento de Procesos Tecnológicos e Industriales, Instituto Tecnológico y de Estudios Superiores de Occidente, Anillo Perif. Sur Manuel Gómez Morín 8585., San Pedro Tlaquepaque C.P. 45604, Mexico; aarana@iteso.mx

4 División de Control y Sistemas Dinámicos, Instituto Potosino de Investigación Científica y Tecnológica, Camino a la Presa San José 2055, Lomas 4a Sección., San Luis Potosi C.P. 78216, Mexico; rfemat@ipicyt.edu.mx

* Correspondence: eherrera@ciatej.mx

† Laboratorio para la Innovación en Bioelectrónica e Inteligencia Artificial, LINBIA®, Biotecnología Industrial, Centro de Investigación y Asistencia en Tecnología y Diseño del Estado de Jalisco A.C., Camino Arenero 1227, Col. El Bajío del Arenal, Zapopan C.P. 45019, Jalisco, Mexico

Citation: Barbosa-Hernández, E.J.; Pliego-Sandoval, J.E.; Gschaedler-Mathis, A.; Arrizon-Gaviño, J.; Arana-Sánchez, A.; Femat, R.; Herrera-López, E.J. Monitoring β-Fructofuranosidase Activity through *Kluyveromyces marxianus* in Bioreactor Using a Lab-Made Sequential Analysis System. *Fermentation* **2023**, *9*, 963. https://doi.org/10.3390/fermentation9110963

Academic Editor: Ricardo Aguilar-López

Received: 16 October 2023
Revised: 30 October 2023
Accepted: 31 October 2023
Published: 10 November 2023

Abstract: The yeast *Kluyveromyces marxianus* has shown the potential to produce β-fructofuranosidases, which are enzymes capable of hydrolyzing β-fructofuranosides links of fructans to obtain fructooligosaccharides. The thriving market for fructose syrup and the quality standards imposed by food and pharmaceutical industries have generated an increased search for improved, monitored, and controlled production processes. Monitoring β-fructofuranosidase activity in a bioprocess requires the use of adequate sensors and the processing of information using efficient software algorithms; nevertheless, currently, such a sensor does not exist for this purpose. In this contribution, a sequential injection analysis system (SIA) developed in our laboratory was adapted to monitor at-line β-fructofuranosidase activity produced by the yeast *K. marxianus*. Samples were taken out automatically from the bioreactor and analyzed using 3,5-dinitrosalicylic (DNS). An algorithm was designed to operate the overall components of the lab-made SIA system. The enzymatic activity error obtained with the automatic SIA compared to the off-line laboratory determinations varied from 0.07% at high enzyme concentrations to 20.39% at low β-fructofuranosidase activity. Further development is required to improve the performance of the lab-made SIA system; nevertheless, such a device must be considered as a potential method for monitoring β-fructofuranosidase activity in real time.

Keywords: *Kluyveromyces marxianus*; β-fructofuranosidase; monitoring; at-line activity; sequential injection analysis; lab-made system

1. Introduction

Kluyveromyces marxianus, a non-*Saccharomyces* thermotolerant yeast, has the potential to grow in a wide variety of substrates, at high specific growth rates, and displays a significant metabolite secretory capacity [1,2]. This yeast has been widely used for the production of aromatic compounds in ethanol fermentation [3], in simultaneous saccharification and fermentation processes [4], as a biocatalyst of renewable chemicals and for lignocellulosic ethanol production [5,6], and other applications in the food and biotechnology industry [7–10]. *K. marxianus* can assimilate inulin [11,12], and *Agave tequilana* fructans

(ATF) as substrate [4,13], and has the secretory capacity to synthetize β-fructofuranosidases. The fructooligosaccharides (FOS) used in producing fructose syrup are obtained from the hydrolysis of fructans. Interest in inulin has increased worldwide due to the growing demand for dietary supplements enriched with prebiotics and the synthesis of fructose as a sweetener [12,14]. Agave fructans are relevant for the production of tequila, which today is one of the most popular alcoholic beverages in the world [15]. Therefore, from an economic point of view, FOS production is relevant since the estimated market will be worth USD 3.52 billion by 2024 [16].

The most common method to determine β-fructofuranosidase activity at the laboratory is through using 3,5-dinitrosalicylic reducing sugars (DNS) [17]. Nevertheless, the standard DNS assay is carried out in a manual way, which is time-consuming, monotonous, and generates considerable waste. In the context of this issue, automatic analyzers such as flow injection analysis systems (FIAs) have been proposed, which support routine determinations that demand frequent sampling [18]; another solution is the use of sequential injection analysis systems (SIAs), which allow discontinuous or intermittent modes of operation reducing reagents and sample consumption [19]. DNS methodologies have been applied in diverse flow systems to detect glucose content in soft drinks and wines [20] to detect L-lactate during lactic acid fermentation [21], for monitoring and controlling a lactose production process [22], and for cell culture applications [23]. SIA systems have been applied in bioprocesses to evaluate enzyme activity such as proteases [24], phospholipases [25], horseradish peroxidase [26,27], glucose oxidases [28], and lipases and esterase [29], among other applications [30,31].

Regarding β-fructofuranosidase activity, this enzyme has been detected by an SIA system coupled to Fast Fourier infrared spectroscopy [32,33]. The SIA system was used to prepare a standard mixture of products where it was possible to determine the enzyme activities of two enzymes acting on two different substrates using the FTIR, although the authors stated that care had to be taken since the reactions were monitored off-line. An electrochemical sensor based on the oxidation of the carbonyl group with ferricyanide ions in a rotating disk electrode was used to detect agave tequila fructans. The method was able to detect concentrations of oligosaccharides as low as 0.71 mM [34]; however, this sensor detected FOS rather than β-fructofuranosidase activity.

FIA and SIA systems can be acquired from different commercial suppliers; however, these devices can be quite expensive. As an alternative, researchers can design and build their own SIA systems. This approach requires one to design the system, purchase and integrate the components, and write the control algorithm. Diverse algorithms to control flow injection systems have been reported in the scientific literature. An FIA system to determine lactose was designed in [22]. The system was controlled with commercial software called CAFCA™ (Computer Assisted Flow Control and Analysis). This software is available as a professional version (ANASYS, Hannover, Germany), and was designed in Borland Pascal 7.0; the system runs under the MS-DOS environment [35]. A methodology to measure glucose and lactate for immobilized cells in FIA systems by means of C++ was designed in [21]; the device used a manufactured electrode with an amperometric detector. An algorithm in Python was developed to control an injection valve Cavro XP3000 and a pH meter [36]; however, these types of systems are not suitable for hardware reconfiguration. The software LabVIEW™ (Austin, TX, USA) also has been used to control the SIA systems, where its operation was validated determining morphine [37], hydroquinone in plant tissue culture media [38,39], thiamine, and 1,10-phenanthroline [40].

Monitoring enzymes in a bioprocess requires the use of specialized instrumentation to measure the desired bioproduct accurately and simultaneously accomplish the strict high-quality standards imposed by the food and pharmaceutical industries. The search for specialized sensors to monitor enzyme activity in a bioprocess is currently an open field of research. To our best knowledge, SIA systems have not been used to detect β-fructofuranosidase from at-line measurements taken out from the bioreactor. DNS could be considered as a potential method to determine β-fructofuranosidase activity using a SIA system. However, this technique is not easy to implement in such devices since it requires a complex process that involves sampling, combining substrate with reactants, homogenizing, heating, cooling, reading the mixture at a specific wavelength, and correlating the spectrum with the enzyme activity [28,41]. In addition, at high enzyme concentrations, the sample must be diluted. All these activities must be performed in an accurate and sequential reproducible way, that needs a computer algorithm to strictly control the routines, execution times, flow management, signal acquisition, and data processing [30].

In this contribution, a Lab-made SIA system previously designed in our laboratory [29] was modified and adapted to determine at-line β-fructofuranosidase activity. The SIA system now has the capability to cool, stir, and perform dilutions to samples automatically taken from the bioreactor; this way, it was possible to determine at-line enzymatic activity by means of the reducing sugar (DNS) method. In addition, we emphasize the LabVIEW™ algorithm designed to operate the components of the lab-made SIA system and describe the graphical user interface. The performance of the lab-made SIA system was evaluated by monitoring at-line β-fructofuranosidase activity produced by the yeast *K. marxianus* in an ongoing bioprocess. The β-fructofuranosidase activity determined during at-line measurements was validated through comparing the samples to regular laboratory measurements.

2. Materials and Methods

2.1. Microorganism

The yeast *Kluyveromyces marxianus* SLP1 belongs to the microorganism collection of the Centro de Investigation y Asistencia en Tecnología y Diseño del Estado de Jalisco; A.C was used as a case study for β-fructofuranosidase production. The strain was stored at 4 °C and subcultured every month in Petri dishes with YPDA (g/L): 20 yeast extract, 10 glucose, 20 bactopeptone, and 20 agar for maintenance.

2.2. Culture Media

The strain was grown in mineral medium (DMM) containing (g/L): 20.0 glucose, 3.0 KH_2PO_4, 3.0 $(NH_2)SO_4$, 1.5 $Na_2HPO_4{\cdot}2H_2O$, 1.0 glutamate, 0.4122 $MgCl_2{\cdot}6H_2O$, 0.0192 $ZnCl_2$, 0.0174 $CaCl_2$, 0.0117 $FeCl_2{\cdot}4H_2O$, 0.0044 $MnCl_2{\cdot}4H_2O$, 0.0006 $CuCl_2{\cdot}2H_2O$, 0.0005 $CoCl_2{\cdot}6H_2O$, 0.0004 $(NH_4)_6Mo_7O_{24}{\cdot}4H_2O$, 0.003 H_3BO_3. Vitamin solution (g/L): 0.000012 biotin, 0.005 thiamine HCl, 0.005 pyridoxine, 0.005 pantothenic acid, 0.005 nicotinic acid, 0.125 myoinositol, and 0.001 4-aminobenzoic acid.

2.3. Inoculums Conditions

Two sterile 500 mL flasks with 100 mL of YPD (YPDA without agar) medium were inoculated with two CFUs of the *K. marxianus* SLP1 obtained from properly conserved Petri dishes. The flasks were placed in a New Brunswick® Innova 44 rotary orbital for 12 h, with a controlled temperature of 30 °C and an agitation speed of 250 rpm. Afterward, two 500 mL flasks with 100 mL of DMM were inoculated with 1 mL of the previous culture for 10 h at the same operational conditions. After incubation, the flasks had approximately 4×10^8 cells/mL.

2.4. Bioreactor Conditions

Yeast propagation was carried out in a 3 L Applikon bioreactor, prepared with 1 L of DMM. The bioreactor was sterilized at 121 °C for 15 min. The following physical variables were controlled: pH 4.5, temperature 34 °C, and agitation were varied automatically depending on the dissolved oxygen saturation (from 500 to 800 rpm). The aeration was kept constant during the kinetics at 1.6 L/min (the air was supplied by a fish tank compressor and filtered by a 0.22 mm membrane for sterilization). The initial substrate concentration was 10 g/L. The fed-batch culture began when the substrate was depleted; afterwards, the bioreactor was fed at a constant flow of 70 mL/h with a carbon source concentration of 100 g/L of glucose.

2.5. Biomass Determination

Biomass was determined by dry weight. From each sampling, 5 mL was centrifuged for 15 min at 5554× g. Pellets were washed twice with 5 mL of distilled water and centrifuged under the above conditions. Subsequently, pellets were dried at 50 °C for 24 h and then placed in a desiccator until constant weight was attained.

2.6. Reducing Sugars Determination

The reducing sugar concentration in the medium was determined using 3,5-dinitrosalicylic acid reagent [17].

2.7. Off β-Fructofuranosidase Activity Determination at the Laboratory

β-fructofuranosidase enzymatic activity was determined in our laboratory using the reducing sugar method described in [42]. A sample taken out manually from a bioreactor was centrifuged to separate enzyme extract from the cells. A measure of 50 µL of supernatant was put in a microtube with 50 µL of substrate (100 mM sodium acetate + 100 mM acetic acid + 1 g/L sucrose, pH 5.0), and the sample was homogenized. The mixture was incubated at 50 °C for 15 min in a Thermo-Shaker® MS-incubator 100, the reaction was stopped by placing the samples in ice for 2 min. A measure of 100 µL of the DNS reagent was added to the samples and homogenized, in addition, 50 µL of enzyme extract was added to the blank. The mixture was placed in a water bath at 95 °C for 5 min, then put on ice for 5 min to stop the reaction. A measure of 800 µL of distilled water was added to the microtubes and then were homogenized. A measure of 200 µL of the described mixture was placed in the well of a microplate to be read at 540 nm in an ×Mark® microplate spectrophotometer from Bio-Rad® (Hercules, CA, USA) with endpoint determination. The sample was analyzed in triplicate and compared against a calibration curve of reducing sugars. In each experiment, a new calibration curve was constructed with an adjustment > 0.98. Equation (1) was used to calculate the enzymatic activity units:

$$Activity = \frac{U}{mL} = \frac{\mu mol}{min \cdot mL} = \frac{F \cdot V_{rx}}{M_w \cdot t \cdot V_e} \quad (1)$$

where F = glucose concentration; V_{rx} = reaction volume; M_w = glucose molecular weight; t = incubation time; V_e = enzymatic extracted volume.

2.8. General Description of the Lab-Made SIA System

The hardware components integrating the lab-made SIA system [29] are a mini peristaltic pump S2 Laboratory, Watson-Marlow, (Wilmington, MA, USA), a holding coil, two interconnected multiposition valves of ten ports C25-3180EMH-FL, Valco (Houston, TX, USA). A reaction coil FT-COIL90 with a heating system. A spectrophotometric detector VIS-NIR USB4000 of Ocean Optics (Dunedin, FL, USA), with source light Tungsten-Halogen HL-2000-LL, and a flow cell (FIA-Z-SMA-SS) with 10 mm path length of stainless steel. An algorithm was designed in LabVIEW™ 11.0 to control the SIA system, installed in an assembled personal computer (W7 home premium, 2009 processor AMD Athlom™ X4 640 processor 3.00 GHz, 8 Gb Ram), as can be seen in Figure 1. The software is described in detail in the results section.

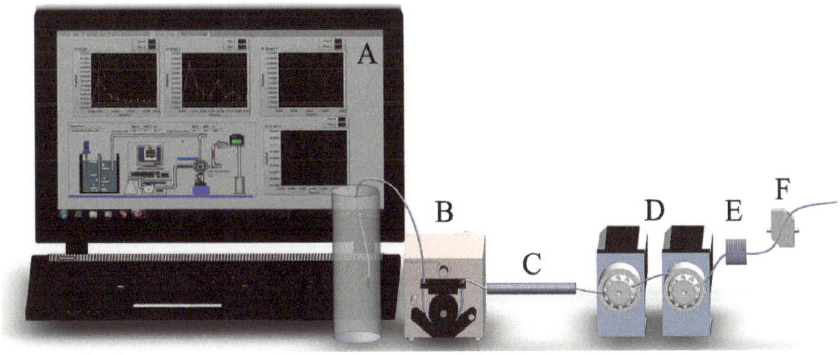

Figure 1. Main components of the SIA System with UV/visible spectrophotometer; (**A**) graphical user interface, (**B**) peristaltic pump, (**C**) holding coil, (**D**) multiposition valves, (**E**) reaction coil, and (**F**) flow cell.

2.9. β-Fructofuranosidase Activity Set Up in the Lab-Made SIA System

Figure 2 shows the configuration and description of the components of the SIA system that were used during the implementation of the methodology to monitor on-line *β*-fructofuranosidase activity.

- Free cell samples supernatant (m) was taken out automatically from the bioreactor at selected times and pumped into the holding chamber of the SIA system.
- An automatic dilution with the carrier water (a) was performed depending on the time of the culture and it was homogenized in the mixing chamber.
- The diluted sample (ds) was mixed in equal parts with the substrate (s) by suction cycles ds/s/ds/s.
- The mixture was injected into the incubation chamber, where it was maintained at 50 ± 2 °C for 15 min.
- The incubated sample (mi) was sent to the retention chamber and mixed with the reagent DNS (r) in suction cycles mi/r/mi/r. Due to the corrosive nature of phenol, this compound was not used in the preparation of the DNS reagent.
- The mixture was injected into the heating chamber, where it was maintained at 93 ± 2 °C for 5 min.
- Afterwards, the mixture was injected into the cooling chamber submerged on ice where it was kept for 1 min.
- The mixture was automatically diluted in a 1:4 ratio with a carrier and homogenized in the mixing chamber.
- Finally, the sample was injected into the detector where it was read at 540 nm. To eliminate any trace of the previous sample, a cleaning cycle was carried out after each analysis. All these hardware sequences were controlled with an algorithm designed with the software LabVIEW™. One second of operation of injection/suction is equivalent to a flow rate of 20 µL/s, with a standard deviation of 6%.

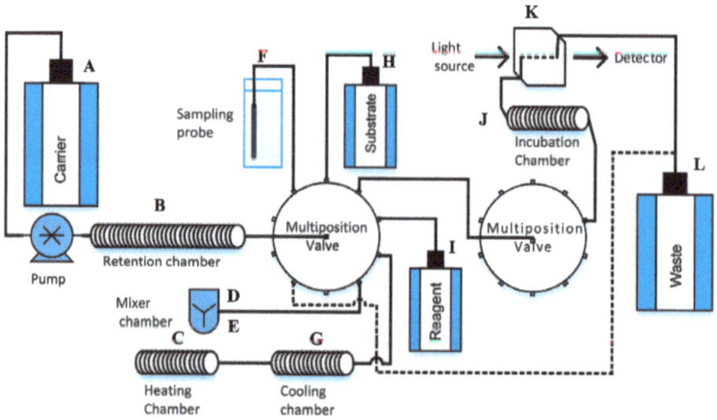

Figure 2. Specific components of the lab-made model used to determine $\beta-$fructofuranosidase activity. (**A**) Carrier, (**B**) retention chamber, (**C**) heating chamber, (**D**,**E**) mixer chambers, (**F**) bioreactor and sampling probe, (**G**) cooling chamber, (**H**) substrate, (**I**) reagents, (**J**) incubation chamber, (**K**) spectrophotometric detector, and (**L**) waste container.

2.10. Calculating β-Fructofuranosidase Activity

Following the steps described in Figure 2, a spectrum is obtained. The resulting area under the curve is directly proportional to the β-fructofuranosidase activity. The spectrum data were exported to the software Matlab™ 2015, where it was analyzed with the command "trapz", which returns the approximate integral of a function through the trapezoidal method. The calculated area was compared with a calibration curve performed in the SIA system. The units of β-fructofuranosidase activity were calculated with Equation (1).

2.11. Validation and Statistical Comparison

At-line β-fructofuranosidase measurements were compared with off-line microplate determinations, and their mean values were analyzed to find statistical differences.

3. Results

3.1. Lab-Made SIA Hardware Modifications to Determine β-Fructofuranosidase

To set up the DNS β-fructofuranosidase activity methodology, the lab-made SIA system reported in [29] was modified to include a cooler chamber to stop the chemical reaction produced by the DNS. To homogenize the samples, a mixer chamber controlled with an electronic Arduino UNO card was also integrated into the SIA system. On the other hand, the flow restrictor FR-902 was eliminated from the device to allow the return of the sample. The software was modified to include automatic dilution options.

3.2. Virtual Code to Control the Lab-SIA System

The software LabVIEW™ is known as a virtual instrument (VI), in which code is created using the graphical programming language G [43]. In LabVIEW, the programmer does not need to develop typing code; instead, the VI is used to create virtual code from interconnecting diverse functional icons. Due to its versatility and functionality, it was decided to use this software to control the SIA system. The algorithm designed in LabVIEW™ is composed of a front panel and the block diagram window. The front panel comprises all the information needed by the user to configure, enable, and operate the SIA system to determine enzyme activity. It also shows the status of the variables, tables, graphs, and indicators. The block diagram window contains the code to control the hardware components of the lab-made SIA system, such as the peristaltic pump, the multiposition valves, and the USB4000 spectrophotometer, which are briefly described below.

3.3. Virtual Code to Control the Peristaltic Pump

The peristaltic pump carries sample/reagents along the different components of the SIA system. The peristaltic pump was controlled enabling/disabling the pins 4/7 of the RS-232 port. The RTS/DTR submenu software controls the request to send (RTS) and data terminal ready (DTR) signals for the RS-232 serial communications interface for hardware handshaking. The STR/DTR signals allowed the interface to operate in a continuous way, as well as to automatically execute suction/injection of the sample/reagents and carrier, all functions were synchronized time-based. The functional block diagram to control the peristaltic pump is shown in Figure 3A.

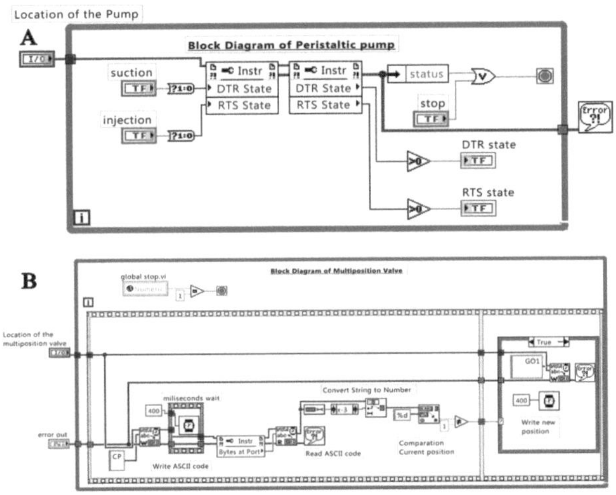

Figure 3. Virtual code diagram to control (**A**) the peristaltic pump and (**B**) the multiposition valves.

3.4. Virtual Code to Control the Multiposition Valves

The multiposition valve allows the user to select a specific port that may be connected via tubing to reagents, buffers, or other substances to be transported by the peristaltic pump to a specific component of the SIA system, i.e., holding coil or to the detector. The multiposition valves were controlled by means of an ASCII communication protocol used through pins 2–3 of the RS-232 port. The serial port requests the current position of the valve using ASCII code. The system transforms data from a string type to a numeric value to make a comparison between the current position and the location requested by the user. The block diagram to control the multiposition valves is shown in Figure 3B.

3.5. Spectrophotometer Control

To evaluate the analyte concentration in the SIA system the USB4000 spectrophotometer read the processed sample within the detector flow cell. This module was redesigned from the existing virtual instrument based in [44]. A Savitzky–Golay filter was implemented along the sampling periods, with wavelength filter selectors to smooth the signal obtained from the spectrophotometer. The filters were configured to be used at two different wavelengths. The designed algorithm allows the activation and deactivation at precise times of the spectrophotometer. Sampling intervals will be calculated according to the time interval required in each methodology. After the completion of each experiment, the information collected through the software was sent to an Excel™ spreadsheet (Microsoft 2016, Redmond, Washington, DC, USA).

3.6. General Virtual Code to Control the SIA System

The virtual code to control the overall components of the SIA system is integrated into a general block diagram window that is divided into six main parts, Figure 4. The "flat sequence" included in Figure 4A resets all the entries to zero, including graphs, synchronization times, tables, graphical and on/off indicators, and run, stop, and pause buttons. A "global stop" button synchronized with the SIA controller was included in all the sections of the control panels of the SIA system, Figure 4B. The block diagram of Figure 4C contains the addresses of the ports USB, and RS-232. In addition, it accounts for the initial settings of the system such as operating times, sequences for turning on and off the device, selection of wavelengths, enable/disable of automatic dilutions, and all the information is stored in proper arrays. Figure 4D, is related to the general software to manipulate the peristaltic pump, the multiposition valves, and the spectrophotometer USB4000 virtual instrument. This section was based on two main sub-virtual instruments: "VI of cut" and "VI of order". The first one considers the inclusion of a general matrix table displaying the sequences or steps to operate the peripherals. In addition, this VI sets the required time that a peristaltic pump must be enabled. The versatility of the software allows to change the order of the sequence within the action line. In Figure 4E, 21 sequences are contained as a case structure. This section allows the user to select a specific port and its configuration, i.e., the peristaltic pump selection actions such as suction, injection, stop, or execute a specific action with the multiposition valve or obtain a read from the spectrophotometer USB4000. To control the movement of a sample through the SIA components the VI located in Figure 4F is used, which is independently configured. Finally, Figure 4G closes the ports and stores all the information in a text document. All the virtual algorithms described previously need to be operated in a perfect synchronization sequence to carry out robust determination of the analyte.

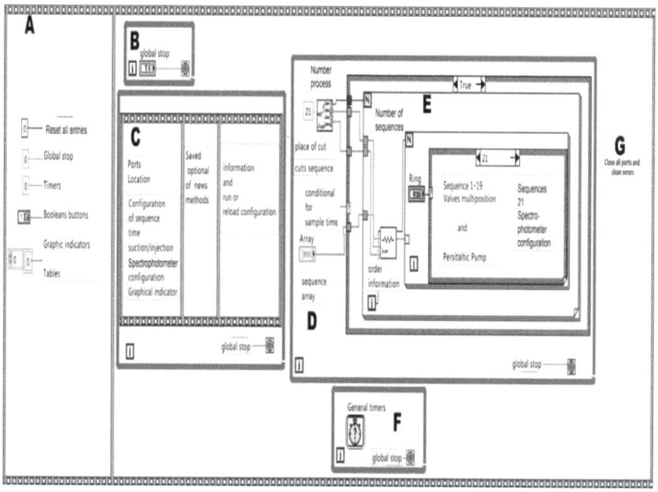

Figure 4. Virtual code to control the overall components of the SIA system. (**A**) initialization, (**B**) global stop, (**C**) USB port configuration, (**D**) control of the actuators, (**E**) sequences to activate components, (**F**) control of the sample, and (**G**) saving data.

3.7. Description of the User Interface That Controls the Lab-Made SIA System

To configure the operation of the hardware components of the SIA system a friendly user interface was designed in the front panel, which contained four different screens denoted as: control panel, setting panel, experiment status panel, and overall monitoring panel (see Figure 5). In the control panel Figure 5A, the user configures the components of the SIA system to be used in the determination of the enzyme. It is important that the selected methodology is set up by the technician who commonly determines the enzymatic activity off-line at the laboratory, and consequently understands the technique. This window allows the user to set the appropriate sequence for the sample and reactants to be transported from a specific location to a selected position. For this purpose, the diverse inputs and outputs of the multiposition valve can be selected, enabled, and associated with the operation of a peristaltic pump. The spectrophotometer wavelengths can also be set in the control window, as well as the conversion factor between absorbance and the variable of interest that is displayed in this panel. The duration of the experiment and the sampling time can be set in this window. There is a section in the control panel in which a suitable dilution could be planned for the experiments.

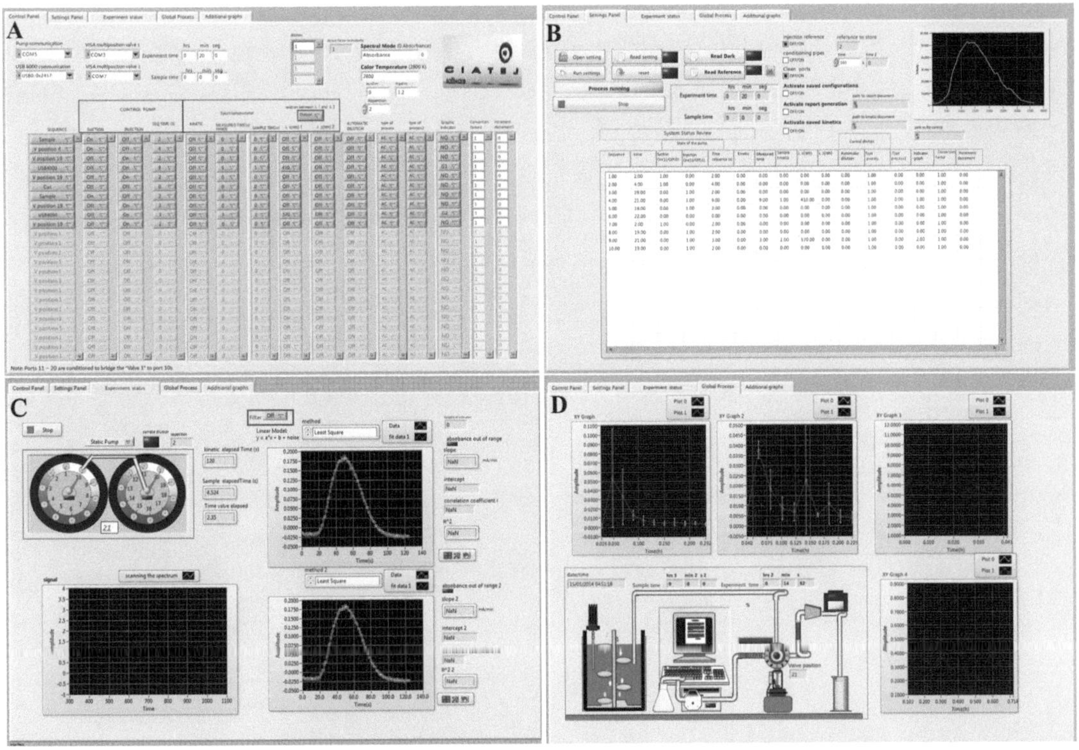

Figure 5. Front panel of the graphical user interface: (**A**) control panel, (**B**) settings panel, (**C**) experiment status, and (**D**) global process.

The setting panel shown in Figure 5B it is intended to load and save the diverse methodologies created in the SIA system. In this window, it is possible to produce the baseline for the spectrophotometer. It can also generate a report in Microsoft Excel. The sequence of operating components configured in the control panel is shown in the setting panel as it is executed by the SIA system. In the experiment status window Figure 5C the user can observe which input of the multiposition valve is enabled. The metabolite being measured can be seen as an end-point or as a kinetic, and the results are depicted in a graph in the same panel, in which it is possible to set a filter to eliminate the Schlieren effect [45], with the assignment of the wavelength of interest and the filter wavelength. Finally, Figure 5D shows one of the two windows developed in the software to monitor the overall measurements performed by the SIA system. The data are displayed in duplicate considering their respective standard deviation bars.

The SIA system is flexible in the sense that the user must configure the components of the device system according to the methodology to be implemented or alternatively, an already saved predefined technique can be loaded by the user. The operator must set the baseline and define the wavelengths of the measurements. In the second stage, the port to operate the inputs of the multiposition valves is selected, then the corresponding action of suction or injection performed by the peristaltic pump is specified, along with other possible actions. The algorithm repeats the sequence as many times as set by the technician corresponding to the sampling events. The results are displayed in diverse graphs with the possibility of generating a report.

3.8. *β-Fructofuranosidase Activity Determination Using the Lab-Made SIA System*

As already described, diverse hardware modifications were performed in the SIA system that allowed us to set up the DNS methodology in this device. Determination of the β-fructofuranosidase activity with the SIA system requires to perform the following steps.

3.8.1. Calibration Curve

Firstly, it was necessary to set up in the SIA system the DNS methodology to determine β-fructofuranosidase activity described in the methodology. Calibration curves were generated, relating the response of the system to the concentration of reducing sugars in a sample. The curve considered five known concentrations of glucose: 0.0, 0.5, 1.0, 1.5, and 2.0 g/L. Flow rate was set to 20 µL/s. The DNS methodology adapted to the SIA system was repeated for each point of the curve considering three repetitions for every determination. Figure 6 shows that each group of curves for a given concentration was close to each other denoting the repeatability of the method. The coefficient of determination was 0.997. Due to the limits imposed by the calibration curve, the methodology developed for the determination of β-fructofuranosidase was able to measure enzymatic activity in the linear range of 0.01–1.4 U/ml. Enzymatic activities outside that range are required to dilute or concentrate the sample.

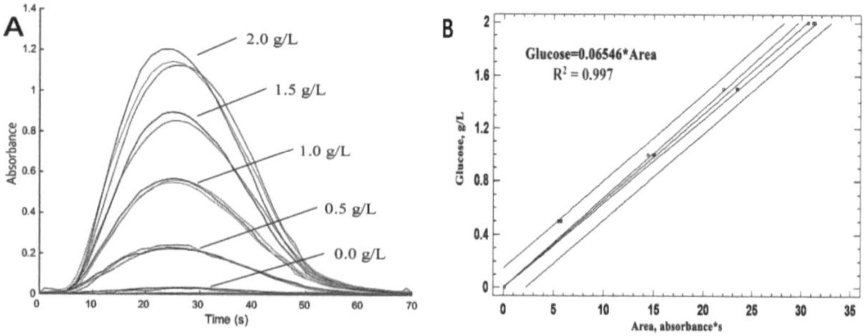

Figure 6. Response from SIA: (**A**) response of the SIA system in front of different substrate concentrations; (**B**) calibration curves.

3.8.2. Sequence Followed in the SIA System to Determine β-Fructofuranosidase Activity

To identify the most appropriate sequence to detect enzymatic activity in the SIA system, diverse configurations of injection and suction times were carried out. Table 1 details the parameters programmed in the flow system for the determination of β-fructofuranosidase activity from a sample taken manually from the bioreactor and processed with the SIA system.

The holding coil of the SIA system allowed us to obtain dilutions up to 10 times; however, for sample dilutions greater than that, it was necessary to include a dilution module to achieve proportions of 1:100 or even 1:1000, where it was required to implement and repeat the sequence shown in Table 2. The dilution module included storage of the sample, the dilution process, and the washing of the system to avoid contamination with undiluted samples.

Table 1. Protocol for the determination of β−fructofuranosidase activity in the SIA system.

Described Action	Sequence	Valve Port Position	Pump Operation	Time (s)
Sample	0	2	Suction	4
Dilution 1:10	1	7	Injection	40
Air	2	8	Suction	2
To mixer chamber	3	7	Injection	4
Agitation	4	22	Stop	30
		Dilution stage if this is required 1:10		
To retention chamber	5	7	Suction	5
Supernatant	6	1	Suction	1
To retention chamber	7	7	Suction	1
Supernatant	8	1	Suction	1
Air	9	8	Suction	2
To incubation chamber	10	10	Injection	35
To retention chamber	11	7	Suction	40
Waste	12	5	Injection	55
Cleaning mixer system *	13–16		Cleaning process	280
Washing chamber **	17	8	Injection	120
To retention chamber **	18	8	Suction	65
Waste **	19	5	Injection	70
To retention chamber **	20	8	Suction	20
Waste **	21	5	Injection	30
Incubation 50 C	22	10	Stop	200
To retention chamber	23	10	Suction	30
Reagent DNS	24	9	Suction	1
To retention chamber	25	10	Suction	1
Reagent DNS	26	9	Suction	1
To retention chamber	27	10	Suction	1
Reagent DNS	28	9	Suction	2
To retention chamber	29	10	Suction	3

*—mix chamber washing process; **—washing process for the heating and cooling chamber.

Table 2. Protocol description for the dilution module 1:10.

Described Action	Sequence	Valve Port Position	Pump Operation	Time (s)
To retention chamber	5	7	Suction	8
Air	6	8	Suction	2
To storage	7	10	Injection	8
To retention chamber	8	7	Suction	40
Waste	9	5	Injection	55
Cleaning mixer system	10	7	Injection	180
To retention chamber	11	7	Suction	65
Waste	12	5	Injection	75
To retention chamber	13	10	Suction	8
Air	14	7	Injection	44
Dilution 1:10	15	8	Suction	2
To mixing chamber	16	7	Injection	4
Agitation	17	22	-	30
Waste	18	10	Injection	60

3.8.3. Automatic β-Fructofuranosidase Activity Determination

Diverse β-fructofuranosidase activity determinations were performed with the lab-made SIA system during its configuration process. Several samples were taken manually from shake flasks and from running bioreactors. The samples were analyzed by the SIA system and the results were compared to laboratory determinations concluding that the device had a satisfactory performance.

To demonstrate the potential of the lab-made SIA system to determine β-fructofuranosidase activity at-line, selected samples were taken automatically from a fed-batch bioreactor. Four culture samples taken at times 1 h (A1), 2 h (A2), 7 h (B1), and 8 h (B2), were extracted automatically from the bioreactor with a specialized probe that included a ceramic filter that retained cells just providing supernatant, Figure 7. The automatic sampling was performed with the sequence shown in Table 3. The samples were processed with the SIA system and the resulting enzymatic measurements were compared to microplate determinations.

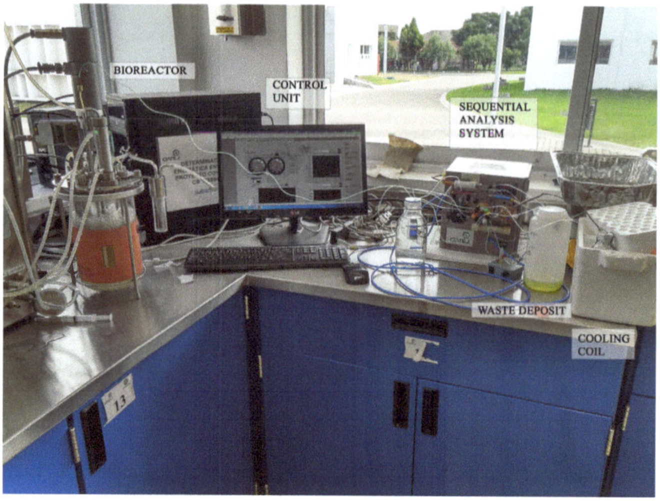

Figure 7. At-line β-fructofuranosidase activity determination in a real bioprocess.

Table 3. Protocol for the suction of supernatant from the bioreactor using the sampling probe.

Described Action	Sequence	Valve Port Position	Pump Operation	Time (s)
Air	0	3	Suction	1
From bioreactor	1	2	Suction	60
Waste	2	5	Injection	80
Air	3	3	Suction	1
From bioreactor	4	2	Suction	60
Waste	5	5	Injection	80
Air	6	3	Suction	1
From bioreactor	7	2	Suction	60
Waste	8	5	Injection	90

4. Discussion

The yeast *K. marxianus* has the potential to produce β-fructofuranosidases, which are enzymes capable of hydrolyzing β-fructofuranosides links of fructans to obtain fructooligosaccharides. It is important to understand the dynamics associated with the production of the enzyme under favorable and inhibited conditions in the bioreactor [46,47]. The DNS methodology has been applied in diverse flow systems [20–22], i.e., to detect sugar content in beverages or to validate self-made amperometric sensors. Fructose is a reducing sugar that reacts with free amino groups giving the Maillard reaction [48]. The DNS method applied for enzymatic activity is based on the detection of fructose produced by β-fructofuranosidase which reduces 3,5-Dinitrosalicylic acid (DNS) to 3-amino-5-nitrosalicylic acid, which has a maximum absorption at 540 nm and can be read spectrophotometrically. The increasing absorption is proportional to the production of 3-amino-5-nitrosalicylic acid and consequently to fructose production [49].

To study the accuracy of the lab-made SIA system, the β-fructofuranosidase activity, performed in microplates, was measured against the reaction in the sequential injection system in a kinetic of 8 h. The values obtained by both methods showed a correlation of 0.9999%. The precision was determined with the standard deviation of the samples with a ($n = 2$). The standard deviation shown in this study was 6.5% for samples with low activity (A1–A2) and 3.56% for samples with high activity (B1–B2), with a mean of 5.03%. Compared to the standard deviation of 8.75%, the maximum error in this investigation was approximately 20.39% in samples with low activity (A1–A2), which is attributable to the enzymatic activity. The SIA system loses sensitivity since Miller's method has low sensitivity at low concentrations [50,51]. The precision and accuracy of the method depend on the analyte reagent molar ratio, the changes and reaction times, and temperatures [17,52,53]. In another study, the accuracy of the use of a DNS in a spectrophotometric method and the accuracy of enzymatic assays are compared, showing variations in glucose dependence with an error of 5–35% [54]. The error could be decreased if the SIA system is coupled to Raman or FTIR spectroscopies.

Comparing the average activity between both techniques, the lower the activity, the greater the degree of separation, with up to 21% difference, as in sample A2. It turns out that as the activity in the sample increases, the difference between the averages of the two techniques decreases, Table 4. The difference in standard deviation is associated with the sensitivity of the designed equipment, although it is worth mentioning that samples B1 and B2 showed larger enzymatic activity. The results obtained demonstrated that the DNS methodology implemented in the SIA systems has the potential to be used as an at-line process to determine β-fructofuranosidase activity in samples taken out automatically from a bioreactor Figure 8. Nevertheless, the apparition of bubbles in the tubing during the processing of the sample provoked perturbations in the measurements, a problem that must be considered in future determinations to improve repeatability. Syringe injection results in lower standard deviation among the sample due to the decrease in pulses caused by the peristaltic pump [39]; this could in part explain the repeatability obtained achieving standard deviations fluctuating from 0 to 21%. Nevertheless, the use of multiposition valves and peristaltic pumps makes the SIA system versatile allowing the use of multiple reactants to determine diverse analytes in a bioprocess.

Table 4. Validation of microplate vs. SIA technique.

Sample	Microplate Enzymatic Activity (U/mL)	Std Desv.	SIA Enzymatic Activity (U/mL)	Std Desv.	% Error SIA vs. Microplate
A1	8.45	1.20	7.20	3.56	14.79
A2	10.47	0.80	8.34	2.18	20.39
B1	74.45	1.21	74.50	5.33	0.07
B2	83.70	1.95	83.70	6.50	0.00

The automation of the SIA system with the software designed in this manuscript presented substantial improvements to what was reported in [36,37]. The algorithms have the advantage of being easily reconfigurable, with the option to save new methodologies of different sequences, sample auto-dilution, and the opportunity to perform kinetics under a stop–flow and endpoint with a continuous flow or stopped flow. In addition, it is possible to select and manage up to two wavelengths, scanning, and monitoring at wavelengths in the range of 345–1000 nm, and real-time graphs of the variables measured; all this is presented in a friendly, versatile user interface which is easy to manipulate. This is relevant since the new trends in bioprocess are related to the use of micro bioreactors for enzymatic determination [55,56], which will require samplings with less volume from the culture medium. On the other hand, it will be required to monitor more complex bioprocesses with multiple metabolites to draw information about the physiological state of the cells [57,58], with the SIA system being a strategic tool to develop better control algorithms.

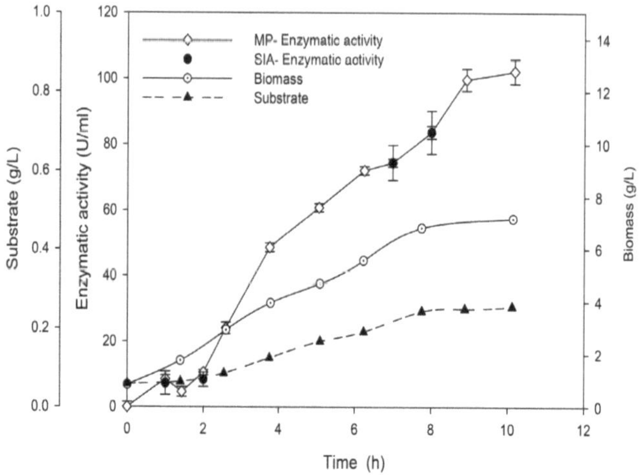

Figure 8. Comparison of β-fructofuranosidase activity determination at selected point with low and high activity in a fed-batch culture.

As a difference between this research and the SIA system reported in [29], it can be stated that in the former manuscript, a flow restrictor was used to pressurize the sequential injection system line at 0.2 MPa. This accessory allows the reduction of bubbles in the SIA line; however, the use of the flow restrictor under the current configuration of the equipment (at the end of the flow cell) does not allow the return of the sample. The modification made in this system was to remove the flow restrictor and include a mixing chamber and a cooling chamber whose purpose is to stop the reaction with the DNS ("quenching reaction") reagent. With respect to the at-line methodology, the determination of the area under the siagram curve is made, which allows the measurement of the generated chromophore, thus reducing the loss of concentration due to the concentration gradient (dilution factor) [29]. On the other hand, in this new system in each determination of reducing sugars during at-line measurement, a calibration curve is created since the DNS continuously degrades. Regarding SIA systems diverse LabVIEW™ algorithms have been reported [37–40]. As a difference to our study, Wagner et al. (2002) [40] reported up to 40 software instructions to control the flow system compared to the 22 commands used in our algorithm. However, in our approach, we can measure samples with the UV-VIS detector reading up to two wavelengths (filter entry), and at-line analysis of the sample, with the possibility to perform analysis in continuous or stopped flow (enzymatic kinetics). Another difference is that in this research we used multiposition valves while in other studies Cavro XP3000 syringe pumps are considered [38–40].

Designing a lab-made SIA system can be quite a challenge, from the point of view of integrating the components, designing the algorithm, and the configuration and validation stages. The built system can be used to monitor different types of metabolites in a bioreactor at the laboratory level in universities, research centers, or even in industry. Designing an SIA system is a challenging research project for Ph.D. students, in which it will be necessary to develop interdisciplinary strategies such as electronics, software development, mechanics, and of course biotechnology resources.

5. Conclusions

A lab-made SIA system was designed to detect at-line β-fructofuranosidase activity. The SIA was controlled with a LabVIEW™ algorithm allowing the user to configure and set up new methodologies in the SIA system from already developed off-line determinations of metabolites in a bioprocess. The system is a potentially useful tool for real-time monitoring of metabolites since it can automatically sample from the bioreactor, increasing efficiency and lowering the need for manual intervention. The evaluation of the SIA system and the software allowed us to conclude that the device was able to determine the enzymatic activity of β-fructofuranosidase, showing a standard deviation below 7% at activities lower than 11 U/mL with standard deviations below 4% and errors below 21% in comparison with the measurement performed off-line. These experiments demonstrated that the SIA system can perform enzymatic kinetics and end point, under a clever scheme of auto configuration according to the conditions that the culture media showed; however, the performance of the flow device must be improved to decrease the determination times in the presence of dilution and to enhance repeatability.

Author Contributions: Conceptualization, J.E.P.-S. and E.J.H.-L.; methodology, E.J.B.-H., J.A.-G., J.E.P.-S. and A.A.-S.; software, J.E.P.-S. and E.J.H.-L.; validation, E.J.B.-H., A.A.-S., J.E.P.-S. and E.J.H.-L.; writing—original draft preparation, J.E.P.-S. and E.J.H.-L.; writing—review and editing, R.F., A.G.-M., J.E.P.-S. and E.J.H.-L.; funding acquisition and Resources, E.J.H.-L.; project administration E.J.H.-L. All authors have read and agreed to the published version of the manuscript.

Funding: This research was funded by Mexican Consejo Nacional de Humanidades Ciencia y Tecnología (CONAHCYT) project 319269.

Institutional Review Board Statement: Not applicable.

Informed Consent Statement: Not applicable.

Data Availability Statement: Data are contained within the article.

Acknowledgments: E.J.B.-H. thanks, CONACYT for the Master scholarship grant 577098.

Conflicts of Interest: The authors declare no conflicts of interest.

Abbreviations

The following abbreviations are used in this manuscript:

DNS	3,5-dinitrosalicylic acid
FIA	flow injection analysis
FOS	fructooligosaccharides
Mp	microplate technique
SIA	sequential injection analysis

References

1. Fonseca, G.G.; Heinzle, E.; Wittmann, C.; Gombert, A.K. The yeast *Kluyveromyces marxianus* and its biotechnological potential. *Appl. Microbiol. Biotechnol.* **2009**, *79*, 339–354. [CrossRef] [PubMed]
2. Lane, M.M.; Morrissey, J.P. *Kluyveromyces marxianus*: A yeast emerging from its sister's shadow. *Fungal Biol. Rev.* **2010**, *24*, 17–26. [CrossRef]
3. Rajkumar, A.S.; Morrissey, J.P. Rational engineering of *Kluyveromyces marxianus*to create a chassis for the production of aromatic products. *Microb. Cell Factories.* **2020**, *19*, 207. [CrossRef] [PubMed]
4. Flores, J.A.; Gschaedler, A.; Amaya-Delgado, L.; Herrera-López, E.J.; Arellano, M.; Arrizon, J. Simultaneous saccharification and fermentation of Agave tequilana fructans by *Kluyveromyces marxianus* yeasts for bioethanol and tequila production. *Bioresour. Technol.* **2013**, *146*, 267–273. [CrossRef]
5. Leonel, L.V.; Arruda, P.V.; Chandel, A.K.; Felipe, M.G.A.; Sene, L. *Kluyveromyces marxianus*: A potential biocatalyst of renewable chemicals and lignocellulosic ethanol production. *Crit. Rev. Biotechnol.* **2021**, *41*, 1131–1152. [CrossRef]
6. Baptista, M.; Domingues, L. *Kluyveromyces marxianus* as a microbial cell factory for lignocellulosic biomass valorisation. *Biotechnol. Adv.* **2022**, *60* , 108027. [CrossRef]
7. Varela, J.A.; Gethins, L.; Stanton, C.; Ross, P.; Morrissey, J.P. Applications of *Kluyveromyces marxianus*in Biotechnology. In *Yeast Diversity in Human Welfare*; Satyanarayana, T., Kunze, G., Eds.; Springer: Singapore, 2017; pp. 439–454. [CrossRef]
8. Karim, A.; Gerliani, N.; Aïder, M. *Kluyveromyces marxianus*: An emerging yeast cell factory for applications in food and biotechnology. *Int. J. Food Microbiol.* **2020**, *333*, 108818. [CrossRef]
9. Homayouni-Rad, A.; Azizi, A.; Oroojzadeh, P.; Pourjafar, H. *Kluyveromyces marxianus* as a probiotic yeast: A mini-review. *Curr. Nutr. Food Sci.* **2020**, *16*, 1163–1169. [CrossRef]

10. Bilal, M.; Ji, L.; Xu, Y.; Xu, S.; Lin, Y.; Iqbal, H.; Cheng, H. Bioprospecting *Kluyveromyces marxianus* as a robust host for industrial biotechnology. *Front. Bioeng. Biotechnol.* **2022**, *10*, 851768. [CrossRef]
11. Barranco-Florido, E.; Garcıa-Garibay, M.; Gómez-Ruiz, L.; Azaola, A. Immobilization system of *Kluyveromyces marxianus* cells in barium alginate for inulin hydrolysis. *Process Biochem.* **2001**, *37*, 513–519. [CrossRef]
12. Singh, R.S.; Singh, T.; Hassan, M.; Kennedy, J.F. Updates on inulinases: Structural aspects and biotechnological applications. *Int. J. Biol. Macromol.* **2020**, *164*, 193–210. [CrossRef] [PubMed]
13. García-Aguirre, M.; Sáenz-Álvaro, V.A.; Rodríguez-Soto, M.A.; Vicente-Magueyal, F.J.; Botello-Álvarez, E.; Jimenez-Islas, H.; Cárdenas-Manríquez, M.; Rico-Martínez, R.; Navarrete-Bolaños, J.L. Strategy for Biotechnological Process Design Applied to the Enzymatic Hydrolysis of Agave Fructo-oligosaccharides To Obtain Fructose-Rich Syrups. *J. Agric. Food Chem.* **2009**, *57*, 10205–10210. [CrossRef] [PubMed]
14. Ricca, E.; Calabrò, V.; Cursio, S.; Iorio, G. The state of the art in the production of fructose from inulin enzymatic hydrolysis. *Crit. Rev. Biotechnol.* **2007**, *27*, 129–145. [CrossRef] [PubMed]
15. Waleckx, E.; Mateos-Diaz, J.C.; Gschaedler, A.; Colonna-Ceccaldi, B.; Brin, N.; García-Quezada, G.; Villanueva-Rodríguez, S.; Monsan, P. Use of inulinases to improve fermentable carbohydrate recovery during tequila production. *Food Chem.* **2011**, *124*, 1533–1545. [CrossRef]
16. FOS. Market Worth 3.52 Billion By 2024, 2019. Available online: https://markets.businessinsider.com/news/stocks/fructo-oligosaccharides-fos-market-size-worth-3-52-billion-by-2024-hexa-research-1027578303 (accessed on 1 October 2023).
17. Miller, G.L. Use of Dinitrosalicylic Acid Reagent for Determination of Reducing Sugar. *Anal. Chem.* **1959**, *31*, 426–428. [CrossRef]
18. Ruzicka, J.; Hansen, E.H. Flow injection analyses: Part I. A new concept of fast continuous flow analysis. *Anal. Chim. Acta* **1975**, *78*, 145–157. [CrossRef]
19. Ruzicka, J.; Marshall, G.D. Sequential injection: A new concept for chemical sensors, process analysis and laboratory assays. *Anal. Chim. Acta* **1990**, *237*, 32–343. [CrossRef]
20. Cántizares-Macías, P.; Hernández-Garciadiego, L.; Gómez-Ruíz, H. An Automated Flow Injection Analysis Procedure for the Determination of Reducing Sugars by DNSA Method. *J. Food Sci.* **2001**, *66*, 407–411. [CrossRef]
21. Kumar, M.A.; Thakur, M.S.; Senthuran, A.; Senthuran, V.; Karanth, N.G.; Hatti-Kaul, R.; Mattiasson, B. An automated flow injection analysis system for on-line monitoring of glucose and L-lactate during lactic acid fermentation in a recycle bioreactor. *World J. Microbiol. Biotechnol.* **2001**, *17*, 23–29. [CrossRef]
22. Ferreira, L.S.; Trierweiler, J.O.; De Souza, M.B., Jr.; Folly, R.O.M. A lactose fia-biosensor system for monitoring and process control. *Braz. J. Chem. Eng.* **2004**, *21*, 307–315. [CrossRef]
23. Wongsa, C.; Udomsom, S.; Budwong, A.; Kiwfo, K.; Grudpan, K.; Paengnakorn, P. Sequential injection amperometric system coupling with bioreactor for in-line glucose monitoring in cell culture application. *Molecules* **2022**, *27*, 6665. [CrossRef] [PubMed]
24. Ruzicka, J. Lab-on-valve: Universal microflow analyzer based on sequential and bead injection. *Analyst* **2000**, *125*, 1053–1060. [CrossRef]
25. Araujo, A.R.T.S.; Gaspar, D.; Lúcio, M.; Reis, S.; Saraiva, M.L.M.F.S.; Lima, J.L.F.C. Sequential injection system for phospholipase A2 activity evaluation: Studies on liposomes using an environment-sensitive fluorescent probe. *Talanta* **2009**, *79*, 1125–1129. [CrossRef]
26. Pinto, P.C.A.G.; Saraiva, M.L.M.F.S.; Lima, J.L.F.C. Sequential injection analysis as a tool for implementation of enzymatic assays in ionic liquids. *Talanta* **2008**, *77*, 479–483. [CrossRef]
27. Vidigal, S.S.M.P.; Tóth, I.V.; Rangel, A.O.S.S. Sequential Injection Lab-on-Valve System for the Determination of the Activity of Peroxidase in Vegetables. *J. Agric. Food. Chem.* **2010**, *58*, 2071–2075. [CrossRef]
28. Sandoval-Ventura, O.; Cañizares-Macías, M.P. Evaluation of the Enzymatic Activity of Glucose Oxidase Immobilized on Multiwalled Carbon Nanotubes and on Controlled Pore Glass by Sequential Injection Analysis. *Anal. Lett.* **2016**, *49*, 639–653. [CrossRef]
29. Pliego, J.; Mateos, J.C.; Rodriguez, J.; Valero, F.; Baeza, M.; Femat, R.; Camacho, R.; Sandoval, G.; Herrera-López, E.J. Monitoring lipase/esterase activity by stopped flow in a sequential injection analysis system using p-nitrophenyl butyrate. *Sensors* **2015**, *15*, 2798–2811. [CrossRef]
30. Silvestre, C.I.C.; Pinto, P.C.A.G.; Segundo, M.A.; Saraiva, M.L.M.F.S.; Lima, J.L.F.C. Enzyme based assays in a sequential injection format: A review. *Anal. Chim. Acta* **2011**, *689*, 160–177. [CrossRef]
31. Kurbanoglu, S.; Unal, M.A.; Ozkan, S.A. Recent developments on electrochemical flow injection in pharmaceuticals and biologically important compounds. *Electrochim. Acta* **2018**, *287*, 135–148. [CrossRef]
32. Schindler, R.; Le Thanh, H.; Lendl, B.; Kellner, R. Determination of enzyme kinetics and chemometric evaluation of reaction products by FTIR spectroscopy on the example of β-fructofuranosidase. *Vib. Spectrosc.* **1998**, *16*, 127–135. [CrossRef]
33. Schindler, R.; Lendl, B. Simultaneous determination of enzyme activities by FTIR-spectroscopy in an one-step assay. *Anal. Chim. Acta* **1999**, *391*, 19–28. [CrossRef]
34. Herrera, A.; Arrizon, J.; Barcena-Soto, M.; Soltero, J.; Mateos-Díaz, J.; Casillas, N. Amperometric Titration of Fructan Oligosaccharides of Agave Tequilana Webber, Blue Variety, in a Rotating Disk Electrode. *ECS Trans.* **2011**, *36*, 351–362. [CrossRef]
35. Busch, M.; Höbel, W.; Polster, J. Software FIACRE: Bioprocess monitoring on the basis of flow injection analysis using simultaneously a urea optode and a glucose luminescence sensor. *J. Biotechnol.* **1993**, *31*, 327–343. [CrossRef] [PubMed]

36. Cocovi-Solberg, D.J.; Miró, M. CocoSoft: Educational software for automation in the analytical chemistry laboratory. *Anal. Bioanal. Chem.* **2015**, *407*, 6227–6233. [CrossRef]
37. Lenehan, C.E.; Barnett, N.W.; Lewis, S.W. Design of LabVIEW®-based software for the control of sequential injection analysis instrumentation for the determination of morphine. *J. Autom. Methods Manag. Chem.* **2002**, *24*, 99–103. [CrossRef]
38. Sklenarova, H.; Svoboda, A.; Solich, P.; Polasek, M.; Karlícek, R. Simple laboratory-made automated sequential injection analysis (SIA) device. II. SIA operational software based on LabVIEW® programming language. *Instrum. Sci. Technol.* **2002**, *30*, 353–360. [CrossRef]
39. Solich, P.; Svoboda, A.; Sklenárova, H.; Polasek, M.; Karlícek, R. Simple laboratory-made automated Sequential Injection Analysis (SIA) device. I. Design and testing of the hardware component. *Instrum. Sci. Technol.* **2002**, *30*, 13–20. [CrossRef]
40. Wagner, C.; Armenta, S.; Lendl, B. Developing automated analytical methods for scientific environments using LabVIEW. *Talanta* **2010**, *80*, 1081–1087. [CrossRef]
41. Hernández-Maya, F.M.; Cañizares-Macías, M.P. Evaluation of the activity of β-glucosidase immobilized on polydimethylsiloxane (PDMS) with a microfluidic flow injection analyzer with embedded optical fibers. *Talanta* **2018**, *185*, 53–60. [CrossRef]
42. Míguez, N.; Gimeno-Pérez, M.; Fernández-Polo, D.; Cervantes, F.V.; Ballesteros, A.O.; Fernández-Lobato, M.; Ribeiro, M.H.; Plou, F.J. Immobilization of the β-fructofuranosidase from *Xanthophyllomyces dendrorhous* by Entrapment in Polyvinyl Alcohol and Its Application to Neo-Fructooligosaccharides Production. *Catalysts* **2018**, *8*, 201. [CrossRef]
43. Moore, J.H. Artificial intelligence programming with LabVIEW: Genetic algorithms for instrumentation control and optimization. *Comput. Methods Programs Biomed.* **1995**, *47*, 73–79. [CrossRef]
44. Instrument Driver Network. *Ocean Optics 2000 4000, Certified LabVIEW Plug and Play (Project-Style) Instrument Driver*; National Instruments: Austin, TX, USA, 2016.
45. Zagatto, E.A.G.; Arruda, M.A.Z.; Jacintho, A.O.; Mattos, I.L. Compensation of the Schlieren effect in flow-injection analysis by using dual-wavelength spectrophotometry. *Anal. Chim. Acta* **1990**, *234*, 153–160. [CrossRef]
46. Santharam, L.; Samuthirapandi, A.B.; Easwaran, S.N.; Mahadevan, S. Modeling of exo-inulinase biosynthesis by *Kluyveromyces marxianus* in fed-batch mode: Correlating production kinetics and metabolic heat fluxes. *Appl. Biochem. Biotechnol.* **2017**, *101*, 1877–1887. [CrossRef] [PubMed]
47. Corona, R.; Morales-Burgos, A.M.; Pelayo Ortiz, C.; Arias, J.; García-Sandoval, J. Substrates' and products' inhibition in fructanase production by a new *Kluyveromyces marxianus* CF15 from Agave tequilana fructan in a batch reactor. *Bioprocess Biosyst. Eng.* **2019**, *42*, 1779–1791. [CrossRef] [PubMed]
48. Dills, W.L., Jr. Protein fructosylation: Fructose and the Maillard reaction. *Am. J. Clin. Nutr.* **1993**, *58*, 779S–787S. [CrossRef] [PubMed]
49. Negrulescu, A.; Patrulea, V.; Mincea, M.M.; Ionascu, C.; Vlad-Oros, B.A.; Ostafe, V. Adapting the reducing sugars method with dinitrosalicylic acid to microtiter plates and microwave heating. *J. Braz. Chem. Soc.* **2012**, *23*, 2176–2182. [CrossRef]
50. Gusakov, A.V.; Kondratyeva, E.G.; Sinitsyn, A.P. Comparison of two methods for assaying reducing sugars in the determination of carbohydrase activities. *Int. J. Anal Chem.* **2011**, *2011*, *283658*. [CrossRef]
51. Shao, Y.; Lin, A.H.M. Improvement in the quantification of reducing sugars by miniaturizing the Somogyi-Nelson assay using a microtiter plate. *Food Chem.* **2018**, *240*, 898–903. [CrossRef]
52. Wood, I.P.; Elliston, A.; Ryden, P.; Bancroft, I.; Roberts, I.N.; Waldron, K.W. Rapid quantification of reducing sugars in biomass hydrolysates: Improving the speed and precision of the dinitrosalicylic acid assay. *Biomass Bioenergy* **2012**, *44*, 117–121. [CrossRef]
53. Başkan, K.S.; Tütem, E.; Akyüz, E.; Özen, S.; Apak, R. Spectrophotometric total reducing sugars assay based on cupric reduction. *Talanta* **2016**, *147*, 162–168. [CrossRef]
54. Xu, H.; Leng, X.; Wang, M.; Zhang, G. Glucose Measurement in the Presence of Tea polyphenols. *Food Anal. Methods* **2012**, *5*, 1027–1032. [CrossRef]
55. Urban, P.L.; Goodall, D.M.; Bruce, N.C. Enzymatic microreactors in chemical analysis and kinetic studies. *Biotechnol. Adv.* **2006**, *24*, 42–57. [CrossRef] [PubMed]
56. Alhadeff, E.M.; Salgado, A.M.; Cos, O.; Pereira, N.; Belkis, V.; Valero, F. Enzymatic microreactors for the determination of ethanol by an automatic sequential injection analysis system. *Appl. Biochem. Biotechnol.* **2007**, *137*, 17–25. [CrossRef] [PubMed]
57. Flores-Cosío, G.; Herrera-López, E.J.; Arellano-Plaza, M.; Gschaedler, A.; Sánchez, A.; Amaya-Delgado, L. Dielectric property measurements as a method to determine the physiological state of *Kluyveromyces marxianus* and *Saccharomyces cerevisiae* stressed with furan aldehydes. *Appl. Microbiol. Biotechnol.* **2019**, *103*, 1–10. [CrossRef] [PubMed]
58. Flores-Cosío, G.; Herrera-López, E.J.; Arellano-Plaza, M.; Gschaedler-Mathis, A.; Kirchmayr, M.; Amaya-Delgado, L. Application of dielectric spectroscopy to unravel the physiological state of microorganisms: Current state, prospects and limits. *Appl. Microbiol. Biotechnol.* **2020**, *104*, 6101–6113. [CrossRef] [PubMed]

fermentation

Article

Design Optimization of a Tray Bioreactor for Solid-State Fermentation: Study of Process Parameters through Protein Modification of By-Products

Pau Sentís-Moré [1,2], María-Paz Romero-Fabregat [1], Cristina Rodríguez-Marca [2], Antonio-Jesús Guerra-Sánchez [3] and Nàdia Ortega-Olivé [2,*]

[1] Food Technology Department, AGROTECNIO Center, University of Lleida, 25198 Lleida, Spain; pau.sentis@udl.cat (P.S.-M.); mariapaz.romero@udl.cat (M.-P.R.-F.)
[2] Eurecat, Centre Tecnològic de Catalunya, Unitat de Nutrició i Salut, 43204 Reus, Spain; cristina.rodriguez@eurecat.org
[3] Eurecat, Centre Tecnològic de Catalunya, Advancing Manufacturing Systems Unit, 08290 Cerdanyola, Spain; antonio.guerra@eurecat.org
* Correspondence: nadia.ortega@eurecat.org; Tel.: +34-977300431

Abstract: This study investigated the design of a tray bioreactor for solid-state fermentation, applying *Rhizopus oryzae* to oilseed meals as the substrate. Two process variables were continuously monitored in the bioreactor to ensure precise control of the environmental conditions: temperature and relative humidity (RH). The comprehensive analysis covered the effects of different fermentation conditions on the protein content, technological properties, and molecular distribution of the samples. The study revealed that the configuration factors suffered a stratification within the three trays of the bioreactor. Notably, the upper tray registered the largest dispersion, with a range of 1.5 °C. When analyzing the differences between sensors within each tray, the largest difference was found in the lower tray (10.9%). Furthermore, higher EAI (Emulsifying Activity Index) values were observed in the upper tray (T3) for rapeseed. As for ESI (Emulsion Stability Index) values, no differences were observed between the trays or fermentation periods. Using the changes induced by *Rhizopus oryzae* fungal enzymes, the study quantitatively examined the changes in the by-product valorization. While the bioreactor factors did not affect the protein quantity itself, they had significant impacts on specific changes within the molecular weight protein fraction. The findings of this study offer significant insights into the complex dynamics of solid-state fermentation processes. The outcomes of this study not only advance understanding of solid-state fermentation but also offer practical guidance for the design and operation of fermenters in industrial applications.

Keywords: configuration; temperature; relative humidity; technological properties; protein fraction

Citation: Sentís-Moré, P.; Romero-Fabregat, M.-P.; Rodríguez-Marca, C.; Guerra-Sánchez, A.-J.; Ortega-Olivé, N. Design Optimization of a Tray Bioreactor for Solid-State Fermentation: Study of Process Parameters through Protein Modification of By-Products. *Fermentation* **2023**, *9*, 921. https://doi.org/10.3390/fermentation9100921

Academic Editor: Ricardo Aguilar-López

Received: 21 September 2023
Revised: 19 October 2023
Accepted: 21 October 2023
Published: 23 October 2023

1. Introduction

Solid-state fermentation (SSF) is emerging as an attractive and alternative process for the valorization of by-products due to its numerous benefits, such as increased productivity, reduced wastewater consumption, lower risk of substrate contamination, and decreased energy requirements [1,2]. The lower water activity requirement (a_w) of SSF for fungal growth (0.5–0.6), compared to that needed by bacteria (around 0.8–0.9), makes SSF more suitable for mimicking the natural growth environment [1]. Currently, SSF has demonstrated its efficacy in the production mainly of enzymes and other products such as biopolymers, biosurfactants, organic acids, and pigments [3,4]. In the current context of protein demand, there is a growing interest to investigate the potential of fungal SSF to produce enriched protein ingredients using solid by-products as substrates.

In the context of SSF, the design of the bioreactor is crucial for creating a controlled environment for microorganism growth and also facilitates the transfer of nutrients and oxygen to the substrate. While many processes have been investigated in the laboratory, conducted in conical flasks, reagent bottles, and plastic bags, there are still relatively few examples of the successful implementation of large-scale SSF processes to produce these new products [5–7]. Selecting a suitable bioreactor and optimizing operating conditions becomes crucial when upscaling the production process [8]. One of the limiting factors has been the relatively poor knowledge base regarding the design and operation of large-scale SSF bioreactors. Among several critical challenges, moisture and the nature of the solid substrate play a significant role; the reason for this is because the thermal properties of a continuous aqueous phase, for example, the thermal conductivity and heat capacity of liquid water, are superior to those of a bed of wet solids with air between particles [9]. Therefore, providing a unique environment for the growth of the microorganisms is essential and requires the standard design of the bioreactor.

When analyzing various types of bioreactors for SSF, it is important to note that different designs have been explored, each with unique characteristics and advantages. Two of the most studied designs are packed-bed bioreactors and tray bioreactors; both are simple configurations because they keep the substrate static. In the packed-bed design, the substrate is placed in a column and has forced aeration through the fermentation bed. In the tray design, the substrate is placed in individual trays with layers of 1 to 5 cm thick, and there is no forced aeration through the sample [10]. There are also other more complex configurations, such as the fluidized bed bioreactor design, which employs a continuous flow of gas or liquid to suspend and mix the solid substrate, promoting better aeration and heat transfer. Finally, another option is the rotating drum bioreactor, where the substrate is placed in a rotating cylindrical drum to achieve a homogenous mixture [11].

Some works have studied and compared multiple bioreactor configurations, from small-scale laboratory [12] to mid-sized pilot-scale experiments [13]. These studies focused primarily on enzyme production and compared the two simpler configurations [5,14]. Some studies concluded that the tray configuration was the best in their case for many reasons, such as the rapid growth of the filamentous fungi due to the greater exposed surface area in the air, minimal mechanical stress, and simple operation and construction [13]. In addition, it is already the preferred type of SSF bioreactor for producing many industrial enzymes [4].

A tray bioreactor configuration comprises a chamber that houses individual trays, each crafted from a variety of materials, including metal or plastic. The trays exhibit open upper sections and, in some cases, are perforated. When stacked in layers with interspaces to improve airflow, these trays facilitate efficient air circulation. Operating as static beds, these trays require minimal or no agitation. The chamber is designed to introduce controlled levels of air, which circulates amongst the trays, maintaining optimal humidity and temperature conditions [15,16].

Therefore, despite certain limitations common to all SSF bioreactors, such as the desiccation and rising temperatures due to the inadequate removal of the internal heating and O_2 supply, the tray bioreactor represents a scalable and promising option, making it the primary focus of investigation [8,16,17].

Rhizopus oryzae is a common filamentous fungus in SSF studies, and it has already been tested in the production of enzymes like proteases using by-products of the bakery sector as a substrate [18]. One of the more explored groups of by-products are oilseed meals from the oil industry, due to the high amount of the product produced worldwide [19]. SSF has already been applied in oilseed meals, especially for the improvement of their nutritional fraction [20–22]. One of the fractions that is affected in the SSF process is the protein fraction, and although *Rhizopus oryzae* does not make significant changes in protein content [23–26], there are changes in the protein fraction and its properties due to the action of the fungal proteases [27,28].

The aim of this study is to explore the potential of SSF, focusing particularly on its implementation within a tray bioreactor. The main objective is to investigate the influence of key process variables, specifically relative humidity and temperature, within a laboratory-scale tray bioreactor configuration. The study focuses on improving fungal proliferation in a multi-tray bioreactor through the changes the microorganism *Rhizopus oryzae* makes in the substrate—rapeseed meal in this case. This investigation includes a comprehensive analysis of protein fraction and aims to elucidate how fermentation process variables impact the functional properties of the resulting products. By achieving these objectives, this study will contribute significantly to the advancement of SSF as a sustainable bioprocess and provide valuable insights into the practicality and potential of tray bioreactors for various fungal fermentation applications, drawing the pathway to a pilot-scale bioreactor.

2. Materials and Methods

2.1. Laboratory Tray Bioreactor Design Optimisation

Solid-state fermentation was carried out using a custom-designed tray bioreactor configuration with a size of 33.5 × 37.5 × 37.5 cm (Figure 1). A set of 3 trays was placed inside a forced air incubator (AXI-6000, ICT, SL, Erandio, Spain) to maintain them at the desired temperature during fermentation. Each tray had a size of 24.5 × 33 × 1 cm, and they were spaced 11.5 cm apart.

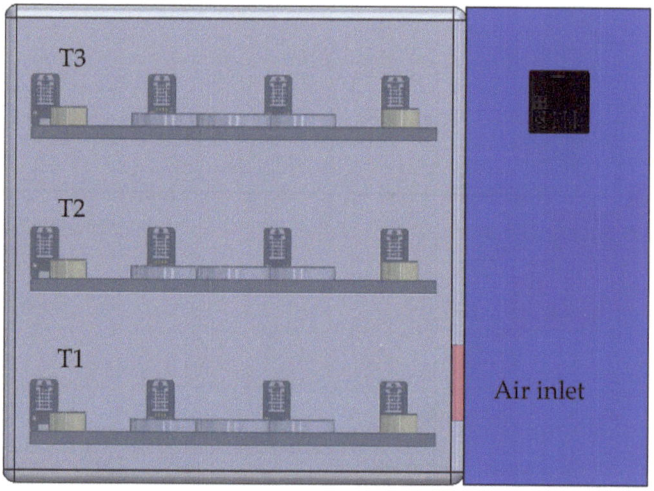

Figure 1. Custom-designed tray bioreactor configuration and distribution of sensors in each of the three trays: T1 (lower tray), T2 (central tray), and T3 (upper tray), and where the air inlet is located.

In each tray, 4 DHT22 sensors (AM2302) were placed, integrating a capacitive humidity sensor and a thermistor to measure the surrounding air. The sensors were connected to an Arduino Mega 2560 (Somerville, MA, USA) microcontroller board for logging temperature and relative humidity values using an Arduino Genuino 1.8.15 (Somerville, MA, USA) connected to Microsoft Excel (Redmond, WA, USA) to obtain real-time values.

2.2. By-Products

Rapeseed meal and sunflower meal were provided by two oil refining companies and obtained through solvent extraction. The by-products were characterized with moisture by heating to 105 °C, and the crude protein content by Kjeldahl combustion in a Bloc Digest and distilled in a PRO-NITRO A distiller (Selecta, Barcelona, Spain).

The pretreatment applied to the by-products was as follows: they were ground with an M20 Universal mill (IKA, Staufen, Germany), sieved at 0.5 mm, and sterilized by autoclaving at 121 °C for 20 min. Following sterilization, the samples were moistened to achieve humidity levels of 60% with sterilized distilled water.

2.3. Solid-State Fermentation (SSF) Process

2.3.1. Microorganism, Culture Media, and Propagation

A commercial culture of *Rhizopus oryzae* culture (ATCC 56536) was acquired from ATCC (Manassas, VT, USA) in lyophilized form and stored at −20 °C until use. To rehydrate the lyophilized *Rhizopus oryzae* culture (ATCC 56536), 1.0 mL of sterile distilled water was added to the pellet, and the mixture was stirred to obtain a suspension. The suspension was then transferred to a test tube containing sterile distilled water and left undisturbed at room temperature (25 °C) for a minimum of 2 h to facilitate rehydration and revival of the fungus's viability. After rehydration, the suspension of *Rhizopus oryzae* was mixed, and several drops were inoculated into Potato Dextrose Agar (PDA) (Sigma-Aldrich, Sant Louis, MO, USA) for 5 days at 25 °C.

2.3.2. Inoculation

Fermentation was initiated by inoculating prepared spores of *Rhizopus oryzae*. Specifically, 2 mL of spore suspension containing 10^6 spores/mL, quantified using a Thoma Pattern counting chamber (Braubrand®, Brand, Wertheim, Germany), was added to autoclaved and prehumidified by-product sources. Each preconditioned and inoculated by-product source, weighing 20 g, was placed in a 90 mm Petri dish (Fischer Scientific, Waltham, MA, USA) in the tray bioreactor, maintained at 25 °C with 70% air humidity for a fermentation period of 72 and 120 h to perform 3 days and 5 days of the fermentation process, respectively. Four Petri dishes were distributed in each tray, with two containing non-inoculated samples (control) and two containing inoculated samples. An oversaturated salt solution (52 g of sodium chloride in 100 mL of distilled water) was prepared and distributed in two beakers in each tray to maintain humidity levels during the fermentation period. After fermentation, the samples were stored in an oven at 50 °C for 72 h to inactivate the fungus. Then, the samples were stored in refrigeration before analysis.

2.4. Analytical Determinations

2.4.1. Crude Protein Content

Crude protein content was determined by Kjeldahl combustion in a Bloc Digest and PRO-NITRO A distiller (Selecta, Barcelona, Spain).

2.4.2. Molecular Weight Distribution

The molecular weight distribution was analyzed by high-performance liquid chromatography (Waters, Milford, MA, USA) as described by Sentís-Moré et al. [29]. Briefly, an XBridge BEH 125Å SEC 3.5 µm column (7.8 × 300 mm) (Waters, Milford, MA, USA) was used with acetonitrile 30% and TFA 0.1% as the mobile phase. Peak signals were detected at 280 nm with a Waters 2996 Photodiode Array Detector (Waters, Milford, MA, USA). Chymotrypsin (25,000 Da), ribonuclease A (13,700 Da), aprotinin (6511 Da), insulin (5733 Da), insulin chain B (3495 Da), angiotensin (1046 Da), and L-tryptophan (204 Da) were used as molecular weight standards. The calibration curve and data were obtained with Empower 3 software (Waters, Milford, MA, USA). The results of the MWD in all samples are expressed as percentages on groups of different molecular weights (MW): (i) >5000 Da, (ii) 5000 to 3000 Da, (iii) 3000 to 1000 Da, and (iv) 1000 to 500. All the samples were measured at least in duplicate.

2.4.3. Determination of Emulsion Activity and Stability Indexes

Emulsion properties were determined according to Pearce and Kinsella [30], with some modifications. In brief, 120 mg of the sample was solubilized to 12 mL of distilled water using a vortex mixer. Sunflower oil (4 mL) was added, and the mixture was emulsified with a homogenizer Polytron PT 10–35 (Kinematica, Malters, Switzerland) at 14,000 rpm. Then, 50 µL of the lower part of the emulsion was added to 10 mL of 0.1% (*w*/*v*) sodium dodecyl sulphate (SDS) and the absorbance was measured in the spectrophotometer at 500 nm, at times 0 and

10 min, to obtain Abs0 and Abs10, respectively. The Emulsifying Activity Index (EAI) and Emulsifying Stability Index (ESI) were calculated using Equations (1) and (2), respectively.

$$EAI\left(\mathrm{m}^2/\mathrm{g}\right) = \frac{2 \times 2.303 \times Abs_0 \times DF}{C \times \varphi \times 10000} \tag{1}$$

$$ESI\ (\mathrm{min}) = \frac{Abs_0}{Abs_0 - Abs_{10}} \times (\Delta t_{10} - \Delta t_0) \tag{2}$$

where DF is the dilution factor of the samples, C is the protein mass, and $= \varphi$ is the volume fraction of the oil in the emulsion.

2.5. Statistical Analysis

The data are presented as the mean of two replicates. The statistical analysis of the full factorial was carried out using JMP® Pro 16.0.0 (SAS Institute, Cary, NC, USA). Appropriate least square means were compared using the t-test after the F-tests were performed. The difference between samples was significant when $p < 0.01$.

3. Results and Discussion

In a tray bioreactor, relative humidity (RH) and temperature play a crucial role in influencing fungal growth and, therefore, the results of fermentation. RH is a key factor affecting water activity and moisture content within the trays; the availability of moisture profoundly impacts the growth rate and metabolism of microorganisms and the overall productivity of the fermentation process [31]. By controlling RH, we can optimize growing conditions to meet specific fungal requirements and achieve optimal yields. Temperature, on the other hand, governs the kinetics of fungal growth and may influence the enzymatic activity and metabolic rates of the fungi within the trays [32]. Different fungal strains have unique temperature optima for growth. By carefully adjusting and maintaining the temperature within the desired range, it can enhance the growth rate and quality of the fungal biomass.

Our approach involves deploying sensors in the laboratory-scale tray bioreactor, where these critical fermentation factors can be motorized. This data is invaluable for designing a pilot-scale tray bioreactor that can efficiently replicate the conditions necessary for successful fungal growth, addressing both scalability and homogeneity concerns. The ability to maintain optimal conditions in these parameters significantly influences the success of the fermentation process so that fermentation can be optimized and yields and product quality improved.

3.1. Fermentation Monitorization Factors

Temperature and RH monitoring employed four sensors in each of the three trays of the bioreactor. No significant variation in deviation was observed; all sensors were consistently kept below 0.5 °C for temperature and 1% for relative humidity during the 3- and 5-day fermentation period. Accordingly, we calculated average values for each sensor to create a thermal and relative humidity map of the bioreactor and to further examine sensor differences (Figure 2).

The temperature and RH monitoring data reveal different patterns. The highest temperature was consistent in the upper tray, reaching a maximum of 26.2 °C, while the lowest temperature was detected in the lower tray, which measured a minimum of 22.6 °C. It is important to note that this temperature behavior remained consistent between 3 and 5 days and between the two substrates used. By looking deeper into the temperature data, variations could be observed within each tray. The upper tray registered the largest dispersion, with a range of 1.5 °C, followed by the lower tray at 1.0 °C, and finally, the central tray was 0.6 °C. Interestingly, a closer analysis reveals that the sensors on the extreme sides of each tray displayed greater temperature deviation compared to the two central sensors, which maintained a more consistent temperature profile.

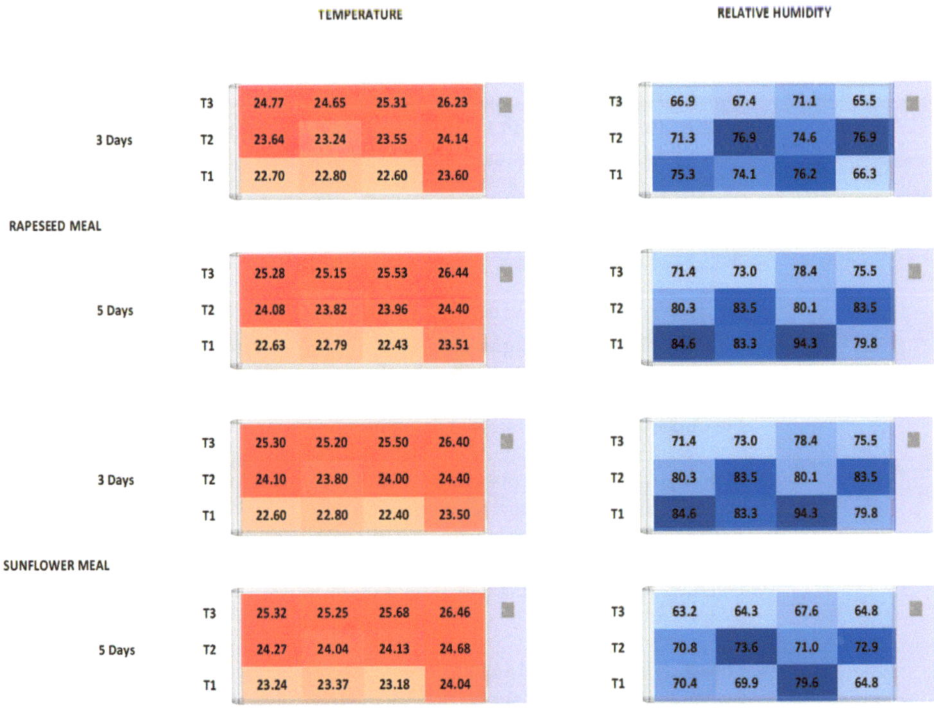

Figure 2. Representation of the thermal and RH map for each tray of bioreactor for fermentations carried out at 3 and 5 days for rapeseed and sunflower: T1 (lower tray), T2 (central tray), and T3 (upper tray). The values displayed at each point represent the average reading recorded during the respective fermentation period. Red colours correspond to temperature and blue colours for RH. Darker colours correspond to higher number and lighter colours to lower ones.

Regarding the average RH values recorded by the sensors after 3 and 5 days (Figure 2), a contrasting pattern could be observed. The highest values were found in the lower tray (94.3%) and the lowest in the upper tray (63.2%). This RH behavior, with stratification in the temperature factor but in reverse, remained constant during the fermentation periods of 3 and 5 days and for both substrates. When analyzing the differences between sensors within each tray, the largest difference was found in the lower tray (10.9%) and the lowest in the central tray (2.8%). In this case, as previously observed with temperature, the sensors located on the extreme sides of each tray also exhibited greater RH deviation compared to the two central sensors. In fact, it is interesting to note that inside the lower tray (T1), the sensor located near to the air inlet consistently recorded the lowest values for RH.

The observed temperature variation, particularly the higher temperatures in the upper tray (T3), can be attributed to fundamental heat dynamics within a confined space. Heat rises naturally, and in the upper tray, the right zone is closer to the heat source at the lower right of the bioreactor and tends to accumulate more heat [33]. In addition, restricted airflow at the upper compared to the lower trays may contribute to heat buildup, creating a thermal gradient across the trays. It is worth noting that RH can influence these temperature variations; RH reflects moisture content in the air, and moisture is a key factor in heat transfer and thermal regulation. Higher RH levels can enhance heat retention, which can exacerbate temperature differences between trays. This interaction between temperature and RH emphasizes the importance of comprehensive environmental control within the bioreactor.

As far as our knowledge, there are no works studying the temperature and HR distribution in SSF tray bioreactors with different sensors. The only study with information on temperature records is by Sala et al. [14], where there was also a stratification of the temperature during 11 days of fermentation, with the upper tray always having more temperature records than the lower tray. In another work by Demir and Tari [32], the differences in the production of polygalacturonase enzyme by *Aspergillus sojae* in different relative humidity were studied, ranging from 70% to 90%; in their case, no significant differences were observed. Therefore, achieving consistent and optimal conditions for microbial growth and product quality requires careful control of these variables, especially in large-scale bioprocesses.

3.2. Process Variable Impact on Fermented Products

The bioreactor configuration affects the fermentation parameters, including temperature and RH, and can potentially affect fungal growth and its action towards the substrates. This study used the growth of *Rhizopus oryzae* in rapeseed and sunflower meal to analyze the impact that the two bioreactor factors may have on fungal growth.

Results of the crude protein content and emulsifying properties of activity and stability of the two substrates are presented in Table 1. Based on the full factorial analysis performed (Table 2), all variables showed statistical differences ($p < 0.01$) in at least one determination unless the interaction was among time (days), tray, and inoculation. Consequently, in order to assess the impact of the solid-state fermentation process, the variables were studied together, considering the different trays of the bioreactor and fermentation period for both by-products.

Table 1. Results of control and inoculation samples obtained from SSF using rapeseed meal and sunflower meal substrates. Results from the crude protein content (g/100 g dm), emulsifying activity index (m^2/g), and emulsifying stability index (min) for each of the three different trays of bioreactor: T1 (lower tray), T2 (central tray), and T3 (lower tray). The results are presented for both 3-day and 5-day fermentation periods.

Determinations	3 Days						5 Days						SED
	Control			Inoculation			Control			Inoculation			
	T1	T2	T3	T1	T2	T3	T1	T2	T3	T1	T2	T3	
Rapeseed Meal													
Crude Protein Content (g/100 g dm)	37.4 ^{ab}	38.9 ^{a}	38.0 ^{ab}	38.2 ^{ab}	38.0 ^{ab}	37.4 ^{ab}	36.8 ^{ab}	36.9 ^{ab}	35.9 ^{b}	36.8 ^{ab}	37.3 ^{ab}	36.6 ^{ab}	0.24
Emulsifying Activity Index (m^2/g)	5.2 ^{d}	3.5 ^{d}	3.7 ^{d}	21.5 ^{bc}	25.1 ^{ab}	27.1 ^{a}	5.7 ^{d}	6.0 ^{d}	6.9 ^{d}	17.5 ^{c}	24.5 ^{ab}	26.4 ^{a}	0.47
Emulsifying Stability Index (min)	44.0 ^{a}	43.8 ^{a}	42.1 ^{a}	11.9 ^{c}	13.1 ^{c}	13.2 ^{c}	36.1 ^{b}	36.9 ^{b}	35.1 ^{b}	14.2 ^{c}	11.7 ^{c}	12.3 ^{c}	0.31
Sunflower Meal													
Crude Protein Content (g/100 g dm)	33.9 ^{b}	33.9 ^{b}	33.1 ^{b}	33.5 ^{b}	31.8 ^{b}	36.6 ^{a}	29.5 ^{c}	28.9 ^{cd}	28.4 ^{cd}	27.6 ^{cd}	27.1 ^{d}	29.5 ^{c}	0.19
Emulsifying Activity Index (m^2/g)	7.6 ^{e}	8.6 ^{e}	9.3 ^{e}	21.9 ^{bc}	26.3 ^{a}	24.0 ^{ab}	8.9 ^{e}	8.7 ^{e}	8.4 ^{e}	20.1 ^{c}	16.3 ^{d}	13.0 ^{d}	0.39
Emulsifying Stability Index (min)	45.9 ^{a}	44.4 ^{a}	42.9 ^{a}	13.8 ^{b}	15.4 ^{b}	13.5 ^{b}	44.0 ^{a}	44.2 ^{a}	43.6 ^{a}	16.4 ^{b}	14.5 ^{b}	14.9 ^{b}	0.48

The results are expressed as the mean of measurements. Results not connected by the same letter are significantly different ($p < 0.01$). Statistics made by row. SED = standard error of the difference.

Oilseed meals contain a substantial protein content; in the present study, rapeseed meal contained 38.3 g/100 g dm, and sunflower meal contained 37.0 g/100 g dm. This content positions them as a promising resource for fermentation, with the potential to recover valuable functional and nutritional benefits. If we analyze the crude protein content, no differences were observed between inoculated and control samples in the case of rapeseed for either of the two fermentation periods (3 and 5 days), nor between the trays. However, differences in protein content were observed for sunflower in the fermented samples from the upper tray (T3) of the 3-day fermentation, which could highlight the higher values for temperature and the lower values for RH. This majority of non-significant results of the crude protein content are in concordance with other works with the same fungal strain, *Rhizopus oryzae*, where no differences were stated in this determination in other by-products, even at more fermentation days [25,34].

Table 2. Statistical results of F ratio and *p*-value of full factorial analysis of fermentation (days), tray and inoculation effects from rapeseed meal and sunflower meal SSF.

Effects	Crude Protein Content		Emulsifying ActivityIndex		Emulsifying StabilityIndex	
	F	*p*-Value	F	*p*-Value	F	*p*-Value
			Rapeseed Meal			
Time (days)	13.69	**0.0030**	0.05	0.8282	71.24	**<0.0001**
Tray	1.95	0.1846	9.85	**0.0004**	1.48	0.2406
Inoculation	0.03	0.8584	782,05	**<0.0001**	3875.74	**<0.0001**
Time (days) Tray	0.14	0.8745	2.10	0.1376	0.89	0.4214
Time (days) Inoculation	0.84	0.3787	8.34	**0.0065**	71.34	**<0.0001**
Tray Inoculation	0.37	0.6955	11.72	**0.0001**	1.99	0.1518
Time (days) Tray Inoculation	0.99	0.4012	0.09	0.9117	2.92	0.0667
			Sunflower Meal			
Time (days)	370.87	**<0.0001**	46.37	**<0.0001**	0.15	0.7048
Tray	9.09	**0.0039**	1.92	0.1614	1.24	0.3016
Inoculation	0.94	0.3516	450.92	**<0.0001**	1861.73	**<0.0001**
Time (days) Tray	1.38	0.2889	10.19	**0.0003**	0.48	0.6239
Time (days) Inoculation	5.44	0.0379	49.22	**<0.0001**	1.25	0.2713
Tray Inoculation	22.95	**<0.0001**	3.40	0.0444	0.13	0.8826
Time (days) Tray Inoculation	2.01	0.1764	4.53	0.0176	1.37	0.2667

p-values in bold are significant ($p < 0.01$).

In relation to the technological properties tested, it can be observed that there were differences in both activity and stability indexes between inoculated and control samples for both sources at 3- and 5-day fermentation (Table 1). Those values were higher in the emulsifying activity for the fermented samples and higher in the emulsifying stability for the control samples. Both were significantly higher ($p < 0.01$) (Table 2). When analyzing among trays, significantly ($p < 0.01$) higher EAI values were observed in the upper tray (T3) for rapeseed, both with 3- and 5-day fermentation, which was correlated with higher values of temperature. Conversely, no differences were identified between the central tray (T2) and the lower tray (T1). In the case of sunflower, a different trend was observed, as the values were higher in the lower tray (T1) and were only significant with the central tray (T2) and upper tray (T3) with the 5-day fermentation ($p < 0.01$). For ESI values, no differences were observed between trays or fermentation periods for either of the two sources studied.

Microorganisms involved in the fermentation process are known to produce enzymes as a secondary metabolite during their growth [35]. The changes in the technological properties of the inoculated samples can be attributed to the action of the protease enzymes produced by *Rhizopus oryzae*, which can result in the hydrolysis of the protein fraction [27,28]. Other studies have also corroborated that smaller proteins result in better results for emulsifying activity and bigger proteins in better emulsifying stability [36].

To verify the changes in the protein fraction, the molecular weight distribution of the protein fraction was analyzed from the soluble fraction of the samples. The results are presented in Figure 3 for rapeseed meal and in Figure 4 for sunflower meal. We can clearly see that the molecular weight distribution has changed in both sources and fermentation days when the by-products were inoculated. The action of the protease enzyme from *Rhizopus oryzae* broke down the bigger molecular weight groups, principally above 5000 Da, into middle and smaller molecular weight groups, from 3000 to 500 Da. In the case of the rapeseed meal, this effect was higher with 5 days of fermentation, but not in the case of sunflower meal. However, no differences were identified in the MWD within the same source among different trays. These results prove that the technological results are affected by the *Rhizopus oryzae* fermentation.

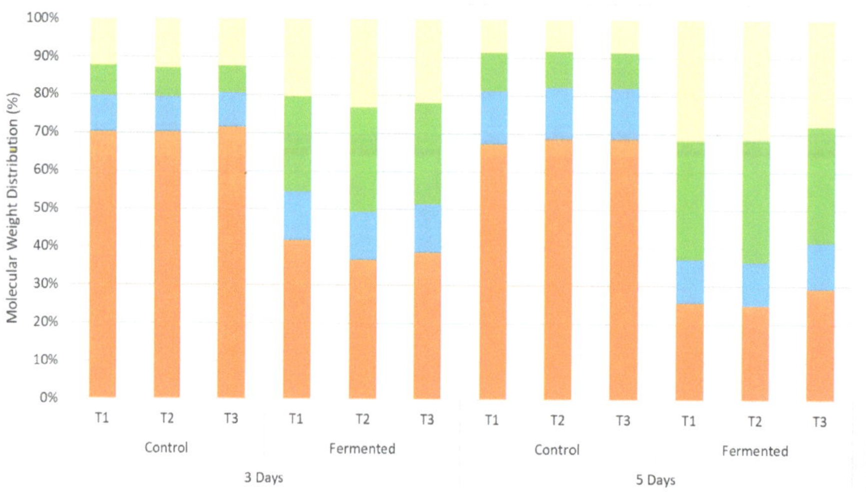

Figure 3. Results of molecular weight distribution (%) by fractions: > 5000 Da, 5000 to 3000 Da, 3000 to 1000 Da, and 1000 to 500 Da, of control and fermented samples from rapeseed meal for three different trays of the bioreactor: T1 (lower tray), T2 (central tray) and T3 (lower tray) and for both 3-day and 5-day fermentation periods.

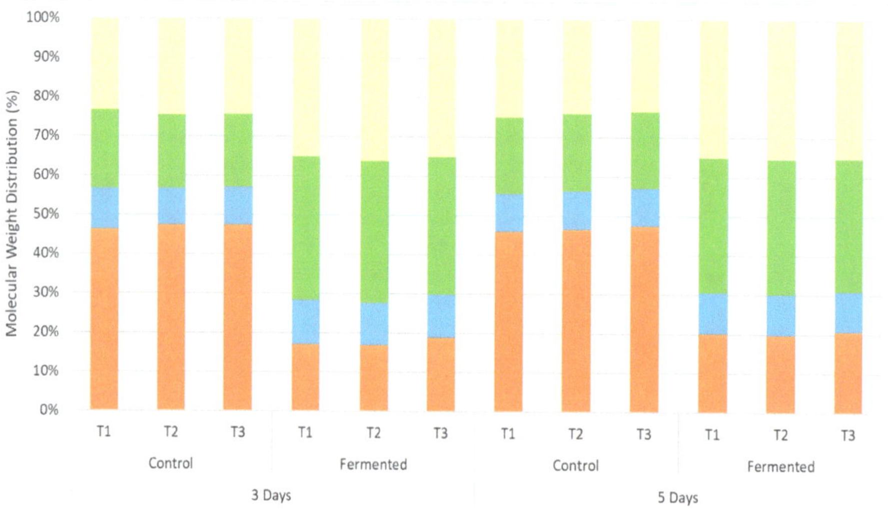

Figure 4. Results of molecular weight distribution (%) by fractions: > 5000 Da, 5000 to 3000 Da, 3000 to 1000 Da, and 1000 to 500 Da, of control and fermented samples from sunflower meal for three different trays of the bioreactor: T1 (lower tray), T2 (central tray) and T3 (lower tray) and for both 3-day and 5-day fermentation periods.

The statistical observations of this study were supported by the principal component analysis (PCA) performed with all the data from the study. The findings provide valuable insights into the complex interplay of environmental factors (temperature and RH) and key variables (crude protein content, EAI, and ESI) in the SSF process carried out in both substrates (Figure 5). The PCA showed that there are no important differences between the samples of the two by-products tested, and also not with different fermentation times. The temperature and RH showed an inverse relationship in the PCA plot. As the temperature increased, RH tended to decrease. This suggests that these environmental factors are closely linked, and changes in one can impact the other, as we have seen in the values registered in the upper and lower trays (T3 and T1, respectively). The observed relationships highlight the importance of RH control for optimizing *Rhizopus oryzae* growth and protein content. Changes in RH appear to have more influence on protein content variation than changes in temperature, as we have observed for sunflower substrates after 5 days of fermentation, although the influence is not strong. Finally, PCA also highlights that technological properties mainly vary with the fungal inoculation, as EAI is correlated on the right side of the graph with the inoculated samples, and ESI is correlated with the control samples on the left side of the graph.

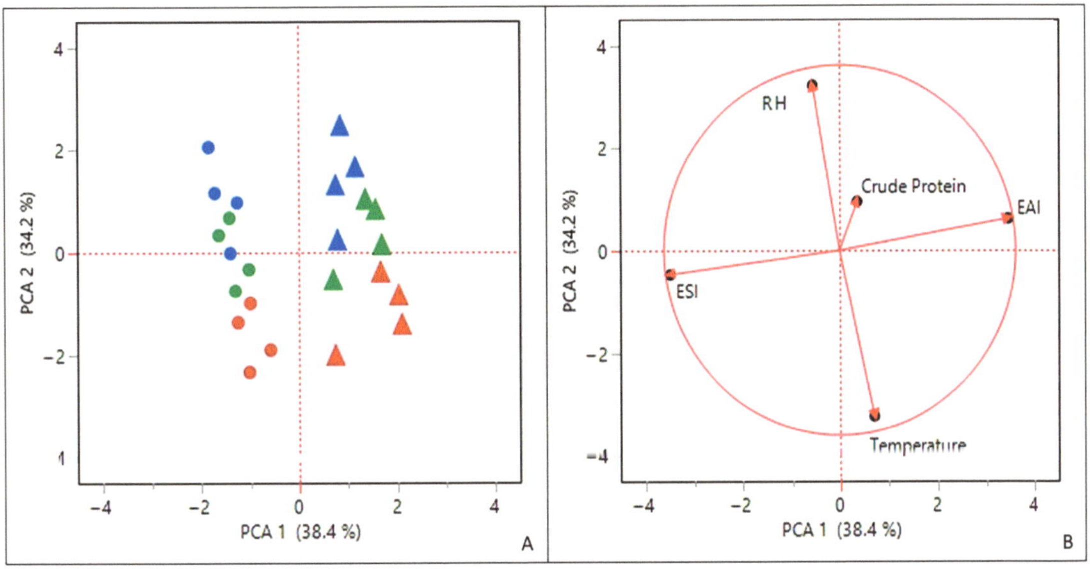

Figure 5. (**A**) Principal component analysis (PCA) containing all the samples of fermented products, grouped by: ● controls tray 1, ● controls tray 2, ● control tray 3, ▲ inoculation tray 1, ▲ inoculation tray 2, and ▲ inoculation tray 3. (**B**) Principal component analysis (PCA) of the variables analyzed in the bioreactor and the fermented products: temperature, relative humidity (RH), crude protein, Emulsifying Activity Index (EAI), and Emulsifying Stability Index (ESI).

3.3. *Design of Pilot Scale Tray Bioreactor*

The design of a pilot-scale tray bioreactor should consider several critical factors that have emerged from this study. Temperature control is of importance, as evidenced by the significant temperature variations observed among the different trays. To address this, the bioreactor design should prioritize precise temperature control mechanisms that ensure uniformity across all trays. Improved heat distribution methods and adaptive temperature regulation can help maintain stable and consistent conditions.

In addition to temperature control, humidity regulation is another crucial consideration. The variations in RH levels observed between trays highlight the need for a comprehensive humidity control system. Achieving uniform RH levels throughout the bioreactor is essential for creating an environment conducive to optimal microbial growth. This may involve optimizing airflow patterns and moisture distribution mechanisms within the trays.

To facilitate precise control over the temperature and humidity, the incorporation of advanced environmental monitoring systems is recommended. Multiple sensors placed strategically within each tray can provide real-time data on temperature and RH, enabling operators to fine-tune environmental conditions and ensure homogeneity. These monitoring systems should also integrate adaptive control algorithms that can dynamically respond to changes in environmental parameters, maintaining stability and consistency in the fermentation process.

The design of the trays themselves should also be optimized to minimize temperature and humidity variations. Factors such as heat distribution and airflow within the trays should be carefully considered to create an environment where environmental conditions remain consistent. Furthermore, scalability should be a key consideration during the design process. The successful conditions achieved at the pilot scale should be replicable at a larger industrial scale, ensuring that the bioreactor can efficiently handle increased production volumes without compromising product quality. Incorporating data analytics and advanced modeling tools, often associated with artificial intelligence (AI), into the design can be invaluable. These AI-driven tools have the capability to analyze vast datasets and complex interactions, allowing for the prediction and optimization of the environmental conditions required for specific fermentation processes. By harnessing AI, operators can ensure not only the stability but also the adaptability of the system, enabling consistent product quality and yields even in the face of varying conditions. This forward-looking approach empowers the bioreactor to respond dynamically to changing environmental factors, further enhancing the efficiency and effectiveness of the fermentation process.

4. Conclusions

This study sheds light on the critical importance of controlling temperature and relative humidity in a tray bioreactor to optimize the fermentation process. It has observed how variations in temperature and RH can have a significant impact on microbial growth and, therefore, on the quality of fermentation products. These findings highlight the need for precise environmental control in pilot-scale biotechnological processes. Furthermore, the study has highlighted significant differences in the technological properties of fermented products, emphasizing the importance of carefully considering these variables in process design and control. Future research, focused on the molecular weight distribution of protein fraction, holds promise for providing deeper insights into a microorganism's enzymatic activity and protein hydrolysis, which could drive further advancements in this field of study.

Author Contributions: Conceptualization, P.S.-M., M.-P.R.-F., A.-J.G.-S. and N.O.-O.; methodology, P.S.-M., N.O.-O., A.-J.G.-S. and C.R.-M.; validation, P.S.-M. and M.-P.R.-F.; investigation, P.S.-M.; resources, N.O.-O.; writing—original draft preparation, P.S.-M.; writing—review and editing, M.-P.R.-F. and N.O.-O.; supervision, M.-P.R.-F. and N.O.-O.; funding acquisition, N.O.-O. All authors have read and agreed to the published version of the manuscript.

Funding: This research was financially supported by the GENERALITAT DE CATALUNYA through the funding grant ACCIÓ-EURECAT, project INNOPROT. P.S.-M. is supported by a fellowship from the Vicente López Program (EURECAT).

Institutional Review Board Statement: Not applicable.

Informed Consent Statement: Not applicable.

Data Availability Statement: The data presented in this study are available on request from the corresponding author. The data are not currently publicly available due to privacy and trademark.

Conflicts of Interest: The authors declare that the research was conducted in the absence of any commercial or financial relationships that could be construed as potential conflicts of interest.

References

1. Chilakamarry, C.R.; Sakinah, A.M.M.; Zularisam, A.W.; Sirohi, R.; Khilji, I.A.; Ahmad, N.; Pandey, A. Advances in Solid-State Fermentation for Bioconversion of Agricultural Wastes to Value-Added Products: Opportunities and Challenges. *Bioresour. Technol.* **2022**, *343*, 126065. [CrossRef] [PubMed]
2. Javourez, U.; Rosero Delgado, E.A.; Hamelin, L. Can Agrifood Co-Products Do Better? Life Cycle Platform for Solid Fermentation. *Nat. Food* **2022**, *3*, 911–920. [CrossRef] [PubMed]
3. Aguilar, C.N.; Gutiérrez-sánchez, G.; Rado-Barragán, P.A.; Rodríguez-Herrera, R.; Martínez-Hernandez, J.L.; Contreras-Esquivel, J.C. Perspectives of Solid State Fermentation for Production of Food Enzymes. *Am. J. Biochem. Biotechnol.* **2008**, *4*, 354–366. [CrossRef]
4. Thomas, L.; Larroche, C.; Pandey, A. Current Developments in Solid-State Fermentation. *Biochem. Eng. J.* **2013**, *81*, 146–161. [CrossRef]
5. Belén Díaz, A.; Alvarado, O.; de Ory, I.; Caro, I.; Blandino, A. Food and Bioproducts Processing Valorization of Grape Pomace and Orange Peels: Improved Production of Hydrolytic Enzymes for the Clarification of Orange Juice. *Food Bioprod. Process.* **2013**, *91*, 580–586. [CrossRef]
6. Rodríguez Couto, S.; López, E.; Sanromán, M.Á. Utilisation of Grape Seeds for Laccase Production in Solid-State Fermentors. *J. Food Eng.* **2006**, *74*, 263–267. [CrossRef]
7. Pallín, M.Á.; González, S.; Gemma, R.; María, E.; Abelairas, L. Towards Industrial Application of Fungal Pretreatment in 2G Biorefinery: Scale—up of Solid—State Fermentation of Wheat Straw. *Biomass Convers. Biorefinery* **2022**. [CrossRef]
8. Wang, J.; Huang, Z.; Jiang, Q.; Roubík, H.; Xu, Q.; Cai, M.; Yang, K.; Sun, P. Fungal Solid-State Fermentation of Crops and Their by-Products to Obtain Protein Resources: The next Frontier of Food Industry. *Trends Food Sci. Technol.* **2023**, *138*, 628–644. [CrossRef]
9. Kumar, V.; Ahluwalia, V.; Saran, S.; Kumar, J.; Patel, A.K.; Singhania, R.R. Recent Developments on Solid-State Fermentation for Production of Microbial Secondary Metabolites: Challenges and Solutions. *Bioresour. Technol.* **2021**, *323*, 124566. [CrossRef]
10. Durand, A. Bioreactor Designs for Solid State Fermentation. *Biochem. Eng. J.* **2003**, *13*, 113–125. [CrossRef]
11. Krishania, M.; Sindhu, R.; Binod, P.; Ahluwalia, V.; Kumar, V.; Sangwan, R.S.; Pandey, A. Design of Bioreactors in Solid-State Fermentation. In *Current Developments in Biotechnology and Bioengineering*; Pandey, A., Larroche, C., Soccol, C.R., Eds.; Elsevier B.V.: Amsterdam, The Netherlands, 2018; pp. 83–96, ISBN 9780444639905.
12. Gutarra, M.; Cavalcanti, E.; Castilho, L.; Freire, D.; Sant'Anna, G. Lipase Production by Solid-State Fermentation. *Appl. Biochem. Biotechnol.* **2005**, *121*, 105–116. [CrossRef] [PubMed]
13. Rodríguez Couto, S.; Moldes, D.; Liébanas, A.; Sanromán, A. Investigation of Several Bioreactor Configurations for Laccase Production by Trametes Versicolor Operating in Solid-State Conditions. *Biochem. Eng. J.* **2003**, *15*, 21–26. [CrossRef]
14. Sala, A.; Echegaray, T.; Palomas, G.; Boggione, M.J.; Tubio, G.; Barrena, R. Insights on Fungal Solid-State Fermentation for Waste Valorization: Conidia and Chitinase Production in Different Reactor Configurations. *Sustain. Chem. Pharm.* **2022**, *26*, 100624. [CrossRef]
15. Ashok, A.; Doriya, K.; Rao, D.R.M.; Kumar, D.S. Design of Solid State Bioreactor for Industrial Applications. An Overview to Conventional Bioreactors. *Biocatal. Agric. Biotechnol.* **2017**, *9*, 11–18. [CrossRef]
16. Mitchell, D.A.; de Lima Luz, L.F.; Krieger, N.; Berovič, M. Bioreactors for Solid-State Fermentation. In *Comprehensive Biotechnology*; Moo-Yong, M., Ed.; Elsevier B.V.: Amsterdam, The Netherlands, 2011; Volume 2, pp. 347–360. ISBN 9780080885049.
17. Vaseghi, Z.; Najafpour, G.D.; Mohseni, S.; Mahjoub, S. Production of Active Lipase by *Rhizopus oryzae* from Sugarcane Bagasse: Solid State Fermentation in a Tray Bioreactor. *Int. J. Food Sci. Technol.* **2013**, *48*, 283–289. [CrossRef]
18. Benabda, O.; M'Hir, S.; Kasmi, M.; Mnif, W.; Hamdi, M. Optimization of Protease and Amylase Production by *Rhizopus oryzae* Cultivated on Bread Waste Using Solid-State Fermentation. *J. Chem.* **2019**, *2019*, 3738181. [CrossRef]
19. FAOSTAT FAO Statistical Database. Available online: https://www.fao.org/faostat/en/#data/QV (accessed on 12 January 2022).
20. Wongsirichot, P.; Gonzalez-Miquel, M.; Winterburn, J. Recent Advances in Rapeseed Meal as Alternative Feedstock for Industrial Biotechnology. *Biochem. Eng. J.* **2022**, *180*, 108373. [CrossRef]
21. Arrutia, F.; Binner, E.; Williams, P.; Waldron, K.W. Oilseeds beyond Oil: Press Cakes and Meals Supplying Global Protein Requirements. *Trends Food Sci. Technol.* **2020**, *100*, 88–102. [CrossRef]
22. Lücke, F.K.; Fritz, V.; Tannhäuser, K.; Arya, A. Controlled Fermentation of Rapeseed Presscake by *Rhizopus*, and Its Effect on Some Components with Relevance to Human Nutrition. *Food Res. Int.* **2019**, *120*, 726–732. [CrossRef]
23. Sousa, D.; Salgado, J.M.; Cambra-López, M.; Dias, A.C.P.; Belo, I. Degradation of Lignocellulosic Matrix of Oilseed Cakes by Solid-State Fermentation: Fungi Screening for Enzymes Production and Antioxidants Release. *J. Sci. Food Agric.* **2022**, *102*, 1550–1560. [CrossRef]
24. Šelo, G.; Tišma, M.; Martinovi, J. Bioconversion of Grape Pomace with *Rhizopus oryzae* under Solid-State Conditions: Changes in the Chemical Composition and Profile of Phenolic Compounds. *Microorganisms* **2023**, *11*, 956. [CrossRef] [PubMed]
25. Sukma, A.; Anwar, H.; Ikhsanudin, A. Effect of *Rhizopus oryzae* Fermentation on Proximate Composition, Anti-Nutrient Contents, and Functional Properties of Banana Peel Flour. *Int. Food Res. J.* **2022**, *29*, 1205–1214. [CrossRef]

26. Mohd Firdaus, O.; Rohaya, M.H.; Miskandar, M.S.; Astimar, A.A. Nutrient Enhancement of Palm Kernel Cake via Solid State Fermentation by Locally Isolated *Rhyzopus oryzae* ME01. *J. Oil Palm Res.* **2022**, *34*, 92–103. [CrossRef]
27. Li, C.; Shi, D.; Stone, A.K.; Wanasundara, J.P.D.; Tanaka, T.; Nickerson, M.T. Effect of Canola Meal Fermentation and Protein Extraction Method on the Functional Properties of Resulting Protein Products. *J. Am. Oil Chem. Soc.* **2023**, *100*, 437–448. [CrossRef]
28. Ling Chin, Y.; Fei Chai, K.; Ning Chen, W. Upcycling of Brewers' Spent Grains via Solid-State Fermentation for the Production of Protein Hydrolysates with Antioxidant and Techno-Functional Properties. *Food Chem. X* **2022**, *13*, 100184. [CrossRef] [PubMed]
29. Sentís-Moré, P.; Ortega-Olivé, N.; Mas-Capdevila, A.; Romero-Fabregat, M.-P. Impact of Centrifugation and Vacuum Filtration Step on the Yield and Molecular Weight Distribution of Protein Hydrolysates from Rapeseed and Sunflower Meals. *LWT-Food Sci. Technol.* **2022**, *165*, 113741. [CrossRef]
30. Pearce, K.N.; Kinsella, J.E. Emulsifying Properties of Proteins: Evaluation of a Turbidimetric Technique. *J. Agric. Food Chem.* **1978**, *26*, 716–723. [CrossRef]
31. Ratkowsky, D.A.; Lowry, R.K.; McMeekin, T.A.; Stokes, A.N.; Chandler, R.E. Model for Bacterial Culture Growth Rate throughout the Entire Biokinetic Temperature Range. *J. Bacteriol.* **1983**, *154*, 1222–1226. [CrossRef]
32. Demir, H.; Tari, C. Bioconversion of Wheat Bran for Polygalacturonase Production by *Aspergillus Sojae* in Tray Type Solid-State Fermentation. *Int. Biodeterior. Biodegrad.* **2016**, *106*, 60–66. [CrossRef]
33. Mitchell, D.A.; Berovič, M.; von Meien, O.F.; Luz, L.F.L., Jr. Basics of Heat and Mass Transfer in Solid-State Fermentation Bioreactor. In *Solid-State Fermentation Bioreactors*; Mitchell, D.A., Berovič, M., Kreiger, N., Eds.; Springer: Berlin/Heidelberg, Germany, 2006.
34. Šelo, G.; Planinić, M.; Tišma, M.; Tomas, S.; Koceva Komlenić, D.; Bucić-Kojić, A. A Comprehensive Review on Valorization of Agro-Food Industrial Residues by Solid-State Fermentation. *Foods* **2021**, *10*, 927. [CrossRef]
35. Tamang, J.P.; Shin, D.H.; Jung, S.-J.; Chae, S.-W. Functional Properties of Microorganisms in Fermented Foods. *Front. Microbiol.* **2016**, *7*, 578. [CrossRef] [PubMed]
36. Sentís-Moré, P.; Ortega-Olivé, N.; Robles-Rodríguez, I.; Royo-Esnal, A.; Romero-Fabregat, M.-P. Protein Hydrolysis of *Camelina Sativa* Meals: A Study of Molecular Weight Distribution and Emulsifying Properties. *Food Biosci.* **2023**, *56*, 103062. [CrossRef]

fermentation

MDPI

Article

Acquisition, Characterization, and Optimization of Distilled Bioethanol Generated from Fermented Carrot (*Daucus carota*) Residues

Abraham Palacios-Velásquez [1], Violeta Quispe-Coquil [1], Enzo Martín Casimiro-Soriano [2,*], Karla Milagros Tapia-Zarate [1] and Alex Rubén Huamán-De la Cruz [2]

1 Faculty of Chemical Engineering, Universidad Nacional del Centro del Perú, Av. Mariscal Castilla No. 3909, Huancayo 12004, El Tambo, Peru; apalacios@uncp.edu.pe (A.P.-V.); violetaqc@uncp.edu.pe (V.Q.-C.); e_2018100819H@uncp.edu.pe (K.M.T.-Z.)

2 Faculty of Environmental Engineering, Universidad Nacional Intercultural de la Selva Central Juan Santos Atahualpa, Jirón Los Cedros No. 141, La Merced 12856, Chanchamayo, Peru; ahuaman@uniscjsa.edu.pe

* Correspondence: vpinvestigacion@uniscjsa.edu.pe

Abstract: Bioethanol is a liquid biofuel produced from the digestion of biomass and usable waste of organic origin. The objective of this research was to obtain bioethanol from carrot (*Daucus carota*) residues of the Peruvian Chantenay variety, with a high content of lignocellulosic substances. The in-batch process method of enzymatic hydrolysis, with *Aspergillus niger* amyloglucosidase, and fermentation, with *Saccharomyces cerevisiae* yeast, was applied. The ferment was steam distilled and chemically characterized. The process was evaluated by controlling pH and enzyme/yeast mass ratio through the response surface optimization. The optimum conditions for the best values of TSS and % ethanol content for the distilled product were a time of 300 min, yeast/enzyme mass ratio of 24.0, and pH of 4.98. The results showed a significant decrease in sugars in the hydrolysis and fermentation stages, optimum alcohol content in the distilled product of 92.48% (*v*/*v*), lower organic compound content, and net calorific value of 23.82 MJ/kg, which is higher than those reported in the literature.

Keywords: bioethanol; *Daucus carota*; enzymatic hydrolysis; fermentation

Citation: Palacios-Velásquez, A.; Quispe-Coquil, V.; Casimiro-Soriano, E.M.; Tapia-Zarate, K.M.; Huamán-De la Cruz, A.R. Acquisition, Characterization, and Optimization of Distilled Bioethanol Generated from Fermented Carrot (*Daucus carota*) Residues. *Fermentation* 2023, 9, 867. https://doi.org/10.3390/fermentation9100867

Academic Editors: Konstantinos G. Kalogiannis and Ricardo Aguilar-López

Received: 25 August 2023
Revised: 18 September 2023
Accepted: 23 September 2023
Published: 25 September 2023

1. Introduction

Fossil fuels currently meet more than 80% of the world's energy demand, with a production of 55 million barrels (mb) per day and a projection of 25 mb per day by 2035 [1]. Their combustion directly affects human health, contributes to the release of large amounts of soot, and acts as the main driver of climate change [2].

By comparison, during recent decades, biofuels based on organic matter substitutes have been developed as cheap, renewable, safe, and cleaner energy sources [3]. For this purpose, organic wastes are used as feedstock in the production of bioethanol, biodiesel, or biohydrogen, through biomass fermentation and pyrolysis in solid state and liquid state [4,5].

Bioethanol (CH_3CH_2OH) is a clean, safe, and renewable biofuel [6], produced from lignocellulosic biomass due to its low cost and easy availability [7,8], in addition to its low consumption of water, chemical reagents, and yeast, which lowers the conversion cost [9,10]. Its addition to conventional gasoline (at a ratio of 5–25%) has been regularly employed in Europe and the United States [11,12].

Different sources of fermentable organic matter, such as agro-industrial waste, food waste [13], fruit and vegetable discards [14], and other substances with high cellulose, lignin, and/or hemicellulose content [15], have been used in their acquisition.

For bioethanol production, pretreatment is required to optimize sugar extraction, followed by enzymatic hydrolysis and subsequent alcoholic fermentation [6]. Hydrolysis consists of the chemical or enzymatic degradation of polysaccharides to fermentable sugars [16] (Equation (1)), while alcoholic fermentation is carried out by the action of yeasts and bacteria to transform these sugars and other nutrients into ethanol and carbon dioxide [4,7] (Equation (2)). Both processes are exothermic, and the efficiency depends on the type of raw material used [10,17].

$$[C_6H_{10}O_6]_n + H_2O \overset{cat.}{\rightarrow} nC_6H_{12}O_6;\ \Delta H_h = -323.18\ KJ/mol \quad (1)$$

$$[C_6H_{10}O_6]_n \overset{cat.}{\rightarrow} CO_2 + C_2H_5OH;\ \Delta H_f - 70.9\ KJ/mol \quad (2)$$

The different modifications to bioethanol production processes aim to improve the chemical or biological activity of the participating organisms and increase the overall yield at low cost [10,18]. In the same way, optimization technologies based on multivariate analysis and the response surface have been applied [19,20]. However, the overall alcohol content of lignocellulose transformation into bioethanol does not exceed 50% [12].

Carrot (*Daucus carota*) pulp and pomace, being frequent residues in juice and food preparation, are important second-generation sources for bioethanol production due to their high content in weight of celluloses (20.8%), sugars (27.6%), and pectins (4.2%) [21]. Regarding carrots, hydrolysis optimization with different enzymes [22,23], nitrogen addition [24], and additional sugar sources [25] have been studied to improve fermentation, as well as modification of the fermenting agent [26]. Despite the significant number of studies performed, there is a considerable gap in the assessment of the optimization measures, characterization, and energy evaluation of products.

Therefore, the present study aims to obtain bioethanol from carrot residues, characterize the product, optimize the parameters of time, yeast/enzyme mass ratio, and pH in the re-reduction of sugar content during fermentation, and energetically evaluate biodiesel through net calorific value.

2. Materials and Methods

2.1. Biomass Collection and Analysis of Raw Material

Discarded carrot samples of the Chantenay variety were collected from a packing shed in the province of Chupaca (74°49′37.74″ W; 12°31′15.46″ S), Junín region, Peru, between April and July 2021. The samples were washed with water and placed in a shed at ambient conditions (5–20 °C; 5–10% relative moisture).

The moisture content was determined gravimetrically in the discarded carrot pulp to express all results on a dry weight basis (DWB). The composition of the dry pulp was determined according to the method of Ramos-Andres et al. [27] on discarded carrots. A 100.00 g sample of dried and pulverized carrot pulp was subjected to two consecutive Soxhlet extractions (the first with water and the second with hexane). Subsequently, the aqueous fraction was hydrolyzed with acid to fractionate it into insoluble material (lignin and ash) and soluble material (cellulose, hemicellulose, pectin, and lignin). The acid-soluble lignin was quantified by UV spectroscopy (UV2802SH-type, UNICO) at 250 nm and the acid-insoluble lignin was measured gravimetrically.

Polysaccharides were hydrolyzed in their monomers for analysis and quantified through HPLC (LC30 NEX-ERA, Shimadzu, Canby, OR, USA), as described by Ramos-Andres et al. [27].

First, 20.0 mL of ultrapure water, 5.0 mL of the liquid sample, and 1.0 mL of H_2SO_4 (72.1%) were mixed. The digestion process was carried out under stirring in a sealed vessel at 125 °C for 1 h. The hydrolyzed sample was cooled to room temperature in a desiccator and neutralized with Na_2CO_3. Impurities were separated with filter paper (pore size 0.22 mm, diameter 47 mm, mixed cellulose esters; Millipore, Burlington, MA, USA). The column of polystyrene divinylbenzene (PSDVB) SH1011 (6 um, 8.0 × 300 mm, Shimadzu, Kyoto, Japan) was maintained at 50 (±0.1) °C and the mobile phase had a flow of 0.95 mL/min of 0.01 N H_2SO_4.

Sugars were identified and quantified with a RID 10A detector, using sugar standards from Sigma-Aldrich: sucrose (99.0%), glucose (99.0%), fructose (99.0%), galacturonic acid

(97.0%), galactose (99.0%), and arabinose (99.0%). The concentration of hemicelluloses was corrected for galactose and arabinose at 0.90 and 0.88, respectively. For pectin, the factor of 0.90 was used for galacturonic acid.

2.2. *Bioethanol Acquisition I: Enzymatic Hydrolysis*

For the preparation of bioethanol, 5 kg of samples from the shed were selected, with individuals larger than 5 cm and presenting minimal areas contaminated by microorganisms. The selected samples were transferred to the laboratory and stored in areas without the presence of light to preserve them and ensure stable points of interest; α = 1.68179 [28,29].

For enzymatic hydrolysis, the initial acidity of the carrot should be conditioned by adding HCl diluted to a pH of 4.5 and controlled using a potentiometer (model B193528 096, SI Analytics), according to the measures suggested by Aimaretti et al. [30] and Yu et al. [26].

The acidified wort was heated to 70 °C for 2 min in a 2.5 L Pyrex beaker to hydrolyze the most complex polysaccharides. It was then cooled and poured into a batch reactor (BioFlo 510, Eppendorf, Hamburg, Germany), with automatic stirring and temperature control.

Then, 0.7 ± 0.1 mL of amyloglucosidase enzyme (Spirizime fuel, Sigma Aldrich, St. Louis, MO, USA) of Aspergillus niger origin was added at a dose of 0.25% *v*/*v*. The closed reactor was stirred at 150 rpm and maintained at a constant temperature of 30 °C for 1 h, as described by Aimaretti et al. [30]. Samples were taken every 30 min to evaluate the quantity of sugar, which was measured using a refractometer (HI96801, Hanna Instruments, Villafranca Padovana, Italy).

2.3. *Bioethanol Acquisition II: Alcoholic Fermentation*

Saccharomyces cerevisiae CCUB yeast cells were stored in a closed container for four days, at 4 °C and approximately 40.0% relative humidity, and without the addition of nutrients. A quantity of 9.0 g of yeast was added to the previously hydrolyzed wort in the batch reactor. The reactor was kept under constant agitation at 50 rpm and 55 ± 2.5 °C, with a time control of up to 5 h, based on the response surface model. Fermentation was controlled by monitoring CO_2 release, temperature, pH, and reducing sugar (RS) concentration, as described by Aimaretti et al. [30] and Demiray et al. [24], who used the same yeast. The sugars present in the ferment were quantified using HPLC, as described in Section 2.1.

2.4. *Determination of TSS and Alcohol Content in Distilled Product*

The fermented wort sample was settled and the supernatant was stored at −20 °C. The final concentration of total soluble solids (TSS) in °Brix was measured using a refractometer. Subsequently, the supernatant was separated and distilled at 75 °C with steam equipment. The distilled alcohol was then isolated for chemical characterization. In addition, a fraction of the broth was separated to determine the alcohol content. Statistical and comparison analyses were based on distilled alcohol.

2.5. *Statistical Analysis and Response Surface*

Before optimization, the variables were evaluated through a single factor, taking into account the publications of De Vrije et al. [21], Aimaretti et al. [23], Demiray et al. [24], and Khosko [25]. The relevance of the variables fermentation time, yeast masses, enzymatic mass, pH, and time were significant ($p < 0.05$), and the fermentation temperature was controlled at approximately 55 °C.

The relationships and effects of fermentation time (X_1), yeast mass/enzyme ratio (X_2) and pH (X_3) concerning response variables such as total suspended solids (Y_1) and percentage alcohol content (Y_2) were optimized by applying the response surface methodology.

The relationship between the variables was studied using the second order polynomial model, as shown in Equation (3)

$$Y = \beta_0 + \sum_{j-1}^{k} \beta_j X_j + \sum_{j=1}^{k} \beta_{jj} X_j^2 + \sum_{i}\sum_{j}^{k} \beta_{ij} X_i X_j + e_i \quad (3)$$

where Y (as Y_1 and Y_2 responses) are the predicted answers; β_0 is the intercept; β_j, β_{jj}, and β_{ij} are the coefficients of the linear, quadratic, and interaction terms, respectively; X_i and X_j are the factors between $-\alpha$ and α; and e_i is the error relative to the measurements. This model was considered due to the presence of significant curvature in the usual optimization systems for biofuels [20].

The parameters were analyzed with the response surface technique using STATGRAPHICS 16 software, considering the R^2 coefficient values for the adjustment of coefficients. For the validation of the model, the significance test and analysis of variance (ANOVA), and curve fitting, with R^2 greater than 75% or $p < 0.05$ with a confidence level of 95%, consistent with Ngomade et al. [29], was used.

2.6. Chemical Analysis

The bioethanol that had the highest alcohol content after the experiments was used for chemical analysis. All chemical analyses were performed in triplicate, considering the ethanol sample distilled from the fermented must.

1. Relative density and viscosity were performed according to ASTM D4052-04 [31], which covers the determination of density, relative density, and API gravity of petroleum distillates and viscous oils, using a bulb density meter. Relative viscosity was measured in a U-type viscometer as the difference in flow time for water flow.
2. Aldehyde, carboxylic acid, and ketone analyses were performed using an 8860 GC gas chromatograph (Agilent, Wilmington, DE, USA), equipped with an FID Headspace detector and a 30 m × 0.25 mm packed column. The procedure was performed based on Medina et al. [32] for the determination of volatiles in alcoholic beverages. The conductive gas was hydrogen (flow rate of 1.5 mL/min). The temperature was programmed gradually from 50 °C (1 min), with a gradual increase of 4 °C/min up to 180 °C, and 8 °C/min up to 250 °C, with final maintenance for 5 min. Acetaldehyde, acetic acid, and acetone were used as standard. Aldehyde concentration was expressed as mg of acetaldehyde per 100 mL of anhydrous alcohol (AA). Carboxylic acid concentration was expressed as mg of acetic acid per 100 mL AA and ketones as parts per million (ppm).
3. Superior alcohol and methanol analyses were performed using the same chromatograph and column as in the previous section. The analysis was guided according to the European standard BS EN 1572:2013 [33] and Zhou et al. [34]. The conductive gas was helium of high purity (flow rate of 1.0 mL/min). The temperature was programmed gradually from 40 °C (2 min), with a gradual increase of 5 °C/min, up to 230 °C, with final holding for 3 min. The intensity of the individual peaks detected was related to the GC reference library to methanol, 1-propanol, 1-butanol, 2-butanol, isobutanol, 2-methylbutanol, and 3-methylbutanol.
4. Total phenol content was determined using the Folin–Ciocalteu spectrophotometric method compared with a standard gallic acid (GAE) curve as a reference. A quantity of 2 mL of the bioethanol was transferred to a flask and made up to 10 mL with a 10.75% (*m*/*v*) ethanolic solution of Na_2CO_3 and 1 mL of Folin–Ciocalteu reagent [35]. The sample was scanned in a UV/vis spectrophotometer at 760 nm; its absorbance was determined through the reference curve and reported as g/mL of solution.

2.7. Lower Heating Value (LHV)

LHV is the difference between the total energy released per unit of mass during the combustion process and that invested in the evaporation of the water it produced and contained in the sample. Calorimetric equipment (BC-CMA-511, Malvern Panalytical, Oregon, Malvern, UK) was used according to the dynamic method of combustion in an adiabatic pump and oxygen atmosphere, considering the ASTM E711-87 standard [36] for waste-based fuels.

3. Results and Discussion

3.1. *Raw Material Characterization*

Discarded carrot pulp of the Chantenay variety used for bioethanol generation had a moisture content of 81.15%. For the characterization of the pulp on a dry basis, the average cellulose (12.65%), hemicellulose (5.85%), pectin (6.15%), and lignin (8.01%) contents were determined. The structural polysaccharide content is in the range reported by De Vrije et al. [21] and Khoshkho et al. [25]. Likewise, a high cellulose content is observed, which is the main input for ethanol generation.

3.2. *Bioethanol Acquistion*

The bioethanol acquisition process occurred through four steps: (i) breaking complex bonds in carrot must by the action of amyloglucosidase to produce cellulose and hemicellulose; (ii) depolymerization of carbohydrate chains into fermentable monosaccharides and disaccharides; (iii) controlling the conversion of pentoses and hexoses to pyruvate and similar molecules by glycolysis; and (iv) metabolization of pyruvate to acetaldehyde under anaerobic conditions and then reduction to ethanol by yeast dehydrogenase [15,37].

It was observed that the addition of a hydrolytic enzyme favors the degradation of sugars for ethanol production. In the case of yeast, it was found that, from 10.0 g of added agent, there is no more significant reduction in sugar content. It was determined that the final content of polysaccharides was made up of cellulose (1.38%), hemicellulose (0.52%), pectin (1.51%), and lignin (2.60%) of the original dry base. The fermentation broth presented a final alcohol concentration of 30.30% (23.90 g/L and 0.08 g alcohol/g yield sugar). This was higher than that found by Aimaretti et al. [30], who reported maximum alcohol content of 19.52% (concentration of 15.4 g/L and yield of 0.10 g alcohol/g sugar), and lower than the ethanol obtained by Aimaretti and Ybalo [23], with a maximum of 36.95% (concentration of 29.15 g/L and yield of 0.19 g alcohol/g sugar), using carrot discards and controlling only the enzymatic agent of the pretreatment. The comparison indicates that an efficient hydrolysis process was developed. Monitoring of yeast cell counts was not performed during the experiment.

At the end of distillation, bioethanol was obtained at a concentration between 68.15% and 92.48% (concentrations from 53.77 to 72.97 g/L, and yields from 0.34 to 0.47 g alcohol/g sugar), which indicates the feasibility of using carrot discards in bioethanol production, confirming the findings of Aimaretti and Ybalo [23]. These results are in the range determined for other lignocellulosic materials, with ethanol contents higher than 85% (concentration of 67.06 g/L, and 0.43 g alcohol/g sugar of yield) [8], and higher than those found by Yu et al. [26], with an alcohol content of 46% (concentration of 37.0 g/L, and yield of 0.23 g alcohol/g sugar), using carrot pulp and carrot peels, respectively.

The results also correspond to those found by Aimaretti et al. [22], for the production of bioethanol with an inoculum of 1011 cells/L of waste yeast and initial pH adjusted to 4.5, who determined an ethanol content of 80.0% (concentration of 63.12 g/L and 0.41 g alcohol/g sugar) and productivity of 10.40 g/L.h. Moreover, Khoshkho et al. [25] evaluated fermentation with the addition of beet molasses inoculum, finding a direct relationship between the alcohol concentration and additive, water, and dry residues used.

The results show that the programmed fermentation reaction reaches its optimum maximum at around 120–250 min, after which it declines rapidly. It is observed that the higher the value of the yeast/enzyme mass ratio, the faster the maximum TSS value is reached. The growth in TSS responds to the increase in monosaccharides after delignification, while the decrease corresponds to their transformation into ethanol [38].

The decreases in progressive TSS content are consistent with those described by Zabed et al. [15] and Tse et al. [37], which indicate that high substrate concentrations inhibit yeast growth and reduce fermentation for ethanol production as a result of high osmotic pressure producing glycerol as an osmoprotectant [4].

On the other hand, in the trials performed, there was no variation in fermentation yield with substrate concentrations, ensuring that sugar and ethanol inhibition did not limit the efficiency of the process, depending mainly on the variables of the amount of yeast and enzyme used in hydrolysis [23,39]. Since a differentiated treatment was employed for the same carbohydrate source, the substrate mass did not act as a differentiator. In this sense, the efficiency of enzymatic hydrolysis and the amount of yeast used in fermentation are considered important factors [4,38], since they are directly related to the availability of fermentable sugars transformed into ethanol, as highlighted by Manojkumar et al. [20] in different plant sources used to prepare bioethanol.

Regarding fermentation pH, as stated by Aimaretti and Ybalo [23] and Aimaretti et al. [30], values between 4 and 6 were used, with an optimum value of 5.5. Similar results were found by Clementz et al. [38] using nanometrically fixed yeasts. Unlike other vegetables and similar residues that work in basic media, carrot requires an acidified medium for its hydrolysis because of the density of lignocellulose in its cell walls, compared to other primary carbohydrate sources [4,40].

3.3. Statistical Analysis and Response Surface

The results of the TSS quantification (Y_1) and ethanol content (Y_2), relating to the variation in fermentation time (X_1), yeast/enzyme mass ratio (X_2), and pH (X_3), are shown in Table 1. A narrow variation was found in the range of 6.52 and 6.92 °Brix as TSS, while the alcohol content fluctuated between 82.26% and 88.73%. These ranges are consistent with those found in alcohols generated with second-generation carbohydrate sources [37] and significantly lower than those found by Vicente et al. [19], which were in the range of 86–100%, which modified the temperature and yeast/substrate mass ratio.

Table 1. Experimental design responses for TSS and ethanol content in the distilled product, by experiment conducted.

Exp.	Time (min), X_1	W_Y/W_E (g_{yeast}/g_{enzime}), X_2	pH, X_3	TSS (°Brix), Y_1	Ethanol Content (%), Y_2
1	180	6	5.0	6.73	82.26
2	120	12	5.5	6.87	82.89
3	120	12	4.5	6.86	82.92
4	180	15	6.0	6.85	83.37
5	180	15	4.0	6.83	83.44
6	240	12	5.5	6.67	83.48
7	240	12	4.5	6.66	83.51
8	60	15	5.0	6.92	83.82
9	180	15	5.0	6.72	84.41
10	180	15	5.0	6.71	84.42
11	180	15	5.0	6.72	84.43
12	300	15	5.0	6.52	84.99
13	120	18	5.5	6.83	85.05
14	120	18	4.5	6.82	85.08
15	240	18	5.5	6.63	85.63
16	240	18	4.5	6.62	85.67
17	180	24	5.0	6.60	88.73

It was found that, at the end of the designed experiments, the concentration of total soluble solids decreased significantly, while the percentage concentration of alcohol increased.

On the other hand, Table 2 shows the ANOVA analysis parameters for the set of variables analyzed in the second-order polynomial model. Significant variables in the regression ($p < 0.05$) were determined to be time, yeast/enzyme mass ratio, pH, and the quadratic relationships of the latter; the least significant relationships were then discarded.

In the correlation analysis of variables, a not very significant relationship (R^2 = 0.28) was found between the yeast/enzyme mass ratio and fermentation pH.

Table 2. ANOVA analysis for the response variables TSS and alcohol content (%) in the distilled product.

Variable	Sum of Squares	Df	Mean Squares	F-Relation	*p*-Value
		Total Soluble Solids Content TSS (°Brix)			
Time (min)-X_1	0.16	1	0.16	86092.60	0.0000
W_Y/W_E (g/g)-X_2	0.00185548	1	0.00185548	998.40	0.0000
pH-X_3	0.02015460	1	0.02015460	10844.78	0.0000
X_2^2	0.00451098	1	0.00451098	2427.26	0.0000
X_3^2	0.02056800	1	0.02056800	11067.22	0.0000
Total error	0.00002044	11	0.00000186		
Total correlation	0.205494	16			
R^2 = 0.90		R^2 adjusted = 0.89			
		Ethanol content (%)			
Time-X_1	0.05139200	1	0.0513920	1683.50	0.0000
W_Y/W_E (g/g)-X_2	0.01318220	1	0.0131822	431.82	0.0000
pH-X_3	1.22437000	1	1.2243700	40107.98	0.0000
X_1^2	0.00026785	1	0.0002679	8.77	0.0142
X_2^2	1.42777000	1	1.4277700	46770.84	0.0000
X_3^2	1.23625000	1	1.2362500	40497.20	0.0000
Total error	0.00030527	10	0.00003053		
Total correlation	36.0878	16			
R^2 = 0.95		R^2 adjusted = 0.90			

The polynomial functions presented in Equations (4) and (5), respectively, represent the regression for TSS and % content of alcohol. In both cases, coefficients of determination (R^2) higher than 90% are observed, indicating an excellent relationship of the studied variables in the range of the experimental results. The determination showed a curvature consistent with the optimizations for biofuel preparation by second-generation residues [20]. According to the analysis and values of $p < 0.05$, greater relevance is observed in the variables of pH and enzyme/substrate ratio on the fermentation time.

$$\begin{aligned} Y_1 = 9.92234 - 1.66667 \times 10^{-3} * X_1 + 0.0134409 * X_2 - 1.18987 * X_3 \\ -6.83072 \times 10^{-4} * X_2^2 + 0.119987 * X_3^2; R^2 = 0.90 \end{aligned} \quad (4)$$

$$\begin{aligned} Y_2 = 55.8971 + 5.2589 \times 10^{-3} * X_1 - 0.03902 * X_2 + 10.1156 * X_3 \\ -1.03746 \times 10^{-6} * X_1^2 + 0.0132836 * X_2^2 - 1.01494 \\ * X_3^2; R^2 = 0.95 \end{aligned} \quad (5)$$

For the same experimental design, Ngomade et al. [29] determined the relevance of fermentation time and yeast mass applied in the regression equation for the optimization of response in ethanol content, with an R^2 between 0.83. Previously, Vicente et al. [19] determined the relationship of temperature and yeast/substrate mass ratio variables for the percentage ethanol concentration with an R^2 = 0.95.

It is important to mention that the variables studied have opposite effects on TSS and the ethanol content obtained. The present research shows a higher degree of correlation with both processes, highlighting the importance of time and pH in the 4.5–5.0 range in fermentation [23,38,40], as well as the improvement in the system response after the addition of a controlled amount of enzyme in the pretreatment. The importance of enzymatic pretreatment was previously exposed by Tse et al. [37] and Aimaretti and Ybalo [23] in the preparation of bioethanol from second-generation sources, due to the increase in the concentration of available fermentable sugars, longer yeast lifetime, and optimal control of pH, temperature, and oxygen variables in the reaction medium to preserve the hydrolytic properties of amylases [20].

The comparison of the theoretical and experimental results in obtaining bioethanol, applying Equations (4) and (5), as well as the optimized experimental values, are shown in Table 3. A general deviation in the range of 0.5–4% of the experimental data for the theoretical values was observed.

Table 3. Comparison of theoretical and experimental results in TSS and percentage ethanol content in distilled product.

Exp.	SST Theo. (°Brix)	SST Exp. (°Brix)	Relat. Deviation SST (%)	Alcohol Content Theo. (%)	Alcohol Content Exp. (%)	Relat. Deviation Alcohol Content (%)
1	6.93	6.73	2.89	81.96	82.26	0.37
2	7.12	6.87	3.51	82.76	82.89	0.16
3	7.02	6.86	2.28	82.79	82.92	0.16
4	7.15	6.85	4.20	83.06	83.37	0.37
5	6.95	6.83	1.73	83.13	83.44	0.37
6	6.92	6.67	3.61	82.94	83.48	0.65
7	6.82	6.66	2.35	82.97	83.51	0.65
8	7.12	6.92	2.81	83.78	83.82	0.05
9	6.92	6.72	2.89	84.11	84.41	0.36
10	6.92	6.71	3.03	84.11	84.42	0.37
11	6.92	6.72	2.89	84.11	84.43	0.38
12	6.72	6.52	2.98	84.15	84.99	1.00
13	7.07	6.83	3.39	84.91	85.05	0.16
14	6.97	6.82	2.15	84.94	85.08	0.16
15	6.87	6.63	3.49	85.09	85.63	0.63
16	6.77	6.62	2.22	85.13	85.67	0.63
17	6.80	6.60	2.94	88.42	88.73	0.35
Optimal	6.40	6.20	3.13	89.30	92.48	3.56

The optimum point was determined with X_1 = 300 min, X_2 = 24.0 g/g, and X_3 = 4.98. The experimental optimum result was better than that calculated through the equations, obtaining an ethanol content of 92.48% and a TSS content of 5.90 °Brix, due to an increase in the fermentation time, high enzyme/yeast ratio, and pH close to 5. It is important to mention that the effect of fermentation time is always constant and directly related to ethanol production, with the main yeast/enzyme mass ratio and pH being subject to optimization.

The small deviation found between the theoretical and experimental data is similar to that found by Ngomade et al. [29] and Del Aguila et al. [28] when applying surface response modeling using vegetable oil sources. In the case of other fermentable sugar sources, the percentage is similar to that found in seeds, which showed high cellulose content [20]. The optimized result found in the present study was similar to those reported by Aimaretti et al. [30], Aimaretti and Ybalo [23], and Khoshkho et al. [25], whose ranges vary from 95 to 100%, when using carrot discard, peels, and pulp, respectively.

Considering an average sugar concentration contained in the must of 93.1 g/L and the final ethanol content at 92.48%, the results of the experiment were comparable to those obtained by Aimaretti et al. [30], who used carrot discards for alcohol content of 35.6 g/L.day. They were also in agreement with the bioethanol concentrations obtained by Khoshkho et al. [25] at 51.5 mL/L (40.63 g/L), where mixtures of carrot pulp, sugar inoculum, and water were controlled.

While authors such as Aimaretti and Ybalo [23] focus on the enzyme preparation in the pretreatment, Khoshkho et al. [25], Yu et al. [26], and Demiray et al. [24], have optimized based on the fermentation conditions, independently. In the present study we address both spectra together through the variable X_2 (yeast/enzyme mass ratio), since they are factors with a greater contribution to productivity than temperature [19].

3.4. *Bioethanol Chemical Analysis*

The result of the chemical analysis of the optimized bioethanol is shown in Table 4, compared to ASTM D4806 (and its complementary regulations) with characteristics required as an additive (the data were taken from Obeta et al. [41].

Table 4. Physicochemical analysis of bioethanol on distilled product compared to the ASTM standard for alcohol used as an additive.

Parameter	Bioethanol (This Study)	Standard Ethanol	ASTM
Ethanol content (% *v*/*v*) on distilled product	92.48	-	>92.00
Density at 15 °C (g/cm^3)	0.89	0.794	0.80
Specific gravity	0.90	--	--
Viscosity at 40 °C (mm^2/s)	1.65	1.30	1.34
Flashpoint (°C) of distilled product	14.5	12.5	18.60
Aldehydes (mg/100 mL)	1.30	--	--
Ketones (ppm)	0.10	--	--
Acidity (mg/100 mL acetic acid)	0.90	--	>0.70
Superior alcohols (mg/100 mL)	2.30	--	--
Methanol content (% m/m)	0.01	--	<0.50
Phenol—water ratio (g/mL)	0.20	--	--
Moisture content (%)	2.50	--	20.00
Sugar content (% m/v)	0.40	--	--

Traces of impurities from amino acids, minerals, and organic acids, as heating residues, were observed in the analysis. The determination of aldehydes, ketones, acetic acid, and higher alcohols in minimal quantities within the final product correspond to traces of enzymes, yeasts, and volatile compounds that could have contaminated the ferment before steam distillation [42].

Regarding the concentration of the bioethanol obtained, several studies with lignocellulosic sources have designed variants in the pretreatment and fermentation processes, with bioethanol contents between 75% and 95% after enzymatic pretreatment [4,15]. For the present study, the ethanol content (92.40%) showed higher percentages than those found in rice husks (82%), corn stover (90%), rapeseed husks (91%), Miscanthus (88%), and other forms of grasses (62–74%), pretreated with H_2SO_4, alkali, and enzymes [6,15]. The highest percentages of ethanol concentrations probably correspond to the enzymatic pretreatments (cellulases, accelerates, glucosidases, and *Aspergillus niger*), that were applied in the present study.

Regarding the other bioethanol properties, the characterization results were found to be within the ranges specified by the US Standard ASTM D4806 (and its complementary regulations) and the European Standard EN14214 for bioethanol and biofuels [29].

Density and viscosity are those variables that directly affect fuel distribution, transport, and storage processes. In addition, they affect the production of waste gases after combustion. In the case of biofuels, Tüccar et al. [43] found a direct relationship between CO_2 and NO_X production, while CO volume was reduced. The bioethanol obtained in our study had higher density and specific gravity (0.89 g/cm^3) than the standard ethanol (0.79 g/cm^3) and that stated in the ASTM standard for use as an additive (0.80 g/cm^3), as a result of the content of other oxygenated chemical species of higher molecular mass than that condensed during distillation. These indicators suggest sufficient content of chemical species with the capacity to burn completely through a stoichiometric relationship with the available air [44].

In the same sense, the viscosity of bioethanol at 1.65 mm^2/s is sufficient for pulverization and atomization, thus preventing carbonaceous deposits from forming after combustion [29].

The magnitude found is higher than that established in the D6751 standard for biodiesel in combustion engines (1.9–2.6 mm^2/s), which indicates its direct use should be avoided. Likewise, the density of the ethanol obtained was higher than the standard and that required according to D4806 for use as a gasoline additive (1.30–1.34 mm^2/s). The higher viscosity is probably due to the formation of dissolved esters and aldehydes of higher molecular weight that were generated during fermentation.

Of the other oxygenated compounds (higher alcohols, phenols, aldehydes, and ketones), their low concentration reflects good product quality, high homogeneity during combustion, and higher oxidation potential, unlike pure ethanol and other hydrocarbons present in fossil fuels [28].

The flash point at 14.5 °C was higher than that found in high-purity ethanol samples (12.5 °C) and lower than that recommended by the ASTM standard. In addition, a low methanol content ensures safe combustion and storage. The experimental inflation point found was lower than that reported using sugarcane bagasse at 19.20 °C [45], Abrus seed meal at 18.35 °C [41], corn cob at 16.50 °C [46], rice straw at 20.37 °C [47], and Dioscorea rotundata lentils at 17.5 °C [48], among others. These values indicate greater ease of incineration from other sources. The low phenolic index indicates that the distillation and storage of the product were sufficient to prevent its humidification and potential hydrolysis to generate esters and oxidizing fatty acids.

The intermediate characteristics described above demonstrate that the bioethanol obtained has the potential to be used as a gasoline additive in low proportions (10–20%) [11] due to its high alcohol content, low formation of residual carbonaceous compounds, and low proportion of oxidizing compounds [12].

3.5. Energy Assessment

The calorific potential found in distilled bioethanol was 23.82 MJ/kg, lower than that of standard ethanol of 28.58 MJ/kg, but within the range of 10.2–30.0 MJ/kg established in ASTM D4806 [41]. The calorific potential obtained compared to other secondary sources of lignocellulosic biomass is shown in Table 5.

Table 5. Comparison between the calorific potential of bioethanol obtained by different biomass sources.

Source	LHV (MJ/kg)	Reference
Rice husk	14.9	[49]
Wheat straw	17.0–18.9	[50,51]
Rice straw	14.5–15.5	[51,52]
Cotton stalk	17.3	[49]
Sorghum stalk	16.9	[49]
Corn stover	16.2–16.5	[51,53]
Mustard stalk	15.9	[49]
Sugarcane bagasse	18.61–18.73	[45,54]
Corn cob	15.5	[49]
Carrot residues	23.82	This study

The main differences between the sources compared lie mainly in the pretreatment medium applied before fermentation. According to Das et al. [39], the best yields in the hydrolysis of lignin, celluloses, and xyloses occur when enzymatic degradation is applied, followed by acid and basic hydrolysis. Combined degradation of acids and enzymes improves the degradation of complex sugars [4], which was corroborated in the present experiment with higher energy potential. This may also be due to the low content of oxidizing compounds identified in the chemical analysis, which increased the oxidation potential of the bioethanol generated [6].

The aforementioned characteristics of the bioethanol obtained give it the capacity to be used as an additive with regular gasoline in proportions close to 10% to obtain an expected combined calorific value of 40 MJ/kg [11].

For the energy balance, it was considered that the only product in the enzymatic hydrolysis of complex carbohydrates was glucose, disregarding the concentration of intermediate dextrins, as presented in Equation (1). On the other hand, in the fermentation, it was estimated that all the glucose was consumed by the bacteria for the generation of ethanol, as shown in Equation (2).

Since the process developed was biological and irreversible, there were significant thermodynamic limitations, limited only by pH and temperature. The overall balance of the process resulted in +1411 W, generating more energy than is consumed during ethanol production.

4. Conclusions

Bioethanol was obtained from carrot residues, considering a combined enzymatic pretreatment and acid degradation, fermentation with *Saccharomyces cerevisiae*, and distillation of the product. The process was optimized via the response surface based on the control of fermentation time, yeast/enzyme mass ratio, and fermentation pH in a central compound factorial design. The optimum conditions found were 300 min, yeast/enzyme mass ratio of 24.0, and pH of 4.98, obtaining an alcohol content of 92.48% and TSS content of 5.90 °Brix. The physicochemical and energetic characterization of the optimum product was found to be within the range accepted by ASTM standards for its use as a gasoline additive and of higher magnitudes than those found with other biomass sources reported in the literature.

Author Contributions: Conceptualization, V.Q.-C. and A.P.-V.; methodology, V.Q.-C. and K.M.T.-Z.; formal analysis, V.Q.-C. and E.M.C.-S.; investigation, V.Q.-C., K.M.T.-Z. and A.R.H.-D.l.C.; resources, A.P.-V.; data curation, E.M.C.-S.; writing—original draft preparation, V.Q.-C., K.M.T.-Z. and E.M.C.-S.; writing—review and editing, E.M.C.-S. and A.R.H.-D.l.C. All authors have read and agreed to the published version of the manuscript.

Funding: This research was funded by Universidad Nacional del Centro del Perú.

Data Availability Statement: Data available on request due to privacy restrictions.

Acknowledgments: We thank the General Research Institute of the Universidad Nacional del Centro del Perú, through its managers, Engineers Edgar Rojas, and Evelyn Tinoco, for their invaluable support in the acquisition of materials and equipment.

Conflicts of Interest: The authors declare no conflict of interest.

References

1. Miller, R.; Sorrell, S. The future of oil supply. *Phil. Trans. R. Soc.* **2014**, *372*, 20130179. [CrossRef] [PubMed]
2. Lelieveld, J.; Klingmüller, K.; Pozzer, A.; Burnett, R.; Haines, A.; Ramanathan, V. Effects of fossil fuel and total anthropogenic emission removal on public health and climate. *Proc. Natl. Acad. Sci. USA* **2019**, *116*, 7192–7197. [CrossRef] [PubMed]
3. Singh, S.; Singh, D. Biodiesel production through the use of different sources and characterization of oils and their esters as the substitute of diesel: A review. *Renew. Sustain. Energy Rev.* **2010**, *14*, 200–216. [CrossRef]
4. Dhungana, P.; Prajapati, B.; Maharjan, S.; Joshi, J. Current Trends in Lignocellulosic Bioethanol Production. *Int. J. Appl. Sci. Biotechnol.* **2022**, *10*, 1–11. [CrossRef]
5. Jarboe, L.; Wen, Z.; Choi, D.; Brown, R. Hybrid thermochemical processing: Fermentation of pyrolysis-derived bio-oil. *Appl. Microbiol. Biotechnol.* **2011**, *91*, 1519–1523. [CrossRef]
6. Rezania, S.; Oryani, B.; Cho, J.; Talaiekhozani, A.; Sabbagh, F.; Hashemi, B.; Mohammadi, A. Different pretreatment technologies of lignocellulosic biomass for bioethanol production: An overview. *Energy* **2020**, *199*, 117457. [CrossRef]
7. Khandaker, M.; Qiamuddin, K.; Majrashi, A.; Dalorima, T. Bio-Ethanol Production from Fruit and Vegetable Waste by Using *Saccharomyces cerevisiae*. In *Bioethanol Technologies*; Intech-Open: KwaZulu-Natal, Sudáfrica, 2018. [CrossRef]
8. Kumar, A.; Singh, J.; Baskar, C. Lignocellulosic biomass for bioethanol production through microbes: Strategies to improve process efficiency. *Prospect. Renew. Bioprocess. Future Energy Syst.* **2019**, *10*, 357–386. [CrossRef]
9. Chen, J.; Zhang, B.; Luo, L.; Zhang, F.; Yi, Y.; Shan, Y.; Lü, X. A review on recycling techniques for bioethanol production from lignocellulosic biomass. *Renew. Sustain. Energy Rev.* **2021**, *149*, 111370. [CrossRef]
10. Bender, L.; Lopes, S.; Gomes, K.; Devos, R.; Colla, L. Challenges in bioethanol production from food residues. *Bioresour. Technol. Rep.* **2022**, *19*, 101171. [CrossRef]
11. Khan, O.; Yadav, A.; Khan, M.; Parvez, M. Characterization of bioethanol obtained from *Eichhornia Crassipes plant*; its emission and performance analysis on CI engine. *Energy Sources Part A* **2021**, *43*, 1793–1803. [CrossRef]

12. Kang, Q.; Appels, L.; Tan, T.; Dewil, R. Bioethanol from lignocellulosic biomass: Current findings determine research priorities. *Sci. World J.* **2014**, *1*, 298153. [CrossRef] [PubMed]
13. Milano, J.; Ong, H.; Masjuki, H.; Silitonga, A.; Kusumo, F.; Dharma, S.; Sebayang, A.; Cheah, M.; Wang, C. Physicochemical property enhancement of biodiesel synthesis from hybrid feedstocks of waste cooking vegetable oil and beauty leaf oil through optimized alkaline-catalysed transesterification. *Waste Manag.* **2018**, *80*, 435–449. [CrossRef]
14. Candama, M.; Duque, S.; Cadena, E. Optimization of enzymatic pretreatments to obtain fermentable sugars from fruit and vegetable waste. *Waste Biomass-Valorization* **2020**, *11*, 5991–6002. [CrossRef]
15. Zabed, H.; Sahu, J.; Boyce, A.; Faruq, G. Fuel ethanol production from lignocellulosic biomass: An overview on feedstocks and technological approaches. *Renew. Sust. En. Rev.* **2016**, *66*, 751–774. [CrossRef]
16. Anwar, M.; Ma, H.; Yue, S.; Wang, Q.; Tu, M. Concise review on ethanol production from food waste: Development and sustainability. *Environ. Sci. Pollut. Res.* **2018**, *25*, 28851–28863. [CrossRef]
17. Panahi, H.; Dehhaghi, M.; Guillemin, G.; Gupta, V.; Lam, S.; Aghbashlo, M.; Tabatabaei, M. Bioethanol production from food wastes rich in carbohydrates. *Curr. Opin. Food Sci.* **2022**, *43*, 71–81. [CrossRef]
18. Broda, M.; Yelle, D.; Serwanska, K. Bioethanol Production from Lignocellulosic Biomass— Challenges and Solutions. *Molecules* **2022**, *27*, 8717. [CrossRef]
19. Vicente, G.; Coteron, A.; Martinez, M.; Aracil, J. Application of the factorial design of experiments and response surface methodology to optimize biodiesel production. *Ind. Crops Prod.* **1998**, *8*, 29–35. [CrossRef]
20. Manojkumar, N.; Muthukumaran, C.; Sharmila, G. A comprehensive review on the application of response surface methodology for optimization of biodiesel production using different oil sources. *J. King Saud Univ. Eng. Sci.* **2020**, *34*, 198–208. [CrossRef]
21. De Vrije, T.; Budde, M.; Lips, S.; Bakker, R.; Mars, A.; Claassen, P. Hydrogen production from carrot pulp by the extreme thermophiles *Caldicellulosiruptor saccharolyticus* and *Thermotoga neapolitana*. *Int. J. Hydrog. Energy* **2010**, *35*, 13206–13213. [CrossRef]
22. Aimaretti, N.; Clementz, A.; Codevilla, A.; Rojas, M.; Yori, J. Sustainable fermentation processing of two revalorized agro-industrial discards: Carrot and brewer's yeast. *Int. J. Energy Environ. Eng.* **2013**, *4*, 24. [CrossRef]
23. Aimaretti, N.; Ybalo, C. Valorization of carrot and yeast discards for the obtention of ethanol. *Biomass-Bioenergy* **2012**, *42*, 18–23. [CrossRef]
24. Demiray, E.; Karatay, S.; Dönmez, S.; Dönmez, G. The usage of carrot pomace for bioethanol production. *J. Chil. Chem. Soc.* **2016**, *61*, 2996–2998. [CrossRef]
25. Khoshkho, S.; Mahdavian, M.; Karimi, F.; Karimi-Maleh, H.; Razaghi, P. Production of bioethanol from carrot pulp in the presence of *Saccharomyces cerevisiae* and beet molasses inoculum; a biomass based investigation. *Chemosphere* **2022**, *286*, 131688. [CrossRef]
26. Yu, C.; Jiang, B.; Duan, K. Production of bioethanol from carrot pomace using the thermotolerant yeast *Kluyveromyces marxianus*. *Energies* **2013**, *6*, 1794–1801. [CrossRef]
27. Ramos-Andrés, M.; Aguilera-Torre, B.; García-Serna, J. Hydrothermal production of high-molecular weight hemicellulose-pectin, free sugars and residual cellulose pulp from discarded carrots. *J. Clean. Prod.* **2021**, *290*, 125179. [CrossRef]
28. Del Águila, N.; Mendocilla, A.; Villalobos, V. Evaluación por el método de superficie de respuesta del efecto de la temperatura y tiempo de transesterificación en el rendimiento y poder calórico del biodiesel obtenido a partir del aceite de piñón (*Jatropha curcas*). *Agroindust. Sci.* **2011**, *1*, 63–72. [CrossRef]
29. Ngomade, S.; Tchuifon, R.; Tagne, R.; Ngueteu, M.; Patai, H.; Nche, G.; Anagho, S. Optimization by Response Surface Methodology of Biodiesel Production from *Podocarpus falcatus* Oil as a Cameroonian Novel Nonedible Feedstock. *J. Chem.* **2022**, *1*, 3786602. [CrossRef]
30. Aimaretti, N.; Ybalo, C.; Rojas, M.; Plou, F.; Yori, J. Production of bioethanol from carrot discards. *Bioresour. Technol.* **2012**, *123*, 727–732. [CrossRef]
31. *D4052-04*; Standard Test Method for Density, Relative Density, and API Gravity of Liquids. ASTM International: West Conshohocken, PA, USA, 2004.
32. Medina, G.; Juárez, R.; Peña, A. Identification and Quantification of Aldehydes in Mezcal by Solid Phase Microextraction with On-fiber Derivatization-Gas Cromatography. *J. Mex. Chem. Soc.* **2011**, *55*, 84–88.
33. *European Standard [ES] IP 571*; Ethanol as a Blending Component for Petrol—Determination of Higher Alcohols, Methanol and Other Impurities—Gas Chromatographic Method. European Committee for Standardization: Brussels, Belgium, 2013.
34. Zhou, Z.; Ni, W.; Ji, Z.; Liu, S.; Han, X.; Li, X.; Mao, J. Development of a rapid method for determination of main higher alcohols in fermented alcoholic beverages based on dispersive liquid-liquid microextraction and gas chromatography-mass spectrometry. *Food Anal. Meth.* **2020**, *13*, 591–600. [CrossRef]
35. Blainski, A.; Lopes, G.; De Mello, J. Application and analysis of the folin ciocalteu method for the determination of the total phenolic content from *Limonium brasiliense* L. *Molecules* **2013**, *18*, 6852–6865. [CrossRef] [PubMed]
36. *E711*; Standard Test Method for Gross Calorific Value of Refuse-Derived Fuel by the Bomb Calorimeter. ASTM International: West Conshohocken, PA, USA, 2004.
37. Tse, T.; Wiens, D.; Reaney, M. Production of bioethanol—A review of factors affecting ethanol yield. *Fermentation* **2021**, *7*, 268. [CrossRef]
38. Clementz, A.; Aimaretti, N.; Manuale, D.; Codevilla, A.; Yori, J. Optimization of ethanol fermentation from discarded carrots using immobilized *Saccharomyces cerevisiae*. *Int. J. Energy Environ. Eng.* **2015**, *6*, 129–135. [CrossRef]

39. Das, N.; Jena, P.; Padhi, D.; Kumar, M.; Sahoo, G. A comprehensive review of characterization, pretreatment and its applications on different lignocellulosic biomass for bioethanol production. *Biomass Convers. Biorefin.* **2021**, *13*, 1503–1527. [CrossRef]
40. Li, A.; Antizar, B.; Khraisheh, M. Bioconversion of municipal solid waste to glucose for bio-ethanol production. *Bioproc. Biosyst. Eng.* **2007**, *30*, 189–196. [CrossRef]
41. Obeta, J.; Ossai, E.; Njoku, O. Optimization and characterization of bioethanol production from Abrus seed flour. *Int. J. Energy Res.* **2021**, *45*, 3883–3898. [CrossRef]
42. Sánchez, C.; Santos, S.; Sánchez, R.; Lienemann, C.; Todolí, J. Profiling of Organic Compounds in Bioethanol Samples of Different Nature and the Related Fractions. *ACS Omega* **2020**, *5*, 20912–20921. [CrossRef]
43. Tüccar, G.; Tosun, E.; Uludamar, E. Investigations of effects of density and viscosity of diesel and biodiesel fuels on NOx and other emission formations. *J. Eng. Sci.* **2018**, *6*, 81–85. [CrossRef]
44. Todoruţ, A.; Molea, A.; Barabás, I. Predicting the Temperature and Composition–Dependent Density and Viscosity of Diesel Fuel–Ethanol Blends. *Period. Polytech. Chem. Eng.* **2020**, *64*, 213–220. [CrossRef]
45. Saka, A.; Afolabi, A.; Ogochukwu, M. Production and Characterization of Bioethanol from Sugarcane Bagasse as Alternative Energy Sources. World Congress on Engineering WCE 2015, pp. 876–880. Available online: http://www.iaeng.org/publication/WCE2015/WCE2015_pp876-880.pdf (accessed on 24 August 2023).
46. Harrison, O.; Ekene, C.; Nathaniel, I. Production and Characterization of Bioethanol from Acid Catalysed Hydrolysis of Cellulosic Biomass (*Maize Cob*). *J. Energy Environ. Chem. Eng.* **2022**, *7*, 66–70.
47. Rabiu, A.; Elinge, C.; Ambursa, M.; Rabiu, A.; Samaila, D. Characterization of Bioethanol Fuel from Rice and Corn Straws: A Comparative Study. *Equity J. Sci. Technol.* **2021**, *8*, 74–78. [CrossRef]
48. Bashir, A.; Baba, N.; Akpomie, T. Process Optimization and Characterization of Bioethanol from Yam (*Dioscorea rotundata*) Peels. *Int. J. Sci. Res. Pub.* **2022**, *12*, 223–229. [CrossRef]
49. Raj, T.; Kapoor, M.; Gaur, R.; Christopher, J.; Lamba, B.; Tuli, D.; Kumar, R. Physical and chemical characterization of various Indian agriculture residues for biofuels production. *Energy Fuels* **2015**, *29*, 3111–3118. [CrossRef]
50. Bridgeman, T.; Jones, J.; Shield, I.; Williams, P. Torrefaction of reed canary grass, wheat straw and willow to enhance solid fuel qualities and combustion properties. *Fuel* **2008**, *87*, 844–856. [CrossRef]
51. Kumar, S.; Paritosh, K.; Pareek, N.; Chawade, A.; Vivekanand, V. De-construction of major Indian cereal crop residues through chemical pretreatment for improved biogas production: An overview. *Renew. Sustain. Energy Rev.* **2018**, *90*, 160–170. [CrossRef]
52. Worasuwannarak, N.; Sonobe, T.; Tanthapanichakoon, W. Pyrolysis behaviors of rice straw, rice husk, and corncob by TG MS technique. *J. Anal. Appl. Pyrolysis* **2007**, *78*, 265–271. [CrossRef]
53. Vassilev, S.; Baxter, D.; Andersen, L.; Vassileva, C. An overview of the chemical composition of biomass. *Fuel* **2010**, *89*, 913–933. [CrossRef]
54. Tsai, W.; Lee, M.; Chang, Y. Fast pyrolysis of rice straw, sugarcane bagasse and coconut shell in an induction-heating reactor. *J. Anal. Appl. Pyrolysis* **2006**, *76*, 230–237. [CrossRef]

fermentation

MDPI

Article

Design and Construction of a New Reactor for Flexible Biomethanation of Hydrogen

Kevin Hoffstadt [1,*], Dheeraja Cheenakula [1], Marcell Nikolausz [2], Simone Krafft [1,*], Hauke Harms [2] and Isabel Kuperjans [1]

1 Institute NOWUM-Energy, University of Applied Sciences Aachen, Heinrich-Mussmann-Str. 1, 52428 Juelich, Germany; cheenakula@fh-aachen.de (D.C.); kuperjans@fh-aachen.de (I.K.)

2 Department of Environmental Microbiology Helmholtz Centre for Environmental Research—UFZ, Permoserstr. 15, 04318 Leipzig, Germany; marcell.nikolausz@ufz.de (M.N.); hauke.harms@ufz.de (H.H.)

* Correspondence: k.hoffstadt@fh-aachen.de (K.H.); krafft@fh-aachen.de (S.K.); Tel.: +49-241-6009-53079 (K.H.); +49-241-6009-53022 (S.K.)

Abstract: The increasing share of renewable electricity in the grid drives the need for sufficient storage capacity. Especially for seasonal storage, power-to-gas can be a promising approach. Biologically produced methane from hydrogen produced from surplus electricity can be used to substitute natural gas in the existing infrastructure. Current reactor types are not or are poorly optimized for flexible methanation. Therefore, this work proposes a new reactor type with a plug flow reactor (PFR) design. Simulations in COMSOL Multiphysics ® showed promising properties for operation in laminar flow. An experiment was conducted to support the simulation results and to determine the gas fraction of the novel reactor, which was measured to be 29%. Based on these simulations and experimental results, the reactor was constructed as a 14 m long, 50 mm diameter tube with a meandering orientation. Data processing was established, and a step experiment was performed. In addition, a k_La of 1 h^{-1} was determined. The results revealed that the experimental outcomes of the type of flow and gas fractions are in line with the theoretical simulation. The new design shows promising properties for flexible methanation and will be tested.

Keywords: methanation; plug flow reactor; bubble column; bio-methane; power-to-gas; P2G

Citation: Hoffstadt, K.; Cheenakula, D.; Nikolausz, M.; Krafft, S.; Harms, H.; Kuperjans, I. Design and Construction of a New Reactor for Flexible Biomethanation of Hydrogen. *Fermentation* **2023**, *9*, 774. https://doi.org/10.3390/fermentation9080774

Academic Editor: Ricardo Aguilar-López

Received: 29 June 2023
Revised: 14 August 2023
Accepted: 17 August 2023
Published: 19 August 2023

1. Introduction

The climate crisis is about to reveal its dramatic consequences for all life on earth. Carbon emissions must be halted as soon as possible to counteract human-induced climate change [1]. Therefore, the transition of energy systems to renewable technologies is essential. The number of wind turbines and photovoltaic (PV) systems and their share in electricity production will further increase in the upcoming years. As a result, electricity production will become more dependent on weather conditions [2]. This can lead to instability in the electricity grid [3]. Increasing e-mobility and electrification of the heat sector further challenge grid stability [4,5].

Energy storage systems help maintain grid stability and reduce the curtailment of wind and PV systems through grid control measures. Electrochemical, mechanical, thermal, chemical, electrical, and hybrid systems are used to store energy [6,7]. An energy storage can be centralized or distributed. Distributed energy storage is primarily found in homes, commercial buildings, and industrial facilities. It is used to achieve various goals, including increasing self-generation, reducing grid dependency, promoting energy independence, lowering costs, and reducing fossil fuel consumption. Centralized energy storage is installed at strategic locations on the grid to support the overall electricity system and to provide operational flexibility, peak shaving, grid stability, and cost savings. It also supports the integration of renewable energy by providing backup power during periods of low generation [8]. Thus, centralized energy storage is critical to overall grid stability, while distributed energy storage provides support at the local level. It is also important to distinguish between short-term storage, with storage periods ranging from seconds to days, and long-term storage, with storage periods ranging from weeks to seasons.

While there are many different short-term storage systems, long-term storage is limited to a few pumped hydro and thermal storage systems, as well as power-to-gas (P2G) and power-to-liquids storage [9]. The advantage of these types of storage is that they can also be used to supplement fuel for vehicles or heating systems. This can help decarbonize existing mobility and heating systems by ensuring they transition to fully electrified energy systems [10]. The most common P2G applications use electricity to electrolyze water into oxygen and hydrogen. The hydrogen can either be directly stored or processed into other gases or liquids. Methanation describes the conversion of hydrogen and carbon dioxide to methane, with methane serving as a substitute for natural gas. Conversion to methane is less efficient than directly using hydrogen, but methane is cheaper to transport because of its higher volumetric energy density. In addition, many countries have well-established natural gas networks with a storage capacity that can be used. However, converting a natural gas network to a hydrogen network requires significant time and financial investment, and there is still a lack of understanding of the options for converting existing pipelines [11,12].

Chemical or biotechnological methods can be used to perform methanation. Chemical methanation uses catalysts in the Sabatier process. The biotechnological approach uses microorganisms called methanogenic archaea that are capable of producing methane. Biomethanation can be carried out either directly by hydrogenotrophic methanogens from hydrogen and carbon dioxide or indirectly by homoacetogens producing acetate, which is further converted by acetoclastic archaea [13]. The direct route is advantageous because acetoclastic methane production releases carbon dioxide. Methanation can occur directly in a biogas plant by injecting hydrogen, called in situ methanation. However, in situ methanation can seriously inhibit the digestion of the biogas substrate if the hydrogen flow is too high [14,15]. When biomethanation is performed in a separate reactor that is fed with hydrogen and a carbon dioxide source, it is called ex situ methanation. Ex situ methanation is easier to operate and can achieve higher methane production rates than in situ methanation [15,16].

There are several reactor concepts used for biomethanation, of which the most relevant systems are briefly described below. Continuous stirred tank reactors (CSTRs) have agitators and can be supplemented with spargers. Gas can be supplied either through the headspace or via gas injection at the bottom of the reactor [17]. Mass transfer is primarily dependent on agitation of the system. CSTRs use high-speed agitators and, therefore, have high energy consumption. Trickle bed reactors typically consist of a packed bed covered with a biofilm that is irrigated to provide nutrients and to maintain moisture. In these reactors, the large volumetric interfacial area created by the biofilm growing on the packed bed covered by a thin layer of liquid is advantageous for mass transfer. Membrane reactors contain a porous membrane that separates the gas and liquid phases. Gas is introduced through the membrane. These reactors do not require additional mixing, but the membrane pores can become clogged due to biofilm formation [18]. Plug-flow reactors (PFRs) are tubular reactors. The tubular design allows for the use of high pressures. Reactor length, diameter, and fluid flow rate define the residence time of the PFR. Thus, the conversion rate of a PFR depends on its length. PFRs are currently not widely used in methanation processes [19]. Bubble column reactors are a special type of PFR used for gas fermentation. They use gas bubbles to facilitate mixing and to enhance mass transfer. The use of smaller gas bubbles results in a larger volumetric interfacial area. In addition, agitators and optimized recirculation can be used to improve the mixing process [17,18]. The most common systems for hydrogen biomethanation are CSTRs and trickle bed reactors [20,21]. Overcoming the limitations of hydrogen mass transfer is a key challenge in methanation, and the volumetric mass transfer coefficient k_La can be used to compare the efficiency. It can be increased by decreasing the bubble size, which results in an increased volumetric interfacial area and can be achieved by sparging or agitation [22]. It has recently been proposed that the mass transfer for thin biofilms may not be dependent on the k_La but on a Fick-like diffusion, leading to an advantage for trickle bed reactors with thin biofilms [18]. Bubble column reactors, membrane reactors, and trickle bed reactors seem to be favorable for use in ex situ methanation. Trickle bed reactors can be used to achieve high hydrogen uptake and conversion rates with low energy consumption when the mass transfer is the main limitation [18].

If hydrogen for methanation is produced from renewable energy sources with fluctuating hydrogen production rates and downtime due to a lack of wind or sun, the reactor used for methanation should be adapted to the fluctuating hydrogen feed. Therefore, either hydrogen storage is needed to avoid downtime, or the methanation reactor design must be sufficient to avoid long start-up times due to the lag phase of the microorganisms. However, it was shown in a previous study that microbial communities can be resilient upon starvation, and even after 14 days of downtime, reactivation without lag phase can be achieved [23]. For trickle bed reactors, it has been reported that the time for recovery after downtimes of 12 h to 24 h is between 1.5 h and 7 h [24,25]. PV plant downtimes of $\geq$12 h can occur. Existing reactors face challenges, particularly when the recovery time exceeds the duration of the power supply, making them unsuitable for shorter operating periods, such as when power is derived from PV systems. This work aims to develop a reactor optimized for fast recovery after downtimes. Therefore, the aim is to shorten start-up phases. This can be achieved by increasing the travel distance of the gas phase in the reactor, either by cascading or by increasing the height of the reactors. Cascading common reactor systems increases investment costs as the number of cascades directly affects the required construction components. Furthermore, increasing the height of bioreactors on an industrial scale poses challenges to structural integrity and mixing, requiring robust construction materials and techniques to withstand the increased weight and pressure while ensuring efficient mixing and uniform nutrient distribution throughout the reactor volume. This limits the use of bubble column reactors, for example, because the travel distance of the gas phase is limited by the height of the reactor. Bubble column reactors are vertical tubes containing a liquid, a gas, and sometimes a solid phase. Bubble column reactors tend to be larger in diameter than PFR reactors. There are many ways to improve the properties of a bubble column reactor, including static mixers [26]. In addition, the bubble column reactor is designed for bubble-to-slug flow but not for laminar-stratified flow [27].

Contrarily, PFRs can provide long travel distances of the gas phase without losing its ability to be operated under increased pressure. They are well-established for chemical applications, especially when aiming for high conversion rates [28]. The PFR design has already been tested for methanation with a biofilm PFR [19]. In contrast, the reactor design described in this paper is a meandering orientation PFR with a liquid phase carrying the microorganisms and a gaseous phase carrying the substrate and the product, similar to a bubble column reactor. Since the mass transfer of hydrogen is less limited in biofilm reactors, lower methane production rates can be expected in our system, but nutrients can be easily supplied, and the risk of clogging is lower compared with that in the biofilm reactor. Packed tubes for trickle bed operation were considered too challenging, as the bed could lead to high-pressure drops in long tubular reactors [20]. Static mixers can be used to improve the mixing and dispersion of gas–liquid fluids with laminar flow in PFR [29]. Therefore, a static mixer was designed and integrated into the reactor. In addition, the proposed reactor design with an extra-long meandering tube would extend the residence time to counteract the negative effect of lag phases after shutdowns.

2. Materials and Methods

The reactor design consists of a 50 mm diameter polyvinyl chloride tube, an integrated static mixer in the form of a helical structure, hereafter referred to as a helical structure, to further improve the properties of the reactor, a gas analysis unit, and a data processing unit. The helical inlays were first designed, modeled, and simulated in COMSOL Multiphysics®, and then tested in an experimental setup. Finally, the reactor with helical inlays was installed for characterization and testing, as shown in Figure 1.

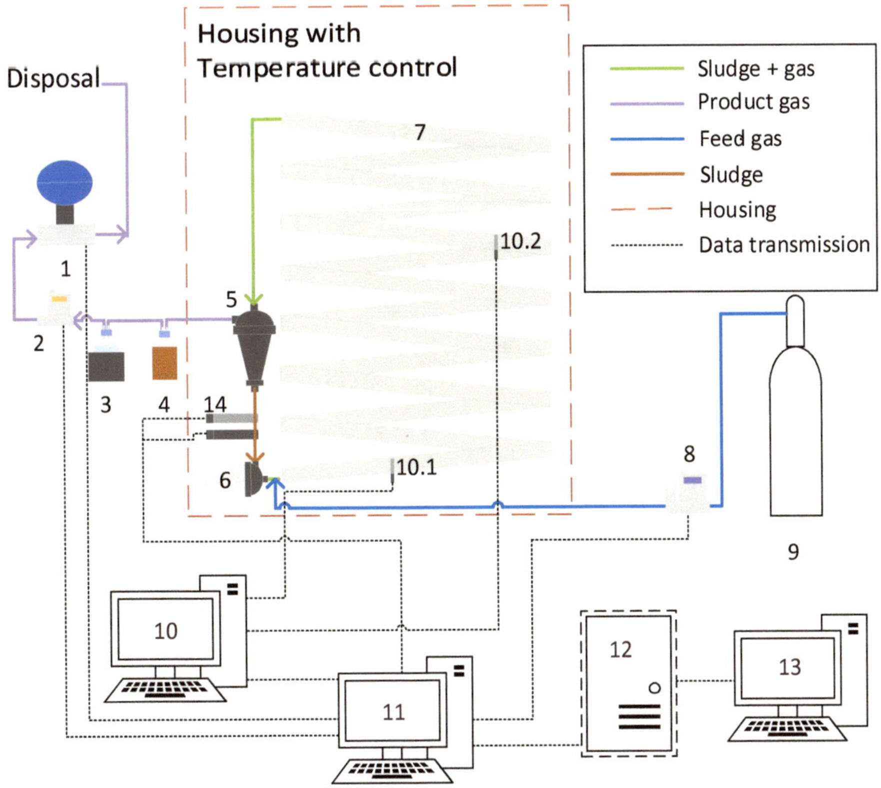

Figure 1. Schematic diagram of the reactor. 1: gas analyzer (BCP-H_2, BlueSens gas sensor GmbH, Herten, Germany); 2: gas flow meter (F-101EI-AGD-00-K, Bronkhorst Deutschland Nord GmbH, Kamen, Germany); 3: chiller 5 °C (WineCase One, CASO, Arnsberg, Germany), 1 L borosilicate bottle (VWR International GmbH, Darmstadt, Germany); 4: 0.5 L borosilicate bottle as sludge container (VWR International GmbH, Darmstadt, Germany); 5: gas–liquid separator (Hydrocyclone Filter 1″, Alfaturbo, Plastica Alfa, Caltagirone, Italy); 6: pump (LS543238, Lilie, GmbH & Co. KG, Besigheim, Germany); 7: tubular reactor with integrated helical structure; 8: gas flow controller (D-6311-DR, Bronkhorst Deutschland Nord GmbH, Kamen, Germany); 9: gas bottle (80% H_2, 20% CO_2, Westfalen AG, Muenster, Germany); 10: raspberry Pi 4 Model B for temperature measurement; 10.1: temperature sensor (ds18b20); 10.2: temperature sensor (ds18b20); 11: raspberry Pi 4 Model B for data processing; 12: data server; 13: computer for monitoring; 14: dissolved hydrogen sensor (AMT Analysemesstechnik GmbH, Rostock, Germany).

2.1. Computational Model

For the simulation, two domain models of the meandering column reactor with and without helical structures were modeled in COMSOL Multiphysics® 6.1. The helical structures were imported from a Solid Works® 2021 model. The mass transfer rate of the liquid (water) and gas (80% H_2 + 20% CO_2) mixture was simulated based on these domain models. Both domains comprised a reactor with a cylindrical geometry of 0.5 m in length and 0.06 m in diameter. A helical structure obtained from Solid Works® 2021 was integrated into domain 2, possessing a spiral geometry with a width of 0.05 m. To obtain the model of the system, the "Two-phase flow, laminar model" under fluid flow in COMSOL Multiphysics® was chosen. This model is a special case of two-phase flow. The level-set technique was used for both domain systems. A time-resolved study was carried out.

Physics: Table 1 lists the liquid and gas properties, as well as the magnitude of the gravity component. Boundary conditions: There are four faces present bounding the calculation domain, which are the inlet boundaries for liquid and gas, the outlet boundary, and the wall boundary. Table 1 presents the boundary conditions for the simulation.

Table 1. Properties, settings, and boundary conditions of the two computational domain systems in COMSOL Multiphysics®.

Properties and Settings		Boundary Conditions	
Variable	**Value**	**Boundary**	**Velocity (V)**
Temperature	T = 313.15 K	Inlet A (liquid)	$v_1 = 0.02$ m/s
Liquid density	$\rho_1 = 992.63$ kg/m^3	Inlet B (gas)	$v_2 = 0.1$ m/s
Liquid dynamic viscosity	$\mu_1 = 6.66 \times 10^{-4}$ Pa·s	Wall	No slip condition, $v_3 = 0$
Gas density	$\rho_2 = 0.441$ kg/m^3		
Gas dynamic viscosity	$\mu_2 = 1.05 \times 10^{-5}$ Pa·s		
Gravity (y-component)	g = −9.806 m/s^2		

2.2. Mesh Independence Test and Model Validation

A mesh dependence test for the static mixer in the form of a helical mixer was performed to ensure that the node density was sufficient. Since the goal of the simulation is limited to estimating the flow pattern and mixing properties based on the streamlines, the focus was on pressure drop and velocity. The mesh was applied with a higher density at the helical structure and the pipe wall. Figure 2 shows that the influence of the mesh was small under the given conditions, although the pressure drop increased slightly with an increasing number of elements. Empirical data on pressure drop, velocity, and mixing characteristics should be collected in the future to validate the model better. However, the model is sufficient for its purpose and has been used to design the static mixer in the form of a helical structure and to estimate its basic properties. The model can be further developed in the future.

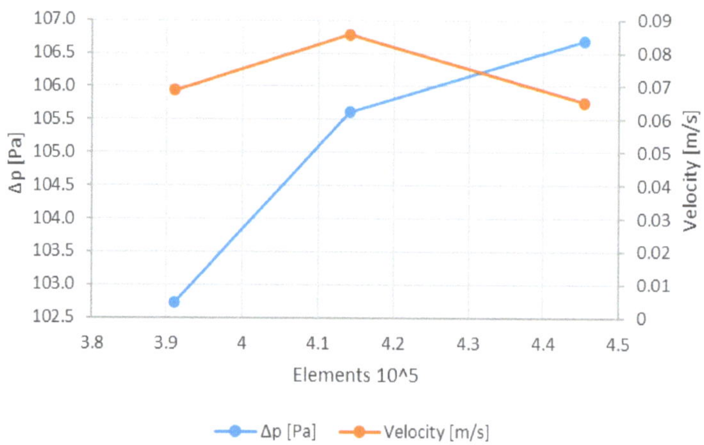

Figure 2. Mesh independence test of the helical model on pressure drop and velocity after 20 s.

Meshes were designed to simulate the streamline flow and velocity distribution of the two domains described in 2.1. Domain 1 (Figure 3a bottom) had 267,116 solid elements,

3684 surface elements, and 365 line elements, resulting in 44,930 degrees of freedom. Instead, domain 2 (Figure 3b bottom) had 35,552 solid elements, 36,616 surface elements, and 6824 line elements, resulting in 379,280 degrees of freedom.

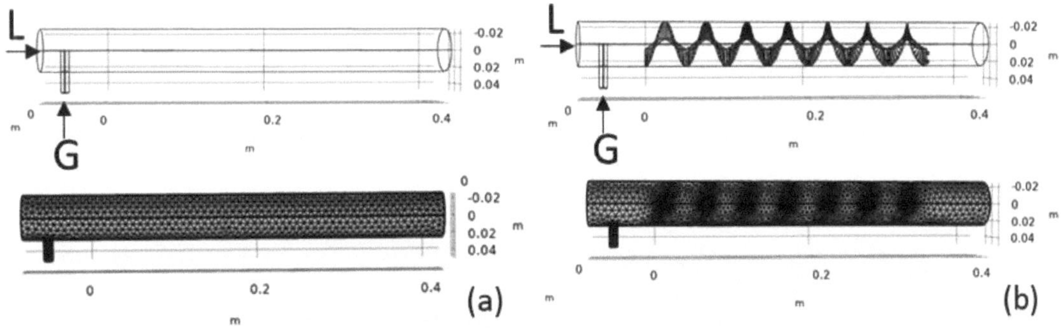

Figure 3. Computational domain 1 (**a**) without helical structure with the applied mesh design, and computational domain 2 (**b**) with helical structure with the applied mesh design. L = input liquid phase; G = input gas phase.

The liquid (L) enters the reactor on the left side of the reactor column, while the gas (G) enters the reactor perpendicular to the liquid. The mesh design used for the simulation is shown at the bottom of Figure 3a. The model of domain 2 is shown in Figure 3b. The column is the same as in domain 1, but the helical structure is integrated into the column. This results in a different mesh design with a more detailed mesh at the edges of the helix.

Despite the mesh, both computational domain systems were given the same dimensions, properties, settings, and conditions during simulation.

2.3. Experimental Setup

The helical structures were tested in an experimental setup with the same dimensions and characteristics as in the simulations discussed in 2.1. An acrylic glass tube was used to visually monitor the gas–liquid phases inside the reactor. The helical structures were 3D-printed with an acrylnitrile-butadiene-styrene copolymer filament (ABS, 3D Composite GmbH, Cologne, Germany) with a helix pitch of 50 mm. However, the helix was approximately 8 mm thick, reducing the outer helix pitch to 42 mm. Since there were small gaps between the outer edge of the printed helical structures and the inner diameter of the reactor column, PTFE strips were used as a seal. The tube was filled with tap water and supplied with air, while the liquid phase was pumped in a loop. The laminar flow of the liquid phase was adjusted inside the reactor column (6 L/min). When the water level did not change any further, the volume of the gas phase was calculated. Therefore, the water level was measured via image processing using the Fiji software, as shown in Figure 4 [30].

The volume of the liquid phase V_{liquid} was calculated based on Equation (1):

$$V_{liquid} = L \cdot \left(r^2 \cdot arccos\left(\frac{r-h}{r}\right) - (r-h) \cdot \sqrt{2 \cdot r \cdot h - h^2} \right) \quad (1)$$

$V_{liquid} = Volume\ liquid\ phase;\ L = Tube\ length = Helix\ pitch = 0.042$ m;
$r = Radius = 0.025$ m; $h = water\ level$

The gas volume fraction was calculated by subtracting the volume of the liquid phase (Equation (1)) from the total volume (Equation (3)) of the tube, neglecting the volume of the helix according to Equation (2).

$$Vol.\%_{gas} = \frac{V_{total} - V_{liquid}}{V_{total}} \cdot 100\% \tag{2}$$

$$V_{total} = \pi r^2 \times L \tag{3}$$

$Vol.\%_{gas} = Gas\ volume\ fraction;\ V_{total} = Total\ volume;$
$V_{liquid} = Volume\ liquid\ phase;\ L = Tube\ length$

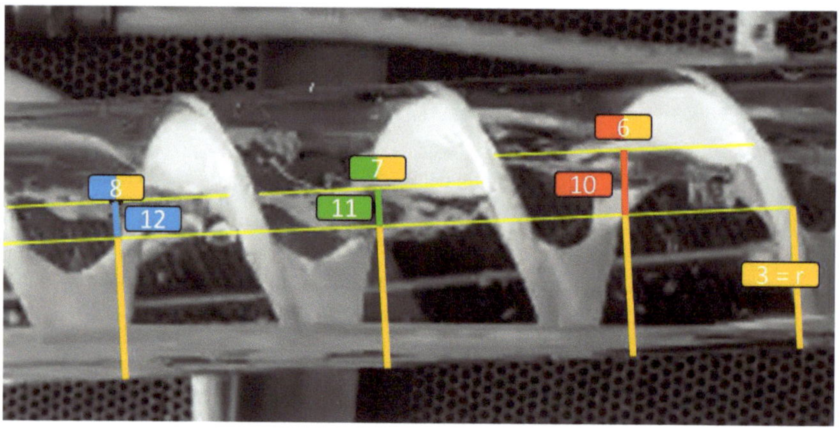

Figure 4. Water level estimation in the experimental setup with Fiji 3 = radius (r); 10, 11, and 12 = distance from center; 6, 7 (h_c), and 8 = estimated water level ($h = r + h_c$).

2.4. Construction of the Meandering Column Reactor

Based on the results of the simulations and the experiments, a meandering column reactor that was approximately 14 m in length and 22.5 L in volume was designed. Figure 1 provides a schematic diagram of the reactor. The meandering reactor was constructed from PVC tubing mounted in a frame with tube brackets. Three dimensionally printed helical structures of ABS (3D Composite GmbH, Cologne, Germany) were integrated into the reactor (Figure 1, No. 7). Ethylene-propylene-diene monomer rubber seals (EPDM, V11, SMI—Gräwe & Sohn GmbH, Brandenburg, Germany) were used to prevent unwanted flow patterns. The reactor was housed in an expanded polystyrene (EPS, 60 mm, WLG 035) enclosure. Four temperature controllers (ITC-308, Inkbird, Shenzhen, China) with 100 W thermos cables (10 m, Lucky reptile) each were used. The thermoelectric cables were wrapped around the tubes. A pump (12 V, cut-off pressure 6.9 bar, max. 6.8 L/min, LS543238, Lilie GmbH & Co. KG, Besigheim, Germany, Figure 1, No. 6) circulated the liquid phase. A gas flow controller (D-6311-DR, Bronkhorst Deutschland Nord GmbH, Kamen, Germany, Figure 1, No. 8) was used to control the gas flow, which was injected into the liquid at the bottom of the reactor. The gas–liquid mixture was transported to the top of the reactor, where the gas was separated from the liquid phase via a cyclone (Alfaturbo Hydrocyclone Filter 1, Plastica Alfa, Caltagirone, Italy, cyclone detached from the vessel, max. operating pressure 5 bar, Figure 1, No. 5). The separated gas is the product gas. Water is formed during methanation, so excess liquid must be removed. The excess liquid was discharged with the product gas flow from the gas separator and collected in a 0.5 L borosilicate bottle (VWR International GmbH, Darmstadt, Germany, Figure 1,

No. 4). The product gas was passed through a 1 L borosilicate bottle (VWR International GmbH, Darmstadt, Germany) and cooled to 5 °C using a wine cooler (WineCase One, CASO, Arnsberg, Germany, Figure 1, No. 3) to condense water. The product gas was then quantified using a gas flow meter (F-101EI-AGD-00-K, Bronkhorst Deutschland Nord GmbH, Kamen, Germany, Figure 1, No. 2). The hydrogen content of the gas was measured with a gas analyzer (BCP-H2, BlueSens gas sensor GmbH, Herten, Germany, Figure 1, No. 1). Data from all sensors were collected using a Raspberry Pi 4 and stored on a server in an InxluxDB database. A Grafana dashboard was used to monitor the data.

2.5. Step Experiment

The reactor described in 2.4 was used to perform the step experiment. First, methane was injected into the reactor; then, a mixture of 20% CO_2 and 80% H_2 was injected at a flow rate of 12 L/h at a temperature of 8.2 °C. The gas composition was measured to determine the residence time distribution. The flow rate of the recirculated liquid phase was 4.3 L/min. The flow directions of the liquid and gas phases were identical.

The different velocities of the liquid and gas phases lead to a slip, which can be calculated using Equation (4). The velocities of the gas phase and the liquid phase can be calculated using Equations (5) and (6) [31].

$$v_S = v_G - v_L \tag{4}$$

$$v_G = \frac{q_G}{A_G} \tag{5}$$

$$v_L = \frac{q_L}{A_L} \tag{6}$$

$v_L = \textit{Liquid phase velocity};\ v_G = \textit{Gas phase velocity};$
$q_L\ q_G = \textit{Gas phase Volumetric flow gas phase};\ A_L = \textit{Cross section area liquid phase};$
$A_G = \textit{Cross section area gas phase}$

The PFR-like design and the laminar flow in this system indicate that the model for CSTR cascades taken from Equation (7) can be used to determine the residence time distribution $(F(\frac{t}{\tau}))$. The mean residence time can be calculated using Equation (8).

$$F\left(\frac{t}{\tau}\right) = 1 - e^{-\frac{K}{\tau}*t}\sum\nolimits_{k=1}^{K} \frac{\left(K*\frac{t}{\tau}\right)^{k-1}}{(k-1)!} \tag{7}$$

$$\tau = \frac{V_R}{\dot{V}} \tag{8}$$

$K = \textit{Amount of cascades};\ t = \textit{Time};\ \tau = \text{Mean residence time};$
$\dot{V} = \textit{Volume flow};\ V_R = \textit{Reactor volume}$

To determine the k_La, dissolved hydrogen was measured with a dissolved hydrogen sensor (AMT Analysemesstechnik GmbH, Germany). A two-point calibration was performed with methane at 0% dissolved hydrogen and with 80% hydrogen, and 20% carbon dioxide at 100% dissolved hydrogen. The k_La was determined in the exponential phase of the step experiment by calculating the ln of the quotient of the difference between the maximal dissolved hydrogen concentration (C^*) and the dissolved hydrogen concentration at t_0 (C_0) and the difference between the maximal dissolved hydrogen concentration and the dissolved hydrogen concentration at t_n (C_n, Equation (9), and plotting it against the time difference (t_n- t_0). The slope of the regression line from the regression analysis expresses the k_La value [32].

$$ln\left(\frac{C^*-C_0}{C^*-C_n}\right)$$
$$C^* = Maximal\ dissolved\ hydrogen\ concentration;$$
$$C_0 = Dissolved\ hydrogen\ concentration\ at\ t_0; \quad (9)$$
$$C_n = Dissolved\ hydrogen\ concentration\ at\ t_n$$

3. Results and Discussion

3.1. Computational Model

The simulated streamline flow of the gas liquid phase is shown in Figure 5. Domain 1 (Figure 5a) without an integrated helical structure and domain 2 (Figure 5b) with an integrated helical structure at 20 s are shown. It is clear from Figure 5a that neither of the two streamlines in domain 1 intersected; instead, they were parallel and thus did not form vortices. No disruption or mixing of the streamlines indicates laminar flow. The streamlines are mainly in the lower half and the top of the tube, indicating less flow in the upper half of the tube.

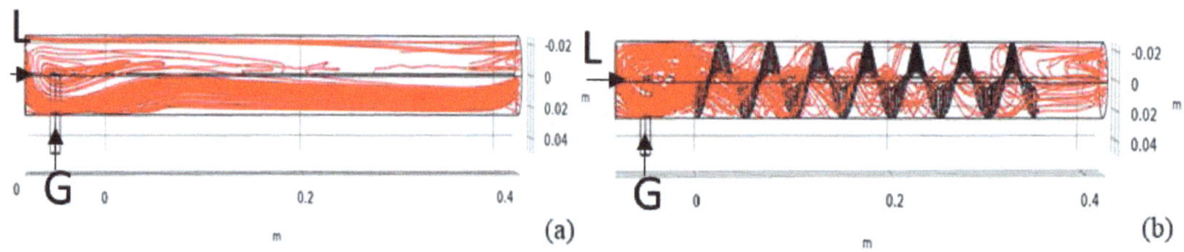

Figure 5. Simulated streamline flow of liquid–gas phase in domain 1 (**a**) without helical structure and domain 2 (**b**) with helical structure at 20 s. L = input liquid phase; G = input gas phase; streamlines in red.

A large part of domain 1 shows smooth laminar flow (Figure 5a). A slightly wavy laminar flow can also be observed at the inlet of domain 1 due to the difference in the inlet flow rate of gas–liquid. When laminar, the liquid–gas displacement pattern can be concentric or segregated depending on the effect of buoyancy forces. Due to buoyancy, the liquid and gas phases completely separate into two continuous phases in domain 1, so the interference between the two phases is relatively smooth. Due to the helical structure in domain 2 (Figure 5b), the streamlines show more vortices compared with those in domain 1. The flow regime in domain 2 is also stratified but segregated by the helical structure. The streamline flow in domain 2 with an integrated helical structure is also assumed to be a laminar flow.

Comparing Figures 5 and 6 shows that waves and ripples appear at the phase boundaries at higher velocities. The waves travel in the direction of the fluid. Similarly, the streamlines in domain 2 spiral along the helix shape in the flow regime towards the exit. Individual vortices formed in the upper part of domain 2, which signifies mixing with the gas phase. The vortex formation also indicates a stratified displacement pattern. The lighter (gas) material tends to occupy the upper part of the tube when buoyancy forces are sufficiently large, resulting in a stratified displacement pattern [33]. In addition, liquid waves reach the top of the tube, cutting off the cross-section of the gas in certain cases at higher velocities. The difference in momentum between the phases (due to different phase velocities) results in sudden pressure changes when the path closes. A larger difference in the momentum of the phases can lead to shocks and vibrations. Nevertheless, vortices at the top of the helical structure in the upper part of domain 2 (Figure 5b) indicate a desirable mixture of liquid and gas phases, which is very important for the biological methanation process.

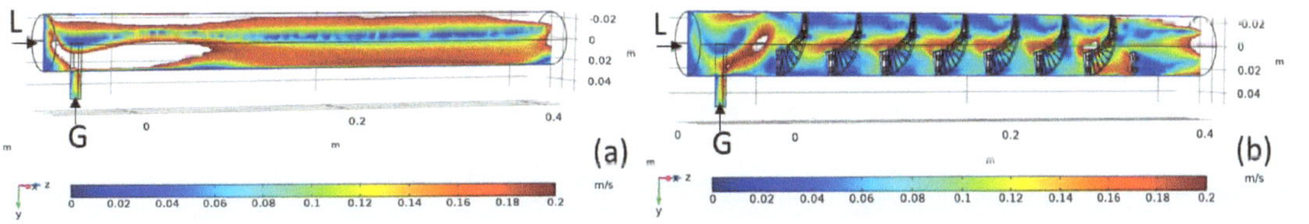

Figure 6. Simulated axial velocity distribution in domains 1 (**a**) without helical structure and 2 (**b**) with helical structure at 20 s. L = input liquid phase; G = input gas phase.

Although both the reactor columns with and without helical inlays were given the same physical characteristics and settings, the distribution of velocity in the two domains differs, as shown in Figure 6a,b. In domain 1, the highest velocities are at the top, driven by the gas phase, and at the bottom, driven by the liquid phase. In the upper center, there is a low-velocity phase. The liquid in domain 2 reaches the highest velocities in the center of the helix, while lower velocities prevail at the upper and lower edge regions. At the inlet and the outlet, the velocity is not equally distributed for domains 1 and 2. The equilibrium of the velocity distribution develops at a shorter tube distance in domain 2 compared with in domain 1.

Figure 7 compares the radial velocity distribution to analyze the influence of the integrated helical structure further. Domains 1 and 2 were intersected by 20 cross-sections spaced 25 mm apart. The radial velocity distribution appears to be equally distributed along domain 1. The radial velocity distribution in domain 1 shows patterns similar to the axial velocity distribution. The velocity is evenly distributed in the x direction, while in the y direction, a higher velocity can be seen at the top (gas driven) and at the bottom (liquid driven). A higher resolution was needed to discuss domain 2 because the more complex helical structure affects the velocity distribution in smaller increments.

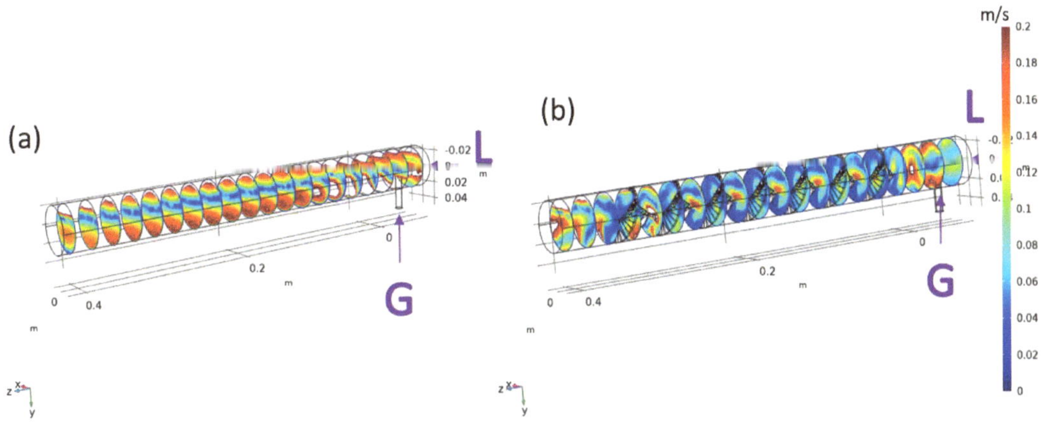

Figure 7. Simulated radial velocity distribution in domain 1 without helical structure at 9 s (**a**) and domain 2 (**b**) with helical structure at 20 s. L = input liquid phase; G = input gas phase.

Figure 8 shows the radial velocity distribution for a single coil of the helix in 5 mm increments. When the intersection of the helical structure is in the upper half of the tube, the radial velocity is almost uniformly distributed. When the intersection of the helical structure enters the lower half of the tube, the velocity increases in the center of the helix. This is because the liquid phase can only flow along the helix or through the center since the upper part of the tube is occupied by the gas phase. It seems that the liquid phase flows through both the center and along the helix as the velocity also increases at the surface of the helical structure, but the velocity in the center appears to be higher than that along the helix. The velocity appears to increase at or near the phase boundary. This would improve the mixing of the gas and liquid phases. In coiled PFR, also known as coiled flow inverters, there are good radial mixing properties due to Dean vortices [34,35]. The helical structure of our study mimics this design, but the hole in the center of the helix also allows axial flow. This limits the effect seen in the coiled flow inverter.

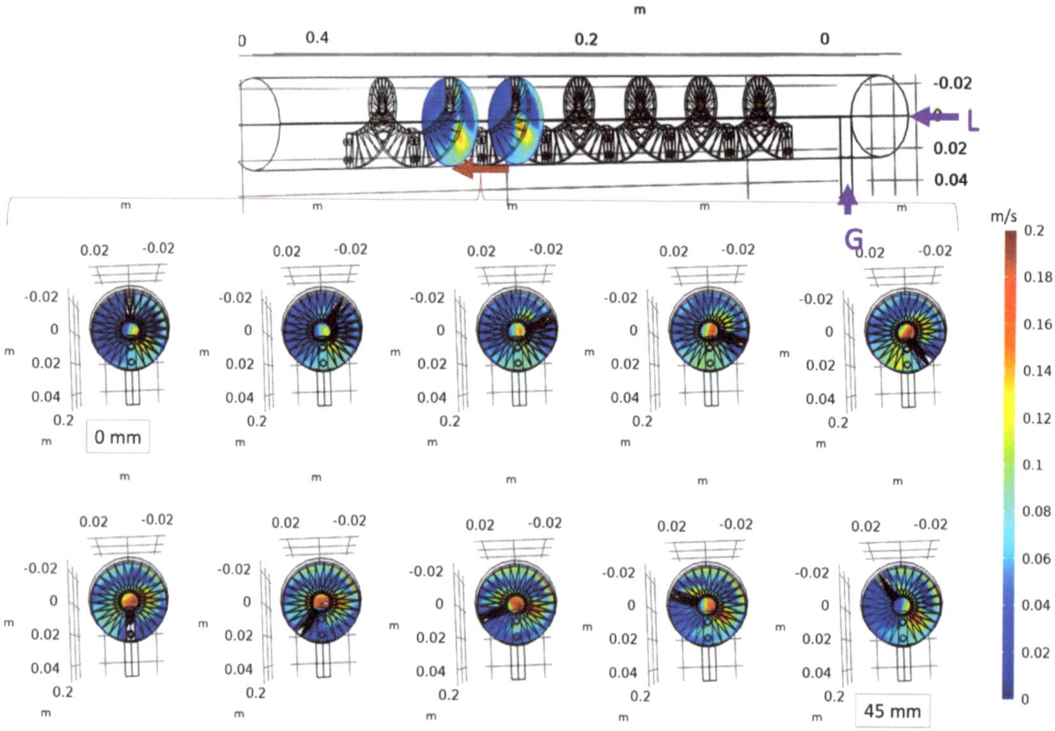

Figure 8. Simulated velocity distribution in domain 2 at 20 s in equidistant sections in 5 mm steps from 0 mm to 45 mm. L = input liquid phase; G = input gas phase.

When comparing the properties of the reactor design with and without an integrated helical structure in the simulation, the mixing properties seem to be improved, especially at the gas–liquid interface. Proper liquid–gas mixing allows for better hydrogen uptake and, thus, improved methane production during biological methanation. The helical structure was selected for further testing based on the simulation data. Compared with the well-established static mixers, it shares some characteristics with a Kenics mixer. However, Kenics mixers are more commonly used for gas–liquid mixing with laminar flow for liquids with higher viscosity compared with water [29,36,37]. For laminar-stratified flow methanation processes, where a low-pressure drop is required to reduce the parasitic energy for process operation, the availability of static mixers is scarce. The proposed static mixer in the form of a helical structure is a good compromise between improved mixing properties and a slightly increased pressure drop.

3.2. Experimental Results

The integrated helical structure leads to the formation of gas cavities, which affects the volume fraction of the liquid and gas phases. The water level of the four cavities of the helical inlays was measured to estimate the volume fraction in the meandering column reactor with helical inlays, as shown in Figure 4. The gas fraction was 29 ± 5% of the total volume and was determined as described in 2.3.

The flow regime observed in the experiments was stratified. The average water level was estimated to be 3.25 cm (average of all h values from Equation (1)). The highest possible water level is 5 cm and is defined by the tube's inner diameter. The distance from the bottom of the tube to the upper edge of the hole in the center of the helical structure is 3.1 cm. The upper edge of the hole defines the limits of the gas cavity since the gas must pass through the center of the helical structure in the axial direction so that the determined water level is consistent with the geometry of the helix structure. Measurements without integrated helical structures could not be evaluated because no cavity formation was observed, and therefore, no decrease in water level could be detected. The size of the gas cavity mainly defines the boundary layer between the gas and liquid phases of the column reactor without an integrated helical structure. The stratified flow was observed with and without helical structures.

The behavior observed in the experiments corresponds well with the behavior observed in the simulations. Furthermore, the volume fraction of the gas and liquid phases was determined, which is needed to ascertain the boundary layer between the liquid and gas phases. In addition, the volume fraction could be used to calculate the residence time of the gas phase.

3.3. Reactor Setup

Assuming that the experimentally determined gas fraction applies to the reactor design, the area of the boundary layer of the gas–liquid phase is 0.7 m^2, with 6.5 L of a gas phase and 16 L of a liquid phase. The helical structure reduces the total volume by approximately 14%. Increasing the area of the boundary layer also increases the hydrogen mass transfer into the liquid phase. Nevertheless, in terms of mass transfer, bubble flow would further increase the k_La and thus the mass transfer [21]. However, the bubble flow regime would have required higher gas and liquid phase velocities, resulting in a higher pressure drop and a more energy-consuming operation [31]. The helical structure avoids back mixing and forms cavities in the tube so that the area of the boundary layer remains large. In addition, the simulation results show good mixing. The cavities can also be viewed as a cascade of small reactors. Since the mixing takes place in each cavity and not in the whole system, which means that the concentration of methane increases with each step, high conversion rates are assumed. The meandering column reactor with integrated helical structures proposes a compromise between the low energy consuming trickle bed reactor and the space-efficient but much more energy-consuming CSTR.

3.4. Step Experiment

Since the flow of the liquid phase is slower than that of the gas phase, a slip occurs. Based on the flow rates of the gas and liquid phases, the slip was calculated to be −0.05 m/s. Due to the slip induced via recirculation of the liquid phase in the same axial direction as the gas phase, dissolved hydrogen is carried faster in the liquid phase than in the gas phase. The dissolved hydrogen can diffuse back into the gas phase in later cavities of the reactor so that a hydrogen sensor signal can be detected earlier than without recirculation. The slip carries only the soluble hydrogen in the reactor. As the archaea will consume hydrogen along the reactor, the overall hydrogen concentration decreases during operation. This suggests that either the slipping hydrogen is directly consumed or a substrate is supplied via the liquid phase to stages with lower hydrogen content in the gas phase, which is favorable. Consequently, there is likely minimal to no dilution of the product gas by hydrogen slipping through the liquid phase. The retention time of the gas mixture is τ = 1.84 h with VR = 22.5 L. If the volume fraction is considered, the retention time is described by τ_g = 0.54 h with V_{RG} = 6.5 L. Thus, the gas phase is exchanged after 32 min.

The washout function of hydrogen, which washes out methane, was used to determine the residence time distribution, shown in Figure 9. A model based on Equations (7) and (8) for cascaded CSTR was applied to estimate the number of theoretical cascades. The residence time distribution behavior is more similar to that of a single CSTR than that of a cascaded CSTR, but there is a short delay in the response at the beginning of the experiment, which is typical of PFR or cascaded reactors. Thus, both CSTR-like and PFR-like behavior can be seen, which can be explained by the novel design of the reactor.

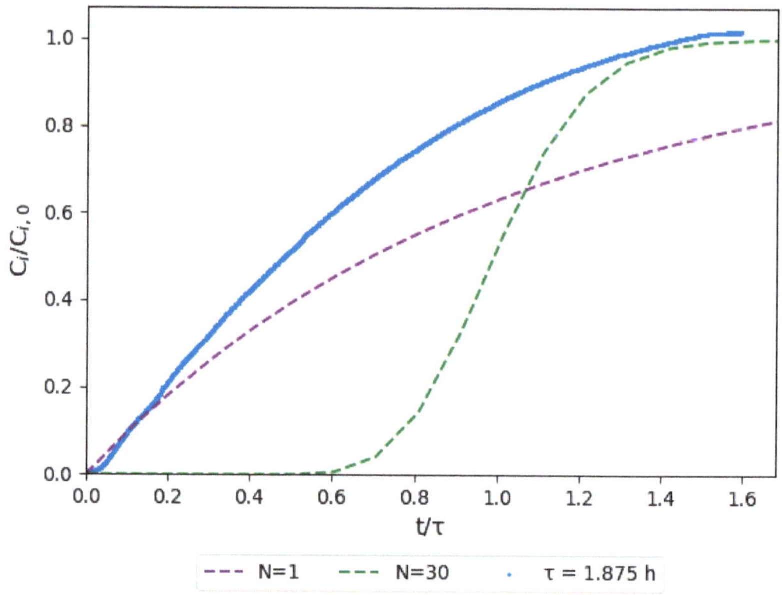

Figure 9. Residence time distribution ($F\left(\frac{t}{\tau}\right) = \frac{C_i}{C_{i,0}}$) at a retention time of τ = 1.84 h. Washout function was determined with a mixture of hydrogen (80%) and carbon dioxide (20%) fed to a reactor, washing out methane. Residence time distribution model for CSTR cascades with N steps with N = 1 (violet) and N = 30 (green).

The CSTR cascade model is not sufficient to model the residence time distribution of the given reactor. More complex models that account for the two phases and the liquid phase recirculation loop may be investigated in the future to model the residence time distribution. This could help predict certain reactor properties when parameters such as gas flow rate, reactor volume, or gas fraction are changed. This could be useful for the technical optimization of the reactor.

To better understand the gas mass transfer from the gas phase into the liquid phase, the k_La was determined during the step experiment. Figure 10 presents the results. The k_La corresponds to the slope of the regression line, and it was 1 h^{-1} in the reactor with helical structures. However, the k_La value measured in the study was not obtained under operating conditions. It is expected that the k_La value may vary under actual operating conditions due to the effect of temperature on k_La. While increasing temperature leads to a decrease in hydrogen solubility, it has recently been discussed that increasing diffusion rates may counteract the decreased solubility and may even lead to an increase in mass transfer at higher temperatures [21]. This effect would lead to slightly higher k_La values under thermophilic conditions. Temperature and pressure are limiting factors, as available sensors for the detection of dissolved hydrogen are not designed for high temperatures or pressures. For example, the dissolved hydrogen sensor used in this work is designed for operating temperatures up to 40 °C and pressures of up to 10 bar. Thus, it is challenging to detect dissolved hydrogen under operating conditions outside of this range [18]. Many biomethanation reactors are operated under thermophilic conditions between 55 and 65 °C [20,21,38].

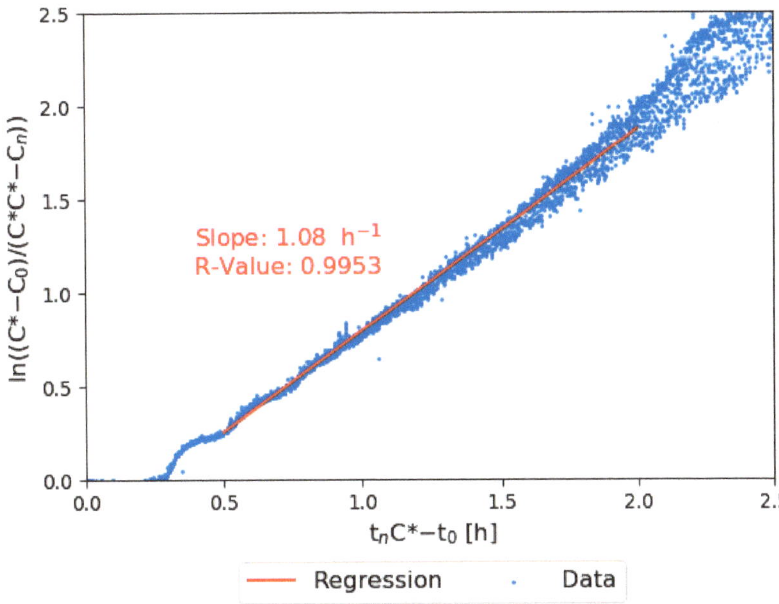

Figure 10. Experimental data for kLa determination at hydrogen feed of 10.24 $\frac{L_N}{L_R*d}$ and a carbon dioxide feed of 2.56 $\frac{L_N}{L_R*d}$.

In the CSTR, k_La values ranging from 1 to 3750 h^{-1} have been obtained at 500 to 1010 rpm under operating conditions [20]. On the downside, it has been suggested that CSTRs may not be sufficient, especially in reactors with high gas volume fractions relative to the total volume flow. A PFR U-loop reactor with similar helical structures integrated and operated under turbulent flow showed k_La values of 400–3000 h^{-1}, which are similar to the k_La values measured in CSTRs. However, to achieve such high k_La values, high-pressure drops of up to 4×10^5 Pa and high energy consumption were also considered [39]. PFR coiled flow inverters could also be a promising approach for sufficient mass transfer, as they show good mixing properties, and a k_La value of 26.6 h^{-1} has been reported [35]. In bubble column reactors, k_La values of up to 210 h^{-1} [18] and, in trickle bed reactors, k_La values of up to 1024 h^{-1} have been reported with low parasitic energy consumption [18]. Thus, the measured k_La is low compared with the k_La reported in the literature. However, the k_La is dependent on many factors, such as temperature, pressure, and feed flow rate, which can make it difficult to compare [32]. The actual performance of the system will be defined by the methane production rate, which will be determined in future experiments.

4. Conclusions

This study successfully constructed a new reactor design and implemented monitoring and data processing. Helical structures were also designed and integrated based on simulations and experimental data. The results of the simulations and experiments corresponded. It was found that a helix pitch of 5 cm in the helical structure is sufficient for a uniform radial velocity distribution. The CFD model was validated and used to understand the basic properties of the reactor, such as mixing properties based on streamlines and velocity distribution.

The step experiments showed that future research should obtain a deeper understanding of the proposed design for flexible methanation. The remaining challenges include the lack of dissolved hydrogen sensors for operating conditions and sufficient modeling of the reactor. Nevertheless, the novel PFR design with reasonable mixing properties indicates good conversion rates. The further advantage of the compact meander design is that it allows a 14 m long reactor to be installed in a 1.3 × 0.3 × 2.0 m space. Therefore, scale-up can be achieved by stacking several reactor modules. Although the k_La values were rather low compared with those in other reactor systems, the PFR design can be advantageous because the residence time is dependent on the tube length, which can lead to improved behavior in the start-up phase. Thus, the new reactor design for flexible biomethanation represents a promising solution to the storage capacity challenges in renewable energy systems. The applicability and advantages of the novel design, especially on flexibility issues, will be tested in bioreactor systems with the implemented reactor design elements.

Author Contributions: Conceptualization: K.H. and I.K.; Data curation: D.C., K.H. and S.K.; Formal analysis: D.C. and K.H.; Funding acquisition: I.K.; Investigation: K.H.; Methodology: D.C. and K.H.; Project administration: I.K.; Resources: I.K.; Software: K.H.; Supervision: H.H., I.K., M.N. and S.K.; Validation: D.C. and K.H.; Visualization: D.C. and K.H.; Writing—original draft preparation: D.C. and K.H.; Writing—review and editing: H.H., I.K., K.H., M.N. and S.K. All authors have read and agreed to the published version of the manuscript.

Funding: This research was funded by the European Regional Development Fund (ERDF), grant number KESW-1-2-032A-B.

Institutional Review Board Statement: Not applicable.

Informed Consent Statement: Not applicable.

Data Availability Statement: The data are contained within the article.

Acknowledgments: Special thanks to the students and research assistants who supported this work: Vivekanantha Kumar, Ali Sadeghzadehgomari, Steven Staudt, Gokul Shivakumar, Abdulaziz Azouz, Axel Joris Diyou Ngoh, Ivan Semchuk, and Marco Karber.

Conflicts of Interest: The authors declare no conflict of interest. The funders had no role in the design of the study; in the collection, analysis, or interpretation of data; in the writing of the manuscript; or in the decision to publish the results.

References

1. IPCC Summary for Policymakers. *Climate Change 2022: Impacts, Adaptation, and Vulnerability*; Contribution of Working Group II to the Sixth Assessment Report of the Intergovernmental Panel on Climate Change 2022; IPCC: Geneva, Switzerland, 2022; *in press*.
2. International Energy Agency. *Electricity Market Report—July 2021*; OECD Publishing: Paris, France, 2021.
3. Johnson, S.C.; Rhodes, J.D.; Webber, M.E. Understanding the Impact of Non-Synchronous Wind and Solar Generation on Grid Stability and Identifying Mitigation Pathways. *Appl. Energy* **2020**, *262*, 114492. [CrossRef]
4. Maurer, F.; Rieke, C.; Schemm, R.; Stollenwerk, D. Analysis of an Urban Grid with High Photovoltaic and E-Mobility Penetration. *Energies* **2023**, *16*, 3380. [CrossRef]
5. Zhang, M.; Millar, M.-A.; Yu, Z.; Yu, J. An Assessment of the Impacts of Heat Electrification on the Electric Grid in the UK. *Energy Rep.* **2022**, *8*, 14934–14946. [CrossRef]
6. Rekioua, D. Energy Storage Systems for Photovoltaic and Wind Systems: A Review. *Energies* **2023**, *16*, 3893. [CrossRef]
7. Hossain, E.; Faruque, H.; Sunny, M.; Mohammad, N.; Nawar, N. A Comprehensive Review on Energy Storage Systems: Types, Comparison, Current Scenario, Applications, Barriers, and Potential Solutions, Policies, and Future Prospects. *Energies* **2020**, *13*, 3651. [CrossRef]
8. Zakeri, B.; Gissey, G.C.; Dodds, P.E.; Subkhankulova, D. Centralized vs. Distributed Energy Storage—Benefits for Residential Users. *Energy* **2021**, *236*, 121443. [CrossRef]
9. Sterner, M.; Stadler, I. (Eds.) *Energiespeicher—Bedarf, Technologien, Integration*; Springer: Berlin/Heidelberg, Germany, 2017; ISBN 978-3-662-48892-8.
10. Ueckerdt, F.; Bauer, C.; Dirnaichner, A.; Everall, J.; Sacchi, R.; Luderer, G. Potential and Risks of Hydrogen-Based e-Fuels in Climate Change Mitigation. *Nat. Clim. Chang.* **2021**, *11*, 384–393. [CrossRef]
11. Ogden, J.; Jaffe, A.M.; Scheitrum, D.; McDonald, Z.; Miller, M. Natural Gas as a Bridge to Hydrogen Transportation Fuel: Insights from the Literature. *Energy Policy* **2018**, *115*, 317–329. [CrossRef]
12. You, Y.; Kim, S.; Lee, J.C. Comparative Study on Ammonia and Liquid Hydrogen Transportation Costs in Comparison to LNG. *Int. J. Nav. Archit. Ocean Eng.* **2023**, *15*, 100523. [CrossRef]

13. Evans, P.N.; Boyd, J.A.; Leu, A.O.; Woodcroft, B.J.; Parks, D.H.; Hugenholtz, P.; Tyson, G.W. An Evolving View of Methane Metabolism in the Archaea. *Nat. Rev. Microbiol.* **2019**, *17*, 219–232. [CrossRef]
14. Wahid, R.; Mulat, D.G.; Gaby, J.C.; Horn, S.J. Effects of H_2:CO_2 Ratio and H_2 Supply Fluctuation on Methane Content and Microbial Community Composition during in-Situ Biological Biogas Upgrading. *Biotechnol. Biofuels* **2019**, *12*, 104. [CrossRef]
15. Logroño, W.; Kleinsteuber, S.; Kretzschmar, J.; Harnisch, F.; De Vrieze, J.; Nikolausz, M. The Microbiology of Power-to-X Applications. *FEMS Microbiol. Rev.* **2023**, *47*, fuad013. [CrossRef] [PubMed]
16. Wahid, R.; Horn, S.J. Impact of Operational Conditions on Methane Yield and Microbial Community Composition during Biological Methanation in in Situ and Hybrid Reactor Systems. *Biotechnol. Biofuels* **2021**, *14*, 170. [CrossRef] [PubMed]
17. Van Hecke, W.; Bockrath, R.; De Wever, H. Effects of Moderately Elevated Pressure on Gas Fermentation Processes. *Bioresour. Technol.* **2019**, *293*, 122129. [CrossRef] [PubMed]
18. Ale Enriquez, F.; Ahring, B.K. Strategies to Overcome Mass Transfer Limitations of Hydrogen during Anaerobic Gaseous Fermentations: A Comprehensive Review. *Bioresour. Technol.* **2023**, *377*, 128948. [CrossRef] [PubMed]
19. Savvas, S.; Donnelly, J.; Patterson, T.; Chong, Z.S.; Esteves, S.R. Biological Methanation of CO_2 in a Novel Biofilm Plug-Flow Reactor: A High Rate and Low Parasitic Energy Process. *Appl. Energy* **2017**, *202*, 238–247. [CrossRef]
20. Rusmanis, D.; O'Shea, R.; Wall, D.M.; Murphy, J.D. Biological Hydrogen Methanation Systems—An Overview of Design and Efficiency. *Bioengineered* **2019**, *10*, 604–634. [CrossRef]
21. Jensen, M.B.; Ottosen, L.D.M.; Kofoed, M.V.W. H_2 Gas-Liquid Mass Transfer: A Key Element in Biological Power-to-Gas Methanation. *Renew. Sustain. Energy Rev.* **2021**, *147*, 111209. [CrossRef]
22. Dehkordi, A.M.; Savari, C. Determination of Interfacial Area and Overall Volumetric Mass-Transfer Coefficient in a Novel Type of Two Impinging Streams Reactor by Chemical Method. *Ind. Eng. Chem. Res.* **2011**, *50*, 6426–6435. [CrossRef]
23. Logroño, W.; Popp, D.; Nikolausz, M.; Kluge, P.; Harms, H.; Kleinsteuber, S. Microbial Communities in Flexible Biomethanation of Hydrogen Are Functionally Resilient Upon Starvation. *Front. Microbiol.* **2021**, *12*, 619632. [CrossRef]
24. Jønson, B.D.; Tsapekos, P.; Tahir Ashraf, M.; Jeppesen, M.; Ejbye Schmidt, J.; Bastidas-Oyanedel, J.-R. Pilot-Scale Study of Biomethanation in Biological Trickle Bed Reactors Converting Impure CO_2 from a Full-Scale Biogas Plant. *Bioresour. Technol.* **2022**, *365*, 128160. [CrossRef] [PubMed]
25. Strübing, D.; Moeller, A.B.; Mößnang, B.; Lebuhn, M.; Drewes, J.E.; Koch, K. Anaerobic Thermophilic Trickle Bed Reactor as a Promising Technology for Flexible and Demand-Oriented H_2/CO_2 Biomethanation. *Appl. Energy* **2018**, *232*, 543–554. [CrossRef]
26. Youssef, A.A.; Al-Dahhan, M.H.; Dudukovic, M.P. Bubble Columns with Internals: A Review. *Int. J. Chem. React. Eng.* **2013**, *11*, 169–223. [CrossRef]
27. Kantarci, N.; Borak, F.; Ulgen, K.O. Bubble Column Reactors. *Process Biochem.* **2005**, *40*, 2263–2283. [CrossRef]
28. Nandagopal, N.S. *Chemical Engineering Principles and Applications*; Springer International Publishing: Cham, Switzerland, 2023; ISBN 978-3-031-27878-5.
29. Valdés, J.P.; Kahouadji, L.; Matar, O.K. Current Advances in Liquid–Liquid Mixing in Static Mixers: A Review. *Chem. Eng. Res. Des.* **2022**, *177*, 694–731. [CrossRef]
30. Schindelin, J.; Arganda-Carreras, I.; Frise, E.; Kaynig, V.; Longair, M.; Pietzsch, T.; Preibisch, S.; Rueden, C.; Saalfeld, S.; Schmid, B.; et al. Fiji: An Open-Source Platform for Biological-Image Analysis. *Nat. Methods* **2012**, *9*, 676–682. [CrossRef]
31. Bahadori, A. Single-Phase and Multiphase Flow in Natural Gas Production Systems. In *Natural Gas Processing*; Elsevier: Amsterdam, The Netherlands, 2014; pp. 59–150. ISBN 978-0-08-099971-5.
32. Shin, W.-S. Application of Scale-Up Criterion of Constant Oxygen Mass Transfer Coefficient (KLa) for Production of Itaconic Acid in a 50 L Pilot-Scale Fermentor by Fungal Cells of Aspergillus Terreus. *J. Microbiol. Biotechnol.* **2013**, *23*, 1445–1453. [CrossRef]
33. Tardy, P.M.; Flamant, N.C.; Lac, E.; Parry, A.; Sutama, C.S.; Almagro, S.P. New Generation 3D Simulator Predicts Realistic Mud Displacement in Highly Deviated and Horizontal Wells. In Proceedings of the Day 2 Wed, The Hague, The Netherlands, 14–15 March 2017; p. D021S011R004.
34. Kockmann, N. Entwurf und Betrieb eines Rohrreaktors mit enger Verweilzeitverteilung. *Chem. Ing. Tech.* **2020**, *92*, 685–691. [CrossRef]
35. Grühn, J.; Behr, A.S.; Eroglu, T.H.; Trögel, V.; Rosenthal, K.; Kockmann, N. From Coiled Flow Inverter to Stirred Tank Reactor—Bioprocess Development and Ontology Design. *Chem. Ing. Tech.* **2022**, *94*, 852–863. [CrossRef]
36. Hobbs, D.M.; Muzzio, F.J. Reynolds Number Effects on Laminar Mixing in the Kenics Static Mixer. *Chem. Eng. J.* **1998**, *70*, 93–104. [CrossRef]
37. Meng, H.; Jiang, X.; Yu, Y.; Wang, Z.; Wu, J. Laminar Flow and Chaotic Advection Mixing Performance in a Static Mixer with Perforated Helical Segments. *Korean J. Chem. Eng.* **2017**, *34*, 1328–1336. [CrossRef]
38. Rafrafi, Y.; Laguillaumie, L.; Dumas, C. Biological Methanation of H_2 and CO_2 with Mixed Cultures: Current Advances, Hurdles and Challenges. *Waste Biomass Valorization* **2021**, *12*, 5259–5282. [CrossRef]
39. Petersen, L.A.H.; Villadsen, J.; Jørgensen, S.B.; Gernaey, K.V. Mixing and Mass Transfer in a Pilot Scale U-Loop Bioreactor: Mixing and Mass Transfer in a Pilot Scale U-Loop Bioreactor. *Biotechnol. Bioeng.* **2017**, *114*, 344–354. [CrossRef] [PubMed]

fermentation

MDPI

Article

Mathematical Modeling of Nitrification in Mixed Cultures: Insights into Nitrite-Oxidizing Bacteria Growth and Ammonia Starvation Effect

Georgios Manthos [1,2], Leila Abbaszadeh [1,2], Dimitris Zagklis [1,2] and Michael Kornaros [1,2,*]

1 Laboratory of Biochemical Engineering & Environmental Technology (LBEET), Department of Chemical Engineering, University of Patras, 26504 Patras, Greece; geomanthos@chemeng.upatras.gr (G.M.); chem.tec.v@gmail.com (L.A.); dimitriszag@chemeng.upatras.gr (D.Z.)

2 Institute of Circular Economy and Environment (ICEE), University of Patras' Research and Development Center, 26504 Patras, Greece

* Correspondence: kornaros@chemeng.upatras.gr

Abstract: Nitrification, a crucial process in wastewater treatment, involves the conversion of ammonium nitrogen to nitrate nitrogen through the sequential activities of ammonia-oxidizing bacteria (AOB) and nitrite-oxidizing bacteria (NOB). In the present study, a comprehensive mathematical model was developed to describe the nitrification process in mixed cultures involving isolated NOB and starved AOB. The growth equation for NOB was divided into anabolism and catabolism, elucidating the key substrates driving their metabolic activities. Considering the ammonia starvation effect, a single cell-based model was developed to capture the mass transfer phenomena across the AOB cell membrane. This addition allowed for a more accurate representation of the biological dynamics during starvation conditions. The model's accuracy was tested using experimental data that was not used in the model calibration step. The prediction's coefficient of determination (R^2) was estimated at 0.9. By providing insights into the intricate mechanisms underlying nitrification, this model contributes to the advancement of sustainable wastewater treatment practices.

Keywords: nitrification; modeling; starvation; AOB; nitrite-oxidizing bacteria (NOB); ammonia accumulation

Citation: Manthos, G.; Abbaszadeh, L.; Zagklis, D.; Kornaros, M. Mathematical Modeling of Nitrification in Mixed Cultures: Insights into Nitrite-Oxidizing Bacteria Growth and Ammonia Starvation Effect. *Fermentation* **2023**, *9*, 681. https://doi.org/10.3390/fermentation9070681

Academic Editor: Ricardo Aguilar-López

Received: 27 June 2023
Revised: 17 July 2023
Accepted: 18 July 2023
Published: 20 July 2023

1. Introduction

Currently, humans are producing approximately 210 Tg of reactive nitrogen per year [1] and more than half of this waste is released into the environment without treatment. Reactive nitrogen is highly mobile and most of it dissipates into the environment and cascades through air, waters and ecosystems [2]. Excess reactive nitrogen not only has a negative impact on human health, but also contributes to air and water pollution, and can lead to complex ecosystems collapsing. Nitrogen is usually present in wastewater in three forms (1) organic nitrogen compounds, (2) ammonium (NH_4^+) or ammonia (NH_3), depending on the pH, and (3) trace amounts of nitrite (NO_2^-) and nitrate (NO_3^-). However, organic fractions such as proteins, amino acids, and amino sugars are quickly degraded to ammonium either in the sewer systems or in the wastewater treatment tanks [3].

The most common method of removing nitrogen from wastewater is biological nitrogen removal (BNR) comprising of nitrification and denitrification, which is considered economical and efficient. In conventional BNR plants, ammonia, which was suggested to be the true substrate for the oxidation process and not ammonium [4], is oxidized to nitrate via autotrophic nitrification followed by its reduction to nitrogen gas via heterotrophic denitrification. Nitrification, the biological oxidation of ammonium to nitrite and nitrate, is essential in nitrogen cycling in wastewater treatment reactors. Groups of organisms known to be involved in this process include autotrophic ammonia-oxidizing bacteria (AOB), and nitrite-oxidizing bacteria (NOB) [5].

AOB are present in most natural aerobic environments, including soils, freshwater, and marine ecosystems [6–8] and some low-oxygen environments and subsurface sediments [9]. AOB cultures are also dominant in many ammonium-rich environments that have been impacted by anthropogenic nitrogen sources such as fertilizers, wastewater, and industrial by-products [7]. Despite its abundance, it is sometimes exposed to stress caused by low substrate concentrations and even its absence.

The starvation behavior of several AOB belonging to different phylogenetic groups has previously been investigated. Nitrogen removal efficiency in an anammox-partial nitrification reactor reached 95% when subjected to repeated starvation and reactivation periods [10]. Laboratory observations can clearly show different strategies of AOB according to N source levels in oligotrophic or N-rich environments [11]. During nitrification, the oxidation of ammonia by AOB is the most decisive process rate, which is catalyzed by two types of enzymes, ammonia monooxygenase (AMO), which leads to hydroxylamine (NH_2OH) as an intermediate, and hydroxylamine reductase (HAO), which oxidizes NH_2OH to nitrite [12]. Starvation stress can affect the level of both enzymes [13]. The effect of short-term ammonia starvation on non-starving cultures of *N. briensis* shows potential ammonia-oxidizing activities of 200 to 250 μM N h^{-1}, and this activity decreased only slowly during starvation up to 10 days. Within 10 min after the addition of fresh NH_4^+-N, 100% of activity was regained. Starvation negatively affected AMO mRNA levels, while during recovery, an increase in amoA mRNA expression was detected simultaneously [14]. In a similar study that was conducted with the enriched culture of freshwater ammonia oxidizers (AOB-G5-7), 16S rRNA and HAO were maintained during starvation, and AMO and mRNA were affected by starvation for 50 days [15].

Nitrosomonas europaea related to *Nitrosomonas* cluster 7 (a group of AOB that has been identified in environments such as wastewater, which contain high concentrations of NH_4^+) was rapidly reactivated after periods of starvation, in the presence of ammonium by batch and retentostat experiments [11,16,17]. Moreover, the *Nitrosomonas cryotolerans* species (marine AOB) have shown a similarly rapid response to the presence of ammonia [18–20]. On the other hand, members of *Nitrosomonas* cluster 6a (*Nitrosomonas oligotrophic* group) are often found in freshwater environments [21–23]. One of these species (*Nitrosospira briensis*), often found in terrestrial habitats, regain their activity slower than *Nitrosomonas europaea* after long-term starvation of 10 weeks or 4 months [11,16]. Experiments conducted in the enriched medium containing *Nitrosomonas eutropha* in CSTR reactors under different steady-state substrate concentrations showed intracellular ammonium concentrations from six different reactors. Intracellular total ammonium nitrogen (TAN) accumulations, gradually increased from a basal value of ~1 M to much higher values (grown under an oligotrophic environment) [4]. In experiments about the physiology of nitrifiers and stress response to optimize the removal of nutrients and design advanced processes, ammonium deprivation for 3 days resulted in fast ammonium/ammonia accumulation upon nitrogen availability, with a maximum uptake rate of 3.87 mmol gprotein^{-1} min^{-1}. Furthermore, a delay in the production of nitrate was observed with increasing starvation periods, resulting in slower recovery and a lower nitrification rate compared to non-starved cells. The maximum accumulation capacity observed was 8.51% (*w/w*) independently of the external nitrogen concentration, at a range of 250–750 mg N L^{-1}, while pH significantly affected ammonia oxidizers' response, with alkaline values enhancing nitrogen uptake [24].

This work aimed to develop a holistic mathematical model that can describe the nitrification process in different substrate concentrations, pH, and starvation conditions. Several authors have developed kinetic models for nitrate production from activated sludge. The main equation that describes microbial growth is the Monod model. Several parameters affect the production rate of biomass, some of them are the temperature, the pH value, and the hydraulic retention time [25]. Other authors developed more fundamental models breaking the ammonium oxidation process into two enzymatic sub-processes (ammonia monooxygenase reaction and hydroxylamine oxidoreductase reaction) with different maximum specific growth rates [26]. Using the proposed model to accurately predict the nitrification process performance can assist nitrification design applications in wastewater treatment facilities and optimizing the operating conditions for the environmental and economic feasibility of full-scale BNR plants.

2. Materials and Methods

2.1. Isolation and Enrichment of Nitrifying Microorganisms

In this study, two kinds of enriched ammonia-oxidizing bacteria (AOB) and purified nitrite-oxidizing bacteria (NOB) were evaluated. The initial sludge consortium was originated from the aeration tank of the biological wastewater treatment plant of the University of Patras (Rio, Patras, Greece). The synthetic growth medium used for the enrichment of nitrifying microorganisms included 0.956 g L^{-1} ammonium chloride (NH_4Cl) as a nitrogen source for AOB and 1.232 g L^{-1} sodium nitrite ($NaNO_2$) for NOB. In addition, 10.52 g L^{-1} potassium hydrogen phosphate (K_2HPO_4) and 4.72 g L^{-1} potassium dihydrogen phosphate (KH_2PO_4) were used both to maintain the pH value in the range of 7.3–7.4 and to provide a phosphorus source to the sludge. A quantity of 3.52 g L^{-1} of sodium hydrogen carbonate ($NaHCO_3$) was added in excess, to ensure that the nitrification process was not limited by alkalinity. Finally, 1 mL L^{-1} trace elements, including 1 g L^{-1} $FeSO_4 \cdot 7H_2O$, 1 g L^{-1} $MgSO_4 \cdot 7H_2O$, 0.25 g L^{-1} $CaCl_2 \cdot 2H_2O$, 0.25 g L^{-1} $Na_2MoO_4 \cdot 2H_2O$, 0.1 g L^{-1} H_3BO_3, and 5 mL L^{-1} H_2SO_4 were added to the medium [24]. During the isolation process which followed, 50 mL of the initial amount of active sludge was mixed with 450 mL of synthetic growth medium in a Duran flask (Schott). The flask was incubated in a stirred water bath, at 25 °C and 100 rpm. To ensure aerobic conditions, air was provided using a ventilation pump under a constant flow rate of 2 L min^{-1}. After the complete oxidation of ammonia to nitrate, biomass was collected through centrifugation and was inoculated in a fresh growth medium.

Enriched activated sludge was used as an initial consortium in order to isolate NOB. The resulting enriched liquid culture was inoculated onto Petri dishes containing curdled growth medium, using agar. The whole isolation process was performed under sterile conditions using a laboratory sterile laminar flow chamber. The inoculated plates were placed in an incubator (BMT Incucell V) at 25 °C for 3 to 4 weeks. Several recultures were performed using the observed colonies in order to purify the bacteria culture, on a solid medium. Following this step, isolated cells were transferred to liquid cultures containing $NaNO_2$ as substrate.

Fifteen different microbial cultures were prepared to examine the nitrification effect and to develop a general mathematical model. More specifically, mixed bacterial cultures with both NOB and AOB were cultivated and monitored in four different pH values (6.5–8 with a step of 0.5) for an initial ammonium nitrogen concentration of 100 mg L^{-1} and 250 mg L^{-1}. Moreover, three different experiments with mixed culture in different initial ammonium nitrogen concentrations (100 mg L^{-1}, and 700 mg L^{-1}) with a pH value of 7.8 were used for model calibration. Regarding the starvation experiments, the enriched nitrifying bacterial culture was cultivated in a nitrogen-depleted medium for 1, 2, 3, 4, and 5 days, respectively, and was subsequently exposed to 250 mg NH_4^+-N L^{-1} in four different pH conditions (6.5 to 8 with a step of 0.5). The pH value was monitored daily with an electronic pH meter (Thermo Scientific, Orion ROSS Ultra Refillable Ph/ATC Triode) and was adjusted manually to the pre-set value, when it was needed. Finally, pure NOB cultures with nitrite ions (from sodium nitrite) in a concentration of 100 mg L^{-1} and both nitrite and ammonium nitrogen (1 mg L^{-1}) as substrate were used to evaluate the kinetic parameters in the different metabolic pathways of the NOB culture. All experiments were performed in duplicate.

2.2. Analytical Techniques

Regarding the nitrification process evaluation, nitrite (NO_2^-) and nitrate (NO_3^-) ions were determined by ion chromatography (DIONEX ICS-3000) equipped with a Dionex IonPac™ AS19 (4 × 250 mm) and a DIONEX conductivity detector. The column temperature was set at 30 °C and detector temperature at 35 °C. The mobile phase used consisted of purified water and HCl 3 M. The flow rate was set at 0.8 mL min^{-1} while the run-time analysis was 30 min. Initially, the eluent was 100% purified water maintained for 18 min. The concentration of HCl 3 M was increased from 15% to 50% for 3 min (18–21 min of the method) and maintained for 4 min (21–25 min of the method). Then, the same eluent was reduced from 50% to 15% for 0.5 min (25–25.5 min of the method). Finally, the concentration of HCl 3 M was slightly increased from 15% to 18% for 4.5 min (25.5–30 min of the method). Ammonium nitrogen was measured based on the Phenate method [27]. Biomass concentration was measured as dry cell weight (DW), according to a modified method of *Standard Methods* (Method 2540) for an estimation of Total Suspended Solids (TSS), using GF/F grade filters [28]. All analytical measurements were performed in duplicate.

2.3. Model Development

The proposed model was based on the well-established model ASM1 which describes the biological wastewater treatment process [29]. This model describes the mass balances among the different forms of nitrogen in the nitrification process (ammonium to nitrate, nitrite to nitrate). Different microorganisms' species were involved in these steps. AOB were involved in the nitrite formation from ammonium nitrogen and NOB were involved in the nitrate formation. Regarding the NOB metabolic pathway, the microbial process was divided into anabolism and catabolism. During anabolism, the NOB cells utilize ammonium nitrogen as the nitrogen source to form new biomass cells. If there is a lack of ammonium nitrogen in the medium, an intracellular conversion of nitrite to ammonium is carried out to cover the microorganism's nitrogen demands. Regarding the energy demands of NOB culture (catabolism), only nitrite is consumed to form nitrate in the medium. A brief description of the major processes included in the proposed model are presented schematically in Figure 1a.

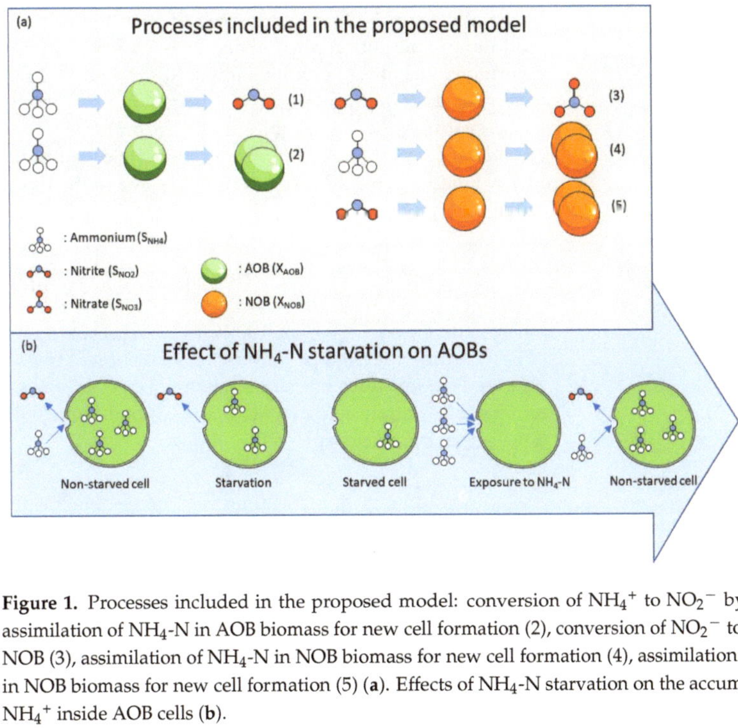

Figure 1. Processes included in the proposed model: conversion of NH_4^+ to NO_2^- by AOB (1), assimilation of NH_4-N in AOB biomass for new cell formation (2), conversion of NO_2^- to NO_3^- by NOB (3), assimilation of NH_4-N in NOB biomass for new cell formation (4), assimilation of NO_2-N in NOB biomass for new cell formation (5) (**a**). Effects of NH_4-N starvation on the accumulation of NH_4^+ inside AOB cells (**b**).

As presented in Figure 1, the ammonium nitrogen (S_{NH4}) of the medium in a mixed AOB-NOB culture is consumed either for AOB (X_{AOB}) (anabolism and catabolism) or NOB anabolism (X_{NOB}). The separation of anabolism and catabolism in AOB growth is expressed mathematically from the parameters $i_{x,b,}$ and Y_{AOB} in Equations (8) and (9), where $i_{x,b}$ represents the fraction of nitrogen in biomass (measured value 3.87 $g_N/g_{biomass}$) and Y_{AOB} denotes the AOB yield [$g_{biomass}/g_N$]. Regarding the growth rates of both AOB and NOB, the widely used Monod equation was implemented in the proposed model. The maximum specific growth rate for each microbial group is presented as μ_{max}.

Regarding the anabolism/catabolism separation in the NOB culture, a new term was implemented in the biomass equation to switch the biomass maximum specific growth rate with the presence or absence of ammonium in the medium. Alongside the new term, a parameter was implemented in the mass balance (K_{NH4}). When the concentration of the ammonium nitrogen (S_{NH4}) in the medium was much greater than the K_{NH4} parameter, the NOB biomass growth rate was ruled from the $\mu_{max,1}$ specific growth rate. On the other hand, when the ammonium nitrogen value was less than K_{NH4}, the biomass growth was determined from the $\mu_{max2,NO2}$. Moreover, a decrease in NOB biomass growth rate was observed when the concentration of ammonium nitrogen in the medium was high. This effect was described with the implementation of the well-established term of Andrews kinetics (i.e., substrate inhibition) for ammonium nitrogen [30].

Regarding the experimental results for the nitrate formation, non-proportional nitrate production was observed compared to the corresponding biomass growth. Hence, a nitrate production rate parameter (q_{max}) was implemented in the model. This parameter was set as an independent parameter concerning biomass's maximum specific growth rate. Moreover, a difference in the nitrate production rate was observed with the presence or absence of ammonium quantities in the pure NOB cultures. In order to express this difference, the maximum nitrate production rate was divided into two different parameters ($q_{max,1}$, $q_{max,2}$) depending on the concentration of ammonium nitrogen in the culture. Besides the inhibition in NOB biomass growth with the excess of ammonium nitrogen in the medium, no inhibition phenomena were observed in nitrate formation when the $q_{max,2}$ determined the nitrate production. For this reason, no implementation of Andrews's term was considered in this mass balance equation.

Regarding the pH inhibition effects, multiple phenomena and assumptions were considered. A partial inhibition in ammonium consumption by AOB was observed in the low pH values. This inhibition was expressed in the model with I_{AOB} term by a sigmoid function (Equation (1)) [31]:

$$I_{AOB} = \frac{1}{1 + \exp(A(K - pH))} \tag{1}$$

where A denotes a fitting parameter and K represents the half-saturation constant for the pH. Regarding the high pH values, an inhibition of free ammonia was considered in the proposed model. The ammonia–ammonium equilibrium was used to estimate the ammonia nitrogen concentration from ammonium concentration (ammonium nitrogen and ammonia nitrogen) in the present pH values (Equation (2))

$$S_{NH3} = S_{NH4} \frac{K_\alpha}{10^{-pK_\alpha} + 10^{-pH}} \tag{2}$$

where K_α represents the equilibrium constant of ammonia–ammonium equilibrium (value 5.6×10^{-10}).

The estimated ammonia concentration was implemented in I_{NOB} inhibition terms involved in biomass growth and nitrate formation. One extra parameter (K_{NH3}) was used to quantify the ammonia inhibition in the two mass balances. The final inhibition terms are presented in Equation (3):

$$I_{NOB} = \frac{K_{NH3}}{K_{NH3} + S_{NH3}} \tag{3}$$

Finally, regarding the modeling of the starvation effect [24], a single cell-based model was used according to Figure 1b. It was assumed that the amount of stored nitrogen inside the cell (X_{Nst}) was in equilibrium with the ammonium nitrogen in the medium, through the semipermanent cell membrane. The equilibrium was carried out with the osmotic pressure on the two sides of the membrane as the driving force. For the calculations, the percentage of moisture inside the cell was set as 70% *w/w* according to [32], and the equilibrium constant k_D [$g_N\ g_{N\text{-}NH4}^{-1}$]. The rate of equilibrium was determined by the k_N parameter and the mass flux. The pH value of the medium affects the starvation effect according to previous experimental work [24]. For this reason, Equation (1) was implemented in the mass balance of internally stored nitrogen in order to inhibit the overall phenomenon at low pH values. The final model equations are summarized in Equations (4)–(11).

$$\frac{dx_{AOB}}{dt} = \mu_{max,NH4}\frac{S_{NH4}}{S_{NH4}+K_{S,NH4}}x_{AOB}I_{AOB} \tag{4}$$

$$\frac{dx_{NOB,NO2}}{dt} = \mu_{max1,NO2}\frac{S_{NO2}}{S_{NO2}+K_{S,NO2}}\frac{K_{NH4}}{S_{NH4}+K_{NH4}}x_{NOB} \tag{5}$$

$$\frac{dx_{NOB,NH4}}{dt} = \mu_{max2,NO2}\frac{S_{NO2}}{S_{NO2}+K_{S,NO2}}\frac{S_{NH4}}{S_{NH4}+K_{S,NH4}+\frac{S_{NH4}^2}{K_{SS,NH4}}}x_{NOB}I_{NOB} \tag{6}$$

$$\frac{dx_{NOB}}{dt} = \frac{dx_{NOB,NO2}}{dt}+\frac{dx_{NOB,NH4}}{dt} \tag{7}$$

$$\frac{dS_{NH4}}{dt} = -\left(i_{xb}+\frac{1}{Y_{AOB}}\right)\frac{dx_{AOB}}{dt} - i_{xb}\frac{dx_{NOB,NH4}}{dt} - \frac{dX_{Nst}}{dt} \tag{8}$$

$$\frac{dS_{NO2}}{dt} = \frac{1}{Y_{AOB}}\frac{dx_{AOB}}{dt} - i_{xb}\frac{dx_{NOB,NO2}}{dt} - \frac{dS_{NO3}}{dt} \tag{9}$$

$$\begin{aligned}\frac{dS_{NO3}}{dt} &= q_{max,1}\frac{S_{NO2}}{S_{NO2}+K_{S,NO2}}\frac{K_{NH4}}{S_{NH4}+K_{NH4}}x_{NOB}I_{NOB} \\ &+ q_{max,2}\frac{S_{NO2}}{S_{NO2}+K_{S,NO2}}\frac{S_{NH4}}{S_{NH4}+K_{S,NH4}}x_{NOB}\end{aligned} \tag{10}$$

$$\frac{dX_{Nst}}{dt} = -k_N\left(k_D S_{NH4}\frac{moist_{biomass}}{1-moist_{biomass}}x_{AOB} - X_{Nst}\right)I_{AOB} \tag{11}$$

2.4. Numerical Methods

Different sets of experimental data were used to train and calibrate the proposed model. In the calibration step, experimental data from both pure NOB and mixed AOB-NOB cultures in different pH and starvation conditions were used. Initial parameters' values were set to start the numerical solution for minimizing the objective function of the sum of the squares of errors normalized with the experimental value (relative error) [33] (Equation (12)):

$$\min_{x}\sum_{i=1}^{n}\left(\frac{y_{exp,i}-y_{sim,i}}{y_{exp,i}}\right)^2 \tag{12}$$

where x denotes the vector of the optimized parameters, $y_{exp,i}$ represents the experimental value in point i, $y_{sim,i}$ represents the theoretical value in point i, and n denotes the length of the experimental point vector.

The optimization algorithm was developed in MATLAB R2018a software, a computing platform used by many engineers and scientists for data analysis and model optimization. The native function *fmincon* was used as a nonlinear programming solver using 'interior-point' as an algorithm, where the *fmincon* sets components of initial values that are equal to the interior of the bound region.

Because of the large number of the parameter vector, certain 'sub-runs' were performed with only the key parameters to be estimated, as explained in the results section. The final model training step included the overall optimization and parameter estimation in a narrow range above and below the final parameter value. Certain experimental data were excluded from the model training step to be used in model validation and testing. The estimated parameters were kept as constants in the model validation process aiming to predict the system behavior for experiments inside the range of the conditions used for optimizing the model parameters.

3. Results

3.1. Determination of Kinetic Parameters—Non-Starved Cultures

The simulated results with the experimental data used for model calibration are presented in Figure 2. Biomass growth, and nitrite and nitrate formation, were observed in the investigated pH range from 7 to 8. A strong inhibition was exhibited in the experiment with a pH value of 6.5 (Figure 2c), where no biomass growth or product formation was observed. The maximum nitrate formation was exhibited when the initial concentration of ammonium nitrogen was 700 mg L^{-1} (Figure 2b), with the maximum nitrate concentration for both the model and experimental results being 800 mg L^{-1}. Regarding the nitrite concentration, almost-zero values were observed for low pH values and initial ammonium nitrogen concentrations. This behavior differs for the high initial ammonium nitrogen concentration (250 mg L^{-1}), with pH values equal to 7 and 8 (Figure 2f,h). A nitrite–nitrogen concentration of 50 mg L^{-1} was exhibited with a rapid consumption rate for a pH value equal to 7 (complete nitrate consumption at 0.5 d). The partial inhibition of this rate was exhibited in a pH value equal to 8, where the nitrite nitrogen elimination was observed at day 5 (Figure 2h). A good fit of model calibration results to experimental data was exhibited (R^2 = 0.7), considering that the proposed model structure describes all process boundaries and limitations for all the investigated parameters (bulk pH value, initial concentration of ammonium and nitrite nitrogen, culture qualitative and quantitative characteristics).

Regarding the isolated NOB kinetics, two different experiments (with and without ammonium–nitrogen addition) were conducted (Figure 3) in order to evaluate the different kinetic parameters for anabolism and catabolism. A slow biomass production rate was observed for both experiments (with and without ammonia) compared to the results that were exhibited in the literature [29,34].

The estimated parameter values are presented in Table 1. The rates for biomass growth and product formation for the NOB were observed significantly higher than the rates concerning AOB (by 50%). This observation has also been reported in other studies. In the work of Liu et al. [35] three different mathematical models were used in order to evaluate the nitrification process. The maximum specific growth for both NOB and AOB was estimated in the same order of magnitude as the results of this study. In another study by Cui et al. [36] the biomass growth rate was estimated as significantly higher comparing the present work (1.95 d^{-1} compared with 0.1 d^{-1}). This fact may be attributed to the higher culture temperature (35 °C) compared to the culture temperature of this work. The same order of magnitude of μ_{max} values was obtained in the work of Thalla et al. [37], even if the parameter estimation was performed using linear regression.

3.2. Determination of Kinetic Parameters—Starved Cultures

Based on the proposed analysis, during the model calibration, the ammonium starvation effect on AOB was examined (Figure 4). The starvation effect was observed during the first day of cultivation (during the first 4 h). The proposed model successfully simulated this effect with the estimation of the parameters of k_N and k_D. The process rate was determined by the parameter k_N with a value equal to 25 d^{-1}, two orders of magnitude higher than the other biological rates. Since the starvation effect affects only the AOB, the pH inhibition was determined through common parameters for the starvation effect and AOB biomass growth. However, when the pH is below neutral or mild alkaline levels, the amount of free ammonia typically decreases. This leads to a decrease in growth, substrate consumption, and enzyme function, as discussed in previous works [24,38].

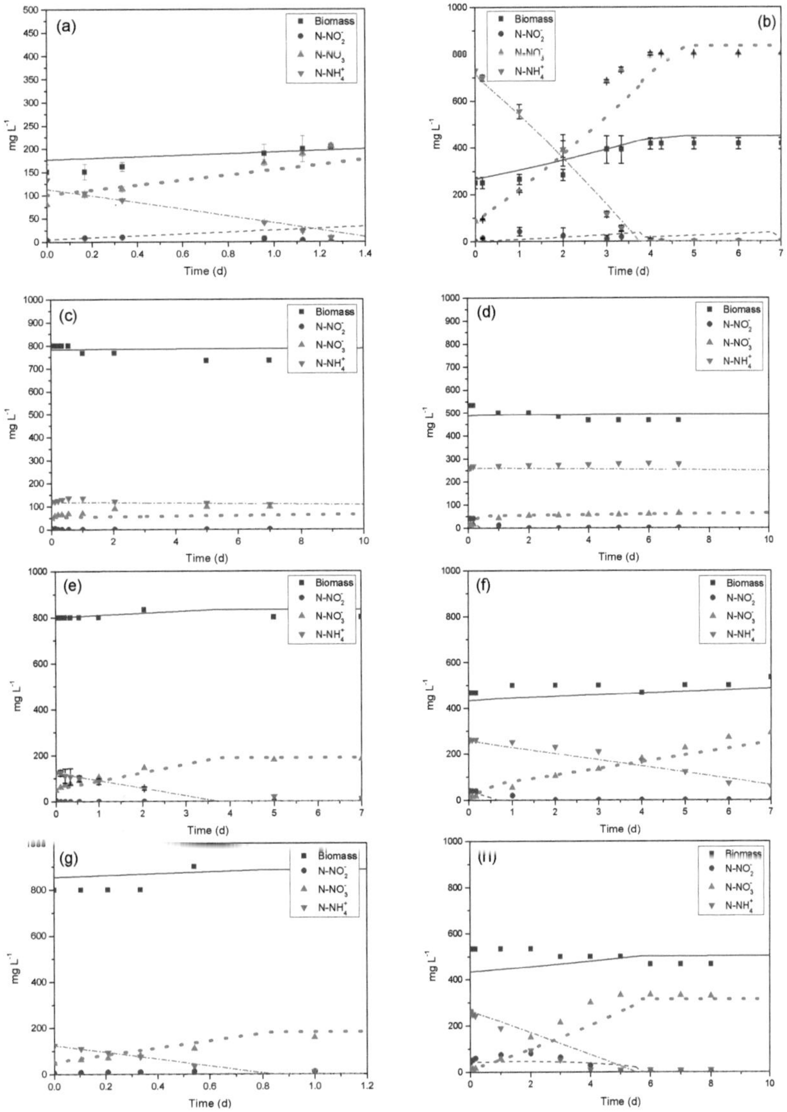

Figure 2. Experimental data and model results (continuous and dotted lines) for nitrification at pH 7.8, mixed cultures (NOB and AOB) and initial ammonium–nitrogen concentration of 100 mg L^{-1} (**a**), initial ammonium–nitrogen concentration 700 mg L^{-1} (**b**), pH 6.5 and initial ammonium–nitrogen concentration of 100 mg L^{-1} (**c**), pH 6.5 and initial ammonium–nitrogen concentration of 250 mg L^{-1} (**d**), pH 7 and initial ammonium–nitrogen concentration of 100 mg L^{-1} (**e**), pH 7 and initial ammonium–nitrogen concentration of 250 mg L^{-1} (**f**), pH 8 and initial ammonium–nitrogen concentration of 100 mg L^{-1} (**g**), and pH 8 and initial ammonium–nitrogen concentration of 250 mg L^{-1} (**h**).

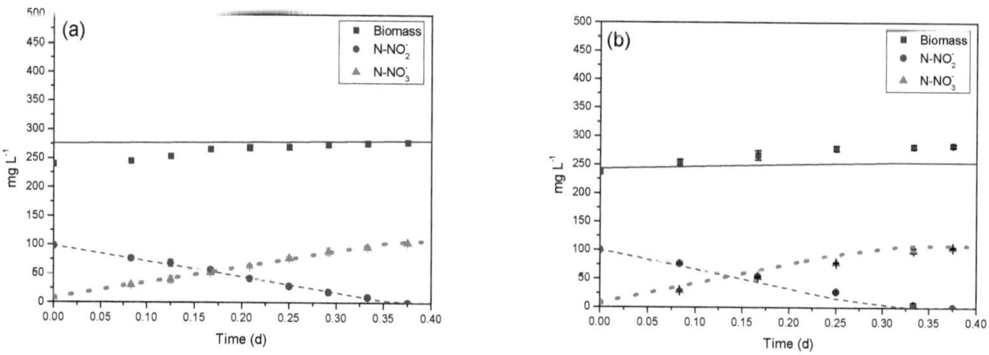

Figure 3. Experimental data and model results (continuous and dotted lines) for nitrification at pH 7.8 of NOB isolated culture with ammonium and nitrite nitrogen as substrate (**a**), and nitrite nitrogen as substrate (**b**).

Table 1. Estimated parameter values for the proposed nitrification model, optimized with the experimental data sets with different pH values, initial substrate concentration, different microorganisms, and starved and non-starved bacteria.

Parameter	Value	Units
$\mu_{max1,NO2}$	0.158	d^{-1}
$\mu_{max2,NO2}$	0.083	d^{-1}
$\mu_{max,NH4}$	0.091	d^{-1}
$q_{max,1}$	1.365	$g_{N\text{-}NO3}\ {g_{biomass}}^{-1}\ d$
$q_{max,2}$	0.788	$g_{N\text{-}NO3}\ {g_{biomass}}^{-1}\ d$
$K_{S,NO2}$	0.003	$g_{N\text{-}NO2}\ L^{-1}$
$K_{S,NH4}$	0.002	$g_{N\text{-}NH4}\ L^{-1}$
Y_{AOB}	0.141	$g_{biomass}\ {g_{N\text{-}NH4}}^{-1}$
K_{NH4}	4×10^{-4}	$g_{N\text{-}NH4}\ L^{-1}$
$K_{SS,NH4}$	7.555	$g_{N\text{-}NH4}\ L^{-1}$
A	6.758	-
K	7.713	-
K_{NH3}	7.819	$g_{N\text{-}NH3}\ L^{-1}$
k_N	25.07	d^{-1}
k_D	0.099	$g_N\ {g_{N\text{-}NH4}}^{-1}$

3.3. *Model Validation*

Based on the proposed analysis, it was deemed necessary to assess the model's accuracy using experimental data that was not used in the model calibration step. Two experiments with intermediate pH conditions (pH value 7.5) were used for this purpose. The main difference between these experiments was the initial concentration of ammonium–nitrogen in the bulk (100 mg L^{-1} and 250 mg L^{-1}, respectively). The results of the model prediction are presented in Figure 5. The maximum concentration of nitrate nitrogen reached the value of 200 mg L^{-1} and 350 mg L^{-1} (obviously as result of the non-starved AOB cells used in this run) for both the experimental data and theoretical simulations in the experiment, with initial ammonium nitrogen concentrations of 100 mg L^{-1} and 250 mg L^{-1}, respectively. The model's prediction R^2 was estimated at 0.9, indicating the high model's accuracy.

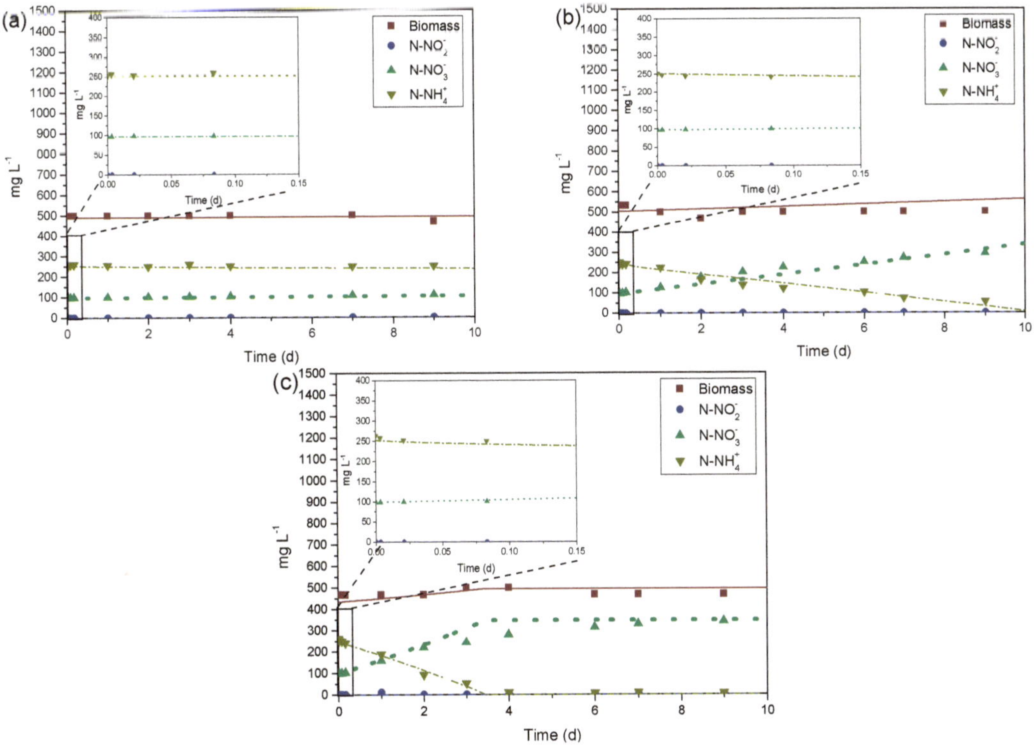

Figure 4. Experimental data and model results (continuous and dotted lines) for the nitrification of starved bacteria at (**a**) pH 6.5, (**b**) pH 7, and (**c**) pH 8.

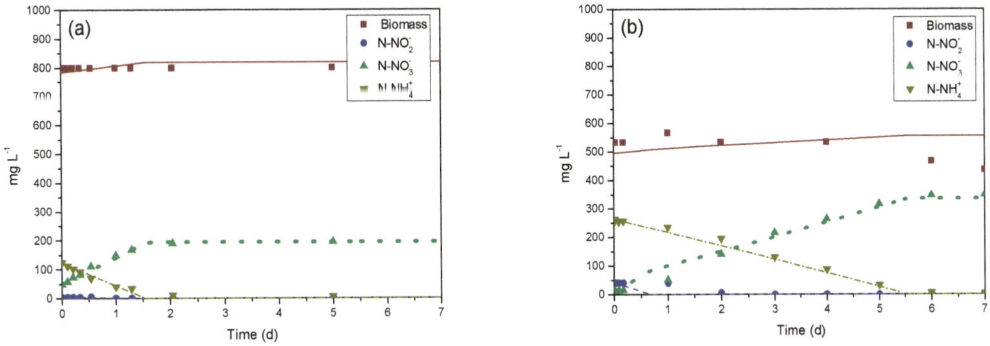

Figure 5. Experimental data and model prediction for nitrification process for mixed culture at pH 7.5 with ammonium nitrogen initial concentration 100 mg L^{-1} (**a**), and 250 mg L^{-1} (**b**).

4. Conclusions

A mathematical model describing the nitrification in mixed AOB-NOB, isolated NOB and mixed ammonium-N-starved AOB-NOB cultures was developed. Regarding the NOB growth equation, the biological process was divided into anabolism and catabolism. The analysis exhibits that ammonium nitrogen is the main nitrogen substrate of anabolism for NOB and nitrite–nitrogen is the secondary substrate that was assimilated by NOB if there is a lack of ammonium nitrogen in the bulk. Regarding the ammonium starvation effect, a new variable (X_{Nst}) and two parameters (k_D and k_N) were implemented in the model to describe the mass transfer through the cell membrane of the AOB. The model could accurately predict microbial growth and product formation in different experiment conditions (pH, initial substrate concentration, microbial consortium) with $R^2 > 0.9$. The proposed model can be useful in the field of wastewater treatment and can be implemented as a tool for process optimization and decision making in full-scale treatment units.

Author Contributions: Conceptualization, G.M.; methodology, G.M.; software, G.M. and D.Z.; validation, G.M., D.Z. and L.A.; formal analysis, G.M. and L.A.; investigation, G.M., L.A. and D.Z.; resources, M.K.; data curation, G.M.; writing—original draft preparation, G.M. and L.A.; writing—review and editing, D.Z.; visualization, G.M.; supervision, M.K.; project administration, M.K. All authors have read and agreed to the published version of the manuscript.

Funding: This research received no external funding.

Institutional Review Board Statement: Not applicable.

Informed Consent Statement: Not applicable.

Data Availability Statement: Available upon request.

Conflicts of Interest: The authors declare no conflict of interest.

References

1. Holmes, D.E.; Dang, Y.; Smith, J.A. Nitrogen Cycling during Wastewater Treatment. *Adv. Appl. Microbiol.* **2019**, *106*, 113–192.
2. Erisman, J.W.; Galloway, J.N.; Seitzinger, S.; Bleeker, A.; Dise, N.B.; Petrescu, A.M.R.; Leach, A.M.; de Vries, W. Consequences of Human Modification of the Global Nitrogen Cycle. *Philos. Trans. R. Soc. B Biol. Sci.* **2013**, *368*, 20130116. [CrossRef]
3. Law, Y.; Ye, L.; Pan, Y.; Yuan, Z. Nitrous Oxide Emissions from Wastewater Treatment Processes. *Philos. Trans. R. Soc. B Biol. Sci.* **2012**, *367*, 1265–1277. [CrossRef]
4. Keerio, H.A.; Bae, W.; Park, J.; Kim, M. Substrate Uptake, Loss, and Reserve in Ammonia-Oxidizing Bacteria (AOB) under Different Substrate Availabilities. *Process Biochem.* **2020**, *91*, 303–310. [CrossRef]
5. Yao, Q.; Peng, D.-C. Nitrite Oxidizing Bacteria (NOB) Dominating in Nitrifying Community in Full-Scale Biological Nutrient Removal Wastewater Treatment Plants. *AMB Express* **2017**, *7*, 25. [CrossRef]
6. Hayden, C.J.; Beman, J.M. High Abundances of Potentially Active Ammonia-Oxidizing Bacteria and Archaea in Oligotrophic, High-Altitude Lakes of the Sierra Nevada, California, USA. *PLoS ONE* **2014**, *9*, e111560. [CrossRef]
7. Kowalchuk, G.A.; Stephen, J.R. Ammonia-oxidizing bacteria: A Model for Molecular Microbial Ecology. *Annu. Rev. Microbiol.* **2001**, *55*, 485–529. [CrossRef]
8. Mullan, G.D.O.; Ward, B.B. Relationship of Temporal and Spatial Variabilities of Ammonia-Oxidizing Bacteria to Nitrification Rates in Monterey Bay, California. *Appl. Environ. Microbiol.* **2005**, *71*, 697–705. [CrossRef]
9. Cao, H.; Hong, Y.; Li, M.; Gu, J.; Cao, H.; Hong, Y.; Li, M.; Gu, J. Lower Abundance of Ammonia-Oxidizing Archaea than Ammonia-Oxidizing Bacteria Detected in the Subsurface Sediments of the Northern South China Sea. *Geomicrobiol. J.* **2012**, *29*, 332–339. [CrossRef]
10. Pedrouso, A.; Tocco, G.; Val del Río, A.; Carucci, A.; Morales, N.; Campos, J.L.; Milia, S.; Mosquera-Corral, A. Digested Blackwater Treatment in a Partial Nitritation-Anammox Reactor under Repeated Starvation and Reactivation Periods. *J. Clean. Prod.* **2020**, *244*, 118733. [CrossRef]
11. Bollmann, A.; Bär-Gilissen, M.J.; Laanbroek, H.J. Growth at Low Ammonium Concentrations and Starvation Response as Potential Factors Involved in Niche Differentiation among Ammonia-Oxidizing Bacteria. *Appl. Environ. Microbiol.* **2002**, *68*, 4751–4757. [CrossRef]
12. Soliman, M.; Eldyasti, A. Ammonia-Oxidizing Bacteria (AOB): Opportunities and Applications—A Review. *Rev. Environ. Sci. Biotechnol.* **2018**, *17*, 285–321. [CrossRef]
13. Geets, J.; Boon, N.; Verstraete, W. Strategies of Aerobic Ammonia-Oxidizing Bacteria for Coping with Nutrient and Oxygen Fluctuations. *FEMS Microbiol. Ecol.* **2006**, *58*, 1–13. [CrossRef]
14. Bollmann, A.; Schmidt, I.; Saunders, A.M.; Nicolaisen, M.H. Influence of Starvation on Potential Ammonia-Oxidizing Activity and AmoA MRNA Levels of Nitrosospira Briensis. *Appl. Environ. Microbiol.* **2005**, *71*, 1276–1282. [CrossRef] [PubMed]
15. French, E.; Bollmann, A. Freshwater Ammonia-Oxidizing Archaea Retain AmoA MRNA and 16S RRNA during Ammonia Starvation. *Life* **2015**, *5*, 1396–1404. [CrossRef]
16. Laanbroek, H.J.; Bär-Gilissen, M.J. Weakened Activity of Starved Ammonia-Oxidizing Bacteria by the Presence of Pre-Activated Nitrobacter Winogradskyi. *Microbes Environ.* **2002**, *17*, 122–127. [CrossRef]
17. Tappe, W.; Laverman, A.; Bohland, M.; Braster, M.; Rittershaus, S.; Groeneweg, J.; Van Verseveld, H.W. Maintenance Energy Demand and Starvation Recovery Dynamics of Nitrosomonas Europaea and Nitrobacter Winogradskyi Cultivated in a Retentostat with Complete Biomass Retention. *Appl. Environ. Microbiol.* **1999**, *65*, 2471–2477. [CrossRef]

18. Jones, R.D.; Morita, R.Y. Survival of a Marine Ammonium Oxidizer Under Energy-Source Deprivation. *Mar. Ecol.* **1985**, *26*, 175–179. [CrossRef]
19. Johnstone, B.H.; Jones, R.D. Recovery of a Marine Chemolithotrophic Ammonium-Oxidizing Bacterium from Long-Term Energy-Source Deprivation. *Can. J. Microbiol.* **1988**, *34*, 1347–1350. [CrossRef]
20. Johnstone, B.; Jones, R. Physiological Effects of Long-Term Energy-Source Deprivation on the Survival of a Marine Chemolithotrophic Ammonium-Oxidizing Bacterium. *Mar. Ecol. Prog. Ser.* **1988**, *49*, 295–303. [CrossRef]
21. Bollmann, A.; Laanbroek, H.J. Continuous Culture Enrichments of Ammonia-Oxidizing Bacteria at Low Ammonium Concentrations. *FEMS Microbiol. Ecol.* **2001**, *37*, 211–221. [CrossRef]
22. Hastings, R.C.; Saunders, J.R.; Hall, G.H.; Pickup, R.W.; McCarthy, A.J. Application of Molecular Biological Techniques to a Seasonal Study of Ammonia Oxidation in a Eutrophic Freshwater Lake. *Appl. Environ. Microbiol.* **1998**, *64*, 3674–3682. [CrossRef]
23. Speksnijder, A.G.C.L.; Kowalchuk, G.A.; Roest, K.; Laanbroek, H.J. Recovery of a Nitrosomonas-like 16S RDNA Sequence Group from Freshwater Habitats. *Syst. Appl. Microbiol.* **1998**, *21*, 321–330. [CrossRef] [PubMed]
24. Abbaszadeh, L.; Koutra, E.; Tsigkou, K.; Gaspari, M.; Kougias, P.G.; Kornaros, M. Nitrification upon Nitrogen Starvation and Recovery: Effect of Stress Period, Substrate Concentration and PH on Ammonia Oxidizers' Performance. *Fermentation* **2022**, *8*, 387. [CrossRef]
25. Gujer, W. Nitrification and Me—A Subjective Review. *Water Res.* **2010**, *44*, 1–19. [CrossRef] [PubMed]
26. Ni, B.-J.; Ruscalleda, M.; Pellicer-Nacher, C.; Smets, B.F. Modeling Nitrous Oxide Production during Biological Nitrogen Removal via Nitrification and Denitrification: Extensions to the General ASM Models. *Environ. Sci. Technol.* **2011**, *45*, 7768–7776. [CrossRef]
27. Rausch, T. The Estimation of Micro-Algal Protein Content and Its Meaning to the Evaluation of Algal Biomass I. Comparison of Methods for Extracting Protein. *Hydrobiologia* **1981**, *78*, 237–251. [CrossRef]
28. Eaton, A.D.; Clesceri, L.S.; Greenberg, A.E.; Franson, M.A.H. *Standard Methods for the Examination of Water and Wastewater*, 22nd ed.; APHA: Washington, DC, USA, 2012.
29. Ostace, G.S.; Cristea, V.M.; Agachi, P.Ş. Extension of Activated Sludge Model No 1 with Two-Step Nitrification and Denitrification Processes for Operation Improvement. *Environ. Eng. Manag. J.* **2011**, *10*, 1529–1544. [CrossRef]
30. Zhang, D.; Cai, Q.; Zu, B.; Bai, C.; Zhang, P. The Influence of Trace NO_2 on the Kinetics of Ammonia Oxidation and the Characteristics of Nitrogen Removal from Wastewater. *Water Sci. Technol.* **2010**, *62*, 1037–1044. [CrossRef] [PubMed]
31. Jiménez, E.; Giménez, J.B.; Ruano, M.V.; Ferrer, J.; Serralta, J. Effect of PH and Nitrite Concentration on Nitrite Oxidation Rate. *Bioresour. Technol.* **2011**, *102*, 8741–8747. [CrossRef]
32. Xie, Y.; Xu, J.; Yang, R.; Alshammari, J.; Zhu, M.-J.; Sablani, S.; Tang, J. Moisture Content of Bacterial Cells Determines Thermal Resistance of Salmonella Enterica Serotype Enteritidis PT 30. *Appl. Environ. Microbiol.* **2021**, *87*, e02194-20. [CrossRef] [PubMed]
33. Tsafrakidou, P.; Manthos, G.; Zagklis, D.; Mema, J.; Kornaros, M. Assessment of Substrate Load and Process PH for Bioethanol Production–Development of a Kinetic Model. *Fuel* **2022**, *313*, 123007. [CrossRef]
34. Rittmann, B.E.; McCarty, P.L. *Environmental Biotechnology: Principles and Applications*; McGraw-Hill Education: New York, NY, USA, 2001; ISBN 1260440591.
35. Liu, X. Comparing Three Mathematical Models Using Different Substrates for Prediction of Partial Nitrification. *Sci. Total Environ.* **2020**, *749*, 141643. [CrossRef] [PubMed]
36. Cui, F.; Park, S.; Mo, K.; Lee, W.; Lee, H.; Kim, M. Experimentation and Mathematical Models for Partial Nitrification in Aerobic Granular Sludge Process. *KSCE J. Civ. Eng.* **2017**, *21*, 127–133. [CrossRef]
37. Thalla, A.K.; Bhargava, R.; Kumar, P. Nitrification Kinetics of Activated Sludge-Biofilm System: A Mathematical Model. *Bioresour. Technol.* **2010**, *101*, 5827–5835. [CrossRef]
38. Prosser, J.I. Autotrophic Nitrification in Bacteria. In *Advances in Microbial Physiology*; Rose, A.H., Tempest, D.W., Eds.; Academic Press: Cambridge, MA, USA, 1990; Volume 30, pp. 125–181, ISBN 0065-2911.

fermentation

Review

Biosynthesis of Nicotinamide Mononucleotide: Current Metabolic Engineering Strategies, Challenges, and Prospects

Shiqi Luo [1,2], Juntao Zhao [1,2], Yangyang Zheng [1,2], Tao Chen [1,2] and Zhiwen Wang [1,2,*]

1 Frontier Science Center for Synthetic Biology and Key Laboratory of Systems Bioengineering (Ministry of Education), Tianjin University, Tianjin 300072, China; 2020207206@tju.edu.cn (S.L.); zhaojuntao@tju.edu.cn (J.Z.); 2018207233@tju.edu.cn (Y.Z.)

2 SynBio Research Platform, Collaborative Innovation Center of Chemical Science and Engineering (Tianjin), School of Chemical Engineering and Technology, Tianjin University, Tianjin 300072, China

* Correspondence: zww@tju.edu.cn; Tel.: +86-22-27893727

Abstract: Nicotinamide mononucleotide (NMN) is an essential precursor of nicotinamide adenine dinucleotide (NAD^+), which is widely applied in the pharmaceutical and biotech industries. The biosynthesis of NMN is currently attracting much attention because it has non-toxic reaction conditions and low amounts of isomers, whereas chemical synthesis has low yields and is not environmentally friendly. This review systematically describes the two biosynthetic pathways of NMN in detail for the first time and introduces the latest studies on NMN production through different pathways using metabolic engineering strategies. NMN accumulation can be improved by optimizing the activity of key enzymes, enhancing the supply of precursors and co-factors, inhibiting the synthesis of byproducts, and promoting product export. Finally, we also discuss the current challenges of producing NMN and possible solutions for the future.

Keywords: nicotinamide mononucleotide; nicotinamide phosphoribosyltransferase; biosynthetic pathway

check for updates

Citation: Luo, S.; Zhao, J.; Zheng, Y.; Chen, T.; Wang, Z. Biosynthesis of Nicotinamide Mononucleotide: Current Metabolic Engineering Strategies, Challenges, and Prospects. *Fermentation* **2023**, *9*, 594. https://doi.org/10.3390/fermentation9070594

Academic Editor: Ricardo Aguilar-López

Received: 24 May 2023
Revised: 23 June 2023
Accepted: 24 June 2023
Published: 26 June 2023

1. Introduction

Nicotinamide mononucleotide (NMN) is an acid- and water-soluble nucleotide containing a pyridine base. Although it exists in α and β anomeric forms, only the β form is the active anomer, which is also termed β-nicotinamide mononucleotide, β-nicotinamide D-ribonucleotide, and β-nicotinamide ribose monophosphate. Inside the cell, NMN is converted into nicotinamide adenine dinucleotide (NAD^+), which is an essential molecule in cells where it functions as an electron carrier in metabolic redox reactions and as a substrate for NAD-dependent signal transduction [1]. Deficiency of NAD^+ can be compensated for with NMN supplementation, which effectively increases NAD^+ levels in various tissues and prevents related metabolic diseases [2]. Recent studies suggested that NMN could recover cognition in Alzheimer's disease model rats and showed a significant protective effect on neurons [3,4]. In addition to improving numerous neuronal functions, NMN was also found to increase resistance to oxidation, improve immunity, and prevent cardiovascular disease [5]. Consequently, NMN is becoming a promising compound for treating neurological disorders and relieving aging-related symptoms.

NMN has a broad market and great application value in medicine and healthcare. To meet this demand, several chemical and biological methods have been developed to synthesize NMN. Chemical synthesis is mainly accomplished through different reaction steps using adenosine monophosphate (AMP), nicotinamide (NAM), and 1,2,3,5-tetra-O-acetyl-D-ribose as raw materials. Compared to chemical synthesis, biological routes have the advantages of mild reaction conditions, non-toxic ingredients, and low amounts of isomers [6]. The biosynthesis of NMN can be subdivided into enzymatic and fermentation-based methods. In vitro enzyme catalysis technology enables NMN synthesis by creating a multi-enzyme cascade biosystem. As early as 1957, Preiss and Handler produced NMN using an in vitro enzymatic method with a yield of 113.64 mg/L [7]. However, this process requires the purification of enzymes for the reactions, as well as the addition of ATP and NADH to provide the energy required for enzymatic catalysis [8]. With the development of metabolic engineering, Sinclair et al. first constructed a recombinant *Saccharomyces cerevisiae* for NMN synthesis from a nucleoside comprising NAM via nicotinamide phosphoribosyltransferase (NAMPT) catalysis [9,10]. *Escherichia coli* is a simple model organism compared to *S. cerevisiae* and has become the main chassis for NMN production. Recently, Huang et al. reconstructed the metabolism of *E. coli* and achieved NMN yields of 16,200 mg/L in a 5 L bioreactor, the highest production reported to date [11].

There are two main metabolic pathways for the biosynthesis of NMN from nicotinate and nicotinamide in nature: the de novo pathway and the salvage pathway [12–15]. Shen et al. summarized the synthesis of NMN via the salvage pathway using 5-phosphoribosyl-1-pyrophosphate (PRPP) and NAM as precursors [6]. Here, we systematically describe the two biosynthetic pathways of NMN, which is the first comprehensive summary of current strategies to promote microbial biosynthesis of NMN. Strategies for regulating key components such as key enzymes, precursors, cofactors, byproducts, and transport proteins through metabolic engineering are introduced. Moreover, the challenges and solutions for increasing the accumulation of NMN are also discussed.

2. Metabolism of Nicotinamide Mononucleotide

Although NMN metabolism is a universal process closely related to NAD^+, there are subtle differences in the cellular pathways of NMN synthesis. The two basic pathways of NMN synthesis are known as the de novo pathway and the salvage pathway.

2.1. De Novo Pathway

In fungi and some bacteria, such as *S. cerevisiae* and *Bacillus subtilis*, NMN is derived from NAD^+ via the de novo pathway catalyzed by a single enzyme, downstream of which many enzymes are involved in the production of NAD^+ (Figure 1). Nicotinic acid mononucleotide (NaMN) is synthesized in three reactions from aspartate (Asp) or six reactions from tryptophan (Trp), after which it is converted into NAD^+ via two enzymatic reactions [16]. Asp is the starting amino acid for the de novo synthesis of NMN in most bacteria. The de novo pathway is characterized by the synthesis of quinolinic acid (QA) from Asp via two enzymatic reactions mediated by L-aspartate oxidase, quinolinate synthase, and spontaneous cyclization. The two enzymes are respectively encoded by the *nadB* and *nadA* genes [17,18]. Quinolinate phosphoribosyltransferase (NADC) then transfers the phosphoribosyl moiety of PRPP to quinolinic acid (QA), which produces NaMN [13]. Next, NaMN adenylyltransferase (NADD) converts NaMN into nicotinic acid adenine dinucleotide (NaAD) via the addition of an AMP moiety from ATP [19]. Finally, NAD^+ synthetase (NADE) converts NaAD into NAD^+. Conversely, the Nudix hydrolase (NUDE) or other pyrophosphatase (USHA and MAGZ) with similar hydrolytic activity can degrade NAD^+ into NMN. However, NAD^+ is involved in intracellular redox reactions and is rarely decomposed directly into NMN. Therefore, the de novo pathway received relatively little attention until Sorci et al. combined a comparative genomic approach with in vitro and in vivo experiments to identify the *nadE* gene from *Francisella tularensis* [20]. This gene encodes NMN synthetase (FtNADE*), which is involved in the direct conversion of NaMN into NMN without NAD^+ synthesis. Moreover, in most cases, this activity was not detected in any of the characteristic members of the NADE family. As shown in Figure 1, the de novo pathway is very long, leading to a slow rate of NMN synthesis. Hence, this pathway is hardly ever chosen for the biosynthesis of NMN.

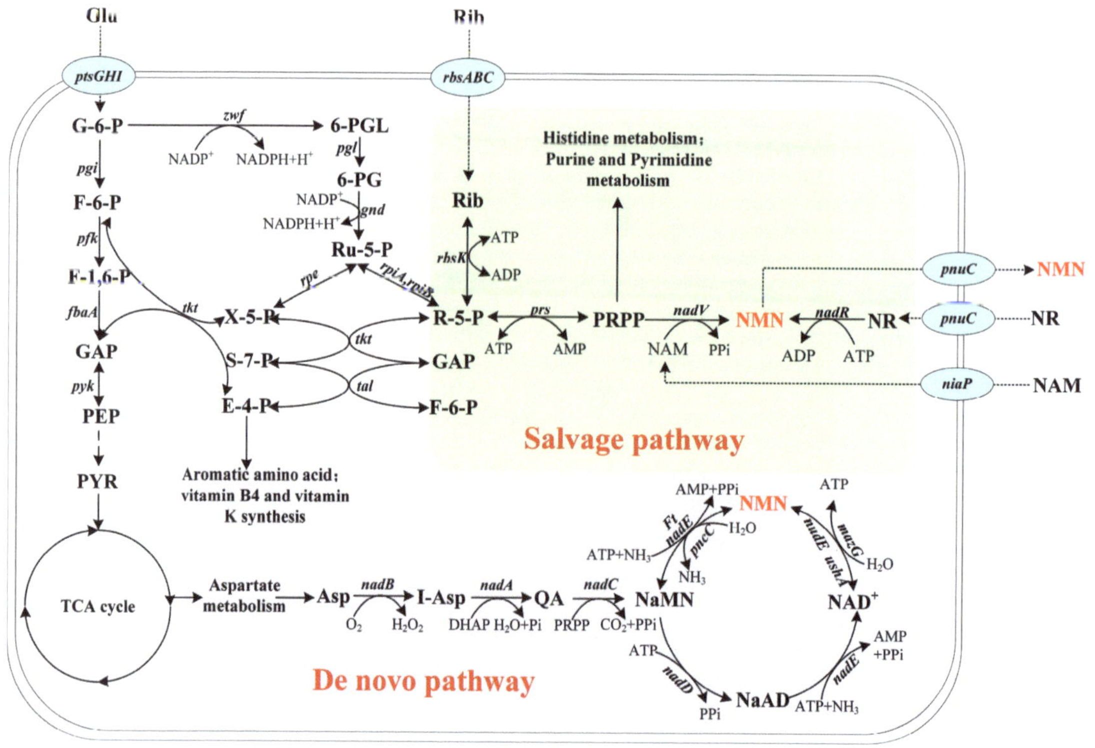

Figure 1. De novo and salvage pathways of nicotinamide mononucleotide synthesis. The de novo synthesis of NMN is mediated by NADB, NADA, and NADC, leading to the production of NaMN. After NAD^+ is generated by the pathway, Nudix hydrolases such as NUDE or other nucleotidases (MAZG and USHA) with similar hydrolytic activity can degrade NAD^+ into NMN. Alternatively, NMN synthetase could directly convert NaMN into NMN. In the salvage pathway, NAM is converted into NMN by NAM phosphoribosyl transferase (NAMPT), whereas NR is converted into NMN by NMN adenylyltransferase (NADR). Abbreviations of NMN intermediates are shown in bold font 12. Asp, aspartate. I-Asp, iminoaspartate. QA, quinolinic acid. NaMN, nicotinic acid mononucleotide. NaAD, deamido-nicotinamide adenine dinucleotide. NAD^+, nicotinamide adenine dinucleotide. NMN, nicotinamide mononucleotide. NAM, nicotinamide. NR, nicotinamide riboside. PRPP, 5′-phosphoribosyl 1-pyrophosphate. ATP, adenosine triphosphate. ADP, adenosine diphosphate. AMP, adenosine monophosphate. DHAP, dihydroxyacetone phosphate. PPi, pyrophosphate. Pi, phosphate. The genes and enzymes associated with the reactions are *nadB*, L-aspartate oxidase; *nadA*, quinolinate synthase; *nadC*, quinolinate phosphoribosyltransferase; *nadD*, NaMN adenylyltransferase; *nadE*, NAD^+ synthetase; *nudE*, NADH hydrolase; *mazG*, nucleoside triphosphate pyrophosphohydrolase; *ushA*, UDP-sugar hydrolase; *pncC*, NMN amidohydrolase; *Ft nadE*, NMN synthase from *Francisella tularensis*; *nadV*, nicotinamide phosphoribosyltransferase; *nadR*, NMN amidohydrolase from *Bacillus subtilis*; *xapA*, xanthosine phosphorylase; and *nadD*, nicotinate nucleotide adenylyltransferase. The production of NMN from NAM and glucose/ribose uses the pentose phosphate pathway or the ribose metabolic pathway. Solid arrows indicate metabolic pathways, whereas dotted arrows indicate the transport directions of transporters. The essential genes and enzymes associated with the reactions are *zwf*, glucose 6-phosphate dehydrogenase; *pgi*, glucose-6-phosphate isomerase; *pgl*, 6-phosphogluconolactonase; *gnd*, 6-phosphogluconate dehydrogenase; *rpiA*, ribose 5-phosphate isomerase A; *rpiB*, ribose 5-phosphate isomerase B; *prs*, ribose-phosphate diphosphokinase; and *rbsK*, ribokinase. Four transporters, *ptsGHI* (glucose transporter), *rbsABC* (D-ribose transporter), *niaP* (niacin

transporter), and *pnuC* (nicotinamide riboside transporter), are shown in blue and purple ovals. Abbreviations of metabolites. Glu, glucose; G-6-P, glucose-6-phosphate; F-6-P, fructose-6-phosphate; F-1,6-P, 1,6-fructose diphosphate; GAP, glyceraldehyde 2-phosphate; PEP, phosphoenolpyruvate; PYR, pyruvic acid; 6-PGL, 6-phosphogluconolactone; 6-PG, 6-phosphogluconic acid; Ru-5-P, ribulose 5-phosphate; X-5-P, D-xylulose 5-phosphate; S-7-P, sedoheptulose 7-phosphate; E-4-P, erythrose 4-phosphate; Rib, ribose; Ru-5-P, ribulose-5-phosphate; R-5-P, ribulose 5-phosphate.

In the de novo pathway, the hydrolysis efficiencies of NAD^+ directly determines the production of NMN. USHA provides most of the pyrophosphatase activity in *E. coli* and showed catalytic efficiencies for the hydrolysis of NAD^+ at 3.7×10^6 $M^{-1}{\cdot}s^{-1}$, much more than MAGZ and NUDE [21]. However, USHA also has a 5′-nuclease activity that decomposes NMN into NAM. Therefore, the most promising route for the de novo synthesis of NMN is the amidation of NaMN catalyzed by FtNADE*. FtNADE* typically use ammonium as an amine nitrogen donor, and the reaction is driven by ATP hydrolysis. The substrate specificity of FtNADE* is very high, as it catalyzes the conversion of NaMN into NMN with an efficiency of 2.5×10^3 $M^{-1}{\cdot}s^{-1}$, 60 times higher than with NaAD as substrate [20]. However, the activity of NAD^+ synthase (NADM) is 1000 times higher than that of FtNADE*. This means that the downstream metabolic pathway for the synthesis of NAD^+ must be blocked to achieve high yields of NMN. In addition, the FtNADE* enzyme is a variant of the NADE family with rare functions [22], and no regulation at the transcriptional level has been reported.

2.2. Salvage Pathway

The salvage pathway is a cost-effective way for eukaryotes and prokaryotes to obtain NMN. It is found in mammals, yeast, and Gram-negative bacteria such as *F. tularensis*. There are two main routes of the salvage pathway: (1) direct biosynthesis of NAM and PRPP by NAMPT, and (2) NR phosphorylation (Figure 1).

Most studies of the salvage pathway investigated the salvageable pyridine base, NAM. It is synthesized via NAM and PRPP catalyzed by NAMPT, which is a rate-limiting enzyme for NMN biosynthesis. [15]. The *nadV* genes encoding NAMPT have been identified in mammals such as mice, as well as in phages and bacteria, including *Shewanella oneidensis*, *Xanthomonas translucens*, *Haemophilus ducreyi* [23], *Ralstonia solanacearum*, *Sphingopyxis* sp. C-1, *Chitinophaga pinensis*, and *Vibrio* Phage KVP40 [24]. The activity of enzymes is closely related to their protein structure, but only a few three-dimensional structures of NAMPTs from different strains have been determined, which greatly limits their rational engineering. PRPP is a precursor in this reaction and can be synthesized from glucose as a substrate. However, this conversion requires a long metabolic pathway to obtain PRPP, whereas the conversion of ribose to PRPP requires only two enzymatic reactions (Figure 1). Common model organisms such as *E. coli* and *B. subtilis* have membrane proteins that transport ribose, and ribose phosphate diphosphokinase (PRS) is considered the most prominent limiting factor for PRPP synthesis. The direct contribution of nicotinamide riboside (NR) to NAD^+ metabolism was first recognized by Bieganowski and Brenner in 2004 [25]. NMN is synthesized from NR via NRK-mediated phosphorylation, bypassing the need for NAMPT [15]. Mammals possess specific NRKs that function to synthesize NAD^+ via NMN in addition to the well-known pathways through NaMN [26].

When NAM is used as a precursor, NMN is formed by NAMPT. NAMPT is found in mammals and some pathogenic microorganisms, and studies on its regulation have focused on mammalian cells such as humans and mice [1,27]. The catalytic activity of human NAMPT could be increased from $1.60 \pm 0.06 \times 10^3$ to $1.8 \pm 0.9 \times 10^6$ $M^{-1}{\cdot}s^{-1}$ by hydrolytic coupling with ATP [28]. Studies on NAMPT in microorganisms have focused on the identification of enzymes [23]. PRS is the key enzyme to produce the essential precursor PRPP. In some bacteria, PRS was complexed with ATP and R-5-P, as well as its four domains for substrate or cofactor recognition (Mg^{2+}, MgATP, Pi, and R5P), and catalytic activity has been studied [29]. In *B. subtilis*, PRS was responsible for the formation of PRPP and purines synthesis, which had K_m values of 4.8×10^{-4} M for R-5-P. The regulation of PRS activity is multi-dimensional and complex. Its activity is affected by negative feedback regulation by some nucleotides, especially ADP and GDP [30]. Furthermore, PRS is also regulated by metal ions and Pi. Only when these ions are present can PRS show good activity [31]. In addition, the precursor PRPP can bind to the purine repressor *purR* and regulate the transcription of the purine pathway, which may cause a poor effect on the binding of PRPP to NAMPT [32].

When NR is used as a precursor, NMN is derived from the phosphorylation of NR in one enzymatic step. In prokaryotes such as *E. coli* and *Haemophilus influenzae*, the full-size multifunctional NADR protein (encoded by *nadR*) is composed of a central nicotinamide mononucleotide adenylyltransferase (NMNAT) domain and a C-terminal NR kinase (NRK) domain, which endow it with NMNAT and NRK enzymatic activities, respectively [33,34]. A new NRK from *Kluyveromyces marxianus* (Klm-NRK) ranks the highest among reported NRKs. The specific activity of purified Klm-NRK was 7.9 U·mg^{-1} protein, and the catalytic efficiencies (k_{cat}/K_m) toward ATP and NR were 5.74×10^4 and 8.44×10^4 M^{-1}·s^{-1}, respectively [35]. In eukaryotes such as yeast, NRK1 (encoding by *nrk1*) catalyzes the reaction of NR with ATP to produce NMN. After purification, NRK from *S. cerevisiae* reached an activity of 2252.59 U·mg^{-1} and K_m values of 5.427×10^{-2} and 1.869×10^{-2} M for ATP and NR, respectively [36]. Human cells have two gene-encoded NRK isoforms: NRK1 and NRK2. Both enzymes convert NR with comparable K_m values of 3.4×10^{-6} and 4.6×10^{-6} M for NRK1 and NRK2, respectively, but also utilize other nucleoside substrates with lower affinity [37,38]. In particular, NRK1 limits the use of exogenous NR for the synthesis of NMN and NAD$^+$ [39]. It is worth noting that NADR may interact with an integral membrane transporter PnuC protein and directly participate in the uptake of exogenous NAD$^+$ precursors [40]. PnuC is a membrane protein and usually regarded as a transporter protein of NMN, but NMN must be dephosphorylated to NR before it can be transported intracellularly [41]. Fortunately, mutant PnuC*290 can transport NMN directly. PnuC*290 has a duplication of the six-base sequence AAAAGC encoding amino acids 108 (K) and 109 (A), which adds K and A residues just before the fourth membrane-panning region [42]. In *Salmonella typhimurium*, transport of NMN requires two proteins: NADR and PnuC. PnuC undertakes the main function of the transport system, whereas NADR is a regulatory protein. PnuC is often clustered with genes for NAD biosynthesis, and in enterobacteria, *pnuC* forms a manipulator with the gene *nadA* (encoding quinolinic acid synthase) and is regulated by NADR [43]. The activity of PnuC* is regulated by intracellular NAD levels. When high concentrations of NAD are sensed by NADR proteins, the PnuC transport system returns to its inactive condition [40]. It was demonstrated that when the internal concentration was high, the PnuC transporter protein was able to export the substrate [44]. Although NMN transporter proteins have not been identified in eukaryotes, the NAD$^+$ transporter protein Ndt1p [45] and NR transporter protein Nrt1 [46] have been identified in *S. cerevisiae*.

3. Metabolic Engineering Strategies for Nicotinamide Mononucleotide Production

NMN is usually produced by microbial fermentation, for example, by constructing a heterologous pathway in *E. coli*. In the salvage pathway, researchers tried to increase the titer and yield of NMN to a certain extent via multiple metabolic engineering strategies, including overexpressing key enzyme NAMPT [11] and optimizing the activity of NAMPT via directed evolution, increasing the supply of key precursors PRPP and NAM by enhancing the carbon flux to PRPP and expressing NAM transporter proteins [47], improving the energy supply of ATP by building an ATP regeneration system [48], eliminating the production of byproducts by knocking out the byproduct pathway [49], and enhancing the output of NMN by overexpressing NMN transporter proteins [50]. Recent advances in the research on NMN biosynthesis are summarized in Table 1.

Table 1. Metabolic engineering strategies for improving the production of NMN.

Chassis	Strategies	Cultivation	Intracellular NMN Production (mg/L)	Extracellular NMN Production (mg/L)	Reference
S. cerevisiae	Overexpression of *nadV*; deletion of *nma1* [1]	Bioreactor [2]	ND [3] (300–350 nmol per g of wet cells)	ND [3]	[9]
E. coli	Overexpression of *nadV*	500 mL benchtop bioreactor	7877.59	10.89	[51]
E. coli	Overexpression of *nadV* and *prs* (with L135I mutation)	500 mL benchtop bioreactor	7563.42	15.42	[51]
E. coli	Overexpression of *nadV* and *nadE*; deletion of *pncC*	2 mL deep-well plate	501.33	ND [3]	[52]
E. coli	Overexpression of *nadV*, *niaP*, *pnuC*, *pig*, *zwf*, *pgl*, *gnd*, *ripA*, *ripB*, and *prs*	2 L fermenter	ND [3]	6.79×10^3	[47]
E. coli	Overexpression of *nadV*, ygcS, *prs* (with L135I mutation), *zwf*, *gnd*, and *adoI*; deletion of *nadR*, *pncC*, *amn*, and *purR* [4]	Flasks [2]	ND [3]	496.2	[53]
E. coli	Overexpression *nadV*, *prs1*, and *prs2*; optimization of the amounts of ribose, Mg^{2+}, phosphate, nicotinamide, and lactose inducer (using response surface methodology)	250 mL Erlenmeyer flask	772.05	ND [3]	[54]
Fructobacillus durionis	Lactic acid bacteria isolated from natural resources cultivated in MRS medium containing 1% D-fructose for 12 h	Flasks [2]	2.1	ND [3]	[55]
E. coli	Overexpression of *nadV*, *prs* (with L135I mutation), and *pnuC*; deletion of *nadR*, *pncC*, *ushA*, and *purR*; controlling the supplementation of nicotinamide and dissolved oxygen level	5 L fermenter	ND [3]	1.62×10^4	[11]
E. coli	Deletion of *tktA* [5], *tktB* [5], and *ptsG* [5]; cascade bioconversion using EcRBSK, EcPRPS, CpNAMPT, CHU0107, and EcPPase	500 mL baffled flask and 10 mL scale bioreactor	ND [3]	284.09	[56]
S. cerevisiae EBY100	Overexpression of *nrk2* [6] (displayed on the cell surface); optimization of the amounts of NR, ATP, and Mg^{2+}; optimization of pH and temperature	30 mL screw vial	ND [3]	1.26×10^4	[57]

[1] *nma1*: encodes nicotinamide mononucleotide adenylyltransferase. [2] Bioreactor, flasks: The size of the vessels used in the literatures are not reported. [3] ND: not determined. [4] *purR*: encodes DNA-binding transcriptional repressor. [5] *tktA* and *tktB*: transketolase; *ptsG*: encodes the glucose-specific IICB component. [6] *nrk2*: NR kinase.

3.1. Selection and Directed Evolution of the Key Enzyme NAMPT

The direct biosynthesis of NAM and PRPP by NAMPT has attracted a lot of attention because of its short metabolic pathway and low metabolic burden. As NAMPT is a key enzyme of the salvage pathway, heterologous metabolic pathways are often constructed in chassis by directly selecting NAMPT derived from different species in nature. Huang et al. first constructed the *E. coli* F004 by deleted four genes (*nadR*, *pncC*, *ushA*, and *purR*) related to the decomposition of NMN, and then they selected eight NAMPT orthologs from different microorganisms and expressed them with the T7 promoter in *E. coli* F004. The results indicated that NAMPT from *Vibrio* bacteriophage KVP4012 (VpNAMPT) showed the highest activity and finally achieved high intracellular NMN production, reaching 81.3 mg/L [11], which made it a potential candidate. Selecting highly active enzymes from nature and directing the carbon flux to the target product could increase the yield of NMN and build a solid foundation for a continuous increase in NMN production [58].

Directed evolution of enzymes is a powerful technology that imitates natural evolution and screens for robust enzymes with mutations, leading to desired properties [59]. The most widely used mutagenesis strategies for NAMPT are error-prone PCR (epPCR) and saturation mutagenesis (SM). NAMPT from *Meiothermus ruber* DSM 1279 (MrNAMPT) was used as the starting enzyme for site-directed mutagenesis. The results suggested that the MrNAMPT carrying the E231Q, D298A, D338E, and D377E mutations showed 6.9 times higher catalytic activity for NAM and PRPP than its parent [60]. However, non-rational strategies such as epPCR are labor-intensive and time-consuming [61]. Therefore, we need to find more efficient methods of modification and selection.

3.2. Improving the Supply of Essential Precursors

The maximum activity of the enzyme is only achieved when the supply of precursors is sufficient. In the salvage pathway, PRPP, NAM, and NR are used as precursors to produce NMN. As the NR-based pathway requires a heterologous kinase that is poorly expressed in recombinant strains, the NAM-based pathway is more commonly chosen in metabolic engineering. Previous studies showed that the accumulation of PRPP in the cytoplasm has a significant impact on the synthesis of NMN [62], and PRPP is mainly synthesized through the pentose phosphate pathway (PPP). As glucose is the most accessible sugar worldwide, it may be an ideal raw material for the synthesis of PRPP if sufficiently high biocatalytic conversion efficacy can be achieved. In order to enhance PRPP synthesis, Shoji et al. selected the genes *pgi*, *zwf*, *pgl*, *gnd*, *rpiA*, *rpiB*, and *prs* from the PPP to construct the artificial operons (Figure 1). The reconstructed strain co-expressing NAMPT from *Chitinophaga pinensis* (CpNAMPT) and the artificial operon achieved 2.5 times higher NMN production (189 mg/L) than the parental strain [47]. Although the construction of artificial operons improved PRPP production, vectors expressing the operons and CpNAMPT constitute a double plasmid system that may cause metabolic burdens on cells [63,64]. Alternatively, PRPP can also be produced from ribose via a short pathway, and many bacteria such as *E. coli* and *B. subtilis* can use ribose as a carbon source [65,66].

In order to promote PRPP synthesis, the activity of PRS needs to be increased. Firstly, the activity of enzyme can be increased by adding cofactors. PRS1 requires phosphate and Mg^{2+} for its activity since the Mg-ATP complex acts as the actual substrate for the enzyme. Maharjan et al. combined the PRS1, PRS2, and NAMPT genes in sequential order on a plasmid and expressed them in *E. coli* [54]. They found that co-expression of PRS1 and PRS2 resulted in higher NMN production (417.78 mg/L) in the presence of Mg^{2+} than without. When both Mg^{2+} and phosphate were present, the NMN titer increased from 200.53 to 524.73 mg/L. Hence, the idea of adding Mg^{2+} and phosphate proved to be beneficial for improving the activity of PRS. Secondly, relieving the negative feedback inhibition of ADP and GDP on PRS can enhance the PRPP supply. Zakataeva et al. discovered that PRS from *Bacillus amyloliquefaciens* strain IAM1523 with the L135I mutation (BaPRS) effectively resists the inhibitory effects of purine nucleotides [67].

NAM is another important precursor in the salvage pathway; the rate of NAM uptake by cells limits the activity of NAMPT. Many microorganisms such as *E. coli* cannot synthesize NAM and instead need to absorb it from the extracellular environment. Accordingly, the first step in strain engineering is to improve the uptake of NAM into cells. Genetic analysis and experimental validation of the niacin transporter (NiaP) protein family revealed that they function as transporters of NAM analogs [68]. Shoji et al. expressed NiaP homologs from six different species, and the results clearly showed that BC-NiaP derived from *Burkholderia cenocepacia* took up NAM at the fastest rate, resulting in an uptake that was up to 25% faster than without expressing the transporter protein [47]. However, NAM is expensive, and its industrial use is not economically viable.

3.3. Constructing ATP Regeneration Systems

In the salvage pathway, PRS transfers two phosphate groups from ATP to R5P for the synthesis of PRPP (Figure 1) [69]. ATP hydrolysis provides a thermodynamic driving force for the reaction and contributes to efficient production of NMN [70]. In order to increase product synthesis in fermentation, the ATP balance is very important. Microorganisms generally synthesize ATP via the purine pathway, which is energy intensive. In *S. cerevisiae*, adenosine kinase (encoded by *ado1*) catalyzes the phosphorylation of adenosine to produce AMP and ATP (Figure 2a) [71]. In order to increase production of ATP and prevent the hydrolysis of AMP into ribose 5-phosphate and adenine, the *amn* gene (encoding AMP nucleosidase) needs to be knocked out [72]. Therefore, strain NMN08 was constructed by integrating the *ado1* gene at the *amn* locus to delete it at the same time. The results suggested that the intracellular concentration of ATP in strain NMN08 was increased, and its NMN titer reached about 220 mg/L after 8 h, which was 22% higher than in the unmodified strain [53]. It has been shown that enhancing the ATP supply can further increase NMN production.

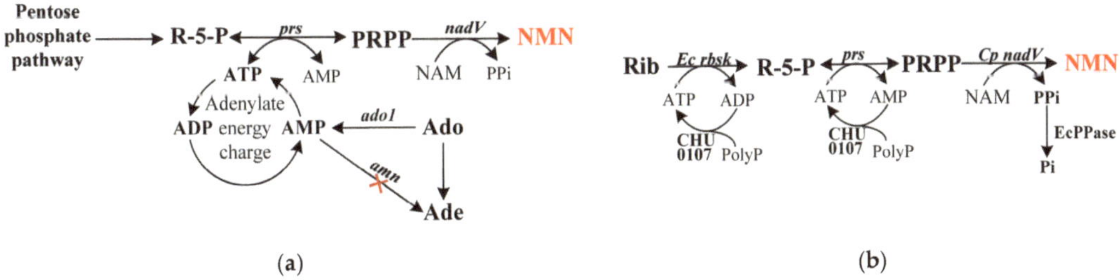

Figure 2. Two types of ATP regeneration systems. (**a**) ATP synthesis via the purine pathway. The red cross represents a deleted pathway. R-5-P, ribose 5-phosphate. PRPP, 5′-phosphoribosyl 1-pyrophosphate. NAM, nicotinamide. NMN, nicotinamide mononucleotide. ATP, adenosine triphosphate. ADP, adenosine diphosphate. AMP, adenosine monophosphate. PPi, pyrophosphate. Ade, adenine; Ado, adenosine. The genes and enzymes associated with the reactions are *amn*, AMP nucleosidase; *ado1*, adenosine kinase (in *S. cerevisiae*); *prs*, ribose-phosphate diphosphokinase; and *nadV*, nicotinamide phosphoribosyltransferase. (**b**) CHU0107 catalyzes the synthesis of ATP from ADP and AMP. The expression of CHU0107 eliminates ADP and promotes ATP production, EcPPase degrades PPi. Pi, inorganic phosphate. The enzymes associated with the reactions are CHU0107, polyphosphate kinase II from *Cytophaga hutchinsonii*; EcPPase, pyrophosphatase from *E. coli*; *EcRbsK*, ribokinase from *E. coli*; and *Cp nadV*, nicotinamide phosphoribosyltransferase from *Chitinophaga pinensis*.

Ngivprom et al. found that CHU0107 consumes AMP or ADP for the biosynthesis of ATP, and inorganic pyrophosphatase from *E. coli* (EcPPase) could hydrolyze PPi generated by CpNAMPT to help drive the reaction (Figure 2b) [56,73]. They constructed *E. coli* MG1655 Δ*tktA*Δ*tktB*Δ*ptsG*, which can metabolize xylose to generate D-ribose. The fermentation supernatant metabolized by the recombinant strain contained D-ribose and was applied to synthesize NMN in the second module, composed of EcRbsK-EcPRS-CpNAMPT. In this system, CHU0107 enables ATP recycling. Finally, a 10 mL optimal cascade bioconversion generated NMN with a good yield of 84% from 150.13 mg/L D-ribose supplied in the supernatant of *E. coli* MG1655 Δ*tktA*Δ*tktB*Δ*ptsG*. This phenomenon indicates that the construction of an ATP regeneration system not only provides sufficient energy for the enzymatic reactions but also reduces the production of ADP and AMP to prevent the feedback inhibition of PRS activity.

Moreover, ATP is also an essential activator of the NAMPT reaction. Hara et al. purified recombinant human NAMPT and measured its K_m value for NAM and PRPP in vitro with or without the addition of ATP [74]. The results showed that the addition of 507.18 mg/L ATP reduced the K_m values for these two substrates by 84% and 98%, respectively. When the concentrations of NAM and PRPP were low, the activity of NAMPT was still significant if the ATP concentration reached millimolar levels. Burgos et al. also found that NAMPT drives its reaction through ATP hydrolysis, allowing the enzymatic system to build up 35-fold higher NMN concentrations than in the absence of ATP [28]. Variations in the substrate and enzyme affinities are also influenced by ATP. Understanding the overall regulatory mechanism of ATP is vital for NMN production.

3.4. Blocking the Formation of Byproducts

NaMN, NR, NAD^+, and other byproducts are generated during NMN metabolism (Figure 3). Suppressing the synthesis of these byproducts has been a focus of bioengineering studies. To this end, researchers have constructed mutants with enhanced production of NMN by blocking the metabolic pathways of byproducts such as NaMN, NR, and NAD^+. The deletion of the *nadR* gene in *Lactococcus lactis* NZ9000 enhanced the accumulation of

NMN by 61% and slightly decreased the intracellular levels of NAD^+ [75]. As previously mentioned, Huang et al. constructed the mutant *E. coli* strain F004 by deleting a set of genes (including *nadR*, *pncC*, *ushA*, and *purR*) to avoid the accumulation of NaMN and NR [11]. Expressing NAMPT from *H. ducreyi* in strain F004, the NMN titer increased 5.3-fold compared with the wild-type one (from 3.6 mg/L to 19.1 mg/L). In the de novo pathway, *pncC*, which encodes an enzyme involved in NaMN production, significantly affects the accumulation of NMN. Expressing FtNADE* and NAMPT from *Ralstonia solanacearum* (RsNAMPT) in a Δ*pncC E. coli* strain resulted in an intracellular NMN level of 501.33 mg/L, a 130-fold increase over the wild-type NMN level [52].

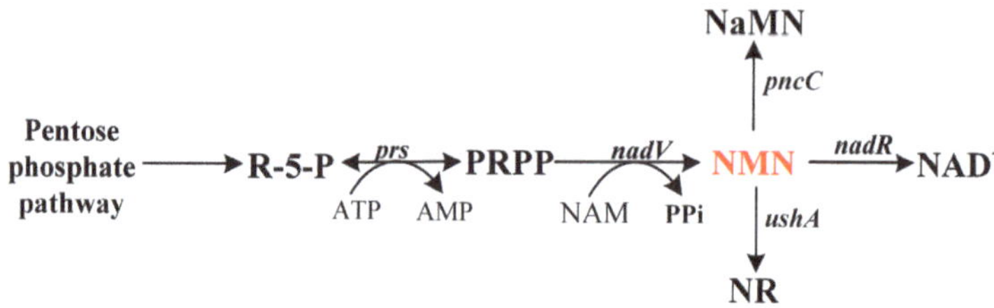

Figure 3. Byproducts of NMN fermentation. During the production of NMN, byproducts such as NAD^+, NR, and NaMN are generated, which influences the final yield. R-5-P, ribose 5-phosphate. PRPP, 5′-phosphoribosyl 1-pyrophosphate. NAM, nicotinamide. NMN, nicotinamide mononucleotide. NR, nicotinamide riboside. NAD^+, nicotinamide adenine dinucleotide. ATP, adenosine triphosphate. AMP, adenosine monophosphate. PPi, pyrophosphate. The enzymes associated with the reactions are *prs*, ribose-phosphate diphosphokinase; *nadV*, nicotinamide phosphoribosyltransferase; *pncC*, NMN amidohydrolase; *nadR*, NMN amidohydrolase; and *ushA*, UDP-sugar hydrolase.

3.5. Expressing Membrane Transporters to Export NMN form the Cell

Excessive intracellular NMN accumulation affects the biological activity of the cells and is detrimental to product synthesis. Even though some model microorganisms such as *E. coli* can spontaneously excrete metabolites out of the cell, additional transporters are needed to accelerate the export of NMN in highly productive engineered strains.

The native substrate of PnuC is generally not NMN but its unphosphorylated precursor NR [76]. However, the transport of NMN was confirmed in a previous study using a PnuC mutant from *Salmonella enterica* [52]. Inspired by this, Shoji et al. screened five PnuC orthologs in *E. coli* and discovered a novel NMN transporter from *Bacillus mycoides*, called BM-PnuC [47]. This transporter was then introduced into recombinant *E. coli* strain NF006, which was derived from *E. coli* strain F004 co-expressing VpNAMPT and PRS from *B. amyloliquefaciens*. After the addition of 200 mg/L NAM, 303.1 mg/L NMN was accumulated extracellularly, which is 2.4 times higher than in the strain without NMN transporter expression. Finally, fine-tuning gene expression and precisely controlling the supplementation of NAM led to an NMN titer of 16,200 mg/L with a conversion ratio of 97.0% from NAM in a 5 L bioreactor, both of which are the highest values reported to date [11]. BM-PnuC can export NMN outside of the cell even when the intracellular production of NMN is low. Therefore, BM-PnuC is the most efficient transporter for NMN reported up to now. Notably, BM-PnuC exhibits the best performance when it is expressed at a comparable or higher level than the enzymes in the corresponding heterologous synthesis pathway.

4. Discussion

Microbial fermentation systems for the synthesis of NMN offer advantages such as greater stability, fewer external additives, and simpler operation. Although significant progress has been made in recent years, further studies are needed to realize the full potential for microbial NMN production. As such, there are several remaining challenges, including: (1) The catalytic activity of the key enzyme NAMPT is insufficient for high production of NMN, (2) the supply of the important precursor PRPP is difficult to enhance through metabolic engineering due to its long and complex synthetic pathway, and (3) the de novo synthesis of NMN in a single-cell system creates a heavy metabolic burden. In order to address these problems, we propose the following potential solutions.

4.1. Utilizing in Silico Analysis and High-throughput Screening to Evolve Key Enzymes

High activity of enzymes could dramatically increase the rate of reactions in the desired pathway [77], and the activity of natural enzymes is generally low. The characterization of more members from the different NAMPT families with the aid of site-directed mutagenesis and in silico methods would provide more insight into the mechanism behind NMN metabolism and would contribute to enhancing the NAMPT titer [78]. However, research on NAMPT from microorganisms is still lacking [79]; in particular, the three-dimensional structure of this enzyme has rarely been reported. With the development of bioinformatics and computational tools, in silico analysis technology provides a more effective approach for predicting the structures of proteins and making the semi-rational design of NAMPT become a reality.

Deep learning-based computational tools such as trRosetta and AlphaFold can be used to predict three-dimensional protein structures of NAMPT based only on amino acid sequence information [80]. To identify protein structures with improved enzymatic activity, Monte Carlo sampling is carried out in the amino acid sequence space to obtain the protein structure of the network-generated protein, which closely matches the real three-dimensional structure [81]. Once the spatial structure of NAMPT is obtained, molecular docking and surface analysis methods are used to analyze the transition state or product binding in the interaction of NAMPT with precursors [82]. The active sites of NAMPT are obtained by analysis of these interactions. After selecting sites based on key amino acid residues, the gene library consisting of NAMPT candidates is constructed by saturation mutagenesis. Notably, Zhang et al. found that the derivatives generated from NMN by simple chemical treatment could emit fluorescence [83]. In droplet-based high-throughput assays, each of the different variants is dispersed into a small droplet, and rapid selection is achieved by detecting the fluorescence of substrates [61]. Perhaps a combination of these two methods could be used for the high-throughput screening of NAMPT variants.

4.2. Enhancing Synergetic Carbon Utilization to Improve Precursor Supply

The supply of precursors is the limiting factor for the maximum activity of enzymes. Therefore, enhancing the flux to precursor synthesis is a key step to improving NMN production. The co-utilization of glucose and ribose makes it possible to increase the carbon flux for the production of PRPP, but the undesirable effects of carbon catabolite repression (CCR) need to be relieved. The main components of CCR include the catabolite control protein A (CcpA) and the catabolite responsive element (CRE), a 14 bp palindromic DNA sequence. Simultaneous mutation of *ccpA* and *spo0A* maximized the intracellular transcription level of the *rbs* operon when glucose and ribose were both added to the medium [66]. CRE is in the upstream region of the *rbs* operon, and synonymous mutation of two bases in this sequence can also alleviate the CCR effect [84]. In addition, it is possible to circumvent CCR. By establishing a nutrient deficient strain, the co-utilization of glucose and ribose could be achieved. As shown in Figure 1, truncating the pathway of glucose into glycolysis by knocking *zwf* and *pfk* results in cells failing to grow [85]. The addition of ribose enables the cell to produce GAP via PPP, allowing the glycolysis pathway to carry on normally. Meanwhile, R-5-P, produced from ribose, synthesizes amounts of PRPP for NMN production via a very short pathway. Moreover, the new optimization algorithm SIMUP was able to predict nutritionally deficient mutants that can be forced to co-utilize glucose and ribose [86]. The analytical algorithm opt-yield-FBA has been applied to describe the dynamic behaviors of microorganisms in a medium comprising a mixture of carbon sources [87]. With the help of the genome-scale metabolic network model, it is possible to better regulate the co-utilization of multiple carbon sources in cells and to increase the carbon flux for NMN production.

4.3. Constructing Artificial Microbial Consortia to Reduce the Metabolic Burden

The direct addition of NAM to fermentation broth is expensive, and the synthesis of NAM using glucose as the substrate can reduce the cost. However, the production of both NAM and NMN in a single-cell system increases the metabolic burden of the cell and suppresses cell growth. A division of labor using microbial consortia could spatially separate different synthetic pathways and distribute metabolic loads [88]. The first step is to construct a strain that can produce NAM. NAD^+ is decomposed into NAM by NAD-dependent protein deacetylase (encoded by *yhdZ*) [89]. If a high NAD^+-producing strain is used as the chassis, expressing the *yhdZ* gene in that strain will produce NAM [19]. Based on this, it is possible to use one recombinant *E. coli* to produce NAM and another strain that produces PRPP and absorbs the NAM to produce NMN.

In constructing this system, attention is first paid to the interactions between the different strains and to identifying the optimal inoculation ratio and product induction time. The separation of microorganisms into independent droplets allows for mixed cultures without knowledge of microbial interactions. A recent paper reported on the design of an invert emulsion system by dispersing the culture medium in a mixture of sunflower oil and surfactant PGPR, which could remain stable for at least 24 h [90]. Secondly, it is important to ensure that NAM can be transported smoothly between cell membranes and absorbed by the NMN-producing strains in a timely way. It becomes important to find a more efficient NAM transporter protein or to select and optimize the already reported transporter proteins. Thirdly, microbial species may naturally evolve into distinct phenotypic subpopulations, and it is necessary to prevent low-yield cheaters from becoming the dominant strain of the colony. Quorum sensing creates an environment more conducive to the survival of cooperative individuals and inhibits the growth of cheaters [91].

Author Contributions: Conceptualization, Z.W.; writing—original draft preparation, S.L.; writing—review and editing, T.C., J.Z., Y.Z. and Z.W.; supervision, Z.W. All authors have read and agreed to the published version of the manuscript.

Funding: This work was financially supported by the National Key Research and Development Program of China (2021YFC2100700) and the National Natural Science Foundation of China (NSFC-22278312).

Institutional Review Board Statement: Not applicable.

Informed Consent Statement: Not applicable.

Data Availability Statement: Not applicable.

Conflicts of Interest: The authors declare no conflict of interest.

References

1. Dölle, C.; Skoge, R.H.; Vanlinden, M.R.; Ziegler, M. NAD biosynthesis in humans--enzymes, metabolites and therapeutic aspects. *Curr. Top. Med. Chem.* **2013**, *13*, 2907–2917. [CrossRef] [PubMed]
2. Okabe, K.; Yaku, K.; Tobe, K.; Nakagawa, T. Implications of altered NAD metabolism in metabolic disorders. *J. Biomed. Sci.* **2019**, *26*, 34. [CrossRef] [PubMed]
3. Campbell, J.M. Supplementation with NAD(+) and Its Precursors to Prevent Cognitive Decline across Disease Contexts. *Nutrients* **2022**, *14*, 3231. [CrossRef] [PubMed]
4. Tang, E.; Shen, X.; Wang, J.; Sun, X.; Yuan, Q. Synergetic utilization of glucose and glycerol for efficient myo-inositol biosynthesis. *Biotechnol. Bioeng.* **2020**, *117*, 1247–1252. [CrossRef]
5. Feng, Z.; Qin, Y.; Huo, F.; Jian, Z.; Li, X.; Geng, J.; Li, Y.; Wu, J. NMN recruits GSH to enhance GPX4-mediated ferroptosis defense in UV irradiation induced skin injury. *Biochim. Biophys. Acta Mol. Basis Dis.* **2021**, *1868*, 166287. [CrossRef]
6. Shen, Q.; Zhang, S.J.; Xue, Y.Z.; Peng, F.; Cheng, D.Y.; Xue, Y.P.; Zheng, Y.G. Biological synthesis of nicotinamide mononucleotide. *Biotechnol. Lett.* **2021**, *43*, 2199–2208. [CrossRef]
7. Preiss, J.; Handler, P. Enzymatic Synthesis of Nicotinamide Mononucleotide. *J. Biol. Chem.* **1957**, *225*, 759–770. [CrossRef]
8. Li, Q.; Meng, D.; You, C. An artificial multi-enzyme cascade biocatalysis for biomanufacturing of nicotinamide mononucleotide from starch and nicotinamide in one-pot. *Enzym. Microb. Technol.* **2022**, *162*, 110122. [CrossRef]

9. Sinclair, D.A. Biological Production of NAD Precursors and Analogs. WO Patent 2015/069860, 14 May 2015.
10. Mills, K.F.; Yoshida, S.; Stein, L.R.; Grozio, A.; Kubota, S.; Sasaki, Y.; Redpath, P.; Migaud, M.E.; Apte, R.S.; Uchida, K.; et al. Long-Term Administration of Nicotinamide Mononucleotide Mitigates Age-Associated Physiological Decline in Mice. *Cell Metab.* **2016**, *24*, 795–806. [CrossRef]
11. Huang, Z.; Li, N.; Yu, S.; Zhang, W.; Zhang, T.; Zhou, J. Systematic Engineering of *Escherichia coli* for Efficient Production of Nicotinamide Mononucleotide From Nicotinamide. *ACS Synth. Biol.* **2022**, *11*, 2979–2988. [CrossRef]
12. Pollard, C.-L.; Younan, A.; Swegen, A.; Gibb, Z.; Grupen, C.G. Insights into the NAD(+) biosynthesis pathways involved during meiotic maturation and spindle formation in porcine oocytes. *J. Reprod. Dev.* **2022**, *68*, 216–224. [CrossRef]
13. Groth, B.; Venkatakrishnan, P.; Lin, S.J. NAD(+) Metabolism, Metabolic Stress, and Infection. *Front. Mol. Biosci.* **2021**, *8*, 686412. [CrossRef]
14. Sharma, S.; Hsieh, Y.C.; Dietze, J.; Bockwoldt, M.; Stromland, O.; Ziegler, M.; Heiland, I. Early Evolutionary Selection of NAD Biosynthesis Pathway in Bacteria. *Metabolites* **2022**, *12*, 569. [CrossRef]
15. Yoshino, J.; Baur, J.A.; Imai, S.I. NAD(+) Intermediates: The Biology and Therapeutic Potential of NMN and NR. *Cell Metab.* **2018**, *27*, 513–528. [CrossRef]
16. Navas, L.E.; Carnero, A. NAD(+) metabolism, stemness, the immune response, and cancer. *Signal. Transduct. Target. Ther.* **2021**, *6*, 2. [CrossRef]
17. Zhu, F.Y.; Pena, M.; Bennett, G.N. Metabolic engineering of *Escherichia coli* for quinolinic acid production by assembling L-aspartate oxidase and quinolinate synthase as an enzyme complex. *Metab. Eng.* **2021**, *67*, 164–172. [CrossRef]
18. Ollagnier-de Choudens, S.; Loiseau, L.; Sanakis, Y.; Barras, F.; Fontecave, M. Quinolinate synthetase, an iron-sulfur enzyme in NAD biosynthesis. *FEBS Lett.* **2005**, *579*, 3737–3743. [CrossRef]
19. Yang, L.; Mu, X.; Nie, Y.; Xu, Y. Improving the production of NAD(+) via multi-strategy metabolic engineering in *Escherichia coli*. *Metab. Eng.* **2021**, *64*, 122–133. [CrossRef]
20. Sorci, L.; Martynowski, D.; Rodionov, D.A.; Eyobo, Y.; Zogaj, X.; Klose, K.E.; Nikolaev, E.V.; Magni, G.; Zhang, H.; Osterman, A.L. Nicotinamide mononucleotide synthetase is the key enzyme for an alternative route of NAD biosynthesis in *Francisella tularensis*. *Proc. Natl. Acad. Sci. USA* **2009**, *106*, 3083–3088. [CrossRef]
21. Wang, L.; Zhou, Y.J.; Ji, D.; Lin, X.; Liu, Y.; Zhang, Y.; Liu, W.; Zhao, Z.K. Identification of UshA as a major enzyme for NAD degradation in *Escherichia coli*. *Enzym. Microb. Technol.* **2014**, *58–59*, 75–79. [CrossRef]
22. De Ingeniis, J.; Kazanov, M.D.; Shatalin, K.; Gelfand, M.S.; Osterman, A.L.; Sorci, L. Glutamine versus ammonia utilization in the NAD synthetase family. *PLoS ONE* **2012**, *7*, e39115. [CrossRef] [PubMed]
23. Martin, P.R.; Shea, R.J.; Mulks, M.H. Identification of a plasmid-encoded gene from *Haemophilus ducreyi* which confers NAD independence. *J. Bacteriol.* **2001**, *183*, 1168–1174. [CrossRef] [PubMed]
24. Lee, J.Y.; Li, Z.; Miller, E.S. *Vibrio* Phage KVP40 Encodes a Functional NAD(+) Salvage Pathway. *J. Bacteriol.* **2017**, *199*, e00855-16. [CrossRef] [PubMed]
25. Bieganowski, P.; Brenner, C. Discoveries of nicotinamide riboside as a nutrient and conserved NRK genes establish a Preiss-Handler independent route to NAD+ in fungi and humans. *Cell* **2004**, *117*, 495–502. [CrossRef] [PubMed]
26. Sonntag, T.; Ancel, S.; Karaz, S.; Cichosz, P.; Jacot, G.; Giner, M.P.; Sanchez-Garcia, J.L.; Pannerec, A.; Moco, S.; Sorrentino, V.; et al. Nicotinamide riboside kinases regulate skeletal muscle fiber-type specification and are rate-limiting for metabolic adaptations during regeneration. *Front. Cell Dev. Biol.* **2022**, *10*, 1049653. [CrossRef] [PubMed]
27. Takahashi, R.; Nakamura, S.; Nakazawa, T.; Minoura, K.; Yoshida, T.; Nishi, Y.; Kobayashi, Y.; Ohkubo, T. Structure and reaction mechanism of human nicotinamide phosphoribosyltransferase. *J. Biochem.* **2010**, *147*, 95–107. [CrossRef]
28. Burgos, E.S.; Schramm, V.L. Weak coupling of ATP hydrolysis to the chemical equilibrium of human nicotinamide phosphoribosyltransferase. *Biochemistry* **2008**, *47*, 11086–11096. [CrossRef]
29. Hove-Jensen, B.; Andersen, K.R.; Kilstrup, M.; Martinussen, J.; Switzer, R.L.; Willemoes, M. Phosphoribosyl Diphosphate (PRPP): Biosynthesis, Enzymology, Utilization, and Metabolic Significance. *Microbiol. Mol. Biol. Rev.* **2017**, *81*, e00040-16. [CrossRef]
30. Shi, T.; Wang, Y.; Wang, Z.; Wang, G.; Liu, D.; Fu, J.; Chen, T.; Zhao, X. Deregulation of purine pathway in *Bacillus subtilis* and its use in riboflavin biosynthesis. *Microb. Cell Factories* **2014**, *13*, 101. [CrossRef]
31. Zakataeva, N.P.; Romanenkov, D.V.; Skripnikova, V.S.; Vitushkina, M.V.; Livshits, V.A.; Kivero, A.D.; Novikova, A.E. Wild-type and feedback-resistant phosphoribosyl pyrophosphate synthetases from *Bacillus amyloliquefaciens*: Purification, characterization, and application to increase purine nucleoside production. *Appl. Microbiol. Biotechnol.* **2012**, *93*, 2023–2033. [CrossRef]
32. Rappu, P.; Pullinen, T.; Mantsala, P. In vivo effect of mutations at the PRPP binding site of the *Bacillus subtilis* purine repressor. *J. Bacteriol.* **2003**, *185*, 6728–6731. [CrossRef]
33. Singh, S.K.; Kurnasov, O.V.; Chen, B.; Robinson, H.; Grishin, N.V.; Osterman, A.L.; Zhang, H. Crystal structure of *Haemophilus influenzae* NadR protein. A bifunctional enzyme endowed with NMN adenyltransferase and ribosylnicotinimide kinase activities. *J. Biol. Chem.* **2002**, *277*, 33291–33299. [CrossRef]
34. Kurnasov, O.V.; Polanuyer, B.M.; Ananta, S.; Sloutsky, R.; Tam, A.; Gerdes, S.Y.; Osterman, A.L. Ribosylnicotinamide kinase domain of NadR protein: Identification and implications in NAD biosynthesis. *J. Bacteriol.* **2002**, *184*, 6906–6917. [CrossRef]
35. Qian, X.-L.; Dai, Y.-S.; Li, C.-X.; Pan, J.; Xu, J.-H.; Mu, B. Enzymatic synthesis of high-titer nicotinamide mononucleotide with a new nicotinamide riboside kinase and an efficient ATP regeneration system. *Bioresour. Bioprocess.* **2022**, *9*, 6906–6917. [CrossRef]

36. He, J.J.; Liu, X.X.; Li, Y.; Wang, Z.; Shi, H.L.; Kan, Y.C.; Yao, L.G.; Tang, C.D. High level expression of nicotinamide nucleoside kinase from *Saccharomyces cerevisiae* and its purification and immobilization by one-step method. *Front. Bioeng. Biotechnol.* **2023**, *11*, 1134152. [CrossRef]
37. Dolle, C.; Ziegler, M. Application of a coupled enzyme assay to characterize nicotinamide riboside kinases. *Anal. Biochem.* **2009**, *385*, 377–379. [CrossRef]
38. Tempel, W.; Rabeh, W.M.; Bogan, K.L.; Belenky, P.; Wojcik, M.; Seidle, H.F.; Nedyalkova, L.; Yang, T.; Sauve, A.A.; Park, H.W.; et al. Nicotinamide riboside kinase structures reveal new pathways to NAD+. *PLoS Biol.* **2007**, *5*, e263. [CrossRef]
39. Ratajczak, J.; Joffraud, M.; Trammell, S.A.; Ras, R.; Canela, N.; Boutant, M.; Kulkarni, S.S.; Rodrigues, M.; Redpath, P.; Migaud, M.E.; et al. NRK1 controls nicotinamide mononucleotide and nicotinamide riboside metabolism in mammalian cells. *Nat. Commun.* **2016**, *7*, 13103. [CrossRef]
40. Zhu, N.; Olivera, B.M.; Roth, J.R. Activity of the nicotinamide mononucleotide transport system is regulated in *Salmonella typhimurium*. *J. Bacteriol.* **1991**, *173*, 1311–1320. [CrossRef]
41. Sauer, E.; Merdanovic, M.; Mortimer, A.P.; Bringmann, G.; Reidl, J. PnuC and the utilization of the nicotinamide riboside analog 3-aminopyridine in *Haemophilus influenzae*. *Antimicrob. Agents Chemother.* **2004**, *48*, 4532–4541. [CrossRef]
42. Grose, J.H.; Bergthorsson, U.; Xu, Y.; Sterneckert, J.; Khodaverdian, B.; Roth, J.R. Assimilation of nicotinamide mononucleotide requires periplasmic AphA phosphatase in *Salmonella enterica*. *J. Bacteriol.* **2005**, *187*, 4521–4530. [CrossRef] [PubMed]
43. Gerasimova, A.V.; Gelfand, M.S. Evolution of the NadR regulon in Enterobacteriaceae. *J. Bioinform. Comput. Biol.* **2005**, *3*, 1007–1019. [CrossRef] [PubMed]
44. Jaehme, M.; Slotboom, D.J. Structure, function, evolution, and application of bacterial Pnu-type vitamin transporters. *Biol. Chem.* **2015**, *396*, 955–966. [CrossRef] [PubMed]
45. Todisco, S.; Agrimi, G.; Castegna, A.; Palmieri, F. Identification of the mitochondrial NAD+ transporter in *Saccharomyces cerevisiae*. *J. Biol. Chem.* **2006**, *281*, 1524–1531. [CrossRef] [PubMed]
46. Belenky, P.A.; Moga, T.G.; Brenner, C. *Saccharomyces cerevisiae* YOR071C encodes the high affinity nicotinamide riboside transporter Nrt1. *J. Biol. Chem.* **2008**, *283*, 8075–8079. [CrossRef] [PubMed]
47. Shoji, S.; Yamaji, T.; Makino, H.; Ishii, J.; Kondo, A. Metabolic design for selective production of nicotinamide mononucleotide from glucose and nicotinamide. *Metab. Eng.* **2021**, *65*, 167–177. [CrossRef]
48. Shen, Y.P.; Liao, Y.L.; Lu, Q.; He, X.; Yan, Z.B.; Liu, J.Z. ATP and NADPH engineering of *Escherichia coli* to improve the production of 4-hydroxyphenylacetic acid using CRISPRi. *Biotechnol. Biofuels* **2021**, *14*, 100. [CrossRef]
49. Liang, B.; Sun, G.N.; Zhang, X.P.; Nie, Q.J.; Zhao, Y.K.; Yang, J.M. Recent advances, challenges and metabolic engineering strategies in the biosynthesis of 3-hydroxypropionic acid. *Biotechnol. Bioeng.* **2022**, *119*, 2639–2668. [CrossRef]
50. Jiang, M.; Hong, K.; Mao, Y.; Ma, H.; Chen, T.; Wang, Z. Natural 5-Aminolevulinic Acid: Sources, Biosynthesis, Detection and Applications. *Front. Bioeng. Biotechnol.* **2022**, *10*, 841443. [CrossRef]
51. Marinescu, G.C.; Popescu, R.G.; Stoian, G.; Dinischiotu, A. beta-nicotinamide mononucleotide (NMN) production in *Escherichia coli*. *Sci. Rep.* **2018**, *8*, 12278. [CrossRef]
52. Black, W.B.; Aspacio, D.; Bever, D.; King, E.; Zhang, L.; Li, H. Metabolic engineering of *Escherichia coli* for optimized biosynthesis of nicotinamide mononucleotide, a noncanonical redox cofactor. *Microb. Cell Fact.* **2020**, *19*, 150. [CrossRef]
53. Liu, Y.; Yasawong, M.; Yu, B. Metabolic engineering of *Escherichia coli* for biosynthesis of beta-nicotinamide mononucleotide from nicotinamide. *Microb. Biotechnol.* **2021**, *14*, 2581–2591. [CrossRef]
54. Maharjan, A.; Singhvi, M.; Kim, B.S. Biosynthesis of a Therapeutically Important Nicotinamide Mononucleotide through a Phosphoribosyl Pyrophosphate Synthetase 1 and 2 Engineered Strain of *Escherichia coli*. *ACS Synth. Biol.* **2021**, *10*, 3055–3065. [CrossRef]
55. Sugiyama, K.; Iijima, K.; Yoshino, M.; Dohra, H.; Tokimoto, Y.; Nishikawa, K.; Idogaki, H.; Yoshida, N. Nicotinamide mononucleotide production by fructophilic lactic acid bacteria. *Sci. Rep.* **2021**, *11*, 7662. [CrossRef]
56. Ngivprom, U.; Lasin, P.; Khunnonkwao, P.; Worakaensai, S.; Jantama, K.; Kamkaew, A.; Lai, R.Y. Synthesis of nicotinamide mononucleotide from xylose via coupling engineered *Escherichia coli* and a biocatalytic cascade. *Chembiochem* **2022**, *23*, e202200071. [CrossRef]
57. He, Z.; Yang, X.; Tian, X.; Li, L.; Liu, M. Yeast Cell Surface Engineering of a Nicotinamide Riboside Kinase for the Production of beta-Nicotinamide Mononucleotide via Whole-Cell Catalysis. *ACS Synth. Biol.* **2022**, *11*, 3451–3459. [CrossRef]
58. Yi, Y.-C.; Shih, I.T.; Yu, T.-H.; Lee, Y.-J.; Ng, I.S. Challenges and opportunities of bioprocessing 5-aminolevulinic acid using genetic and metabolic engineering: A critical review. *Bioresour. Bioprocess.* **2021**, *8*, 100. [CrossRef]
59. Sharma, A.; Gupta, G.; Ahmad, T.; Mansoor, S.; Kaur, B. Enzyme Engineering: Current Trends and Future Perspectives. *Food Rev. Int.* **2019**, *37*, 121–154. [CrossRef]
60. Fu, R.Z.; Zhang, Q. Nicotinamide Phosphoribosyltransferase Mutant and Application Thereof. WO Patent 2018/023206A1, 8 February 2018.
61. Wang, Y.; Xue, P.; Cao, M.; Yu, T.; Lane, S.T.; Zhao, H. Directed Evolution: Methodologies and Applications. *Chem. Rev.* **2021**, *121*, 12384–12444. [CrossRef]
62. Zhou, M.; Li, Y.; Che, H.; Sun, Y.; Wang, S.; Zhan, Y.; Cai, D.; Chen, S. Metabolic Engineering of *Bacillus licheniformis* for the Bioproduction of Nicotinamide Riboside from Nicotinamide and Glucose. *ACS Sustain. Chem. Eng.* **2023**, *11*, 6201–6210. [CrossRef]

63. García-Calvo, L.; Rane, D.V.; Everson, N.; Humlebrekk, S.T.; Mathiassen, L.F.; Mæhlum, A.H.M.; Malmo, J.; Bruheim, P. Central carbon metabolite profiling reveals vector associated differences in the recombinant protein production host *Escherichia coli* BL21. *Front. Chem. Eng.* **2023**, *5*, 1142226. [CrossRef]
64. Kim, S.K.; Kim, H.; Woo, S.G.; Kim, T.H.; Rha, E.; Kwon, K.K.; Lee, H.; Lee, S.G.; Lee, D.H. CRISPRi-based programmable logic inverter cascade for antibiotic-free selection and maintenance of multiple plasmids. *Nucleic Acids Res.* **2022**, *50*, 13155–13171. [CrossRef] [PubMed]
65. Shimada, T.; Kori, A.; Ishihama, A. Involvement of the ribose operon repressor RbsR in regulation of purine nucleotide synthesis in *Escherichia coli*. *FEMS Microbiol. Lett.* **2013**, *344*, 159–165. [CrossRef] [PubMed]
66. Strauch, M.A. AbrB modulates expression and catabolite repression of a *Bacillus subtilis* ribose transport operon. *J. Bacteriol.* **1995**, *177*, 6727–6731. [CrossRef] [PubMed]
67. Zakataeva, N.P.; Romanenkov, D.V.; Yusupova, Y.R.; Skripnikova, V.S.; Asahara, T.; Gronskiy, S.V. Identification, Heterologous Expression, and Functional Characterization of *Bacillus subtilis* YutF, a HAD Superfamily 5′-Nucleotidase with Broad Substrate Specificity. *PLoS ONE* **2016**, *11*, e0167580. [CrossRef]
68. Jeanguenin, L.; Lara-Nunez, A.; Rodionov, D.A.; Osterman, A.L.; Komarova, N.Y.; Rentsch, D.; Gregory, J.F., 3rd; Hanson, A.D. Comparative genomics and functional analysis of the NiaP family uncover nicotinate transporters from bacteria, plants, and mammals. *Funct. Integr. Genom.* **2012**, *12*, 25–34. [CrossRef]
69. Zhou, W.J.; Tsai, A.; Dattmore, D.A.; Stives, D.P.; Chitrakar, I.; D'Alessandro, A.M.; Patil, S.; Hicks, K.A.; French, J.B. Crystal structure of *E. coli* PRPP synthetase. *Bmc Struct. Biol.* **2019**, *19*, 1. [CrossRef]
70. Luo, Z.; Zeng, W.; Du, G.; Chen, J.; Zhou, J. Enhanced Pyruvate Production in Candida glabrata by Engineering ATP Futile Cycle System. *ACS Synth. Biol.* **2019**, *8*, 787–795. [CrossRef]
71. Barrado, P.; Rodriguez, M.J.; Jimenez, A.; Fernandez Lobato, M. Expression in *Escherichia coli* of a recombinant adenosine kinase from *Saccharomyces cerevisiae*: Purification, kinetics and substrate analyses. *Yeast* **2003**, *20*, 1145–1150. [CrossRef]
72. Leung, H.B.; Kvalnes-Krick, K.L.; Meyer, S.L.; deRiel, J.K.; Schramm, V.L. Structure and regulation of the AMP nucleosidase gene (*amn*) from *Escherichia coli*. *Biochemistry* **1989**, *28*, 8726–8733. [CrossRef]
73. Wan, L.; Wang, X.Y.; Hu, Y.H.; Li, Q.; Zhao, Z.K. Gram-scale biocatalytic preparation of the non-natural cofactor nicotinamide cytosine dinucleotide. *Tetrahedron Lett.* **2022**, *88*, 153568. [CrossRef]
74. Hara, N.; Yamada, K.; Shibata, T.; Osago, H.; Tsuchiya, M. Nicotinamide phosphoribosyltransferase/visfatin does not catalyze nicotinamide mononucleotide formation in blood plasma. *PLoS ONE* **2011**, *6*, e22781. [CrossRef]
75. Kong, L.H.; Liu, T.Y.; Yao, Q.S.; Zhang, X.H.; Xu, W.N.; Qin, J.Y. Enhancing the biosynthesis of nicotinamide mononucleotide in *Lactococcus lactis* by heterologous expression of *FtnadE*. *J. Sci. Food Agric.* **2022**, *103*, 450–456. [CrossRef]
76. Panchapakesan, S.S.S.; Corey, L.; Malkowski, S.N.; Higgs, G.; Breaker, R.R. A second riboswitch class for the enzyme cofactor NAD(+). *Rna* **2021**, *27*, 99–105. [CrossRef]
77. Ali, M.; Ishqi, H.M.; Husain, Q. Enzyme engineering: Reshaping the biocatalytic functions. *Biotechnol. Bioeng.* **2020**, *117*, 1877–1894. [CrossRef]
78. Currin, A.; Parker, S.; Robinson, C.J.; Takano, E.; Scrutton, N.S.; Breitling, R. The evolving art of creating genetic diversity: From directed evolution to synthetic biology. *Biotechnol. Adv.* **2021**, *50*, 107762. [CrossRef]
79. Magni, G.; Di Stefano, M.; Orsomando, G.; Raffaelli, N.; Ruggieri, S. NAD(P) Biosynthesis Enzymes as Potential Targets for Selective Drug Design. *Curr. Med. Chem.* **2009**, *16*, 1372–1390. [CrossRef]
80. Ren, F.; Ding, X.; Zheng, M.; Korzinkin, M.; Cai, X.; Zhu, W.; Mantsyzov, A.; Aliper, A.; Aladinskiy, V.; Cao, Z.; et al. AlphaFold accelerates artificial intelligence powered drug discovery: Efficient discovery of a novel CDK20 small molecule inhibitor. *Chem. Sci.* **2023**, *14*, 1443–1452. [CrossRef]
81. Madhavan, A.; Arun, K.B.; Binod, P.; Sirohi, R.; Tarafdar, A.; Reshmy, R.; Kumar Awasthi, M.; Sindhu, R. Design of novel enzyme biocatalysts for industrial bioprocess: Harnessing the power of protein engineering, high throughput screening and synthetic biology. *Bioresour. Technol.* **2021**, *325*, 124617. [CrossRef]
82. Tournier, V.; Topham, C.M.; Gilles, A.; David, B.; Folgoas, C.; Moya-Leclair, E.; Kamionka, E.; Desrousseaux, M.L.; Texier, H.; Gavalda, S.; et al. An engineered PET depolymerase to break down and recycle plastic bottles. *Nature* **2020**, *580*, 216–219. [CrossRef]
83. Zhang, R.Y.; Qin, Y.; Lv, X.Q.; Wang, P.; Xu, T.Y.; Zhang, L.; Miao, C.Y. A fluorometric assay for high-throughput screening targeting nicotinamide phosphoribosyltransferase. *Anal. Biochem.* **2011**, *412*, 18–25. [CrossRef] [PubMed]
84. Nentwich, S.S.; Brinkrolf, K.; Gaigalat, L.; Hüser, A.T.; Rey, D.A.; Mohrbach, T.; Marin, K.; Pühler, A.; Tauch, A.; Kalinowski, J. Characterization of the LacI-type transcriptional repressor RbsR controlling ribose transport in *Corynebacterium glutamicum* ATCC 13032. *Microbiology* **2009**, *155*, 150–164. [CrossRef] [PubMed]
85. Wu, Y.; Wang, J.; Shen, X.; Wang, J.; Chen, Z.; Sun, X.; Yuan, Q.; Yan, Y. Investigating the strategies for microbial production of trehalose from lignocellulosic sugars. *Biotechnol. Bioeng.* **2018**, *115*, 785–790. [CrossRef] [PubMed]
86. Gawand, P.; Hyland, P.; Ekins, A.; Martin, V.J.; Mahadevan, R. Novel approach to engineer strains for simultaneous sugar utilization. *Metab. Eng.* **2013**, *20*, 63–72. [CrossRef]
87. Luo, H.; Li, P.; Ji, B.; Nielsen, J. Modeling the metabolic dynamics at the genome-scale by optimized yield analysis. *Metab. Eng.* **2023**, *75*, 119–130. [CrossRef]

88. Zhang, H.; Wang, X. Modular co-culture engineering, a new approach for metabolic engineering. *Metab. Eng.* **2016**, *37*, 114–121. [CrossRef]
89. Gardner, J.G.; Escalante-Semerena, J.C. In *Bacillus subtilis*, the sirtuin protein deacetylase, encoded by the *srtN* gene (formerly *yhdZ*), and functions encoded by the *acuABC* genes control the activity of acetyl coenzyme A synthetase. *J. Bacteriol.* **2009**, *191*, 1749–1755. [CrossRef]
90. Dijamentiuk, A.; Mangavel, C.; Elfassy, A.; Michaux, F.; Burgain, J.; Rondags, E.; Delaunay, S.; Ferrigno, S.; Revol-Junelles, A.M.; Borges, F. Invert emulsions alleviate biotic interactions in bacterial mixed culture. *Microb. Cell Factories* **2023**, *22*, 16. [CrossRef]
91. Özkaya, Ö.; Xavier, K.B.; Dionisio, F.; Balbontín, R. Maintenance of Microbial Cooperation Mediated by Public Goods in Single- and Multiple-Trait Scenarios. *J. Bacteriol.* **2017**, *199*, e00297-17. [CrossRef]

fermentation

MDPI

Article

Production of Glyoxylate from Glucose in Engineered *Escherichia coli*

Bui Hoang Dang Long , Masahiro Nishiyama, Rintaro Sato, Tomonari Tanaka , Hitomi Ohara and Yuji Aso *

Department of Biobased Materials Science, Kyoto Institute of Technology, 1 Hashigami-cho, Matsugasaki, Sakyo-ku, Kyoto 606-8585, Japan; buihoangdanglong@gmail.com (B.H.D.L.); m1661012@edu.kit.ac.jp (M.N.); sato6r@kit.ac.jp (R.S.); t-tanaka@kit.ac.jp (T.T.); ohara@kit.ac.jp (H.O.)

* Correspondence: aso@kit.ac.jp; Tel.: +81-(0)75-724-7694

Abstract: Glyoxylates are essential intermediates in several metabolic pathways and have a broad range of industrial applications. In this study, we propose a novel method for producing glyoxylate from glucose using engineered *Escherichia coli* BW25113. To direct the production of glyoxylate from glucose, malate synthase A (*aceB*), malate synthase G (*glcB*), glyoxylate carboligase (*gcl*), and glyoxylate/hydroxypyruvate reductase A (*ycdW*) genes were disrupted, and the glyoxylate shunt was reinforced in the disruptants by the overexpression of citrate synthase (*gltA*) and isocitrate lyase (*aceA*). In flask cultivation using M9 medium supplemented with 1% glucose, the disruptant *E. coli* BW25113 Δ*aceB* Δ*glcB* Δ*gcl* Δ*ycdW* produced 0.93 ± 0.17 g/L of glyoxylate. Further overexpression of *gltA* and *aceA* in the disruptant resulted in an improvement in glyoxylate production to 1.15 ± 0.02 g/L. By expressing a heterologous gene, *pyc*, in the engineered *E. coli*, the accumulation of intracellular oxaloacetate remarkably improved, leading to glyoxylate production of up to 2.42 ± 0.00 g/L with specific productivity at 4.22 ± 0.09 g/g-cell. To date, this is the highest reported titer and specific productivity of glyoxylate in *E. coli*.

Keywords: *Escherichia coli*; glucose; glyoxylate; metabolic engineering; pyruvate carboxylase

check for updates

Citation: Long, B.H.D.; Nishiyama, M.; Sato, R.; Tanaka, T.; Ohara, H.; Aso, Y. Production of Glyoxylate from Glucose in Engineered *Escherichia coli*. *Fermentation* **2023**, *9*, 534. https://doi.org/10.3390/fermentation9060534

Academic Editors: Ricardo Aguilar-López and Michael Breitenbach

Received: 2 May 2023
Revised: 19 May 2023
Accepted: 30 May 2023
Published: 31 May 2023

1. Introduction

Escherichia coli has garnered research attention owing to its fast growth rate and straightforward capacity for scale up [1,2] because of its well-documented genome [3]. Gene modification in *E. coli* paves the way for the production of novel products. Recent studies have reported the production of multiple important substances by *E. coli*, including acetate, ethanol, itaconate, lactate, and propanediol [4–8]. These studies demonstrate the advantages of using an *E. coli* model to produce various biochemicals.

As a carboxylate, glyoxylate is of considerable interest owing to its functional properties [9,10]. Typical glyoxylate molecules harboring both aldehyde and carboxyl groups exhibit flexible chemical interactions. This stimulates pathways that produce various biochemical products including anticancer agents such as bestatin [11], anti-inflammatory substances [12], and antihypertensive agents such as atenolol [13]. One of the most popular applications of glyoxylates is the production of vanillin, a well-known aroma derivative used in the perfume and food industries [14]. Glyoxylate is chemically synthesized from malate in a three-step process [15]. Although maleate synthesis is complex, this approach produces glyoxylate with 97% purity [15]. Another approach involves the production of glyoxylate from oxalate via a reduction reaction or glyoxal via anodic oxidation [16].

The glyoxylate shunt serves as an alternative to the tricarboxylic acid (TCA) cycle and benefits bacteria through various biochemical processes [17]. First, this shunt enables bacteria to utilize acetate, fatty acids, and ethanol to recover TCA cycle intermediates, which are required for gluconeogenesis and other biosynthetic processes [18]. Second, the metabolites derived from the glyoxylate shunt are mainly organic acids such as glycolate and tartronate semialdehyde, which have high potential for application as industrial chemicals [19]. However, a considerable drawback of the glyoxylate shunt in bacteria is the production of multiple byproducts, such as lactate and malate [7,20]. Glyoxylate is also synthesized by glyoxylate oxidases in plant leaves and animal livers, with hydrogen peroxide as a by-product [21–24]. Although chemical production would facilitate the large-scale production of glyoxylate, this is associated with a large amount of physical and economic effort owing to the requirement of malate, oxalate, and glyoxal, as discussed above [15,16].

Recently, Li et al. produced 0.74 g/L of glyoxylate from xylose via a glyoxylate shunt using engineered *E. coli* K-12 [20]. Overexpression of *dte*, *fucK*, *fucA*, *aldA*, and *glcDEF* assimilated xylose to glyoxylate and disruption of *aceB*, *glcB*, *gcl*, and *ycdW* accumulated glyoxylate at higher concentrations. However, the conversion of xylose to glyoxylate resulted in a limited titer (0.74 g/L). Despite successful attempts to produce glycolate from glucose via the glyoxylate shunt in *E. coli*, resulting in high glycolate accumulation [25], related studies on the conversion of glucose to glyoxylate are currently lacking. The application of a glyoxylate shunt with positive results suggests the application of this pathway from glucose to glyoxylate.

Recent studies have attempted to improve the operation of the TCA cycle by introducing a heterologous pyruvate carboxylase gene (*pyc*) into *E. coli*. The expression of *pyc* has positive effects on the production of various chemicals in the TCA cycle, such as succinate [26], malate [27], and fumarate [28]. In a study by Chen et al. (2020), the expression of *pyc* in *E. coli* significantly improved the operation of the glyoxylate shunt, leading to an increase in fumarate concentration [28]. This suggests the expression of *pyc* would activate the glyoxylate shunt in *E. coli*. However, no study has demonstrated an improvement in glyoxylate production by expression of *pyc* in *E. coli*.

The present study demonstrated the production of glyoxylate from glucose in *E. coli* BW25113 engineered by disrupting *aceB*, *glcB*, *gcl*, and *ycdW*, along with the expression of *gltA*, *aceA*, and *pyc*, to achieve a higher production titer of glyoxylate (Figure 1). As a result, for the first time, glyoxylate was produced from glucose with the highest reported titer (2.42 ± 0.00 g/L) and productivity (4.22 ± 0.09 g/g-cell). These results could also help improve the bioproduction of value-added chemicals derived from glyoxylates.

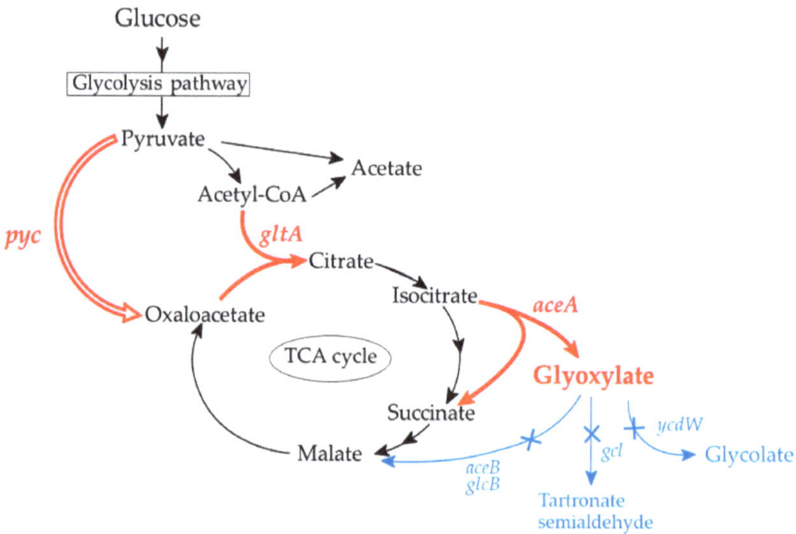

Figure 1. Production of glyoxylate from glucose in engineered *Escherichia coli* BW25113. Malate synthase G (*glcB*), malate synthase A (*aceB*), glyoxylate carboligase (*gcl*), and glyoxylate/hydroxypyruvate

reductase A (*ycdW*) were disrupted, and citrate synthase (*gltA*) and isocitrate lyase (*aceA*) were overexpressed. Pyruvate carboxylase (*pyc*) from *Corynebacterium glutamicum* NBRC 12168 was also expressed. Red and blue arrows indicate reinforced and disrupted pathways, respectively.

2. Materials and Methods

2.1. Gene Disruption

The bacterial strains and plasmids used in this study are listed in Table 1. *Escherichia coli* BW25113 cells were obtained from the NITE Biological Resource Center (NBRC, Chiba, Japan). Gene disruption was performed using the tetA-sacB disruption method [29]. Specifically, DNA fragments containing the tetA-sacB cassette were amplified using the following primer sets: aceB-F-tetA and aceB-R-sacB for aceB, glcB-F-tetA and glcB-R-sacB for glcB, gcl-F-tetA and gcl-R-sacB for gcl, and ycdW-F-tetA and ycdW-R-sacB for ycdW (Table S1). These primers were designed with homologous 50-bp upstream and downstream regions of the target disrupted genes, using the tetA-sacB cassette encoded on the genomic DNA of *E. coli* T-SACK [29] as the template. Polymerase chain reaction (PCR) was performed under the following conditions: denaturation at 98 °C for 30 s, 35 cycles of denaturation at 98 °C for 10 s, annealing at 60 °C for 30 s, and elongation at 72 °C for 2 min. All PCR master mixes were formulated using the Q5 High-Fidelity PCR Kit (New England Biolabs, Inc., MA, USA). The amplified fragments were introduced into *E. coli* BW25113 harboring pKD46 [30] by electroporation (2500 V, 200 Ω, 25 μF), resulting in a series of *E. coli* strains carrying the *tetA-sacB* cassette. The upstream and downstream regions of the target genes were amplified via PCR using the following primer sets: aceB-up-F, aceB-up-R, aceB-dn-F, and aceB-dn-R for *aceB*; glcB-up-F, glcB-up-R, glcB-dn-F, and glcB-dn-R for *glcB*; gcl-up-F, gcl-up-R, gcl-dn-F, and gcl-dn-R for *gcl*; and ycdW-up-F, ycdW-up-R, ycdW-dn-F, and ycdW-dn-R for *ycdW*. PCR was performed under the following conditions: denaturation at 98 °C for 30 s, 35 cycles of denaturation at 98 °C for 10 s, annealing at 60 °C for 30 s, and elongation at 72 °C for 2 min. The amplified upstream and downstream regions were connected by SOEing PCR [31] and introduced into the resulting mutants, followed by screening on Luria-Bertani (LB) agar medium [32] containing 6% sucrose to eliminate the *tetA-sacB* cassette from their genomes. Finally, pKD46 was removed by overnight incubation at 45 °C [30], resulting in the construction of *E. coli* EG_1, EG_2, EG_3, and EG_4.

Table 1. Strains and plasmids used in this study.

Strains and Plasmids	Description	Reference
Strains		
Escherichia coli BW25113		NBRC
E. coli EG_1	BW25113 Δ*aceB*	This work
E. coli EG_2	BW25113 Δ*aceB* Δ*glcB*	This work
E. coli EG_3	BW25113 Δ*aceB* Δ*glcB* Δ*gcl*	This work
E. coli EG_4	BW25113 Δ*aceB* Δ*glcB* Δ*gcl* Δ*ycdW*	This work
E. coli EG_5	BW25113/pSR13	This work
E. coli EG_6	BW25113 Δ*aceB* Δ*glcB* Δ*gcl* Δ*ycdW*/pSR13	This work
E. coli EG_7	BW25113 Δ*aceB* Δ*glcB* Δ*gcl* Δ*ycdW*/pSR13/pLB6	This work
Corynebacterium glutamicum NBRC 12168		NBRC
Plasmids		
pGV3	Expression vector	[6]
pTV118N	Expression vector	Takara Bio, Japan.
pSR13	pGV3 harboring *gltA* and *aceA*, Δ*oprI′*	This work
pLB6	pTV118N harboring *pyc*	This work
pKD46	λ-red recombinase expressing helper plasmid	[30]

2.2. Plasmid Construction

For the construction of the pSR13 plasmid, *gltA* and *aceA* were amplified from the *E. coli* BW25113 genome using gltA-F, gltA-R, aceA-F, and aceA-R primers and were ligated with the fragment of the pGV3 expression vector [6] without *oprI'*, which was amplified using pGV3-F and pGV3-R primers. The pLB6 plasmid was prepared by ligation with PCR amplicons of *pyc* from *Corynebacterium glutamicum* NBRC 12168 using the pyc-F and pyc-R primers and its genomic DNA as the template, and the pTV118N expression vector (Takara Bio Inc., Shiga, Japan) using the pTV118N-pyc-F and pTV118N-pyc-R primers and the vector as the template. The ligation was performed using the Gibson assembly technique [33]. Thereafter, *E. coli* ECOS DH5α (Nippon Gene, Tokyo, Japan) was transformed with the mixture using the heat shock method [34]. Cells were grown in LB medium for 1 h and plated on LB agar containing 100 μg/mL spectinomycin and 50 μg/mL carbenicillin for pSR13 and pLB6, respectively. The resulting plasmids were extracted from DH5α cells using the MagExtractor Plasmid kit (Toyobo Co., Ltd., Osaka, Japan), and *E. coli* BW25113 and its disruptants were transformed with the constructed plasmids by electroporation, resulting in the construction of *E. coli* EG_5, EG_6, and EG_7.

2.3. Fermentation Production

For pre-culture, all strains were grown overnight in LB medium. When required, 100 μg/mL of spectinomycin and 50 μg/mL of carbenicillin were added to the medium. For cultivation in a flask, 1 mL of *E. coli* preculture was transferred to flasks with 100 mL of M9 medium containing 1% glucose, 10 g/L glucose, 6 g/L Na_2HPO_4, 3 g/L KH_2PO_4, 0.5 g/L NaCl, 1 g/L NH_4Cl, 2 mM $MgSO_4$, 0.2 mM $CaCl_2$, and 20 mg/L thiamine [7]. When required, 1 g/L of yeast extract was added to the medium. To analyze glyoxylate toxicity, 0–1.5% (*w*/*v*) sodium glyoxylate was prepared in the M9 medium. *Escherichia coli* BW25113 was pre-cultured in LB medium and inoculated into glyoxylate-supplemented M9 medium. Optical density at 600 nm (OD600) was checked at 24-h intervals (Figure S1). For fermentation, flasks were capped with aerobic caps and shaken at 120 rpm and 30 °C under aerobic conditions. Supplementation with 5 mM of isopropyl-β-D-thiogalactopyranoside (Apollo Scientific, Stockport, UK) was performed for the induction of gene expression when OD600 reached 0.4. Cultures were sampled at appropriate intervals to determine the OD600 and to analyze the metabolite and residual glucose concentrations.

2.4. Analytical Methods

Culture supernatants were analyzed using a high-performance liquid chromatography (HPLC) system equipped with an ion exclusion column (Aminex HPX-87H; Bio-Rad, Hercules, CA, USA) and a refractive index detector (RID-20A; Shimadzu Corporation, Kyoto, Japan) for acetate, lactate, and formate quantification. Five millimolars of H_2SO_4 was used as the mobile phase with a 0.4 mL/min flow rate at 65 °C. Glyoxylate in the culture supernatant was derivatized with phenylhydrazine reagent [35] and analyzed by HPLC. Briefly, 200 μL of glyoxylate sample (0.01–2 g/L) was mixed with 200 μL of 0.4 M phosphate buffer (pH 8.0) prepared by mixing K_2HPO_4 and NaH_2PO_4 in 70% (*v*/*v*) ethanol. Then, 20 μL of 5% (*v*/*v*) phenylhydrazine in 0.4 M phosphate buffer was added to the samples. Subsequently, the reaction occurred in mixing at 37 °C for 15 min. Then, the derivatized samples were injected into an HPLC system. The glyoxylate concentration was determined using an HPLC system equipped with a Cosmosil 5C18-AR-II (Nacalai Tesque, Inc., Kyoto, Japan) and a prominent diode array detector (SPD-M20A) at 324 nm using a 5% ethanol solution as the mobile phase in isocratic mode at a flow rate of 0.4 mL/min. The HPLC profiles of glyoxylate are shown in Figure S2. Glucose was quantified using a Glucose CII Test Kit (Fujifilm Wako Co., Osaka, Japan).

The correlation between cell weight (g/L) and OD600 was determined by the following method: *E. coli* cells were grown in a 5 mL test tube containing LB medium overnight. Then, 1 mL of cells was sampled, centrifuged to collect the cells, and washed three times with physiological saline water. Cell densities were prepared at different OD600 values by dilution with physiological saline water. Then, 1 mL of each sample at different OD600 values was completely dried overnight at 70 °C, and the cell weight was measured. Subsequently, the cell weight was measured at OD600 using the correlation equation (1 OD600 = 0.33 g-cell/L).

Intracellular oxaloacetate was extracted using the methanol freeze-thaw method [36]. Bacterial cells (1 mL) were collected from the cultures and centrifuged at 15,000 rpm for 5 min. The cells were washed once with 1 mL saline solution. Subsequently, 250 µL of 50% methanol precooled at −40 °C was added to the cells. Samples were mixed, incubated in liquid nitrogen for 5 min, and thawed on ice for 5 min. The experiment was conducted in triplicate. The samples were then analyzed at 210 nm using a Hitachi LaChrom Elite HPLC System (Hitachi High-Tech Corp., Tokyo, Japan) equipped with a Cosmosil 5C18-AR-II column and UV detector (L-2400; Hitachi High-Tech Corp.). HPLC was performed in gradient mode with acetonitrile and water supplemented with 0.01% trifluoroacetic acid as the mobile phase. From 0 to 20 min, the concentration of acetonitrile containing trifluoroacetic acid increased from 0% to 100%. The flowrate was set at 1 mL/min and the temperature was stabilized at 25 °C. The standard samples were prepared with 0 to 2.5 g/L fresh standard oxaloacetate solutions (Tokyo Chemical Industry, Tokyo, Japan). Oxaloacetate was detected at a retention time of 3.2 min (Figure S3). All fermentation samples were diluted with water to ensure that the oxaloacetate concentration was within the quantifiable range (0–2.5 g/L).

All data were analyzed in duplicate and are presented as averages with standard errors.

3. Results and Discussion

3.1. *Effects of Gene Disruption on Glyoxylate Production*

Glyoxylate can be toxic because of its highly reactive properties and accumulation inside cells as an aldehyde [37]. In this study, low (0.47 ± 0.06 g-cell/L) and no cell growth was noted in the presence of 1% and 1.5% glyoxylate, respectively (Figure S1). Possible solutions to overcome the toxicity of glyoxylate to *E. coli* growth may be the utilization of extractive fermentation or continuous fermentation to avoid the accumulation of glyoxylate in the culture. Furthermore, appropriate channel proteins would be improved to efflux extracellular glyoxylate. In this study, glyoxylate production of up to 5 g/L did not negatively affect *E. coli* growth. As an intermediate metabolite in *E. coli*, the secreted concentration of glyoxylate in wild-type *E. coli* is theoretically low. The wild-type BW25113 produced 0.01 ± 0.00 g/L glyoxylate after 48 h of cultivation (Figure 2A).

To improve glyoxylate production, the competing genes were disrupted. Sequential disruption of *aceB*, *glcB*, *gcl*, and *ycdW* led to an increase in the final glyoxylate content. *Escherichia coli* EG_1, EG_2, and EG_3 produced 0.52 ± 0.07, 0.62 ± 0.12, and 0.71 ± 0.05 g/L of glyoxylate after 48 h of cultivation, respectively (Figure 2B–D). The highest production of glyoxylate was achieved in *E. coli* EG_4 with 0.93 ± 0.17 g/L (Figure 2E). Previously, a deletion of *aceB*, *glcB*, and *gcl* in *E. coli* K-12 was reported to stimulate glyoxylate production from xylose [20]. Of note, in the previous study, the production of glyoxylate in a flask was lower (0.74 g/L) than that in the present study. These results suggested that glucose is a better carbon source than xylose for glyoxylate production by *E. coli*. Further disruption of *ycdW* and the use of glucose as a carbon source positively affected glyoxylate production.

A significant decrease in glyoxylate content was observed after 48 h of cultivation, although tertiary and quaternary gene disruptions were attempted. This may be owing to the central role of glyoxylate in *E. coli* metabolism, which converts glyoxylate into other metabolites. A potential side pathway is the conversion of glyoxylate to 4-hydroxyoxoglutarate, which is catalyzed by an enzyme encoded by the 2-keto-4-hydroxyglutarate aldolase gene (*eda*) [38]. This gene limits the accumulation of glyoxylate and drives its conversion to 4-hydroxyoxoglutarate. A possible solution to overcome the assimilation of glyoxylate conferred by *eda* is to limit the accumulation of pyruvate, as pyruvate is required for condensation with glyoxylate to form 2-keto-4-hydroxyglutarate [38]. We found that the expression of *pyc* was a key technique for reducing glyoxylate consumption by the rapid conversion of pyruvate to oxaloacetate.

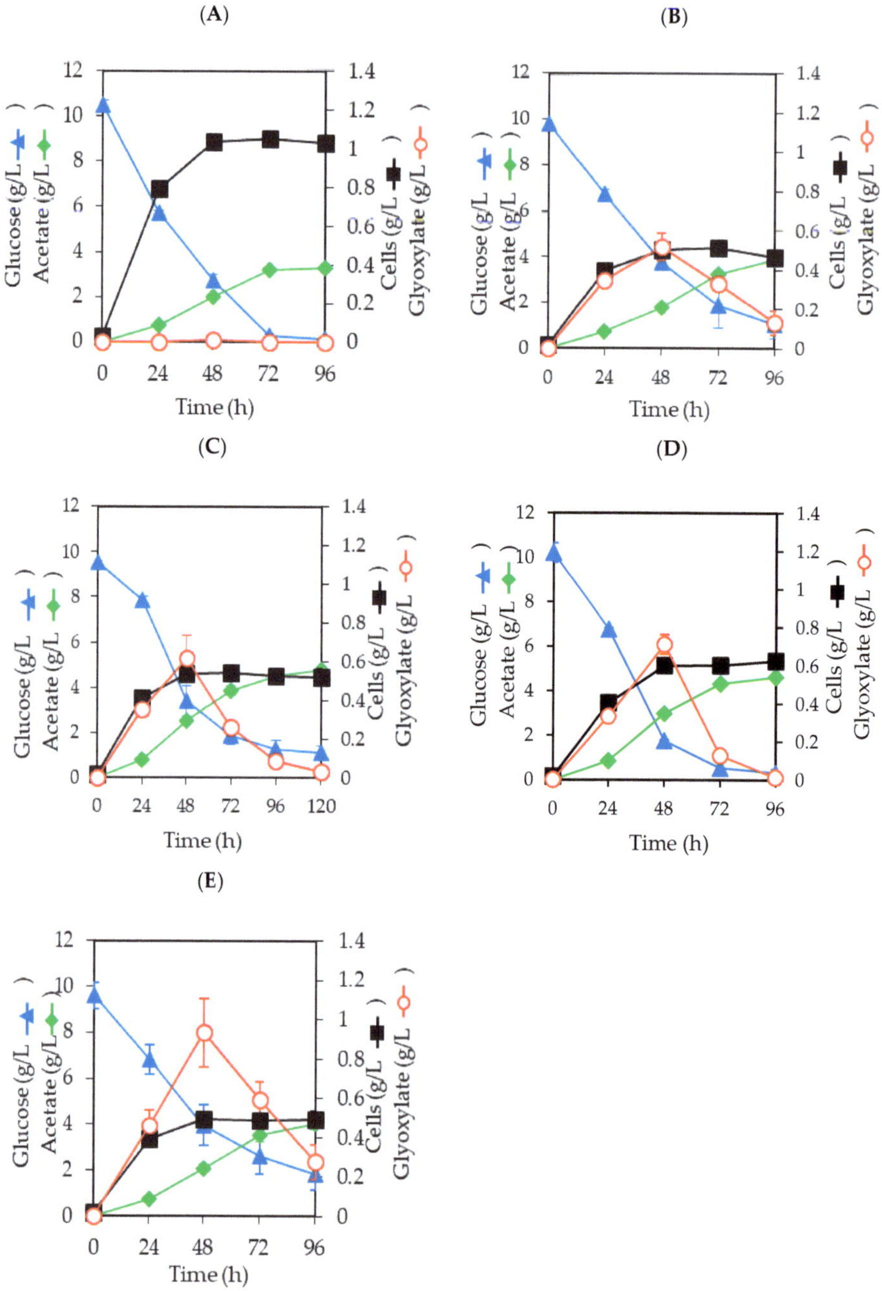

Figure 2. Fermentation production of glyoxylate in wild-type and disruptant *E. coli* BW25113 in a flask. (**A**) BW25113; (**B**) EG_1; (**C**) EG_2; (**D**) EG_3; (**E**) EG_4. *Escherichia coli* strains were cultured in 100 mL of M9 medium containing 1% glucose at 30 °C under aerobic condition. The experiment was performed in duplicate and the average is presented with error bars.

As shown in Figure 2, EG_1 (0.51 ± 0.02 g-cell/L), EG_2 (0.54 ± 0.03 g-cell/L), EG_3 (0.60 ± 0.02 g-cell/L), and EG_4 (0.49 ± 0.03 g-cell/L) showed a lower growth at 72 h than BW25113 (1.05 ± 0.01 g-cell/L). This may be because of the effect of gene disruption on metabolism. Disruption of *aceB* results in a significant decrease in cell growth. In fact, the disruption of *aceB* and *glcB* can interfere with the glyoxylate shunt assimilating acetate in *E. coli* [39]. This is compatible with the increase in the residue acetate concentration observed in EG_2 (4.82 ± 0.14 g/L) compared to that in the wild-type BW25113 (3.31 ± 0.03 g/L).

Among the disruptants, the deletion of *ycdW* created a significant impact on *E. coli* growth, with a final cell biomass of 0.50 ± 0.04 g-cell/L. Although the effects of *ycdW* on cell growth are unclear, an attempt at gene disruption of *ycdW* results in 10% lower cell biomass [40]. Since the *eda* gene plays an important role in the bacterial Entner-Doudoroff pathway, further disruption of *eda* was not performed in the present study to avoid possible effects on cell growth because glyoxylate is produced during cell growth.

An increase in the specific productivity of glyoxylate was observed with an increase in the number of disrupted genes (Table 2). Among the tested strains, the specific productivity of EG_4 was the highest (1.92 ± 0.32 g/g-cell) compared to BW25113 (0.01 ± 0.00 g/g-cell), EG_1 (1.01 ± 0.08 g/g-cell), EG_2 (1.12 ± 0.12 g/g-cell), and EG_3 (1.18 ± 0.06 g/g-cell).

Table 2. Glyoxylate production by engineered *Escherichia coli* strains.

Strains and Conditions	Highest Glyoxylate Titers (g/L)	Specific Productivities (g/g-Cell)	Other Products			
			Acetate (g/L)	Formate (g/L)	Lactate (g/L)	Cell Biomass (g/L)
BW25113, M9 medium	0.01 ± 0.00	0.01 ± 0.00	1.98 ± 0.09	0.20 ± 0.04	0.01 ± 0.00	1.03 ± 0.02
EG_1, M9 medium	0.52 ± 0.07	1.01 ± 0.08	1.82 ± 0.04	0.09 ± 0.00	0	0.50 ± 0.03
EG_2, M9 medium	0.62 ± 0.12	1.12 ± 0.12	2.53 ± 0.18	0.09 ± 0.01	0.03 ± 0.00	0.54 ± 0.05
EG_3, M9 medium	0.71 ± 0.05	1.18 ± 0.06	2.99 ± 0.04	0.07 ± 0.00	0	0.60 ± 0.01
EG_4, M9 medium	0.93 ± 0.17	1.92 ± 0.32	2.09 ± 0.83	0.04 ± 0.02	0.01 ± 0.01	0.49 ± 0.03
EG_5, M9 medium	0.12 ± 0.00	0.14 ± 0.00	2.63 ± 0.02	0.03 ± 0.00	0.38 ± 0.00	0.87 ± 0.01
EG_6, M9 medium	1.15 ± 0.02	2.88 ± 0.02	1.83 ± 0.04	0.05 ± 0.00	0	0.40 ± 0.01
EG_7, M9 medium	1.30 ± 0.11	4.90 ± 0.57	2.45 ± 0.39	0.04 ± 0.01	0	0.28 ± 0.06
EG_7, M9 medium, yeast extract	2.42 ± 0.00	4.22 ± 0.09	1.72 ± 0.04	0.05 ± 0.01	0	0.57 ± 0.01

As the major by-product, acetate was produced at relatively high concentrations in BW25113 (3.31 ± 0.03 g/L), EG_1 (3.90 ± 0.02 g/L), EG_2 (4.02 ± 0.14 g/L), EG_3 (4.63 ± 0.10 g/L), and EG_4 (4.06 ± 0.28 g/L) (Figure 2). Gene disruption had no significant effect on acetate accumulation in any strain. Pinhal et al. (2019) studied *E. coli* growth on glucose and found that the overflow metabolism of acetate was considered a fermentative inhibitory agent because acetate lowered the pH levels and was toxic at high concentrations [41].

3.2. *Effects of Gene Overexpression on Glyoxylate Production*

To further improve glyoxylate production, the glyoxylate shunt was enhanced by overexpressing *gltA* and *aceA* using plasmid pSR13. Overall, glyoxylate production increased with an increase in the number of disrupted genes. The maximum titers of glyoxylate in *E. coli* EG_5 and EG_6 were 0.12 ± 0.00 and 1.15 ± 0.02 g/L, respectively (Figure 3). Among these, *E. coli* EG_6 showed better glyoxylate production than the other *E. coli* EG_5. *Escherichia coli* EG_6 showed decreased glyoxylate content at the end of the cultivation period. This trend may have originated from the potential conversion of glyoxylate into other compounds, as discussed above.

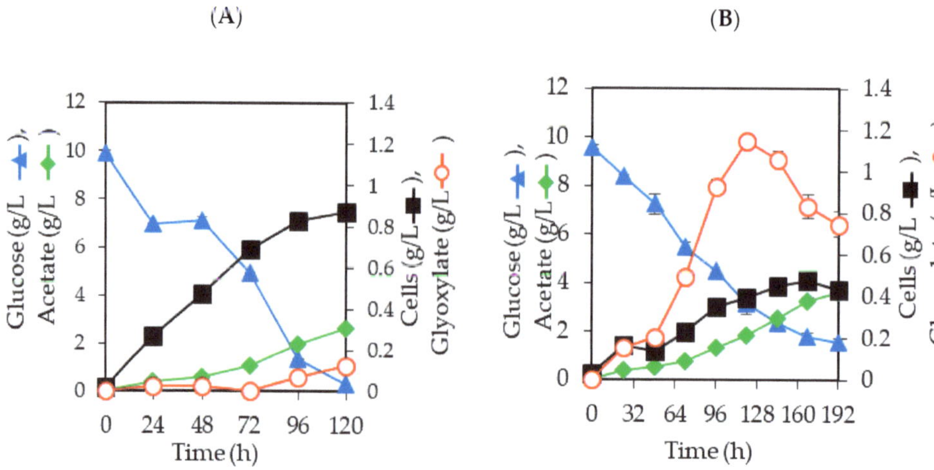

Figure 3. Fermentation production of glyoxylate in disruptant *E. coli* BW25113 harboring pSR13 in a flask. (**A**) EG_5; (**B**) EG_6. *Escherichia coli* strains were cultured in 100 mL of M9 medium containing 1% glucose at 30 °C under aerobic condition. The experiment was performed in duplicate and the average is presented with error bars.

Among the evaluated strains, *E. coli* EG_6 showed lower cell growths at the end of the cultivation, corresponding to 0.43 ± 0.01 g-cell/L than *E. coli* EG_5 (0.87 ± 0.01 g-cell/L). This was consistent with the lower growth rates of EG_4 than that of *E. coli* BW25113, as *E. coli* EG_6 shared the same disrupted genes as *E. coli* EG_4. The overexpression of *gltA* and *aceA* showed no negative effect on the growth rate of *E. coli*.

The overexpression of *gltA* and *aceA* further benefits *E. coli* BW25113 in the improvement of the titer and specific productivity of glyoxylate (Table 2). Among these strains, *E. coli* EG_6 showed the highest specific productivity at 2.88 ± 0.02 (g/g-cell). Deng et al. (2015) also reported that the production of glycolate from glyoxylate via a glyoxylate shunt could be reinforced by the overexpression of *aceA* [42].

We investigated the antagonistic effects of gene overexpression on acetate production. All of the strains equipped with the glyoxylate shunt reinforced by gene overexpression produced less acetate; EG_5 and EG_6 produced acetate at 2.62 ± 0.01 and 3.61 ± 0.17 g/L, respectively, at 72 h. These titers were lower than those of BW25113, EG_1, EG_2, and EG_3 (Figures 2 and 3). Renilla et al. (2012) showed that the disruption of genes involved in the glyoxylate shunt affects *E. coli* growth, and that the reinforced glyoxylate shunt can reduce acetate [43].

As shown in Figure 3, the residual glyoxylate at the end of fermentation of the overexpressed strains EG_5 and EG_6 was higher than that of BW25113 and EG_4, respectively, indicating that the overexpression of *gltA* and *aceA* not only enhanced glyoxylate production but also limited glyoxylate assimilation. In particular, although the majority of the produced glyoxylate was consumed in the fermentation of *E. coli* EG_4 (Figure 2), more than 70% glyoxylate concentration remained at the end of *E. coli* EG_6 fermentation with the residue glyoxylate noted at 0.74 ± 0.06 g/L compared to that of *E. coli* EG_4 with 0.28 ± 0.09 g/L (Figure 2). These results demonstrate that the overexpression of *gltA* and *aceA* is an efficient method to overcome glyoxylate consumption.

Similarly, the glyoxylate productivities of all strains were significantly improved compared to non-overexpressed strains with specific productivities of glyoxylate in EG_5 and EG_6 at 0.14 ± 0.03 and 2.88 ± 0.02 g/g-cell, respectively (Table 2).

3.3. Effects of *pyc* Expression on Glyoxylate Production in *E. coli*

Recent studies have demonstrated an improvement in chemical production via the glyoxylate shunt by improving the flow of pyruvate into the TCA cycle. Here, we reinforced glyoxylate production by expressing the heterologous gene *pyc* from *C. glutamicum*, which helps to convert pyruvate to oxaloacetate. Figure 4A shows the fermentation profile of *E. coli* EG_7 with the expression of *pyc* using pLB6 plasmid.

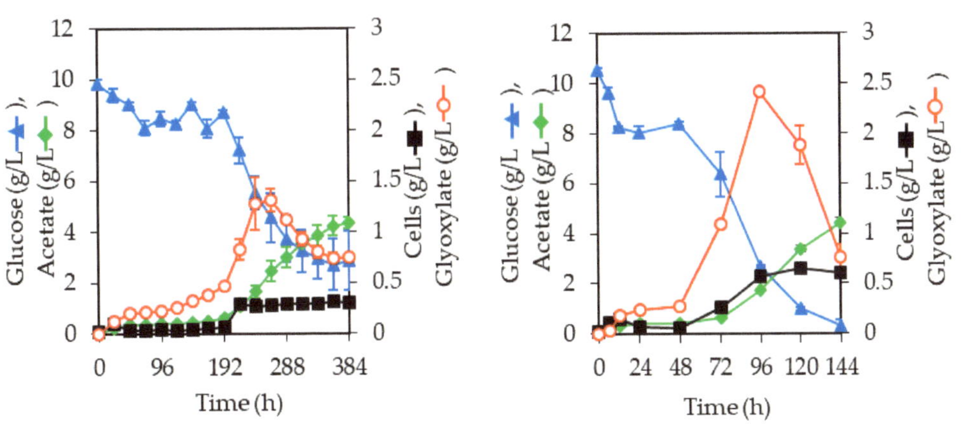

Figure 4. Fermentation production of glyoxylate in *Escherichia coli* EG_7 in 100 mL of M9 medium supplemented with (**A**) 10 g/L of glucose or (**B**) 10 g/L of glucose and 1 g/L of yeast extract. The experiment was performed in duplicate and the average is presented with error bars.

Although the expression of *pyc* slowed *E. coli* growth, this strategy helped increase the glyoxylate concentration to 1.31 ± 0.11 g/L. The positive effects of *pyc* expression on succinate [26], malate [27], and fumarate production [28] have been demonstrated in recent studies. These studies concluded that the expression of *pyc* could activate the glyoxylate shunt of *E. coli* and improve the production of these organic acids. As shown in Figure 4A, EG_7, equipped with *pyc*, grew more slowly than *E. coli* EG_6 and stopped using glucose at the end of fermentation.

To improve the growth of *E. coli* EG_7, we conducted fermentation in a medium supplemented with 1 g/L yeast extract (Figure 4B). As a result, *E. coli* EG_7 rapidly grew with yeast extract supplementation and the final cell biomass reached 0.61 ± 0.01 g-cell/L compared to a cell biomass of 0.30 ± 0.04 g-cell/L cells in the non-supplemented medium. In addition, glyoxylate production reached the highest at 2.42 ± 0.00 g/L with specific productivity at 4.22 ± 0.09 g/g-cell (Table 2) at 48 h. In this study, glucose was completely consumed after 144 h. Yeast extract can support *E. coli* growth as a source of amino acids.

In theory, glyoxylate production from glucose via the glyoxylate shunt follows the equation: 1 glucose + 6 H_2O = 2 glyoxylate + 2 CO_2 + 20 H + 1 O_2. Therefore, 1 g of glucose can generate 0.82 g of glyoxylate under the optimal condition. In Figure 4B and Table 2, the highest glyoxylate concentration was 2.42 ± 0.00 g/L at 48 h with 1.72 ± 0.04 g/L acetate, 0.57 ± 0.01 g/L cells, and 0.05 ± 0.01 g/L formate from 7.85 ± 0.07 g/L consumed glucose. Malate and succinate were not detected in the cultures (data not shown). The total quantifiable products accounted for 60.6% of the consumed glucose mass, reaching 37.6% theoretical yield in mass and 0.30 mol-glyoxylate/mol-glucose. It was suggested that the assimilation of glyoxylate and the generation of non-detected metabolites, such as CO_2, caused this decrease in the yield. The production from glucose in this study was higher than the yield from xylose, with a 30.0% yield compared to the theory and 0.30 mol-glyoxylate/mol-xylose in the previous study [20]. On the other hand, the related study reported that malate was accumulated when boosting the glyoxylate shunt [44]. In contrast, the production level of malate was negligible in this study. This may be due to the disruption of *glcB* and *aceB* involving the conversion of glyoxylate to malate.

In a previous study on *pyc* expression in *E. coli* for the production of succinate, the increase in succinate production was due to an increase in oxaloacetate concentration, which accelerates glyoxylate production [26]. To understand the effects of *pyc* expression on *E. coli* metabolism, we quantified intracellular oxaloacetate in *E. coli* EG_6 and EG_7 during fermentation (Figure 5). As a result, the highest intracellular oxaloacetate was noted in *E. coli* EG_7 at 327.4 ± 46.5 mg/g-cell, which is higher than that of *E. coli* EG_6 (51.5 ± 10.1 mg/g-cell). During the first 24 h of induction by isopropyl-β-D-thiogalactopyranoside, the intracellular oxaloacetate content was undetectable in both *E. coli* EG_6 and EG_7. The accumulation of intracellular oxaloacetate was quickly improved after gene induction by isopropyl-β-D-thiogalactopyranoside, which indicated the effects of the introduced *pyc* gene on oxaloacetate production in *E. coli*. As shown in Figure 4B, the cell biomass and glyoxylate concentration steadily increased after 48 h, followed by a decrease in the concentration of intracellular oxaloacetate (Figure 5), indicating that the assimilation of intracellular oxaloacetate improved glyoxylate production in *E. coli*.

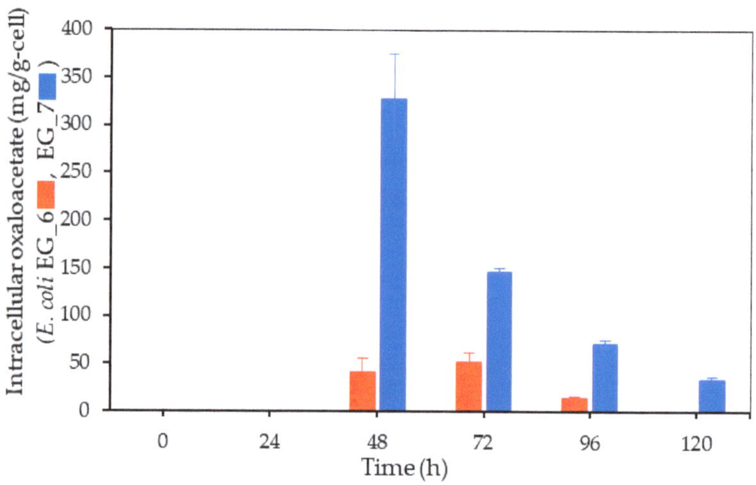

Figure 5. Intracellular oxaloacetate produced by *Escherichia coli* EG_6 and EG_7. *Escherichia coli* EG_6 and EG_7 were cultivated in 100 mL of M9 medium supplemented with 10 g/L of glucose and 1 g/L of yeast extract. The experiment was performed in duplicate and the average is presented with error bars.

Figure 4A also indicates a lower growth of *E. coli* EG_7, as the highest cell biomass reached 0.30 ± 0.04 g-cell/L, 30% lower than that of *E. coli* EG_6. One possible reason for poor cell growth is the accumulation of intracellular oxaloacetate, consequently causing the feedback inhibition of malate dehydrogenase, as reported in a recent study [45]. Oxaloacetate is considered a branch point that controls amino acid synthesis via lysine metabolism and the TCA cycle via the phosphoenolpyruvate-pyruvate-oxaloacetate node in bacteria [3]. Furthermore, the expression of *pyc* in *E. coli* was suggested to generate competitive effects on the production of acetyl-CoA from pyruvate. A possible solution is the overexpression of acetyl-CoA synthetase (*acs*) to recover acetyl-CoA from acetate since acetate concentrations were remarkable during the fermentation (Figure 4). Nevertheless, the expression of *pyc* can be a valuable technique for improving glyoxylate production.

As discussed above, the assimilation of glyoxylate was noted during the stationary phase of *E. coli* growth, which may be due to a decrease in TCA cycle operation and an increase in the accumulation of pyruvate [46], a precursor for *eda* function in reducing glyoxylate.

In this study, pH-controlled jar fermentation was conducted; however, the glyoxylate titer was not improved (data not shown). One possible solution to overcome the assimilation of glyoxylate is to apply fermentation optimization to extend the cell growth phase using DO-stat fermentation [47]. This approach limits the operation of the glycolytic pathway, which controls pyruvate accumulation [48]. In addition, DO-stat cultivation can effectively control the pH and the production of organic acids, such as acetate, lactate, and formate, which enable higher cell growth [47] and glyoxylate production.

Another disadvantage of the fermentation in the present study was the accumulation of acetate as the major by-product, with the final content generated by *E. coli* EG_7 at 4.42 ± 0.18 g/L. Acetate, the major by-product, accumulates at a high concentration in the cultures of engineered *E. coli*. According to recent studies, overflow metabolism originating from a high pyruvate content results in high acetate production and can affect *E. coli* growth [38]. A possible solution for acetate accumulation is the overexpression of the acetyl-CoA synthetase gene (*acs*), because Lin et al. (2006) showed that *acs* overexpression results in the reduction of acetate in *E. coli* [49]. Another approach was reported by Negrete et al. (2013) using the overexpression of *sgrS*, which works as a small RNAi to slow down the glucose uptake rate and could decrease acetate by 80% in *E. coli* [50]. These results provide promising insights into improving glyoxylate production from glucose in future studies.

4. Conclusions

This study demonstrated an improvement in glyoxylate production from glucose in *E. coli* BW25113. Glyoxylate concentrations of up to 5 g/L did not affect *E. coli* growth. The disruption of *aceB*, *glcB*, *gcl*, and *ycdW*, along with the overexpression of *gltA* and *aceA*, improved the glyoxylate production titer and specific productivity at 1.15 ± 0.02 g/L and 2.88 ± 0.02 g/g-cell, respectively, which were much higher than those of the wild-type (0.01 ± 0.00 g/L and 0.01 ± 0.00 g/g-cell, respectively). In addition, the expression of *pyc* significantly enhanced glyoxylate production to achieve the highest titer and specific productivity at 2.42 ± 0.00 g/L and 4.42 ± 0.09 g/g-cell, respectively, which is the highest reported to date.

Supplementary Materials: The following supporting information can be downloaded at: https://www.mdpi.com/article/10.3390/fermentation9060534/s1, Figure S1: Effects of glyoxylate concentrations on Escherichia coli BW25113 growth; Figure S2: HPLC chromatograms of glyoxylate after derivatization with phenylhydrazine; Figure S3: HPLC chromatograms of oxaloacetate; Table S1: Sequence information of primers used in this study.

Author Contributions: Conceptualization, Y.A. and R.S.; methodology and formal analysis, M.N. and B.H.D.L.; investigation and writing—original draft preparation, B.H.D.L. and M.N.; writing—review and editing, B.H.D.L. and Y.A.; supervision, H.O., Y.A. and T.T. All authors have read and agreed to the published version of the manuscript.

Funding: This research received no external funding.

Institutional Review Board Statement: Not applicable.

Informed Consent Statement: Not applicable.

Data Availability Statement: Data presented within the article.

Acknowledgments: We would like to express special thanks to the National BioResource Project (National Institute of Genetics, Japan) and the NITE Biological Resource Center (NBRC, Chiba, Japan) for sharing *E. coli* BW25113 and *C. glutamicum* NBRC 12168. We are also grateful to the Coli Genetic Stock Center (Yale University, USA) for providing us with pKD46.

Conflicts of Interest: The authors declare no conflict of interest.

References

1. Skarstad, K.; Boye, E.; Steen, H.B. Timing of initiation of chromosome replication in individual *Escherichia coli* cells. *EMBO J.* **1986**, *5*, 1711–1717. [CrossRef] [PubMed]
2. Castiñeiras, T.S.; Williams, S.G.; Hitchcock, A.G.; Smith, D.C. *E. coli* strain engineering for the production of advanced biopharmaceutical products. *FEMS Microbiol. Lett.* **2018**, *365*, fny162. [CrossRef] [PubMed]
3. Sauer, U.; Eikmanns, B. The PEP-pyruvate-oxaloacetate node as the switch point for carbon flux distribution in bacteria. *FEMS Microbiol. Rev.* **2005**, *29*, 765–794. [CrossRef]
4. Aso, Y.; Tsubaki, M.; Long, B.H.D.; Murakami, R.; Nagata, K.; Okano, H.; Dung, N.T.P.; Ohara, H. Continuous production of D-lactic acid from cellobiose in cell recycle fermentation using β-glucosidase-displaying *Escherichia coli*. *J. Biosci. Bioeng.* **2019**, *127*, 441–446. [CrossRef]
5. Förster, A.H.; Gescher, J. Metabolic engineering of *Escherichia coli* for production of mixed-acid fermentation end products. *Front. Bioeng. Biotechnol.* **2014**, *2*, 16. [PubMed]
6. Okamoto, S.; Chin, T.; Nagata, K.; Takahashi, T.; Ohara, H.; Aso, Y. Production of itaconic acid in *Escherichia coli* expressing recombinant α-amylase using starch as substrate. *J. Biosci. Bioeng.* **2015**, *119*, 548–553. [CrossRef] [PubMed]
7. Sato, R.; Tanaka, T.; Ohara, H.; Aso, Y. Engineering *Escherichia coli* for direct production of 1,2-propanediol and 1,3-propanediol from starch. *Curr. Microbiol.* **2020**, *77*, 3704–3710. [CrossRef]
8. Sato, R.; Tanaka, T.; Ohara, H.; Aso, Y. Disruption of *glpF* gene encoding the glycerol facilitator improves 1,3-propanediol production from glucose via glycerol in *Escherichia coli*. *Lett. Appl. Microbiol.* **2021**, *72*, 68–73. [CrossRef]
9. Gupta, N.K.; Vennesland, B. Glyoxylate carboligase of *Escherichia coli*: A flavoprotein. *J. Biol. Chem.* **1964**, *239*, 3787–3789. [CrossRef]
10. Pozdniakov, M.A.; Zhuk, I.V.; Lyapunova, M.V.; Salikov, A.S.; Botvin, V.V.; Filimoshkin, A.G. Glyoxylic acid: Synthesis, isolation, and crystallization. *Russ. Chem. Bull.* **2019**, *68*, 472–479. [CrossRef]
11. Nishizawa, R.; Saino, T.; Suzuki, M.; Fujii, T.; Shirai, T.; Aoyagi, T.; Umezawa, H. A facile synthesis of bestatin. *J. Antibiot.* **1983**, *36*, 695–699. [CrossRef] [PubMed]
12. Liu, L.; He, A.; Li, X. Synthesis of Allantoin Catalyzed by SO_4^{2-}/La_2O_3-SiO_2-ZrO_2. *Asian J. Chem.* **2012**, *24*, 2298–2300.
13. Mattioda, G.; Christidis, Y. Glyoxylic Acid. In *Ullmann's Encyclopedia of Industrial Chemistry*, 6th ed.; Elvers, B., Ed.; Wiley-VCH: Weinheim, Germany, 2000; pp. 89–92.
14. Kalikar, R.G.; Deshpande, R.S.; Chandalia, S.B. Synthesis of vanillin and 4-hydroxybenzaldehyde by a reaction scheme involving condensation of phenols with glyoxylic acid. *J. Chem. Technol. Biotechnol.* **1986**, *36*, 38–46. [CrossRef]
15. Sun, Z.C.; Eli, W.; Xu, T.Y.; Zhang, Y.G. Oxidation of glyoxal with hydroperoxide compounds prepared from maleic acid by ozonation to produce glyoxylic acid. *Ind. Eng. Chem. Res.* **2006**, *45*, 1849–1852. [CrossRef]
16. Jin, J.; Tan, T.; Wang, H.; Su, G. The expression of spinach glycolate oxidase (GO) in *E. coli* and the application of GO in the production of glyoxylic acid. *Mol. Biotechnol.* **2003**, *25*, 207–214. [CrossRef] [PubMed]
17. Berg, J.M.; Tymoczko, J.L.; Stryer, L. Section 17.4: The Glyoxylate Cycle Enables Plants and Bacteria to Grow on Acetate. In *Biochemistry*, 5th ed.; Berg, J.M., Tymoczko, J.L., Stryer, L., Eds.; W. H. Freeman: New York, NY, USA, 2002.
18. Dunn, M.F.; Ramírez-Trujillo, J.A.; Hernández-Lucas, I. Major roles of isocitrate lyase and malate synthase in bacterial and fungal pathogenesis. *Microbiology* **2009**, *155*, 3166–3175. [CrossRef] [PubMed]
19. Sneeden, R.P.A. 50.2—Organic Syntheses where Carbon Monoxide is the Unique Source of Carbon. In *Comprehensive Organometallic Chemistry*; Wilkinson, G., Stone, F.G., Abel, E.W., Eds.; Pergamon: Oxford, UK, 1982; pp. 19–100.
20. Li, L.K.; Shi, L.L.; Hong, P.H.; Tan, T.W.; Li, Z.J. Metabolic engineering of *Escherichia coli* for the production of glyoxylate from xylose. *Biochem. Eng. J.* **2018**, *129*, 113–118. [CrossRef]
21. Foyer, C.H.; Bloom, A.J.; Queval, G.; Noctor, G. Photorespiratory metabolism: Genes, mutants, energetics, and redox signaling. *Annu. Rev. Plant Biol.* **2009**, *60*, 455–484. [CrossRef]
22. Rojas, C.M.; Mysore, K.S. Glycolate oxidase is an alternative source for H_2O_2 production during plant defense responses and functions independently from NADPH oxidase. *Plant Signal. Behav.* **2012**, *7*, 752–755. [CrossRef]
23. Rojas, C.M.; Senthil-Kumar, M.; Wang, K.; Ryu, C.M.; Kaundal, A.; Mysore, K.S. Glycolate oxidase modulates reactive oxygen species-mediated signal transduction during nonhost resistance in *Nicotiana benthamiana* and *Arabidopsis*. *Plant Cell* **2012**, *24*, 336–352. [CrossRef]
24. Gavagan, J.E.; Fager, S.K.; Seip, J.E.; Payne, M.S.; Anton, D.L.; DiCosimo, E. Glyoxylic acid production using microbial transformant catalysts. *J. Org. Chem.* **1995**, *60*, 3957–3963. [CrossRef]
25. Zhu, T.; Yao, D.; Li, D.; Xu, H.; Jia, S.; Bi, C.; Cai, J.; Zhu, X.; Zhang, X. Multiple strategies for metabolic engineering of *Escherichia coli* for efficient production of glycolate. *Biotechnol. Bioeng.* **2021**, *118*, 4699–4707. [CrossRef]
26. Martínez, I.; Bennett, G.N.; San, K.Y. Metabolic impact of the level of aeration during cell growth on anaerobic succinate production by an engineered *Escherichia coli* strain. *Metab. Eng.* **2010**, *12*, 499–509. [CrossRef] [PubMed]
27. Jiang, Y.; Zheng, T.; Ye, X.; Zheng, T.; Ye, X.; Xin, F.; Zhang, W.; Dong, W.; Ma, J.; Jiang, M. Metabolic engineering of *Escherichia coli* for L-malate production anaerobically. *Microb. Cell Fact.* **2010**, *19*, 165. [CrossRef] [PubMed]
28. Chen, X.; Ma, D.; Liu, J.; Luo, Q.; Liu, L. Engineering the transmission efficiency of the noncyclic glyoxylate pathway for fumarate production in *Escherichia coli*. *Biotechnol. Biofuels.* **2020**, *13*, 132. [CrossRef]

29. Li, X.T.; Thomason, L.C.; Sawitzke, J.A.; Costantino, N.; Court, D.L. Positive and negative selection using the *tetA-sacB* cassette: Recombineering and P1 transduction in *Escherichia coli*. *Nucleic Acids Res.* **2013**, *41*, e204. [CrossRef]
30. Datsenko, K.A.; Wanner, B.L. One-step inactivation of chromosomal genes in *Escherichia coli* K-12 using PCR products. *Proc. Natl. Acad. Sci. USA* **2000**, *97*, 6640–6645. [CrossRef]
31. Higuchi, R.; Krummel, B.; Saiki, R. A general method of in vitro preparation and specific mutagenesis of DNA fragments: Study of protein and DNA interactions. *Nucleic Acids Res.* **1988**, *16*, 7351–7367. [CrossRef]
32. Bertani, G. Studies on lysogenesis. I. The mode of phage liberation by lysogenic *Escherichia coli*. *J. Bacteriol.* **1951**, *62*, 293–300. [CrossRef]
33. Gibson, D.G.; Young, L.; Chuang, R.Y.; Venter, J.C.; Hutchison, C.A.; Smith, H.O. Enzymatic assembly of DNA molecules up to several hundred kilobases. *Nat. Methods* **2009**, *6*, 343–345. [CrossRef]
34. Froger, A.; Hall, J.E. Transformation of plasmid DNA into *E. coli* using the heat shock method. *J. Vis. Exp.* **2007**, *6*, 253.
35. Lange, M.; Mályusz, M. Fast method for the simultaneous determination of 2-oxo acids in biological fluids by high-performance liquid chromatography. *J. Chromatogr. B Biomed.* **1994**, *662*, 97–102. [CrossRef] [PubMed]
36. Canelas, A.B.; ten Pierick, A.; Ras, C.; Seifar, R.M.; van Dam, J.C.; van Gulik, W.M.; Heijnen, J.J. Quantitative evaluation of intracellular metabolite extraction techniques for yeast metabolomics. *Anal. Chem.* **2009**, *81*, 7379–7389. [CrossRef]
37. Lassalle, L.; Engilberge, S.; Madern, D.; Vauclare, P.; Franzetti, B.; Girard, E. New insights into the mechanism of substrates trafficking in glyoxylate/hydroxypyruvate reductases. *Sci. Rep.* **2016**, *6*, 20629. [CrossRef]
38. Nishihara, H.; Dekker, E.E. Purification, substrate specificity and binding, β-decarboxylase activity, and other properties of *Escherichia coli* 2-keto-4-hydroxyglutarate aldolase. *J. Biol. Chem.* **1972**, *247*, 5079–5087. [CrossRef] [PubMed]
39. Jo, M.; Noh, M.H.; Lim, H.G.; Kang, C.W.; Im, D.K.; Oh, M.K.; Jung, G.Y. Precise tuning of the glyoxylate cycle in *Escherichia coli* for efficient tyrosine production from acetate. *Microb. Cell Fact.* **2019**, *18*, 57. [CrossRef]
40. Jing, P.; Cao, X.; Lu, X.; Zong, H.; Zhuge, B. Modification of an engineered *Escherichia coli* by a combined strategy of deleting branch pathway, fine-tuning xylose isomerase expression, and substituting decarboxylase to improve 1,2,4-butanetriol production. *J. Biosci. Bioeng.* **2018**, *126*, 547–552. [CrossRef]
41. Pinhal, S.; Ropers, D.; Geiselmann, J.; de Jong, H. Acetate Metabolism and the Inhibition of Bacterial Growth by Acetate. *J. Bacteriol.* **2019**, *201*, e00147-19. [CrossRef]
42. Deng, Y.; Mao, Y.; Zhang, X. Metabolic engineering of *E. coli* for efficient production of glycolic acid from glucose. *Biochem. Eng. J.* **2015**, *103*, 256–262. [CrossRef]
43. Renilla, S.; Bernal, V.; Fuhrer, T.; Castaño-Cerezo, S.; Pastor, J.M.; Iborra, J.L.; Sauer, U.; Cánovas, M. Acetate scavenging activity in *Escherichia coli*: Interplay of acetyl-CoA synthetase and the PEP-glyoxylate cycle in chemostat cultures. *Appl. Microbiol. Biotechnol.* **2012**, *93*, 2109–2124. [CrossRef]
44. Hua, Q.; Yang, C.; Baba, T.; Mori, H.; Shimizu, K. Responses of the central metabolism in *Escherichia coli* to phosphoglucose isomerase and glucose-6-phosphate dehydrogenase knockouts. *J. Bacteriol.* **2003**, *185*, 7053–7067. [CrossRef]
45. Takahashi-Íñiguez, T.; Aburto-Rodríguez, N.; Vilchis-González, A.L.; Flores, M.E. Function, kinetic properties, crystallization, and regulation of microbial malate dehydrogenase. *J. Zhejiang Univ. Sci. B* **2016**, *17*, 247–261. [CrossRef]
46. Kováč, L.; Berta, F.; Pšenák, M.; Slezáriková, V. Metabolic differences between *Escherichia coli* cultures growing aerobically and anaerobically in the presence of fluoroacetate. *Folia Microbiol.* **1966**, *11*, 263–270.
47. Riesenberg, D.; Schulz, V.; Knorre, W.A.; Pohl, H.D.; Korz, D.; Sanders, E.A.; Roß, A.; Deckwer, W.D. High cell density cultivation of *Escherichia coli* at controlled specific growth rate. *J. Biotech.* **1991**, *20*, 17–27.
48. Causey, T.B.; Shanmugam, K.T.; Yomano, L.P.; Ingram, L.O. Engineering *Escherichia coli* for efficient conversion of glucose to pyruvate. *Proc. Natl. Acad. Sci. USA* **2004**, *101*, 2235–2240. [PubMed]
49. Lin, H.; Castro, N.M.; Bennett, G.N.; San, K.Y. Acetyl-CoA synthetase overexpression in *Escherichia coli* demonstrates more efficient acetate assimilation and lower acetate accumulation: A potential tool in metabolic engineering. *Appl. Microbiol. Biotechnol.* **2006**, *71*, 870–874. [PubMed]
50. Negrete, A.; Majdalani, N.; Phue, J.N.; Shiloach, J. Reducing acetate excretion from *E. coli* K-12 by over-expressing the small RNA *SgrS*. *New Biotechnol.* **2013**, *30*, 269–273. [CrossRef]

fermentation

MDPI

Article

Improving the Functionality of Lentil–Casein Protein Complexes through Structural Interactions and Water Kefir-Assisted Fermentation

Mohammad Alrosan [1,2,*], Thuan-Chew Tan [1,3,*], Azhar Mat Easa [1], Muhammad H. Alu'datt [4], Carole C. Tranchant [5], Ali Madi Almajwal [6], Sana Gammoh [4], Sofyan Maghaydah [4,7], Mohammed Ali Dheyab [8], Mahmood S. Jameel [8] and Ali Al-Qaisi [9]

1 Food Technology Division, School of Industrial Technology, Universiti Sains Malaysia, USM 11800, Penang, Malaysia
2 Applied Science Research Center, Applied Science Private University, Amman 11937, Jordan
3 Renewable Biomass Transformation Cluster, School of Industrial Technology, Universiti Sains Malaysia, USM 11800, Penang, Malaysia
4 Department of Nutrition and Food Technology, Faculty of Agriculture, Jordan University of Science and Technology, Irbid 22110, Jordan
5 School of Food Science, Nutrition and Family Studies, Faculty of Health Sciences and Community Services, Université de Moncton, Moncton, NB E1A 3E9, Canada
6 Department of Community Health Sciences, College of Applied Medical Sciences, King Saud University, P.O. Box 10219, Riyadh 11433, Saudi Arabia
7 Department of Human Nutrition and Dietetics, College of Health Sciences, Abu Dhabi University, Zayed City, Abu Dhabi P.O. Box 59911, United Arab Emirates
8 School of Physics, Universiti Sains Malaysia, USM 11800, Penang, Malaysia
9 Department of Agricultural Biotechnology, Faculty of Agricultural Sciences and Technology, Palestine Technical University-Kadoorie (PTUK), Jaffa Street, Tulkarm P.O. Box 7, Palestine
* Correspondence: mohammad.alrosan@hotmail.com (M.A.); thuanchew@usm.my (T.-C.T.)

check for updates

Citation: Alrosan, M.; Tan, T.-C.; Easa, A.M.; Alu'datt, M.H.; Tranchant, C.C.; Almajwal, A.M.; Gammoh, S.; Maghaydah, S.; Dheyab, M.A.; Jameel, M.S.; et al. Improving the Functionality of Lentil–Casein Protein Complexes through Structural Interactions and Water Kefir-Assisted Fermentation. *Fermentation* **2023**, *9*, 194. https://doi.org/10.3390/fermentation9020194

Academic Editor: Ricardo Aguilar-López

Received: 29 January 2023
Revised: 14 February 2023
Accepted: 15 February 2023
Published: 20 February 2023

Abstract: Highly nutritious lentil proteins (LP) have recently attracted interest in the food industry. However, due to their low solubility, extensive application of LP is severely limited. This study describes a new and successful method for overcoming this challenge by improving the nutritional–functional properties of LP, particularly their solubility and protein quality. By combining protein complexation with water kefir-assisted fermentation, the water solubility of native LP (~58%) increases to over 86% upon the formation of lentil–casein protein complexes (LCPC). Meanwhile, the surface charge increases to over −40 mV, accompanied by alterations in secondary and tertiary structures, as shown by Fourier-transform infrared and UV-vis spectra, respectively. In addition, subjecting the novel LCPC to fermentation increases the protein digestibility from 76% to over 86%, due to the reduction in micronutrients that have some degree of restriction with respect to protein digestibility. This approach could be an effective and practical way of altering plant-based proteins.

Keywords: casein proteins; lentil proteins; structural interaction; protein quality; solubility; water kefir-assisted fermentation

1. Introduction

Population expansion has recently boosted the focus on highly nutritious plant-based proteins. Plant-based proteins, particularly those from legumes, have been utilized to replace protein from animal sources. The main components of lentil proteins (LP) are globulins, albumins, glutelins, and prolamins, representing about 70, 16, 11, and 3%, respectively [1]. The limited use of LP in food industries is due to their low water solubility, i.e., ~58% [2], and their poor protein digestibility, i.e., ~76% [3]. Many features make proteins useful, but one of the most significant is their water solubility. Comprehensive investigations into the production of soluble biopolymers based on protein–protein interactions (PPIs) have emphasized the increase in water solubility [4–6].

The pH of an aqueous solution is also a major factor in the solubility of the protein. Molecular forces govern interactions between proteins, which are electrostatic interactions, hydrogen bonds, and hydrophobic interactions; as a result, these interactions can modify water solubility [4,6] and the emulsion of the proteins [7].

The water solubility of protein increases during the protein–protein interaction process, based on the higher activity of electrostatic repulsion more than hydrophobic interactions between the polymers of proteins. Hydrophobic interactions in an aqueous solution can also enhance PPI. Different types of protein, such as casein proteins (CP), are remarkably affected by the exposed hydrophobic amino acids between the non-polar groups of the protein [8]. PPI in solution is classified as one of the most effective methods for improving the functionality of plant-based proteins. Food manufacturers are increasingly turning to plant-based proteins for their low impact on the environment and low cost [4]. As a result, several researchers are interested in enhancing the water solubility of lentils [2] and rice protein [5].

Protein digestibility is widely regarded as the most important means of evaluating protein quality, because it influences amino acid absorption, availability, and hydrolysis. Therefore, proteins with a higher digestibility have higher nutritional value than proteins with a lower digestibility because they provide more dietary value, including the ability to have more amino acids available for absorption. According to Azi et al. [9] and Alrosan et al. [10], water kefir-assisted fermentation plays a major role in modifying the bioavailability and bioaccessibility of proteins and micronutrients. These modifications depend on the type of fermenting microorganisms (e.g., *Streptococcus*, *Lactococcus*, *Leuconostoc*, and *Lactobacillus* spp.) and their enzymes, which can alter the level of nutritive and non-nutritive compounds during the fermentation [11].

Water kefir grains are the most popular source of bacteria used in fermented compounds, including protein, carbohydrates, and food matrices, because of the presence of many lactic acid bacteria, acetic acid bacteria, as well as yeasts. Thus, this study aimed to investigate the combination of two main techniques. In the first stage, PPI was investigated to prepare soluble protein complexes based on LP and CP complexation. Secondly, water kefir-assisted fermentation was carried out on the lentil–casein protein complexes (LCPC) generated to enhance their nutritional characteristics. Analyses were studied in detail to investigate the mechanism of the formation of novel LCPC and the structure-function relationship of the fermented LCPC.

2. Materials and Methods

Lentil seeds, CP, and kefir seeds were obtained from iHerb (Moreno Valley, CA, USA). These materials were transported to the laboratories appropriately, as suggested by the seller, and kept at 4 °C until needed.

2.1. Extraction of LP

LP were extracted according to Jarpa-Parra et al. [1]. The fine lentil flour was produced by grinding the lentil seeds in an ultra-centrifugal mill (RETSCH, ZM 200, Visalia, CA, USA). The fine lentil flour was then mixed with distilled water at a ratio of 1:10 (w/v). The pH of the slurry was then adjusted to pH 9.5 using 0.1 M NaOH on a stirring apparatus (Joan Lab, SH-4, Huzhou City, China) for 2 h. The slurry was centrifuged (CN Meditech, CNME060222, Nanjing, China) for 15 min at 8500× g. The pH of the supernatant was adjusted to pH 4.2 using 0.1 M HCL and left to precipitate for 24 h before centrifuging at 1590× g for 30 min to separate the insoluble particles. The precipitate was then lyophilized (Hawach Scientific, ILFD55EH-20A, Shanxi, China). The lyophilized LP were kept at 4 °C. The protein content of the LP (62.91 ± 1.82%) was then determined using the Kjeldahl method [12].

2.2. Protein Complexation

Protein complex (1%, w/v) was prepared from LP and CP with distilled water (Figure 1). The percentage of CP in the protein suspension was 10, 33, and 50%. The pH of the protein suspension was adjusted to 12.0 using 0.5 M NaOH and left on an SH-4 stirrer for 60 min, and then the pH was readjusted to 7.0 using 0.05 M HCL. After that, the protein suspension was centrifuged at 7000× g for 10 min. The collected supernatant was then lyophilized. The control was prepared using LP and was subjected to the same protein complexation process as described above, but without the addition of CP, to evaluate the impact of pH recycling on LP.

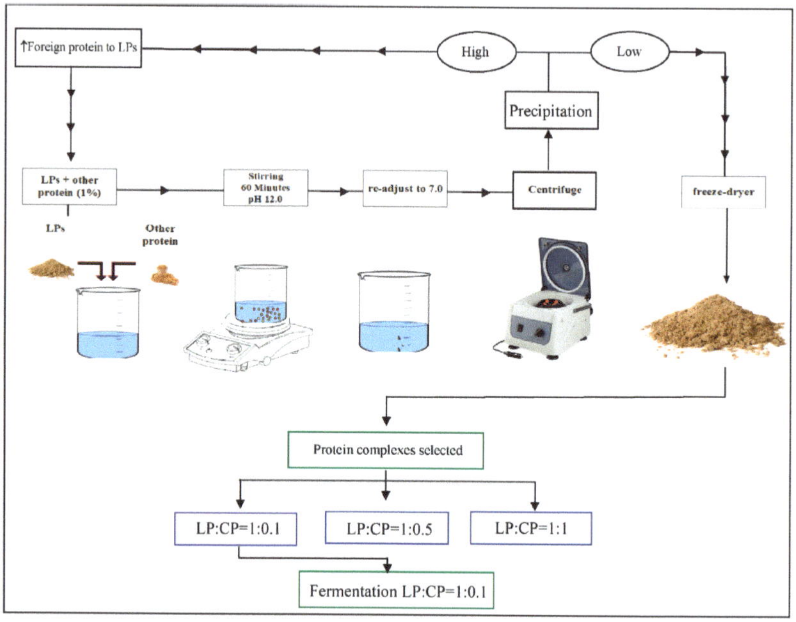

Figure 1. Schematic diagram of evaluation of fermentation treatment of lentil–casein protein complexes (LCPC) generated by structural interactions.

2.3. Water Solubility

The water solubility of protein was investigated using the methods described by Morr et al. [13]. The protein sample (200 mg) was mixed with distilled water (18 g), and then the pH was adjusted to pH 7.0 (using 0.1 M HCL or NaOH), followed by stirring at 1000 rpm for 60 min using the SH-4 stirrer. Ten minutes before the end of stirring, the weight of the protein solution was adjusted to 1% using distilled water. The Kjeldahl method [12] was used to determine the nitrogen content. The water solubility was calculated using Equation (1).

$$\text{Water solubility (\%)} = (N_S/N_T) \times 100 \quad (1)$$

where N_S is the amount of nitrogen in the supernatant and N_T is the amount of nitrogen in the sample before centrifugation.

2.4. Spectral Acquisition

2.4.1. Fourier-Transform Infrared Spectroscopy (FTIR)

The amide I group of LP, CP, and LCPC was determined using FTIR spectra, as described by Alrosan et al. [3]. The FTIR spectra (amide group I) were analyzed for β-sheets (at 1600–1639 cm^{-1}), random coils (RC) (at 1640–1649 cm^{-1}), α-helices (at 1650–1660 cm^{-1}), and β-turns (at 1661–1699 cm^{-1}).

2.4.2. Spectrofluorometry

The protein samples were prepared with distilled water at a ratio of 0.001% (*w*/*v*) and scanned using a fluorescence spectrophotometer (Agilent, Cary Eclipse, Santa Clara, CA, USA). The wavelengths of intrinsic fluorescence and excitation of spectra were set at a range of 300 to 450 nm and 280 nm, respectively. In addition, the bandwidths of emission and excitation were set at 10 nm.

2.4.3. Non-Covalent Forces

The contributions of hydrogen bonds, hydrophobic interactions, and electrostatic interactions were obtained according to Alrosan et al. [2]. First, 10 mM sodium dodecyl sulfate (SDS), thiourea, and NaCl were added separately to the protein suspension (1%, *w*/*v*) with the distilled water to determine the hydrophobic interactions, hydrogen bonding, and electrostatic interactions, respectively. Then, the pH was adjusted to 12.0 for 60 min, readjusted to 7.0, and the protein solution was scanned using the Cary Eclipse fluorescence spectrophotometer. The wavelengths of emission and excitation of spectra were set at a range of 300 to 450 nm and 280 nm, respectively. In addition, the bandwidths of emission and excitation were set at 10 nm.

2.4.4. Surface Hydrophobicity (H_0)

The surface hydrophobicity of protein samples (at different pH and ratios of LP:CP) was obtained according to the methods of Johnston et al. [14] with slight modifications. The procedure involved the addition of 100 mg of each protein sample to sodium phosphate (10 mM) in a beaker, followed by stirring on the SH-4 magnetic stirrer for 120 min at room temperature. Then, the calibration curve was prepared by diluting each protein solution from 0.1 to 0.01% (*w*/*v*). In a centrifuge tube, each serially diluted protein sample (4 mL), sodium phosphate (10 mM), and 8-anilino-1-naphthalene sulfonic acid (ANS; 20 μL, 8 mM) was added and then vortexed for 10 s. Finally, samples were transferred to a dark place for 15 min before injecting them. The emission and excitation wavelengths of the fluorescence spectra are 470 and 390 nm, respectively; the slit wavelength of emission and excitation was set at 1 nm. In addition, protein solutions of each concentration were prepared without ANS and blank ANS to calculate the fluorescence intensity (FI) of each calibration curve value concentration by subtracting it from the FI of each sample that contained ANS for all calibration curve values. The linear regression of FI for a sample against protein concentration was measured, which has been utilized as an indicator of the average H_0 of each protein sample.

2.4.5. Ultraviolet-Visible Spectroscopy

In this study, a UV-vis spectrophotometer (Shimadzu, UV-3600, Kyoto, Japan) was used to measure the unfolding and folding of proteins in control samples and protein complexes (different ratios of the protein complex and different pH values) between the wavelengths of 190 and 350 nm.

2.5. Zeta Potential

Zeta potential analyzer (Malvern Panalytical, Mastersizer 2000, Malvern, UK) was used to determine the surface charge of protein samples (0.05%, *w*/*v*) based on the procedure described by Johnston et al. [14]. The dispersant was distilled water with a refractive index of 1.330, while the protein sample had a refractive index of 1.450.

2.6. Scanning Electron Microscopy (SEM)

The surface morphology of protein samples was obtained based on the SEM (Leo Supra 50, Carl Zeiss, Oberkochen, Germany) under vacuum conditions (5–10 kV). Platinum layers (10 nm) were used to cover the metal substrates on which the protein powders were cast.

2.7. Preparation of Water Kefir

In brief, brown sugars (100 g) and kefir seeds (50 g) were combined with distilled water (1000 mL). The mixture was then fermented in a refrigerated incubator (Faithful, SPX-70 BIV, Shanghai, China) at 25 °C for 72 h. The mixture was shaken three times a day (every 8 h) during the incubation to keep the kefir seeds viable. Using a sterile sieve, the water kefir was isolated from the kefir seeds.

2.8. Preparation of Fermented Lentil–Casein Protein Complex

Lentil–casein protein complex at a ratio of 1.0:0.1 (LCPC 1.0:0.1) was selected to study the effects of water kefir-assisted fermentation on its pH, composition (sugars and phenolic compounds), protein quality (protein digestibility and secondary protein components), and microbiological qualities. The fermented protein mixture, consisting of LCPC 1.0:0.1 (1%, *w*/*v*), distilled water (95%), and water kefir (5%), was placed in a 250 mL flask and incubated for 5 days at 25 °C in the SPX-70 BIV refrigerated incubator. The mixture was shaken three times a day (every 8 h) during the incubation.

2.9. pH and Total Soluble Solids (TSS)

A pH meter (Apera Instruments, PH820, Columbus, OH, USA) and a digital refractometer (Hanna Instruments, HI96841, RI, USA) were used to determine the pH and TSS (expressed as °Brix) of the unfermented and fermented LCPC, respectively.

2.10. Protein Digestibility

The protein digestibility of unfermented and fermented LPCP was measured using the procedure used by Almeida et al. [15]. Fermented samples were collected every 24 ± 1 h. Samples (250 mg) and pepsin (1.5 mg/mL) were dispersed in HCl (15 mL, 0.1 M) before being heated at 37 °C for 3 h using a water bath (Memmert, WB22, Schwabach, Germany). To suppress microorganisms' growth in the protein, the mixtures were added with 1 mL of sodium azide (0.005 M) and 7.5 mL of NaOH (0.5 M). Pancreatin (10 mg) and 10 mL of phosphate buffer (0.2 M, pH 8.0) were added to the mixtures. Finally, the mixtures were incubated at 37 °C for 24 h. After the incubation, the mixtures were centrifuged at 10,000× *g* for 20 min using the CNME060222 centrifuge. The protein digestibility (expressed in %) of fermented and unfermented LPCP was determined based on the Kjeldahl method [12] and calculated according to Equation (2).

$$\text{Protein digestibility} = [(N_S - N_B)/N_T] \times 100\% \quad (2)$$

where N_T represents the nitrogen of the sample before centrifugation, N_B represents the nitrogen in the blank sample, and N_S represents the nitrogen in the supernatant of the sample after centrifugation.

2.11. Determination of the Nutrients of Fermented Protein Complexes

2.11.1. Phenolic Compounds

Phenolic compounds, such as catechin, sinapic acid, chlorogenic acid, quercetin, rutin, caffeic acid, gallic acid, epicatechin, ferulic acid, and ferulic acid, in the unfermented and fermented LCPC were measured based on the procedure by Alrosan et al. [3]. In brief, protein dispersions (1 mL) blended with methanol (8 mL) were prepared. The mixtures were then sonicated (Elma Electronic, EP10H, Hamburg, Germany) for 3 min at 35 °C. After sonication, the mixtures were kept at 4 °C until the residues turned white. Then, the mixtures were centrifuged at 10,000× *g* for 15 min using the CNME060222 centrifuge. The supernatants collected were filtered using a syringe filter (0.22 µm) before HPLC analysis. Sample preparation was carried out in a dark environment.

The phenolic components were analyzed using HPLC (Agilent, 1200 series, East Brunswick, NJ, USA) based on a Plus C18 column (4.6 mm × 250 mm) to separate the phenolic compounds with flow rate (0.7 mL/min) and injection volution (40 µL). Acetonitrile was used as mobile phase A, and acetic acid (1%) in distilled water was used as mobile phase B. The profile setting of HPLC was 95% mobile phase A (0 to 24 min), 85% mobile phase A (25 to 41 min), 78% mobile phase A (42 to 60 min), and 95% mobile phase A (65 min). Phenolic compounds were measured at two different wavelengths, 254 and 272 nm.

2.11.2. Total Phenolic Content (TPC) and Total Saponin Content (TSC)

A UV-3600 UV-vis spectrophotometer was used to read the TPC of unfermented and fermented LCPC based on the procedure of Alrosan et al. [3]. every 24 h for 5 days. Protein samples (100 μL) were combined with Folin–Ciocalteu reagent (500 μL) and distilled water (8.4 mL) in test tubes, followed by a 4 min vortex. Then, 1 mL of sodium carbonate (5%) was added, followed by the mixtures and vortex for another 4 min. The mixtures were kept in the dark for 1 h. The absorbance of the samples was read at 725 nm. The TPC was expressed as mg of gallic acid equivalent per 100 g (mg GAE/100 g).

The TSC content was measured using the UV-3600 UV-vis spectrophotometer based on the procedure by Alrosan et al. [3]. In brief, protein samples were mixed with (400 μL), perchloric acid (800 μL), and vanillin–glacial acetic acid (5%, 200 μL) in glass tubes and then heated in a water bath at 70 °C for 15 min. The heated mixtures were then cooled in an ice bath. After cooling, 500 μL of glacial acetic acid was added. The absorbance of the samples was read at wavelength 546 nm. The calibration curve range was between 6.25 to 600 μg/mL, using oleanolic acid as a reference. TSC was expressed as mg of oleanolic acid per 100 g (mg OAE/100 g).

2.11.3. Determination of Sugars

The glucose, sucrose, and fructose contents in the unfermented and fermented LCPC were measured using the Agilent 1200 series HPLC based on Alrosan et al. [3]. Samples (1 mL) were mixed with distilled water (1 mL) and vortexed for 10 min before centrifugation (Kubota, S700TR, Tokyo, Japan) at 15,000× *g* for 10 min. The supernatants were filtered using syringe filters (0.45 m). These simple sugars were separated using a Cosmosil Sugar-D column (4.6 mm × 250 mm) at 40 °C. A mixture of acetonitrile and distilled water (3:1, *v/v*) was used as the mobile phase. The injection volume and flow rate were set at 20 μL and 1.2 mL/min, respectively.

2.12. *Microbiological Quality*

Enumeration of yeasts, lactic acid bacteria (LAB), and acetic acid bacteria (AAB) in the unfermented and fermented protein complexes was performed using the spread plate method. Each sample was diluted step by step, and 1 mL of each dilution was used to infect a solid medium by spreading it twice. Potato dextrose agar (PDA) under aerobic conditions at 25 °C for 48 h was used to determine the yeasts content, while MRS agar at 37 °C for 24 h under anaerobic conditions was used to determine the LAB and AAB contents, respectively.

2.13. *Statistical Analysis*

The data analysis was conducted using SPSS program version 23.0 (Chicago, IL, USA). Duncan's multiple range test and one-way ANOVA were used; differences were considered significant at $p < 0.05$.

3. Results and Discussion

3.1. *Solubility of Lentil–Casein Protein Complexes (LCPC)*

The fundamental limitation of applying LP in the food sector is its low solubility in water. The first purpose of this research was to generate soluble protein complexes based on LP through protein complexation with CP. After the complexation of LP (90%) with CP (10%), the solubility of the LCPC jumped to over 86.5%. The water solubility of the control sample was ~68.6% and continued to increase to over 91.4% when the proportion of CP in the protein complexes was increased to 50%. Upon exceeding 50%, the addition of more CP resulted in an insignificant increase ($p > 0.05$) in the water solubility of the LCPC (Figure 2A). Meanwhile, when the proportion of CP in the LCPC was less than 10%, the complexes formed were mostly precipitated. They could be seen visually even before centrifugation. Consequently, LCPC comprising <10% and >50% CP was omitted from this study.

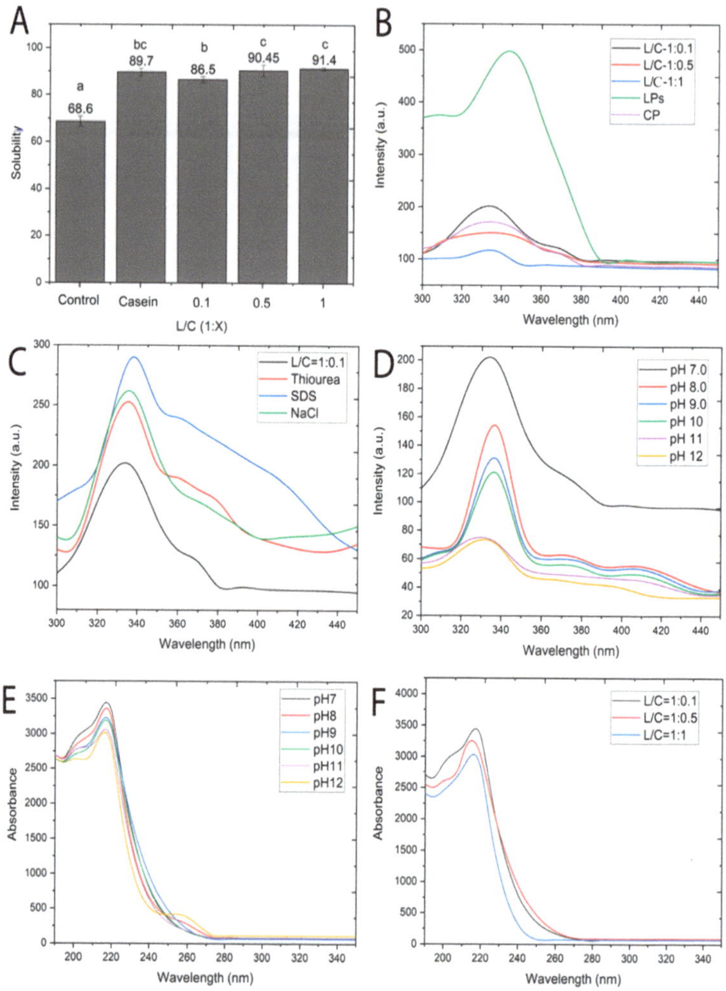

Figure 2. Spectroscopic analysis of structural interactions. (**A**) Evaluation of the nitrogen solubility index of lentil proteins (LP) and lentil–casein protein complexes (LCPC) with various proportions. (**B**) Fluorescence absorption of LP with various LP to casein proteins (CP) at pH 7. The small picture represents the absorption spectra of LCPC with various LP:CP ratios at pH 7. (**C**) Fluorescence intensity spectrum of LCPC at a ratio of 1.0:0.1 (LCPC 1.0:0.1) at various pH levels (pH 7 to 12). (**D**) Fluorescence intensity spectrum of LCPC 1.0:0.1 in the presence of foreign compounds. (**E**) The ultraviolet-visible wavelength description of LCPC 1.0:0.1 at pH levels ranging from 7 to 12. (**F**) Profiles of the ultraviolet-visible spectra of LCPC 1.0:0.1 at pH 7. Bars with different letters differ significantly ($p < 0.05$).

3.2. LP and CP Interaction

CPs have been utilized as co-proteins to increase the solubility of plant-based proteins, such as rice proteins, soya proteins, and LPs, through PPI [4]. The generation of a new protein structure was demonstrated by analyzing the protein structure of protein complexes. The emission and excitation of tryptophan residues in protein complexes at 340 and 280 nm, respectively, was used to acquire spectra to quantify the interactions between the proteins. The fluorescence spectra of the LP show that the maximum peak intensity (F_{max}) was at emission and excitation wavelengths of 340 and 280 nm, respectively. After LP interacted with CP, the spectrophotometric intensity was reduced (Figure 2B). The spectrophotometric intensity of LCPC decreased following protein complexation with increasing proportions of CP. PPI has been proven to decrease the fluorescence intensity of protein structure formation [6]. Therefore, the emission shift after the LP with CP interaction shows the existence of protein interactions in the development of protein complexes. The fluorescence intensity of protein complexes dropping to less than that of the control sample could be due to electrons being transmitted to electron-deficient groups from electron-rich aromatic amino groups [4,6].

Furthermore, observations using FTIR spectroscopy revealed a change in the components of the secondary protein structure of the LCPC (Table 1). Protein complexation between LP and CP was demonstrated in this study. Molecular forces are vital in binding proteins, and understanding the molecular forces involved in forming protein complexes is of much interest in this study. The protein solution contained foreign components, such as NaCl, SDS, and thiourea, to measure the contributions of the electrostatic forces, hydrophobic forces, and hydrogen bonds, respectively. As a result, of the interplay, the stabilization of the structure improved the fluorescence (Figure 2C). These results suggest that these foreign compounds facilitated interconnections between LP and CP and, at the same time, controlled hydrogen bonds and electrostatic and hydrophobic interactions. The F_{max} of the enriched protein complex suspension decreased in the order of SDS > NaCl > thiourea. The F_{max} was at a maximum for LCPC containing SDS. Thus, hydrophobic bonds, electrostatic forces and hydrogen bonds significantly impact the interaction between the complexation of LP with CP. Hence, it can be hypothesized that protein complexes are affected by hydrogen bonds, as well as electrostatic and hydrophobic bonds, to a lesser extent.

Table 1. Evaluation of the proportion of secondary protein components of lentil proteins (LP), casein proteins (CP) and lentil–casein protein complexes (LCPC).

Secondary Protein Components	Peak (cm^{-1})	Protein Samples					p-Value
		LP	CP	LCPC 1.0:0.1	LCPC 1.0:0.5	LCPC 1:1	
β-Sheet							
	1614.42	9.07	13.23	11.30	12.09	12.28	
	1622.13	7.65	8.00	8.54	8.81	9.06	
	1633.71	11.04	10.75	11.60	11.82	12.07	
β-Sheet (Σ)		27.76 ^{a}	31.97 ^{a}	31.44 ^{a}	32.72 ^{a}	33.40 ^{a}	>0.05
Random coils	1645.28	15.78 ^{d}	16.00 ^{e}	15.04 ^{b}	14.88 ^{a}	15.16 ^{c}	<0.05
α-Helix	1654.07	18.48 ^{d}	13.48 ^{c}	9.76 ^{b}	9.48 ^{a}	9.30 ^{a}	<0.05
β-Turn							
	1668.43	10.42	8.18	12.31	11.61	11.55	
	1681.93	11.11	13.82	11.10	10.79	10.74	
	1693.50	16.45	16.55	20.34	20.52	19.84	
β-Turn (Σ)		37.98 ^{a}	38.55 ^{a}	43.75 ^{a}	42.91 ^{a}	42.13 ^{a}	>0.05

Means (n = 3) with different superscripts in the same row differ significantly ($p < 0.05$). LCPC 1:0.1, LCPC 1:0.5, and LCPC 1:1 represent lentil–casein protein complexes at a ratio of 1:0.1, 1:0.5, and 1:1, respectively.

3.3. Structural Folding of Protein Complexes

The fluorescence spectrum of protein complexes can reveal information about their structural microenvironment. An alteration in the novel protein complex structure (especially tertiary structure) between LP and CP might be represented using fluorescence emission with excitation of tryptophan residues at 280 nm [16]. Usually, the tryptophan residues present in non-polar environments of proteins have a maximum emission (F_{max}) of <330 nm. LCPC 1.0:0.1 remained neutral in an alkaline environment (above pH 11) (Figure 2D). The results showed that tryptophan could be exposed to solvents disregarding the pH variations. These outcomes are determined by the level of binding between both proteins [4,8]. The fluorescence intensity gradually increased as the protein solution readjusted the pH to 7.0 (Figure 2D). The proteins, however, were reconstituted into relatively high structures of novel LCPC [2,4,8]. The increased co-compounds in the protein complexes formed resulted in a decrease in the F_{max} [4–6]. In addition, PPI reduced fluorescence intensity as the ratio of CP in protein complexes increased (Figure 2B).

Protein complexes made of LP and CP exhibited significant ($p < 0.05$) modification, especially for α-helices and RC (Table 1). Protein interfaces and multilayer interfaces depend on their α-helix components, which are dependent on molecular forces between the component of secondary protein structures [4,17]. Tomczyńska-Mleko et al. [18] explained that in the association between solution pH and the α-helix component of whey protein isolate, pH plays a major role in the increased unfolding and surface activity of proteins and decreases their α-helix components. The amount of α-helix components decreased after complexation between LP and CP, decreasing with increasing ratio of CP in the protein complexes. The percentage of β-sheets and β-turns made up of amino acid residues for each component is approximately two-thirds. The β-turns and β-sheets presented no significant differences ($p > 0.05$) after complexation with CP (Table 1), suggesting that the β-structure could be amphipathic, changing hydrophobic and hydrophilic residues that produce hydrophobic and hydrophilic subunits, respectively.

UV spectra can detect protein conformations of protein complexes. The high degree of folding in protein structures has a reciprocal association with an increase in the absorbance at 230 nm (A_{230}) [2,4–6], whereby the A_{230} increased with decreasing pH value of the protein suspension, indicating that the protein structure had been successfully refolded (Figure 2E). The reconstruction of LCPC might be enabled by decreasing the A_{230} for pH recycling (from pH 12 to 7), whereas A_{230} of all LCPC increased on neutralization of the protein solution (decreasing in the pH of the protein solution), as observed in Figure 2E. The most significant development happened whenever the pH was reduced from pH 8 to 7, since the structure around these pH values was responsible for the most refolding. Consequently, incorporating CP rendered the LP robust to refolding (Figure 2F).

With an increase in the proportion of CP, the extent of the tertiary structure of protein complexes decreases when the pH reaches 7.0. Due to the contribution of various synergistic effects, e.g., structural interaction between LP and CP occurring during the protein complexation, which varies depending on secondary protein structural components and tertiary structure, the protein complexation was not even begun by layering CP on the surface of LP. Synergistic interactions or PPIs result in the generation of a more consistent structure with each protein separately [2,6].

The mechanisms of PPI between LP and CP by structural interactions are illustrated in Figure 3. Negatively charged sites in proteins react electrostatically, removing all protons from the surface of proteins, resulting in restriction of some of the molecular forces, such as hydrophobic and ionic interactions in an alkaline environment [2,4]. Under the neutral pH of the protein solution, molecular forces, such as hydrophobic and electrostatic interactions and hydrogen bonds, were active during neutralization. Based on our findings, these molecular forces significantly affect the formation of protein complexes made of LP and CP.

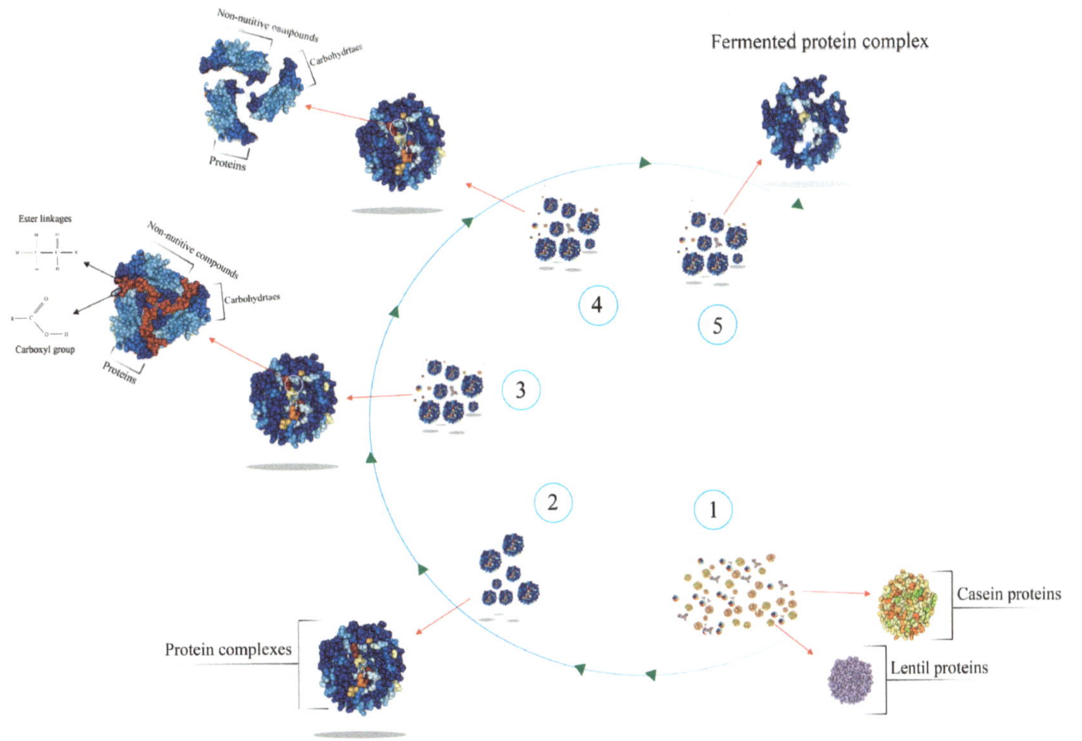

Figure 3. Schematic diagram of the mechanism of dual technology (based on protein–protein interaction and fermentation) to generate lentil–casein protein complexes (LCPC) with improved nutrition and protein functionalities. (1) The protein solution (1% *w*/*v*) contains lentil proteins (LP) and casein proteins (CP) at a ratio of 1:0.1 in distilled water. The pH of the protein solution was adjusted to 12 for 60 min, then was readjusted to 7.0. (2) Soluble protein composites with novel protein structures were formed based on the structural interaction of lentil proteins and casein. (3) Fermentation was performed for 5 days at 25 °C with a protein complex of (1%, *w*/*v*), water kefir (5%, *v*/*v*), and distilled water (95%, *v*/*v*). (4) microorganism that synthesizes enzymes capable of breaking ester links and consequently releases free soluble phenols. (5) Fermented protein complexes have high digestibility, nutritional value, and soluble proteins.

3.4. Surface Morphology of LCPC

The surface morphology of the LP was significantly aggregated, resulting in extensive particle morphologies (Figure 4A), while the microstructures of the CP were notably smaller and more distinct, comparable to silt, with no definite angular edges (Figure 4B). Surprisingly, after protein complexation between LP and CP, the formed LCPC had their self-aggregation diminished, and they exhibited a smooth surface morphology. The addition of 10% CP to LP resulted in the formation of LCPC, which were compounds with many cube-shaped molecules and sharp edges. Meanwhile, when the proportion of CP reached 33%, it formed polygons with somewhat varying particle diameters between the protein complexes.

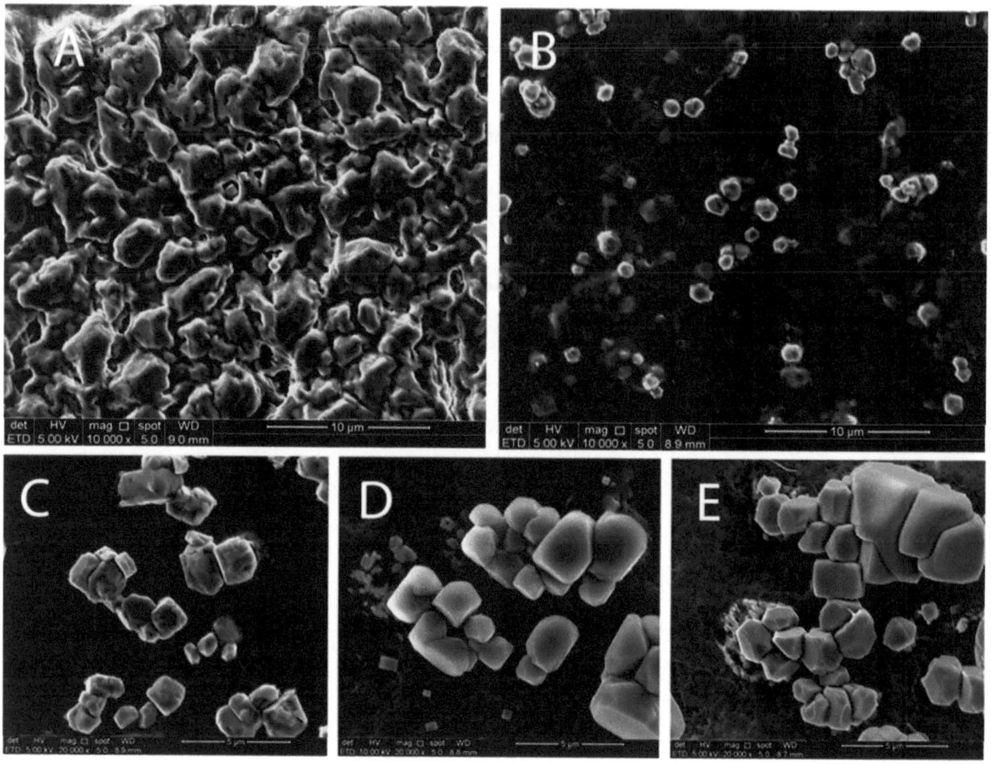

Figure 4. Morphology of the surface of (**A**) lentil proteins (LP), (**B**) casein proteins (CP), and lentil–casein protein complexes (LCPC) with various LP:CP ratios; (**C**) LCPC 1.0:0.1, (**D**) LCPC 1.0:0.5, and (**E**) LCPC 1:1.

The surface morphology of LP, CP, and LCPC differed, indicating the protein interaction of the individual proteins, i.e., LP and CP. Consequently, surface morphological alterations were caused by adding CP to create LCPC, thus affecting their water solubility. These modifications include the reduction in aggregation between independent components and effects on the surface morphology of LCPC. Consequently, the complexation between LP and CP occurred in the formation of LCPC, which was further studied better understand the protein complexation mechanism.

3.5. *Protein Interfacial Characteristics Resulting from Protein Complexation*

Because of the polymeric nature of proteins, surface hydrophobicity has a greater impact on their functional characteristics than their hydrophobicity. Protein aggregation, adsorption behavior, physical stability, and solubility are all influenced by the surface hydrophobicity of the protein [2,8]. Fluorescent dyes are useful in determining the degree of protein denaturation and surface hydrophobicity. Acidification improved the surface hydrophobicity of novel LCPC (Figure 5A). The main reason for the rise in hydrophobic groups was that the co-folded protein molecules enabled non-polar groups to create hydrophobic caverns accessible to the ANS probes. The zeta potential increased with pH (Figure 5C), indicating that most loaded units remained at the interfaces of the newly synthesized LCPC.

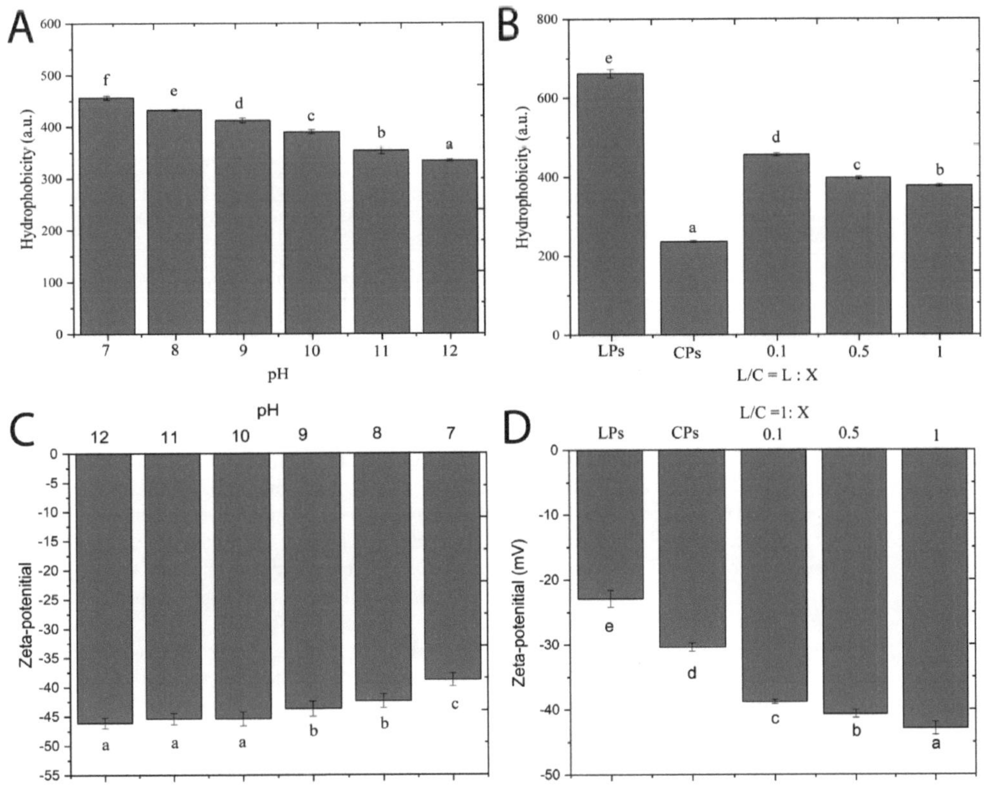

Figure 5. Surface characteristics of lentil proteins (LP) and lentil-casein protein complexes (LCPC). (**A**) Surface hydrophobicity (H_o) of LCPC 1.0:0.1 at a range of pH 7 to 12. (**B**) H_o of LP, CP, and LCPC at pH 7. (**C**) Zeta potential of LPCP 1.0:0.1 at a range of pH 7 to 12. (**D**) Zeta potential of LP, CP, and LCPC at various LP:CP ratios. Different letters indicate statistically significant differences ($p < 0.05$).

In general, an increased ratio of CP in LCPC resulted in a decrease in surface hydrophobicity (Figure 5B). We discovered that the zeta potential decreased in the same way, although to a considerably lower percentage than hydrophobicity (Figure 5C). The increased surface charge of LCPC was attributed to the increased complexation between LP and CP due to an increase in the proportion of CP. The aggregation and dispersion of proteins are strongly influenced by their surface charge [19].

The surface charge of the control sample was around ~22.1 mV. The increased charges on the surface of proteins resulted in appropriate electrostatic repulsions, resulting in increased stabilization and resistance to aggregation of protein complexes after PPI. Consequently, the LCPC formed is more stable, indicating the presence of enough self-repulsive externals in the protein complexation.

3.6. *Effects of Water Kefir-Assisted Fermentation on the pH and TSS of Fermented Lentil–Casein Protein Complex at a Ratio of 1.0:0.1 (LCPC 1.0:0.1)*

Throughout the water kefir-assisted fermentation, the pH and TSS of the fermented samples declined significantly ($p < 0.05$) (Table 2). The pH of the fermented LCPC 1.0:0.1 decreased significantly ($p < 0.05$) from 7.09 ± 0.03 to 34.04 ± 0.05 on Day 2. Finally, the pH value reached 3.83 ± 0.01 on Day 5. These findings suggest that the release of ammonium (NH_4^+) and amino acids is resulted from the protein hydrolysis by LAB, AAB, and yeast during the kefir fermentation [20].

Table 2. Evaluation of the pH, total soluble solids (TSS, Brix), protein digestibility (%), total saponin content (TSC, mg of oleanolic acid per 100 g), and sugar profile (g/L) of the unfermented and fermented lentil–casein protein complex at a ratio of 1.0:0.1 (LCPC 1.0:0.1).

	Fermentation Period						p-Value
	Day 0	Day 1	Day 2	Day 3	Day 4	Day 5	
pH	7.09 ± 0.03 [a]	4.53 ± 0.03 [b]	4.04 ± 0.05 [c]	3.94 ± 0.01 [d]	3.89 ± 0.01 [e]	3.83 ± 0.01 [f]	<0.05
TSS	2.13 ± 0.05 [a]	1.40 ± 0.00 [b]	1.30 ± 0.00 [c]	1.20 ± 0.00 [d]	1.20 ± 0.00 [d]	1.10 ± 0.00 [e]	<0.05
Protein digestibility	79.53 ± 0.43 [b]	80.60 ± 0.79 [b]	84.42 ± 1.47 [a]	85.33 ± 0.88 [a]	86.39 ± 1.80 [a]	86.79 ± 0.43 [a]	<0.05
TSC	46.20 ± 0.05 [a]	45.30 ± 1.11 [a]	41.23 ± 0.60 [b]	38.50 ± 0.51 [c]	37.93 ± 0.64 [cd]	37.13 ± 0.92 [d]	<0.05
Sugars							
Fructose	0.59 ± 0.02 [c]	2.43 ± 0.09 [a]	1.11 ± 0.04 [b]	0.50 ± 0.02 [d]	0.24 ± 0.01 [e]	0.07 ± 0.01 [f]	<0.05
Glucose	ND	1.24 ± 0.02 [b]	2.72 ± 0.04 [a]	1.05 ± 0.02 [c]	0.42 ± 0.01 [b]	0.20 ± 0.00 [a]	<0.05
Sucrose	5.41 ± 0.14 [a]	1.06 ± 0.02 [b]	0.14 ± 0.01 [c]	0.07 ± 0.00 [cd]	ND	ND	<0.05

Data represent the mean ± standard deviation (n = 3). Means with different superscripts in the same row differ significantly ($p < 0.05$). ND: not detected.

Furthermore, the drop in pH throughout the fermentation period and the production of lactic acid could be due to the accumulation of lactic acid caused by microbial activity [3,10,21,22]. These results are in agreement with the findings reported by Tu et al. [23], Azi et al. [9], and Jia et al. [22], whereby *Lactobacillus* spp. are responsible for the reduction in the pH solution during the fermentation. During the water kefir-assisted fermentation, there were significant variations ($p < 0.05$) in the pH during the last 3 days.

The TTS of the fermented LCPC 1.0:0.1 decreased significantly ($p < 0.05$) during the water kefir-assisted fermentation, reducing from 2.13 ± 0.05 to 1.10 ± 0.00 °Brix. These results refer to the microbial activity of LAB, AAB, and yeasts during fermentation. Comparably, Tu et al. [23] showed that the TSS of whey-soy reduced significantly during the first 2 days of kefir fermentation, from 9.20 to 4.43 °Brix after 5 days. Furthermore, dos Santos et al. [24] also reported that the TSS of soymilk dropped from 1.88 to 1.45 °Brix during 5 days of kefir fermentation at 25 °C.

3.7. *Effects of Water Kefir-Assisted Fermentation on the Protein Quality of Fermented LCPC 1.0:0.1*

3.7.1. Protein Digestibility

The nutritional value of protein depends on the digestibility and bioavailability of the protein. In this research, the protein digestibility of the unfermented LCPC 1.0:0.1 was ~79.53% (Table 2). Throughout the water kefir-assisted fermentation, the protein digestibility of fermented protein complexes significantly increased ($p < 0.05$) to ~86.79% on Day 5 of the fermentation. The protein digestibility of fermented LCPC 1.0:0.1 increased due to the presence of yeasts (*Kluyveromyces*, *Candida*, and *Saccharomyces*), LAB (*Lactobacillus*, *Streptococcus*, *Leuconostoc*, and *Lactococcus*), and AAB [3,9,10,23] in the water kefir. Pranoto et al. [25] reported that the protein digestibility of sorghum flour increased from 40 to 80% after fermentation with *Lactobacillus plantarum*. In another study, by Chandra-Hioe et al. [11], the protein digestibility of lyophilized yogurt fermented with cultures (*Streptococcus bulgaricus* and *Lactobacillus*) increased from 70.5 to over 77.2%.

There were no significant differences ($p > 0.05$) in protein digestibility of the fermented LCPC 1.0:0.1 during the first 2 days of water kefir-assisted fermentation (Table 2). This insignificance could be due to the decrease in the protein cross-linking and amount of micronutrient compounds, such as phenolic acids, saponins, and tannins [11,21]. On the other hand, Pranoto et al. [25] reported that *L. plantarum* could hydrolyze proteins into smaller fragments (e.g., peptides) and amino acids during the kefir fermentation, thus resulting in partially digestible proteins. In addition, *Lactobacillus* has also been attributed to the hydrolysis of proteins due to cell-envelope proteinase activity during kefir fermentation [7,26]. Jia et al. [22] reported that fermentation could release small protein fragments into ovomucoid and ovalbumin because of peptide bond breakdown. Furthermore, these results are in agreement with Çabuk et al. [21] and Ayala-Nino et al. [27], whereby the protein digestibility increased after *Lactobacillus* fermentation.

3.7.2. Secondary Protein Structure

It was reported by Carbonaro et al. [28] that increasing the proportion of amid group II (1600 and 1039 cm^{-1}) reduced the protein digestibility. The components of the secondary protein structure of unfermented LCPC 1.0:0.1; β-turns (43.87%), β-sheets (30.90%), random coil (RC, 15.32%), and α-helices (9.90%), were determined in this study (Table 3). The proportions of β-turns and β-sheets were not significantly different ($p > 0.05$) throughout the water kefir-assisted fermentation. In contrast, significant changes ($p < 0.05$) were observed for the ratio of α-helices and RC components. In this study, the percentage of α-helices in the fermented LCPC 1.0:0.1 decreased significantly ($p < 0.05$) from 9.90 to 6.58%, with a greater reduction in the first 24 h of the 5 days of water kefir-assisted fermentation. A drop in the proportion of α-helices in protein indicates the improvement of protein digestibility [29].

Table 3. Evaluation of the proportion of secondary protein components of the unfermented and fermented lentil–casein protein complex at a ratio of 1.0:0.1 (LCPC 1.0:0.1).

Secondary Protein Components	Peak (cm^{-1})	Fermentation Period						*p*-Value
		Day 0	Day 1	Day 2	Day 3	Day 4	Day 5	
β-Sheet								
	1614.42	8.51	11.30	11.48	11.50	11.28	11.25	
	1622.13	11.58	8.91	8.98	9.06	8.88	8.83	
	1633.71	15.32	11.76	11.85	11.80	11.51	11.58	
β-Sheet (Σ)		30.90 ^{a}	31.97 ^{a}	32.31 ^{a}	32.34 ^{a}	31.67 ^{a}	31.66 ^{a}	>0.05
RC (Σ)	1645.28	15.32 ^{f}	15.83 ^{e}	17.65 ^{d}	18.85 ^{c}	20.43 ^{b}	21.67 ^{a}	<0.05
α-Helix (Σ)	1654.07	9.90 ^{a}	9.71 ^{b}	7.71 ^{c}	7.63 ^{d}	7.25 ^{e}	6.58 ^{f}	<0.05
β-Turn								
	1668.43	12.29	12.41	13.23	13.38	13.03	13.51	
	1681.93	11.35	11.73	12.69	12.85	12.70	11.21	
	1693.50	20.24	18.33	16.40	14.94	14.90	15.3	
β-Turn (Σ)		43.87 ^{a}	42.47 ^{a}	42.32 ^{a}	41.17 ^{a}	40.63 ^{a}	40.07 ^{a}	>0.05
Ratio (α-helix:β-sheet)		32.04	30.38	23.87	23.58	22.90	20.81	

Means (n = 3) with different superscripts in the same row differ significantly ($p < 0.05$).

Another change in one of the secondary protein structure components, i.e., RC, was observed during the water kefir-assisted fermentation on LCPC 1.0:0.1, whereby a significant increase ($p < 0.05$) in the RC was recorded, from 15.32 to 21.67%. This upward trend suggests that the fermented LCPC 1.0:0.1 had accumulated. These outcomes are consistent with the current findings, whereby a rise in the RC proportion is paired with a decrease in the α-helix proportion. The degree of protein restructuring in this study was larger than in a past investigation by Wang et al. [29]. As a result, it is hypothesized that the effects of LAB, AAB, and yeast on the structure of fermented LCPC are much more beneficial than those of thermal or pressure treatments, such as extrusion, frying and pelleting.

Various previous investigations have revealed that microbes fermenting has a major impact on the α-helix proportion and the RC proportion of fermented protein [3,10,30]. These modifications are remarkable and advantageous for enhancing fermented protein functionality [30]. Consequently, our results showed that fermented proteins have improved protein quality. A previous study by Salazar-Villanea et al. [30] showed that increased protein digestibility is associated with a decrease in the α-helix-to-β-sheet ratio. The α-helix-to-β-sheet ratio declined from 32.04 to 23.87% on Day 2 of the water kefir-assisted fermentation and remained at this value (Table 3).

3.8. Effects of Water Kefir-Assisted Fermentation on the Nutrients of Fermented LCPC 1.0:0.1

3.8.1. Phenolic Compounds

Saponins and phenolic compounds have been reported to have an adverse effect on protein digestibility [10]. Some of these phenolic compounds can link with macronutrients, such as carbohydrate and protein molecules, which could hinder enzymatic hydrolysis on these macromolecules. The TPC of fermented LCPC 1.0:0.1 increased significantly ($p < 0.05$) after the fermentation, to 458.33 ± 11.51 mg GAE/100 g on Day 3, and then decreased significantly ($p < 0.05$) during the last 3 days (Table 4). This increase might be attributed to the dissociation of bound phenols [31]; by microbial fermentation [10]. These results are consistent with the conditions reported by Azi et al. [9] and Tu et al. [23], whereby some phenolic compounds were reduced during the kefir fermentation. In another study, by Adebo et al. [32], *Lactobacillus* strains significantly reduced phenolic compounds.

Table 4. Evaluation of total phenolic content (TPC, mg GAE/100 g) and phenolic compounds (mg/100 g) during water kefir-assisted fermentation of lentil–casein protein complex at a ratio of 1.0:0.1 (LCPC 1.0:0.1).

	Fermentation Period [Day]						p-Value
	0	1	2	3	4	5	
TPC	394.46 ± 3.72 ^{d}	516.83 ± 8.95 ^{b}	624.88 ± 7.23 ^{a}	458.33 ± 11.51 ^{c}	411.17 ± 11.74 ^{d}	405.80 ± 14.21 ^{d}	<0.05
Phenolic Compounds							
Catechin	34.03 ± 0.48 ^{f}	61.90 ± 0.54 ^{b}	63.08 ± 0.77 ^{a}	59.53 ± 0.21 ^{c}	56.49 ± 0.14 ^{d}	51.74 ± 0.39 ^{e}	<0.05
Chlorogenic	84.93 ± 0.98 ^{e}	89.61 ± 0.76 ^{bc}	105.03 ± 0.42 ^{a}	90.62 ± 0.29 ^{b}	88.45 ± 1.11 ^{cd}	87.34 ± 0.76 ^{d}	<0.05
Epicatechin	106.85 ± 0.54 ^{f}	127.87 ± 0.57 ^{b}	157.55 ± 0.87 ^{a}	122.05 ± 0.67 ^{a}	116.31 ± 0.25 ^{d}	112.33 ± 0.28 ^{e}	<0.05
Quercetin	14.05 ± 0.68 ^{c}	14.16 ± 0.44 ^{c}	15.07 ± 0.18 ^{c}	14.55 ± 0.56 ^{bc}	16.05 ± 0.34 ^{a}	3.04 ± 0.10 ^{d}	<0.05
Rutin	2.43 ± 0.05 ^{c}	1.90 ± 0.08 ^{d}	2.27 ± 0.04 ^{cd}	4.50 ± 0.23 ^{a}	4.37 ± 0.07 ^{a}	3.69 ± 0.49 ^{b}	<0.05
Caffeic acid	ND	ND	ND	ND	4.10 ± 0.05 ^{b}	5.29 ± 0.04 ^{a}	<0.05
Ferulic acid	3.77 ± 0.05 ^{b}	3.86 ± 0.07 ^{a}	4.14 ± 0.04 ^{a}	4.04 ± 0.04 ^{a}	3.83 ± 0.11 ^{b}	3.81 ± 0.08 ^{b}	<0.05
Gallic acid	11.76 ± 0.90 ^{e}	19.44 ± 0.43 ^{b}	20.51 ± 0.39 ^{b}	27.67 ± 0.59 ^{a}	15.85 ± 0.84 ^{c}	14.02 ± 0.44 ^{d}	<0.05
Sinapic acid	0.00	1.61 ± 0.04 ^{ab}	1.41 ± 0.11 ^{a}	1.15 ± 0.03 ^{ab}	1.00 ± 0.03 ^{ab}	0.90 ± 0.02 ^{b}	<0.05
Synergic acid	46.90 ± 0.97 ^{b}	46.96 ± 0.51 ^{b}	50.27 ± 0.48 ^{a}	47.60 ± 0.87 ^{b}	47.45 ± 1.16 ^{b}	47.28 ± 2.50 ^{b}	<0.05
Phenolic Compounds (Σ)	304.71 ^{f}	367.30 ^{c}	419.33 ^{a}	371.72 ^{b}	353.88 ^{d}	329.46 ^{e}	<0.05

Data represent the mean ± standard deviation (n = 3). Means with different superscript letters within the same row are significantly different from each other ($p < 0.05$). ND: not detected.

Rutin, caffeic acid, quercetin, catechin, chlorogenic, epicatechin, sinapic acid, gallic acid, ferulic acid, and syringic acid were among the phenolic compounds determined in the fermented proteins during the water kefir-assisted fermentation (Table 4). All phenolic compounds increased during the fermentation period. The level of catechin, gallic acid, and quercetin rise with increasing the fermentation period. Adebo and Gabriela Medina-Meza [32] observed a rise in phenolic compounds during fermentation. Caffeic acid was detected on Day 3 of the fermentation, producing a high level of phenolic compounds on Day 3. Furthermore, rutin levels dropped from 2.43 ± 0.05 to 1.90 ± 0.08 mg/100 g on Day 1 and then increased to 4.50 ± 0.23 mg/100 g on Day 3. The reduction in phenolic compounds could be attributed to the *Lactobacillus* strains, which can degrade and hydrolyze phenolic compounds [32]. Phenolic compounds can form linkages with carbohydrates and proteins in nature, leading to the formation of more complex compounds and phenolics that are less soluble. These phenolics are connected with ester linkages through the hydroxyl groups of proteins and the carboxylic groups of carbohydrates [3]. In this study, the findings show that phenolic compounds significantly increased ($p < 0.05$) in the fermented LCPC 1.0:0.1 compared to in the unfermented sample (Day 0).

3.8.2. Total Saponin Content (TSC)

The saponins found in the outer layers of cereals and legumes give them a bitter taste that may have anti-nutritional implications, resulting in lower acceptability [10]. Saponins are a complicated group of compounds with constructions with a carbohydrate molecule connected to a steroid or triterpenoid aglycone [33]. Because of their toxicity and hemolytic behavior, these phytochemicals have traditionally been recognized as unacceptable. Saponins are responsible for the bitterness and astringency of grains [34]. Del Hierro et al. [35] discovered that lentils contain 110–1269 mg/kg saponins. In this study, the TSC in LCPC 1.0:0.1 was around 74.52 ± 0.35 mg OAE/100 g. Chan et al. [36] reported that the TSC in samples depends on the extraction solvent, which could be due to the different polarities of the extraction solvent.

In this study, TSC was present in LCPC 1.0:0.1 during water kefir-assisted fermentation (Table 2). After fermentation, the TSC of protein complexes dropped significantly ($p < 0.05$), from 46.20 ± 0.05 to 41.23 ± 0.60 mg OAE/100 g on Day 2, and reached 37.13 ± 0.92 mg OAE/100 g on Day 5. The decrease in TSC might be attributed to the degradation of saponins connected with protein or carbohydrate molecules through fermentation. These discoveries are consistent with several investigations showing that these micronutrients decrease during fermentation [9,23].

Similarly, Lai et al. [37] showed that fermentation with LAB could decrease the TSC by around 46% in fermented soy. Past studies have reported that fermentation with *Bacillus* spp. or fungal cultures, such as *Rhizopus stolonifer* or *Aspergillus oryzae*, could result in the cleavage of saponins that are cross-linked with macronutrients, such as carbohydrates and proteins [3]. Such cleavage has been reported to enhance protein digestibility.

3.8.3. Sugars

Brown sugar has typically been widely utilized to enhance kefir seeds' functional activity [3,9,10,23]. Fructose, glucose, and sucrose are the main components of brown sugar, accounting for ~85% of the brown sugar composition [24]. The concentrations of fructose, glucose, and sucrose in the fermented LCPC 1.0:0.1 were determined during the 5 days of water kefir-assisted fermentation (Table 2). The level of sucrose reduction from 5.41 ± 0.14 to 0.14 ± 0.01 g/L from the unfermented sample to Day 2 of the fermentation, respectively, while the glucose and fructose contents rose to 2.72 ± 0.04 and 1.11 ± 0.04 g/L, respectively. Starting from Day 3 of the fermentation, the glucose and fructose contents began to decrease. Sucrose was no longer detected after Day 4 of the fermentation. Previous results support our findings that glucose, fructose, and sucrose levels are reduced during the kefir fermentation since they are considered the primary energy source for fermenting microorganisms [25].

3.9. Effects of Water Kefir-Assisted Fermentation on the Microbiological Qualities of Fermented LCPC 1.0:0.1

Figure 6 illustrates the dynamics of LAB, AAB, and yeasts during the water kefir-assisted fermentation of LCPC 1.0:0.1. The number of LAB colonies increased to over 6.7 log CFU/mL after 2 days of the fermentation. In contrast, the number of AAB and yeast colonies increased to over 7 log CFU/mL. Kefir seeds have an excellent composition of various beneficial microorganisms, such as LAB (*Streptococcus, Leuconostoc, Lactococcus,* and *Lactobacillus)* and AAB, as well as yeasts (*Saccharomyces, Candida,* and *Kluyveromyces*) [9,23]. However, the nutritional composition of complex proteins provides sufficient support for microbial growth and metabolism. Yeasts play a major role in kefir fermentation by producing the enzymes responsible for the degradation of sucrose into fructose and glucose, as well as the production of ethanol as primary metabolites [10]. AAB utilized glucose and fructose to produce ethanol, whereas LAB used these as carbon sources. This unique symbiotic communication allows the yeasts, AAB, and LAB to collaborate and develop together in the water kefir consortium [38].

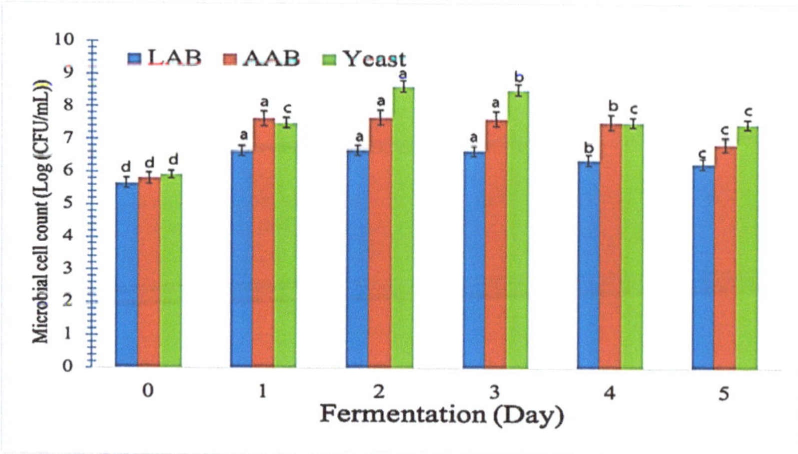

Figure 6. Developments in acetic acid bacteria (yellow bar), acetic acid bacteria (grey bar), and yeast (black bar) microbiological activity (white bar) during the water kefir-assisted fermentation of fermented and unfermented lentil–casein protein complexes at a ratio of 1.0:0.1 (LCPC 1.0:0.1). Bars with different letters differ significantly within the same color bar ($p < 0.05$).

4. Conclusions

The demand for the highly functional properties of legume-based proteins is increasing. Because of this, modifications to LP to improve their functional and nutritional properties are of utmost importance in delivering more innovative combined methods to increase the solubility and digestibility of LP and other plant-based proteins. The soluble protein composites formed through PPI with a new protein structure and protein quality, microstructure, solubility in water, and secondary and tertiary protein structure, as well as the interfacial properties of the novel LCPC, were thoroughly investigated. This study describes the impact of secondary and tertiary protein structures on the water solubility of LCPC. The protein complexation managed to alter the secondary protein structures. Interactions of LP with CP are governed by non-covalent interactions, i.e., hydrophobic interactions, hydrogen bonding, and electrostatic interactions. These interactions increased the water solubility from 55 to over 86.5% after complexation between LP and CP. This study proves that PPI and water kefir-assisted fermentation can favorably alter the protein structure, protein digestibility, and micronutrients of LCPC. These alterations indicate the rearrangement of the degraded protein complexes that occurred during the water kefir-assisted fermentation.

Author Contributions: Conceptualization, C.C.T., M.H.A. and S.G.; methodology, A.M.A.; validation, S.M. and M.A.D.; formal analysis, M.A. and M.S.J.; writing—original draft preparation, M.A.; writing—review and editing, A.M.E.; supervision, T.-C.T. and A.M.E.; project administration, M.A.; funding acquisition and software, T.-C.T. and A.A.-Q. All authors have read and agreed to the published version of the manuscript.

Funding: This research was funded by Malaysia's Fundamental Research Grant Scheme (FRGS/1/2019/STG01/USM/02/8). The research was partially funded by the Researchers Supporting Project number (RSP2023R502), King Saud University, Riyadh, Saudi Arabia.

Institutional Review Board Statement: Not applicable.

Informed Consent Statement: Not applicable.

Data Availability Statement: The data presented in this study are available on request from the corresponding author.

Acknowledgments: We would additionally like to thank the reviewers for their helpful comments and suggestions that improved the quality of the manuscript.

Conflicts of Interest: The authors declare no conflict of interest.

References

1. Jarpa-Parra, M.; Bamdad, F.; Wang, Y.; Tian, Z.; Temelli, F.; Han, J.; Chen, L. Optimization of lentil protein extraction and the influence of process pH on protein structure and functionality. *LWT* **2014**, *57*, 461–469. [CrossRef]
2. Alrosan, M.; Tan, T.-C.; Easa, A.M.; Gammoh, S.; Alu'datt, M.H. Mechanism of the structural interaction between whey and lentil proteins in the unique creation of a protein structure. *J. Food Sci.* **2021**, *86*, 5282–5294. [CrossRef] [PubMed]
3. Alrosan, M.; Tan, T.-C.; Easa, A.M.; Gammoh, S.; Alu'datt, M.H. Effects of fermentation on the quality, structure, and nonnutritive contents of lentil (*Lens culinaris*) proteins. *J. Food Qual.* **2021**, *2021*, 5556450. [CrossRef]
4. Alrosan, M.; Tan, T.-C.; Easa, A.M.; Gammoh, S.; Alu'datt, M.H. Molecular forces governing protein-protein interaction: Structure-function relationship of complexes protein in the food industry. *Crit. Rev. Food Sci. Nutr.* **2022**, *62*, 4036–4052. [CrossRef]
5. Wang, R.; Xu, P.; Chen, Z.; Zhou, X.; Wang, T. Complexation of rice proteins and whey protein isolates by structural interactions to prepare soluble protein composites. *LWT* **2019**, *101*, 207–213. [CrossRef]
6. Wang, T.; Chen, X.; Zhong, Q.; Chen, Z.; Wang, R.; Patel, A.R. Facile and efficient construction of water-soluble biomaterials with tunable mesoscopic structures using all-natural edible proteins. *Adv. Funct. Mater.* **2019**, *29*, 1901830. [CrossRef]
7. Wang, Y.H.; Wang, J.M.; Wan, Z.L.; Yang, X.Q.; Chen, X.W. Corn protein hydrolysate as a new structural modifier for soybean protein isolate based O/W emulsions. *LWT* **2020**, *118*, 108763. [CrossRef]
8. He, J.; Wang, R.; Feng, W.; Chen, Z.; Wang, T. Design of novel edible hydrocolloids by structural interplays between wheat gluten proteins and soy protein isolates. *Food Hydrocoll.* **2020**, *100*, 105395. [CrossRef]
9. Azi, F.; Tu, C.; Rasheed, H.A.; Dong, M. Comparative study of the phenolics, antioxidant and metagenomic composition of novel soy whey-based beverages produced using three different water kefir microbiota. *Int. J. Food Sci. Technol.* **2020**, *55*, 1689–1697. [CrossRef]
10. Alrosan, M.; Tan, T.-C.; Koh, W.Y.; Easa, A.M.; Gammoh, S.; Alu'datt, M.H. Overview of fermentation process: Structure-function relationship on protein quality and non-nutritive compounds of plant-based proteins and carbohydrates. *Crit. Rev. Food Sci. Nutr.* **2022**, 1–15. [CrossRef]
11. Chandra-Hioe, M.V.; Wong, C.H.M.; Arcot, J. The potential use of fermented chickpea and faba bean flour as food ingredients. *Plant Foods Hum. Nutr.* **2016**, *71*, 90–95. [CrossRef] [PubMed]
12. Official Methods of Analysis of AOAC. *Method 930.29*, 19th ed.; AOAC International: Rockville, USA, 2012.
13. Morr, C.V.; German, B.; Kinsella, J.E.; Regenstein, J.M.; Van Buren, J.P.; Kilara, A.; Lewis, B.A.; Mangino, M.E. A collaborative study to develop a standardized food protein solubility procedure. *J. Food Sci.* **1985**, *50*, 1715–1718. [CrossRef]
14. Johnston, S.P.; Nickerson, M.T.; Low, N.H. The physicochemical properties of legume protein isolates and their ability to stabilize oil-in-water emulsions with and without genipin. *J. Food Sci. Technol.* **2015**, *52*, 4135–4145. [CrossRef] [PubMed]
15. Almeida, C.C.; Monteiro, M.L.G.; da Costa-Lima, B.R.C.; Alvares, T.S.; Conte-Junior, C.A. In vitro digestibility of commercial whey protein supplements. *LWT* **2015**, *61*, 7–11. [CrossRef]
16. Liu, W.; Zhang, Z.-Q.; Liu, C.-M.; Xie, M.-Y.; Tu, Z.-C.; Liu, J.-H.; Liang, R.-H. The effect of dynamic high-pressure microfluidization on the activity, stability and conformation of trypsin. *Food Chem.* **2010**, *123*, 616–621. [CrossRef]
17. Jarpa-Parra, M.; Bamdad, F.; Tian, Z.; Zeng, H.; Temelli, F.; Chen, L. Impact of pH on molecular structure and surface properties of lentil legumin-like protein and its application as foam stabilizer. *Colloids Surf. B* **2015**, *132*, 45–53. [CrossRef] [PubMed]
18. Tomczyńska-Mleko, M.; Kamysz, E.; Sikorska, E.; Puchalski, C.; Mleko, S.; Ozimek, L.; Kowaluk, G.; Gustaw, W.; Wesołowska-Trojanowska, M. Changes of secondary structure and surface tension of whey protein isolate dispersions upon pH and temperature. *Czech J. Food Sci.* **2014**, *32*, 82–89. [CrossRef]
19. Song, X.; Zhou, C.; Fu, F.; Chen, Z.; Wu, Q. Effect of high-pressure homogenization on particle size and film properties of soy protein isolate. *Ind. Crops Prod.* **2013**, *43*, 538–544. [CrossRef]
20. Tepari, E.A.; Nakhla, G.; Haroun, B.M.; Hafez, H. Co-fermentation of carbohydrates and proteins for biohydrogen production: Statistical optimization using Response Surface Methodology. *Int. J. Hydrogen Energy* **2020**, *45*, 2640–2654. [CrossRef]
21. Çabuk, B.; Nosworthy, M.G.; Stone, A.K.; Korber, D.R.; Tanaka, T.; House, J.D.; Nickerson, M.T. Effect of fermentation on the protein digestibility and levels of non-nutritive compounds of pea protein concentrate. *Food Technol. Biotechnol.* **2018**, *56*, 257–264. [CrossRef]
22. Jia, J.; Ji, B.; Tian, L.; Li, M.; Lu, M.; Ding, L.; Liu, X.; Duan, X. Mechanism study on enhanced foaming properties of individual albumen proteins by Lactobacillus fermentation. *Food Hydrocoll.* **2021**, *111*, 106218. [CrossRef]
23. Tu, C.; Azi, F.; Huang, J.; Xu, X.; Xing, G.; Dong, M. Quality and metagenomic evaluation of a novel functional beverage produced from soy whey using water kefir grains. *LWT* **2019**, *113*, 108258. [CrossRef]
24. dos Santos, D.C.; de Oliveira Filho, J.G.; Santana, A.C.A.; de Freitas, B.S.M.; Silva, F.G.; Takeuchi, K.P.; Egea, M.B. Optimization of soymilk fermentation with kefir and the addition of inulin: Physicochemical, sensory and technological characteristics. *LWT* **2019**, *104*, 30–37. [CrossRef]

25. Pranoto, Y.; Anggrahini, S.; Efendi, Z. Effect of natural and *Lactobacillus plantarum* fermentation on in-vitro protein and starch digestibilities of sorghum flour. *Food Biosci.* **2013**, *2*, 46–52. [CrossRef]
26. Klaenhammer, T.R.; Barrangou, R.; Buck, B.L.; Azcarate-Peril, M.A.; Altermann, E. Genomic features of lactic acid bacteria effecting bioprocessing and health. *FEMS Microbiol. Rev.* **2005**, *29*, 393–409. [CrossRef]
27. Ayala-Niño, A.; Rodríguez-Serrano, G.M.; Jiménez-Alvarado, R.; Bautista-Avila, M.; Sánchez-Franco, J.A.; González-Olivares, L.G.; Cepeda-Saez, A. Bioactivity of peptides released during lactic fermentation of amaranth proteins with potential cardiovascular protective effect: An in vitro study. *J. Med. Food* **2019**, *22*, 976–981. [CrossRef]
28. Carbonaro, M.; Maselli, P.; Nucara, A. Relationship between digestibility and secondary structure of raw and thermally treated legume proteins: A Fourier transform infrared (FT-IR) spectroscopic study. *Amino Acids* **2012**, *43*, 911–921. [CrossRef]
29. Wang, Z.; Li, Y.; Jiang, L.; Qi, B.; Zhou, L. Relationship between secondary structure and surface hydrophobicity of soybean protein isolate subjected to heat treatment. *J. Chem.* **2014**, *2014*, 475389. [CrossRef]
30. Salazar-Villanea, S.; Hendriks, W.H.; Bruininx, E.; Gruppen, H.; Van Der Poel, A.F.B. Protein structural changes during processing of vegetable feed ingredients used in swine diets: Implications for nutritional value. *Nutr. Res. Rev.* **2016**, *29*, 126–141. [CrossRef]
31. Liyana-Pathirana, C.M.; Shahidi, F. Importance of insoluble-bound phenolics to antioxidant properties of wheat. *J. Agric. Food Chem.* **2006**, *54*, 1256–1264. [CrossRef]
32. Adebo, O.A.; Gabriela Medina-Meza, I. Impact of fermentation on the phenolic compounds and antioxidant activity of whole cereal grains: A mini review. *Molecules* **2020**, *25*, 927. [CrossRef]
33. Liu, Q.; Wang, C.; Guo, G.; Huo, W.J.; Zhang, Y.L.; Pei, C.X.; Zhang, S.L.; Wang, H. Effects of branched-chain volatile fatty acids supplementation on growth performance, ruminal fermentation, nutrient digestibility, hepatic lipid content and gene expression of dairy calves. *Anim. Feed Sci. Technol.* **2018**, *237*, 27–34. [CrossRef]
34. Heiniö, R.-L.; Noort, M.W.J.; Katina, K.; Alam, S.A.; Sozer, N.; De Kock, H.L.; Hersleth, M.; Poutanen, K. Sensory characteristics of wholegrain and bran-rich cereal foods–A review. *Trends Food Sci. Technol.* **2016**, *47*, 25–38. [CrossRef]
35. Del Hierro, J.N.; Herrera, T.; García-Risco, M.R.; Fornari, T.; Reglero, G.; Martin, D. Ultrasound-assisted extraction and bioaccessibility of saponins from edible seeds: Quinoa, lentil, fenugreek, soybean and lupin. *Food Res. Int.* **2018**, *109*, 440–447. [CrossRef] [PubMed]
36. Chan, K.W.; Iqbal, S.; Khong, N.M.H.; Ooi, D.-J.; Ismail, M. Antioxidant activity of phenolics–saponins rich fraction prepared from defatted kenaf seed meal. *LWT* **2014**, *56*, 181–186. [CrossRef]
37. Lai, L.-R.; Hsieh, S.-C.; Huang, H.-Y.; Chou, C.-C. Effect of lactic fermentation on the total phenolic, saponin and phytic acid contents as well as anti-colon cancer cell proliferation activity of soymilk. *J. Biosci. Bioeng.* **2013**, *115*, 552–556. [CrossRef]
38. Gulitz, A.; Stadie, J.; Wenning, M.; Ehrmann, M.A.; Vogel, R.F. The microbial diversity of water kefir. *Int. J. Food Microbiol.* **2011**, *151*, 284–288. [CrossRef]

MDPI AG
Grosspeteranlage 5
4052 Basel
Switzerland
Tel.: +41 61 683 77 34

Fermentation Editorial Office
E-mail: fermentation@mdpi.com
www.mdpi.com/journal/fermentation

www.ingramcontent.com/pod-product-compliance
Lightning Source LLC
Chambersburg PA
CBHW041347210926
51850CB00013B/3014
9783725825424